A BIBLIOGRAPHY OF STAINED GLASS

A
BIBLIOGRAPHY
OF
STAINED
GLASS

David Evans

D.S. BREWER

© David Evans 1982

First published 1982 by D.S. Brewer
240 Hills Road, Cambridge

an imprint of Boydell & Brewer Ltd
PO Box 9, Woodbridge, Suffolk IP12 3DF
and by Biblio Distribution Services
81 Adams Drive, Totowa, N.J. 07512, U.S.A.

ISBN 0 85991 087 3

British Library Cataloguing in Publication Data

Evans, David
   A bibliography of stained glass.
   1. Glass painting and staining—Bibliography
   I. Title
   016.7485   Z5956.G5

   ISBN 0-85991-087-3

Printed in Great Britain by
St.Edmundsbury Press,Bury St.Edmunds Suffolk

C O N T E N T S

PREFACE   vii

BIBLIOGRAPHY   1

  Supplement   179

GENERAL INDEX   181

TOPOGRAPHICAL INDEX: England   190

                             Europe   196

Stained glass windows have been the object of scholarly research and popular exposition for a considerable time, though advances in knowledge have not been made systematically and the history of this branch of learning tends to be a record of the contributions of a relatively small number of scholars, often separated by lengthy periods of time. It is not too much to say that the subject remains at the level of 'primitive accumulation' - to borrow a phrase from another context - and the slow progress being made at recording the mediaeval glass of England would seem to indicate that no rapid advances are in prospect.

In these circumstances there appears to be a need for a book which begins to indicate what has been committed to print. Many of the more valuable contributions have appeared in scholarly journals and other periodicals, and the task of finding out just what (if anything) has been written about a particular place can be very time-consuming. The only full-dress bibliography of the subject which has appeared so far (Brady & Serban), though extraordinarily useful to students of modern American stained glass, has the self-imposed restrictions of dealing only with books (with the exception of some entries in Stained Glass and the Journal of the British Society of Master Glass-Painters), and books written in English at that.

A truly complete bibliography of the subject is perfectly conceivable, but the expense of the resulting volumes would doubtless make the project impractical. This preliminary bibliography gives examples of the kinds of material which remain to be quarried: letters to the Times, articles in provincial newspapers, obituaries, passing references in the Gentleman's Magazine, etc. One very important source, familiar to all workers in the field of nineteenth century glass, has deliberately not

been touched: the <u>Builder</u>.   A full index to that work would be an
invaluable set of volumes, and one which will not be compiled by me.
Readers should not be too downcast, though, for I can reveal that a
thorough index of the stained glass entries in the <u>Ecclesiologist</u> is
being compiled by Dr. Chris Brooks of Exeter University, which will
be an indispensable supplement to this work.   The grosser omissions
from this source are:

       Ancient Heraldry, vol. 1 (1841-2) pp. 138-140

       An Anglo-Saxon Church, <u>ibid</u>. pp. 190-192

       Foreign Stained Glass, <u>ibid</u>. pp. 207-208

       Stained Glass in York, vol. 2 (1842-3) p.47

Other sources have not been mentioned: not in this case
because of the daunting prospect, but because they are unlikely to
be overlooked.   Such books are County guides, VCH and RCHM volumes,
the Pevsner series, Murray's guides, etc.   It is not to be supposed
that this restriction has been scrupulously observed.

The range of material covered has been deliberately kept as broad
as possible: a certain proportion of the entries may appear impossibly
trivial but they are of some value as indications of the ways in which
popular journalism has dealt with the subject, and the formation of public
taste.   One work of outright fiction has been included: Maurice Drake's
novel <u>The Doom Window</u>.   <u>The Treasure of Abbot Thomas</u> was reluctantly
excluded, but under the M.R. James entry can be found - by those who do
not already know - the original of Lord D's private chapel.   More
'oddities' might have been included with advantage: the reader who wishes
to find out where to see portraits in glass of United States labour
'leaders' of the ilk of John L. Lewis will have to comb the post-war
volumes of <u>Stained Glass</u> for himself.   'Stained glass for Stalin' was
allowed in by virture of the superior dignity of the recipient.
(Anyone who travels to Georgia in the hope of encountering Socialist
realism in glass will be disappointed.)

The topographical index should prove useful, though it must be
remembered that only specific articles or books have been indexed under
particular locations: the reader should in all cases first consult the
general entry (where it exists).   Some of the subject headings are
very generalised.   In most case this has proved unavoidable, and the
sheer number of entries makes them rather unwieldy.   Often, however,
the date of the entry will afford a valuable clue to its interest.

Thanks are due to the staffs of the Victoria & Albert Museum
Library, York Minster Library, Canterbury Cathedral Library, the
British Library, Birmingham University Library, the Barber Institute
Library, Birmingham Reference Library, the Bodleian Library,
Cambridge University Library, Exeter University Library, the
Devon & Exeter Institution Library, Exeter Cathedral Library and
the North Devon Athenaeum.

Special thanks go to Barbara (for prodding), to Mary Hill
for heroic feats of typing, to Hanns Makosch and Dr Feargus McGanran
for German proof-reading, to Andy Clark for topographical information,
and to Betty and Reg Shepard for providing a congenial working
environment.

Abbreviations

Journal of the British Society of Master Glass Painters :   JMGP
Stained Glass :   SG
In the index, (S) indicates the presence of an entry in the Supplement.

to Bill & Joan

(Abbey Folk Park, New Barnet)
Early Stained Glass Panels at Abbey Folk Park.
The Times, Oct. 2, 1934.

(Acquisition of domestic panels)
in News and Notes, J.M.G.P., vol. 7, no. 4 (April, 1939), p. 153.

(Abingdon)
County Hall, Abingdon. The Armorial Windows (formerly in St.
Nicholas' Church).
Abingdon, 1939.

ABEL, Charles
L'Oeuvre du Peintre Verrier Hermann.
Metz, 1865.

(Acezat collection sale catalogue)
Vente après décès A. Ancienne collection de M. Michel Acezat.
Vitraux Français, vitraux Cisterciens, vitraux héraldiques, etc.
Hôtel Drouot, Nov. 24, 25, 1969.
Paris (Nov. 1969).

ACOMB, H.W.
The Flemish Glass at Earsham.
in Supplement to Blomefield's Norfolk, 1929.

ADAM, Paul, and BANNIER, Ingeborg
Les vitraux du choeur de l'église Saint-Georges.
Publications de la Société des Amis de la Bibliothèque de
Sélestat (1968), pp. 11-31.

ADAM, Stephen
Ecclesiastical Stained Glass. (Excerpts from an address).
Transactions of the Glasgow Ecclesiological Society, vol. 1,
1894 (1895), pp. 6-11.

(On the Glasgow stained glass windows: contained in)
TODD, G.E., The Book of Glasgow Cathedral. A History and
Description.
Glasgow, 1898.

ADAMS, Doug
The Chagall Windows as Choreography: Stained Glass as
Inspiration for Dance in Worship.
Stained Glass, vol. 69, nos. 1 and 2 (Spring-Summer, 1974),
pp. 4-7.

ADAMS, Henry
Mont-Saint-Michel and Chartres.
Boston, 1905.

ADAMS, Henry B.
The Stained Glass of John La Farge.
American Art Review, (July-August, 1975), pp. 41-63.

ADAMS, Maxwell
A Brief Account of Ashton Church and Some of the Chudleighs
of Ashton.
Transactions of the Devonshire Association, vol. 31 (1899),
pp. 185-198.

Some Notes on the Churches and the Manors of East and West Ogwell.
Transactions of the Devonshire Association, vol. 32 (1900).
(Glass in East Ogwell Church; pp. 231-232.)

Some Notes on the Church and Parish of Churston Ferrers.
Transactions of the Devonshire Association, vol. 36 (1904).
(Glass, pp. 509-510.)

ADLOW, Dorothy
(The Heinz Chapel Windows, Pittsburgh University.)
Stained Glass, vol. 33, no. 2, (Autumn-Winter, 1938), pp. 64-67.

AHNE, Paul
Les Vitraux de la Cathédrale de Strasbourg.
(with BEYER, Victor)
Strasbourg, 1960.
Reviewed by AUBERT, Marcel, Bulletin Monumental, vol. 118 (1960),
p. 237.

(Aikman, William)
Obituary (by BUSS, A.E.)
J.M.G.P., vol. 13, no. 1 (1960), pp. 364-365.

AITKEN, W.C.
Francis Eginton.
Transactions of the Birmingham and Midland Institute
Archaeological Section, vol. 111 (1872), pp. 27-43.

ALAUZIER, M.L.D'.
Les Vitraux de Junies (Lot.).
Bulletin de la Société des Etudes Littéraires, Scientifiques et
Artistiques du Lot, Part I (1962).

ALCAIDE, Victor Nieto
El "Tratado de la Fabrica del Vidrio" per Juan Danis, y el "Modo"
de hacer vidrierias de Francisco Herranz.
Archivo Espanol del Arte (1967), pp. 273-303.

Las Vidrieras de la Catedral de Sevilla.
(CVMA, Spain I.)
Madrid, 1969.

La Vidriera del Renacimiento en España.
Madrid, 1970.

Les Vidrieras de la Catedral de Granada.
(CVMA. Spain, vol. 2.)
Madrid, 1973.

ALDER, J.
Couverte.
(Letter to the Editor.)
J.M.G.P., vol. 4, no. 2 (Oct., 1931), p. 104.

ALEXANDER, W.C.
Painted Glass from a Window in the Church of St. Thomas a
Becket, Brightling, Sussex.
Sussex Archaeological Collections, vol. 45 (1902), pp. 180-185.

ALLCHIN, A.M.
Review of CAVINESS, M.H.,
The Early Stained Glass of Canterbury Cathedral.
Canterbury Cathedral Chronicle, no. 73 (April, 1979), pp. 53-54.

ALLEAUME, A.A.
Les Vitraux de Saint-Mars-sur-Colmont, et les Frères de Heemsee.
Bulletin de la Commission Historicale et Archéologice de la
Mayenne Laval, (séries 2), vol. 3 (1897), pp. 104-111.

ALLEN, W. Godfrey
Report to the Friends of Exeter Cathedral on the Progress at St.
James' Chapel and the Muniment Room.
21st Annual Report of the Friends of Exeter Cathedral, 1950 (1951).
(Future of the Drake Memorial glass, p. 18.)

1

ALLOU, Bishop

  Notice Historique et Descriptive sur la Cathédrale de Meaux.
  (2nd. ed.) Meaux, 1871.

(Allt-yr-yns Mansion and Walterstone Church, Herefordshire.)

  (Armorial Glass.)

  Transactions of the Woolhope Naturalists' Field Club, 1905,
  1906, 1907, vol. 19 (1911), p. 258.
  See also
  Cecil Arms from Allt-yr-Ymis.
  Ibid. 1918, 1919, 1920 (1921), p.183.

ALMY, Ruth Case

  Simulated Stained Glass for Amateurs.
  New York, 1949.

  (Letter to the Editor suggesting how the work of the Stained
  Glass Association of America might be improved.)
  Stained Glass, vol. 48, no. 2, (Summer 1953), pp. 98-101.

ALOI, Roberto

  Esempi di Decorazione Arte e Arredi Sacri.
  Milan, 1950.

(Altenberg Abbey)

  (Glass from Altenberg exhibited at the Egyptian Hall. Originally
  purchased for Hitchin church, but the parishioners would not pay
  up. Now exposed for sale.)
  The Gentleman's Magazine, vol. 102 (1832, Part II), p. 63.
  (Letter alleging they were designed by Dürer) Ibid. p. 400.
  (A further letter agreeing, and describing the windows) Ibid.,
  p. 517-518.

(Altenberg Abbey, Contd.)

  Stained Glass Windows at Altenberg. By K.P.D.E.
  (Request for information on their whereabouts.)
  Notes and Queries, 4th series, vol. 8 (Aug. 19, 1871), pp. 146-147.
  Replied to by WEALE, W.H. James, Ibid. (Nov. 25, 1871), p. 444.

AMÉ, Emile

  Recherches sur les Anciens Vitraux Incolorés.
  Bulletin de la Société des Sciences Historiques et Naturelles de
  l'Yonne, vol. 7 (1853), pp. 243-252.

  Recherches sur les Anciens Vitraux Incolorés du Département de
  l'Yonne.
  Paris, 1854.

  Monogramme d'un Peintre-Verrier de XVe Siècle et Decription du
  Vitrail de la Sainte Vierge de l'Eglise de Cravan (Yonne).
  Paris, 1854.

(Amiens Cathedral)

  The Stained Glass of Amiens. By R.L.
  (Report of loss of some glass removed during the war in a
  subsequent fire, and request for information.)
  Notes and Queries, vol. 149 (Oct. 24, 1925), p. 299.

(Amman, Jost)

  (With a reproduction of his woodcut Der Glasmaler.)
  Stained Glass, vol. 33, no. 2 (Autumn-Winter, 1938), pp. 50-51.

AMSLER and RUTHARDT

  Entwürfe zu Glasfenstern.
  In Originalzeichnungen alter Glasmaler des 16 und 17 Jahrhunderts.
  Berlin, 1895.

Ancient French Treasures Saved (during the War and Liberation).
  Stained Glass, vol. 39, no. 4 (Winter, 1944), pp. 130-132.

ANDERES, Bernhard

  Die spätgotische Glasmalerei
  In Freiburg in B. Ein Beitrag zur Geschichte der schweizerischen
  Malerei.
  Freiburg, 1963.

ANDERSON, Charles

  On Stained Glass.
  Reports and Papers of the Associated Architectural Societies,
  vol. 1 (1850-1851), pp. 100-109.

ANDERSON, David

  A Sketch of the History and Characteristics of Stained Glass.
  A Paper read to the Glasgow Architectural Association, Feb. 1,
  1885.
  Summarised in
  The Architect, Feb. 14 (1885), p. 98.

ANDERSSON, Aron

  (with CHRISTIE, Sigrid, NORDMANN, Carl-Axel, ROUSSEL, Aage.)
  Die Glasmalereien des Mittelalters in Skandinavien.
  (CVMA, Scandinavia.)
  Stockholm, 1964.
  Reviewed by GRODECKI, Louis:
  Bulletin Monumental, vol. 123 (1965), pp. 358-361.

  Medieval Stained Glass on the Island of Gotland.
  J.M.G.P., vol. 15, no. 1 (1972-1973), pp. 41-62.

ANDRAE, F.W.

  Gedanken, Studien und Erfahrungen auf dem Gebiete der
  Glasmalerei.
  Leipzig, 1880.

ANDRAL, B.G.

  Les Vitraux de la Chapelle du Grand Seminaire de Bayonne.
  Reprinted from:
  Revue Historique et Archeologique du Bearn et du Pays Basque.
  Pau, 1925.

ANDRÉ, A.

  De la Verrerie et des Vitraux Peints dans l'Ancienne Province
  de Bretagne.
  Rennes, 1878.

ANDRÉ, J. Lewis

  Compton Church.
  Surrey Archaeological Collections, vol. 12 (1895).
  Glass, pp. 11-12.

  Battle Church.
  Sussex Archaeological Collections, vol. 42 (1899).
  Glass, pp. 223-224.

ANDREWS, H.C.

  Some Armorial Glass of Northamptonshire: Cosgrove Church.
  Notes and Queries, vol. 184 (June 19, 1943), p. 380.

ANGEL, G. Arnand D'.

  L'Art Religieux Moderne.
  Grenoble, 1935.

ANGOULVENT, P.J.

  The Church of Brou.
  Paris, 1930.

ANGUS-BUTTERWORTH, L.M.

The Chemistry of Glass Coloration.
Endeavour (July, 1947).

English Heritage of Stained Glass.
Transactions of the Ancient Monuments Society (new series),
vol. 9 (1961), pp. 57-72.

ANNAN, Thomas

The Painted Windows of Glasgow Cathedral.
Glasgow. 1867.

ANSELME, M.

L'Art Cistercien, France
La Pierre-qui-Vire (Yonne), 1972.

ANSELME DE PUYSAYE, J. d'

Les Vitraux de la Cathédrale de Tunis et l'Esprit Religieux de
Notre Temps.
Paris, 1909.

ANSTAING, Le Maistre d'

Notice sur les Vitraux Placés à l'Abside Méridionale du Transept
de la Cathédrale de Tournai.
Tournai, n.d. (c. 1855).

('Antique' Glass)

Die Kathedralglas-Fabrikation.
By St.
Sprechsaal, vol. 33 (1900), pp. 684, 718.

ANTOINE, H.

L'Eglise Saint-Germain d'Argentan.
Argentan, 1913.

(Apedale)

Heraldic Glass at Apedale.
Transactions of the North Staffordshire Field Club, vol. 67.

APLIGNY, Le Pileur d'

Traité des Couleurs Materielles, et de la Manière de Colorer
Relativement aux Différens Arts et Métiers.
Paris, 1779.
Translated into German:
Abhandlung von den Farben . . .
Leipzig, 1779.

(Apprenticeship)

Report of the National Joint Apprenticeship Committee for
Stained Glass.
Stained Glass, vol. 44, no. 1 (Spring 1949), pp. 17-21.

(Arborfield)

Stained Glass from Old Arborfield Church.
Berkshire Archaeological Journal, vol. 38, no. 1.

ARCHER, M.

Seventeenth Century Painted Glass at Little Easton.
Essex Journal, vol. 12, part 1 (1977), pp. 3-

ARCHER, Michael

Stained Glass.
London, 1979.

The Architect Looks at Stained Glass.
A Symposium.
Contributions by WALKER, H.L.
            CELLARIUS, C.F.
            BELLUSCHI, P.
            WHITEHOUSE, H.C.
Stained Glass, vol. 48, no. 1. (Spring 1953), pp. 20-27.

ARDAGH, J.

Stained Glass Windows to Fictitious Characters.
Notes and Queries, vol. 171 (Dec. 12, 1936), p. 425.

ARENAS José Fernandez

Las Vidrieras de la Catedral de Léon.
Madrid. 1976.

ARENDT, C.H.

Analyse d'un Manuscrit de 1565 Traitant de la Technique de la
Peinture sur Verre.
18th Congress, Féderation Archeologique et Historique de Belgique.
Mons, 1904.

ARMAND, G.

L'Art Religieux Moderne.
Grenoble, 1936.

ARMITAGE, E. Liddall

The Qualities of Stained Glass.
Transactions of the Ecclesiological Society, new series, vol. 2,
part 2 (1949), pp. 84-86.

Stained Glass.
London, 1959.
Reviewed by LAFOND, Jean, in The Archaeological Journal, vol.
cxvi, for 1959, pp. 271-272.
Reviewed by KIRBY, H.T., J.M.G.P., vol. 13, no. 1 (1960), pp.
374-375.
Reviewed by SKINNER, Orin E., Stained Glass, vol. 55, no. 1
(Spring, 1960), p. 39.

(Letter indicating the reasons for the usual size of pieces of
glass in a window.)
J.M.G.P., vol. 14, no. 1 (1964), pp. 87-88.

Review of LAFOND, Jean; Le Vitrail.
J.M.G.P., vol. 14, no. 3 (1967), pp. 178-179.

ARNOLD, Hugh (with SAINT, Lawrence)

Stained Glass of the Middle Ages in England and France.
London, 1913.

ARNOLD, Hugh

The Glass in Balliol College Chapel.
Oxford, 1914.

An Account of the Special Meeting Held March 31, 1916, by the
Art Workers' Guild.
Privately printed, n.d.

(Art Workers' Guild)

Papers on Stained Glass Read at the Art Workers' Guild.
(By FISHER, Alfred, and others.)
J.M.G.P., vol. 14, no. 3 (1967), pp. 159-160.

ARTHUR, Henry

Chartres (Interior).
Sainte-Marie de la Pierre-qui-Vire (Yonne), n.d.

(Artificial Gemstones of Glass)

Ancient Glass Imitations of Precious Stones.
The Antiquary, vol. 1 (1880), p. 138.

(The Arts and Crafts Exhibition, 1893)

The Studio, vol. 2 (1894).
(Stained glass designs, pp. 11-13.)

(The Arts and Crafts Exhibition, 1906)
The Studio, vol. 37 (1906).
(Stained glass designs, pp. 48-59.)

Art's Master-piece, or a Companion for the Ingenious of either Sex.
By C.K.
London, 1697. (Several subsequent editions.)

(Arundel Castle)
Catalogue of Pictures Painted on Glass Containing Principally
the Great Norfolk Window for the Baron's Hall of Arundel
Castle. Exhibited at Mr. J. Backler's Stained Glass Works,
no. 18 Newman Street, Oxford Street, London.
London, 1817.

The Antiquities of Arundel Castle.
London. 1838. (1st ed. c. 1832.)

(Window for Arundel by BACKLER depicting the signing of Magna
Carta exhibited.)
The Gentleman's Magazine, vol. 87, part 1 (1817), p. 272.

ASCENZO, Nicola D'
Stained Glass in the Pennsylvania Museum.
Stained Glass, vol. 27, no. 3 (March, 1932), pp. 85-89.

Traditionalism and Modernism.
Stained Glass, vol. 36, no. 1 (Spring, 1941), pp. 4-8.

(Ascenzo, Nicola D'.,Snr.)
Obituary.
Stained Glass, vol. 48, no. 4 (Winter, 1953-1954), pp. 204-205.

ASHDOWN, C.H.
History of the Worshipful Company of Glaziers, of the City of
London, otherwise the Company of Glaziers and Painters of Glass.
London, 1919.

ASHLEY, John
The Art of Painting on, and Annealing in Glass, with the True
Receipts of the Colours, the Ordering of the Furnace and the
Secrets Thereunto Belonging, as Practised about the Year 1500.
London. 1801.

(Ashridge Park, Herts.)
(Announcement of sale of the Ashridge House windows.)
The Times, June 5, 1928.
(Letter to the Editor suggesting that the windows be purchased
for Guildford Cathedral.)
The Times, July 11, 1928.
(Sold for £27,000.)
The Times, July 13, 1928.
(Donated to the Victoria and Albert Museum.)
The Times, July 26, 1928.

Sale of the Sixteenth Century Glass from the Chapel of Ashridge
Park. Herts.
J.M.G.P., vol. 2, no. 4 (Oct. 1928), pp. 210-211.

ASSIER, Alex.
Les Arts et Les Artistes dans l'ancienne Capitale de la
Champagne.
Paris, 1866.

(Association of German Glass Painting)
Verbandstag deutscher Glasmalereien im München.
Keramische Rundschau. vol. 20 (1912), p. 306.

(Assy Church)
Assy, Miracle d'Art Sacré Moderne.
L'Illustration (Christmas, 1950).

(Assy Church Contd)
More About Assy.
The Catholic Art Quarterly, Pentecost, 1951.

ATALONE, A.P.
Profils Messins: Charles Laurent Maréchal.
Paris, 1911.

(Atcham Church, Shropshire)
(Glass removed from Bacton Church, Herefordshire.)
Transactions of the Woolhope Naturalists' Field Club, 1895.
1896, 1897, vol. 15 (1898), pp. 23-24.

Blanche Parry Windows.
Transactions of the Woolhope Naturalists' Field Club, 1912,
1913, vol. 21 (1916), pp. 60-61.

ATHOE, G.B.J.
Stained Glass in Churches.
(A contribution to the correspondence started by J.M.G.P.,
April 1936 (q.v.) recommending sculptured plain glass as an
alternative.)
Notes and Queries, vol. 170 (May 16, 1936), p. 354.

Stained Glass Windows to Fictitious Characters.
Notes and Queries, vol. 171 (Dec. 12, 1936), p. 425.

ATKINSON (William) and Co. New York
The Artists, Painters and Glass Stainers' Coats of Arms and
Crest Book of 1871.
New York, 1871.

(Atrocious offer made by a glass stainer)
(To supply a church window in exchange for its fragmentary
ancient glass.)
The Ecclesiologist, vol. 4 (1845), p. 247.

AUBER, Abbé
Histoire de la Cathédrale de Poitiers, Contenant la Théorie
de ses Vitraux Peints.
2 vols, Poitiers and Paris, 1849.

Des Verrières Peintes et de Quelques Amateurs qui en Devisent.
Bulletin Monumental, vol. 24 (1858), pp. 524-

The Crucifixion Window at Poitiers.
(Translated by LAVANOUX, Maurice, from Histoire de la
Cathédrale de Poitiers.)
Stained Glass, vol. 27, no. 12 (Dec. 1932), pp. 335-337.

AUBERT, Marcel
Stained Glass in Chartres Cathedral.
Burlington Magazine, vol. 42 (Jan.-June, 1923), pp. 266-272.

Les Vitraux d'Emmanuel Vigeland à Stockholm.
Art et Décoration, (Aug. 1923), pp. 51-58.
Translated in Stained Glass, vol. 33, no. 2 (Autumn-Winter,
1938), pp. 39-46.

Saint-Wandrille.
Congrès Archéologique de France, (Rouen), vol. 89 (1927), pp.
566-567.

Une Verrière du XIVe Siècle à la Trinité de Fécamp.
Gazette des Beaux-Arts (June 1, 1928), pp. 165-166.

Les Vitraux.
Contained in La Cathédrale de Metz.
Paris, 1931, pp. 215-248.

Le Vitrail du XIIe au XVIe Siècle.
L'Art Sacré (May, 1936), pp. 143-148.

La Protection des Verrières de la Cathédrale de Chartres.
Bulletin de la Société Nationale des Antiquaries de France
(1936), pp. 82-83.

AUBERT, Marcel (Contd.)

Les Vitraux des Cathédrales de France aux XIIe et XIIIe Siècles.
Paris, 1937.
(With a preface by CLAUDEL, Paul.)
(2nd ed. 1947)
Reviewed by RACKHAM, Bernard, Burlington Magazine, vol. 72
(Feb. 1938).

Stained Glass of the XIIth and XIIIth Centuries. From French
Cathedrals.
(Introduction by COULTON, G.G.)
London, n.d. (1939?).
Reviewed by FELL, H. Granville, The Connoisseur, vol. 103 (May,
1939), p. 292.

Review of LAFOND, Jean;   Pratique de la Peinture sur Verre . . .
Suivie d'un Essai Historique sur la Jaune d'Argent . . .
Bulletin Monumental, vol. 103 (1945), pp. 298-299.

Le Vitrail en France.
Paris, 1946.
Reviewed by SALET, Francis, in Bulletin Monumental, no. 105 (1947)
p. 289.
Reviewed by RACKHAM, Bernard, J.M.G.P., vol. 10, no. 1 (1948),
pp. 44-47, and in Burlington Magazine, vol. 90 (Jan.-Dec. 1948),
pp. 54-55.

Review of COUFFON, R.; La Peinture sur Verre en Bretagne,
Origine de Quelques Verrières du XVIe Siècle.
Bulletin Monumental, vol. 104 (1946), pp. 138-140.

L'Architecture Cistercienne en France.
2 vols., Paris, 1947.
(Glass, vol. 1, pp. 311-313.)

Review of BRUYNE, Edgar De; Etudes d'Esthetique Mediévale.
Bulletin Monumental, no. 105 (1947), pp. 161-162.

Le Vitrail Moderne dans les Eglises.
France Illustration (Christmas, 1947).

Le Vitrail aux XIIe et XIIIe Siècles.
Visages du Monde, no. 90 (1948).
(Le Vitrail en France, pp. 6-9.)

Suger.
Editions de Fontenelle, Abbaye de Saint-Wandrille, 1950.
Reviewed by SALET, Francis, in Bulletin Monumental, vol. 109
(1951), pp. 341-342.

Review of ROOSVAL, Johnny; Gotländsk Vitriarius.
Bulletin Monumental, vol. 109 (1951), pp. 230-231.

La Cathédrale de Chartres.
Paris, 1952.

Review of BEER, Ellen; Die Rose der Kathedrale von Lausanne . . .
Bulletin Monumental, vol. 111 (1953), pp. 202-203.

Les Vitraux de la Cathédrale du Mans.
Une Cathédrale en son Pays.
VIIe Centenaire de la Cathédrale du Mans (1954), pp. 23-27.

Emile Mâle. Nécrologie.
Bulletin Monumental, vol. 113 (1955), pp. 47-49.

Review of MARCHINI, Guiseppe; Le Vetrate Italiane.
Bulletin Monumental, no. 114 (1956), pp. 77-78.

Review of BEER, Ellen; CVMA vol. 1 (Switzerland).
Bulletin Monumental, no. 114 (1956), pp. 148-149.

La Bible Illustrée des Verrières de la Sainte-Chapelle.
Bible et Vie Chrétienne (Sept.-Nov., 1957), pp. 28-34.

AUBERT, Marcel (Contd.)

Review of LAFOND, Jean; Le Vitrail Civil Français a l'Eglise
et au Musée.
Bulletin Monumental, no. 115 (1957), pp. 73-74.

Le Vitrail Français.
(With CHASTEL, A., GRODECKI, L., GRUBER J.-J., LAFOND, J.,
MATHEY, F., TARALON, S., VERRIER, J.)
Paris, 1958.
Reviewed by SALET, Francis, in Bulletin Monumental, no. 116 (1958),
p. 226.

Les Vitraux de Notre-Dame et de la Sainte-Chapelle de Paris.
(With GRODECKI, Louis, LAFOND, Jean)
CVMA France I. Département de la Seine I.)
Paris, 1959.

La Lumière dans les Eglises au Début de l'Epoque Gothique.
Archives de l'Art Français, nouvelle période, t.22.
(Mélanges Gaston Brière.) 1959, pp. 27-32.

Review of COUFFON and LE BARS; Répertoire des Eglises . . . de
Quimper et de Léon.
Bulletin Monumental, no. 117 (1959), pp. 241-242.

Review of BIBOLET, F.; Les Vitraux de Saint-Martin-ès-Vignes.
Bulletin Monumental, no. 117 (1959), p. 242.

Review of AHNE and BEYER; Les Vitraux de la Cathédrale de
Strasbourg.
Bulletin Monumental, vol. 118 (1960), p. 237.

(Obituaries.)
Bulletin Monumental, vol. 121 (1963), pp. 9-19.

(Austria)

Austrian Glass-Paintings of the Fourteenth Century and Grisaille
Glass-Paintings of the Fifteenth and Sixteenth Centuries.
Victoria and Albert Museum Annual Review, (1930), pp. 26-29.

(Auxerre Cathedral)

The Glory of Mediaeval Glass: A Thirteenth-Century Window.
(From Auxerre Cathedral.)
Illustrated London News, (Oct. 22, 1932), pp. 617-618.

(Ayston Church)

Ayston Church, Rutland: Glass.
(Grant to restore the east window.)
The Pilgrim Trust, 43rd Annual Report (1973), p. 14.

AZEGLIO, V.T.D'.

An Exhibition of Artistic Painted Glass from the Fourteenth to
the Nineteenth Century. (Burlington Fine Arts Club.)
London, 1876.

BAAR, Armand

Verrerie des Flandres, Fabrication Anversoise.
Revue Belge d'Archeologie et d'Histoire de l'Art, no. 3 (1938),
p. 214.

BABEAU, Albert

L'Eglise Saint-Pantaléon de Troyes; Sa Construction et Ses
Objets d'Art.
Annuaire de L'Aube (1881), pp. 33-74.

Linard Gontier et ses Fils, Peintres-Verriers.
Annuaire de l'Aube (1888).

BACH, E., BLONDEL, Louis, BOVY, Adrien

La Cathédrale de Lausanne.
Les Monuments d'Art et d'Histoire de la Suisse, vol. 16, Basle (1942).

BACH, E.

Monuments d'Art et d'Histoire.
Vaud II. Les Vitraux de la Cathédrale de Lausanne.
1944, pp. 245-265.

BACHER, Ernst

Die Ornamentscheiben aus Spitz.
Osterreichische Zeitschrift für Kunst und Denkmalpflege, vol. 21
(1967), pp. 191-192.

Die Glasgemälde der Deutschordenskirche in Graz.
In 8e Colloque du Corpus Vitrearum Medii Aevi.
Paris ?, 1972, p. 42.

Zu aktuellen Fragen der Konservierung mittelalterlicher
Glasgemälde.
In Akten des 10 Internationalen Colloquiums des CVMA.
Stuttgart, 1977, pp. 52-53.

BACK, Friedrich

Hessisches Landesmuseum Darmstadt. Kunst-u. historische
Sammlungen. Die Glasmalereien.
Mit 5 Holzchn. von W. Harwerth nach Scheiben aus d.
Ritterstiftskirche in Wimpfen am Neckar.
Darmstadt, 1923.

BACON, Percy C. Haydon

Fifteenth Century Jesse Window at St. Margaret's Church,
Margaretting.
The Essex Review, vol. 27, no. 105 (Jan. 1918), pp. 1-7.

Ancient Stained Glass in Essex.
Transactions of the Essex Archaeological Society, (new series),
vol. 15, 1918-1920 (1921), pp. 230-234.

Fifteenth Century Jesse Window at St. Margaret's Church,
Margaretting.
J.M.G.P., vol. 1, no. 3 (Oct. 1925), pp. 3-11.

Some Stained Glass Windows Executed Within the Past Twenty
Years.
London, 1930.

BADDELEY, St. Clair

A Brief Account of the Stained and Painted Glass at
Toddington House.
Transactions of the Bristol and Gloucestershire Archaeological
Society, vol. 23 (for 1900), pp. 162-192.

The Stained Glass Art of the Fourteenth Century.
Transactions of the Bristol and Gloucestershire Archaeological
Society, vol. 26 (for 1903), pp. 150-161.

The Stained Glass of Prinknash.
Letters to The Times, Dec. 8, 1927, Jan. 26, 1928.

BADERMANN, G.

Die Deutsche Glasmalerei im dreizehnten Jarhundert.
Glashütte, no. 61 (1931), pp. 6-7.

BAESCHLIN, J.H.

Schaffhausen Glasmaler des 16 und 17 Jahrhunderts.
Neujahrsblätter des Kunstvereines in Schaffhausen für 1879.
Schaffhausen, 1880.

(Bagendon Church, Glos.)

(Some glass replaced in the Church.)
Wiltshire and Gloucestershire Standard, Sept. 20, 1924.

BAIGENT, Francis J.

On Ibberton Church, Dorsetshire, and the Painted Glass Remaining
There.
Archaeologia, vol. 48 (1885), pp. 347-354.

BAILEY, George

The Stained Glass at Norbury Manor House.
Transactions of the Derby Archaeological and Natural History
Society, vol. 4 (1882), pp. 152-158
                vol. 5 (1883), pp. 64-68.

On a Painted Glass Window in Morley Church, Derbyshire.
Ibid., vol. 8 (1886), pp. 143-149.

Stained Glass in the Old Commandery at Worcester.
The Antiquary, vol. 23 (1893), pp. 205-206.

BAILLARGEAT, M.

Les Vitraux de la Collegiale Saint-Martin de Montmorency.
Paris et Ile-de-France. Mémoires publiés par la Fédération des
Sociétés Historiques et Archéologiques de Paris et de l'Ile de
France.
t. 7, 8.

BAILLARGEAT, René

L'Eglise Saint-Acceul d'Ecouen.
Bulletin de la Société de l'Histoire de l'Art Francais, 1951,
pp. 52-60.

BAILLET, Auguste

Les Maîtres Verriers à Orleans.
Bulletin Monumental, 1919.

BAILLIE, Thomas and Co.

Concise Account of Some of the Ecclesiastical and Domestic
Painted and Stained Glass Windows, etc. Designed by T.B. and Co.
London, 1875.

BAIN, Joseph

Notes on the East Window of the Choir of Bothwell Church and its
Armorial Shields.
Proceedings of the Society of Antiquaries of Scotland, vol. 8
(1868-1870), pp. 395-403.

Notes on a Piece of Painted Glass Within a Genealogical Tree of
the Family of Stewart.
The Archaeological Journal, vol. 35 (1878), pp. 399-401.

BAKER, Charles Albert

Obituary.
Stained Glass, vol. 31, no. 1 (Spring-Summer, 1936), pp. 32-33.

BAKER, James W.

An Old-Timer.
(On stained-glass firms in the U.S.A. in the late nineteenth
century.)
Stained Glass, vol. 37, no. 4 (Winter, 1942), pp. 127-129.
Reprinted from The Ornamental Glass Bulletin, Sept. 1913.

BAKER, John, and LAMMER, Alfred.
  English Stained Glass. With an Introduction by Herbert Read.
  London, 1960.
  Reviewed by Jean Lafond in The Archaeological Journal, vol. cxvi
  (for 1959), pp. 274-276.
  Reviewed in Oxoniensia, vol. xxvi/vii for 1961/1962 (1963), pp.
  353-354.

  Reviewed by EDWARDS, Carl.
  The Studio, vol. 160 (1960), pp. 229-232.

  Reviewed by KIRBY, H.T.
  in J.M.G.P., vol. 13, no. 1 (1960), pp. 375-376,
  and also in The Connoisseur, vol. 147 (Feb. 1961), pp. 48-49.
  Reviewed in Stained Glass, vol. 56, no. 2 (Summer, 1961), p. 35.

BAKER, John, with LAMMER, Alfred
  English Stained Glass of the Medieval Period.
  London, 1978.

BAKER, Stanley
  Salisbury Glass. An Act of Vandalism in 1790.
  (Letter to the Editor) The Times, Nov. 3, 1932.

  Digging for Salisbury's Lost Cathedral Glass.
  Illustrated London News, Dec. 3, 1932.

BALET, Leo
  Schwäbische Glasmalerei.
  Stuttgart, 1912.

BALL, H.W.
  Notes on William Fowler and his Work.
  North Lincolnshire Monthly Illustrated Journal, April, 1869.

BALL, W.E.
  Stained-Glass Windows of Nettlestead Church.
  Archaeologia Cantiana, vol. 28   (1909), pp. 157-249.

BALLANTINE, James
  Treatise on Painted Glass Showing its Applicability to Every
  Style of Architecture.
  London, 1845.
  Translated by GRAUSS, H.:
  Gefärbtes Glas in seiner Anwendung auf alle Baustyle . . . .
  Weimar, 1847.
  Reviewed in The Ecclesiologist, vol. 5 (1846), pp. 194-195.

  A Short History of Church Stained Glass.
  Transactions of the Scottish Ecclesiological Society, vol. 3,
  part 3, 1911-1912 (1912), pp. 347-354.

(Baltimore)
  Five Memorial Windows in Grace Church, Baltimore.
  Baltimore, 1888.

BALTRUSAITIS, J.
  Le Moyen Age Fantastique: Antiquités et Exotismes dans l'Art
  Gothique.
  Paris, 1955.

BAMPS, C.
  Les Vitraux de l'Ancienne Eglise Abbatiale des Dames Nobles de
  Herckenrode.
  Bulletin des Commissions Royales d'Art et d'Archéologie, no. 13
  (1874).

  Débris des Vitraux Limbourgeois du Début au XVIIe Siècle
  Conservés au Musée de Cluny à Paris.
  Ancien Pays de Looz, nos. 8, 9. 10 (1905).

BANCEL, E.M.
  Jehan Perreal. Recherches sur sa Vie et son Oeuvre.
  Paris, 1885.
  (Glass at Brou.)

BANNISTER, W.G.
  Stained and Painted Glass in the Windows of Tewkesbury Abbey
  Church.
  Tewkesbury (n.d.).

(Banwell Church)
  Stained Glass. By Notsa.
  (Request for an account of some medallions, and a mention of
  their having been moved.)
  Notes and Queries, 2nd series, vol. 10 (Oct. 27, 1860), p. 326.

BARBER, E.
  The Ancient Glass in the Church of St. Mary-on-the-Hill.
  Journal of Architectural and Archaeological History for the
  County and City of Chester, new series, vol. 10 (1904), pp. 53-56.

BARBIER DE MONTAULT, Xavier
  Le Vitrail de la Crucifixion à la Cathédrale de Poitiers.
  Bulletin Monumental, vol. 51 (1885), pp. 17-45, 141-168.

  L'Arbre de Jessé et la Vie du Christ. Vitraux du XIIIe Siècle
  à la Cathédrale d'Angers.
  Angers, 1887.

(Bardwell Church, Suffolk)
  Painted Glass at Bardwell Church.
  The Gentleman's Magazine, vol. 95, part 2 (1825), pp. 21-22.

BARFF, Frederick S.
  On Silicates, Silicides, Glass and Glass Painting.
  Journal of the Society of Arts, vol. 20 (1872), pp. 765, 855.

BARILIFT, Louis
  Some General Views on the Present State of French Glass
  Craftsmen.
  (Translated by HUNTER, Gertrude F.)
  Stained Glass, vol. 42, no. 3, (Autumn, 1947).

BARKER, H.R.
  West Suffolk Illustrated.
  Bury St. Edmunds, 1907.

BARKER, W.R.
  St. Mark's or the Mayor's Chapel, Bristol.
  Bristol, 1892.

BARNARD, E.A.B.
  Church and Rectory of Buckland.
  Transactions of the Bristol and Gloucester Archaeological
  Society, vol. 45 (for 1923).
  (Glass, pp. 77-80.)

BARNARD, Jabez and Son
  Diaphanie for Church, Hall and other Windows. With Instructions
  for Transparency Painting.
  (8th ed.) London, 1865.

  Designs of Different Styles for Windows to be Executed in
  Diaphanie by the Improved Transparency Process.
  London, n.d. (c. 1874).

BARNARD, William
  Stained Windows and Painted Glass by the Transparency Process
  or Diaphanie.
  (2nd ed.) London, 1863.

BARNES, W.M.

    (Glass at Bradford Peverell.)

    The Archaeological Journal, vol. 48 (1891), p. 434.

(Barnwell Church)

    Barnwell Church, Northamptonshire: Glass.

    (Grant towards cleaning and re-leading a window.)

    The Pilgrim Trust, 43rd Annual Report (1973), p. 15.

BARRAUD, Abbé

    Descriptions des Vitraux de la Cathédrale de St. Etienne de
    Beauvais. (3 parts.)

    Beauvais, 1850, 1855, 1856.

    Vitraux des Chapelles de la Cathédrale de Beauvais.

    Mémoires de la Société Académique de l'Oise, vol. 3 (1856),
    pp. 50-86.

BARRAULT, A.

    L'Eglise Saint-Aspais de Melun.

    Meaux, 1964.

BARREAU, J.L.

    Guide au Voyageur dans la Ville de Bourges et Specialement
    dans la Cathédrale.

    Bourges, 1863.

BARRELET, James

    La Verrière en France.

    Paris, 1953.

BARRITT, Thomas

    (Glass from Healey Hall, Lancashire. Recently bought in the
    Low Countries.)

    The Gentleman's Magazine, vol. 61, part 2 (1791), p. 697.

    (Two more roundels from Healey Hall.)

    The Gentleman's Magazine, vol. 63, part 1 (1793), p. 225.

BARROW, John

    Dictionarium Polygraphicum, or the Whole Body of Arts Regularly
    Digested.

    London, 1735.

    (Article on glass-painting.)

BARTHÉLEMY, A. de

    Lettre sur les Anciens Peintres sur Verre de Tréguier.

    Bulletin Monumental, vol. 13 (1847), pp. 577.

    Notice sur Quelques Peintres-Verriers de Bretagne.

    Bulletin de l'Archaeologique Association Bretonne (1849).

BARTHELEMY, Edmond Marie de

    Les Vitraux des Eglises de Châlons-sur-Marne. Etude et
    Description.

    Travaux de l'Académie Imperiale, Reims, vol. 26 (1856-1857), p. 48.

BARWICK, J.

    Mercurius Belgieus, or a briefe chronologie of the battails,
    sieges, conflicts . . . of this warre, to the 25th of March,
    1646.

    Oxford, 1646 (also 1647, 1685).

    (Also includes Bruno Ryves' Mercurius Rusticus.)

(Basel Cathedral)

    Ancient Painted Windows of the Early Part of the Sixteenth
    Century, Originally Forming a Portion of one of the Windows in
    the Cathedral of Basle.

    London, n.d.

BASSERMANN-JORDAN, Ernst von

    Die Antiken Gläser des Herrn Oskar Zettler zu München.

    Munich, 1908.

BASSUK, Bertram L.

    Observations in the Light of Stained Glass in Synagogue
    Architecture.

    Stained Glass, vol. 58, no. 1 (Spring, 1963), pp. 7-19.

BATES, Cadwallader John

    The Armorial Glass in the Windows of Montacute House.

    Proceedings of the Somersetshire Archaeological and Natural
    History Society, vol. 32 (for 1886), 1887, part 2, pp. 90-111.

BATES, William

    Fairford Windows.

    Notes and Queries, 4th series, vol. 2 (Oct. 10, 1868), pp.
    pp. 352-354.

BATHURST, W.R.S.

    The City Parish Church of St. Stephen, Bristol.

    Gloucester, 1958.

    Glass, pp. 17-19.

BATISSIER, Louis

    Histoire du Verre et des Vitraux Peints.

    Le Cabinet de l'Amateur et de l'Antiquité, no. 2 (1843), pp.
    49-128.

    Des Procédés de la Peinture sur Verre, et des Ouvrages relatifs
    a l'Art de la Verrerie.

    Ibid., pp. 531-539.

    Histoire de l'Art Monumental dans l'Antiquité et au Moyen Age,
    Suivie d'un Traité de la Peinture sur Verre.

    Paris, 1845.

BATT, N.G. and NEW, H.

    Report on the Portraits of the Abbots of Evesham in the Windows
    of Preston-on-Stour Church.

    Journal of the British Archaeological Association, vol. 32
    (1876), pp. 502-503.

BATTEN, H.H.

    Acorn Bank, Temple Sowerby.

    (Description of Seventeenth Century Armorial Glass.)

    Transactions of the Cumberland and Westmorland Antiquarian and
    Archaeological Society, new series, vol. 9 (1909), p. 163.

BATTERSBY, R. St. John

    Heraldry of the Churches of Wiltshire.

    The Wiltshire Archaeological and Natural History Magazine, no.
    150 (June, 1929), pp. 360-371; no. 151 (Dec. 1929), pp. 418-428;
    no. 153 (Dec. 1930), pp. 147-155.

BAUDOT, Marcel, with DUBUC, René

    Les Verrières de la Cathédrale d'Evreux: Cinq Siècles d'Histoire.

    Nouvelles de l'Eure, no. 27, Evreux, pp. 26-55.

BAUDOT, Marcel, with THIRION, Jacques

    Vitraux et Boiseries de la Cathédrale d'Evreux.

    (Numero Special de Nouvelles de l'Eure.)

    Evreux, 1967.

    Reviewed by GRODECKI, Louis, in Revue de l'Art, no. 10 (1970), p. 98.

BAUDOT, Marcel

    Les Vitraux de la Cathédrale d'Evreux.

    (An exchange of articles with GRODECKI, Louis, and DUBUC, René.)

    Bulletin Monumental, no. 126 (1968), pp. 65-71.

BAUDOT, Marcel, with LAFOND, Jean

    Eglises et Vitraux de la region de Pont-Audemer.

    Nouvelles de l'Eure, Evreux (1969).

    Reviewed by GRODECKI, Louis, Revue de l'Art, no. 10 (1970), p. 98.

BAUDRY, F. Paul
L'Eglise Paroissiale de St. Vincent de Rouen.
Reprinted from Gazette de Normandie, Rouen, 1875.

L'Eglise Paroissiale de Saint-Patrice de Rouen. Description
des Vitraux.
Rouen, 1896 (2nd ed.)

BAUER, W.P.
Untersuchung Nr. 1. Analysen der Malfarben auf Glasproben des
Chorfensters Nord II der Stiftskirche in Heiligenkreuz.
Österreichische Zeitschrift für Kunst und Denkmalpflege, vol. 21
(1967), pp. 201-202.

Untersuchung Nr. 2. Analysen von Acht Glasproben des Chorfensters
Nord II der Stiftskirche in Heiligenkreuz.
Ibid., pp. 203-205.

Der Einfluss von Reinigungsmethoden auf die Glasoberfläche.
(Actes du IXe Colloque du CVMA, Paris, Sept. 8-12, 1975.)
Verres et Réfractaires, Numéro Spécial, vol. 30, no. 1 (Jan.-
Feb. 1976), pp. 62-64.

(Baum, Herman Josef)
Herman Josef Baum, a Versatile Young Artist.
Das Munster (Nov.-Dec., 1969).

BAUX, J.
Recherches Historiques et Archéologiques sur l'Eglise de Brou.
Paris, Lyons and Bourg, 1844.

BAYEUX ——.
Les Vitraux de l'Eglise de Brienne-le-Château.
69e Congrès Archéologique (Troyes), Troyes (1903), p. 350.

BAYLESS, J.H.
Jewels of Light, Stained Glass at Washington Cathedral.
Washington, 1975.

BAYLEY, T.D.S. and STEER, Francis W.
Glass at Stanley Hall, Pebmarsh (Essex).
J.M.G.P., vol. 12, no. 3 (1958), pp. 183-190.

(W. Bazeley Collection)
Stained Glass. By R.B.
(Mentioning that the Rev. W. Bazeley of Matson, Gloucs., has a
fine collection of ancient glass.)
Notes and Queries, 8th series, vol. 12 (July 31, 1897), p. 92.

BEACH, G.C.
Short Popular History of the Churches and Parish of St. Martin-
cum-Gregory, York.
York, 1927.

BEAMAN, Richard B.
Vitrail Reconsidered.
(A criticism of some of Viollet-le-Duc's theories.)
Stained Glass, vol. 62, no. 3 (Autumn, 1967), pp. 8-11.

BEARD, Charles R.
Armorial Window, Pickering, Yorkshire.
The Connoisseur, vol. 103 (March,1939), p. 11.

BEATTIE, E.H.
The Parish Church of St. Mary-the-Virgin, Ross.
Ross-on-Wye (n.d.)
(Glass, pp. 6-8 [unnumbered])

BEAUDRY, Yvonne
A New Demand for an Old Art.
(On the Heinigke firm, with some account of its history.)
Stained Glass, vol. 47, no. 1 (Spring, 1952), pp. 16-23.

BEAUMONT, William, and RYLANDS, John
An Attempt to Identify the Arms Formerly Existing in the Window
of the Parish Church and Austin Friary at Warrington.
Warrington, 1878.

BEAUREPAIRE, Eugène de
Les Vitraux Peints de la Cathédrale de Bourges.
Bulletin Monumental, vol. 62 (1897), pp. 355-396.

Les Vitraux Peints de l'Eglise Abbatiale de Bourges.
Caen, 1898.

BEAZELEY, Alex
Jesse Window.
Notes and Queries, 8th series, vol. 8 (July 27, 1895), p. 75.

BECK ——.
Beitrage zur Geschichte des Maschenbaus.
Berlin, 1900.

BECK, Elizabeth N.
The Heritage of Stained Glass.
Stained Glass, vol. 48, no. 4 (Winter, 1953-1954), pp. 134-140.

BECKMANN, Johann
Beyträge zur Geschichte der Erfindungen.
(5 vols.) Leipzig, 1782-1805.
Partial English translation, 3 vols., London, 1797.
4th ed. revised and enlarged by FRANCIS, W., and GRIFFITH, J.W.,
2 vols., London, 1846 (Bohn's Lib.).

BECKSMANN, Rüdiger
Die architektonische Rahmung des hochgotischen Bildfensters.
Untersuchung zur oberrheinischen Glasmalerei von 1250 bis 1350.
Berlin, 1967.
Reviewed by BLOCK-WILD, Christiane, Bulletin Monumental, no. 127
(1969), pp. 56-57,
and by CAVINESS, M.H., Art Bulletin, vol. 52 (1970), pp. 432-434.

Das Hausbuchmeisterproblem in der mittelrheinischen Glasmalerei.
Pantheon, 1968, pp. 352-367.

Die ehemalige Farbverglasung der Mauritiusrotunde des
Konstanzer Münsters. Erkenntnisse aus einer historisierenden
Restaurierung.
Jahrbuch der staatlichen Kunstsammlungen in Baden-Württemburg.
Bd. 5, (1968), pp. 57-82.

Das Jesse-Fenster aus dem spätromanischen Chor des Freiburger
Münsters. Ein Beitrag zur Kunst um 1200.
Zeitschrift des deutschen Vereins für Kunstwissenschaft.
Bd. 23, Heft 1/4. Berlin, 1969, pp. 8-43.

Das Schwarzacher Köpfchen. Ein ottonischer Glasmalereifund.
Kunstchronik, I (1970), pp. 3-9.

Bericht über die Arbeitsstelle CVMA in Stuttgart.
In 7^e Colloque du Corpus Vitrearum Medii Aevi.
Florence?, 1970, pp. 31-32.

Zur Werkstattgemeinschaft Peter Hemmels in den Jahren 1477-1481.
Pantheon, vol. 28, 3 (1970), pp. 183-197.

The Stylistic Problems of the Freiburg Jesse Window.
In The Year 1200, A Symposium.
New York, 1975, pp. 361-372.

(With WAETZOLDT, S., and GAMBKE, G.)
Vitrea Dedicata: Das Stifterbild in der deutschen Glasmalerei
des Mittelalters.
Berlin, 1975.

9

BECKSMANN, Rüdiger (Contd.)

Zum Werk des Walburger Meisters von 1461.
Beiträge zur Kunst des Mittelalters. Festschrift für Hans
Wentzel.
Berlin, 1975.

(Glass from Münster museum.)
Die Zeit der Staufer.
(Exhibition catalogue.)
Stuttgart, 1977, t.1. pp. 278-279, t.2. p. 202.

Vorwort.
In Akten des 10. Internationalen Colloquiums des CVMA.
Stuttgart, 1977, pp. 5-6.

Architekturbedingte Wandlungen in der deutschen Glasmalerei
des 13.Jahrhunderts.
Ibid., pp. 19-20.

BEEBY, W.T.

Ancient Painted Glass in the Parish Church of St. John,
Cirencester.
Transactions of the Bristol and Gloucestershire Archaeological
Society, vol. 39, (for 1916), pp. 201-231.

BEEH-LUSTENBERGER, Suzanne

Glasmalerei um 800-1900 im Hessischen Landesmuseum in Darmstadt
Frankfort-am-Main, 1967.
Reviewed by GRODECKI, Louis, Revue de l'Art, no. 10 (1970), p. 98.

BEER, Ellen J.

Die Rose der Kathedrale von Lausanne und der kosmologische
Bilderkreis des Mittelalters.
Berne, 1952.
Reviewed by AUBERT, Marcel, Bulletin Monumental, vol. iii (1953)
pp. 202-203.

Die Glasmalereien der Schweiz vom 12. bis zum Beginn des 14.
Jahrhunderts.
(CVMA, Switzerland, vol. 1.)
Basel, 1956.
Reviewed by LAFOND, Jean, The Archaeological Journal, vol. 113
(for 1956), pp. 170-172.
Reviewed by AUBERT, Marcel, Bulletin Monumental, no. 114 (1956),
pp. 143-149.
Reviewed by GRODECKI, Louis, Gazette des Beaux-Arts (Oct. 1958),
pp. 252-255.

Wiedergefundene Fragmente aus der Chorverglasung der Zisterze
Hautrive.
CIBA-Blätter (Dec.,1958), pp. 25-29.

Medaeval Swiss Stained Glass. An Artistic Interplay that
Transcended Frontiers.
The Connoisseur, vol. 152 (1963), pp. 94-101.

Die Bedeutung der Farbe in der Gotischen Glasmalerei.
Palette, 20, pp. 3-10.
Basel, 1965.

Die Glasmalereien der Schweiz aus dem 14. und 15. Jahrhundert
ohne Königsfelden und Berner Münsterchor.
(CVMA, Switzerland, III.)
Basel, 1965.
Reviewed by GRODECKI, Louis, Bulletin Monumental, no. 125 (1967),
pp. 452-455.

Le Vitrail Médiéval à l'Abbatiale de Payerne.
L'Abbatiale de Payerne (Bibliothèque Historique Vaudoise),
vol. 39.
Lausanne, 1966.
Pp. 189-202.

Nouvelles Réflexions sur l'Image du Monde dans la Cathédrale de
Lausanne.
Revue de l'Art, no. 10 (1970), pp. 57-62.

BEETS, Nicolas

Dirick Jacobsz Vellert, Schilder van Antwerpen.
Onze Kunst, vol. 10 (1906), p. 137-
              11 (1907), p. 109-
              13 (1908), p. 165-
              22 (1912), p. 133-
              40 (1922), p. 85-
French version:
Art Flamand et Hollandais, vol. 6 (1906), p. 133-
                           7 (1907), p. 105-
                          10 (1908), p. 89-
                          12 (1912), p. 129-
La Revue de l'Art, vol. 26 (1925), p. 116-

Dirick Vellert and the Windows in King's College Chapel.
Burlington Magazine, vol. 12 (Oct., 1907-March, 1908), pp. 33-39.

(With JACOBSZ, Dirick
Vellert, Peintre d'Anvers.
L'Art Flamand et Hollandais, vol. 26 (1925), pp. 131-139.

BÉGIN, E.A.

Histoire de la Cathédrale de Metz.
2 vols., Metz, 1843.

BÉGULE, Lucien

Monographie de la Cathédrale de Lyon.
Lyon, 1880.

(With BERTAUX, Emile)
Un Vitrail Profane du XVe Siècle. (Provenant de Villefranche-
sur-Saone.)
Gazette des Beaux-Arts (Nov., 1906), pp. 407-416.

Les Vitraux du Moyen Age et de la Renaissance de la Région
Lyonnaise.
Lyon, 1911.

(Beine)

Les Vitraux de l'Eglise de Beine. By G.J.
Céramique et Verrerie, 46th year, no. 773, (Nov. 25, 1926),
pp. 450-452.

(Belgium)

L'Art Ancien Belge.
Brussels, 1882.

BELL, C. Farrar

Heraldry in the Great West Window, Exeter Cathedral.
The Coat of Arms, vol. 2, no. 13 (Jan. 1953), pp. 180-182.

BELL, J. Clement

The Introduction of the Glazier's Diamond.
(Letter to the Editor.)
J.M.G.P., vol. 1, no. 2 (Apr., 1925), pp. 52-53.

Decoration in Opus Sectile for Grangetown Cathedral, Demerara.
The Builder (June 5, 1925).

Ancient Stained Glass of Alsace.
J.M.G.P., vol. 4, no. 4 (Oct., 1932), pp. 163-170.

W.E. Chance and the Revived Manufacture of Coloured Glass.
(Letter to the Editor.)
J.M.G.P., vol. 6, no. 1 (Apr., 1935), p. 58.

BELL, M.C. Farrar
Reginald Bell. (Obituary.)
J.M.G.P., vol. 10, no. 4 (1951), pp. 214-215.

Stained Glass Windows: the Problems of Design.
The Studio, vol. 148 (1954), pp. 48-51.

Windows of the Twelfth and Thirteenth Centuries.
J.M.G.P., vol. 14, no. 5 (1970-1971), pp. 255-258.

BELL, Reginald
Review of 'The Art and Craft of Stained Glass' by E.W. TWINING.
J.M.G.P., vol. 3, no. 1 (Apr., 1929), pp. 43-44.

Stained Glass Windows.
Church of England Newspaper (Supplement), vol. 37, no. 1886,
(Apr. 11, 1930).

Copyright Regarding Sketches for Stained Glass.
(Letter to the Editor.)
J.M.G.P., vol. 3, no. 3 (Apr., 1930), pp. 146-148.

(Bell, Reginald)
Reginald Bell, 1886-1950. Artist in Stained Glass.
The Studio, vol. 141 (1951), pp. 148-151.

Obituary, by BELL, M.C. Farrar.
J.M.G.P., vol. 10, no. 4 (1951), pp. 214-215.

BELL, R. Anning
A Lecture on Stained Glass.
London, n.d. (1922).

Design for Two-Light Window. (Coloured plate only.)
The Studio (June, 1926).

Obituary.
J.M.G.P., vol. 5, no. 3 (Apr. 1934), pp. 153-154.

BELL AND GOULD (OF YORK)
Selections of Painted and Stained Glass from York.
Weale's Quarterly Papers on Architecture, no. 2 (1844), pp. 33-37.

BELTJES, P.J.W.
De Culemborgse 'Glaesmaker' Antonis Evertszoon.
In Jaarboek van Hoogstraten's Oudheidkundige Kring, vol. 16.
Hoogstraten, 1948.

BEMDEN, Yvette van den
L'Influence Italienne dans le Vitrail Belge.
In 7e Colloque du Corpus Vitrearum Medii Aevi.
Florence ?, 1970, p. 30.

Review of WAYMENT, CVMA, England, I.
Art Bulletin, vol. 55 (Dec. 1973), pp. 635-636.

Contemporary Stained Glass in Belgium.
J.M.G.P., vol. 15, no. 3 (1974-1975), pp. 23-33.

BENEZÉ, Emil.
Bossanyi Ervin.
Magyar Imparmüvészet, 33, (1930), pp. 99-105.

BENSON, George
Handbook to the Cathedral Church of St. Peter York . . . Being
Notes on the Architecture, Stained Glass, Shields and
Monuments.
York, 1893. (Several subsequent edns.)

The Ancient Painted Glass Windows in the Minster and Churches
of the City of York.
York, 1915.

The Old Painted Glass in the Parish Churches of York.
Journal of the Royal Society of British Architects, 3rd series,
vol. 21 (1916), pp. 10- .

BENSON, George (Contd.)
John Browne, 1793-1877, Artist and the Historian of York Minster.
Annual Report of the Yorkshire Philosophical Society for 1917.
York, 1918.

A Delineator of Ancient Painted Glass, John Browne of York,
1793-1877.
J.M.G.P., vol. 1, no. 5 (Oct., 1926), pp. 12-14.

BENTLEY, William
Notes on the Musical Instruments Figured in the Windows of the
Beauchamp Chapel, St. Mary's Church, Warwick.
Transactions of the Birmingham Archaeological Society, vol. 53
for 1928 (1931), pp. 167-172.
Reprinted Oxford, 1931.

BENTON, G. Montague, and LEWER, H.W.
A Fifteenth Century Panel of Stained Glass Described as
"Probably a Portrait of Richard III".
Transactions of the Essex Archaeological Society, new series,
vol. 16, 1921-1923 (1923), pp. 298-300.

BENTON, G. Montague
Armorial Glass Formerly in Clavering Church.
Transactions of the Essex Archaeological Society, new series,
vol. 17, 1923-1925 (1926), p. 50.

Heraldic Glass Formerly at Bicknacre Priory.
Transactions of the Essex Archaeological Society, new series,
vol. 19, 1927-1930 (1930), pp. 48-50.

BERGHOFF, Guy
Background to the Principles of Color Dynamics.
Stained Glass, vol. 41, no. 2, (Summer, 1946), pp. 45-53.

BERLEPSCH, H.E. Von
Die Glasgemälde im Kreuzgange des Ehemaligen Klosters Wettingen.
Kunstgewerbebl (Munich), 1886.

Die Entwicklung der Glasmalerei in der Schweiz.
Zeitschrift für Kunstgewerbevereins, (Munich), 1886.

(Berlin Museum)
Vorbildliche Glasmalereien aus dem späten Mittelalter und der
Renaissancezeit.
Berlin, 1911-1915.

Glasgemälde des Königlichen
Kunstgewerbemuseums in Berlin.
2 vols., Berlin, 1913.

BERNARD, Abbé
Notice Descriptive et Historique sur les Vitraux de l'Eglise
de l'Huître (Haute Marne).
Paris, 1897.

BERNDT, Ruth Rose
A Stained Glass Workshop in Guatemala.
Stained Glass, vol. 40, no. 4, (Winter, 1945), pp. 109-112.

BERNIER, Rosamond
Matisse Designs a New Church.
Vogue, Feb. 15, 1949.

BERRY, Warren T.
Buried Treasure.
(Nineteenth-century glass excavated on the site of the Sandwich
(Mass.) glass factory.)
Stained Glass, vol. 29, no. 3 (Autumn, 1934), pp. 82-85.

BERTHELOT, M.P.E.

    Histoire des Sciences et la Chimie au Moyen-Âge.
    3 vols., Paris, 1893.

BERTRAM, R.J.S., HAMILTON THOMPSON, A., HUNTER BLAIR, C.H.
    Notes on Old Glass in St. John's Church, Newcastle-upon-Tyne.
    Archaeologia Aeliana, vol. 19, third series (1922), pp. 35-49.

BERTRAND, L.

    Peinture sur Verre. Notice sur les Travaux de Vincent Larcher . . .
    et Martin Hermannowske.
    Troyes, 1845.

BESBORODOV, M.A.

    Comptes Rendus (Doklady) de l'Académie des Sciences de l'URSS.
    (Deals with Lomonosov's experiments in glassmaking at about 1750.)
    Lenningrad, n.d.

BESNARD, A.

    L'Eglise de Saint-Germer . . .
    Paris, 1913.

BEST, Harold

    The Abbey Church of St. Peter and St. Paul, Dorchester, Oxon.
    Huntingdon, n.d.
    (Glass, pp. 7-11.)

BÉTHUNE, Baron de

    Quelques notes sur l'art de la Vitrerie Selon la Tradition
    Médiévale.
    Bulletin des Commissions Royales d'Art et d'Archeologie (1900,
    1902, 1905).

BETJEMAN, John

    Report of Speech to Annual Dinner of British Society of Master
    Glass-Painters.
    J.M.G.P., vol. 12, no. 1 (1956), pp. 63-64.

BETTEMBOURG, Jean-Marie

    Nettoyage par Voie Chimique et par Ultra-sons des Verres de
    Vitraux.
    In 8e Colloque du Corpus Vitrearum Medii Aevi.
    Paris ?, 1972, p. 47.

    Essais de Collage des Vitraux Brisés.
    Ibid., p. 53.

    Composition et Altération des Verres de Vitraux Anciens.
    (Actes du IXe Colloque du CMVA, Paris, Sept. 8-12, 1975.)
    Verres et Réfractaires, numéro spécial, vol. 30, no. 1 (Jan.-
    Feb., 1976), pp. 36-42.

    (With PERROT, Françoise.)
    La Restauration des Vitraux de la Façade Occidentale de la
    Cathédrale de Chartres.
    Verres et Réfractaires, numero special, 1976.

    Problèmes de la Conservation des Vitraux de la Façade de la
    Cathédrale de Chartres.
    In Les Monuments Historiques de la France, no. 1 (1977),
    pp. 7-13.

    Les Problèmes de la Conservation des Vitraux de la Cathédrale
    de Bourges.
    In Akten des 10. Internationalen Colloquiums des CVMA.
    Stuttgart, 1977, p. 48.

    Degrédation et Conservation des Vitraux Anciens.
    Les Dossiers de l'Archéologie, no. 26 (Jan.-Feb., 1978), pp.
    102-111.

BEUCHER, Monique

    Les Verrières du Choeur d'Evreux. L'influence de Paris au
    XIVe Siècle.
    Les Dossiers de l'Archéologie, no. 26 (Jan.-Feb., 1978), pp.
    63-75.

(Beverley Minster)

    Beverley Minster Glass.
    (An appeal for money to remove the East window for safety.)
    The Yorkshire Archaeological Journal, vol. 35 (1943), p. 6

BEYER, Victor

    Eine Strassburgische Glasmaler-Werkstätte des 13. Jahrhunderts
    und Ihre Beziehungen zu den Rheinlanden.
    Saarbrucker Hefte, no. 4 (1956).
    Reviewed in Bulletin Monumental, no. 115 (1957), pp. 228-229.

    (Les vitraux)
    In La Cathédrale de Strasbourg
    By HAUG, H., AHNE , P., WILL, R., REIGER, T., BEYER, V.
    Strasbourg, 1957.

    La Dépose de Vitraux de l'Eglise des Dominicains et la Verrière
    de la Vie de Saint Barthélemy.
    Cahiers Alsaciens d'Archéologie, d'Art et d'Histoire, I (1957),
    pp. 143-162.
    Reviewed in Bulletin Monumental, no. 116 (1958), p. 154.

    Les Roses de Réseau des Bas-côtés de la Cathédrale et l'Oeuvre
    d'un Atelier Strasbourgeois du XIIIe Siècle.
    Bulletin de la Societé des Amis de la Cathédrale de Strasbourg,
    no. 7 (1960).

    Un Atelier Strasbourgeois du XIIIe Siècle.
    Bulletin de la Societé des Amis de la Cathédrale de Strasbourg
    (1960), pp. 63-96.

    Les Vitraux de la Cathédrale de Strasbourg.
    (With AHNE, Paul.)
    Strasbourg, 1960.
    Reviewed by AUBERT, Marcel, Bulletin Monumental, vol. 118 (1960)
    p. 237.

    Offenbarung der Farbe.
    Ettal, 1963.
    Translated as Stained Glass Windows
    Ed. RICE, David Talbot, Tr. HERZFELD, M. von, and GAZE, R.
    Edinburgh and London, 1964.
    Reviewed by KIRBY, H.T., J.M.G.P., vol. 14, no. 2 (1965), p. 136.

    Les Vitraux des Musées de Strasbourg.
    Strasbourg, 1965.

    La Verrière du Jugement Dernier à l'Ancienne Eglise des
    Dominicains de Strasbourg.
    Hommage à Hans Haug. Cahiers Alsaciens d'Archéologie, d'Art
    et d'Histoire (1967), pp. 33-48.

    Das Strassburger Münster.
    Augsburg, 1969.

    La Cathedrale de Strasbourg.
    Paris, 1970.

    Un Vitrail du XVIe Siècle à la Cathédrale de Strasbourg.
    Revue de l'Art, no. 10 (1970), pp. 73-76.

    Les Vitraux du Collatéral Sud de la Cathédrale de Strasbourg.
    Cahiers Alsaciens d'Archéologie, d'Art et d'Histoire (1971),
    pp. 123-134.

    Les Roses de l'Ancien et du Nouveau Testament au Transept de
    la Cathédrale de Strasbourg.
    In 8e Colloque du Corpus Vitrearum Medii Aevi.
    Paris ?, 1972, p. 45.

    Le Zackenstil à Strasbourg.
    In Akten des 10. Internationalen Colloquiums des CVMA.
    Stuttgart, 1977, pp. 24-25.

(Bibliography of Stained Glass)

    Proc. Antiq. Ges.(Zurich), no. 22 (1837), pp. 259-

    Indicateur d'Antiquités Suisses (1900), pp. 69-

    A Brief Annotated Bibliography of Stained Glass.
    Liturgical Arts, vol. 6, 2nd quarter (1937).

    (Library of Books on Stained Glass.)
    (Books in the Library of the Society of Master Glass-Painters
    and some in the R.I.B.A.)
    J.M.G.P., vol. 11, no. 3 (1954), pp. 178-179.
    J.M.G.P., vol. 12, no. 2 (1957), p. 148.

    J.M.G.P., vol. 12, no. 3 (1958), p. 231.

BIBOLET, Françoise
    Les Vitraux de Saint-Martin-ès-Vignes.
    Troyes, 1959.
    Reviewed by AUBERT, Marcel, Bulletin Monumental, no. 117
    (1959), p. 242.

BICKERSTETH Julian
    New Stained Glass in the Cathedral.
    (The Bossanyi Windows.)
    32nd Annual Report of the Friends of Canterbury Cathedral
    (1959), pp. 47-49.

(Bicton Church, Devon)
    Bicton Church. By L.A.G.
    Exeter, 1850.

BIDAUT, Jacques
    L'Eglise Sainte-Radegonde de Poitiers.
    Congrès Archéologique, 109 (1951), pp. 114-

BIDET, Alfred
    Brou.
    Fontenay-le-Comte, n.d. (? 1959).

BIELENBERG, Fred
    Architektur und Glasmalerei.
    Diamant, 52nd year, no. 2 (Jan. 11, 1930).

BIGLAND, R.
    An Account of the Parish of Fairford, with a Description of
    the Stained Glass in the Church.
    London, 1791.

BILLINGTON, Tom
    The Parish Church of St. Mark, Worsley. A Souvenir Handbook.
    (Possible South German glass, pp. 14-18.)
    n.d. (1954), n.p.

BILSON, John
    Gilling Castle.
    Yorkshire Archaeological Journal, vol. 19 (1907).
    (Glass, pp. 149-170.)

    Gilling Castle. Stained Glass.
    The Archaeological Journal, vol. 19 (1907), pp. 149-170.

    Gilling Castle, Glass.
    Yorkshire Archaeological Journal, vol. 26 (1922), pp. 307-308.

BINDER, R., LIEB, N., ROTH, T.
    Der Dom zu Augsburg.
    Augsburg, 1965.

BINGLEY, A.H.
    The Armorial Window at Cranleigh Church.
    Surrey Archaeological Collections, vol. 39.

BINNALL, P.B.G.
    William Fowler, Artist and Antiquary.
    J.M.G.P., vol. 2, no. 4 (Oct. 1928), pp. 176-182.

    Early Painted Glass in Messingham Church.
    J.M.G.P., vol. 4, no. 1 (Apr., 1931), pp. 14-16.

    The Remaining Painted Glass in Tattershall Church,
    Lincolnshire.
    J.M.G.P., vol. 7, no. 2 (Apr., 1938), pp. 80-85.

    The East Window of Redbourne Church, Lincolnshire.
    (With a technical note by KING, Dennis.)
    J.M.G.P., vol. 13, no. 2 (1961), pp. 408-410.

    The Collegiate Church of the Holy Trinity, Tattershall,
    Lincolnshire.
    Gloucester, 1962.

    The Nineteenth Century Stained Glass in Lincoln Minster.
    Lincoln, 1966.

    Notes on Victorian Stained Glass in Devon.
    Devon and Cornwall Notes and Queries, vol. 31 (1968-1970),
    pp. 112-115.

    The Adelaide Memorial Window in Worcester Cathedral.
    J.M.G.P., vol. 15, no. 2 (1973-1974), pp. 42-45.

BIRCH, G.H.
    St. Margaret's. Westminster.
    Transactions of the St. Paul's Ecclesiological Society,
    vol. 2 (1886-1890).
    (The East window, pp. 108-109.)

BIRCH, Walter de Gray
    The Lady Anne Percy's Portrait in Stained Glass at Long
    Melford.
    Journal of the British Archaeological Association, vol. 40
    (1884), pp. 400-408.

    The Legendary Life of St. Nicholas.
    Ibid, vol. 42 (1886), pp. 185-201.
          vol. 44 (1888), pp. 222-234.

BIRGLIN, M.E.
    Les Vitraux de M. Maréchal à la Chapelle du Sacré-Coeur de la
    Cathédrale de Metz.
    Mémoires de la Société des Lettres et des Sciences, Bar-le-Duc,
    no. 7 (1877), pp. 133-139.

(Birkin, St. Mary's Church)
    (York Glaziers Trust restore glass from St. Mary's, Birkin.)
    Yorkshire Evening Press, August 27,1977.

Birmingham Glass Painters before Pugin.
    English Illustrated Magazine, London (1886).

(Birmingham, Glass Painters of)
    J.M.G.P., vol. 2, no. 2 (Oct., 1927), part 1, pp. 63-71.
    J.M.G.P., vol. 2, no. 3 (Apr., 1928), part 2, pp. 131-135.

(Birmingham Museum and Art Gallery)

    Catalogue of a Loan Collection of Tapestries and Laces.
    Designs for Stained Glass and Wall Decorations.
    Birmingham, 1895.

(Bishop, Morchard) (pseudonym)

    Maurice Drake.
    The West Country Magazine, vol. 6, no. 1 (Spring, 1951), pp. 28-32.

BIVER, P.

    Modes d'Emploi des Cartons par les Peintres-Verriers du XVIe
    Siècle.
    Bulletin Monumental, vol. 77 (1913), pp. 101-125.

    French Glass-Painters' Methods of Using Cartoons during the
    Sixteenth Century.
    J.M.G.P., vol. 3, no. 3 (Apr., 1930), pp. 112-117.
    J.M.G.P., vol. 3, no. 4 (Oct., 1930), pp. 173-180.
    J.M.G.P., vol. 4, no. 1 (Apr., 1931), pp. 24-31.

    L'Ecole Troyenne de Peinture sur Verre.
    Paris, 1925.

BLACKHAM, R.J.

    Martin Travers. Stained Glass Artist and Beautifier of
    Churches.
    (Obituary)
    J.M.G.P., vol. 10, no. 2 (1949), pp. 106-107.

BLACKING, W.H. Randoll

    Notes on Fragments of Painted Glass in St. Michael's Church,
    Basingstoke.
    J.M.G.P., vol. 10, no. 1 (1948), pp. 34-35.

BLAKEWAY, J.B.

    (Ed. by Mrs. BALDWYN CHILDE.)
    Notes on Kinlet.
    Transactions of the Shropshire Archaeological and Natural
    History Society, 3rd series, vol. 8 (1908).
    (Glass, pp. 105-106.)

(Blatherwycke, Holy Trinity, Northamptonshire.)

    (Theft of Armorial Glass.)
    News and Notes, J.M.G.P., vol. 14, no. 1 (1964), p. 8.

BLAVIGNAC, J.D.

    Histoire de l'Architecture Sacrée . . . de Genève, Lausanne
    et Sion.
    Paris, 1853.

(Blecha, Frank J.)

    (Obituary)
    Stained Glass, vol. 38, no. 1 (Spring, 1943), p. 34.

BLENKO, William

    (Letter to the Editor on glass-making techniques and the
    stability of the colours.)
    Stained Glass, vol. 27, no. 5 (May, 1932), p. 159.

    Antique Glass.
    Stained Glass, vol. xxviii (Winter, 1933-1934), pp. 195-198.

    (With WILLET, H.L., CUMMINGS, H.W. and others.)
    Technical Aspects of Stained Glass with Emphasis on Faceted Glass.
    (A Symposium).
    Part 1: Stained Glass, vol. 56, no. 3 (Autumn, 1961), pp. 30-39.
    Part 2: Ibid., vol. 56, no. 4 (Winter, 1961-1962), pp. 34-45.
    Part 3: Ibid., vol. 57, no. 1 (Spring, 1962), pp. 14-21.

BLES, Arthur de

    The Pictorial Element in Stained Glass.
    Art and Archaeology, vol. 20, no. 5 (Nov., 1925), p. 263-276.

BLISS, Douglas Percy

    The Painted Glass of Glasgow Cathedral.
    (Reprinted from Glasgow Herald.)
    J.M.G.P., vol. 12, no. 1 (1956), pp. 39-41.

BLOCHERER, Karl

    Glasfenster zu Erbendorf.
    In Die Christliche Kunst (1924-1925), Munich, p. 45.

(Saint-Lomer de Blois)

    Le Vitrail de la Saussaye à Saint-Lomer de Blois.
    Mémoires de la Societe des Sciences et Lettres de Loir-et-Cher
    (1949).
    Quoted in Bulletin Monumental, vol. 109 (1951), p. 93.

BLOMME, A.

    Rapport sur le Mémoire de M. Cl. van Cauwenberghs Intitulé
    Notice Historique sur les Peintres-Verriers d'Anvers du XVe
    au XVIIe Siècle.
    Bulletin de l'Academie d'Archeologie de Belgique (1891), pp. 96-98.

BLOXAM, R.N.

    The Church of All Saints, Ockham, Surrey.
    Surrey Archaeological Collections, vol. 45 (1937),
    (Glass, pp. 30-33.)

BLUME, Mary

    Have the French been shockingly negligent of their greatest
    artistic glory? Restoration of Stained Glass in Chartres
    Cathedral.
    Art News, no. 77 (Feb., 1978), pp. 36-40.

BOASE, T.S.R.

    English Art 1100-1216.
    Oxford, 1953.
    (Stained Glass, p. 237, 291-293.)

BODNÁR, Eva

    Szobotka Imre, Magyar Nemzeti Galéria Catalogue.
    Budapest, 1971.

BOECKLER, A.

    Die romanischen Fenster des Augsburger Domes und die Stilwende
    vom 11 zum 12 Jahrhunderts.
    Zeitschrift des deutschen Vereins fur Kunstwissenschaft, 10,
    fasc. 3/4 (1943).

BOESCH, Paul

Die Zugerischen Glasgemälde in der Sammlung von Nostell Church.
Zug, 1936.

The Swiss Stained Glass Panels in Wragby (Nostel) Church.
Yorkshire Archaeological Journal, vol. 32, 1934-1936 (1936),
pp. 443-450.

Schweizerische Glasgemälde im Ausland. Englische Sammlungen.
(Descriptions of the panels in the Bowes Museum, Barnard
Castle; the F.E. SIDNEY Collection; and the G. WÜTHRICH
Collection.)
Anzeiger für Schweizerische Altertumskunde, Band 38,
Heft 1 (1936), pp. 40-50.

Schweizerische Glasgemälde im Ausland. Die Sammlung in Nostell
Church.
Anzeiger fur Schweizerische Altertumskunde (1937), Heft 1, pp.
1-22; Heft 2, pp. 103-123.

The Glass-Painters, Hans Caspar and Hans Balthazar Gallati.
Anzeiger für Schweizerische Altertumskunde, Band 38 (1936).

Die Schweizer Glasmalerei.
Bazel, 1955.

Lord St. Oswald's Collection of Swiss Glass-Paintings.
(Condensed from his 1937 article in Anzeiger für Schweizerische
Altertumskunde.)
J.M.G.P., vol. 13, no. 1 (1960), pp. 310-312.

BOESWILWALD, E.

Vitrail de la Chapelle de St. Germer.
Annales Archéologique, vol. 22 (1862).

BOISSERÉE, S.

Anlichten, Risse und einzelne Theile des Doms von Köln, mit
Ergänzungen nach dem Entwurf des Meisters.
Stuttgart, 1821.

Histoire et Description de la Cathédrale de Cologne.
Munich, 1842-1843.

BOISSIER, G.R.

Stained Glass, Stoke Golding.
The Ecclesiologist, vol. 3 (1844), pp. 91-92.

BOISSONOT, Henri

Histoire et Description de la Cathédrale de Tours.
Paris, 1920.

Les Verrières de la Cathédrale de Tours. Dessins et
Aquarelles de Melle de Costigliole.
Paris, 1936.

BOISTHIBAULT, D. de
Les Verrières de Notre Dame de Chartres.
Revue Archéologique, no. 14 (1857-1858), p. 477.

(Boldre Church, Hants.)
(On the vanished glass.)
Letter to the Editor from PERKINS, Elizabeth.
J.M.G.P., vol. 11, no. 2 (1953), p. 123.

BOLTON, W.J.
(Paper on the Painted Glass in King's College Chapel, read to
the Archaeological Institute.)
The Gentleman's Magazine, vol. 42, new series, part 2 (1854),
pp. 282-284.

King's College Chapel Windows, Cambridge.
Archaeological Journal, vol. 12, (1855), pp. 153-172.

(Bolton, W.J. and J.)
The Stained Glass of the Brothers William Jay Bolton and John
Bolton.
Compiled from articles by BOLTON, R.P., MAXON, J.M., HEINIGKE, O.,
HEINIGKE, O.W.
Stained Glass, vol. 31, no. 1 (Spring-Summer, 1936), pp. 8-20.

(Bolton, William Jay)
William Jay Bolton of Bolton Priory.
Stained Glass, vol. 39, no. 2 (Summer, 1944), pp. 43-48.

BOMBE, W.
Die Peruginer Glasmalerei, vom 14 bis 16 Jahrhundert.
Zeitschrift für alte und neue Glasmalerei. 1914, p. 74.

BON, G. Le
La Civilisation des Arabes.
Paris, 1884.
(Contains Vitraux du Sanctuaire de la Mosquée El-Acza à
Jerusalem.)

BONNEAU, Abbé
Description des Verrières de la Cathédrale d'Auxerre.
Bulletin de la Société des Sciences Historiques et Naturelles
de l'Yonne, vol. 39 (1885), pp. 296-348.
Reprinted Paris, 1885.

Les Verrières de l'Eglise de Saint-Bris.
Ibid, vol. 52 (1899), p. 359-370.

BONNENFANT, Chanoine
Verrières de Croth (Eure).
Evreux, n.d.

Notre Dame d'Evreux.
Paris, 1939.

BONTEMPS, Georges
Peinture sur Verre au 19e Siècle. Les Secrets de cet Art,
Sont-ils Retrouvés?
Paris, 1845.

Vitraux.
(In Report of Exhibition, London, 1862.)
13 vols., Paris, 1862.

Guide du Verrier.
Paris, 1868.

(With BOESWILWALD, M.)
Report on Stained Glass at Paris Exhibition, 1867. Rapports du
Jury International.
London, 1868 (Vol. 3.).

BOOM, A. van der
Ontwikkeling en Karakter der Oude Monumentale Glasschilderkunst.
Amsterdam, 1944.
Reviewed by RACKHAM, Bernard, Burlington Magazine, vol. 89
(Jan.-Dec., 1947), p. 171.

Review of HELBIG, J.
De Glasschilderkunst en Belgie.
Burlington Magazine, vol. 89 (Jan.-Dec., 1947), pp. 109-110.

BOOM, A. van der (Contd.)

Een Nederlandse Glasschilder in den Vreemde, Aert Ortkens
van Nijmegen.
Nederland Kunsthistorisch Jaarboek, 1948-1949 (The Hague, 1949),
pp. 90-91.

Florentine Painted Glass.
(Defines and gives examples of a vidimus.)
Letter to the Editor, Burlington Magazine, vol. 91 (Jan.-Dec.,
1949), p. 114.

Monumentale Glasschilderkunst in Nederland.
The Hague, 1950.

De Kunst der Glazeniers in Europa 1100-1600.
Amsterdam, 1960.
Reviewed by GRODECKI, Louis, Bulletin Monumental, vol. 119 (1961),
pp. 293-294.

BORDEAUX, R.

Principes d'Archéologie Pratique . . . de la Conservation et du
Rétablissement des Verrières Peintes.
Bulletin Monumental, vol. 17 (1851), p. 634.

BOREHAM, F.

Stained Glass Windows in Cornwall.
Journal of the Royal Institute of Cornwall, (new series), vol. 3,
part 1 (1957), pp. 43-47.

BORENIUS, Tancred

St. Thomas Becket in Art.
London, 1932.

Review of RUSHFORTH, Medieval Christian Imagery . . .
The Archaeological Journal, vol. 92 (for 1935), pp. 364-365.

(Borthwick, A.E.)

A Scottish Stained Glass Artist. (Captain A. E. Borthwick.)
The Connoisseur, vol. 76, no. 301 (Sept. 1926).

BOSLAND, James A.

The Evolution of a Stained Glass Window.
Church Property Administration (Milwaukee). (May-June, 1947).

(Bossanyi, Ervin)

Stained Glass Art.
(Notice of Ervin Bossanyi's Exhibition), The Morning Post.
Oct. 15, 1935.

A Stained Glass Exhibition of Work by Ervine Bossanyi.
The Builder, Oct. 18, 1935.

Ervin Bossanyi: Encounter with an Artist.
Beacon (supplement), Spring, 1974.

Obituary by BAYLESS, John.
Stained Glass, vol. 20, no. 2 (Summer, 1975), p. 86.

Catalogue of an Exhibition of his Works in the Ashmolean Musuem.
Oxford, 1979.

BOSSCHERE, Jean de

Les Vitraux de Notre Dame d'Anvers.
L'Art Flamand et Hollandais, part 4, no. 8 (1905), pp. 46-53;
no. 9, pp. 72-80.

Les Vitraux de Lierre et d'Anvers.
L'Art Flamand et Hollandais, fasc. 9, no. 4 (1908), pp. 117-129;
fasc. 10, no. 7, pp. 1-18.

BOSTOCK, Mary E.

A Short History of Stained Glass.
Bulletin of the Stained Glass Association of America,
vol. 23, no. 10, (Nov., 1928)
no. 11, (Dec., 1928)
vol. 24, nos. 1-4 (Jan.-Apr., 1929).

(Boston, Lincs.)

St. Botolph's Church, Boston.
Boston, n.d.
(Glass - modern - pp. 15-18.)

BOUCHIER, E.S.

Notes on the Stained Glass of the Oxford District.
Oxford, 1918.

Old Stained Glass in Oxfordshire.
J.M.G.P., vol. 4, no. 3 (Apr., 1932), pp. 123-133.

BOUCHON, Chantal, BRISAC, Catherine, LAUTIER, Claudine, ZALUSKA, Yolanta

La 'Belle-Verrière' de Chartres.
Revue de l'Art, no. 46 (1979), pp. 16-24.

(Boughton Aluph, Kent)

The Church of All Saints, Boughton Aluph.
Ashford, n.d.
(Glass, pp. 2, 3. Unpaged pamphlet.)

BOUILLET, Abbé

L'Eglise Sainte-Foy de Conches (Eure) et ses Vitraux.
Bulletin Monumental (1888).
Reprinted Caen, 1889.

BOULAY HILL, A. du. and GILL, Harry

Beauvale Charterhouse.
Transactions of the Thoroton Society, vol. 12 for 1908 (1909).
(Glass in Beauvale Manor Farm, pp. 92-93.)

BOUMPHREY, R.S.

(With introduction by BAGOT, Annette.)
The Heraldry at Levens Hall, Westmorland.
Transactions of the Cumberland and Westmorland Antiquarian and
Archaeological Society, new series, vol. 72, (1972), pp. 205-215.

The Braddyll Heraldry at Conishead Priory and in the Braddyll
Chapel in St. Mary's Church, Ulverston.
Transactions of the Cumberland and Westmorland Antiquarian and
Archaeological Society, new series, vol. 73, (1973), pp. 148-160.

The Heraldry in Queen's Hall and in the Council Chamber at the
Town Hall, Barrow-in-Furness.
(With MELVILLE, J.)
Ibid., pp. 161-169.

Heraldry at Holker Hall.
Transactions of the Cumberland and Westmorland Antiquarian and
Archaeological Society, new series, vol. 74, (1974), pp. 103-104.

Heraldry at Graythwaite Hall.
Ibid, pp. 105-108.

Heraldry at Rydal Hall.
Transactions of the Cumberland and Westmorland Antiquarian and
Archaeological Society, new series, vol. 75, (1975), pp. 132-135.

BOURASSÉ, J.-J., MANCEAU, Abbé, MARCHAND, J.

Verrières du Choeur de l'Eglise Métropolitaine de Tours.
Paris and Tours, 1849.

BOURASSÉ, J.-J., MANCEAU, Abbé, MARCHAND, J. (Contd)

Dictionnaire d'Archéologie Sacrée: L'Architecture, les
Vitraux Peints, etc.
2 vols., Paris, 1851.

La Touraine-Histoire et Monuments.
Tours, 1855.

BOURDEAUT, A.

Le Vitrail de St. Pierre de Montrelais.
Bulletin de la Société Archéologique de Nantes et de la Loire-
Inférieure, vol. 69.

(Bourges, Saint Etienne)

Saint-Etienne de Bourges. Architecture et Vitraux.
Bourges, 1960.

(Bourges, Cathedral)

Dépose des Vitraux de la Cathédrale de Bourges.
Mémoires de la Société des Antiquaires du Centre (1941-1943).
Quoted in Bulletin Monumental, no. 105 (1947), pp. 279-280.

(Bourges)

Les Vitraux de Jean Lécuyer dans la Cathédrale de Bourges.
Bulletin Mensuel de la Société des Antiquités du Centre (Dec.
1947).
Quoted in Bulletin Monumental, no. 106 (1948), p. 182.

BOURKE, Patricia

The Stained Glass Windows of the Church of St. Neot, Cornwall.
Devon and Cornwall Notes and Queries, vol. 33 (1974-1976), pp.
65-68.

BOURNE, W.H.

The Church of All Saints, Woodchurch, Kent.
(Printed) Bethersden, 1938.
(Glass, p. 5.)

BOVINI, G.

Gli Antichi Vetri da Finestra della Chiesa di S. Vitale.
Felix Ravenna, series 3, no. 91 (1965), pp. 98-108.

Les Anciens Vitraux de l'Eglise Saint-Vital à Ravenne.
Annales 3e Congrès des 'Journées Internationales du Verre'
14-24 novembre, 1964.
Liège, 1966, pp. 85-90.

BOWE, Nicola Gordon.

Harry Clarke. Ireland's Magical Stained Glass Artist.
Stained Glass, vol. 73, no. 4 (Winter, 1978-1979), pp. 270-274.

BOWMAN, Henry. and HADFIELD, James

The Ecclesiastical Architecture of Great Britain from the Conquest
to the Reformation. Part 1, Norbury Church, Derbyshire.
London, 1844.

BOYER, Jean

Guillaume Dombet, verrier, est-il le 'Maître de l'Annonciation
d'Aix'?
Connaissance des Arts, (Feb., 1958), pp. 39-43.

BRABAZON, T.

Old British and Continental Glass in American Windows.
Arts Decoration, no. 4 (May, 1914), pp. 263-265.

BRADFORD J.G.

The Armorial Glass and Badges in Harlow Church.
Transactions of the Essex Archaeological Society, new series,
vol. 11, 1908-1910 (1911), pp. 347-361.

(Bradninch)

The New Parish Room, Bradninch.
(Glass by Drake and Sons.)
Devon and Cornwall Notes and Queries, vol. 6 (1911), pp. 33-38.

BRAKSPEAR, Harold

(Revised and extended by HICK, E.M.)
The Cathedral Church of St. Peter and St. Paul at Bath, now
generally known as Bath Abbey.
Gloucester, n.d.

(Brangwyn, Frank)

Stained Glass Designs by Frank Brangwyn.
The Studio, vol. 16 (1899), pp. 252-259.

BRAYLEY, E.W. and BRITTON, John

History of the Ancient Palace and Late Houses of Parliament at
Westminster.
London, 1836.

BREMEN, Walther

Die alten Glasgemälde und Hohlgläser der Sammlung Bremen in
Krefeld.
Cologne and Graz.
Reviewed by C(HARLESTON), R.J., Burlington Magazine, vol. 109
(Jan., 1967), p. 40.

BRETON, G. Le

Essai Iconographique sur Saint-Louis.
Paris, 1880.

Les Médaillons des Mois du Musée de Rouen.
Bulletin Monumental, vol. 47 (1881), p. 63.

BREWSTER, David

On the Structure and Optical Phenomena of Ancient Decomposed
Glass.
Transactions of the Royal Society of Edinburgh, no. 23 (1863),
pp. 193-204.

BRICE, A.H.M.

Glass of Tewkesbury Abbey. A Complete Restoration.
J.M.G.P., vol. 13, no. 4 (1963), pp. 569-571.
(Reprinted from The Times, March 25, 1925.)

BRIDGEMAN, C.G.O.

(On the Morris Dance Window from Betley Hall.)
Transactions of the William Salt Archaeological Society (1923).

BRIDGES. Harold Stephen

Blessed James of Ulm.
Stained Glass, vol. 32, no. 2 (Autumn, 1937), pp. 48-50.

Some Reflections on the Stained Glass in the Cloisters.
Stained Glass, vol. 33, no. 1 (Spring-Summer, 1938), pp. 12-14.

Mostly About Stained Glass. By Sergeant 35123762.
Stained Glass, vol. 38, no. 4 (Winter, 1943), pp. 126-129.

BRIDGES, Stephen

Some New Ideas in an Old Church.
(On the glass at Gouda.)
Stained Glass, vol. 45, no. 2 (Summer, 1950), pp. 63-69.

Jesse's Tree.
Stained Glass, vol. 45, no. 3 (Autumn, 1950), pp. 99-106.

Carved Glass.
Stained Glass, vol. 50, no. 1 (Spring, 1955), pp. 13-14.

(With FREI, Robert, SKINNER, Orin E., and others.)
What Makes for Good Stained Glass Design? (A Symposium.)
Stained Glass, vol. 55, no. 4 (Winter, 1960-1961), pp. 16-27.
Part 2: Ibid, vol. 56, no. 1 (Spring, 1961), pp. 38-47.

(With GOODMAN, P., ATKINSON, Harry, RAMBUSCH, Robert, BATES, Harold.)
Stained Glass as Architects Consider It. (A Symposium.)
Stained Glass, vol. 59, no. 4 (Winter, 1964-1965), pp. 24-31.

(Review of JOHNSON, J.R.)
The Radiance of Chartres.
Stained Glass, vol. 60, no. 3 (Autumn, 1965), p. 31.

Blessed James of Ulm.
Stained Glass, vol. 64, no. 1 (Spring, 1969), pp. 23-25.

Review of SEWTER, A.C., The Stained Glass of William Morris and his Circle.
Stained Glass, vol. 71, no. 2 (Summer, 1976), pp. 102-103.

(Bridges, Stephen)
Obituaries.
Stained Glass, vol. 72, no. 2 (Summer, 1977), pp. 82, 83, 115.

BRIDGES, Stephen
John Ruskin's Window in St. Giles' Church, Camberwell.
J.M.G.P., vol. 15, no. 3 (1974-1975), pp. 35-38.

BRIEGER, Peter H.
Principles of French Classic Painting.
(Refers to Sixteenth Century Glass-Painting.)
Art Bulletin, vol. 20, no. 4 (Dec., 1938), pp. 339-358.

English Art 1216-1307.
Oxford, 1957.
(Stained Glass, pp. 24, 94-95, 129-130.)

BRIGGS, Albert E.
Jesse Windows.
(Identifies the Ettington Park windows as those from Winchester College.)
Notes and Queries, 7th series, vol. 10, (Nov. 29, 1890), p. 429.

BRIGHT, Hugh
The Herkenrode Windows in Lichfield Cathedral.
Lichfield, 1932.

Lichfield Cathedral, The Lady Chapel Windows.
Lichfield, 1950.
(Revised edition with an additional note by Sir Eric Maclagan.)

BRIGHTON, J.T.
The Heraldic Window in the Frecheville Chapel, Stavely Church.
Derbyshire Archaeological Journal, vol. 53 (1960), pp. 98-104.

The Painted Glass in Gray's Court, York.
The Yorkshire Archaeological Journal, vol. 41, 1963-1966 (1966), pp. 709-725.
Addendum: Ibid., vol. 42, 1967-1970, (1971), pp. 61-62.

William Peckitt, the Greatest of the Georgian Glasspainters.
York Georgian Society Annual Report (1967-1968), pp. 14-24

BRIGHTON, J.T. (Contd.)
Cartoons for York Glass - Henry Gyles.
Preview, vol. 21 (1968), pp. 772-775.

Cartoons for York Glass - William Peckitt.
Preview, vol. 22 (1969), pp. 779-783.

Seventeenth Century Painted Glass in Witherslack Church.
Transactions of the Cumberland and Westmorland Antiquarian and Archaeological Society, new series, vol. 71 (1971), pp. 90-96.

York's Car of Justice Pursued.
J.M.G.P., vol. 15, no. 3 (1974-1975), pp. 17-22.

Henry Gyles' Guildhall Window.
York History, vol. 3 (1977), pp. 109-117.

BRILL, R.H. and MOLL, S.
The Electronbeam Probe Microanalysis of Ancient Glass.
Recent Advances in Conservation, London, 1961, pp. 145-151.

BRILL, R.H.
The Record of Time in Weathered Glass.
Archaeology, no. 14 (1961), pp. 18-22.

(With HOOD, H.P.)
A New Method for Dating Ancient Glass.
Nature, no. 189 (1961), pp. 12-14.

Ancient Glass.
Scientific American, (Nov. 1963), pp. 120-130.

Lead Isotopes in Ancient Glass.
Annales du 4e Congrès des Journées Internationale du Verre.
Ravenna-Venice (May 13-20, 1967), pp. 255-261.
Reprinted 1969.

The Scientific Examination of Ancient Glasses.
8th International Congress on Glass, London (July 1-6, 1968).
Society of Glass Technology, Sheffield, pp. 47-68.

Scientific Studies of Stained Glass: A Progress Report.
Journal of Glass Studies, vol. 12 (1970), pp. 185-192.

A Request for Help in the Conservation of Early Stained Glass Windows.
Compte Rendu du IXe Congrès International du Verre, Versailles (1971), pp. 51-56.

Incipient Crizzling in Some Early Glasses.
IIC Bulletin, no. 12 (1972), pp. 46-47.

Some Notes on Conservation Treatments.
In 8e Colloque du Corpus Vitrearum Medii Aevi, Paris? (1972), pp. 35-41.

BRINDLEY, H.H. and MOORE, A.H.
The Ship in the Windows of King's College Chapel, Cambridge.
Proceedings of the Cambridge Antiquarian Society, new series, vol. 8, 1909-1910 (1910), pp. 87-110.

BRINDLEY, H.H.
The Ship in the St. Christopher Window in Thaxted Church, with remarks on early methods of reefing sails.
Proceedings of the Cambridge Antiquarian Society, new series, vol. 9, 1910-1911 (1911), pp. 26-41.

The Fishing Boats in a Window of 1552 in Auppegard Church, Normandy.
Proceedings of the Cambridge Antiquarian Society, new series, vol. 10, 1911-1912 (1912), pp. 118-121.

BRINDLEY, H.H. (Contd.)

Mediaeval and Sixteenth Century Ships in English Churches.
Proceedings of the Cambridge Antiquarian Society, new series,
vol. 11, 1912-1913 (1914), pp. 139-145.

Ships in the Cambridge 'Life of the Confessor'.
(Gives references to ships in windows at Auxerre, Canterbury,
Sens.)
Proceedings of the Cambridge Antiquarian Society, new series,
vol. 12, 1913-1914 (1915), pp. 67-75.

BRINLEY, D. Putnam

Three-Light Window in Thirteenth Century Style.
International Studio. (Jan. 1926), p. 57.

BRISAC, Catherine

La Verrière du Champrès-Froges.
Bulletin Mensuel de l'Académie Delphinale, 8e series, 12e annee
(1973), pp. 204-211.

Les Vitraux de l'Etage Inférieur du Choeur de Saint-Jean-de-
Lyon.
3 vols., Paris, 1977.

La Peinture sur Verre à Lyon.
Les Dossiers de l'Archéologie, no. 26, (Jan.-Feb., 1978), pp. 38-49.

Grisailles Romanes des Anciennes Abbatiales d'Obazine et de
Bonlieu.
102e Congrès National des Sociétés Savantes. Limoges, 1977.
Paris, 1979, pp. 129-143.

(With BOUCHON, Chantal, LAUTIER, Claudine, ZALUSKA, Yolanta.)
La 'Belle-Verrière' de Chartres.
Revue de l'Art, no. 46 (1979), pp. 16-24.

Review of GRODECKI, Louis, PERROT, Françoise, TARALON, Jean.
Recensement des Vitraux de Paris, de la Région Parisienne,
de la Picardie, du Nord et du Pas-de-Calais.
(CVMA, France, supplementary series, no. 1).
Bulletin Monumental, vol. 138, no. 1 (1980), pp. 109-111.

La 'Tête Gérente'.
Revue de l'Art, no. 47 (1980), pp. 72-75.

B.B.C.

Pictures in Windows.
B.B.C. Radiovision. Notes for the teacher, N. 218.
London, 1970.
Stained Glass, Ibid., N. 240.

British Society of Master Glass-Painters

Some Stained Glass Windows Executed (by Fellows of the Society)
within the past Twenty Years.
London, 1930.

A Directory of Stained Glass Windows within the past Twenty
Years.
London, 1939.

A Directory of Stained Glass Windows Executed within the past
Twenty Years.
London, 1955.

A Directory of Stained Glass Windows.
London, 1958.

A Directory of Stained Glass Windows.
London, 1966.

Directory of Master Glass-Painters.
(Ed. THOMAS, Brian, and RICHARDSON, Eileen.)
Newcastle-on-Tyne, 1972.

B.S.M.G.P. (Contd.)

Examples of Contemporary Work in Stained Glass by Members of
the Society.
(East Window, Balsham Church, by NICHOLSON, A.K. and SMITH, G.E.R.;
East Window of Lady Chapel, Chew Magna, by HUTCHINSON, G.P., and
POWELL, J., and Sons; Cartoon by BELL, Reginald, for the Old
Guild Hall of St. Mary, Coventry.)
J.M.G.P., vol. 5, no. 2 (Oct., 1933), pp. 69-70.

Examples of Contemporary Work in Stained Glass Executed by
Members of the Society.
(North Aisle of Llanidloes Church, by WEBB, Geoffrey; High
Church, Linlithgow, by MEIKLE, William, and Sons; St. Olave's
Church, City of London, by SPEAR, Francis, H.; Welwyn Parish
Church, by LAWSON, William.)
J.M.G.P., vol. 5, no. 3 (Apr., 1934), p. 116.

Examples of Contemporary Work in Stained Glass Executed by
Members of the Society.
(In St. Mary's Hall, Coventry, by BELL, Reginald; West Window,
Hayle, Cornwall, by BELL, Reginald; Paisley Abbey, by WEBB,
Christopher; St. Chad's, Rochdale, by HUTCHINSON, G.P.)
J.M.G.P., vol. 5, no. 4 (Oct., 1934), pp. 185-186.

Reports of Meetings of the Council of the Society (unless noted).

J.M.F.G., vol. 1, no. 2 (Apr., 1925), pp. 29-31.

J.M.G.P., vol. 1, no. 3 (Oct., 1925), pp. 32-34.

J.M.G.P., vol. 1, no. 4 (Apr., 1926), pp. 45-46.

J.M.G.P., vol. 1, no. 5 (Oct., 1926), pp. 41-44.

(Report of the Council.) J.M.G.P., vol. 1, no. 5 (Oct., 1926),
pp. 47-50.

J.M.G.P., vol. 2, no. 1 (Apr., 1927), pp. 49-50.

J.M.G.P., vol. 2, no. 2 (Oct., 1927), pp. 103-104.

J.M.G.P., vol. 2, no. 3 (Apr., 1928), p. 159.

J.M.G.P., vol. 3, no. 3 (Apr., 1930), p. 141.

J.M.G.P., vol. 3, no. 4 (Oct., 1930), pp. 201-202.

J.M.G.P., vol. 4, no. 1 (Apr., 1931), pp. 45-46.

J.M.G.P., vol. 4, no. 2 (Oct., 1931), pp. 98-99.

(Report of the Council.) J.M.G.P., vol. 4, no. 2 (Oct., 1931),
pp. 101-102.

J.M.G.P., vol. 4, no. 3 (Apr., 1932), pp. 157-158.

(Report of the Council.) J.M.G.P., vol. 4, no. 4 (Oct., 1932),
pp. 205-206.

(Annual General Meeting and Dinner, with Report of Speech by
Sir Edwin LUTYENS.) J.M.G.P., vol. 5, no. 2 (Oct., 1933), pp.
93-98.

(Report of the Council.) J.M.G.P., vol. 5, no. 2 (Oct., 1933),
pp. 99-101.

(Annual General Meeting: the President's Address by the Earl
of Crawford and Balcarres.) J.M.G.P., vol. 5, no. 4 (Oct., 1934),
pp. 199-200.

J.M.G.P., vol. 6, no. 2 (Oct., 1935), pp. 102-103.

(Annual General Meeting and Report of the Council.) J.M.G.P.,
vol. 7, no. 3 (Oct., 1938), pp. 146-147.

B.S.M.G.P. (Contd.)

    (Annual General Meeting and Dinner; Address by H.S. GOODHART-
RENDEL.) J.M.G.P., vol. 8, no. 1 (Oct., 1939), pp. 26-29.

    (Annual Report.) J.M.G.P., vol. 8. no. 1 (Oct., 1939), pp. 30-31.

    (Notes by the Hon. Secretary /on arrangements to continue the
Society during the war7.) J.M.G.P., vol. 8, no. 2 (Apr., 1940),
pp. 84-86.

    (Annual General Meeting.) J.M.G.P., vol. 10, no. 4 (1951), p. 216.

    (Annual Dinner.) J.M.G.P., vol. 11, no. 1 (1952), pp. 22-24.

    (Annual General Meeting) J.M.G.P., vol. 11, no. 2 (1953), pp.
108-111.

    (Report of the Hon. Secretary and Annual Dinner) J.M.G.P., vol. 11,
no. 2 (1953), pp. 112-113.

    (Annual General Meeting; Hon. Secretary's Report; Annual Dinner,
with speech by RICHARDSON, A.E.) J.M.G.P., vol. 11, no. 4 (1955),
pp. 235-240.

    (Annual General Meeting; Report of Hon. Secretary; Annual Dinner,
with report of speech by BETJEMAN, John.) J.M.G.P., vol. 12,
no. 1 (1956), pp. 61-65.

    (Hon. Secretary's Report) J.M.G.P., vol. 12, no. 2 (1957), pp.
148-149. (Annual Dinner) Ibid, pp. 151-153.

    (Annual General Meeting; Hon. Secretary's Report; Annual Dinner.)
J.M.G.P., vol. 12, no. 3 (1958), pp. 206-212.

    (Hon. Secretary's Report.) J.M.G.P., vol. 12, no. 4 (1959), pp.
254-255. (Annual Dinner, Annual General Meeting.) Ibid., pp.
257-260.

    (Hon. Secretary's Report.) J.M.G.P., vol. 13, no. 1 (1960),
pp. 344-345. (Annual Dinner.) Ibid, pp. 345-346.

    (Annual General Meeting.) J.M.G.P., vol. 13, no. 2 (1961), pp.
411-414. (Annual Dinner.) Ibid., pp. 415-418.

    (Hon. Secretary's Report.) J.M.G.P., vol. 13, no. 3 (1962), p. 479.
(Council Meeting.) Ibid, pp. 480-482. (Annual General Meeting.)
Ibid, pp. 483-486. (Annual Dinner.) Ibid., p. 487.

    (Annual General Meeting.) J.M.G.P., vol. 13, no. 4 (1963), pp.
558-560. (Reports of speeches by KENDRICK, Sir Thomas, and
REYNTIENS, Patrick, Annual Dinner.), Ibid., pp. 579-581.

    (Annual General Meeting.) J.M.G.P., vol. 14, no. 1 (1964), pp.
17-19. (Annual Dinner.) Ibid., pp. 52-53.

    (Annual General Meeting.) J.M.G.P., vol. 14, no. 2 (1965), pp.
114-116. (Annual Dinner.) Ibid., pp. 122-123.

    (Annual General Meeting,) J.M.G.P., vol. 14, no. 4 (1968-1969),
p. 191.

    (Annual Dinner.) J.M.G.P., vol. 15, no. 2 (1973-1974), pp. 68-70.

Recent and Current Work by Members.
(Contributions by LEE, Lawrence, SKEAT, Francis, NEW, Kenneth,
HAYWARD. John, HOLLOWAY, A.V., and others, including the
Whitefriars Studio.)
(Articles by HOLLOWAY, A.V. on restoring glass at St. Mary's
Shrewsbury, and ROBINSON, Geoffrey, on restoring glass at St.
Thomas', Salisbury, and Banwell, Somerset.)
J.M.G.P., vol. 14, no. 3 (1967), pp. 163-174.

B.S.M.G.P. (Contd.)
    Recent and Current Work by Members.
    (Includes contributions by ROBINSON, G.A.K.. SKEAT, Francis,
HAYWARD, John, Whitefriars Studio, and others.)
    J.M.G.P., vol. 14, no. 4 (1968-1969), pp. 207-214.

(British Society of Master Glass-Painters, Journal of)
    J.M.G.P., vol. 3.
    Noticed in 'Memorabilia' Notes and Queries. vol. 149
    (Oct. 3. 1925), p. 235.

    J.M.G.P. (Apr., 1926).
    Noticed in 'Memorabilia'. Notes and Queries. vol. 150 (Apr. 24.
    1926), p. 290.

    J.M.G.P. (Oct., 1927)
    Noticed in 'Memorabilia'. Notes and Queries. vol. 153 (Oct. 15.
    1927), p. 271.

    J.M.G.P. (Apr., 1930)
    Noticed in 'Memorabilia'. Notes and Queries. vol. 158 (May 24.
    1930), p. 361.

    J.M.G.P.,(Oct.,1930)
    Noticed in 'Memorabilia', Notes and Queries. vol. 159 (Oct. 11.
    1930), p. 253.

    J.M.G.P. (Apr., 1931)
    Noticed in 'Memorabilia'. Notes and Queries. vol. 160 (May 2,
    1931). pp. 307-308.

    J.M.G.P. (Oct.,1931)
    Noticed in 'Memorabilia'. Notes and Queries. vol. 161 (Oct. 24.
    1931), p. 280.

    J.M.G.P. (Apr., 1932)
    Noticed in 'Memorabilia'. Notes and Queries. vol. 162 (Apr. 16.
    1932), p. 271.

    J.M.G.P. (Oct., 1932)
    Noticed in 'Memorabilia'. Notes and Queries. vol. 163 (Oct. 29.
    1932), p. 307.

    J.M.G.P. (Apr., 1933)
    Noticed in 'Memorabilia'. Notes and Queries. vol. 164 (Apr. 29.
    1933), p. 280.

    J.M.G.P. (Oct.,1934)
    Noticed in 'Memorabilia', Notes and Queries. vol. 167 (Dec. 15.
    (1934), p. 416.

    J.M.G.P.,(Apr., 1936)
    Noticed in 'Memorabilia', Notes and Queries. vol. 170 (Apr. 18,
    1936), p. 271.
    (Discusses recent attacks on stained glass by an Anglican bishop.
    Correspondence ensues. See WULCKO, C.T. (May 2, 1936), pp. 320-
    321; ATHOE, G.B.J. (May 16, 1936), p. 354; F.H.C. (May 30, 1936),
    pp. 392-393.

    J.M.G.P. (Nov., 1937)
    Noticed in 'Memorabilia', Notes and Queries, vol. 173 (Nov. 6,
    1937). p. 326.

    J.M.G.P., (Oct. 1937)
    Noticed in 'Memorabilia', Notes and Queries. vol. 175 (Oct. 29,
    1938), pp. 307-308.

    J.M.G.P. (Oct., 1943)
    Noticed in 'Memorabilia', Notes and Queries, vol. 185 (Oct. 9,
    1943), p. 212.

    J.M.G.P. (Spring, 1946)
    Noticed in 'Memorabilia', Notes and Queries, vol. 190 (March 19,
    1946). p. 89.

    J.M.G.P. (Nov., 1950)
    Noticed in 'Memorabilia', Notes and Queries, vol. 195 (Nov. 11,
    1950), p. 485.

B.S.M.G.P.. Journal of (Contd.)
    J.M.G.P. (Apr. 1953)
        Noticed in 'Memorabilia', Notes and Queries, vol. 198 (Apr., 1953),
        p. 137.

    J.M.G.P. (Apr., 1954)
        Noticed in 'Memorabilia'. Notes and Queries, new series, vol. 1
        (May, 1954), p. 185.

    J.M.G.P.,(Apr., 1955)
        Noticed in 'Memorabilia'. Notes and Queries, new series, vol. 2
        (May, 1955), p. 185.

    J.M.G.P. (1956)
        Noticed in 'Memorabilia', Notes and Queries, new series, vol. 3
        (June, 1956), p. 231.

    J.M.G.P. (1958)
        Noticed in 'Memorabilia', Notes and Queries, new series, vol. 5
        (June 1958), p. 232.

    J.M.G.P. vol. 12, no. 4 (1958-1959)
        Noticed in 'Memorabilia', Notes and Queries, new series, vol. 6
        (March, 1959), p. 85, and vol. 13, no. 5 (Oct., 1959), p. 344.

    J.M.G.P., vol. 13, no. 2
        Noticed in 'Memorabilia', Notes and Queries, new series, vol. 8
        (Aug., 1961), p. 282.

    (The Future of the Journal.)
        J.M.G.P., vol. 13, no. 3 (1967), p. 147.

    (Another editorial on the future of the Journal.)
        J.M.G.P., vol. 14, no. 4 (1968-1969), p. 181.

(Brittany)
    Le Vitrail Breton.
    (MUSSAT, A., GRUBER, J.-J., BARRIE R., MOIREZ-DUBIEF, D.)
    Arts de l'Ouest, no. 3 (1977), Rennes.
    Reviewed by BRISAC, Catherine. Bulletin Monumental, vol. 136
    (1978), pp. 370-371.

BRITTON, John
    Illustrations of Fonthill Abbey.
    London, 1823.

BRIVIO, E.
    Le Vetrate del Duomo di Milano.
    In Il Duomo di Milano.
    Cassa di Risparmio delle Provincie Lombarde, 1973.
    (pp. 233-244.)

BRIZIO, Anna Maria
    Le Vetrate della Cattedrale e della Collegiata di S. Orso
    ad Aosta.
    Congresso Storico Subalpine, 1956.

BROAD, Harold T.
    Reminiscences of Miller, Beale and Hider Ltd.
    J.M.G.P., vol. 17, no. 2 (1978-1979), pp. 73-74.

BROCHARD, Louis
    Saint-Gervais.
    Paris, 1938.
    (Contains material on the Pinaigrier family.)

BROCHMANN, Odd
    Glassmalerei i Norden. (Utgitt av A/S Drammens Glassverk.)
    Copenhagen, 1966.

BROCK, E.P. Loftus
    Ancient Stained Glass in Westbere Church.
    Archaeologia Cantiana, vol. 17 (1887), pp. 1-4.

BROCKINGTON, Allen
    The Five Sisters at York.
    (Letter to the Editor.)
    The Times, Dec. 2, 1933.

BROCKWELL, M.W.
    Scrap Windows.
    Notes and Queries, vol. 181 (Nov. 8, 1941). p. 262.
    Ibid., (Dec. 6, 1941), p. 320.

BROMLEY, James
    The Heraldry of Ormskirk Church.
    Transactions of the Historic Society of Lancashire and Cheshire,
    new series, vol. 22 for 1906 (1907), pp. 64-90.
    (Very little on glass.)

BROOKES, H.E.
    The Washington Memorial Window at All Saints', Maldon.
    The Essex Review, (Jan., 1929).

BROWN, G.P.
    A Plantagenet Observed?
    (Portraiture in the East Window.)
    Beverley, 1973.

    A Te Deum of Light.
    (The Great East Window of Beverley Minster.)
    Beverley, 1973.

BROWN, S.L.
    The Structure of Lead as Related to Stained Glass.
    J.M.G.P., vol. 2, no. 3 (Apr., 1928). pp. 123-128.

BROWN, William
    Heraldic Glass from Ingleby Arncliffe and Kirby Sigston Churches.
    The Yorkshire Archaeological Journal, vol. 22 (1913), pp. 138-144.

BROWNE, John
    History of the Metropolitan Church of St. Peter, York.
    2 vols., London, 1838-1847.

    . . . Notes on the Painted Glass (of York).
    Proceedings of the Archaeological Institute (July, 1846), York.
    (London, 1848)
    Incorporated in J.H. PARKER'S Architectural Notes of the
    Churches and other Ancient Buildings in the City and
    Neighbourhood of York, pp. 1-48 (articles irregularly
    paginated).

    Description . . . of the Windows of York Minster.
    (1859, published 1915.)

    A Description of the Representation and Arms on the Glass in the
    Windows of York Minster, also the Arms on Stone.
    Edited with a biographical notice by PUREY-CUST, Dean A.P.
    Leeds, 1917.

BRUCK, Robert
    Die Elsässische Glasmalerei.
    Strasbourg, 1901.

    Die Elsässische Glasmalerei vom Beginn des XII bis zum Ende des
    XVII Jahrhunderts.
    Strasbourg, 1902.

BRUCK, Robert (Contd.)

Der Traktat des Meisters Antonio von Pisa über die Glasmalerei.
Repertorium für Kunstwissenschaft, vol. 25 (1902).

Die Sophienkirche in Dresden: Ihre Geschichte und Ihre
Kunstschätze.
Dresden, 1912.

BRUCKMANN, F.

Deutsche Glasmalkunst.
Munich, 1927.

BRUECKNER, Margarethe, and HAETGE, Ernst

Der Zyklus der farbigen Glasfenster im Chor des Erfurter Domes.
Kunstdenkmale d. Provinz Sachsen, Bd. 1, pp. 145-224.
Burg, 1929.

BRUNER, Louise

Glass Workshop.
American Artist (Feb. 1969).

BRUNET, E.

The Replacing of the Eighteenth-Century Glass in the Sanctuary
Windows of Chartres Cathedral.
Les Monuments Historiques de la France, vol. 1, fascicule 3.

BRUSHFIELD, T.N.

The Execution of Sir Walter Raleigh and the Events that
Followed It.
Devonshire Association for Science, Literature and Art, vol. 39
(1907), pp. 242-263.
(Accounts of windows representing Raleigh.)

(Brussels Exhibition, 1880)

Exposition Nationale: Catalogue Officiel.
Brussels, 1880.

(Brussels Cathedral)

La Cathédrale Saint-Michel. Trésors d'Art et d'Histoire.
Brussels, 1975.

BRUYN, H. de

Trésor Artistique de la Collégiale de Sainte-Gudule, à Bruxelles -
Verrières.
Bulletin des Commissions Royales d'Art et d'Archéologie, no. 10
(1871), p. 110.

Notice sur les Anciennes et les Nouvelles Verrières de l'Eglise
de Notre Dame au Sablon, à Bruxelles.
Brussels, 1866.
Ibid., no. 11 (1872), p. 130.

Trésor Artistique de l'Eglise Notre Dame au Sablon à Bruxelles.
Brussels, 1872.

BRUYNE, Edgar de
Etudes d'Esthétique Médiévale.
3 vols., Bruges, 1946.
Reviewed by AUBERT, Marcel, Bulletin Monumental, no. 105 (1947),
pp. 161-162.

BRYANS, Herbert W.

Stained Glass from the Earliest Period of the Renaissance.
Oxford, 1910.

BRYANT, T.H.

Norfolk Churches.
N.d., n.p.

BRŻUSKI, Henryk

Witraze Sreduiowieczne
w Kosciele N.P. Marji w Krakowie.
Cracow, 1926.

BUCKERIDGE

(Extract from a paper 'The Production of Modern Stained Glass
Windows' read at a meeting of the Oxford Architectural Society.)
The Ecclesiologist, vol. 19 (1858), pp. 119-120.

BUCKINGHAM, F.F.

Stained Glass Windows in Doddiscombsleigh Church.
Devon and Cornwall Notes and Queries, vol. 13 (1925), pp. 193-195.

BUCKLEY, Francis

Advertisements of Seventeenth and Eighteenth Century Glass-
Painters.
Antiquaries Journal, vol. 6, no. 2 (Apr. 1926), p. 193.

BUCKLEY, M.J.C.

The Ancient Stained Glass of St. Canice's Cathedral, Kilkenny.
Journal of the Royal Society of Antiquaries (Ireland), 5th
series, no. 6 (1896), pp. 240-244.

BUCZKOWSKI, K.

Dawne szkla artystyczne w Polsce. (Le verre ancien en
Pologne.)
Cracow, 1958.

BUDRYS, Stasys.

Lietuviuvitrazas.
Vilno, 1968.

BUEK, Julius von

Polnische Glasmalerkunst.
Diamant, vol. 34 (1912), pp. 900-902, 1008, 1010, 1116-1118,
1217, 1218, 1249, 1250.

BUENO, Luis Pérez

Vidrios y vidrieras.
Barcelona, 1942.

BULTEAU, Abbé

Description de la Cathédrale de Chartres Suivie d'une Courte
Notice sur les Eglises Saint-Pierre, Saint-André et Saint-
Aignan de la Même Ville.
Chartres, 1850.

Petite Monographie de la Cathédrale de Chartres et des Eglises
de la Même Ville.
Cambrai, 1872.

Monographie de la Cathédrale de Chartres.
3 vols., Chartres, 1887.

BUMPUS, T.

    Stained Glass in England since the Gothic Revival; with some
    account of the churches referred to.
    The Architect, vol. 62 (1899)
                       63
                       64
                       65
                       66 (1901)

BURBURE, Leo de

    Toestand der Beeldende Kunsten in Antwerpen Omtrent 1454.
    Antwerp, 1854.

BURCKHARDT, A.

    Glasgemälde der Mittelaltischen Sammlung zu Basel.
    Basel, 1885.

    Die Gotischen Glasgemälde der Ehemaligen Karthäuserkirche zu
    Basel.
    Basel, 1915.

BURGES, William

    Art Applied to Industry. A Series of Lectures.
    Oxford and London, 1865.
    (Glass, pp. 13-26.)

BURGESS, I.J.

    Modern Stained Glass.
    American Homes, no. 11 (Nov., 1914), pp. 369-370.

BURGKMAIER, Hans

    Der Einfluss Hans Burgkmaiers des Älteren auf die Augsburger
    Glasmalerei.
    Zeitschrift fur alte und neue Glasmalerei (1912), p. 24.

(Burlison and Grylls)

    Memorial Window to Lord Leverhulme, St. George's Congregational
    Church, Thornton Hough, Cheshire.
    Progress (Lever Bros. Magazine), (July, 1926), p. 36.

BURMAN, P.A.T.

    Report of CVMA meeting on Sept. 30th, 1972: Canterbury
    Cathedral Glass.
    J.M.G.P., vol. 15, no. 1 (1972-1973), pp. 27-33.

BURN, John S.

    Representation of the First Person of the Trinity.
    (In a destroyed window at St. Edmund's, Salisbury.)
    Notes and Queries, 4th series, vol. 3 (March 27., 1869), p. 299.

(Burne-Jones, Edward)

    VALLANCE, Aymer, Sir Edward Burne-Jones' Designs for Painted
    Glass.
    The Studio, vol. 51 (1911), pp. 91-103.

BURNHAM, W.H.

    Stained Glass: Construction and Detail.
    Architectural Forum, (Feb., 1924). (? Subsequent months as well.)

    What constitutes a Good Window?
    (BURNHAM's comments on the six 'yardsticks' adopted by the
    Chapter of Washington Cathedral.)
    Stained Glass, vol. 30, no. 1 (Spring-Summer, 1935), pp. 4-9.

    (An account of the successful struggle to allow lead to be
    supplied to stained glass firms in wartime.)
    Stained Glass, vol. 37, no. 1 (Spring, 1942), pp. 1-3.

    The Maid of Orleans Lives Again in Stained Glass.
    The Cathedral Age (Washington D.C.), (Summer, 1942).

    Two Boston Studios Collaborate on Washington Cathedral Apse
    Windows.
    (With REYNOLDS, J.G.)
    Stained Glass, vol. 38, no. 3 (Autumn, 1943), pp. 83-87.

    Creating the Apse Windows.
    The Cathedral Age (Washington D.C.), (Spring, 1943).

    The Spiritual Significance of a Stained Glass Window.
    The Cathedral Age (Washington, D.C.), (Easter, 1945).

    Stained Glass Windows.
    Design (Dec., 1946).

(Bury St. Edmunds, St. James')

    (Restoration of the 'Susanna' Window by Clayton and Bell.)
    The Times, July 25, 1925.

BUSHNELL, A.J. de Havilland

    Storied Windows: A Traveller's Introduction to the Study of
    Old Glass from the Twelfth Century to the Renaissance,
    especially in France.
    Edinburgh, 1914.

BUSK, R.H.

    Jesse Windows.
    Notes and Queries, 7th series, vol. 10 (Nov. 29, 1890), pp. 428-429.

BUTCHER, C.H.

    Some Heraldic Glass in North-West Essex.
    The Essex Review, vol. 30, no. 120 (Oct., 1921), pp. 193-199.

BUTLER, Herman J.

    The Rathenau Codex and Theophilus.
    Stained Glass, vol. 32, no. 3 (Winter, 1937-1938), pp. 82-85.

BUTTERWORTH, L.M.A.

    Review of S.E. WINBOLT's 'Wealden Glass'.
    Journal of the Society of Glass Technology, vol. 18,   no. 72,
    (Dec., 1934).

BUTTERWORTH, Walter

    Characteristics of Stained Glass.
    Manchester City News, Feb. 20, 1926.

    Renaissance Glass.
    Journal of the Society of Glass Technology, vol. 12 (1928),
    pp. 119-128.

    Renaissance Glass.
    J.M.G.P., vol. 4, no. 4 (Oct., 1932), pp. 172-182.

BUTTRESS, Donald Reeve

    An Architect's Notebook.
    J.M.G.P., vol. 16, no. 1 (1976-1977), pp. 41-45.

BUZAS, Stanislaus

    The Stained Glass of Osmund Caine.
    The Studio, vol. 139 (1950), pp. 80-81.

BYE, Arthur Edwin

    Stained Glass Panels from the Workshop of Dirk Vellert in
    the Goldman Collection.
    Art Bulletin, vol. 11, no. 2 (1929), pp. 125-145.

BYRNE, Barry

    Contemporary Glass.
    Stained Glass, vol. 43, no. 1 (Spring, 1948), pp. 3-4.

L.S.Colchester

    Stained Glass in Wells Cathedral.
    Wells, 1952. Revised ed. 1956.

CACHEUX, Paul le

    La Cathédrale de Coutances.
    in Notre Millénaire, Coutances, 1933.

CADWALLADER, Charles G.

    Thomas Godfrey. Philadelphia Glazier, Mathematician, Inventor.
    Stained Glass, vol. 39, no. 1 (Spring, 1944), pp. 25-26.

CAHIER, C.

    Monographie de la Cathédrale de Bourges.
    (with MARTIN. A.)
    2 vols., Paris, 1841-1844.
    (Livraisons 1-11, reviewed by WINSTON, Charles, and F.B. in
    The Archaeological Journal, vol. 1 (1845), pp. 169-176.)

CALDWELL, J.M.C.

    Cathedral Church of Christ, Canterbury. Notes on the Old Glass.
    Canterbury, 1931.

(Caldwell, Samuel)

    (Interview with Samuel Caldwell.)
    The Daily Telegraph (April 8, 1950).

CALDWELL, Samuel

    Memories of a Craftsman.
    24th Annual Report of the Friends of Canterbury Cathedral (1951),
    pp. 22-23.
    25th Annual Report of the Friends of Canterbury Cathedral (1952),
    pp. 22-23.

(Caldwell, Samuel)

    Samuel Caldwell.
    J.M.G.P., vol. 12, no. 3 (1958), p. 208.

    (Obituary.)
    J.M.G.P., vol. 14, no. 1 (1964), pp. 26-27.
    Reprint of RACKHAM, Bernard's, Times Obituary, Sept. 16, 1963.

CALKINS, Robert G.

    Monuments of Medieval Art.
    Oxford, 1979.
    (Stained glass, pp. 167-174.)

(Camberwell, St. Giles)

    (New windows by Lavers and Barrand.)
    Art Journal (1860), p. 223.

(Cambridge, Jesus College)

    (New windows by Hardman.)
    The Ecclesiologist, vol. 14 (1853), pp. 370-371.

(Cambridge, King's College Chapel)

    King's College Chapel Windows. By C.W.G.
    (Story about the financing of the windows.)
    Notes and Queries, vol 5 (March 20, 1852), p. 276.
    Discussed further by T.A.L. and COOPER, C.H., Ibid, (March 27,
    1852), pp. 308-309.

(Cambridge, St. Peter's College)

    Munich Glass at St. Peter's College Chapel.
    The Ecclesiologist, vol. 16 (1855), pp. 221-222.

    (More, much poorer windows inserted.)
    Ibid, vol. 19 (1858), pp. 139-140.

(Cambridge, Trinity College)

    (Window by Wailes inserted.)
    The Ecclesiologist, vol. 14 (1853), p. 371.

CAMES, G.

    Les plus anciens Vitraux de la Cathédrale de Strasbourg.
    Cahiers Alsaciens d'Archéologie, d'Art et d'Histoire (1964),
    8, pp. 101-126.

CAMESINA, Albert von

    Die ältesten Glasgemälde des Chorherren-Stiftes Klosterneuburg
    und die Bildnisse der Babenberger in der Cistercienser-Abtei
    Heiligenkreuz.
    Vienna, 1857.

    Glasgemälde aus dem zwölften Jahrhunderte im Kreuzgange des
    Cistercienser - Stiftes Heiligenkreuz im Wiener Walde.
    Vienna, 1859.

CAMM. T.W.

    Some Notes on Old Stained Glass Windows.
    Transactions of the Birmingham Midland Institute, vol. 15, for
    1888 (1890), pp. 95-106.

CANAVAN, James

    The Glass Medallions of Carl Paulson.
    American Artist, (August, 1969).

CANÉTO, F.

    Sainte-Marie d'Auch. Atlas Monographique de cette Cathédrale;
    les Vitraux, etc.
    Paris, 1857.

(Canterbury Cathedral)

    (A correspondent reports on glass which has disappeared within
    the last twenty years.)
    The Ecclesiologist, vol. 11 (1850), p. 152.

    Notes on the Painted Glass in Canterbury Cathedral.
    Aberdeen, 1887.

    Edward IV's Windows at Canterbury.
    Notes and Queries, series 2, vol. 12 (Dec. 4, 11, 1915).

    The Rose Window. By a Lover of Ancient Glass.
    Canterbury Cathedral Chronicle, no. 1 (Oct., 1928), pp. 10-12.

    Royal Arms, and Figure of an Archbishop. Fourteenth and
    Fifteenth Century. By a Lover of Ancient Glass.
    Ibid., no. 2 (April, 1929). pp. 10-12.

    A Royal Window: Its Donor and its Destruction.
    Ibid., no. 4 (Oct. 1929), pp. 11-16.

    (Notice of insertion of old and new glass in the Water Tower.)
    Third Annual Report of the Friends of Canterbury Cathedral
    (1930), p. 25.

    (Releading of the Martyrdom Window. Reglazing of the Water
    Tower.)
    4th Annual Report of the Friends of Canterbury Cathedral (1931)
    pp. 21-22.

    Notes on Queen Elizabeth Wydville's Flowers. (Letter to the Editor.)
    Canterbury Cathedral Chronicle, no. 11 (Apr. 1932), pp. 10-12.

(Canterbury Cathedral Contd.)

    (The releading of part of the Royal Window and completion of
Water Tower glass.)
5th Annual Report (1932), p. 24.

    (The Royal Window. Progress of work.)
6th Annual Report (1933), pp. 27-28.

    Order of Service for the Unveiling of the Royal Window of
Edward IV. Saturday, June 10, 1933.
Canterbury, 1933.

    The Princes in the Tower - Canterbury's Royal Window Portraits.
Illustrated London News, Dec. 23, 1933.

    English History in Glass.
Canterbury Cathedral Chronicle, vol. 22 (Oct. 1935), pp. 3-5.

    Programme of Work During 1936. (South Transept Window.)
9th Annual Report (1936), p. 49.

    The 'Miracle' Glass in Canterbury Cathedral.
Canterbury Cathedral Chronicle, vol. 25 (Oct. 1936), pp. 4-6.

    Glass Seven Hundred Years Old. Panels Renovated (Choir of
Canterbury Cathedral).
The Daily Telegraph, Oct. 25, 1937.

    Ancient Glass at Canterbury. Secrets of Early Craftsmen.
The Daily Telegraph, Aug. 2, 1939.

    (Various Restoration jobs.)
12th Annual Report (1939), pp. 28-29.

    (On the recent cleaning of the Methuselah panel.)
In News and Notes, J.M.G.P., vol. 8, no. 1 (Oct., 1939), p. 1.

    (Re-leading Borders of Twelfth Century Glass.)
13th Annual Report (1940), p. 20.

    (Re-leading glass removed for the duration.)
Ibid., p. 22.

    (Various re-leading jobs.)
14th Annual Report (1941), pp. 17-18.

    (Replacement of the glass.)
19th Annual Report (1946), p. 16.

    (Restoration of the South Rose.)
22nd Annual Report (1949), pp. 20-21.

    Postcards in Colour of the Ancient Glass.
Canterbury Cathedral Chronicle, no. 45 (Aug.,1950), p. 3.

    Canterbury Cathedral. (Insertion of glass from the Hearst
collection.)
J.M.G.P., vol. 13, no. 1 (1960), p. 339.

    Latest Addition to the Ancient Glass.
(From the Hearst Collection at St. Donat's.)
34th Annual Report (1961), p. 25.

    Canterbury Cathedral: Glazier's Workshop.
(Grant to set up a glazier's workshop for the restoration.)
The Pilgrim Trust, 43rd Annual Report (1973), p. 10.

    (Grant towards restoration of the glass.)
The Pilgrim Trust, 44th Annual Report (1974), p. 11.

    (Grant towards the restoration of the glass.)
The Pilgrim Trust, 48th Annual Report (1978), p. 9.

(Canterbury Cathedral Contd.)

    Cathedral Appeal Report.
    Fabric Restoration and Stained Glass Exhibition, New York.
    Canterbury Cathedral Chronicle, no. 72 (Apr. 1978), pp. 11-13.

(Canterbury Royal Museum)

    Catalogue of two Dutch Paintings and Stained Windows in the
Royal Museum and Free Library of Canterbury.
Canterbury, 1899.

CANTORE, Enrico

    Genetical Understanding of Science; Some Considerations About
Optics.
Archives Internationales d'Histoire des Sciences. vol. 19 (1966),
p. 333-363.

CAPRONNIER, J.B.

    Les Vitraux de la Cathédrale de Tournai, Dessinés par J.B.
Capronnier, et Mis sur Pierre par J. de Keghel, avec un Texte
Historique et Descriptif . . .
Brussels, 1848.

    Histoire de la Peinture sur Verre.
(With LEVY, Edmond.)
Brussels, 1860.

    Peinture sur Verre. Exposition Nationale de 1880.
Brussels, 1880.

    Vitraux, Verres Grès. L'Art Ancien à l'Exposition Nationale
Belge.
Brussels, 1881.

(Capronnier Collection)

    Catalogue of the Valuable Collection of Cartoons of Glass
Painting Works by the late Mn J.B. Capronnier of Brussels.
Brussels, 1892.

CARBONELL, Francis R.

    Handbook to Fairford Church and its Windows.
Oxford, 1893.

    Fairford Church Windows.
Christian Art, vol. 4 (Oct. 1908), pp. 35-46.

CARBONIER, A.

    Catalogue of Glass Objects and Glass Paintings in the Museum
of Stieglitz Central School of Design.
(In Russian.) St. Petersburg, 1893.

(Carcassonne)

    Monographie Religieuse de l'Eglise de la Cité de Carcassonne.
Description de Plusieurs Vitraux du XIVe Siècle.
Carcassonne, 1875.

(Cardiff Castle)

    William Burges, A.R.A., 1827-1881: Exhibition of Stained Glass
Cartoons from the . . . Castle Collection.
Cardiff?, 1977.

A Career in Stained Glass.
    The Washington (D.C.) Star-Sunday Magazine, Dec. 17, 1967.

CARLI, Enzo

    Vetrate Duccesca.
Florence, 1946.

CARPENTER, Herbert

    Painted Glass.
The Builder, no.   (Feb. 27, 1892).

CHALONS, J. de Chateau (pseudonym of CARRÉ DE BUSSEROLLE, Joseph Xavier)
Un Air de Guitare Archéologique sur les Vitraux de Champigny.
Tours, 1885.

CARSALADE DU PONT, M. de
Les Verrières des Nefs de la Cathédrale d'Auch.
Société Archaeologique de Gers (1897).

CARTER, John
Specimens of the Ancient Sculpture and Painting now Remaining
in England from the Earliest Period to the Reign of Henry VIII.
(2 vols.) London, 1780-1794.
(New ed. 2 vols. London, 1838.)

Observations on Mr. Hawkins's 'History of Gothic Architecture'.
The Gentleman's Magazine, vol. 85, part 2 (1815), pp. 305-306.
(Deals with stained glass.)

CARTER, Owen B.
A Series of the Ancient Painted Glass at Winchester Cathedral.
London, 1845.

CARTER, T.J.P.
King's College Chapel, Cambridge.
London and Cambridge, 1867.

(Cartmel Priory)
(Grant towards restoring and rearranging the glass in the East
Windows.)
33rd Annual Report of the Pilgrim Trust (1963), p. 15.

CARTWRIGHT, Leo
Harry Clarke: Artist and Craftsman.
Stained Glass, vol. 28, no. 1 (Spring, 1933), pp. 29-32.

CARY, Elisabeth Luther
Stained Glass now in the Metropolitan Museum, New York.
Stained Glass, vol. 27, no. 12 (Dec. 1932), pp. 338-340.

CASSELL'S Technical Educator
An Encyclopaedia of Technical Education.
(4 vols.) London, 1870-1872.
(Stained glass is in vols. 3, 4.)
Another ed. London, 1879-1881.

New Technical Educator, 6 vols., London, 1892-1895.

CASSIE, Guy
Glimpses of Modern Continental Windows on a Return Journey
from Holiday.
J.M.G.P., vol. 12, no. 1 (1956), pp. 57-60.

CASTEELE, D. van de
Lettre à M.S. sur l'Ancienne Verrerie Liègeoise.
2nd.ed. Liège, 1890.

CASTELNUOVO, Enrico
Le vetrate della Cattedrale di Chartres.
Milan, 1965.

(Catalogue of a Sale of Stained Glass in 1804)
(In Norwich and London.)
J.M.G.P., vol. 12, no. 1 (1956), pp. 22-29.

CAUMONT, de
A Panel of Glass by De Caumont, Glass-Painter of Louvain,
recently restored to the Abbey of Parc by Wilfred Drake.
J.M.G.P., vol. 2, no. 3 (Apr. 1928), pp. 129-130.

CAUTON, M.G.R., and HAINSSELIN, M.P.
Etudes sur les Vitraux de Picardie.
Bulletin Trimensuelle de la Société des Antiquaires de Picardie,
part 3 (1956).

CAUWENBERGHS, C. Van
Notice Historique sur les Peintres-Verriers d'Anvers du XVe au
XVIIIe Siècle.
Antwerp, 1891.

CAVINESS, Madeline Harrison
A Life of St. Edward the Confessor in Early Fourteenth-Century
Stained Glass at Fécamp in Normandy.
Journal of the Warburg and Courtauld Institutes, vol. 26 (1963),
pp. 22-37.

A Panel of Thirteenth Century Stained Glass from Canterbury in
America.
Antiquaries Journal, no. 45 (1965), pp. 192-199.

(With GRODECKI, Louis)
Les Vitraux de la Sainte-Chapelle.
Revue de l'Art, 1-2 (1968), pp. 8-16.

Review of BECKSMANN, Rüdiger, Die architektonische Rahmung . . .
Art Bulletin, vol. 52 (1970), pp. 432-434.

French Thirteenth Century Stained Glass at Canterbury. A Fragment
from the Sainte Chapelle of Paris in St. Gabriel's Chapel.
Canterbury Cathedral Chronicle, no. 66 (Autumn, 1971), pp. 35-41.

Saving Canterbury's Medieval Glass.
Country Life (Sept. 1972), pp. 739-740.

Canterbury Stained Glass.
Arts in Virginia, no. 13 (1973), pp. 4-15.

A Lost Cycle of Canterbury Paintings of 1220.
Antiquaries Journal, no. 54:1 (1974), pp. 66-74.

The Canterbury Jesse Window.
In The Year 1200, Part III.
New York (1975), pp. 373-398.

Review of MARCHINI, CVMA Italy. I.
Art Bulletin, vol. 58 (March, 1976), pp. 124-126.

New Observations on the Channel School: A French Glass-Painter
in Canterbury.
In Aktendes 10. Internationalen Colloquiums des CVMA.
Stuttgart, 1977, pp. 30-31.

The Early Stained Glass of Canterbury Cathedral.
Princeton, 1977.
Reviewed by ALLCHIN, A.M. in Canterbury Cathedral Chronicle,
no. 73 (Apr., 1979), pp. 53-54.
Reviewed in J.M.G.P., vol. 17, no. 2 (1978-1979), pp. 79-81.
Reviewed by WEIS, Helene, Stained Glass, vol. 74, no. 2 (Summer,
1979), pp. 139-141.

Louis Grodecki and the Corpus Vitrearum.
Stained Glass, vol. 74, no. 2 (Summer, 1979), pp. 137-138.

CECCHELLI, C.
Vetri di finestra del San Vitale.
Felix Ravenna, n.s. 35 (1930), pp. 14-20.

CERF, T. le
Notice Historique sur l'Eglise Saint-Martin d'Argentan.
Caen, 1856.

CHABOT-KARLEN, Ch.

    (Auction catalogue of the collection.)

    Katalog der Kunstsammlung des Herrn Ch. Chabot-Karlen, früher
    in Fontenay-le-Comte, (Vendée).

    Abgeschlossene Glas-Sammlung, Glas-Malereien, u.s.w.

    Cologne, 1898.

CHADWICK, S.J.

    The Old Painted Glass in Dewsbury Church.

    The Yorkshire Archaeological Journal, vol. 15 (1898), pp. 211-223.

(Chagall, Marc)

    Chagall: Vitraux pour Jérusalem.

    (Catalogue of exhibition at the Musée des Arts decoratifs.)

    Paris, 1961.

(Challock, Kent)

    St. Cosmas and St. Damien, Challock.

    N.p., n.d. (Glass, pp. 2-3)(unnumbered pages of pamphlet).

(Châlons-sur-Marne)

    Iconographie des Vitraux de Châlons-sur-Marne.

    Bulletin Monumental, vol. 112 (1954), pp. 379-381.

(Chamber Family)

    The Chamber Family, Glass Painters of York.

    Notes and Queries, series 12, vol. 8 (Feb. 12, 1921), p. 127.

CHAMBERLAIN, T.

    (Discussion on 'The Principles on which Stained Glass should be
    Designed for Use in Churches') with other contributions from
    MILLARD, J.E.; MEYRICK, F.; PARKER, J.; WALTON, H.B.; etc.
    WINSTON is criticised.

    The Ecclesiologist, vol. 16 (1855), pp. 121-123.

    (A reply to CHAMBERLAIN.)

    Ibid., pp. 131-133.
    (CHAMBERLAIN replies)
    Ibid, pp. 196-197.

CHAMBON, R.

    L'Histoire de la Verrerie en Belgique du 11ᵐᵉ Siècle à nos Jours.

    Brussels, 1955.

CHAMOREL and NAEF

    La Cathédrale de Lausanne.

    Lausanne, 1929.

CHAMOREL. G

    Les Vitraux de la Cathédrale de Lausanne.

    Gazette de Lausanne, (Aug. 1930), nos. 227-228.

CHAMPIER, Victor

    Catalogue Illustré de l'Union Centrale des Arts Decoratifs.

    Paris, 1884.

    (Glass and glass painting, pp. 136-147.)

CHAMPIGNEULLE. Charles

    Le Vitrail. Conférence Faite au Palais de l'Industrie, Paris.

    Paris, 1895.

CHAMPOLLION-FIGEAC, M.

    Peinture sur Verre, Mosaique, Émaux.

    Paris, 1851.

CHANCE BROS. & CO. LTD.

    Designs for Ornamental Enamelled Window Glass.

    Birmingham, n.d.

    Designs for Ornamental Enamelled Window Glass Registered Oct. 3,
    1855.

    Birmingham, 1855.

CHARAVAY. Etienne

    La Corporation des Peintres Verriers de Paris en 1585.

    Revue des Documents Historiques.

    Paris, 1879, pp. 156-164.

CHARD, T.D.

    Stained Glass Window in Cadbury Church.

    Devon and Cornwall Notes and Queries, vol. 13 (1925), p. 152.

CHARDON DU RANQUET, Henry

    Les Vitraux de la Cathédrale de Clermont-Ferrand.(XIIᵉ, XIIIᵉ,
    XIVᵉ, XVᵉ Siècles.)

    Clermont-Ferrand, 1932.

CHARLES, B.

    Un Atelier de Peintre-Verriers à Montoire au XVIᵉ Siècle.

    Bulletin de la Société Archéologique et Scientifique
    Vendômois, (1879).

CHARLES, George H.

    Stained and Painted Glass in American Churches.

    (In the same author's American Churches, 2 vols., New York, 1915.)

CHARLES, Léopold

    Atelier de Verriers à La Ferté-Bernard à la Fin du Quinzième
    Siècle et au Seizième.

    Le Mans, 1851.

    De la Conservation et de la Restauration des Anciens Vitraux.

    Bulletin Monumental, vol. 24 (1858), p. 638.

    La Peinture sur Verre au XVIᵉ Siècle et à Notre Epoque.

    Le Mans, 1860.

    Verriers et Vitraux au XVIᵉ Siècle à Propos du Peintre Jean Cousin.

    Bulletin Monumental, vol. 39 (1873), p. 502.

    Extraits d'une Notice sur les Vitraux de l'Eglise de La Ferté-
    Bernard (Sarthe) et sur l'Atelier des Verriers qui a Existé
    dans cette Ville Pendant près de cent cinquante années.

    Paris, 1857.

    Reprinted from Bulletin du Comité de la Langue, de l'Histoire
    et des Arts de la France, vol. 4.

CHARLESTON, R.J.

    Lead in Glass.

    Archaeometry, vol. 3 (1960), pp. 1-4.

(Chartham Church)

    A History of St. Mary's Church, Chartham.

    (Printed) Chatham, 1954.

    (Glass, p. 8.)

(Chartres Cathedral)

    The Famous Glass of Chartres.

    (Plans for the removal of it in case of air raids.)

    The Observer, Feb. 16, 1936.

    French Glass in War Danger.

    Stained Glass, vol. 33, no. 2 (Autumn-Winter, 1938), pp. 59-60.

    (A Petition to remove the air base from Chartres.)

    J.M.G.P., vol. 7, no. 4 (Apr., 1939), p. 155.

    (Article and illustrations on the West window.)

    Time, Dec. 24, 1951.

CHASTEL, André

    Paris Summer.

    (On the stained glass exhibition at the Pavillion de Marsan.)

    Art News, vol. 52, no. 4 (June, July, August, 1953).

CHASTEL, André

Le Vitrail Français.
(With AUBERT, M.; GRODECKI, L.; GRUBER, J.-J., LAFOND, J.;
MATHEY, F.; TARALON, J.; VERRIER, J.)
Paris, 1958.
Reviewed by SALET, Francis, in Bulletin Monumental, no. 116
(1958), p. 226.

CHATWIN, Philip B.

Some notes on the Painted Windows of the Beauchamp Chapel,
Warwick.
Transactions of the Birmingham Archaeological Society, vol. 53
for 1928 (1931), pp. 158-166.
Reprinted Oxford, 1931.

Wixford Church, Warwickshire: its Brass and Painted Glass.
Transactions of the Birmingham Archaeological Society, vol. 55
for 1931 (1933), pp. 48-56.

Medieval Glass from Kinwarton Church, Warwickshire.
Transactions of the Birmingham Archaeological Society, vol. 59
for 1935 (1938), p. 1.

Medieval Stained Glass from the Cathedral, Coventry.
Transactions of the Birmingham Archaeological Society, vol. 66,
p. 1.
Reprinted Oxford, 1950.

CHAUBRY, De Froncenord

Recherches sur les Peintres-Verreriers Champenois.
Châlons, 1857.

CHEETHAM, F.H.

The Church of St. Michael-on-Wye in Amounderness.
Transactions of the Historic Society of Lancashire and Cheshire,
new series, vol. 30 for 1914 (1915).
(Glass, pp. 202-205.)

(Chelsea Old Church)

(Exhibition of proposed restoration by Maurice DRAKE.)
The Daily Telegraph, Nov. 4, 1922.
The Daily Telegraph, Nov. 7, 1922.
The Times, Nov. 7, 1922.

CHESNEAU, G.

Contribution à l'Etude Chimique des Vitraux du Moyen Age.
Comptes Rendus de l'Academie de Science, vol. 160 (1915),
pp. 622-624.

Etude Chimique des Vitraux de l'Eglise Saint-Remi de Reims.
Comptes Rendus de l'Académie de Science, vol. 178 (1924), p. 852.

Contribution à l'Etude de la Technique des Vitraux du Moyen-Age.
Bulletin Monumental, vol. 42, part 3 (1933), pp. 265-295.

(Chester Cathedral)

(Announcement of auction of glass supposedly from the Chapter
House at Chester, and subsequently at Atherstone.)
The Gentleman's Magazine, vol. 87, part 2 (1817), pp. 443-444.

CHESTER, Grenville J.

A Brief Account of the Painted Glass in Wells Cathedral.
Proceedings of the Somersetshire Archaeological and Natural
History Society, vol. 6 for 1855 (1856), part 2, pp. 125-130.

CHEVREUL, M.E.

De la Loi du Contraste Simultané des Couleurs, et de
l'Assortment des Objets Colorés Considéré d'Après cette Loi
dans ses Rapports avec la Peinture . . . les Vitraux
Colorés . . . etc.
Paris, 1839.
Translated into English:
The Principles of Harmony and Contrast of Colours, and their
Applications to the Arts . . .
London, 1854. (Subsequent editions 1855, 1859).
Another edition based on the first English edition, with
introduction and notes by BIRREN, F., New York, 1967.

Chimie Appliquée aux Beaux-arts. Mémoire sur les Vitraux Peints.
Comptes Rendus, vol. 57 (1863), pp. 655-666.

(Chilwell House, Notts.)

(Reference to a window, destroyed, representing viticulture.)
Notes and Queries, 11th series, vol. 11 (May 1, 1915), p. 335.

CHITTY, Herbert

John Prudde, King's Glazier.
Notes and Queries, 12th series, vol. 3 (Sept., 1917), pp. 419-421.

C(HITTY), H(erbert)

Barnard Flower, the King's Glazier.
Notes and Queries, 12th series, no. 3 (Oct., 1917), pp. 436-437.

Devils Blowing Horns or Trumpets.
(Iconography of the Last Judgement: refers to Winchester window.)
Notes and Queries, 12th series, vol. 4 (Nov., 1918), pp. 308-309.

Shield in Winchester Stained Glass.
Notes and Queries, 12th series, vol. 4 (Aug., 1918), pp. 225-226.

Representations of the Blessed Trinity.
(Refers to Winchester College Chapel.)
Notes and Queries, 12th series, vol. 4 (Dec., 1918), pp. 331-332.

Winchester Stained Glass.
(Letter to the Editor.)
Times Literary Supplement (Nov. 23, 1920).

Thurbern's Chantry at Winchester College.
(With HARVEY, John)
Antiquaries Journal, vol. 42 (1962), pp. 208-225.

(Christie's Ltd.)

Sale Catalogue, June 16, 1808.
Reprinted in J.M.G.P., vol. 10, no. 4 (1951), pp. 181-188.

Catalogue of a Sale by Auction of Ancient Stained Glass at
Christie's in 1816.
J.M.G.P., vol. 6, no. 4 (Apr., 1937), pp. 217-220.

Catalogue of a Sale of Stained Glass at Christie's in 1816.
J.M.G.P., vol. 8, no. 1 (Oct., 1939), pp. 15-17.

Catalogue of a Sale by Auction of Ancient Stained Glass at
Christie's in 1820.
J.M.G.P., vol. 6, no. 3 (Apr., 1936), pp. 129-131.

The Stevenson Collection of Books, Oriental Porcelain, Ancient
Stained Glass, etc. Offered for Sale at Christie's Sale Rooms.
London (with Buyers and Prices).
London, 1921.

Lord Manton's Collection . . . (including) early English and
German stained glass . . . removed from the chapel at Compton
Verney, Warwickshire.
Catalogue of Sale, July 30, 1931.

(Sales of designs and drawings for stained glass.)
News and Notes, J.M.G.P., vol. 15, no. 2 (1973-1974), p. 54.

(Christie's Ltd., Contd.)

(Sales of drawings and cartoons.)
News and Notes, J.M.G.P., vol. 15, no. 3 (1974-1975), p. 54.

(Sales of stained glass.)
Editorial, J.M.G.P., vol. 17, no. 1 (1978-1979), pp. 9-14.

CHRISTY, Miller
Some Old Roothing Farmhouses.
(Roundels of Labours of the Months.)
The Essex Review, vol. 12. no. 47 (July, 1903), pp. 129-144.

Chronological List of English Glass-Paintings of known date compiled
with a view to displaying the uninterrupted continuity of the
art of Glass-Painting in England from the Middle Ages until the
present day.
J.M.G.P., vol. 6, no. 1 (Apr., 1935), pp. 50-57.
J.M.G.P., vol. 6, no. 3 (Apr., 1936), pp. 164-175.
Additions in the Letters to the Editor, J.M.G.P., vol. 6, no. 4
(Apr., 1937), pp. 227-228, and J.M.G.P., vol. 7, no. 1 (Oct.,
1937), pp. 57-58.

(Additions.)
J.M.G.P., vol. 7, no. 2 (Apr., 1938), p. 106.
J.M.G.P., vol. 7, no. 3 (Oct., 1938), p. 152.
J.M.G.P., vol. 8, no. 1 (Oct., 1939), p. 35.
J.M.G.P., vol. 8, no. 2 (Apr., 1940), p. 83.
J.M.G.P., vol. 13, no. 1 (1960), pp. 340-343.

CHUTE, Chaloner W.
A History of the Vyne in Hampshire.
Winchester and London, 1888.

(Cilcain Church, Flint)
(A note on the glass by RIDGWAY, M.H.)
Archaeologia Cambrensis, vol. 99 (1947), pp, 350-351.

(Cingria, Alexandre)
A Pioneer in the Swiss Modern Stained Glass Movement.
L'Artisan et les Arts Liturgiques, nos. 2, 3 (1946).

CLARK, J.W.
A Description of the East Room of the University Library,
Cambridge, as built by Bishop Rotheram, written by William
COLE, M.A., in 1759.
(With an appended comment by JAMES, M.R.)
Proceedings of the Cambridge Antiquarian Society, new series,
vol. 4, 1898-1903 (1904), pp. 419-425.

CLARKE, David T-D.
Painted Glass from Leicester.
Leicester, 1962.

CLARK, William S.
Stained Glass and the Liturgy.
Stained Glass, vol. 58, no. 3 (Autumn, 1963), pp. 5-15.
Replied to by SADWITH, Lucille:
From the Artist's Point of View: A Rebuttal.
Stained Glass, vol. 58, no. 4 (1963-1964), pp. 38-40.
Replied to in turn by PRATHER, Odell:
Another Point of View as to Liturgical Art and the Artist's
Responsibilities.
Stained Glass, vol. 59, no. 2 (Summer, 1964), pp. 23-25.

CLARKE, Juliet and Florence
The Ancient Heraldic Glass at Ronaele Manor.
International Studio (Jan., 1930).

CLARKE, Kate M.
St. Catherine's, Polsloe.
(Suggesting that some of the Polsloe glass was inserted in the
East Window of Exeter Cathedral.)
Devon Notes and Queries, vol. 3 (1905), p. 219.

CLARKE, Lady
The Home Industries of Chipping Campden and its Individualistic
Artist-Craftsmen.
Illustrated London News, (Dec., 18, 1931).

CLARKE. W.E.H.
Madley Church.
Transactions of the Woolhope Naturalists' Field Club, vol. 22,
for 1914, 1915, 1916, 1917 (1918),
(Glass, pp. 110-111.)

CLAUDEL, Paul
Les Vitraux des Cathédrales de France.
(With AUBERT. Marcel).
Paris, 1936.

The Eye Listens.
New York, n.d. (? 1949).

CLAY. Ernest C.
Ancient Glass in Buckland Church.
Surrey Archaeological Collections, vol. 41 (1933), pp. 123-124.

CLAY, John W.
Elland Church.
Yorkshire Archaeological Journal (Leeds), vol. 10 (1889), pp.
104-116, 205-216.

(Clayton and Bell)
Clayton and Bell. (Anon.)
J.M.G.P., vol. 4, no. 3 (Apr., 1932), pp. 142-145.

(George Payne's Indenture Papers to Clayton and Bell printed.)
Stained Glass, vol. 28, no. 1 (Spring, 1933), pp. 61-63.

CLAYTON. Gerald W.
John Richard Clayton. Some Notes on his Lesser-Known Works.
J.M.G.P., vol. 12 no. 1 (1956), pp. 36-38.
(Error pointed out by BELL, M.C. Farrar, Letter to the Editor,
J.M.G.P., vol. 12, no. 2 (1957), p. 166.
Acknowledged by CLAYTON, G.W., Ibid.)

Forty Years of Stained Glass Painting (By Clayton and Bell).
J.M.G.P., vol. 12, no. 3 (1958), pp. 191-195.

CLAYTON, John R.
The Fairford Windows.
The Builder, vol. 26 (Nov. 7, 1868), p. 818.
(Replies to a letter by TAYLOR, Tom, Ibid., Nov. 14, 1868).

Cleaning Old Stained Glass.
Notes and Queries, 2nd series, vol. 12 (1861), pp. 9, 59.

Cleaning and Restoration of Museum Exhibits.
3rd Report of Investigations Conducted at the British Museum.
(For the Department of Scientific and Industrial Research.)
London, 1926.

CLEMEN, Paul (Editor)
Belgische Kunstdenkmäler.
Vol. 2, Munich, 1923.

CLEMENT, S.
Vitraux de Bourges.
Vitraux du XIIIe Siècle de la Cathédrale de Bourges.
(With GUITARD, A.)
Bourges, 1900.

CLEMENTS, H.J.B.
The Donors of the St. William Window, York Minster.
(A reply).
Notes and Queries, vol. 163, no. 25 (   ), p. 446.

CLIFTON-TAYLOR, Alec
An Event in Stained Glass.
Country Life, (Oct. 22, 1948), p. 839.

Review of LEWIS, Mostyn's;
Stained Glass in North Wales.
The Connoisseur, vol. 177 (June, 1971), p. 151.

CLOSE——.
Les Gentilshommes Verriers du Pays de Charleroi.
Namur, 1928.

CLOWES, HUGHES and BAILEY
A Description of the East Window of St. Martin's, Windermere.
Kendal, 1874.

COBB, F.W.
Medieval Glassmakers.
(Mentions window at Chiddingfold church composed of local glass.)
(Letter to the Editor.)
The Times, Sept. 10, 1930.

COBURN, F.W.
Harry E. Goodhue, Worker in Stained Glass.
International Studio, vol. 41 (Aug., 1910), supplement, pp. 37-40.

COCHARD, Th.
Les Verrières de Notre-Dame-de-Pitie à Sully-sur-Loire.
Société Archéologique et Historique de l'Orléannais, vol. 31 (1907)
pp. 165-201.

COCHET, J.B.D.
Les Eglises de l'Arrondissement de Dieppe.
2 vols., Dieppe, 1846-1850.

COCK, F. William
Glazier's Arms.
(In Appledore Church.)
Notes and Queries, vol. 161 (Aug.22, 1931), p. 135.
Further instance (the Chester Glaziers' Arms) given by R.S.B.,
Ibid., (Sept. 5, 1931), pp. 177-178.

(With HUMPHRY, G.W.)
Notes on Appledore Church, Kent.
9th issue, 1938, n.p.
(Glass, p. 8.)

CODALÁ, Manuel Rodriquez
Algo de Maestros Pintores de Vidrios y Notas Sobre Vidrieras de
Colores.
Barcelona, 1944.
(Reprinted from Memorias de la Real Academia de Ciencias y Artes
de Barcelona, vol. 27, no. 8.)

COFFIN, Richard
A Description of the Great West Window in the Cathedral Church
of St. Peter, at Exeter.
Bristol, n.d.

COFFINET, Abbé
Les Peintres-Verriers de la Ville de Troyes Pendant Trois Siècles,
1375-1690.
Annales Archéologiques, vol. 18 (1858), pp. 125, 212.

COHN, Werner
A Glass-Painting by the Master E.S.
Burlington Magazine, vol. 70 (Jan.-June, 1937), pp. 71-77.

Two Glass Panels after Designs by Hans Holbein.
Burlington Magazine, vol. 75 (1939), pp. 115-121.

Zur Ikonographie der Glasfenster von Orsanmichele.
Mitteilungen des Kunsthistorischen Instituts in Florenz. 9. (1959),
pp. 1-12.

COLE, William C.
The Flemish Roundel in England.
J.M.G.P., vol. 15, no. 2 (1973-1974), pp. 16-27.

Old Stained Glass.
Antique Collector, no. 48 (July, 1976), pp. 14-18.

COLEMAN, Caryl
Windows of Gouda.
The Architectural Review, vol. 10 (1901), pp. 225-227.

Jesse Tree.
Ibid, vol. 21 (1907), pp. 361-370.

COLLIER, C.V. and LAWRENCE, H.
Ancient Heraldry in the Deanery of Harthill.
The Yorkshire Archaeological Journal, vol. 26, (1921), pp. 93-143.

Ancient Heraldry in Yorkshire.
The Yorkshire Archaeological Journal, vol. 28 (1924).
(Deanery of Ryedale, pp. 25-33.)
(Deanery of Cleveland, pp. 34-47.)
(Deanery of Richmond, pp. 67-79.)

Ancient Heraldry in the Deanery of Catterick.
The Yorkshire Archaeological Journal, vol. 29, 1927-1929, (1929),
pp. 202-231.

COLLIER, Mrs.
The Church and Painted Glass at Bowness-on-Windermere.
Journal of the British Archaeological Association, vol. 53 (1897),
pp. 122-133.

St. Christopher and some Representations of Him in English Churches.
Ibid., new series, vol. 10, pp. 130-145.

John Halle, Merchant and Mayor of Salisbury.
(With an account of the heraldic glass in the Hall of John Halle.)
Journal of the British Archaeological Association, new series,
vol. 14,(Dec., 1908), pp. 221-242.

(Collins——.)
(Collins' Window for St. Peter's Church, Calcutta.)
The Gentleman's Magazine, vol. 98, part 1 (1828), p. 72.

COLLONGUES, Robert, PEREZ Y JORBA, M., TILLOGA, G., DALLAS, J.P.
Nouveaux Aspects du Phénomène de Corrosion des Vitraux Anciens
des Eglises Françaises.
Verres et Réfractaires, numéro spécial, vol. 30, no. 1 (Jan.-Feb.,
1976).

30

COLLONGUES, R., and PEREZ Y JORBA, M.
  Recherches récentes sur le Processus de Corrosion des Vitraux.
  In *Akten des 10. Internationalem Colloquiums des CVMA.*
  Stuttgart, 1977, p. 47.

COLLONGUES, Robert
  La Corrosion des Vitraux.
  Les Monuments Historiques de la France, no. 1 (1977), pp. 14-16.

(Cologne glass)
  Ancient Stained Glass from Cologne.
  By Ithuriel.
  Notes and Queries, 2nd series, vol. 10 (Oct. 6, 1860), p. 266.
  (Subsequent history of the glass given by J.G.N.)
  Ibid., (Nov. 17, 1860), p. 395.
  (And final destination, Shrewsbury, given by LEIGHTON, W.A.)
  Ibid., (Dec. 1, 1860), pp. 438-439.

(Cologne Cathedral)
  The Newest Windows in Cologne Cathedral.
  The Ecclesiologist, vol. 29 (1868), pp. 349-353.
  (Translated from *Organ für Christliche Kunst*.)

  Legendenfenster in der Stephanskapelle des Domes zu Köln, um 1300.
  Zeitschrift für alte und Neue Glasmalerei (1912), p. 12

(Cologne: German Trades Exhibition)
  Modernes Ausstellungswesen und das dekorative Kunstgewerbe,
  insonderheit die Glasmalerei. Die Ausstellung des deutschen
  Werkbundes in Köln.
  Zeitschrift für alte und neue Glasmalerei (1914), pp. 81, 103.

(Cologne)
  Glasmalerei in der Jahrtausend-Ausstellung in Köln.
  Diamant (Sept. 21, 1925).

  Von den Kölner Domfenstern.
  Diamant, 48th year, no. 28 (Oct. 1, 1926), pp. 542-543.

  Repairing Cologne Glass.
  Stained Glass, vol. 42, no. 4 (Winter, 1947), p. 112.

(Color and Light)
  Exploring New Dimensions in Color and Light. A Symposium.
  Contributions from COOLEY, W.
              DOUAIRE, R.
              FREI, R.
              NOONAN, E.
              WILLET. C.
              LINCOLN. J.
              RIORDAN, J.
  Stained Glass, vol. 61, no. 4 (Winter, 1966-1967)
            vol. 62, no. 1 (Spring, 1967), pp. 25-30.

COLUM, Padraic, and DAVID, John
  The Art of Stained Glass in Ireland.
  Stained Glass. vol. 27, no. 11 (Nov., 1932), pp. 315-317.
  (Reprinted from *Keltia*, Summer, 1931.)

(Columbus Guild of Window Makers)
  (Report of its organisation.)
  Stained Glass, vol. 28 (Winter, 1933-1934), pp. 199-200.

(Comper, Ninian)
  Obituary (by KIRBY, H.T.).
  J.M.G.P., vol. 13, no. 2 (1961), pp. 447-448.

(Compton Verney Glass)
  Stained Glass Returns.
  (To the Warwick Museum.)
  The Connoisseur, vol. 133 (March, 1954), p. 188.

  (Glass purchased for Warwick Museum.)
  News and Notes, *J.M.G.P.*, vol. 11. no. 4 (1955), p. 192.

COMYNS —— .
  Stained Glass.
  (Stained glass sales catalogue.)
  London and Norwich, c. 1804.

CONDY, Nicholas
  Cotehele, on the Banks of the Tamar, the seat of the Earl of
  Edgcumbe.
  London, c. 1850.
  (Chapel Windows, p. 17.)

CONNICK, Charles Jay
  Windows of Old France.
  International Studio.(Dec., 1923
              Jan., 1924
              Feb., 1924
              July, 1924).

  Modern Glass - A Review.
  International Studio (Oct., 1924).

(Connick, Charles Jay)
  The Work of Charles J. Connick at Newport Exposition.
  Revue du Vrai et Beau, 3rd year, no. 52 (Jan. 25, 1925)
              4th year, no. 62 (June 25, 1925).

  Stained Glass in Modern Style at the Paris Exhibition.
  New York Times Magazine (Nov. 1, 1925).

  Christopher Whall, Artist Craftsman.
  J.M.G.P., vol. 1, no. 4 (Apr., 1926), pp. 9-13.

  Modern Stained Glass at the Paris Exhibition. 1925.
  J.M.G.P., vol. 2, no. 1 (1927), pp. 12-17.

  Stained Glass Windows - Coloured Sunlight.
  The American Magazine of Art, vol. 18, no. 5 (May, 1927),pp.
  240-248.

  Stained Glass. An Artist's Medium in Light and Colour.
  The American Lutheran, vol. 10, no. 6, (June, 1927).

  Colour in Light.
  Architectural Progress (Nov., 1929).

  Review of Delaporte and Houvet's 'Les Vitraux de la Cathédrale
  de Chartres'.
  J.M.G.P., vol. 2, no. 2 (Oct., 1927), pp. 96-98.

  The Curious Power of Glass.
  Bankers' Monthly (Jan., 1930).

(Connick, Charles Jay)
  History in Glass.
  (Deals with the work of CONNICK, C.J.)
  The Studio (Feb., 1930), pp. 125-127.

CONNICK, Charles Jay
  By Way of Introduction (to the position of Stained Glass in the
  U.S.A.)
  Stained Glass, vol. 26, no. 2 (Feb., 1931), pp. 23-27.

  The Beautiful Window's Message for Glass Men. (La Belle Verrière.)
  Stained Glass, vol. 27, no. 1 (Jan., 1932), p. 7.

CONNICK, Charles Jay (Contd.)

    The Tree of Jesse Window (Chartres).
    Stained Glass, vol. 27, no. 2 (Feb., 1932), p. 39.

    The Life of Our Lord. The Central Window of the Western Group,
    Chartres.
    Stained Glass, vol. 27, no. 3 (March, 1932), p. 71.

    The Passion Window of the Western Group, Chartres.
    Stained Glass, vol. 27, no. 4 (Apr., 1932), p. 107.

    'La Belle Verrière' of Infinite Variety.
    Stained Glass, vol. 27, no. 5 (May, 1932), pp. 137-140.
    (Reprinted from American Magazine of Art, vol. 24, no. 3, March,
    1932.)

    The Good Samaritan Window at Bourges.
    Stained Glass, vol. 27, no. 7 (July, 1932), p. 201.

    The Riches of York in Stained Glass.
    Stained Glass, vol. 27, no. 8 (August, 1932), p. 236.

(Connick, C.J.)

    (Reprints of editorial comments on the occasion of an M.A. being
    conferred by Princeton on CONNICK.)
    Stained Glass, vol. 27, no. 8 (Aug., 1932), pp. 251-252.

CONNICK, Charles Jay

    Rose Window in the Cathedral of St. John the Divine, New York City.
    Creative Art Magazine (New York), vol. 11, no. 2 (Oct., 1932).

    Ancient Colors in Sandwich Glass.
    Stained Glass, vol. 27, no. 11 (Nov., 1932), pp. 309-311.

    The Crucifixion Window, Poitiers.
    Stained Glass, vol. 27, no. 12 (Dec., 1932), p. 333.

    Light and Colour in the Church School.
    Church School Journal (Cincinatti, Ohio), (Dec., 1932), pp. 659-662.

    Boston Stained Glass Craftsmen.
    Stained Glass, vol. 28, no. 2 (Summer, 1933), pp. 84-93.

    Windows in Grace Cathedral.
    Architect and Engineer (San Francisco), (Dec., 1934).

    Adventures of Light and Colour.
    New York, 1937.
    Reviewed by FELL, H. Granville, The Connoisseur, vol. 101 (Apr.,
    1938), pp. 219-220.
    Reviewed by YOUNG, Stark, The New Republic (Dec.,29, 1937).
    Reviewed by RACKHAM, Bernard, Burlington Magazine, vol. 72
    (Jan.-June, 1938), p. 246.
    Reviewed in The Sunday Times (Nov. 14, 1937).
    Reprinted in Stained Glass, vol. 32, no. 3 (Winter, 1937-1938),
    pp. 99-100.

    Brother Sun's Workshop.
    World Horizons (Feb., 1938).

    Adventures in Light and Colour.
    Eastern Arts Association Bulletin (New York), (Oct., 1938).

    Christian Art's Worst Enemy.
    The Churchman (New York), (Oct. 15, 1938).

    Sermons in Light and Colour.
    Holy Cross Magazine (West Park, New York), (Nov., 1938).

    Gloom is no longer Respectable.
    The Churchman (Apr. 1, 1939).

    Poetry, Light and Color.
    Bostonia (May, 1939).

CONNICK, Charles Jay (Contd)

    My Friend, J. Horace Rudy.
    Stained Glass, vol. 35, no. 1 (Spring, 1940), pp. 4-12.

    What Does Color Mean to You?
    The Church School Journal (Apr., 1940).

    Stained Glass Windows.
    The Modern Hospital (Chicago), (Sept., 1940).

    St. Clement's Glass.
    St. Clement's Quarterly (Philadelphia), (Spring, 1941).

    Is there a Language of Color?
    Bostonia (Boston), (July, 1941).

    The Unpublished Ralph Adams Cram.
    Stained Glass, vol. 37, no. 4 (Winter, 1942), pp. 108-115.

    Messages of Light and Color.
    Classmate (Cincinnati), (Dec., 1942).

    The Language of Stained Glass.
    Advance (Crawfordsville, Indiana), (Apr., 1944).

    Stained Glass for Tomorrow and the Post-War Years.
    Catholic Buyers' Guide (New York), vol. 9 (1944).

    Stained Glass Windows.
    Church Arts (1944).

    Jewelled Windows in Wartime Europe.
    Classmate (Cincinnati), (Sept., 1944).

    The Stained Glass Window is a Natural.
    The Borromean (Catonsville, Maryland), (Nov., 1945).

    The Creative Spirit and the Restorer.
    The Christian Advocate (Chicago), (June 27.,1946).

    Obituaries in
    Stained Glass, vol. 41, no. 1 (Spring, 1946),
    By CUMMINGS, H.W. (pp. 1-4)
        BLOCK, K.M.   (pp. 5-6)
        CASSIDY, J.E. (pp. 7-9)
        MAGINNIS, C.D. (pp. 10-11)
        CLEVELAND. F.E.(pp. 12-15)
        BUXTON. F.W.   (pp. 15-16)
        HEINIGKE, O.W. (pp. 20-21)
    By WILBERT, H.G., Stained Glass, vol. 41, no. 3 (Autumn. 1946),
    pp. 76-79.
    By SKINNER, O.E., Church Property Administration (Milwaukee),
    (May-June, 1946).
    (Anonymous), Cowley, Quarterly Review of the Society of St. John
    the Evangelist (Cambridge, Mass.), (Spring, 1946).
    (Anonymous), American Glass Review, vol. 65, no. 15 (Jan. 5, 1946),
    p. 21.

(Conyers, Georgia, Cistercian Abbey)

    Cistercian Glass. By the monks of the Abbey's Stained Glass
    Department.
    Stained Glass, vol. 55, no. 2 (Summer, 1960), pp. 5-14.

COOK, Jean M.

    A Fragment of Early Medieval Glass from London.
    Medieval Archaeology. 2 (1958), pp. 173-177.

COOK, Leland A.

    Photographing Stained Glass. Part 2.
    Stained Glass, vol. 70, nos. 3, 4 (Fall and Winter, 1975), pp.
    110-112.
    (Also see ROENN, Kenneth von, 1975.)

COOLEY, William M.
    A Critical View of Stained Glass.
    Christian Art (Aug., 1966).

COOPER, C.
    On Stained Glass Windows. A Paper read before the Royal
    Society of Arts, Jan. 27, 1847.
    London, 1847.

COOPER, T.P.
    The Story of a Lost Window, The Guildhall, York.
    J.M.G.P., vol. 4, no. 2 (Oct., 1931), pp. 94-96.

COPE, E.E. (Mrs Hautenville Cope)
    Some Stained Glass at Hurst House, Berks.
    The Connoisseur, vol. 64 (Sept.-Dec., 1922), p. 182.

    Some Stained Glass at the West Gate, Winchester.
    The Connoisseur, vol. 65 (Jan.-Apr., 1923), p. 44.

    Lost Stained Glass Windows.
    (With the supposed arms of Owen Glendower.)
    Notes and Queries, vol. 155 (Dec. 15, 1928), pp. 420-421.

    Heraldry in Old Glass Windows.
    Notes and Queries, vol. 168 (Feb. 16, 1935), pp. 114-115.

COPE, W.H.
    On the History of Ancient Ecclesiastical Stained Glass.
    Journal of the British Archaeological Association, vol. 38 (1882),
    pp. 249-267.

    Ancient Ecclesiastical Stained Glass.
    London, 1897.

(Copper Wire Ties)
    Copper Wire Ties Falling Off.
    (Letter to the Editor asking for the reason.)
    J.M.G.P., vol. 9, no. 3 (1945), p. 100.

CORNELIUS, C. Fryer
    Fittings, Furnishings and Finishings of the Ancient Devon Parish
    Churches Within a Ten Mile Radius of Newton Abbot.
    Transactions of the Devonshire Association, vol. 79 (1947),
    (Glass. p. 87 - very brief.)

(CVMA)
    7e Colloque du Corpus Vitrearum Medii Aevi.
    Compte Rendu.
    Florence ?, 1970.

    8e Colloque du Corpus Vitrearum Medii Aevi.
    Compte Rendu.
    Paris ?, 1972.

    (Work in progress in England.)
    J.M.G.P., vol. 15, no. 3 (1974-1975), p. 53.

    Actes du IXe Colloque International du Corpus Vitrearum Medii
    Aevi, Paris, Sept. 8-12, 1975.
    Verres et Réfractaires, numéro spécial, (1976). pp. 15-187.

    (9th Colloquium)
    (Thirty pieces of York glass sent to Paris for the Colloquium.)
    Yorkshire Evening Press, Sept. 19, 1975.

    Akten des 10. Internationalen Colloquiums des Corpus Vitrearum
    Medii Aevi.
    Stuttgart, 1977.

(CVMA)
    Work in Progress in England.
    J.M.G.P., vol. 16, no. 1 (1976-1977), p. 7.

CORROYER, E.
    Description de l'Abbaye du Mont-Saint-Michel.
    Paris, 1877.

COTTLE, Basil
    St. Mary Redcliffe, Bristol.
    Bristol, 1957.

COTTON, R.W.
    The Powell MSS.
    (In Second Report of the Committee on Devonshire Records.)
    (Contains descriptions from 1811 of Devonshire glass in B.M.
    Add. MSS 17459.)
    Transactions of the Devonshire Association, vol. 22 (1890), pp.
    61-63.

COUFFON, René
    Contribution à l'Etude des Verrières Anciennes du Départment
    des Côtes-du-Nord.
    Bulletin de la Societé d'Emulation des Côtes-du-Nord, tome 67
    (1935), pp. 65-228.
    Reviewed in Diamant, (Nov. 11, 1937).

    La Peinture sur Verre en Bretagne, Origine de Quelques Verrières
    du XVIe Siècle.
    Rennes, 1945.
    (Reprinted from Mémoires de la Société d'Histoire et d'Archeologie
    de Bretagne, t. 25, pp. 27-64.)
    Reviewed by AUBERT, Marcel, Bulletin Monumental, vol. 104 (1946),
    pp. 138-140.

    (With LE BARS, A.)
    Répertoire des Eglises et Chapelles du Diocèse de Quimper et de
    Léon.
    Saint-Brieuc, 1959.
    Reviewed by AUBERT, Marcel, Bulletin Monumental, no. 117, (1959)
    pp. 241-242.

COULTON, G.G.
    (With AUBERT, Marcel)
    Introduction to Stained Glass of the Twelfth and Thirteenth
    Centuries in France.
    London, n.d. (? 1939).

COUNCER, C.R.
    The Medieval Painted Glass at Mersham.
    Archaeologia Cantiana, vol. 48 (1936), pp. 81-90.

    The Medieval Painted Glass of Boughton Aluph.
    Archaeologia Cantiana, vol. 50 (1938), pp. 131-139.
    Reprinted in J.M.G.P., vol. 9, no. 3 (1945), pp. 80-86.

    The Medieval Painted Glass of Teynham.
    J.M.G.P., vol. 8, no. 2 (Apr., 1940), pp. 63-67.

    The Medieval Painted Glass of Chilham.
    Archaeologia Cantiana, vol. 58 (1945), pp. 8-13.

    The Medieval and Renaissance Painted Glass of Eastwell.
    Archaeologia Cantiana, vol. 59 (1946), pp. 109-113.

    Glass and Monuments Formerly in the Church of Gillingham.
    Archaeologia Cantiana, vol. 61 (1948), pp. 160-179.

COUNCER, C.R. (Contd.)

    The Medieval Painted Glass of West Wickham, Kent.
    J.M.G.P., vol. 10, no. 2 (1949), pp. 67-73.

    Glass and Monuments Formerly in Gillingham Church. A Postscript.
    Archaeologia Cantiana, vol. 62 (1949), pp. 148-149.

    Review of RACKHAM, Bernard, The Ancient Glass of Canterbury
    Cathedral.
    Archaeologia Cantiana, vol. 63 (1950), pp. 156-158.

    The Ancient Glass from Petham Church, now in Canterbury Cathedral.
    Archaeologia Cantiana, vol. 65 (1952), pp. 167-170.

    (With HILL, D. Ingram.)
    Ancient Heraldic Glass at Wickham Court, West Wickham, Kent.
    J.M.G.P., vol. 11, no. 2 (1953), pp. 94-104.

    Heraldic Painted Glass in the Church of St. Lawrence, Mereworth.
    Archaeologia Cantiana, vol. 77 (1962), pp. 48-62.

    Painted Glass at Cranbrook and Lullingstone.
    Archaeologia Cantiana, vol. 86 (1971), pp. 35-54.

COUSIN, Jean
    Recueil des Oeuvres Choisies de J. Cousin.
    Paris, 1873.

COUSSEMAKER, I. de
    Les Anciens Vitraux de Flêtre.
    (n.d., n.p.)

    Vitraux Peints et Incolorés des Eglises de la Flandre Maritime.
    Annales du Comité Flamand de France, part 5 (1860).

COUTEUR, John Dolbel Le
    Notes on the Great North Window of Canterbury Cathedral.
    Archaeologia Cantiana, vol. 29 (1911), pp. 323-332.

    Barnard Flower: Bishop Fox of Winchester.
    (Request for information about Flower.)
    Notes and Queries, 12th series, no. 2 (Oct. 21, 1916), p. 330.

    John Prudde: King's Glazier.
    (Request for information.)
    Notes and Queries, 12th series, vol. 2 (Nov. 26, 1916), pp. 430-431.
    Replied to by HULME, E. Wyndham (q.v.).

    Representations of the Blessed Trinity.
    (Request for information of similar iconographical treatments to
    that found in Winchester College.)
    Notes and Queries, 12th series, vol. 3 (March 3, 1917). p. 168.
    Replied to by TURPIN, P. (q.v.)
          'St. Swithin' (March 24, 1917), p. 232.
          SUMMERS, M.   (March 24, 1917), p. 232.
          KNOWLES, J.A. (March 24, 1917), p. 232.
          FYNMORE, R.J. (March 24, 1917), p. 232.
          CHITTY, H. (q.v.)

    Stained Glass: Its Importation Forbidden.
    (Request for information about the repeal of a 1483 Act.)
    Notes and Queries, 12th series, no. 3 (Oct., 1917), p. 446.
    Replied to by T.F.D.,
          PROSSER, G., Ibid. (Nov., 1917), p. 485.

    Shield in Winchester Stained Glass.
    (Request for information on a shield in the Close.)
    Notes and Queries, 12th series, no. 4 (July, 1918), p. 188.
    Replied to by CHITTY, Herbert (q.v.)

    Winchester College Chapel: Stained Glass Painter.
    (Query if there are any other portraits comparable to that of
    Thomas of Oxford.)
    Notes and Queries, 12th series, no. 4 (Aug., 1918), p. 216.

COUTEUR, J.D. Le (Contd.)

    Barnard Flower, the King's Glazier.
    (On Malvern glass compared with St. Margaret's, Westminster.)
    Notes and Queries, 12th series, no. 4 (Sept., 1918), p. 247.

    Old Stained Glass.
    (On the fate of glass from New College, Winchester College, and
    Betton and Evans' work.)
    Notes and Queries, 12th series, vol. 6 (May 22, 1920), pp. 231-232.
    (A continuation of the subjects.)
    Ibid., June 19, 1920, pp. 314-315.

    Ancient Glass in Winchester.
    Winchester, 1920.
    Reviewed by THOMPSON, A. Hamilton in
    The Archaeological Journal, vol 67 (1920), pp. 313-314,
    The Connoisseur, vol. 58 (Sept.-Dec., 1920), p. 252.

    Notes on the East Window of the College Chapel (Winchester).
    The Wykehamist, no. 626 (1923).

    A Note Upon Some Ancient Glass in Timsbury Church, Hants.
    J.M.G.P., vol. 1, no. 2 (Apr., 1925), pp. 36-37.

    (With CARTER, P.H.M.)
    Notes on the Shrine of St. Swithin, (Winchester).
    Papers and Proceedings of the Hampshire Field Club Archaeological
    Society, vol. 9 (1925), pp. 370-384.

    The Medieval Glass Painter as Copyist.
    J.M.G.P., vol. 1, no. 3 (Oct., 1925), pp. 15-19.

(Couteur, J.D. Le)
    Obituary.
    The Times, Aug. 17, 1925.

    English Mediaeval Painted Glass.
    London, 1926.

    Long Melford Church, Suffolk, and its Portrait Glass. A
    Medieval Portrait Gallery.
    J.M.G.P., vol. 2, no. 2 (Oct., 1927), pp. 74-77.

COUTURE, Léonce
    Les Vitraux Peints de M.J. Villiet à l'Eglise Saint-Gervais de
    Lectoure.
    Bulletin de la Comité Historique et Archéologique de la Province
    Ecclesiastique d'Auch, vol. 3 (1862), pp. 440-444.

COUTURIER, Marie-Alain
    Stained Glass and Ecclesiastical Timidity.
    Liturgical Arts, vol. 9 (Oct., 1940).

    A Modern French Church in the Alps. (Rouault Window.)
    Harper's Bazaar (Dec., 1947).

    Religious Art and the Modern Artist.
    Magazine of Art (Nov., 1951).

(Couturier, Marie-Alain)
    Obituary.
    Stained Glass, vol. 48, no. 4 (Winter, 1953-1954), p. 206.

(Couverte)
    The Employment of Couverte on the Windows of Chartres Cathedral.
    J.M.G.P., vol. 5, no. 1 (Apr., 1933), pp. 35-36.
    (A free translation of some passages from:
    Mémoires de la Société Archéologique d'Eure et Loir.
    Chartres, 1909, pp. 459-462.)

(Coventry, St. Mary's Hall)

The Gentleman's Magazine, part 1 (May, 1827), pp. 317-320.
Reprinted in The Gentleman's Magazine Library, vol. 2, part 2,
pp. 240-246.
London, 1891.

Photographs of Tapestry and Stained Glass at St. Mary's Hall,
Coventry.
London, 1920.

(Coventry, Trinity Church)

(Window by David Evans installed.)
The Gentleman's Magazine, vol. 2, new series, part 2 (1834), p. 407.

COWELL, Jack

(Script of a broadcast on stained glass given in South Africa.)
Stained Glass, vol. 39, no. 1 (Spring, 1944), pp. 30-32.

COWEN, Painton

Rose Windows.
London, 1979.
Reviewed by WEIS, Helene, Stained Glass. vol. 74, no. 2 (Summer,
1979), pp. 130-131.

COWLES, Genevieve

Building a Stained Glass Window.
The Craftsman, vol. 15 (Oct., 1908), pp. 97-103.

(Cox and Sons)

Illustrated Catalogue of Church Furniture, Painted Glass, etc.
London, 1865.

Illustrated Catalogue of Designs for Stained Glass Windows for
Churches and Domestic Use. (Ecclesiastical Warehouse, Southampton.)
London, 1870.

COX, G.A., and POLLARD, A.M.

X-ray Fluorescence Analysis of Ancient Glass: The Importance of
Sample Preparation.
Archaeometry, vol. 19, part 1 (Feb., 1977), pp. 45-54.

A Craftsman's Portfolio. Examples of Fine Craftsmanship. XVII, Modern
Stained Glass.
The Architectural Review, vol. 62, no. 370 (Sept., 1927).

CRAIG, John

A Note on Stained Glass in the United States.
J.M.G.P., vol. 11, no. 3 (1954), pp. 157-159.

(Craigweil House, Bognor, Sale)

(Sixteenth Century glass, some supposedly from Hampton Court.)
The Connoisseur, vol. 90 (July-Dec., 1932), p. 279.

CRAM, Elizabeth Carrington

Singing Windows.
The Horn Book Magazine (Boston), (Sept.-Oct., 1938).

CRAM, Ralph Adams

Stained Glass: An Art Restored.
Arts and Decoration, vol. 20 (Feb., 1924).

Stained Glass from the Architect's Point of View.
National Glass Budget (July 11, 1925).

Personal Recollections of Harry Wright Goodhue.
Stained Glass, vol. 27, no. 9 (Sept., 1932), pp. 263-272.

(Report of his address at the 31st Convention of the Stained Glass
Association of America.)
Stained Glass, vol. 34, no. 2 (Autumn, 1939), pp. 42-44.

CRAMP, Rosemary J.

Decorated Window-Glass and Millefiori from Monkwearmouth.
Antiquaries Journal, vol. 50 (1970), pp. 327-335.

Glass Finds from the Anglo-Saxon Monastery of Monkwearmouth and
Jarrow.
Studies in Glass History and Design, Sheffield, 1970, pp. 16-19.

Window Glass from the Monastic Site of Jarrow.
Journal of Glass Studies, vol. 17 (1975), pp. 88-96.

CRANE, George W.

Case K-121.
(A grotesque 'psychological' analysis of the effect of stained
glass windows.)
Stained Glass, vol. 33, no. 2 (Autumn-Winter, 1938), pp. 61-63.
An exchange of letters between CONNICK, C.J. and this 'academic'
occupies pp. 35-38 of the same number.

(Cranwell, Lenox, Mass.)

A New Concept in Stained Glass at Cranwell School.
Stained Glass, vol. 62, no. 4 (Winter, 1967-1968), pp. 8-13.

CRAWFORD, J.E.

The Travers School of Glass.
J.M.G.P., vol. 14, no. 2 (1965), pp. 102-104.

CRAZANNES, Chaudruc de

Notice sur les Vitraux Peints de Quelques Eglises du
Département du Lot.
Bulletin Monumental, vol. 7 (1841), p. 32.

CREAGER, Kathryn and MONT, Virginia Le

French Glassmen of this Century.
Stained Glass, vol. 37, no. 2 (Summer, 1942), pp. 59-61.

CRESSWELL, Beatrix

Notes on Ancient Glass in Devonshire Churches.
n.p., n.d., prob. 1911.
(DUNCAN, G.S. (q.v.) recorded a copy of this privately printed
book with ms. notes by DRAKE, Maurice, in Exeter Public Library
before the war. This was presumably destroyed during the war
and the only copy now held in the West Country Studies Library
is CRESSWELL'S typescript.)

Exeter Churches.
Devon Notes and Queries, vol. 5, part 2 (1908).
(A whole volume, little on glass.)

Notes on the Churches of the Deanery of Kenn, Devon.
Devon and Cornwall Notes and Queries, vol. 7, part 2 (1912).

Milles' Parochial Collections for Devon.
(7 vols. of Ms. in the Bodleian Library.)
Devon and Cornwall Notes and Queries, vol. 11 (1921).
(Refers to his notes on stained glass, p.323.)

Stained Glass Window in Cadbury Church.
Devon and Cornwall Notes and Queries, vol. 13 (1925), pp. 195-196.

CROOME, W.I.

Frederick Charles Eden F.S.A., F.R.I.B.A.
J.M.G.P., vol. 13, no. 4 (1963), pp. 554-557.

The Stained Glass of Cirencester Parish Church.
J.M.G.P., vol. 14, no. 1 (1964), pp. 31-40.

(Crosby Hall)

(Oriel window executed by Willement.)
The Gentleman's Magazine, vol. 2, new series, part 2 (1834),
pp. 628-629.

C(ROSSLEY), F.H.   ?

   Stained Glass in Churches.
   (Contribution to the correspondence started by J.M.G.P., Apr.,
   1936 (q.v.).
   Notes and Queries (May 30, 1936), pp. 392-393.

CROSSLEY, F.H.

   English Church Craftsmanship.
   London, 1941.
   (The Craft of the Glazier, pp. 64-70.)

(Crosthwaite Church, Cumberland)

   (Windows by Wailes.)
   The Gentleman's Magazine, vol. 31, new series, part 1 (1849)
   (Glass, pp. 376-377.)

(Crotti, Jean)

   New Stained Glass at Last.
   Art News (Feb., 1947).

(Crowmarsh Church, Oxfordshire)

   Crowmarsh Church, Oxfordshire.
   The Church Builder (1866), p. 140.

CROZET, René

   Le Vitrail de la Crucifixion à la Cathédrale de Poitiers.
   Gazette des Beaux-Arts (Apr., 1934), pp. 218-231.

CROZIER, Gladys B.

   Modern Stained Glass: the Revival of a Beautiful Mediaeval Art
   by Artists who are Adapting an Ancient Craft to Latter-day Uses.
   London, 1923.
   (Reprinted from The World's Work, Sept., 1923).

CRUM, J.M.C.

   Cathedral Church of Christ, Canterbury: Notes on the Old Glass.
   Plymouth, 1930.

CUBITT, J.

   Stained Glass: Fairford and Bledington.
   Building News (Feb. 9, 1877).

CUESTA, T.G.

   Las Vidrieras Pintadas de la Catedral de Valencia (Siglo 16).
   Bolletino de Seminario des Estudios de Arte y Arqueoligia, vol.
   24 (1958).

(Culford Manor, Suffolk)

   A Wonder Window. Sixteenth-century Stained Glass Window
   Discovered in an Attic at Culford Manor, Suffolk.
   The Sphere (Dec. 7, 1935).

CULLETON, Leo

   Stained Glass: René, Duc de Bar.
   (Enquiry of present location of window depicting René and
   purchased at Dijon by an Englishman c. 1802.)
   Notes and Queries, 8th series, vol. 11 (Jan. 2, 1897), pp. 7-8.

CUMMINGS, Harold W.

   Stained Glass Looks at its Apprenticeship Problem.
   Liturgical Arts (Nov., 1945).

   Modern Stained Glass in Architecture.
   Architect and Engineer (San Francisco), (Apr., 1946).

CUMMINGS, Harold W.

   President's Message.
   (On the position of stained glass makers in the U.S.A. just after
   the War.)
   Stained Glass, vol. 41, no. 2 (Summer, 1946), pp. 35-38.

   A Blessed James of Ulm Window.
   Stained Glass, vol. 44, no. 3 (Autumn, 1949), pp. 69-71.

   (With BLENKO, W.H., WILLET, H.L., and others.)
   Technical Aspects of Stained Glass with Emphasis on Faceted Glass.
   (A Symposium.)
   Part 1, Stained Glass, vol. 56, no. 3 (Autumn, 1961), pp. 30-39.
   Part 2, Ibid, vol.56, no. 4 (Winter, 1961-1962), pp. 34-45.
   Part 3, Ibid, vol.57, no. 1 (Spring, 1962), pp. 14-21.

CUMMINGS, John

   Finding the Lost Art.
   Stained Glass, vol. 50, no. 3 (Autumn, 1955), pp. 100-106.

CUNO, C.

   Cleaning Old Glass Paintings.
   (Appendix to HERMANN F., Painting on Glass and Porcelain, q.v.)

CURLING, J.

   (Letter suggesting that the Altenberg glass (q.v.) be purchased
   for Crosby Hall.)
   (WILLEMENT offers to present his glass for the Oriel Window.)
   The Gentleman's Magazine, vol. 1, new series, part 1 (1834),
   p. 234.

CURRIVAN, Earl J.

   Adventure in Glass.
   St. Anthony Messenger (Cincinnatti), (Sept., 1944).

Customs Duties Payable on Stained-Glass Windows Overseas.
   J.M.G.P., vol. 5, no. 2 (Oct., 1933), pp. 81-82.

CUTTS, J.E.K.

   Bledington Church (Glos.).
   Transactions of the Bristol and Gloucestershire Archaeological
   Society, vol. 7 (for 1882-1883), pp. 81-86.

CUYPERS, J.T.J.

   Over Kerklijke Glasschilderkunst.
   Van Onzen Tijd, vol. 15 (1914), pp. 23, 29, 48.

CUZACQ, René

   La Cathédrale de Bayonne, les Vitraux Anciens, le Heurtoir et
   la Chaire.
   Mont-de-Marsan, 1954.

(Cylinder Window)

   A Glass Cylinder Window Unique in Annals of Craft.
   National Glass Budget (May 14, 1966).

DAHMEN, Walther

    Gotische Glasfenster. Rhythmus und Strophenbau.
    Forschungen zur Kunstgeschichte Westeuropas hrsg. von Eugen.
    Lüthgen. Band II.
    Bonn and Leipzig, 1922.

DALLAWAY, James

    Anecdotes of the Arts in England; or, Comparative Observations
    on Architecture, Sculpture, and Painting, Chiefly Illustrated by
    Specimens at Oxford.
    London, 1800.
    Reviewed in The Gentleman's Magazine, vol. 70, part 2 (1800).
    (With reference to glass-painting, pp. 1073-1074.)

    Observations on English Architecture . . . including a critical
    itinerary of Oxford and Cambridge, and also historical notices of
    stained glass, etc. . . .
    London, 1806.

    Walpole's Anecdotes of Painting . . . with considerable additions
    by the Rev. J. DALLAWAY.
    Vol. 2, 1826 (n.p.)
    Reviewed in The Gentleman's Magazine, vol. 97, part 1 (1827).
    (Stained glass, pp. 42-43.)

DANCEY, C.H.

    Ancient Painted Glass in Gloucester Cathedral.
    (Gives some account of the restoration of the 1890s.)
    Transactions of the Bristol and Gloucestershire Archaeological
    Society, vol. 34 (for 1911), pp. 97-

DANIELS, Polydore

    A Propos d'un Vitrail Hasseltois de 1624. Verzamelde opstellen
    uitgegewen door den geschied-en oudheid-Kundingen.
    Studien te Hasselt, part 3 (1927).

DANKO, József

    Geschichtliches, Beschreibendes und Urkundliches aus dem Graner
    Domschatz.
    Budapest, 1880.

DARCEL, Alfred

    Salon de 1863. L'Opera; L'Architecture; Les Vitraux.
    Gazette des Beaux-Arts, vol. 15 (1863), p. 136.

    La Peinture Vitrifiée et l'Architecture au Salon de 1864.
    Ibid., vol. 17 (1864), p. 80.

(Darmstadt)

    Alte Glasmalerei in Darmstadt. Eine Neue Abteilung im Hess.
    Landesmuseum.
    Diamant, 54th year, no. 18 (June 21, 1932).

DASSEL, Otto von

    Glasmalereien der Familie Dassel.
    Familiengeschichtenblätter für Adelige und Bürgerliche Geschlechter.
    Bd. II (1903, 1906).

DASSY, L.F.

    L'Abbaye de Saint-Antoine en Dauphiné. Essai Historique et
    Descriptif.
    Grenoble, 1844.

DAVID, John

    The Art of Stained Glass in Ireland.
    (With COLUM, Padraic.)
    Stained Glass, vol. 27, no. 11 (Nov., 1932), pp. 315-317.

Davies, Archibald John)

    Obituary by WHEWELL, George H.
    J.M.G.P., vol. 11, no. 3 (1954), pp. 180-181.

DAVIES, Robert

    Stained Glass of York Minster.
    The Herald and Genealogist, vol. 5 (1870).

    Walks Through the City of York.
    London, 1880.

DAVIS, Derek C., and MIDDLEMAS, K.

    Colored Glass.
    New York, 1969.

DAVIS, John

    A Concise History of the Cathedral Church of St. Andrew in
    Wells.
    Salisbury, 1809.
    (Subsequent editions 1914, 1925.)

DAY, Lewis F.

    Stained Glass Windows as They Were, Are, and Should Be.
    Journal of the Society of Arts, vol. 30 (1882), p. 292.

    The Earliest Cathedral Windows.
    The Magazine of Art (1882), pp. 19-23.

    Glass-Painting in the Fourteenth Century.
    The Magazine of Art (1882), p. 289-294.

    Later Gothic Glass in England.
    The Magazine of Art (1883), pp. 420-424.

    Stained Glass.
    The Architect, part 1 (1886), pp. 50-68.

    From Gothic Glass to Renaissance.
    The Magazine of Art (1887), pp. 282-286.

    Cinque-Cento Picture Windows.
    Ibid., pp. 341-346.

    Glass-Painting: the Beginning of the End.
    Ibid., pp. 377-381.

    Windows: A Book About Stained and Painted Glass.
    London, 1897.

    Reviewed in The Builder (Sept. 24, 1898), pp. 262-264.

    The Making of a Stained Glass Window.
    Journal of the Society of Arts, vol. 46 (1898), pp. 421-430.

    Stained Glass.
    Victoria and Albert Museum Art Handbook.
    London, 1903.

    Stained Glass.
    (Article in Encyclopaedia Britannica, 11th edition, 1910-1911.)

DEANE, Anthony C.

    A Short History of Great Malvern Priory Church . . . with a
    Chapter on the Ancient Glass and Tiles.
    London, 1914.
    (2nd ed., 1916, reprinted 1926.)

DECLOUX and DOURY

    Histoire Archéologique, Descriptive et Graphique de la Sainct-
    Chapelle du Palais.
    Paris, 1865.

(Decoration on Glass)

    Durable Decoration on Glass Without Burning In.
    Diamant, no. 22 (1924).

DEDEKAM, H.

    Glasmaleriets Eshetik og Histoire.
    Kristiana, 1908.

DELAMOTTE, Philip H.

    Choice Examples of Art Workmanship Selected from the Exhibition of
    Ancient and Medieval Art of the Society of Arts. Drawn and
    Engraved Under the Superintendence of P. de la Motte.
    London, 1851.

    The Art of Glass-Painting.
    In Practical Application of the Fine Arts. Cassell's Technical
    Educator, 4 vols., London, 1870-1872. (In vols. 2, 3.)

DELAPORTE, Yves

    Les Vitraux de la Cathédrale de Chartres.
    (With HOUVET, Emile.)
    4 vols., Chartres, 1926.
    (With a preface by AUBERT, Marcel.)

    The Jesse Tree, Chartres.
    (Translated and abridged from Les Vitraux de la Cathédrale de
    Chartres, by PEASE, Murray.)
    Stained Glass, vol. 27, no. 2 (Feb. 1932), pp. 41-46.

    La Vie de Notre Seigneur.
    (Translated and abridged from Les Vitraux . . ., by PEASE, Murray.)
    Stained Glass, vol. 27, no. 3 (March, 1932), pp. 72-74.

    The Passion Window.
    (Translated and abridged from Les Vitraux . . ., by PEASE, Murray.)
    Stained Glass, vol. 27, no. 4 (Apr., 1932), pp. 108-110.

    Le Vitrail de Martigny.
    Avranches, 1941.

    La Cathédrale de Chartres et ses Vitraux.
    Paris, 1943.

    L'Art du Vitrail aux XIIe et XIIIe Siècles.
    Chartres, 1963.
    Reviewed by SALET, Francis, Bulletin Monumental, vol. 121 (1963),
    pp. 301-302.

    Review of WITZLEBEN, Elisabeth von, Les Vitraux des Cathédrales
    de France.
    Bulletin des Sociétés Archéologiques d'Eure-et-Loir.
    Chromique 3, 1968, p. 38.

DELIGNIERES, Emile

    Une Peinture sur Verre de 1525 'Fixé Peint' a l'Eglise de Saint
    Vulfran à Abbeville.
    Réunion des Sociétés des Beaux-Arts des Departements (1901), pp.
    272-297.

DELVILLE, Jean

    L'Art du Vitrail en Belgique.
    Bulletin de la Classe des Beaux-Arts, (part 4, 1912), nos. 11 and
    12, pp. 186-203.

    Les Travaux des Vitraux d'Eglises en Belgique.
    Bulletin des Commissiones Royales d'Art et d'Archéologie, vol.
    67 (1928).

DEMAISON, L.

    La Cathédrale de Reims.
    Paris, 1954.

DEMNISE——.

    Analyse des Nouveaux Vitraux de Sainte Maria, Lunéville.
    Nancy, 1855.

(Demotte, Inc.)

    Catalogue of an Exhibition of Stained Glass from the XIth to
    the XVIIIth Centuries.
    New York, 1925.

DEMOTTE, Lucien

    (A brief study of the design and drawing of heads from the XIIth
    to the XVth century.)
    Stained Glass, vol. 29, no. 3 (Autumn, 1934), pp. 77-81.

DENAIS, J.

    La Cathédrale d'Angers.
    (Inventaire général des Richesses d'Art de la France, Province,
    Monuments religieux, vol. 4.)
    Paris, 1907.

DENEUX, H.

    A Thirteenth-Century Mould for Making Calm Lead.
    J.M.G.P., vol. 3, no. 2 (Oct., 1929), pp. 81-84.
    (Originally appeared as Un Moule à Plomb de Vitraux du XIIIe
    Siècle, Bulletin Monumental, vol. 87, nos. 1-2 (1929), pp. 149-
    154.)

DENGLAR, Georg

    Kirchenschmuck, Sammlung von Vorlagen für kirchliche Stickerein,
    Glasmalereien, u.s.w.
    Amberg, 1873.

    Kirchenschmuck. Neue Folge. Sammlung von Vorlagen für
    kirchliche Stickereien, Holz-und Metallarbeiten, und Glasmalerein.
    Vol. 4, part 6, Regensburg, 1895.

(Denton)

    The Denton Glass Excavation.
    Pilkington Glass Museum,
    St. Helens, n.d.

(Denton-in-Wharfedale Church)

    Denton-in-Wharfedale Church, Yorkshire; Glass.
    (Grant towards restoring the glass by GYLES and PECKITT.)
    The Pilgrim Trust, 38th Annual Report (1968), p. 16.

DEREWITSKY, A.

    Das Museum der Kaiserlich Odessaer Gesellschaft für Geschichte
    und Altertumskunde.
    Odessa, 1897-1898.

(Derschau, Hans Albrecht von)

    (Auction catalogue of the Derschau collection. Fifteenth to
    seventeenth century glass-paintings, pp. 24-25.)
    Verzeichniss der Seltenen Kunst-Sammlungen von Gemälden,
    Geschmeltzen Glasmalereyen des . . . H.A. von DERSCHAU . . .
    Nuremberg, 1825.

DESCHAMPS and D'ANSTAING, Le Maistre

    Les Vitraux de la Cathédrale de Tournay.
    Brussels, 1848.

(Designs for stained glass)

Moderne Entwürfe für Kunstverglasung und Glasmalerei.
Berlin, 1910-1912.

DESPIERRES, G.

Portail et Vitraux de Notre-Dame d'Alençon.
Réunion des Sociétés des Beaux-Arts des Départements (1891),
pp. 467-489.
Reprinted Paris, 1891.

DESPRÉAUX, M.

The Windows of Sainte-Odile, Paris.
(By F. Décorchement.)
Stained Glass, vol. 34, no. 1 (Spring-Summer, 1939), pp. 17-19.

DESTRÉE, O.G.

Some Notes on the Stained Glass Windows and Decorative Paintings
of the Church of St. Martin-on-the-Hill, Scarborough.
Savoy (Oct., 1896), pp. 76-90.

(Destruction of Painted Glass)

74 Alte Glasgemälde Vernichtet.
Keramische Rundschau, vol. 19 (1911), p. 340.

(Detroit)

Ancient Glass in Detroit Cathedral.
Stained Glass, vol. 38, no. 3 (Autumn, 1943), pp. 88-89.

DETZEL, H.

Alte Glasmalerei am Bodensee und seiner Umgebung.
Lindau, 1891.

DEVILLE, Etienne

Les Vitraux de la Cathédrale de Lisieux.
(In HARDY, V., La Cathédrale St. Pierre de Lisieux.)
Paris, 1917.

DEVLIEGHER, Luc

Enkele Brugse Glasramen uit het einde van de XVe eeuw.
Belgisch Tijdschrift voor Oudheidkunde en Kunstgeschiedenis,
vol. 23, nos. 3, 4 (1954).

DEY, Muriel Foster

Eugène Yoors, Gourmand of Colour.
Stained Glass, vol. 37, no. 1 (Spring, 1942), pp. 14-21.

DICKINS, Bruce

The 'Owl and the Nightingale' and the St. William Window in York Minster.
Leeds Studies in English and Kindred Languages, no. 5 (1936).

DICKINSON, J.C.

Cartmel Priory Church.
Huntingdon, n.d.
(Glass, pp. 4, 10.)

(Didbrook Church, Glos.)

(Glass Fragments in the East Window.)
Transactions of the Bristol and Gloucestershire Archaeological
Society, vol. 23 (for 1900), pp. 12-13.

DIDIER-LAMBORAY, Anne-Marie

Les Vitraux d'Histoire de Joseph a l'Eglise Saint-Antoine de
Liège et leurs Modèles.
Bulletin de l'Institut Royal du Patrimoine Artistique (1965),
pp. 201-222.

DIDON, Albert

Les Vitraux Disparus de l'Eglise de Moret.
Bulletin de la Société d'Histoire et d'Art du Diocèse de Meaux
(1954), pp. 193-201.

DIDRON, Adolphe Napoléon

Monographie de Notre Dame de Brou, par Louis Dupasquier.
Texte Historique et Descriptive par A.N.D.
Lyon, 1842.

Iconographie Chrétienne.
Paris, 1843.

(With THIBAUD, Emile)
Manufacture de Vitraux.
Paris, 1850.

Les Vitraux du Grand-Andely.
Annales Archéologiques, vol. 22 (1862), pp. 260, 353.

Verrieres de la Rédemption à Notre-Dame de Châlons-sur-Marne.
Paris, 1863.

Verrières Nouvelles à Notre-Dame de Châlons-sur-Marne.
Annales Archéologiques, vol. 23 (1863), p. 69.

Histoire de la Peinture sur Verre en Europe.
Annales Archéologiques, vol. 23 (1863), pp. 45, 201;
vol. 24 (1864), p. 211.

Groupe de Patriarches, Vitrail de Brou, XVI Siècle.
Annales Archéologiques, vol. 24 (1864), p. 145.

(With CLEMANDOT, L.)
Rapport sur les Cristaux, la Verrerie et les Vitraux.
Paris Exposition de 1878.
Paris, 1880.

DIEPOLDER, J.N.

Der Tempelbau. Die bildenden Künste im Dienste der Religion.
Leipzig, 1881.

DIERICK, Alfons

Kirchenfenster von Chartres.
Berne, 1955.

The Stained Glass at Chartres.
Berne, 1961.

Dignity without the Dust of Ancients.
Glass Digest (March, 1962).

DIHL——.

Descriptive Catalogue of the Exhibition of Paintings on Glass.
London, 1819.
(Excerpt, Art of Painting on Glass, printed in The Gentleman's
Magazine, vol. 89 (part 1, 1819), pp. 409-411.)

DILKE, Emilia F.S. (Mrs. Mark Pattison)

The Renaissance of Art in France.
2 vols., London, 1879.
(Glass-painting in vol. 2.)

(Diocesan Advisory Committees)

The Diocesan Advisory Committee System, Faculties and Faculty
Procedure.
J.M.G.P., vol. 10, no. 4 (1951), pp. 175-180.

(A discussion between ABBOTT, J.E.H.; SKEAT, Francis; HAYWARD,
John; and others, on difficulties experienced with Diocesan
Advisory Committees.)
J.M.G.P., vol. 14, no. 4 (1968-1969), pp. 217-218.

DION, A. De
L'Eglise de Montfort-l'Amaury et ses Vitraux.
Tours, 1902.

Directory for the British Glass Industry.
Compiled by DUNCAN, G.S.; edited by TURNER, W.E.S.
Sheffield, 2nd ed., 1928.

(Disappearances of windows.)
(Refers to St. Mary's, Oldham, Stoke Golding, Leicestershire,
St. Martin-le-Grand, Coney St., York.)
News and Notes, J.M.G.P., vol. 12, no. 1 (1956), p. 6.

(Diserth Church, Flint)
Diserth Church.
Archaeologia Cambrensis, vol. 99 (1947), pp. 329-330.

DIVINE, J.A.F., and BLACHFORD, G.
Stained Glass Craft.
London, 1940.

(Divining for lost glass)
Divining for Old Glass.
Yorkshire Evening Press, Jan. 25, 1933.

'Dowsing' for Old Glass.
The Daily Telegraph, Jan. 26, 1933.

DIXON, A.E.
Shields in Ancient Glass in the Church of St. Martin, Stamford
Baron.
With illustrations from drawings made by H.F. TRAYLEN.
Reports and Papers of the Associated Architectural Societies,
vol. 37 (for 1923, 1924, 1925), pp. 316-321.

DIXON, R.W.
Glass-painting.
(Suggested new technique.)
Notes and Queries, 4th series, vol. 4 (Oct. 23, 1869), pp. 332-333.
(Rejected in contributions by HUTCHINSON, P., Ibid. (Dec. 4, 1869),
p. 487, and P.P., Ibid., p. 487-488.)
(He withdraws his suggestion, Ibid., vol. 5 (Feb. 12, 1870).)

DOBIE, Gilbert H.
Mediaeval Stained Glass in Cornwall and Brittany.
J.M.G.P., vol. 4, no. 4 (Oct., 1932), pp. 183-186.

DODGSON, Campbell
Swiss Glass-Paintings and their Designers.
The Connoisseur, vol. 1 (1901), pp. 224-233.

DODSON, W.M.
Old Stained Glass.
(Enquiries about the fate of glass from New College, Winchester
College, and BETTON and EVANS' work.)
Notes and Queries, 12th series, vol. 6 (May 8, 1920), p. 188.
Replied to by COUTEUR, J.D. Le (q.v.).
Request for more information on the same topics, Ibid., (June 5,
1920), pp. 281-282.
(On Ludlow glass) Vol. 7 (July 10, 1920), p. 34.

Twelfth Century Jesse Window, Canterbury Cathedral.
(Letter to the Editor.)
J.M.G.P., vol. 1, no. 4 (Apr., 1926), p. 52.

DOMASLOWSKI, W., KWIATKOWSKI, E., and TORWIRT, L.
(Techniques of restoring stained glass.)
Teka Konserwatorska (Warsaw), vol. 3 (1956), pp. 117-147.

DOMASLOWSKI, W., and KWIATOWSKI, E.
Probleme der Konservierung von Glasmalereien.
Annales du 2e Congrès du Journal Internationale du Verre
(Leyden, June 30-July 4, 1962), pp. 137-151.

(Domestic Stained Glass)
Stained Glass in Domestic Use.
(A correspondence in Notes and Queries, by
H.C., vol. 158 (March 1, 1930), p. 152;
KNOWLES, J.A. (q.v.), (March 15, 1930), pp. 189-190;
R.S.B., Ibid., p. 190;
GAWTHORP, W.E., Ibid.
O.F.B., Ibid.
COCK, F.W. (March 29, 1930), pp. 229-230.

DONNET, Fernand
Notes sur quelques Vitraux Héraldiques des XVIe et XVIIe Siècles.
Annales de l'Académie d'Archéologie de Belgique, part 73 (1911),
pp. 299-356.

Les Vitraux de la Toison d'Or dans l'Eglise Notre-Dame d'Anvers.
Le Chapitre de la Toison d'Or Tenu à Anvers en 1555.
Antwerp, 1924.

(Donors)
(Windows on the continent donated by Englishmen in the fifteenth
and sixteenth centuries.)
News and Notes, J.M.G.P., vol. 12, no. 2 (1957), p. 93.

DOPPELMAYR, J.G.
Historische Nachrichte von den Nürnbergischen Mathematicis und
Künstlern.
Nuremberg, 1730.

(Dorchester Abbey)
(Notice of a proposal to replace the ancient glass in the sedilia
with modern.)
The Ecclesiologist, vol. 6 (1846), p. 160.

Dorchester Abbey, Oxfordshire: Stained Glass.
(A grant to relead and amalgamate the clerestory glass.)
The Pilgrim Trust, 39th Annual Report (1969), p. 17.

DORLING, E.E.
Leopards of England and other Papers on Heraldry.
London, 1912.
Contains
Armorial Glass in Salisbury Cathedral (pp. 57-72);
Two Nevill Shields at Salisbury (pp. 79-88).

DORNON, Armand de Behault
Notice sur deux Anciennes Verrières de l'Eglise Ste. Waudru à
Mons.
Annales du Cercle Archéologique de Mons, no. 20 (1887), pp. 377-389

DORR, C.H.
The Art of Making a Stained Glass Window and the Work of Clara M.
Burd.
Architectural Review, vol. 35 (Feb., 1914), pp. 162-169.

DORREGARAY, J.G.
Museo Espanol de Antiguedades.
7 vols., Madrid, 1871-1876.
(Stained glass in vol. 2.)

DOUBLET DE BOISTHIBAULT
Les Pinaigriers.
Paris, 1854.

DOUGLAS, R.W., and ISARD, J.O.
The Action of Water and Sulphur Dioxide on Glass Surfaces.
Journal of the Society of Glass Technology, vol. 33 (1949), pp.
289-335.

DOWNS, Joseph
Stained Glass by John La Farge.
(Reprinted from the Bulletin of the Metropolitan Museum of Art,
May, 1945).
Stained Glass, vol. 40, no. 4 (Winter, 1945), pp. 123-126.

DOWSING, William
The Journal of William Dowsing . . .
Edited by LODER, R.
Woodbridge, 1786.
New Edition by WHITE, C.H.E., Ipswich, 1885.

DRACHENBERG, E.; MAERCKER, K.-J.; SCHMIDT, C.
Die Mittelalterliche Glasmalerei in Erfurt.
Die Mittelalterliche Glasmalerei in den Ordenskirchen und im
Angermuseum zu Erfurt. (CVMA, German Democratic Republic, no. 1.)
(Erfurt ?), 1976.

(Drake, Daphne)
Woman Glazier's Novel Post: Exeter Cathedral Appointment.
Westminster Gazette, June 7, 1923.

Woman Worker in Stained Glass.
Newcastle Chronicle, June 27, 1923.

A Worker in Stained Glass.
Liverpool Daily Post, June 20, 1923.

(On her work at Chelsea and Exeter.)
Morning Post, June 18, 1923.

DRAKE, Daphne
Frederick Drake, Glass-Painter of Exeter.
J.M.G.P., vol. 3, no. 3 (Apr., 1930), pp. 105-107.

D(RAKE), D(aphne)
Maurice Drake.
J.M.G.P., vol. 4, no. 4 (Oct., 1932), pp. 187-188.

DRAKE, Daphne
Ancient Glass in Exeter Cathedral.
Devon and Cornwall Notes and Queries, vol. 17 (1933), p. 299-302.

Heraldic Glass at Medland Manor, Cheriton Bishop.
Devon and Cornwall Notes and Queries, vol. 18 (1935), pp. 146-147.

Repairing the Ravages of Corrosion.
J.M.G.P., vol. 11, no. 2 (1953), p. 67.

(Letter to the Editor on the early nineteenth century Devonshire
glass-painter Robert BEER.)
J.M.G.P., vol. 13, no. 4 (1963), pp. 602-603.

DRAKE, Francis
Eboracum; or the History and Antiquities of the City of York . . .
London, 1736.

DRAKE, Frederick
The Ancient Stained Glass of Exeter Cathedral.
Transactions of the Exeter Diocesan Architectural Society, 2nd
series, vol. 4 (Oct. 2, 1879), pp. 321-327.
(Reprint with DRAKE, Frederick Morris)
Two Papers on the Ancient Stained Glass in Exeter Cathedral.
Exeter, 1909.

(Drake, Frederick)
(Obituaries.)
Express and Echo (Exeter), Dec. 22, 1920.
Devon and Exeter Gazette, Dec. 28, 1920.
East Devon Gazette, Dec. 28, 1920.
(Funeral.)
Express and Echo, Dec. 29, 1920.

DRAKE, F. Morris
(Usually wrote as DRAKE, Maurice, by which name he is subsequently
referred to.)
Rare Mediaeval Glass in a Devonshire Church.   (Ashton).
Building News (March, 10, 1905).
(Report of Address.)

Heraldic Stained Glass in Ashton Church (Devon).
Transactions of the Exeter Diocesan Architectural Society, 3rd
series, vol. 2 (1907), pp. 167-174.

Votive Figures in Stained Glass.
(Enquiry for whereabouts of donor figures in Devon and Somerset.)
Devon Notes and Queries, vol. 4 (1907), p. 59.

Wages of Mediaeval Craftsmen.
(Letter to the Editor.)
Express and Echo (Exeter), March 7, 1908.

The East Window of Exeter Cathedral.
(In Two Papers Dealing with the Ancient Stained Glass of Exeter
Cathedral. The other is a reprint of DRAKE, Frederick, 1879)
Exeter, 1909.
Reviewed in The Builder (Sept. 29, 1911).

Dartmouth Arms.
Devon Notes and Queries, vol. 5 (1909), p. 222-223.

Seventeenth Century Stained Glass in Upton Pyne Church.
Devon and Cornwall Notes and Queries, vol. 6 (1911), pp. 177-178.
And subsequent note by WERE, F., ibid, p. 196.

The Fourteenth Century Stained Glass of Exeter Cathedral.
Transactions of the Devonshire Association, vol. 44 (1912),
pp. 231-251.

A History of English Glass Painting.
London, 1912.

(Drake, Maurice)
A History of English Glass Painting.
(Announced in Daily Chronicle, Nov. 8, 1912;
          Glasgow Daily Herald, Nov. 10, 1912;
          Glasgow News, Nov. 14, 1912;
          Daily News, Nov. 15, 1912;)
Reviewed: Times Literary Supplement, Nov. 21, 1912;
          Building News, no. 3020 (Nov. 22, 1912);
          Liverpool Daily Post, Jan. 1, 1913;
          Daily News, Jan. 2, 1913;
          The Antiquary (by COX, J. Charles), (Feb., 1913);
          The Athenaeum
          The Morning Post, May 5, 1913;
          The Academy (1912-1913);
          Irish Times, Dec. 6, 1912;
          Saturday Review, Apr. 19, 1913;
          The Tablet, Jan. 10, 1913;
          Glasgow Herald, Feb. 13, 1913;
          Birmingham Daily Post, Jan. 15, 1913;
          Daily Chronicle, Jan. 11, 1913.
          Manchester Guardian, July 25, 1913.

DRAKE, Maurice
English Glass Painting.
Letter to the Editor in reply to a critical review of 'A History
of English Glass Painting'.
Morning Post, May 31, 1913.

DRAKE, Maurice (Contd)

Stained Glass. Devon Specimens.
(Primarily Doddiscombsleigh.)
Devon and Exeter Gazette, July 26, 1913.
(Report of address.)

The Painted Glass of Exeter Cathedral and other Devon Churches.
The Archaeological Journal, vol. 70 (1913), pp. 163-174.

(Reports of a Lecture to the Camera Club.)
Morning Post, Jan. 2, 1914.
Westminster Gazette, Jan. 3, 1914.
Daily Mail, Jan. 5, 1914.
The Architect, (Jan. 9, 1914).
Amateur Photographer (Jan. 12, 1914).

(Reports of Lecture for Exeter Literary Society.)
Devon Gazette, Oct. 30, 1914.
Western Daily Mercury, Oct.31, 1914.

(With DRAKE, Wilfred)
Saints and their Emblems.
London, 1916.
Reviewed in The Connoisseur, vol. 45 (May-Aug., 1916), p. 177.

(Drake, Maurice)

Captain Maurice Drake.
Western Daily Mercury, March 3, 1917.

DRAKE, Maurice

The Costessey Collection of Stained Glass.
(With an introductory article by VALLANCE, Aymer.)
Exeter, 1920.

Story of Stained Glass. Rare Relics in Peril.
(Report of a lecture to the Glaziers' Company.)
Morning Post, July 10, 1920.

Winchester Stained Glass.
(Letter to the Editor.)
Times Literary Supplement, Oct. 9, 1920.

Fourteenth Century Stained Glass Windows in Exeter Cathedral.
(Chapter 13 of The Building of the Cathedral Church of St. Peter
in Exeter, by BISHOP, H.E., and PRIDEAUX, F.K., Exeter, 1922,
pp. 146-156.)
Stained Glass.
Morning Post, Aug. 8, 1922.
(Second part.)
Ibid., Aug. 15, 1922.
(Third part.)
Ibid., Aug. 22, 1922.

A Stained-Glass Hobby.
Daily Mail, Aug. 9, 1922.

(Drake, Maurice)

Notice of 'A Stained-Glass Hobby'.
The Architects' Journal (Aug. 16, 1922).

(Exhibition of a proposed restoration of glass discovered in
Chelsea Old Church.)
Daily Telegraph, Nov. 4, 1922.
The Times, Nov. 7, 1922.
Daily Telegraph, Nov. 7, 1922.

DRAKE, Maurice

Windows You Can Put in Your Pocket.
(Miniature Swiss windows.)
Daily Mail, Nov. 18, 1922.

(Drake, Maurice)

The Doom Window.
(Announcement of serialisation of the book with an account of
his career.)
The Queen, (Dec. 30, 1922).

DRAKE, Maurice (Contd.)

Stained Glass by Reginald Bell.
The Studio, vol. 85 (1923), pp. 190-196.

The Making of a Stained Glass Window.
London, 1923.

Stained Glass Forgeries.
Evening News, Jan. 4, 1923.

The Making of Stained Glass Windows.
The Builder (Feb. 16, 1923), p. 286.

(Drake, Maurice)

(Obituaries.)
Express and Echo (Exeter), Apr. 30, 1923.
Daily Mail, Apr. 30, 1923.
Western Morning News, Apr. 30, 1923.
The Morning Post, Apr. 30, 1923.
Daily Telegraph, Apr. 30, 1923.
The Star, Apr. 30, 1923.
Liverpool Post, Apr. 30, 1923.
Birmingham Post, Apr. 30, 1923.
The Times, May 1, 1923.
Architects' Journal (May 2, 1923).
The Teignmouth Post, May 4, 1923.
The Architects' Journal (May 9, 1923).
The Teignmouth Post, May 11, 1923.
The Architectural Review (May, 1923).
The Studio, (July, 1923).

(Reports of funeral.)
Express and Echo (Exeter), May 2, 1923,
                                   May 3, 1923.

(Will.)
Devon and Exeter Gazette, June 28, 1923.

The Doom Window.
London, n.d. (1923).
(Announced in the Evening Standard, Sept. 2, 1921;
            Weekly Despatch, Sept. 27, 1922;
            John O'London's Weekly, (Oct. 28, 1922;
            The Bookman (March, 1923).
Reviewed in John O'London's Weekly, (March 31, 1923);
            Daily Chronicle, June 25, 1923;
            Westminster Gazette, July 7, 1923;
            Sunday Times, July 8, 1923;
            The Scotsman, July 9, 1923;
            Morning Post, July 11, 1923;
            Aberdeen Free Press, July 11, 1923;
            Times Library Supplement, July 12, 1923;
            Glasgow Herald, July 12, 1923;
            Eastbourne Gazette, July 18, 1923;
            Cassells Weekly, July 18, 1923;
            Evening Standard, July 28, 1923;
            Buxton Advertiser, Aug. 4, 1923;
            Eastbourne Gazette, Aug. 9, 1923;
            John O'London's Weekly (Aug. 12, 1923);
            Weekly Dispatch (Aug. 27,1923);
            John O'London's Weekly (Aug. 31, 1923).
Serialised in The Queen.

The Technique of Painted Glass.
The Archaeological Journal, vol. 85 (for March-Dec., 1928), pp.
80-90.

(Drake, Maurice)
Frederick Drake, Glass Painter of Exeter.
By DRAKE, Daphne.
J.M.G.P., vol. 3, no. 3 (Apr., 1930), pp. 105-107.

Maurice Drake.
By BISHOP, Morchard (pseudonym).
The West Country Magazine, vol. 6, no. 1 (Spring, 1951), pp.
28-32.

(Drake, Maurice), Contd.
    (Centenary of his birth.)
    News and Notes, J.M.G.P., vol. 15, no. 3 (1974-1975), p. 54.

DRAKE, T.
    Stained Glass Windows.
    Transactions of the Leicester Architectural and Archaeological
    Society, vol. 2, (1870), pp. 347-350.

DRAKE, Wilfred
    Ancient Heraldic Glass in Slapton Church.
    Devon and Cornwall Notes and Queries, vol. 6 (1911), p. 149.

    Stained Glass in Bamfylde House, Exeter.
    Devon and Cornwall Notes and Queries, vol. 6 (1911), pp. 225-228.

    Stained Glass at Bamfylde House, Exon.
    Devon and Cornwall Notes and Queries, vol. 7 (1913), p. 45.

    The Badges of King Henry VII.
    (In a window at Bovey House, Beer.)
    Devon and Cornwall Notes and Queries, vol. 7 (1913), p. 57.

    Heraldic Stained Glass of Exeter Cathedral.
    Devon and Cornwall Notes and Queries, vol. 7 (1913), pp. 174-175.

    The Heraldry and Ancient Stained Glass in the Great East Window
    of Exeter Cathedral.
    Devon and Cornwall Notes and Queries, vol. 7 (1913), p. 283.

    Old Glass at Salcombe Regis.
    Devon and Cornwall Notes and Queries, vol. 8 (1915), pp. 140-141.

    (With DRAKE, Maurice.)
    Saints and their Emblems.
    London, 1916.

    Two Panels of English Sixteenth Century Glass.
    (Request for help in identifying the stories depicted.)
    Notes and Queries, 13th series, vol. 146 (Jan. 5, 1924), p. 9.

    Exhibition of French Painted Glass in London, c. 1802.
    Notes and Queries, 13th series, vol. 146 (May 10, 1924), p. 346.

    Portraits in French Seventeenth Century Stained Glass.
    (Request for identification of two figures in a panel.)
    Notes and Queries, vol. 149 (July 18, 1925), p. 44.

    Pedigrees of Families of Glass-Painters.
    J.M.G.P., vol. 5, no. 3 (Apr., 1934), pp. 130-132.

    Chronological List of English Glass-Paintings (Additions).
    (Letter to the Editor.)
    J.M.G.P., vol. 6, no. 4 (Apr., 1937), p. 227.

    Chronological List of English Glass-Paintings (Additions).
    (Letter to the Editor.)
    J.M.G.P., vol. 7, no. 1 (Oct., 1937), p. 58.

    The Stained Glass of St. George's Chapel, Windsor Castle.
    J.M.G.P., vol. 8, no. 4 (1942), pp. 149-151.

    The Stained Glass of the Tower of London.
    J.M.G.P., vol. 9, no. 1 (1943), pp. 24-25.

(Drake, Wilfred)
    Obituary.
    J.M.G.P., vol. 10, no. 2 (1949), p. 105.

DRAKE, Wilfred
    A Dictionary of Glasspainters and 'Glasyers' of the Tenth to the
    Eighteenth Centuries.
    New York, 1955.
    Reviewed by RACKHAM, Bernard, J.M.G.P., vol.12, no. 2 (1957), pp.
    161-162.

(Drake, Wilfred)
    RORIMER, J.J.
    Letter to the Editor concerning the state of readiness of DRAKE,
    Wilfred's Dictionary . . . for the press.
    J.M.G.P., vol. 12, no. 2 (1957), p. 163.

(Drury, A.J.)
    Obituary.
    J.M.G.P., vol. 8, no. 2 (Apr., 1940), pp. 82-83.

DRURY, Donald V.
    Some Contemporary Stained Glass. A Letter from America.
    J.M.G.P., vol. 13, no. 4 (1963), pp. 576-578.

DRURY, Myles.
    The Reconstruction.
    19th Annual Report of the Friends of Exeter Cathedral, 1948 (1949),
    pp. 15-16.
    (Glass, including restoration of the East window.)

    Further Notes on War Damage and Maintenance Repairs.
    21st Annual Report of the Friends of Exeter Cathedral, 1950 (1951),
    (On the reglazing, p. 20.)

    Report on the War Damage and Maintenance Repairs.
    22nd Annual Report of the Friends of Exeter Cathedral (1952), pp.21-22.
    (The Drake Memorial glass and other re-glazing.)

DRURY, V.J. and WILKINSON, A.L.
    The Conservation of Stained Glass.
    J.M.G.P., vol. 13, no. 4 (1963), pp. 582-584.

DRURY, W.E.
    A Guide to Wilton Parish Church and the Old Church of St. Mary.
    Wilton, 1959.

DUBUC, René
    Les Vitraux de la Cathédrale d'Evreux.
    (An exchange of articles with GRODECKI, Louis, and BAUDOT, Marcel.)
    Bulletin Monumental, no. 126 (1968), pp. 71-73.

DUFAY, Charles J.
    Essai Biographique sur Jehan Perreal, dit Jehan de Paris. Peintre,
    Architecte et Maître Verrier du XV Siècle.
    Lyons, 1864.

DUFOUR, A., and MUGNIER, F.
    Les Verriers-Vitriers du 14e au 19e Siècle en Savois.
    Chambéry, 1894.

DUFTY, A.R.
    Through a Stained Glass Less Darkly.
    The Times, Sept. 23, 1972.

DUGAST-MATINFEUX, C.
    Les Gentilshommes Verriers de Mouchamps en Bas Poitou, 1399.
    Nantes, 1861.

DULEEP SINGH, F.
    Armorial Glass in Old and New Buckenham Churches.
    Norfolk Archaeology, vol. 15 (1904), pp. 324-334.

DUNCAN, Alastair.
    The Technique of Leaded Glass.
    London, 1975.
    Reviewed in J.M.G.P., vol. 15, no. 3 (1974-1975), p. 80.

DUNCAN, G.S.

    Bibliography of Glass.
    (From the earliest records to 1940.)
    Ed. DIMBLEBY, V.
    London, 1960.

DURAND, Georges

    La Peinture sur Verre au 13e Siècle, Cathédrale d'Amiens.
    Bulletin de la Société des Antiquaires de Picardie, vol. 1 (1889).

    Monographie de la Cathédrale d'Amiens.
    Amiens and Paris, 1901.

    Causerie sur la Peinture sur Verre en Picardie.
    Bulletin de la Société des Antiquaires de Picardie (1908), p. 36.

    Description abrégée de la Cathédrale d'Amiens.
    Amiens, 1914.

DURAND, Paul

    Monographie de Notre-Dame de Chartres.
    Paris, 1867-1881.

DURST, Hans

    Vitraux Anciens en Suisse/Alte Glasmalerei der Schweiz.
    Fribourg, 1971.
    Reviewed by O'CONNOR, David, J.M.G.P., vol. 15, no. 2 (1973-1974),
    pp. 75-78.

Dutch Art of Today.
    (Includes two cartoons for stained glass by Joep Nicholas.)
    The Studio (Nov., 1937).

DUTHIE, A.L.

    Decorative Glass Processes.
    London, 1908.

DVORAK, Max

    Idealismus und Naturalismus in der gotischen Skulptur und Malerei.
    Munich, 1918.

    Idealism and Naturalism in Gothic Art.
    Notre Dame, 1967.

DYE, Trudy

    West Virginia Glassmakers.
    (About the Blenko factory.)
    The Country Gentleman (Philadelphia), (Feb., 1948).

DYER-SPENCER, J.

    Les Vitraux de la Sainte-Chapelle de Paris.
    Bulletin Monumental, vol. 91 (1932), pp. 333-407.

DYKES-BOWER, S.E.

    The Rose Window at Lancing.
    J.M.G.P., vol. 17, no. 1 (1978-1979), pp. 31-36.

EAGLE, W.H.

La date du Vitrail du Chevet de la Cathédrale de Dol.
Bulletin Monumental, vol. 88, (1929), pp. 508-513.

(East Harling Church)

Stained Glass, etc., at Ss. Peter and Paul, East Harling, Norfolk.
The Ecclesiologist, vol. 4 (1845), pp. 228-229.

(Easton, George)

The Retirement of a Great Craftsman.
Canterbury Cathedral Chronicle, no. 59 (Autumn, 1964), p. 40.

(Eaton Bishop Church)

Eaton Bishop Church, Herefordshire: Glass.
(Grant towards restoring the East Window.)
The Pilgrim Trust, 38th Annual Report (1968), p. 16.

EBERLEIN, Harold D.

Use of Stained Glass for Windows in Homes.
Suburb Life, vol. 15 (Oct., 1912), pp. 183-185, 226.

ECKHARDT, Wolf von

Translucent Beauty.
A.I.A. Journal (Feb., 1962).

Through the Glass Brightly; Stained Glass Revival.
Horizon (Summer, 1962).

ECKERT, K.

St. Bernard von Clarvaulx, Glasmalerien aus dem Kreuzgang von
Altenberg bei Köln.
Wuppertal, 1953.

EDEN, F.C.

Stained Glass in Milan Cathedral.
(Review of VILLARD, Monneret de, 'Le Vetrate del Duomo di Milano'.)
Journal of the Royal Institute of British Architects, vol. 34,
3rd series, no. 10 (March 19, 1927), p. 338.

Review of VILLARD, Monneret de, 'Le Vetrate del Duomo di Milano'.
J.M.G.P., vol. 2, no. 2 (Oct., 1927), pp. 98-100.

Report of Lecture 'Modern Stained Glass in Relation to
Architecture' read before R.I.B.A. and Subsequent Discussion.
The Builder, (Dec. 18, 1931).

Stained Glass and Architecture.
Journal of the Royal Institute of British Architects, 3rd series,
vol. 39, no. 4 (Dec. 19, 1931).

EDEN, Frederick Sydney

Windows from Church at Trier.
(Inquiry about location of glass sold to an Englishman in early
nineteenth century.)
Notes and Queries, 10th series, vol. 12 (Aug. 7, 1909), p. 109.

Stained and Painted Glass in Essex Churches. (A listing.)
Notes and Queries, 11th series, vol. 2 (Nov. 5, 1910), pp. 361-362.
Ibid. (Dec. 10, 1910), pp. 462-464.
(Elucidation of a subject by L.M.R.)
Ibid. (Dec. 10, 1910), p. 464.
Ibid., vol. 3 (Jan. 21, 1911), pp. 41-42.

EDEN, Frederick Sydney

Review of Nelson's Ancient Painted Glass in England.
Notes and Queries, 11th series, vol. 8 (Dec. 20, 1913), pp. 497-498.

EDEN Frederick Sydney

Ancient Stained and Painted Glass.
Cambridge, 1913.
Revised and enlarged edition, Cambridge, 1933.

(Eden, F.S.)

Ancient Stained and Painted Glass.
Reviewed in Daily News, Jan. 27, 1913.
          Manchester Guardian, July 25, 1913.

Reviews of 2nd edition of Ancient Stained and Painted Glass.
Notes and Queries, vol. 164 (Apr. 22, 1933), p. 288;
By RACKHAM, Bernard, Burlington Magazine, vol. 63 (July-Dec.,
1933), p. 186.
By SKINNER, Orin E., Stained Glass, vol. 28, no. 2 (Summer, 1933),
pp. 112-113.

EDEN, Frederick Sydney

Middlesex: Ancient Painted Glass.
(Request for information about pre-eighteenth century domestic
glass.)
Notes and Queries, 11th series, vol. 9, (Jan. 17, 1914), p. 49.

Old Painted Glass at Maldon, Essex.
Notes and Queries, 11th series, vol. 9 (May 9, 1914), pp. 361-362.

Louvain and Malines: Old Painted Glass.
(Request for references to printed accounts of the glass in these
cities.)
Notes and Queries, 11th series, vol. 10, (Oct. 3, 1914), p. 268.

(Letter to the Editor suggesting that coloured tracings of
exported glass should be deposited in museums before the glass is
permitted to leave the country.)
The Times, March 9, 1922.

Abbot Islip's Glazing Quarries.
The Connoisseur, vol. 68 (Jan.-Apr., 1924), pp. 204-206.

Ancient Stained Glass in the Tower of London.
Bulletin of the Stained Glass Association of America, vol. 19,
nos. 9, 10, (1925).

Ancient Painted Glass in London.
J.M.G.P., vol. 1, no. 2 (Apr., 1925), pp. 18-27.

Ancient Painted Glass Recently Restored to Hereford Cathedral.
Burlington Magazine, vol. 47 (July-Dec., 1925), pp. 115-121.

Stained Glass from Bury St. Edmunds.
(The 'Susanna and the Elders' window repaired by Clayton and
Bell.)
The Connoisseur, vol. 73 (Sept.-Dec., 1925), p. 59.

Ancient Painted Glass in North-West Essex of the Thirteenth and
Fourteenth Centuries.
The Connoisseur, vol. 73 (Sept.-Dec., 1925), pp. 97-102.

(Eden, Frederick Sydney)

Notice of Ancient Painted Glass . . . in . . . Essex.
In 'Memorabilia', Notes and Queries, vol. 149 (Oct. 10, 1925), p. 254.

EDEN, Frederick Sydney

The Twelfth Century Medallions at Rivenhall, Essex.
J.M.G.P., vol. 1, no. 3 (Oct., 1925), pp. 20-23.

Old Painted Glass in Village Churches.
Country Life (Nov. 28, 1925), pp. 816-817.

Heraldic Painted Glass of Knights of the Order of St. John of
Jerusalem.
The Connoisseur, vol. 74 (Jan.-Apr., 1926), pp. 225-227.

The Collection of Heraldic Stained Glass at Ronaele Manor, Elkins
Park, Philadelphia.
Privately printed, London, 1927.

New Painted Glass for Laleham. (By W.M. GEDDES.)
The Connoisseur, vol. 77 (Jan.-Apr., 1927), p. 61.

EDEN, Frederick Sydney (Contd.)

Ancient Painted Glass in the Conventual Buildings, other than the Church, of Westminster Abbey.
The Connoisseur, vol. 77, (Jan.-Apr., 1927), pp. 81-88.

Stained Pressed Glass.
The Connoisseur, vol. 78 (May-Aug., 1927), pp. 34-36.

(Eden, Frederick Sydney)
Notice of 'Stained Pressed Glass'
(The Connoisseur, May, 1927.)
In 'Memorabilia', Notes and Queries, vol. 152 (May 7, 1927), p. 326.

EDEN, Frederick Sydney
Review of SHERRILL, C.H., Stained Glass Tours in Germany, Austria and the Rhine Lands.
The Connoisseur, vol. 79 (Sept.-Dec., 1927), p. 255.

Ancient Painted Glass at Colchester.
The Connoisseur, vol. 80 (Jan.-Apr., 1928), pp. 13-19.

The Bysshe Claim.
(Heraldic Glass at Colchester Castle.)
The Connoisseur, vol. 81 (May-Aug., 1928), pp. 210-214.
(Letter to the Editor, Ibid., vol. 82 (Sept.-Dec., 1928), p. 191.)

Heraldic Painted Glass at the Law Society's Hall, London.
J.M.G.P., vol. 2, no. 4 (Oct., 1928), pp. 183-187.

Belhus and its Heraldic Glass.
Grays and Tilbury Gazette, July 5, 1929
                            Sept. 21, 1929
                            Sept. 28, 1929.

Review of TWINING, E.W., The Art and Craft of Stained Glass.
The Connoisseur, vol. 82 (Sept.-Dec., 1928).

Royal Memorial Window at Pagham Church, Sussex.
(By Wilfred DRAKE.)
The Connoisseur, vol. 85 (Jan.-June, 1930), pp. 58-60.

English Heraldic Glass in America (at Ronaele Manor).
The Connoisseur, vol. 85 (Jan.-June, 1930), pp. 363-364.

Heraldic Glass at Ronaele Manor.
The Connoisseur, vol. 86 (July-Dec., 1930), pp. 30-31.

The Arms of Battle Abbey.
The Connoisseur, vol. 86 (July-Dec., 1930), pp. 174-175.
Ibid., vol. 87 (Jan.-June, 1931), pp. 43-44.

Ancient Painted Glass at Stanford-on-Avon.
J.M.G.P., vol. 3, no. 4 (Oct., 1930), pp. 156-165.

Heraldic Glass at Bramall Hall.
The Connoisseur, vol. 88 (July-Dec., 1931), pp. 253-256.

The Compton Verney Glass.
(Auction at Christie's, July 30, 1931.)
The Connoisseur, vol. 88 (July-Dec., 1931),pp. 354-355.

Verre Eglomisé.
(An example in Upper Shuckburgh Church, Warwickshire.)
The Connoisseur, vol. 89 (Jan.-June, 1932), pp. 393-396.

Heraldic Painted Glass at Horham Hall, Essex.
Apollo (May, 1932).

Vicissitudes of Ancient Stained Glass.
Burlington Magazine, vol. 61 (July-Dec., 1932), pp. 118-125.
(Letter to the Editor giving a correction.)
Ibid., p. 235.

EDEN, Frederick Sydney (Contd.)

New Stained Glass at York Minster.
(By BELL, Reginald.)
The Connoisseur, vol. 91 (Jan.-June, 1933), pp. 337-338.

Heraldic Glass in the City of London.
The Connoisseur, vol. 93 (Jan.-June, 1934), pp. 249-255.

(Eden, Frederick Sydney)
Notice of Heraldic Glass in the City of London (The Connoisseur, Apr., 1934).
'Memorabilia', Notes and Queries, vol. 166 (Apr. 21, 1934), p. 272.

EDEN, Frederick Sydney
Ancient Painted Glass at Old Hall Highgate. (Lord Rochdale's collection.)
The Connoisseur, vol. 94 (July-Dec., 1934), pp. 3-8, 79-84, 266-269.

Stained Glass in Churches.
Dublin Review (Oct., 1935).

(Eden, Frederick Sydney)
Notice of Stained Glass in Churches (Dublin Review, Oct., 1935).
Notes and Queries, vol. 169 (Dec. 21, 1935), p. 434.

EDEN, Frederick Sydney
Armorial Glass Quarries. Heraldry of Yorkshire Families.
The Connoisseur, (Apr., 1936), pp. 213-216.

Review of RUSHFORTH, G. McNeil, Mediaeval Christian Imagery . . .
The Connoisseur, vol. 97 (May, 1936), pp. 291-292.

The Heraldic Stained Glass at Grays Inn. Part I.
The Connoisseur, vol. 98 (July, 1936), pp. 16-22.
Part II. Ibid. (Sept., 1936), pp. 133-139.

Ancient Stained Glass in South-East Essex.
Southend Standard, July 30, 1936.

Review of KNOWLES, J.A., Essays in the History of the York School of Glass-Painting.
The Connoisseur, vol. 99 (Jan., 1939), p. 52.

Heraldic Stained Glass at Gray's Inn. Part III.
The Connoisseur, vol. 100 (July, 1937), pp. 16-20.

Secular Pedigree Windows.
J.M.G.P., vol. 7, no. 1 (Oct., 1937), pp. 18-19.

Oxford Heraldic Quarries.
The Connoisseur, vol. 101 (Feb., 1938), pp. 78-81, 106.

Medieval Heraldry in Painted Glass.
J.M.G.P., vol. 7, no. 2 (Apr., 1938), pp. 63-68.

The Heraldic Stained Glass at Gray's Inn. Part IV.
The Connoisseur, vol. 102 (July, 1938), pp. 21-26.

The Heraldic Stained Glass at Gray's Inn. Part V.
The Connoisseur, vol. 103 (Apr., 1939), pp. 198.

Fifteenth and Sixteenth Century Painted Glass in North-West Essex.
The Connoisseur, vol. 104 (July-Dec., 1939), pp. 22-27.

Ancient Stained Glass in South-East Essex.
The Connoisseur, vol. 105, (Jan.-June, 1940), pp. 148-152.

Ancient Stained and Painted Glass in London.
London, 1939.
Reviewed in J.M.G.P., vol. 8, no. 2 (Apr., 1940), pp. 77-78.

Ancient Stained Glass in South-East Essex.
The Connoisseur, vol. 105 (Apr., 1940), pp. 148-152.

Mediaeval Heraldic Glass in Surrey Churches. Part I.
The Connoisseur, vol. 106 (July-Dec., 1940), pp. 7-9, 18-19.
Part II. Ibid., pp. 143-146, 174.
Part III. The Connoisseur, vol. 107 (Jan.-June, 1941), pp. 28-31, 41.

EDEN, Frederick Sydney (Contd.)

    Ancient Heraldic Glass at Winchester.
    The Connoisseur, vol. 109 (Jan.-June, 1942), pp. 49-53.

    Domestic Stained Glass of the Sixteenth and Seventeenth Centuries:
    Berkshire.
    The Connoisseur, vol. 110 (July-Dec., 1942), pp. 31-33.

(Eden, Frederick Sydney)

    A Bibliography of Works, by Frederick Sydney Eden, Relating to
    Ancient Stained and Painted Glass.
    J.M.G.P., vol. 8, no. 4 (1942), pp. 145-148.

(Edgcote Church)

    Edgcote Church, Northamptonshire: Glass and Monuments.
    (A grant towards repairing and rearranging the sixteenth century
    heraldic glass.)
    The Pilgrim Trust, 39th Annual Report (1969), p. 17.

EDGERTON, Samuel Y.

    Review of PARRONCHI, Alessandro, Studi su la Dolce Prospettiva.
    Art Bulletin, vol. 49 (March, 1967), pp. 77-80.

    Alberti's Colour Theory: A Medieval Bottle Without Renaissance Wine.
    Journal of the Warburg and Courtauld Institutes, vol. 32 (1969),
    pp. 109-134.

(Edinburgh, Walter Scott Monument)

    (Glass painted by Ballantine in the Scott Monument.)
    Art Journal (1857), p. 21.

(Edinburgh, Parliament House)

    (Munich glass window installed.)
    The Builder, vol. 26 (Oct. 17, 1868), pp. 762-763.

(Edington Church)

    Edington Church, Wiltshire: Glass.
    (Grant to restore three windows.)
    The Pilgrim Trust, 28th Annual Report (1958), pp. 15-16.

    (Grant to restore the windows in the North Transept.)
    The Pilgrim Trust, 40th Annual Report (1970), pp. 13-14.

EDWARDS, Carl

    Stained Glass.
    Transactions of the Ecclesiological Society, new series, vol. 2,
    part 4 (1951), pp. 233-236.

    The Beauty of Stained Glass.
    J.M.G.P., vol. 12, no. 1 (1956), pp. 48-56.

EELES, F.C.

    The Fifteenth Century Stained Glass at Clavering.
    Transactions of the Essex Archaeological Society, new series, vol. 16,
    1921-1923 (1923), pp. 77-87.

    Ancient Glass at Carlisle Cathedral.
    Transactions of the Cumberland and Westmorland Antiquarian and
    Archaeological Society, new series, vol. 26 (1926), pp. 312-317.

    Notes on the Medieval Stained Glass at Winscombe and East Brent.
    Proceedings of the Somersetshire Archaeological and Natural History
    Society, vol.75, for 1929, part 2 (1930), pp. 14-25.

    Ancient Stained Glass at Farleigh Hungerford.
    Proceedings of the Somerset Archaeological and Natural History
    Society, vol. 80, for 1934, part 2 (1935), pp. 57-62.

    Ancient Stained Glass at Alford.
    Notes and Queries for Somerset and Dorset, vol. 21 (1935), pp. 219-221.

EELES, F.C. (Contd.)

    (Letter to the Editor about wartime measures taken to protect glass.)
    J.M.G.P., vol. 9, no. 1 (1943), p. 30.

    The Advisory Committee System in Relation to Stained Glass.
    J.M.G.P., vol. 9, no. 2 (1944), pp. 63-67.

    Glass-Painters' Signatures on Windows.
    (Letter to the Editor.)
    J.M.G.P., vol. 9, no. 4 (1946), p. 142.

    The Diocesan Advisory Committee's Directory of Glass Painters.
    (Letter to the Editor.)
    J.M.G.P., vol. 10, no. 1 (1948), p. 54.

    The Restoration of the East Window at Bowness on Windermere.
    J.M.G.P., vol. 10, no. 3 (1950), pp. 147-148.

(Eeles, F.C.)

    Obituary by RALEGH-RADFORD, C.A.
    Proceedings of the Somersetshire Archaeological and Natural History
    Society, vol. 98, for 1953, part 2 (1955), pp. 160-161.

    Obituary by CROOME, W.I.
    J.M.G.P., vol. 11, no. 4 (1955), pp. 241-242.

EELES, F.C.

    The Ancient Stained Glass of Westminster Abbey.
    J.M.G.P., vol. 17, no. 1 (1978-1979), pp. 17-29.

EGGERT, F.X.

    Darstellung aus dem Leben Marias in der Maria Hilfkirche in der
    Münchener Vorstadt Au. Les Peintres sur Verre de la Nouvelle
    Eglise de Notre Dame de Secours, Munich.
    Munich, 1845.

    (Editor.)
    Abbildungen der Glasgemälde in der Salvatorkirche zu Kilndown in
    der Grafschaft Kent.
    Munich, 1852.

(Eginton, Francis)

    List of Works.
    The Gentleman's Magazine, vol. 75, part 1 (1805), pp. 482-483;
    part 2, pp. 606-607, 625, 821-822.

    Obituary.
    The Gentleman's Magazine, vol. 75, part 1 (1805), p. 387.

    (A description of his window at Stationer's Hall.)
    The Gentleman's Magazine, vol. 84, part 2 (1814), p. 417.

    (A window by Eginton presented to the Church of Buckingham by the
    Duke of Buckingham.)
    The Gentleman's Magazine, vol. 93, part 2 (1823), p. 39.

    A Note on Francis Eginton.
    (A listing of his works.)
    Transactions of the Birmingham and Midland Institute, vol. 30,
    for 1904 (1905), pp. 89-92.

    Francis Eginton, the Glass Painter.
    Notes and Queries, series 5, vol. 11 (March 1, 1879), p. 168;
                            (April 5, 1879), p. 273.

EGINTON, W.R.

    References to Works in Stained Glass, by W.R.E.
    Birmingham, 1806.

    Short Account of some of the Works Executed in Stained Glass.
    Edinburgh, 1818.

    Original Drawings and Designs for Stained Glass Windows.
    Birmingham, 1819-1822.

EGLI, Johannes
    Die Glasgemälde des Historischen Museums in St. Gallen. Part I.
    Historische Verein des Kantons St. Gallen (1925).

    Restauration von Glasgemälden in alter Zeit.
    Anzeiger für Schweizerische Altertumskunde, Band 33 (1931), pp. 265-266.

(Egypt)
    Stained Glass in Egypt.
    Stained Glass, vol. 56, no. 2 (Summer, 1961), pp. 38-39.

EITELBERGER VON EDELBERG, Rudolf von
    Quellenschriften für Kunstgeschichte und Kunsttechnik des Mittelalters
    und der Renaissance.
    Vienna, 1871.

EL-SHAMY, T.M., LEWINS, J., DOUGLAS, R.W.
    The Dependence on the pH of the Decomposition of Glasses by
    Aqueous Solutions.
    Glass Technology, 13, no. 3 (1972), pp. 81-87.

(Electric kilns)
    The Electric Kiln in the Service of Glass Painting.
    Diamant, no. 6 (1925).

    An Electric Kiln for Firing Glass.
    J.M.G.P., vol. 5, no. 3 (Apr., 1934), pp. 148-150.

ELLACOMBE, H.T.
    The Parish of Clyst St. George, Devon.
    Transactions of the Exeter Diocesan Architectural Society, vol. 1,
    2nd series (1867).
    (Glass, pp. 107-111.)
    (Including work by Powell using WINSTON'S Formula.)

(Ellesmere Church, Shropshire)
    (Glass by David Evans installed.)
    The Gentleman's Magazine, vol. 99, part 2 (1829), pp. 115-116.

EL-SHAMY, T.M.M., and DOUGLAS, R.W.
    Kinetics of the Reaction of Water with Glass.
    Glass Technology, vol. 13 (1972), pp. 77-80.

EL-SHAMY, T.M.M.
    The Chemical Durability of K_2O-CaO-MgO-SiO_2 Glasses.
    Physical Chemistry of Glasses, vol. 14 (1973), pp. 1-5.

ELSKUS, Albinus, RAMBUSCH, Robert, FREI, Robert
    Contemporary Stained Glass.
    Stained Glass, vol. 60, no. 1 (Spring, 1965), pp. 13-23.

(Ely, window of a prebendal house.)
    (Stained glass panels briefly described: illustrated facing p. 768.)
    The Gentleman's Magazine, vol. 58, part 2 (1788), p. 792.

(Ely Cathedral)
    (Includes an account of the insertion of many windows, including
    some by Wailes and Gerente. Warrington's window is severely
    criticised.)
    The Ecclesiologist, vol. 11 (1850), pp. 155-161.
    WARRINGTON replies:
    Ibid., pp. 266-267.

    (Further windows installed.)
    The Ecclesiologist, vol. 12 (1851), p. 332.

    (Further windows inserted.)
    The Ecclesiologist, vol. 14 (1853), pp. 6-7.
    (More windows.)
    Ibid., p. 370.

(Ely Cathedral Contd.)
    (Wailes' East window inserted.)
    The Ecclesiologist, vol. 17 (1857), p. 196.

    (New windows by Hedgeland.)
    Art Journal (1858), p. 254.

    (Recently inserted windows.)
    The Ecclesiologist, vol. 23 (1862), p. 20.

    Ely Cathedral: Stained Glass Museum.
    (A grant to transport the glass to Ely.)
    The Pilgrim Trust, 42nd Annual Report (1972), pp. 14-15.

    Ely Cathedral: Stained Glass Museum.
    (Grant to aid setting up the museum.)
    The Pilgrim Trust, 45th Annual Report (1975), p. 11.

    Ely Cathedral: Stained Glass Museum.
    (Grant to aid setting up the museum.)
    The Pilgrim Trust, 46th Annual Report (1976), p. 11.

(Ely Stained Glass Museum)
    (Glass rescued recently for the museum.)
    In Editorial, J.M.G.P., vol. 16, no. 1 (1976-1977), p. 7.

(Emblematic Stained Glass)
    (An emblematic roundel described and illustrated.)
    The Gentleman's Magazine, vol. 57, part 2 (1787), p. 349-350.

(Engel-Gros Collection: Auction Catalogue of)
    Catalogue des Vitraux Anciens . . . Vente . . . Hôtel Drouot . . .
    7 Dec., 1922.
    Paris, 1922.

ENGELS, Mathias
    Zur Problematik der Mittelalterlichen Glasmalerei.
    Berlin, 1937.

    Campendonk: Holzschnitte. Werkverzeichnis.
    Stuttgart, 1959.

    Campendonk als Glasmaler. Mit einem Werkverzeichnis.
    Krefeld, 1966.

ENGLISH, Rachel Willet
    Stained Glass Tours: Atlanta.
    Stained Glass, vol. 60, no. 4 (Winter, 1965-1966), pp. 18-25.

(Ennis, George Pearse)
    George Pearse Ennis, 1884-1936, and the Washington Window for
    West Point.
    Stained Glass, vol. 31, no. 2 (Autumn, 1936), pp. 57-58.

    Obituary.
    Stained Glass, vol. 31, no. 2 (Autumn, 1936), pp. 59-60.

ENNS, Abram
    Kunst und Bürgertum, Die Kontroversen der Zwanziger Jahre in Lübeck.
    Hamburg, 1978.

(Epsom Church)
    Some Particulars Relating to the History of Epsom.
    Epsom, 1825-1826.

(Erfurt Cathedral)
    Das Helenafenster im Dome zu Erfurt um 1400.
    Zeitschrift für alte und neue Glasmalerei (1912), p. 71.

ERIKSON, Erik
Step by Step: Stained Glass.
Racine (Wisconsin), 1974.

ERNSBERGER, F.M.
Attack of Glass by Chelating Agents.
Journal of the American Ceramic Society, vol. 42, no. 8 (1959),
pp. 373-375.

ESSENWEIN, A.
Die Mittelalterlichen Kunstdenkmale der Stadt Krakau.
Leipzig, 1869.

ESSENWEIN, August Ritter von
Die Farbige Ausstattung des zehneckigen Schiffes der Pfarr-Kirche
zum heiligen Gereon in Köln durch Wand-und Glasmalerei.
Frankfurt-am-Main, 1891.

ESSEX, R.H., and SMIRKE, S.
Illustrations of the Architectural Ornaments and Embellishments
and Painted Glass of the Temple Church, London.
Weale's Quarterly Papers on Architecture, London, 1844-1845.

EVANS, C.J.
The Heraldry of Norwich Cathedral.
Norfolk Archaeology, vol. 8 (1879), pp. 57-87.

Heraldry in King's College, Cambridge, Windows.
In WILLIS and CLARK's Architectural History of the University of
Cambridge.
Cambridge, 1886. (Vol. 1, pp. 581-583.)

EVANS, Joan
Pattern: a Study of Ornament in Western Europe from 1180-1900.
2 vols., Oxford, 1931.

Review of WOODFORDE Christopher, Stained Glass in Somerset
1250-1830.
The Archaeological Journal, vol. 105 (for 1948), p. 96.

English Art 1307-1461.
Oxford, 1949.

EVANS, Sebastian
Hints on Church Windows. A Series of Designs, Original or
Selected from Ancient Examples.
Smethwick, 1862.

The Glass in Fairford Church, Gloucestershire.
(He justifies his proceedings in 'restoring' away the upper part
of the West window.)
The Ecclesiologist, vol. 26 (1865), pp. 16-18.
q.v. Fairford (1864).

EVEN, Edward van
L'Ancienne Ecole de Peinture de Louvain.
Louvain, 1870.

EVETTS, L.C.
Canterbury Glass.
(Letter to the Editor.)
Daily Telegraph, Aug. 8, 1939.

Genealogical Windows at Canterbury Cathedral. Part I.
Burlington Magazine, vol. 78 (Jan.-June, 1941), pp. 95-98.
Part II, Ibid., pp. 112-118.

EVETTS, L.C. (Contd.)
Medieval Painted Glass in Northumberland.
Archaeologia Aeliana, vol. 20, 4th series (1942), pp. 91-109.

Sixteenth-Century Heraldic Glass at Earsdon, Northumberland.
Archaeologia Aeliania, vol. 37, 4th series (1959), pp. 333-338.

(Window glass excavated at Tynemouth Priory.)
Archaeologia Aeiliana, vol. 45, 4th series (1967), pp. 86-88.

(Evreux Cathedral)
Vitraux du Choeur de la Cathédrale d'Evreux.
Evreux, 1893.

(Exeter Cathedral)
Some Account of the Cathedral Church of Exeter . . .
London, 1797.
Description of the East Window of the Cathedral Choir, Exeter.
Exeter, n.d. (c. 1830).

(On the re-leading and cleaning of two lights in the East window
by Frederick DRAKE.)
In Annual Report. Transactions of the Exeter Diocesan
Architectural Association, vol. 5, new series (1879), pp. 84-85.

The Great West Window of Exeter Cathedral.
Notes and Gleanings, vol. 1 (Dec. 15, 1888), p. 183.

Annual Report, Transactions of the Exeter Diocesan Architectural
and Archaeological Society, vol. 3, 3rd series (1921 ?).
(Refers to the possible return of some heraldic glass from a
London Museum to the Cathedral.)

Notes of the Month. Exeter Cathedral Bulletin (July, 1935).
(Replacing of fragments in the Chapel of St. Edmund, pp. 1, 2.)
(Appeal for donations for fixing, Ibid. (Aug., 1935), p. 1.)

Notes on the Great East Window.
18th Annual Report of the Friends of Exeter Cathedral, 1947 (1948),
p. 16.

(Exhibition of Stained Glass)
Ausstellung von Glasmalereien.
Keramische Rundschau, vol. 19 (1911), p. 374.

(Exhibition of Medieval and Renaissance Glass at Clayton and Bell's Premises)
Exhibition of Antique Stained Glass.
The Connoisseur, vol. 65 (Jan.-Apr., 1923), p. 109

(Exhibition at Pittsburgh)
Drawings of Stained Glass Windows Exhibited at Carnegie Galleries
(Pittsburgh).
National Glass Budget (Pittsburgh), (July 4, 1925).

(Exposition Internationale, Paris, 1937.)
Classe 40. Les Vitraux.
Paris, 1937.

(Exhibition of Gothic Art at Stein-bei-Krems.)
Austellung die Gotik in Niederoesterreich.
Krems-Stein, 1959.

Exposition Mille Ans d'Art du Vitrail.
Strasbourg, 1965.

Exhibitions of Stained Glass (at Loudwater: the Langton Gallery: and
St. Paul's.
J.M.G.P., vol. 15, no. 1 (1972-1973), p. 20.

EXTRACTS of papers read at meetings of the Society of Master Glass-Painters.

1. A Collection of Fifteenth Century Stained Glass /made by Sir
   Thomas Legge/ exhibited at a Meeting of the Society on March
   26, 1924.
   J.M.G.P., vol. 1, no. 2 (Apr., 1925), pp. 40-42.

2. Decay of Mediaeval Stained Glass. /Papers by MELLOR, E.,
   HEATON, N., TURNER, W.E.S./
   J.M.G.P., vol. 1, no. 2 (Apr., 1925), pp. 42-44.

3. Methods of Protecting and Preserving Stained Glass.
   J.M.G.P., vol. 1, no. 2 (Apr., 1925), pp. 44-47.

4. Stained Glass at the Victoria and Albert Museum.
   J.M.G.P., vol. 1, no. 2 (Apr., 1925), pp. 47-49.

5. The Fourteenth Century Glass at Tewkesbury and its Recent
   Repair.
   J.M.G.P., vol. 1, no. 2 (Apr., 1925), pp. 48-49.

(Eyck, Charles)
    A Visit to Charles Eyck Recalled.
    J.M.G.P., vol. 15, no. 2 (1973-1974), pp. 46-48.

(Eydon Church)
    Eydon Church, Northamptonshire. Glass.
    (Grant towards restoring the 1831 heraldic windows.)
    The Pilgrim Trust, 39th Annual Report (1969), pp. 16-17.

(Faculty for a window)

    Procedure for obtaining a Faculty for a Stained Glass Window.
    J.M.G.P., vol. 13, no. 3 (1962), p. 467.

FAHRNGRUBER, Johannes

    Unsere heimische Glasgemälde.
    Berichte für den Alterlichen Verein. Wein, no. 32 (1896), pp. 20-52.

FAIR, M.C.

    Calder Abbey.
    Transactions of the Cumberland and Westmorland Antiquarian and
    Archaeological Society, new series, vol. 53 (1954).
    (The Glass fragments, p. 94.)

(Fairford Church)

    History of Fairford Church.
    Fairford, 1835.

    The Glass in Fairford Church, Gloucestershire, by G.W.
    (A denunciation of the 'restoration' of the glass by Chance
    and Evans.)
    The Ecclesiologist, vol. 25 (1864), pp. 202-203.
    q.v. EVANS, Sebastian (1865).

    The Painted Glass in Fairford Church.
    (Condemns EVANS' 'restoration'.)
    The Ecclesiologist, vol. 27 (1866), pp. 175-176.

    Fairford Windows.
    The Ecclesiologist, vol. 29 (1868), pp. 363-371.

    The Painted Windows at Fairford. By H.N.H.
    (Letter to the Editor.)
    The Times, Aug. 17, 1868.

    (Contribution to the discussion. By F.S.A.)
    Notes and Queries, 4th series, vol. 2 (Aug. 29, 1868), p. 194.
    Ibid (Sept. 26, 1868), p. 307.

    Windows of Fairford Church.
    Church Builder,(Oct. 1868).
    Reprinted in Art Journal (1868), p. 221.

    Report of discussion at the meeting of the Royal Archaeological
    Institute, between
    RUSSELL, J.F. (q.v.)
    WALLER, J.G. (q.v.)
    HOLT, H.F. (q.v.)
    OLDFIELD, E.
    WESTMACOTT, R.
    BURY, T.
    The Archaeological Journal, vol. 26 (1869), pp. 91-92.

    (Miscellaneous notes.)
    Notes and Queries, 4th series, vol. 7 (Jan. 14, 1871), p. 47.

    (Review of the revived question of the authorship of the windows.)
    The Archaeological Journal, vol. 32 (1875), pp. 342-344.

    Restoration of the Fairford Windows. By Z.
    Notes and Queries, 5th series, vol. 5 (June 10, 1876), pp. 464-465.

    The West Window of Fairford Church.
    The Builder, no. 2 (1891), p. 226.

    (Grant towards replacing the windows.)
    The Pilgrim Trust, 15th Annual Report (1945), p. 7.

    (Replacing of windows.)
    News and Notes, J.M.G.P., vol. 10, no. 2 (1949), pp. 58-59.

FARCY, Louis De

    Monographie de la Cathédrale d'Angers.
    Vol. 1: Les Immeubles.
    Angers, 1910.

FARMER, Oscar G.

    Fairford Church and its Stained Glass Windows.
    Bath, 1933.
    (Many subsequent editions.)

(Farndon Church, Cheshire)

    (Notice of a seventeenth century window depicting Cheshire
    gentlemen, in armour, who attended Charles I at the siege of
    Chester, described in the Journal of the Society of Army
    Historical Research.)
    'Memorabilia', Notes and Queries, vol. 151 (Oct. 23, 1926), p. 290.

    (A seventeenth-century panel.)
    Archaeologia Cambrensis, vol. 90 (1935), p. 364-366.

FARR, D.L.A.

    (Evie Hone Memorial Exhibition.)
    Burlington Magazine, vol. 100 (Jan.-Dec., 1958), pp. 331-332.

FARRAR, F.W.

    Notes on the Painted Glass in Canterbury Cathedral,
    Aberdeen, 1897.

FAULKNER, C.

    A Fragment of Painted Glass from a Church (Adderbury) in
    Oxfordshire.
    (With a drawing by Charles WINSTON.)
    The Archaeological Journal, vol. 9 (1852), p. 119.

FAUSSET, Thomas Godfrey

    On a Fragment of Glass in Nettlestead Church.
    Archaeologia Cantiana, vol. 6 (1864-1865), pp. 129-134.
    (Embodies Charles WINSTON's findings on the window with a
    drawing by him.)

FAYOLLE, Marquis de

    La Tentation de Saint Antoine. Verre Peint en Grisaille par
    Nicholas le Pot.
    Caen, 1907.
    (Reprinted from Comptes Rendus du 67e Congrès Archéologique de
    France, Beauvais, 1905.)

(Fécamp Abbey)

    Fécamp Abbey Stained Glass. Restorer's Alleged Confession.
    The Times Nov. 27, Nov. 28, 1933.

    The Fécamp Abbey Glass Mystery: The Window; and the Woman
    Restorer.
    (Mll. Marguerite Huré confessed to having replaced four panels
    with copies. W.R. Hearst purchased the originals.)
    Illustrated London News (Dec. 16, 1933), p. 973.

    Reported Glass Fraud.
    Stained Glass, vol. 28 (Winter, 1933-1934), p. 211-214.

    Court Shows Mercy in French Art Theft.
    New York Evening Journal, Jan. 16, 1936.

FEENY, Patrick A.

    The Heraldic Glass in the Houses of Parliament. Its Early
    History and Recent Restoration.
    J.M.G.P., vol. 12, no. 2 (1957), pp. 142-147.

    Fire and Phoenix at John Hardman Studios.
    J.M.G.P., vol. 14, no. 5 (1970-1971), pp. 259-261.

FEILDEN, Bernard M.

    The Wonder of York Minster.

    York, n.d.

    (Glass, p. 41.)

    (The book deals with the recent- 1970s - restoration.)

FÉLIBIEN DES AVAUX, A.

    Des Principes de l'Architecture et des Arts Qui en Dependent.

    Paris, 1676.

    2nd ed., Paris, 1960.

FENN, E.A.H.

    The Story of English Windows.

    London, 1932.

FENWICK, R.

    Modern French Stained Glass.

    Art Journal (1885), pp. 20-23.

FERGUSON, R.S.

    The East Window, Carlisle Cathedral: Its Ancient Stained Glass.

    (See also LEES, Thomas.)

    Transactions of the Cumberland and Westmorland Antiquarian and

    Archaeological Society, vol. 2 (1876), pp. 296-312.

    Windermere (Bowness) Parish Church, and its Old Glass.

    Transactions of the Cumberland and Westmorland Antiquarian and

    Archaeological Society, vol. 4, 1878-1879 (1880), pp. 44-75.

FERGUSSON, Adam

    The Crumbling of Canterbury.

    Illustrated London News (Jan., 1975), pp. 31-37.

FFYTCHE, May

    The Old Stained Glass in Clavering Church.

    (Its breaking by a drunken half-wit and subsequent restoration.)

    The Essex Review, vol. 31, no. 121 (Jan., 1922), pp. 240-242.

FICKER, Johannes

    Reformatorenbilder. Glasgemälde in der Marktkirche zu Wiesbaden.

    Wiesbaden, 1912.

FIELD, F.J.

    Heraldry at Carlisle Cathedral.

    Transactions of the Cumberland and Westmorland Antiquarian and

    Archaeological Society, new series, vol. 34 (1934), pp. 22-29.

FIELD, Walter

    Stones of the Temple, or Lessons from the Fabric and Furniture

    of the Church.

    London, Oxford and Cambridge, 1871.

FIGEL, Albert

    Neue Glasgemälde.

    In Die Christliche Kunst (1924-1925), p. 29.

FILLON, A.

    Notice sur les Vitraux de Sainte-Radegonde. (Poitiers.)

    Memoires de la Société des Antiquaires de l'Ouest (1844), p. 483.

FINE ART SOCIETY OF LONDON

    Exhibition of Old Stained Glass, Thirteenth to Eighteenth Centuries:

    Descriptive Catalogue.

    London, 1912.

FINNY, W.E. St. Lawrence

    The May Games Window in the Town Hall, Kingston-upon-Thames.

    Journal of the British Archaeological Association, new series,

    vol. 32 (1926), pp. 265-270.

FIOT, Robert

    Jean Fouquet à Notre-Dame-la-Riche de Tours.

    Revue de l'Art, no. 10 (1970), pp. 31-46.

(Firing)

    An Experiment in Glass Firing by Radiation Heat.

    J.M.G.P., vol. 11, no. 4 (1955), pp. 233-234.

FISCHER, J.A.

    Kartons zu den Fenstern der Mariahilf-Kirche in der Au zu München,

    und zu den Glasgemälden des südlichen Seitenschiffes im Dome zu

    Köln.

    Munich, 1891.

FISCHER, J.L.

    Vierzig Jahre Glasmal-Kunst.

    Festschrift des Kgl. Bayer ischen Hofglasmalerei F.X. Zettler.

    Munich, 1910.

    Die ältesten Glasmalereien in Augsburg.

    Zeitschrift für alte und Neue Glasmalerei (1912), p. 1.

    Die Glasmalerei auf der Bayrischen Gewerbeschau.

    Ibid, pp. 63, 77.

    Spätgotische Glasfenster in Langenlois, Niederösterreich.

    Ibid., p. 83.

    Schwäbische Glasmalerei.

    Ibid., p. 85.

    Zur Kenntnis des Schweizer Kunstlebens und der Glasmalereien im

    besondern.

    Ibid., p. 99.

    Die Glasgemälde des Georg Hebensreit in der Michaelshofkirche zu

    München.

    Ibid., p. 107.

    Zur Schwäbisch Tirolischen Glasmalerei in der ersten Hälfte des

    16 Jahrhunderts.

    Ibid., p. 108.

    Wo und Wie Lässt Sich immodernen Privathause Farbiger

    Fensterschmuck Anbringen.

    Ibid., p. 111.

    Die Glasgemälde der St. Paulskirche zu Brandenburg.

    Ibid., p. 119.

    Zwei Glasgemälde in der Viktorskirche zu Xanten, vom Meister

    Jakob von Köln, um 1350.

    Ibid., p. 131.

    Stilharmonie.

    Ibid., p. 134.

    Romanische Formen in der modernen Glasmalerei.

    Ibid.,(1913), p. 5.

    Das Portrait in Glasmalerei und Mosaik.

    Ibid., p. 13

    Moderne Schweizer Glasmaler. Ernst Rinderspacher aus Basel.

    Ibid., p. 18.

FISCHER, J.L. (Contd.)

Glasgemälde und Mosaikschmuck in den Neubauten der Münchener
Universität.
Ibid., p. 25.

Die Entwicklung der Kunstverglasung.
Ibid., pp. 37, 50.

Drei Süddeutsche Glasgemälde aus der Mitte des 15 Jahrhunderts.
Ibid., p. 49.

Das Syndicat der Kunstglasereien und Glasmalerei-eine Zukunftsfrage.
Ibid., p. 52.

Antikes in der Glasmalerei.
Ibid., p. 61.

Königsdarstellungen auf romanischen und frühgotischen Glasgemälden.
Ibid., p. 73.

Glasmalerei und Keramik auf der Internationalen Baufachausstellung
zu Leipzig.
Ibid., pp. 75, 89, 113, 130.

Die Krakauer Kunstanstalt für Glasmalerei-und-Mosaik-ausführungen
G.S. von Zelenski.
Ibid., p. 105.

Zwei Glasgemälde der Schaffhausener Glasmalerfamilie Grimm.
Ibid., p. 121.

Der Neue Stil.
Ibid., p. 125.

Das 'Süssliche' in der Glasmalerei.
Ibid., p. 133.

Die Zeichnung des Kopfes in der Glasmalerei.
Ibid., (1914), pp. 1, 32.

Alte Glasgemälde auf der Marienburg.
Ibid., p. 14.

Die Bedeutung des Schwartzlots in der Glasmalerei als Kontur und
Ueberzug.
Ibid., p. 35.

Das Architektorische Problem in der Glasmalerei.
Ibid., pp. 48, 61, 100, 130, 143.

Zu den Beziehungen des Hans Baldungs Grien zu der Glasmalerei.
Ibid., p. 65.

Die Münchener Glasmalerei der spätgotischen Periode.
Ibid., pp. 87-91.

Altungarische Glasmalereien.
Ibid., p. 115.

Handbuch der Glasmalerei.
Leipzig, 1914.
(2nd ed., 1937).

Krieg. Kriegerische Darstellungslust alter Glasmaler.
Zeitschrift für Alte und Neue Glasmalerei, (1915), p. 1.

Einige unveröffentliche Rheinische Glasgemälde.
Ibid., p. 31.

Wo stand die französische Glasmalerei Beim Ausbruch des Krieges?
Ibid., p. 35.

Am Vorabend neuer künstlerischer Impulse.
Ibid., p. 53.

Wettbewerb zur Erlangung von Entwürfen für Glasmalerei-künstlerisches
Ergebnis.
Ibid., p. 66.

FISCHER, J.L. (Contd.)

William Pütz. Eine Betrachtung zu seinem 60 Oeburtstag.
Diamant, 57th year, no. 24, (Aug. 21, 1935).

Die Tausendjährige Glasmalerei.
Diamant, 59th year, no. 20 (July 11, 1937)
            no. 23 (Aug. 11, 1937).

FISH, Margaret

The Art and Craft of Stained Glass.
Wisconsin Architect (Nov., 1966).

FISHER, Alfred

Observations on Some Recent French Work.
J.M.G.P., vol. 13, no. 3 (1962), pp. 509-513.

Report on Stained Glass to the Federation of British Craft Societies.
J.M.G.P., vol. 14, no. 5 (1970-1971), pp. 243-246.

An Artist's Look at CVMA.
J.M.G.P., vol. 15, no. 1 (1972-1973), pp. 34-40.

FITCHFIELD, P.H.

History of Stained Glass.
Christian Art, vol. 3 (Apr., 1908), pp. 3-22.

FIXOT, M., and PELLETIER, J.-P.

Fouille de Sauvetage au Prieuré de Ganagobie (Alpes de Haute-
Provence).
Archéologie Médiévale, vol. 6 (1976), pp. 287-327.

(Flashed Blue Glass)

(Editorial reply to a query about the date of the introduction of
the technique.)
J.M.G.P., vol. 2, no. 1 (1927), p. 56.

(Flashed Glass)

Revival of Ancient Art of Flashed Glass Reported.
National Glass Budget (Aug. 29, 1964).

(Flemish Glass in England)

Flemish Stained Glass Windows Brought to England.
Notes and Queries, 3rd series, vol. 6 (1864-1865), pp. 472, 541.
            vol. 7, pp. 165, 291.

(Flemish Window of 1780)

For Sale.
News and Notes, J.M.G.P., vol. 14, no. 2 (1965), p. 101.

FLETCHER, J.M.S.

The Stained Glass in Salisbury Cathedral.
The Wiltshire Archaeological And Natural History Magazine, no. 153,
(Dec., 1930), pp. 235-253.

FLETCHER, Rory

An Exhibition of French Painted Glass in London, about A.D. 1802.
Notes and Queries, 13th series, vol. 146 (Apr. 5, 1924), pp. 243-244.

FLETCHER, W.G.D.

The Stained Glass Formerly in Battlefield Church.
Transactions of the Shropshire Archaeological and Natural History
Society, 3rd series, vol. 3 (1903), 'Miscellanea', pp. xix-xxi.

FLEURY, G.

La Cathédrale du Mans.
Paris, n.d.

FLICK, Miriam
    Review of Catalogue of Stained and Painted Glass in Pennsylvania
    Museum. Pennsylvania, 1925.
    Art Bulletin, vol. 10, no. 2 (Dec., 1927), p. 209.

(Florence, Modern Stained Glass Artists)
    Art in Continental States. Florence.
    Art Journal (1870), p. 318.

FLORIVAL, A. De, and MIDOUX, E.
    Les Vitraux de la Cathédrale de Laon. (4 parts.)
    Paris, 1882-1891.

(Foreign Glass Purchased at 97, Pall Mall)
    (The Seven Herckenrode windows purchased. Also foreign glass for
    York, Ely, Tottenham, Stoke Newington, Strelley, Rickmansworth,
    Blithfield, Cholmondeley Castle, Tixhall Chapel and others.)
    The Gentleman's Magazine, vol. 77, part 1 (1807), p. 408.

FORMIGÉ, J.
    L'emploi du verre pour former les baies chez les Romains.
    Bulletin de la Société des Antiquaires de France (1934), pp. 82-84.

FORSETH, Einar.
    Autobiography.
    J.M.G.P., vol. 11, no. 1 (1952), pp. 40-43.

FORSTER, Benjamin
    Some Account of the Church and Windows of St. Neot's in Cornwall.
    London, 1786.

(Forsyth, J. Dudley)
    Obituary.
    J.M.G.P., vol. 2, no. 1 (1927), p. 51.

FOUÉRE-MACÉ, Abbé
    Les Vitraux de l'Eglise Abbatiale de Lehon.
    Rennes, 1897.

FOULKES, Peter
    Musarum Anglicanarum Analecta.
    Oxford, 1699.
    (Latin verses on the East Window, Christ Church. II, 180.)

FOURÈS, E.
    Un Peintre Verrier. Verrière Destinée à la Chapelle du Palais
    de Monaco.
    L'Artiste (Aug., 1882).

FOURNÉE, Jean
    Essai d'Exégèse d'une Oeuvre d'Art: Le Jugement Dernier d'Apres
    le Vitrail de la Cathédrale de Coutances.
    Paris, 1964.
    Reviewed by SALET, Francis, Bulletin Monumental, vol. 124 (1966),
    pp. 453-455.

FOURREY, Renée
    Les Verrières Historiées de la Cathédrale d'Auxerre.
    Bulletin de la Société des Sciences Historiques et Naturelles de
    l'Yonne, vol. 83 (1929), pp. 5-101.

FOWLER, C.H.
    Notes on the Stained Glass of Durham Cathedral.
    Archaeologia Aeliana, new series, vol. 7 (1876), pp. 137-141.

FOWLER, James
    On the Painted Glass at Thornhill.
    Yorkshire Archaeological Journal, vol. 1 (1870), pp. 69-78, 107-109.

    On the Painted Glass at Methley.
    Yorkshire Archaeological Journal, vol. 1 (1870), pp. 214-220,
                                    vol. 2 (1873), pp. 226-245.

    On Representations of the Virgin with Two Children.
    The Sacristy, vol. 1 (1871), p. 27.

    On a Painted Window at Brighouse.
    Ibid., vol. 2 (1872), p. 150.

    On a Window representing the Life and Miracles of St. William of
    York, at the North End of the Eastern Transept, York Minster.
    Yorkshire Archaeological and Topographical Journal, vol. 3, for
    1873-1874 (1875), pp. 198-348.

    On Mediaeval Representations of the Months and Seasons. Windows
    in the Churches of St. Mary, Shrewsbury, and All Saints, Dewsbury.
    Also Glass from the Mayor's Parlour at Leicester.
    Archaeologia, vol. 44 (1873), pp. 137-224.

    An Account of the Representation of the Moon in One Window of
    Herringfleet Church.
    Proceedings of the Society of Antiquaries, 2nd series, no. 6
    (Dec. 16, 1875), p. 459.

    The Great East Window, Selby Abbey.
    Yorkshire Archaeological and Topographical Journal, vol. 5 for
    1877-1878 (1879), pp. 331-349.

FOWLER, James
    On the Process of Decay in Glass and, Incidentally, on the
    Composition and Texture of Glass at Different Periods, and the
    History of its Manufacture.
    Archaeologia, vol. 46 (1880), pp. 65-162.

    Old Stained Glass: Case for Opinions.
    (Request for opinions on the best means of describing disordered
    story windows.)
    Notes and Queries, 5th series, vol. 3 (Jan. 30, 1875), p. 100.

FOWLER, J.T.
    On the St. Cuthbert Window in York Minster.
    Yorkshire Archaeological and Topographical Journal, vol. 4 for
    1875-1876 (1877), pp. 249-376.

    Notes on Some Painted Glass in the Priory Church, Great Malvern.
    Reports and Papers of the Associated Architectural Societies,
    vol. 17 (1883-1884), pp. 115-120.

    On the St. Cuthbert Window in York Minster. (Additional notes.)
    Yorkshire Archaeological and Topographical Journal, vol.11 (1891),
    486-501.

    A Note on a Seventeenth Century Figure in Painted Glass in Stoke
    Poges Church, Bucks.
    Proceedings of the Society of Antiquaries, 2nd series, vol. 19
    (1903), pp. 185-188.

    The Correspondence of William Fowler. (ed.)
    Privately printed (50 copies), 1907.

    Stained Glass.
    In A Dictionary of the English Church, ed. ORCHARD, S.L., and
    CROSSE, Gordon, London, 1912; p. 239.

    On Painted Glass at St. Anthony's Chapel, Cartmel Fell.
    Transactions of the Cumberland and Westmorland Antiquarian and
    Archaeological Society, new series, vol. 12 (1912), pp. 297-311.

FOWLER, J.T. (Contd)

Three Panels of Thirteenth Century Stained Glass from Lanchester
Church. Durham.
Proceedings of the Society of Antiquaries, 2nd series, vol. 27
(1915), pp. 205-

Last Fifteen Days of the World in Mediaeval Art and Literature.
Yorkshire Archaeological Journal, vol. 23 (1915), pp. 313-337.

FOWLER, Joseph
Obituary of William Fowler.
Wesleyan Methodist Magazine (Apr., 1834).

Appendix to H.W. BALL's 'Notes on William Fowler and His Work'.
North Lincolnshire Monthly Illustrated Journal (June, 1869).

FOWLER, William
Mosaic Pavements, and Paintings in Stained Glass.
1804. Appendix, 1809. Second Appendix, 1824.

(Fowler, William)
A Note on William Fowler of Winterton and his Work.
Barton-on-Humber, 1888.

FOX, Cyril
The Design by Miss D. Marion Grant for the East Window of the
Lady Chapel.
22nd Annual Report of the Friends of Exeter Cathedral (1952),
pp. 13-16.

FOX, G.J.B.
A Note on the Glass in the East Window, St. Margaret's Church,
Westminster.
(A useful assembly of authorities.)
Transactions of the St. Paul's Ecclesiological Society, vol. 10
(1931), pp. xxv-xxviii.

FOXLEY-NORRIS, W.
Decoration and Enrichment in Cathedrals.
York Minster Historical Tracts.
London, 1927.

(Foxley-Norris, William)
Obituary.
J.M.G.P., vol. 7, no. 2 (Apr., 1938), pp. 105-106.

FOY, Daniel
Vitraux Découverts dans les Fouilles Médiévales du Sud-Est de la
France.
Annales du VIIe Congrès de l'Association Internationale pour
l'Histoire du Verre. Leipzig, Aug., 1977 (1978).

Lampes de Verre et Vitraux de Ganagobie.
Archéologie Médiévale, vol. 7 (1977).

Les Verres Trouvés dans les Fouilles Archéologiques en France
Méridionale.
Les Dossiers de l'Archéologie, no. 26 (Jan.-Feb., 1978), pp. 115-122.

(Fragments)
Fragments for the Antiquary.
(Remains of a Mediaeval Window.)
Report of the Marlborough College Natural History Society (1932).

(Fragments)
'Scrap' Windows.
(A correspondence in Notes and Queries giving examples of
windows composed of fragments.)
TEKTON, vol. 181 (Aug. 30, 1941), p. 121.
HORNE, E. (q.v.) (Sept. 30, 1941), p. 164.
D.P.Q. (St. Hilda's, Whitby), (Sept. 27, 1941), p. 180.
BROCKWELL, M.W. (q.v.), (Wragby Church, Yorks), (Nov. 8, 1941),
p. 262.
BROCKWELL, M.W. (q.v.), (Rivenhall, Essex), (Dec. 6, 1941), p. 320.
MORRIS, J.E. (Winchester Cathedral), (Dec. 27, 1941), pp. 361-362.

(Frampton, Edward)
Obituary.
J.M.G.P., vol. 3, no. 1 (Apr., 1929), p. 45.

(France: Modern Stained Glass)
(A short listing.)
News and Notes, J.M.G.P., vol. 13, no. 1 (1960), pp. 306-307.

FRANCEN, V.L., and HEINE, R.F.
Fluoro-Chemical Glass Treatments.
Glass Industry, vol. 46 (1965), pp. 594-597, 628-629.

FRANCHET, Louis
Les Émaux et les Couleurs Céramiques du Moyen-Age et de la
Renaissance.
Revue Scientifique, (Jan., 1908).

L'Emaillage et la Peinture sur Verre. Les Différents Moyens.
Revue Scientifique (June, 1908).

FRANCIS, Robert
Visit to a Stained Glass Studio.
Worship and Arts (Apr.-May, 1962).

FRANCOTTE, Gustave
Les Vitraux.
Conférences de la Société d'Art et d'Histoire du Diocèse de Liége,
(1888), pp. 95-119.

FRANK, Sepp
Glasgemälde.
In Die Christliche Kunst, Munich (1924-1925), p. 22.

FRANK, W.G.
Ervin Bossanyi and his Glass.
Johnson Matthey Bulletin, London (Nov.-Dec., 1968), pp. 3-6.

FRANKL, Paul

    Beiträge zur Geschichte der süddeutschen Glasmalerei im 15.
Jahrhundert.
Strasbourg, 1911.

    Die Glasmalerei des 15. Jahrhunderts in Bayern und Schwaben.
Strasbourg, 1912.

    Der Ulmer Glasmaler Hans Wild.
Jahrbücher der Preussischen Kunstsammlungen, vol. 33, Berlin,
1912, p. 31.

    Deutsche Glasmalerei. Der Meister des Speculumfensters von 1480
in der Münchener Frauenkirche.
Berlin, 1932.

    Peter Hemmel, Glasmaler von Andlau.
Berlin, 1956.
Reviewed by LAFOND, Jean, in The Archaeological Journal, vol. 114
(for 1957), pp. 201-203.
Reviewed by GRODECKI, Louis, in Bulletin Monumental, no. 115 (1957),
pp. 74-76.
Reviewed by HAYWARD, Jane, in Art Bulletin, vol. 40 (March, 1958),
pp. 75-78.

    Der Glasmaler Theobald von Lixheim.
Zeitschrift für Kunstwissenschaft, vol. 2, Berlin (1957), pp. 55-90.

    Unnoticed Fragments of Old Stained Glass in Notre-Dame de Paris.
Art Bulletin, vol. 39 (Dec., 1957), pp. 299-300.

    Die Glasmalereien der Wilhelmkirche in Strassburg.
Rekonstruktionen, Datierungen, Attributionen.
Studien zur Deutsche Kunstgeschichte, no. 320, Baden-Baden/
Strasbourg, 1960.

    The Chronology of the Stained Glass in Chartres Cathedral.
Art Bulletin, vol. 45 (Dec., 1963), pp. 301-322.
Reviewed by GRODECKI, Louis, Bulletin Monumental, vol. 122 (1964),
pp. 99-103.

FRANKS, Augustus Wollaston

    Ornamental Glazing Quarries, Collected and Arranged from Ancient
Examples.
Cambridge, 1849.

FREEMAN, A.C.

    Making Leaded Lights.
Illustrated Carpenter and Builder, vol. 106, no. 2745 (March 28,
1930).

FREEMAN, E. Vere

    Littleham Church.
Transactions of the Exeter Diocesan Architectural Association,
vol. 5, new series (1879).
(Stained glass, pp. 93-94.)

(Frei, Emil, Senior)

    Obituary.
Stained Glass, vol. 37, no. 4 (Winter, 1942), p. 136.

(Frei, Emil)

    The Future of Stained Glass. The Workshop and Designs of Emil
Frei. Inc.
Architectural Record (June, 1948).

FREI, Emil Jnr.

    New Methods in Light Control.
Stained Glass, vol. 50, no. 1 (Spring, 1955), pp. 10-11.

    Developments in Stained Glass.
Stained Glass, vol. 52, no. 4 (Winter, 1957-1958), pp. 153-155.

FREI, Emil, Jnr. (Contd.)

    The Modern Stained Glass Artist
Stained Glass, vol. 60, no. 4 (Winter, 1965-1966), pp. 7-11.

(Frei, Emil, Jnr.)

    Obituaries.
(By various hands.)
Stained Glass, vol. 62, no. 1 (Spring, 1967), pp. 20-23.

FREI, Robert

    With BRIDGES, Stephen, SKINNER, Orin E., and others.
What Makes for Good Stained Glass Design? (A Symposium.)
Stained Glass, vol. 55, no. 4 (Winter, 1960-1961), pp. 16-27.

    Part II, Ibid, vol. 56, no. 1 (Spring, 1961), pp. 38-47.

    With RAMBUSCH, Robert, and ELSKUS, Albinus.
Contemporary Stained Glass.
Stained Glass, vol. 60, no. 1 (Spring, 1965), pp. 13-23.

FRENCH, Jennie

    Glass-Works, the Copper Foil Technique of Stained Glass.
Cincinnatti, 1975.
Reviewed by WEIS, Helen, Stained Glass, vol. 70, no. 1 (Spring, 1975),
p. 36.

FRENCH, T.W.

    Observations on Some Medieval Glass in York Minster.
Antiquaries Journal, vol. 51 (1971), pp. 86-93.

    The West Windows of York Minster.
The Yorkshire Archaeological Journal, vol. 47 (1975), pp. 81-85.

FRENZEL, Gottfried

    (Conservation and restoration of grisaille.)
Zeitschrift für Kunstgeschichte (1960), pp. 1-18.

    Entwurf und Ausführung in der Nürnberger Glasmalerei der Dürerzeit.
Zeitschrift für Kunstwissenschaft , Berlin (1961), pp. 31-59.

    With FRODL-KRAFT, Eva.
(A Paper on conservation difficulties read at CVMA meeting, Erfurt,
1962.)
Osterreichische Zeitschrift für Kunst und Denkmalpflege, vol. 17
(1963), pp. 93-114.

    St. Lorenz-Nürnberg.
Augsberg, 1967.

    Glasgemalderestaurierung.
Die Instandsetzung des Kaiser-Fensters und des Rieter-Fensters aus
der St. Lorenzkirche zu Nürnberg.
Verein zur Wiederherstellung der St. Lorenzkirche in Nürnberg, no.
9 (1968), pp. 3-16.
(Decay of the windows.)

    Die Instandstezung des Kaiser-Fensters und des Rieter Fensters
aus der St. Lorenz Kirche zu Nürnberg.
Mitteilungsblatt Neue Folge, no. 9 (July, 1968).

    Problèmes de la Technique et de la Restauration.
(A summary of a discussion between FRODL-KRAFT, Eva, TARALON, Jean,
FRENZEL, Gottfried, KING, Dennis.)
Bulletin du Comité International d'Histoire de l'Art (Jan.-June,
1969), p. 8.

    Die Instandsetzung des Kaiserfensters und des Rieterfensters aus der
St. Lorenzkirche zu Nürnberg.
Osterreichische Zeitschrift für Kunst und Denkmalpflege, vol. 23
(1969), pp. 75-85.

FRENZEL, Gottfried (Contd.)

Bericht über die Erstellung einer Glasmalerei - Schadensatlas
für die Bundesrepublik Deutschland.
In Akten des 10. Internationalen Colloquiums des CVMA, Stuttgart,
1977, p. 51.

Umweltgefahren bedrohen mittelalterliche Glasmalerei.
Kirche und Kunst, vol. 49 (Dec., 1971), pp. 58-60.

La Conservation des Vitraux Anciens. 1. Les Causes de
Degradation - développement et importance.
Glas-Email-Keramo-Technik, vol. 22 (1971), pp. 168-171.

Die letzen Zeugnisse mittelalterlicher Glasmalerei im Untergang.
Glasforum, no. 6 (1971).

FRENZEL, Urzula
'Venedisch Schewen.'
In 7ᵉ Colloque du Corpus Vitrearum Medii Aevi, Florence ?, 1970,
pp. 27-28.

FREUND, Miriam K.
Jewels for a Crown: The Story of the Chagall Windows.
New York, 1963.

FRIEDLANDER, Max
Werk über die Renaissance-Ausstellung.
Berlin, 1898.

Ueber Antwerpener Glasmalerei in der ersten Hälfte des 16.
Jahrhunderts.
Amtliche Berichte aus den Königlichen Kunstsammlungen, part 39,
no. 4 (Jan., 1918), pp. 75-80.

FRIEDLEY, D.
A Renaissance Window of 1531.
Owned by F.T. Ryan.
Art America, vol. 1 (Apr., 1913), pp. 136-140.

FRIESENEGGER, J.
Führer durch den Dom in Augsburg.
Augsburg, 1930.

FRODL, Walter
Glasmalerei in Kärnten, 1150-1500.
Vienna, 1950.

FRODL-KRAFT, Eva
Die Glasgemälde des Hauptchors.
(In St. Stephen's Cathedral, Vienna.)
Osterreichische Zeitschrift für Kunst und Denkmalpflege, parts
1 and 2 (1952), pp. 10-20.

Architektur im Abbild, ihre Spiegelung in der Glasmalerei.
Wiener Jahrbuch für Kunstgeschichte, vol. 17 (1956), pp. 7-13.

Ein Glasgemäldezyklus um 1300.
Alte und Moderne Kunst, no. 6 (1959).

Le Vitrail Médiéval, Technique et Esthétique.
Cahiers de Civilisation Médiévale, no. 10 (1962).

Die mittelalterlichen Glasgemälde in Wien.
(CVMA, Austria, I.), Vienna, 1962.
Reviewed by GRODECKI, Louis, Bulletin Monumental, vol. 121 (1963),
pp. 214-215.

FRODL-KRAFT, Eva (Contd.)

Die Vierte Tagung des Corpus Vitrearum Medii Aevi, 1962, in
Erfurt.
Oesterreichische Zeitschrift für Kunst und Denkmalpflege (1963),
pp. 38-42.

With FRENZEL, Gottfried.
Referate . . . auf der Tagung Corpus Vitrearum Medii Aevi, 1962.
Oesterreichische Zeitschrift für Kunst und Denkmalpflege, vol.
17 (1963), pp. 93-114.

Gotische Glasmalerei aus dom Kreuzgang in Klosterneuburg. (Katalog.)
Klosterneuburg, 1963.

With FRODL, M.W.
Das Problem der Schwarzlotsicherung an mittelalterlichen
Glasgemälden.
Vienna, 1963.

Das 'Flechtwerk' der Frühen Zisterzienserfenster.
Wiener Jahrbuch für Kunstgeschichte (1965), pp. 7-20.

Monumenta Deperdita. Die Geschichte eines Glasgemälde Verkaufs.
Oesterreichische Zeitschrift für Kunst und Denkmalpflege (1965),
pp. 186-190.

Restaurierung und Erforschung, I. Die Süd-rose von Maria
Strassengel.
Oesterreichische Zeitschrift für Kunst und Denkmalpflege, vol. 21
(1967), pp. 192-197.
II. Heiligenkreuz, Chorfenster der Stiftskirche.
Ibid., pp. 197-200.

Problèmes de la Technique et de la Restauration.
(A summary of a discussion between FRODL-KRAFT, Eva, TARALON, Jean,
FRENZEL, Gottfried, KING, Dennis.)
Bulletin du Comité International d'Histoire de l'Art (Jan-June, 1969),
p. 8.

Die Prophetenscheiben von Lorch.
Oesterreichische Zeitschrift für Kunst und Denkmalpflege, vol. 23
(1969), pp. 68-74.

(Report on the 6th Colloquium of the CVMA, at Ulm, Oct., 1968.)
Osterreichische Zeitschrift für Kunst und Denkmalpflege, vol. 23
(1969), pp. 86-89.

Konservierungsprobleme mittelalterlicher Glasmalereien.
Annales du 5ᵉ Congrès du Verre, Prague (July 6-11, 1970), pp.
357-370.

Die Glasmalerei. Entwicklung, Technik, Eigenart.
Vienna, 1970.
Reviewed by GRODECKI, Louis, Revue de l'Art, no. 10 (1970), p. 98.

Zur Restaurierung und Sicherung. Die Bildfenster der
Wasserkirche in Leoben.
Osterreichische Zeitschrift für Kunst und Denkmalpflege, vol. 25
(1971), pp. 70-73.

Untersuchungen und praktische Erfahrungen in der Konservierung
mittelalterlicher Glasgemälde, 1963-1972.
In 8ᵉ Colloque du Corpus Vitrearum Medii Aevi, Paris ? (1972),
p. 52.

Untersuchungen und praktische Erfahrungen in der Konservierung
mittelalterlicher Glasgemälde, 1963-1972.
Osterreichische Zeitschrift für Kunst und Denkmalpflege, vol. 27
(1973), pp. 55-65.

Mittelalterliche Glasmalerei, Erforschung-Restaurierung.
Das 9 Colloquium des Corpus Vitrearum, Paris (Sept., 1975),
Osterreichiche Zeitschrift für Kunst und Denkmalpflege, vol. 29,
parts 3, 4 (1975), pp. 154-158.

FRODL-KRAFT, Eva (Contd.)

Einige Bemerkungen zu Wissenschaft und Handwerkin der
GlasgemÄlde Restaurierung.
Verres et Réfractaires, numéro special (1976).

Zum Werden der 'gotischen' Farbsprache in der Glasmalerei.
In Akten des 10. Internationalen Colloquiums des CVMA.
Stuttgart, 1977, pp. 32-34.

FROIDEVAUX, Yves-Marie

Le Vitrail dans l'Architecture Médiévale.
Les Monuments Historiques de la France, no. 1 (1977), pp. 31-36.

FROMBERG, Emmanuel Otto

Handbuch der Glasmalerei, oder grundliche Anleitung, die
Glaspigmente und Flussmittel darzustellen.
Quendlinburg, 1844.
Translated by CLARKE, H.J., An Introductory Essay on the Art of
Painting on Glass, London, 1845 (Several subsequent editions).

FROST, W.A.

St. George's Chapel, Windsor, East Window.
(Fate of the window by West and Jervais.)
Notes and Queries, 11th series, vol. 10 (Sept. 26, 1914), p. 256.
See also PAGE, J.T.
         PIERPOINT, R.

FRUEH, Erne R., and Florence

Munich Studio Windows at Chicago's Ss. Cyril and Methodius Church.
Stained Glass, vol. 74, no. 2 (Summer, 1979), pp. 109-113.

FRY, Sir Frederick Morris

The Windows of Merchant Taylor's Hall.
(With LLOYD THOMAS, Walter.)
Privately printed, 1934.

FRYER, Alfred C.

Theophilus the Penitent as Represented in Art.
Archaeological Journal, vol. 92, part 2 (for 1935), pp. 327-332.

FULFORD, Francis

Ancient Heraldic Glass in Slapton Church.
Devon and Cornwall Notes and Queries, vol. 6 (1911), p. 215.

Ancient Heraldic Glass in Slapton Church.
Devon and Cornwall Notes and Queries, vol. 7 (1913), p. 46.

FULFORD, J.L.

A Few Remarks on Some Stained Glass in Exeter Cathedral.
Transactions of the Exeter Diocesan Architectural Society, vol. 2
(1847), pp. 133-138.
Reviewed in The Gentleman's Magazine, vol. 28, new series, part 2
(1847), p. 611.

FUMI, L.

Il Duomo di Orvieto.
Rome, 1891.

(Furnace for firing)

Aeusserst beachtenswerte Konstruktion für einen Gasmuffelofen für
einzubrennende Glasmalereien.
Diamant, vol. 39 (1917), p. 339.

FYOT, E.

Les Verrieres et les Verriers d'Autrefois a Dijon.
Bulletin Archeologique, 1930-1931 (1934), pp. 101-102, 571-585.

GAGNIERE, S.; GRANIER, S.
    La Salle de Théologie et les Fouilles de 1967.
    Mémoires de l'Académie de Vaucluse, 2 (1968), pp. 57-65.

    La Salle de Théologie et les Fouilles de 1967, Contribution
    a l'Etude du Palais des Papes.
    Avignon, 1969.

GAHLEN, Clemens
    Goethe und die Glasmalerei.
    Diamant, vol. 50, no. 31 (Nov. 1, 1928), pp. 646-648.

    Glasmalerei und moderne Architektur.
    Diamant, vol. 51, no. 32 (Nov. 11, 1929), pp. 624, 666.

    Die Glasmalerei in der Gegenwart. Von Kunsthistoriker Clemens
    Gahlen.
    Diamant, vol. 51, no. 4, (Feb. 1, 1929), p. 65.

    Die Anfänge der Glasmalerei.
    Diamant, vol. 51 (1929), pp. 688-
             vol. 52 (1930), pp. 8-

    Die Fibel der Glasmalerei.
    Diamant, 52nd year, no. 15 (May 21, 1930).

    Neue Glasmalkunst.
    Leipzig, 1930.

    Glasgemälde in Auxerre.
    Diamant, 53rd year, no. 31 (Nov. 1, 1931).

    Alte Glasmalereien in Goslar.
    Diamant, 56th year, no. 25 (Sept. 1, 1934).

    Zu den Fenster in der Marienburg in Westpreussen.
    Diamant, 57th year (Sept. 21, 1935).

    Vom Ethos in der Glasmalerei.
    Diamant, 58th year, no. 1 (Jan. 1, 1936).

    Neue Möglichkeiten für die Glasmalerei.
    Diamant (Apr. 21, 1936).

GAIGNIÈRES, F.R. de
    Les Dessins d'Architecture de Roger de Gaignières.
    Paris, 1914.
    (Vol. 2, Vitraux.)

GAILHABAUD, Jules
    L'Architecture de Vau XVII Siècle, et les Arts qui en Dépendent;
    la Sculpture, la Peinture, la Peinture sur Verre, etc.
    4 vols., Paris, 1858.

GAILLARD, J.
    Recherches Historiques sur la Chapelle du Saint-Sang.
    Bruges, 1846.

GALABERT
    L'Eglise et les Vitraux de Caylus.
    Montauban, 1881.

GALLINER, Arthur
    Glasgemälde des Mittelalters aus Wimpfen.
    Freiburg, 1932.

GAMLEN, St. J.O.
    Stained Glass from Notley Abbey.
    Oxoniensia, vol. 8-9 (1943-1944), pp. 112-136.

GAMLEN, St. John O. (Contd.)
    Some Local Medieval Window Glass Affinities.
    J.M.G.P., vol. 15, no. 3 (1974-1975), pp. 8-16.

GANAY, M.C. de
    Blessed James of Ulm, Patron of Stained Glass Workers.
    (Translated by PEASE, Murray, from Comment Représenter les Saints
    Dominicains, Autun, 1926).
    Stained Glass, vol. 27, no. 6 (June, 1932), p. 171.

GANDERTON, E.W.
    With LAFOND, Jean.
    Ludlow Stained and Painted Glass.
    Ludlow, 1961.

    Stained Glass as a Hobby.
    J.M.G.P., vol. 14, no. 1 (1964), pp. 68-70.

(Ganderton, E.W.)
    Obituary.
    J.M.G.P., vol. 14, no. 1 (1964), pp. 24-25.

GANTNER, J.
    Kunstgeschichte der Schweiz. Vol. 2, Die gotische Kunst.
    Frauenfeld, 1947.

GANZ, Paul
    Historisches Museum, Basel. Katalog No. 3. Glasgemälde.
    Basel, 1901.

    Die Entwicklung der Basler Malerei im XVI Jahrhundert.
    Basler Jahrbuch (1904), pp. 260-

    Ueber die schweizerische Glasmalerei und ihre Bedeutung für die
    Kunstgeschichte.
    Offentliche Kunst Sammlung in Basel LVIII.
    Basler Jahrbuch (1906), pp. 17-28.

    L'Oeuvre d'un Amateur d'Art. La Collection de M.F. Engel-Gros.
    2 vols., Paris, 1925.

GANZ, Paul Leonhard

    Die Basler Glasmaler der Spätrenaissance und der Barockzeit.
    Basle and Stuttgart, 1966.
    Reviewed by HAYWARD, J.F., Burlington Magazine, vol. 111 (May, 1969),
    pp. 309-310.

GARBER, Josef
    Das gotische Glasfenster in Weitau bei St. Johann in Tirol.
    Museum Ferdinandeum (Innsbruck) Veröffentlichungen, vol. 8, no. 47
    (1928).

GARDNER, Elaine C.
    Music Iconography in Stained Glass.
    Stained Glass, vol. 69, no. 4 (Winter, 1975), pp. 87-92.

GARNER, W.P.
    St. Mary's Parish Church, Willesborough.
    (2nd revised edition) Ashford, 1971.
    (Glass, pp. 4-5, very slight.)

GARROD, H.W.
    Ancient Painted Glass in Merton College, Oxford.
    Oxford, 1931.

(Gascoyne, Alexander)
    Obituary.
    J.M.G.P., vol. 2, no. 3 (Apr., 1928), p. 163.

GATES, Milo Hudson
    The Great Rose Window.
    (At St. John the Divine, New York.)
    Stained Glass, vol. 28, no. 1 (Spring, 1933), pp. 23-26.

GATOUILLAT, Françoise
    A Saint-Sulpice de Favières; des Vitraux Témoins de l'Art Parisien
    au Temps de Saint Louis.
    Les Dossiers de l'Archéologie, no. 26 (Jan.-Feb., 1978), pp. 51-62.

GAUDIN, Félix
    Les Vitraux des Ordres du Grand Seminaire de Besançon.
    (2 parts.) Paris, 1895 and 1905.

    Die Glasmalerei.
    Bulletin de Société Industriale de Mulhouse, vol. 90 (1924), pp.
    388-403.
    Reviewed in Chemical Zentralblatt, vol. 2 (1924), p. 1262.

    Le Vitrail du XIIe Siècle au XVIIIe Siècle en France.
    Paris, 1928.

GAUSSEN, A.
    Portefeuille Archéologique de la Champagne.
    Bar-sur-Aube, 1861.
    (Stained glass, pp. 3-10.)

GAUTHIER, M., and MARCHEIX, M.
    Le Vitrail de Saint Jean-Baptiste à l'Eglise Saint-Michel-des-Lions
    de Limoges.
    Cahiers de la Céramique, du Verre et des Arts du Feu, no. 35 (1964),
    pp. 173-187.

GAYNER, Dr.
    Notes on the East Window of Holy Trinity Church, Goodramgate, York.
    (Privately printed), 1905.

(Geddes, Wilhelmina Margaret)
    Obituary by HOWSON, Joan.
    J.M.G.P., vol. 12, no. 1 (1956), pp. 69-70.

    Notes on a Great Artist. By C.D.
    J.M.G.P., vol. 13, no. 3 (1962), pp. 490-491.

GEE, E.A.
    The Painted Glass of All Saints' Church, North Street, York.
    Archaeologia, vol. 102 (1969), pp. 151-202.
    (With a note by WORMALD, Francis, on the Fifteen Signs of the Last
    Days.)

GEHRIG, O.
    Vom deutschen Mosaik und von deutscher Glasmalkunst.
    Sprechsaal, vol. 60 (1927), p. 1046.

GEIGES, Fritz
    Die alte Fensterschmuck des Freiburger Münsters. 3 parts.
    Freiburg, 1901-1905.

    Das S. Annenfenster im jetzigen S. Alexanderchörlin des Freiburger
    Münsters.
    Freiburger Münsterblätter (1908), pp. 41-

    Der Mittelalterliche Fensterschmuck des Freiburger Münsters, seine
    Geschichte, die Ursachen seines Zerfalles, und die Massnahmen zu
    seiner Wiederherstellung, zugleich ein Beitrag zur Geschichte des
    Baues selbst.
    Freiburg-im-Breisgau, 1931.

GEILMANN, W.
    With JENEMANN, H.
    Der Phosphatgehalt alter Gläser und seine Bedeutung fur die Geschichte
    der Schmelztechnik.
    Glastechnische Berichte, no. 26 (1953), pp. 259-263.

    With BRUCKBAUER, T.
    Beiträge zur Kenntnis alter Glaser. II. Der Mangangehalt alter
    Gläser.
    Glastechnische Berichte, no. 27 (1954), pp. 456-459.

    Beiträge zur Kenntnis alter Glaser. III. Die chemische
    Zusammensetzung einiger alter Gläser inbesondere deutsche Gläser des
    10. bis 18. Jahrhunderts.
    Glastechnische Berichte, no. 28 (1955), pp. 146-156.

    With BERTHOLD, H.T., and TOLG, G.
    Beiträge zur Kenntnis alter Gläser. V. Die Verwitterungsprodukte
    auf Fensterschieben.
    Glastechnische Berichte, no. 33 (1960), pp. 213-219.

    Beiträge zur Kenntnis alter Gläser. VII. Kobalt als Färbungsmittel.
    Glastechnische Berichte, no. 35 (1962), pp. 186-192.

GENAUER, Emily
    Chagall's Stained Glass Windows.
    W.F.M.T. Perspective (Jan., 1962).

(Geneva International Exhibition)
    Die Glasgemälde für das Internationale Arbeitsamt in Geneva. Dr. N.
    Sprechsaal, no. 60 (1927), pp. 10-12.

GENT, Thomas
    The Most Delectable, Scriptural and Pious History of the Famous and
    Magnificent Great Eastern Window (According to Beautiful Portraitures)
    in St. Peter's Cathedral at York.
    York, 1762.

GERICHTEN, Ludwig von
    Founding the Association - A Retrospect.
    (Reminiscences of the founding of the forerunner of the Stained Glass
    Association of America.)
    Stained Glass, vol. 31, no. 3 (Winter, 1936-1937), pp. 73-78.

(Gerichten, Ludwig von)
    Obituary.
    Stained Glass, vol. 40, no. 3 (Autumn, 1945), pp. 96-99.

GÉRIN, Jules
    Le Vitrail de Saint-Louis Peint par Claudius Lavergne pour Nôtre-Dame
    de Senlis. La Chapelle de la Vièrge.
    Comptes rendus de la Comité Archéologique (Senlis), vol. 1 (1864),
    pp. 105-

    Le Vitrail Moderne.
    Senlis, 1875.

    Les Vitraux de la Chapelle de l'Hospice de Beauvais.
    Beauvais, 1879.

GERKE, Friedrich
    Das Lorscher Glasfenster.
    Beiträge zur Kunst des Mittelalters.
    Vorträge der 1. deutschen Kunsthistorikertagung.
    Berlin, 1948. Pp. 186-192.

GERMAIN, L.
    L'Origine de Guillaume de Marcillat, Peintre Verrier du 15e-16^3 Siècle.
    Nancy, 1886.

(German Glass Painters, Association of)
    Verband deutscher Glasmalereien.
    (Meeting of Sept. 7-10, 1907).
    Keramische Rundschau, vol. 19 (1911), p. 307.

(Germany: South-German Glass-Painting)

Aus der Geschichte der Glasmalerei in Süddeutschland. By H.H.
Diamant, vol. 48 (1926), pp. 23-25.

(Germany)

Anregung zur Gründung eines Reichs-Museums für Glasmalerei.
Eine internationale Ausstellung für Glasmalerei in Verbindung mit
der 3.Internationalen Baufach-Ausstellung.
Diamant, 48th year, no. 33 (Nov. 21, 1926), pp. 643-646.

Modern German Stained Glass. (Note.)
Architect's Journal, vol. 69, (Jan. 30, 1929).

GERRARD, Charles R.

Stained Glass.
Drawing and Design (Oct., 1925).

GERSON, H.

Exhibition of Glass-Painting at Gouda.
Burlington Magazine, vol. 73 (July-Dec., 1938), pp. 87-88.

GERSTUNG, W.

Die Glasmalereien in Darmstadt.
Darmstadt, 1923.

GESSERT —— .

Geschichte der Glasmalerei in Deutschland und den Nederlanden,
Frankreich, England, etc.
Stuttgart, 1839.

GEUER, H.J.S.

Grisaillemuster und Mosaiken. Sammlung von Mustern für monumentale
Glasmalerei Nebst Auszug aus der Geschichte der Glasmalerkunst.
Utrecht, 1882.

(The Geyling Firm)

The House of Geyling.
J.M.G.P., vol. 15, no. 2 (1973-1974), pp. 37-41.

GIBB, J.H.P.

Sherborne Abbey.
Huntingdon, 1971.
(Glass, inc. Pugin window, pp. 27-29, 32.)

GIBBS, Herbert Cockayne

The Parish Registers of Himsdon, co. Hertford, 1546-1837, with some
account of the church and parish.
London, 1915.

GIBBS, Roscoe

The Heraldry and Ancient Stained Glass in the Great East Window
of Exeter Cathedral.
Devon Notes and Queries, vol. 3 (1905), pp.1-10.

(Portrait of Bishop Lacy in Paignton Church.)
Devon Notes and Queries, vol. 3 (1905), p. 119.

The Arms of Dartmouth and their Origin.
(Glass, some now destroyed, in St. Saviour's Church.)
Devon Notes and Queries, vol. 5 (1909), pp. 137-142.

The Arms of Dartmouth.
Devon Notes and Queries, vol. 5 (1909), pp. 280-281.

The Heraldry of the Lower Windows in Exeter Cathedral.
Devon Notes and Queries, vol. 5 (1909), pp. 282-288.

GIBSON, A.A.

The Painted Glass of St. Peter's Church, Harrogate.
n.d. (Reprinted from the /Parish/ Magazine, August, 1928.)

GIBSON, Peter

The Stained and Painted Glass of York.
In The Noble City of York.
(Edited by STACPOOLE, Alberic,York, 1972), pp. 67-223.

The Minster's Greatest Window. The Great East Window.
York Minster News, no. 1 (June, 1973), p. 7 (unnumbered).

With NEWTON, R.G.
A Study on Cleaning Painted and Enamelled Glass in an Ultrasonic Bath.
CVMA, Great Britain, Additional Papers, no. 1.
London, 1974, pp. 70-78.

The Restoration of the Stained Glass of York Minster.
47th Annual Report of the Friends of York Minster (1976), pp. 19-29.

The Stained and Painted Glass of York Minster.
Norwich, 1979.

GIBSON, Walter S.

Two Painted Glass Panels from the Circle of Lucas van Leyden.
The Bulletin of the Cleveland Museum of Art (March, 1970), pp. 81-92.

GILBERT, A.P.M.

Déscription Historique de l'Eglise Cathédrale de Nôtre-Dame d'Amiens.
Amiens, 1833.

GILBERT (later GIDDY), Davies

Description of the Windows of St. Neots (Cornwall).
2 parts, London,1830-1831.
Reviewed in The Gentleman's Magazine, vol. 100 (183 , part 1), pp.
332-334.

GILBERT, Edward

A Guide to the Priory Church and Saxon Chapel, Deerhurst,
Gloucestershire.
Tewkesbury, 1956.
(Glass, p. 10.)

GILBERT, Sir John

Fragments Towards the History of Stained Glass and the Sister Arts
of the Middle Ages.
London, n.d. (1842).

GILBERT, M.

A Window in Chiswick Church.
(Letter to the Editor.)
J.M.G.P., vol. 4, no. 3 (Apr., 1932), p. 160.

GILL, Harry

The Church Windows of Nottinghamshire.
Transactions of the Thoroton Society, vol. 20 for 1916 (1917), pp.
93-124.
(List of ancient glass, pp. 120-122.)

GILL, W.W.

Stained Glass Windows to Fictitious Characters.
Notes and Queries, vol. 172 (Jan. 9, 1937), p. 33.

(Gilling Castle)

The Heraldic Glass of Gilling Castle, Yorkshire.
J.M.G.P., vol. 3, no. 2 (Oct., 1929), p. 54.

(Announcement of W.R. Hearst's intent to sell St. Donat's and its
works of art.)
J.M.G.P., vol. 7, no. 4 (Apr., 1939), p. 155.

(Gilling Castle)

(Replacement of glass in the Great Chamber.)
News and Notes, J.M.G.P., vol. 11, no. 2 (1953), pp. 65-66.

GIRARDOT, Auguste Théodore de
With DURAND, Hippolyte.
Monographie Générale de la Cathédrale de Bourges.
Moulins, 1849.

Les Artistes de la Ville et de la Cathédrale de Bourges.
Nantes, 1861.

GIRAUDET, E.
Jehan Courtoys, Peintre-Verrier du XVIᵉ Siècle.
Bulletin Monumental, vol. 46 (1880), pp. 499-509.

Les Artistes Tourangeaux.
Mémoires de la Société Archéologique de Touraine, vol. 33 (1885),
pp. 324-330, 367-368.

GIRKON, Paul
Die Glasmalerei als kultische Kunst.
Berlin, 1927.

Die Glasmalerei als kultische Kunst.
Diamant, vol. 50, no. 2 (Jan. 11, 1928), p. 34.

(Gislingham Church)
The Columbine Window of Rare Glass, Gislingham.
East Anglian Daily Times, May 17, 1928.

The Protection of our English Churches.
(4th report of the Central Council for the Care of Churches, 1928-1929.)

GIUSTO, Egidio Maria
Le Vetrate di San Francesco in Assisi.
Milan, 1911.

(Glasgow Cathedral)
(Ballantine's proposed windows for Glasgow Cathedral.)
Art Journal (1856), p. 321.
(A denial that the Lord Provost had commissioned Ballantine.)
Ibid., pp. 350-351.

The Painted Windows in Glasgow Cathedral.
The Ecclesiologist, vol. 23 (1862), pp. 104-107.
(The East Window completed.)
Ibid., p. 241.

Painted Glass in Glasgow Cathedral.
The Ecclesiologist, vol. 25 (1864), pp. 196-202, 261-264.

(Glasgow Museum)
Stained Glass in the Burrell Collection.
The Glasgow Art Review (Summer, 1947),

Catalogue of Stained and Painted Heraldic Glass in the Burrell
Collection.
Glasgow, 1962.

Catalogue of Stained and Painted Glass in the Burrell Collection
(Figure and Ornamental Subjects).
Glasgow, 1965.

Catalogue of the Touring Exhibition. (Vol. 2.)
London, 1977.

GLAZER, Adolf
Die Basler Glasmalerei im 16. Jahrhundert seit Hans Holbein.
Winterthur, 1937.

(Glass)
Glass as an Art Form.
Glass Digest (Apr., 1966).

Elements of Glass.
Stained Glass, vol. 42, no. 2 (Summer, 1947), pp. 35-47.
(Reprinted from Pittsburgh Plate Products, Sept.-Oct., 1940.)

The Making of Cathedral Glass for Stained Glass Windows: A
Flourishing Craft.
American Glass Review (Apr., 1967).

Glass is an Old Art but a New Science.
National Glass Budget (Nov. 8, 1969).

(Glass cutting)
The Origin of the Steel Wheel Glass Cutter.
Stained Glass, vol. 39, no. 4 (Winter, 1944), pp. 124-127.

Glass Cutting Appliances.
1. The Introduction of the Glazier's Diamond.
2. The Introduction of the Steel Wheel Glass-Cutter.
J.M.G.P., vol. 9, no. 3 (1945), pp. 93-96.

Starting from Scratch.
100th Anniversary of the Steel Wheel Glass Cutter.
Stained Glass, vol. 64, no. 4 (Winter, 1969-1970), pp. 30-32.

(Glass Painters)
Glass-Painters, 1750-1850.
(A biographical listing.)
Part 1, J.M.G.P., vol. 13, no. 1 (1960), pp. 326-338.
Part 2, J.M.G.P., vol. 13, no. 2 (1961), pp. 390-407.
Part 3, J.M.G.P., vol. 13, no. 3 (1962), pp. 514-525.

(Glass-Painters, 19th Century)
Visits to Art Manufactories. No. 2. Stained Glass.
Art Journal, vol. 5 (1859), p. 38.

(Glass Painting)
L'Art de Peindre sur le Verre.
Journal d'Oeconomie (Aug., 1754), pp. 149, 280-289.

Observation sur la Cuisson de Verre Après qu'il a été Peint.
Ibid., (Aug., 1754), pp. 150-152.

Proefkundige Verhandeling van wit en Gecouleurd Platiel Verglas en
Schilderwerk; benevens eene Duidelyke Onderrichting van het Glas-
Schildern . . . door A.F.
S'Gravenhage, 1774.

Geheimnisse der Alten bei der durchsichtigen Glasmalerei, nebst der
Kunst die dazu nöthigen Farben zu verarbeiten und einzubrennen.
By C.S.
Leipzig, 1831.

Remarks on the Character and Application of Ancient and Modern
Stained Glass. By E.T.
Brayley's Graphic Illustrator, London, 1834.

On the Art of Glass Painting. By a Correspondent.
Philosophical Magazine, vol. 9 (Dec., 1836), pp. 455-461.

Recherches sur la Peinture sur Verre. (M. van E.)
Ghent, 1839.

Glass-Painting.
Journal of the Franklin Institute, vol. 42 (1846), pp. 276, 429.

Painted Glass. Art Industries, No. VI.
Building News, vol. 28 (Apr. 23, 1875), pp. 452-453.

(Glass-Painting, Contd.)

Glass Painting and Staining for Amateurs.
London, 1877.

An Introduction to the Study of Painted Glass. By A.A.
London, 1878.

The Art of the Glass Painter.
The Builder, vol. 37 (Nov. 29, 1879), pp. 1307-1309.

Stained Glass from a Modern Point of View.
The Builder, vol. 39 (July 10, 1880), pp. 36-38.

America's Interest in Stained Glass.
American Architecture, vol. 15 (1883), p. 235.

Peinture sur Verre. Vitrail de la Vierge.
Annales Archéologiques, vol. 1 (1884), p. 83.

Stained Glass as an Accessory to Domestic Architecture.
Chambers' Journal (June 7, 1884), p. 359.

Painting the Sunshine. A Chapter on the Stained Glass Revival.
Sunday Chronicle, March 16, 1890.

Zum Stilcharacter der Glasmalerei.
Keramische Rundschau, vol. 2, no. 47 (1894).

Die Glasmalerei des Mittelalters.
St. Lucas (Deutsche Glaser Zeitung), vol. 6 (1895), p. 16.

Glasgemälde neuer Art.
St. Lucas (Deutsche Glaser Zeitung), vol. 7 (1896), p. 336.

Die musivische Fenstermalerei. By W.M.
Sprechsaal, vol. 30 (1897), p. 1489.

Scientific Rationale of Glass Painting. By G.E.W.
The Builder, vol. 74 (1898), p. 388.

Stained Glass and Decoration.
The Builder, vol. 75 (1898), pp. 42, 415.
           vol. 85 (1903), pp. 12, 279.

Glasmalereien und ihre Haltbarkeit.
St. Lucas (Deutsche Glaser Zeitung), vol. 9 (1898), p. 347.
And Keramische Rundschau, vol. 6 (1898), no. 40.

Die moderne Glasmalerei und deren Wiedererwecker.
Sprechsaal, vol. 33 (1900), p. 815.

The Making of Stained Glass.
Current Literature, vol. 31 (Nov., 1901), pp. 547-549.

Eine neue Art der Glasmalerei.
Keramische Rundschau, vol. 9 (1901), no. 48.

Over the Draughting Board; Opinions Official and Unofficial. A
Difficulty and its Solution.
Architectural Record, vol. 11, (Jan., 1902), pp. 110-112.

New Process of Stained Glass.
Scientific American Supplement, vol. 55 (Jan. 17, 1903).

Stained Glass.
International Studio, vol. 33 (Sept., 1904), supplement, pp. 359-363.

Stained Glass and Glass Mosaics.
Current Literature, vol. 36 (March, 1904), pp. 331-333.

Chromobilder auf Glas. By Btu.
Diamant, vol. 29 (1907), p. 219.
And Glasindustrie, vol. 18, no. 11 (1907), p. 1.

Die vier Projektionsmethoden in ihrem Einflusse auf die Architektur-
Glasmalerei.
Diamant, vol. 29 (1907), p. 399.

(Glass-Painting, Contd.)

Eine Neue Art farbiger Hinterglasmalerei. By P.D.
Diamant, vol. 30 (1908), pp. 907, 908, 941-943, 977-978.

Glasmalerei und Glasmosaik. By R.S.
Sprechsaal, vol. 42 (1909), p. 183.

Neu aufgefundenes Heft über Glasmalerei-technik.
Keramische Rundschau, vol. 19 (1911), p. 34.

Die Entstehung eines Glasgemälde.
Keramische Rundschau, vol. 19 (1911), p. 386.

Glasmalerei und Glasmosaik.
Keramische Rundschau, vol. 19 (1911), p. 505.

Imitation de la Peinture sur Verre.
Science Pratique (Vevey), (June, 1911), p. 21.

Glasmalereien.
Keramische Rundschau, vol. 20 (1912), p. 31

Die in alter und neuer Zeit zur Glasbemalung gebrauchten Gläser.
Zeitschrift für alte und neue Glasmalerei, (1912), pp. 42-44.

Der junge Glasmaler.
Nuremberg, 1912.

Aufkochen und Mattwerden von Glasmalerei.
Keramische Rundschau, vol. 21 (1913), pp. 457-458.
(Physical-chemical side of glass-painting.)

Standes-und Wirtschaftsfragen in der Glasmalerei.
(Editorial.)
Zeitschrift für alte und neue Glasmalerei (1914), p. 12.
(Commerce.)

Glasmalerei-Imitationen auf Fensterglas.
Diamant, vol. 37 (1915), p. 205.

Einiges aus der Glasmalerei.
Osterreich Glasindustrie, vol. 6 (1915), nos 2, 4.

Die Glasmalerei als Industrie-und Export-Artikel. By A.R.
Süddeutsche Glaserm, no. 10 (1926), p. 10.
(Commerce.)

Mittelalterliche Bleiverglasung.
Diamant (Aug. 1, 1925).

Glasmalerei als Festsaalschmuck.
Diamant (Feb. 1, 1926), pp. 63-66.

Die Arbeiten der Vereingten Werkstätten für Mosaik und Glasmalerei
zu Berlin-Treptow.
Sprechsaal, vol. 59, no. 6 (Feb. 11, 1926), pp. 96-98.

Glasmalereien auf der Leipziger Messe.
Diamant, 48th year, no. 9 (March 21, 1926).

Eine Anleitung zur Anfertigung von Glasmalerein aus dem 16 Jahrhundert.
By K.H.
Diamant, 49th year, no. 21 (Apr. 21, 1927), p. 229.

Vorbildliche Glasmalereien aus dem Spaeten Mittelalter und der
Renaissancezeit.
4 vols., Berlin, 1927.

Moderne Entwürfe für Kunstverglasung und Glasmalerei.
(25 plates in colour.)
Berlin, n.d.

Das antike Fenster und die Herstellung seines Glases. By A.G. and
H.J.M.
Die Glas-Industrie, 35th year, (1927), pp. 128-130.

Deutsche Glasmal-Kunst.
Jahresheft, Munich (1927).

(Glass-Painting, Contd.)

'Ueber die Haltbarkeit der Grisaille-Glasfarben' von Friedrich Greiner, München.
Diamant, 50th year, no. 28 (Oct. 1, 1928).

Die Frage des Submissionswesens im modernen Kunstgewerbe im allgemeinen und in der Glasmalerei im besonderen.
Zeitschrift für alte und neue Glasmalerei (1912), p. 92.
(See HEINERSDORFF, G., and LINNEMANN, R.)

Einiges von der Glasmalerei. By Dr. E.R.
Diamant, 55th year, no. 29 (Oct. 11, 1933).

Neue Technik der Glasmalerei.
Diamant, 53rd year, no. 35 (Dec. 11, 1931).

Die Glasmalerei, eine deutsche Zukunstskunst.
Diamant, 55th year, no. 34 (Dec. 1, 1933).

Vom Glaser.
Diamant, 56th year, no. 24 (Aug. 21, 1934).

Niederdeutsche Glasmalerei. By M.K.
Diamant, 57th year, no. 10,(Apr. 1, 1935).

Städtebilder in der Glasmalerei. By G.
Diamant, 57th year, no. 29 (Oct. 11, 1935).

Mittelalterliche Glasmalereien.
Diamant, 58th year, no. 3 (Jan. 21, 1936).

Die Glasmalerei in der Ostmark.
Diamant (July 1, 1939).

A Manual of Glass-Painting:Designs and Full Size Drawings.
J.M.G.P., vol. 13, no. 1 (1960), pp. 349-356.

GLUCK, Gustav
Der Wahre Name des Meisters D.V., 'Dirk Vellert'.
Jahrbuch der Kunsthistorischen Sammlungen des allerhöchsten Kaiserhauses, vol. 22, 1 (1901).

GLYNNE, Stephen R.
(Edited by ATKINSON, J.A.)
Notes on the Churches of Lancashire.
The Chetham Society, vol. 27 (1891).

(Edited by ATKINSON, J.A.)
Notes on the Churches of Cheshire.
The Chetham Society, vol. 32 (1894).

GODDARD, E.H.
Additional Notes on the Ancient Glass in Lydiard Tregoze Church.
The Wiltshire Archaeological and Natural History Magazine, no. 117 (June, 1912), pp. 444-447.

A List of Wiltshire Churches Containing Old Glass.
The Wiltshire Archaeological and Natural History Magazine, no. 179 (Dec., 1943), pp. 205-213.

GODFREY, W.H.
Sutton Place, Guildford.
(Renaissance heraldic glass.)
Architectural Review, vol. 34, no. 202 (Sept., 1913).

GODFREY, Walter H.
Hamsey Church. (Panel of Fragments Inserted.)
Sussex Notes and Queries, vol. 13, (1950-1953), p. 289.

GODWIN, Alfred
Examples of Stained Glass Windows for Ecclesiastical and Domestic Purposes.
Philadelphia, 1895.

GODWIN, George
On the Present State of the Art of Glass Painting in England and France, and on the Necessity for Efforts in its Favour.
London, 1840.
Reprinted from Civil Engineer and Architect's Journal (July, 1840).

GOERKE, C.
Die Zisterzienserkloster Mariawald.
Mariawald, 1932.

GOERN, H.
Die gotischen Bildfenster in Dom zu Erfurt.
Dresden, 1961.

GOETHE
Theory of Colours.
Translated by EASTLAKE, Charles.
London, 1840.

GOFFAERTS, Camille
Les Verrières du Cloître à l'Abbaye de Parc.
Revue Belge (Jan.15, 1891, Feb. 1, 1891).

GOLD, Sidney M.
A Short Account of the Life and Work of John Rowell.
Privately printed, 1965.
Reviewed by KIRBY, H.T., J.M.G.P., vol. 14, no. 2 (1965), p. 136.

GOMME, George Laurence (Editor)
Progress of Stained Glass in England.
The Gentleman's Magazine, part 1 (1817), pp. 309-315.
Reprinted in The Gentleman's Magazine Library, vol. 16,London (1894), pp. 147-155.

GOODALL, John A.
A Plan for the Study and Description of Medieval Stained Glass.
J.M.G.P., vol. 14, no. 2 (1965), pp. 131-135.

GOODHART-RENDEL, H.S.
(Speech at A.G.M. of the British Society of Master Glass-Painters.)
J.M.G.P., vol. 8, no. 1 (Oct., 1939), pp. 26-29.

GOODHUE, Harry E.
Stained Glass in Private Homes.
The Architectural Record (New York), vol. 18 (Nov., 1905), pp. 347-354.

Painted Glass and its Problems.
Christian Art, vol. 4 (Nov., 1908), pp. 49-60.

GOODMAN, Percival
Stained Glass.
Stained Glass, vol. 52, no. 3 (Autumn, 1957), pp. 105-107.

With BRIDGES, Stephen, ATKINSON, Harry, RAMBUSCH, Robert, BATES, Harold.
Stained Glass as Architects Consider It. (A Symposium.)
Stained Glass, vol. 59, no. 4 (Winter, 1964-1965), pp. 24-31.

(Goodrich Church)
(Armorial glass.)
Transactions of the Woolhope Naturalists' Field Club, 1914, 1915, 1916, 1917, vol. 22 (1918), p. 199.

GOODYEAR, R.A.H.

 Modern Knights in Stained Glass.
 Yorkshire Evening Post, Jan. 22, 1926.

GOOVAERTS, A.

 Les Ordonnances Données en 1480 à Tournai aux Métiers des Peintres
 et des Verriers.
 Bulletin de la Commission Royale d'Histoire de Belgique, vol. 6, no.1
 (1896), article 23.

GORDON, Ian

 The Great Windows of Liverpool Cathedral.
 J.M.G.P., vol. 7, no. 1 (Oct., 1937), pp. 27-28.
 Reprinted from The Observer, May 23, 1937.

GORDON-CHRISTIAN, J.

 Source Material. The Archives of the Whitefriars Studios, London.
 Artifex, vol. 1 (1968), pp. 35-36.

GOSHAWK, B., and BENNETT, M.

 The Stained Glass of the Firm of William Morris.
 Transactions of the Ecclesiological Society, new series, vol. 3,
 part 3, 1955-1956 (1958), pp. 259-263.

(Goslar)

 Die Restaurierung der Glasmalerei Fenster des ehemaligen Goslarer
 Domes.
 Diamant, 56th year, no. 25, (Sept. 1, 1934).

 Zu dem Gehurtsfenster im ehemaligen Goslarer Dom. By G.
 Diamant, 57th year, no. 9 (March 21, 1935).

GOSSET, A.

 La Cathédrale de Reims.
 Reims, 1894.

GOSTLING, William.

 A Walk in and about the City of Canterbury.
 Canterbury, 1774.
 2nd edition 1777 (extensive additions relative to the windows).

(Gouda)

 Explanation of the Famous and Renowned Glas-Work. Or Painted
 Windows, in the Fine and Eminent Church at Gouda. For the Use
 and Commodity of both Inhabitants and Foreigners that come to
 see this Artificial Work.
 Gouda, 1790.

 Catalogue of Stained Glass at Gouda.
 Antiquarian and Architectural Year Book for 1844, (London), (1845),
 pp. 207-216.

 Reproductie van een der Glasremin in de St. Janskerk te Gouda
 Voorstellende het Redden van het Bellegerde Bethulie, door het
 out Hooften van het Legerhootd Hodfermis.
 Scheltam und Holdema's Bockhandel (Jan., 1913).

 Description of the Stained Glass Windows in Saint John's Church at
 Gouda. A Short Manual for Visitors.
 Gouda, n.d.

GOULD, G.T.S.

 Ancient Glass in St. Bride's Chapel, Douglas, Lanarkshire.
 J.M.G.P., vol. 3, no. 1 (Apr., 1929), pp. 21-24.

 A Panel of Thirteenth-Century Stained Glass; 'The Temptation of
 Christ', in the Royal Scottish Museum, Edinburgh.
 J.M.G.P., vol. 4, no. 1 (Apr., 1931), p. 13.

(Governmental Relations)

 (Import of Stained Glass from Europe. Crisis in the U.S. stained
 glass trade.)
 Stained Glass, vol. 49, no. 2 (Summer, 1954), pp. 74-75.

GOWER, A.F.G. Leveson

 Jesse Windows.
 (St. George's, Hanover Square.)
 Notes and Queries, 8th series, vol. 8 (Aug. 31, 1895), p. 178.

GRABAR, A.

 La Verrerie d'Art Byzantine au Moyen Age.
 Monuments Piot, vol. 57 (1971), pp. 89-127.

GRAEVENITZ, Dr. von

 Freiburg im Breisgau, eine Stadt der Glasmalerei.
 Diamant, 56th year, no. 17 (June 11, 1934).

GRAFLY, Dorothy

 Stained Glass Tomorrow.
 Stained Glass, vol. 41, no. 2 (Summer, 1946), pp. 54-57.

GRAHAM, Henry B.

 (On a fragment from Chartres at Princeton.)
 Record of the Art Museum, Princeton University, vol. 21 (1962),
 pp. 30-45.

GRAHAM, J.G., and Christie, A.

 The Chapel of St. Anthony the Eremite, at Murthly, Perthshire.
 Edinburgh, 1850.

GRANCSAY, Stephen V.

 A Stained Glass Saint Michael in Armour.
 Bulletin of the Stained Glass Association of America, vol. 25, no. 1
 (Jan., 1929).

GRANGE, A. de la, and CLOQUET, L.

 Etudes sur l'Art à Tournai et sur les Anciens Artistes de Cette
 Ville.
 Tournai, 1889.

GRANGE, E.L.

 The Removal of the Glass from Tattershall Church.
 Lincolnshire Notes and Queries, vol. 1 (1889), pp. 1-3.

GRANGES, C. des

 Le Vitrail d'Appartement. Conseils pour Pratiquer la Peinture sur
 Verre, pour la Comprendre, et pour la Juger.
 Paris, 1864. (Subsequent editions, Moulins, 1871, 1876.)

GRAUL, Richard

 Die Glasmalereien in St. Gudula zu Brüssel.
 In Belgische Kunstdenkmäler, vol. 2 (Munich, 1923), (Ed. CLEMEN,
 Paul), p. 47.

GRAVES, James

 Ancient Irish Stained Glass.
 Transactions of the Kilkenny Archaeological Society, vol. 1 (1849),
 pp. 210-214.

GRAVES, Norbert W.

 Stained Glass in the M.H. De Young Museum. (Given by W.R. Hearst.)
 Stained Glass, vol. 35, no. 2 (Summer, 1940), pp. 50-55.

 Heraldic Hints.
 Stained Glass, vol. 36, no. 2 (Summer, 1941), pp. 56-60.

GRAY, Edward F.
> St. Mary's Parish Church, Ripple, Worcestershire.
> (4th edition) Tewkesbury, 1967.
> (Destroyed glass, p. 7.)

(Great Exhibition, London, 1851)
> Painted, Stained and Ornamental Glass in the Exhibition.
> The Illustrated Exhibitor (1851), pp. 375-384.
>
> Glass in the Great Exhibition.
> Ibid, pp. 533-535.
>
> Stained and Painted Glass.
> Illustrated London News (June 14, 1851),
>
> Official Catalogue of the Great Exhibition of the Industries of all
> Nations, London, 1851.
> London, 1851.
>
> Reports of the Juries of the International Exhibition, London, 1851.
> London, 1852.
> (Glass painting, p. 533.)
>
> Catalogue of Articles of Ornamental Art, Selected and Purchased by
> the Government from the International Exhibition, London, 1851.
> London, 1852.

GREEN, Everard
> The Identification of the Eighteen Worthies Commemorated in the
> Heraldic Glass in the Hall Windows of Ockwells Manor House in the
> Parish of Bray, Berkshire.
> Archaeologia, vol. 56 (1899), pp. 323-336.

GREEN, Mary A.
> Old Painted Glass in Worcestershire. I.
> Worcestershire Archaeological Society Transactions, new series,
> vol. 11 (for 1934), pp. 33-63.
>
> Old Painted Glass in Worcestershire. II.
> Transactions of the Worcestershire Archaeological Society, new
> series, vol. 12 (for 1935), pp. 42-55.
>
> Old Painted Glass in Worcestershire. III.
> Transactions of the Worcestershire Archaeological Society, new
> series, vol. 13 (for 1936), pp. 1-10.
>
> Ibid., vol. 15 (for 1938), pp. 10-26.
>
> Ibid., vol. 17 (for 1940), pp. 1-10.
>
> Ibid., vol. 19 (for 1942), pp. 37-44.
>
> Ibid., vol. 21 (for 1944), pp. 30-47.
>
> Ibid., vol. 22 (for 1945), pp. 69-83.
> Ibid., vol. 23 (for 1946), pp. 1-26.
> Ibid., vol. 24 (for 1947), pp. 4-39.
>
> Noticed in 'Memorabilia', Notes and Queries, vol. 182 (Feb. 14, 1942),
> p. 85.

GREEN, Maureen
> New Life for Canterbury's Old Glass.
> Smithsonian (June, 1975), pp. 28-37.

GREEN, W.J.
> Report from the Clerk of the Works, January-December, 1944.
> (Replacement of part of the Great East Window and installation of
> the glass from St. John's, Micklegate.)
> 17th Annual Report of the Friends of York Minster (1945), pp. 31-32.

GREEN, W.J. (Contd.)
> Report from the Clerk of Works, January-December, 1945.
> (Replacement of windows.)
> 18th Annual Report of the Friends of York Minster (1946), p. 38.
>
> Report from the Clerk of Works, January-December, 1946.
> (Replacement and restoration.)
> 19th Annual Report of the Friends of York Minster (1947), p. 42.
>
> Report from the Clerk of Works, January-December, 1947.
> (Replacement and restoration.)
> 20th Annual Report of the Friends of York Minster (1948), p. 38.
>
> Report from the Clerk of Works, January-December, 1948.
> 21st Annual Report of the Friends of York Minster (1949), p. 38.
>
> Report from the Clerk of Works, January-December, 1949.
> 22nd Annual Report of the Friends of York Minster (1950), p. 33.
>
> Report from the Clerk of Works, January-December, 1950.
> (Replacement of the Five Sisters.)
> 23rd Annual Report of the Friends of York Minster (1951), p. 33.
>
> Report from the Clerk of Works, January-December, 1951.
> 24th Annual Report of the Friends of York Minster (1952), p. 34.
>
> Report from the Clerk of Works, January-December, 1952.
> 25th Annual Report of the Friends of York Minster (1953), p. 38.
>
> Report from the Clerk of Works, January-December, 1953.
> (Completion of Great East Window.)
> 26th Annual Report of the Friends of York Minster (1954), p. 28.
>
> Report from the Clerk of Works, January-December, 1954.
> 27th Annual Report of the Friends of York Minster (1955), p. 37.
>
> Report from the Clerk of Works, January-December, 1958.
> 31st Annual Report of the Friends of York Minster (1959), p. 41.
>
> Report from the Clerk of Works, January-December, 1961.
> 34th Annual Report of the Friends of York Minster (1962), p. 34.
>
> Report from the Clerk of Works, January-December, 1962.
> 35th Annual Report of the Friends of York Minster (1963), pp. 28-29.
>
> Report from the Clerk of Works, January-December, 1963.
> 36th Annual Report of the Friends of York Minster (1964), p. 21.
>
> Report from the Clerk of Works, January-December, 1964.
> 37th Annual Report of the Friends of York Minster (1965), p. 40.
>
> The Minster Works Department.
> 38th Annual Report of the Friends of York Minster (1966), p. 31.

(Gresford Church, Denbigh)
> (A table of the contents of the mediaeval windows.)
> Archaeologia Cambrensis, vol. 90 (1935), pp. 352-356.

(Grien, Hans Baldung)
> (Projects for glass-painting and glass-painting.)
> In Exhibition Catalogue, Karlsruhe (1959), pp. 97-117.

GRIEVE, Alastair I.
> Review of SEWTER, A.C., 'The Stained Glass of William Morris and
> his Circle, Vol. I'.
> Art Bulletin, vol. 59 (June, 1977), pp. 293-296.

GRIFFIN, R.
> The Arms of Richard II as Shown in Windows at Westwell and
> Wateringbury.
> Archaeologia Cantiana, vol. 47 (1935), pp. 170-176.

GRIMKÉ-DRAYTON, T.D.

    The East Window of Gloucester Cathedral.
    (With an introduction by RUSHFORTH, G. McNeil.)
    Transactions of the Bristol and Gloucester Archaeological Society,
    vol. 32 (for 1915), pp. 69-97.
    Some notes on the above by WERE, F., (same volume), pp. 220-221.

GRIMME, Ernst G.

    Das Karlsfenster in der Kathedrale von Chartres.
    Aachener Kunstblätter des Museumvereins, nos.19-20 (1961).

GRINLING, C.H.

    Ancient Stained Glass in Oxford.
    Proceedings of the Oxford Architectural and Historical Society,
    new series, vol. 4 (1883), pp. 111-184.

GRINNELL, Robert

    Iconography and Philosophy in the Crucifixion Window at Poitiers.
    Art Bulletin, vol. 28, no. 3 (Sept., 1946), pp. 171-196.

(Grisaille)

    Die Grisaille. By C.O.
    Diamant (May 1, 1936).

GRODECKI, Louis

    Les Vitraux des Eglises de France.
    Paris, 1947.

    A Stained Glass Atelier of the Thirteenth Century.
    A study of windows in the Cathedrals of Bourges, Chartres and
    Poitiers.
    Journal of the Warburg and Courtauld Institutes, no. 11 (1948), pp.
    87-111.

    Le Vitrail et l'Architecture au XIIe et au XIIIe Siècles.
    Gazette des Beaux-Arts (July-Sept, 1949), pp. 5-24.

    The Ancient Glass of Canterbury Cathedral.
    (Letter to the Editor.)
    Burlington Magazine, vol. 92 (Jan.-Dec., 1950), pp. 294-297.
    Q.v. RACKHAM, Bernard, ibid., p. 357.

    The Ancient Glass of Canterbury Cathedral.
    (Letter to the Editor).
    Q.v. RACKHAM, Bernard, ibid., pp. 94-95.
    Burlington Magazine, vol. 93 (Jan.-Dec., 1951), p. 94.

    Suger et l'Architecture Monastique.
    Bulletin des Relations Artistiques France-Allemagne (May, 1951).

    Les Vitraux de la Cathédrale de Poitiers.
    Congrès Archéologique de France, 1951 (Orleans, 1952), pp. 138-163.

    Fragments de Vitraux Provenant de Saint-Denis.
    Bulletin Monumental, vol. 110 (1952), pp. 51-62.

    Quelques Observations sur le Vitrail au XIIe Siècle en Rhenanie et
    en France.
    In Memorial d'un Voyage d'Etudes de la Société Nationale des
    Antiquaires de France en Rhenanie, July 1951.
    Paris, 1953, pp. 241-249.

    Notre-Dame d'Alençon.
    Congrès Archéologique de France, CXIe session tenue dans l'Orne en
    1953.

    Un Vitrail Démembré de la Cathédrale de Soissons. (Vers 1220.)
    Gazette des Beaux-Arts (Oct., 1953), pp. 169-176.

GRODECKI, Louis (Contd.)

    Vitraux de France du XIe au XVIe Siècle.
    In Catalogue de l'Exposition du Musée des Arts Décoratifs.
    Paris, 1953.

    La Restauration des Vitraux du XIIe Siècle Provenant de la
    Cathédrale de Châlons-sur-Marne.
    Mémoires de la Société d'Agriculture, Commerce, Science et Arts
    de la Marne, 2nd series, t. 28 (1953-1954).
    Châlons-sur-Marne, 1954, pp. 322-352.

    Les Problèmes de la Peinture Gothique.
    Critique, no. 98 (July, 1955), pp. 610-624.

    (Glass from Saint-Germain-des-Prés, now in various situations.)
    Bulletin de la Société Nationale des Antiquaires de France, (for
    1956), pp. 82-83.

    Les Verrieres d'Evreux.
    L'Oeil, May, 1957.

    Stained Glass Windows of Saint-Germain-des-Prés.
    The Connoisseur, vol. 140 (Sept., 1957), pp. 33-37.

    Review of FRANKL, Paul, Peter Hemmel, Glasmaler von Andlau.
    Bulletin Monumental, no. 115 (1957), pp. 74-76.

    Le Vitrail Français.
    (With AUBERT, M., CHASTEL, A., GRUBER, J.-J., LAFOND, J., MATHEY, F.,
    TARALON, J., VERRIER, J.)
    Paris, 1958.
    Reviewed by SALET, Francis, Bulletin Monumental, no. 116 (1958), p. 226.

    Les Vitraux de Châlons-sur-Marne et l'Art Mosan.
    In Actes du XIXe Congrès International d'Histoire de l'Art, Paris,
    1958, pp. 183-190.

    Review of WENTZEL, Hans, CVMA, Germany, vol. 1.
    Gazette des Beaux-Arts (Oct., 1958), pp. 252-255.

    Les Vitraux de Notre-Dame et de la Sainte-Chapelle de Paris.
    (With AUBERT, M., LAFOND, J.)
    (CVMA France 1. Département de la Seine 1.)
    Paris, 1959.

    Les Vitraux Soissonais du Louvre, du Musée Marmottan et des
    Collections Américaines.
    Revue des Arts, vol. 10 (1960), pp. 163-178.

    Vidrieras Romanicas.
    Revista Goya, nos. 43-45, Madrid, 1961.

    Vitraux Français du XIIe Siècle.
    Festschrift Hans R. Hahnloser.
    Basel, 1961, pp. 289-298.

    Les Vitraux de la Cathédrale du Mans.
    In Congrès Archéologique de France (Maine), 1961.

    Les Vitraux Allégoriques de Saint-Denis.
    Art de France, no. 1 (1961), pp. 19-46.

    Les Vitraux de la Fin du XIIe ou du Début du XIIIe Siècle à la
    Cathédral de Troyes.
    In Bulletin de la Société Nationale des Antiquaires de France
    (1961), pp. 57-

    Review of BOOM, A. van der, De Kunst der Glazeniers in Europa
    1100-1600.
    Bulletin Monumental, vol. 119 (1961), pp. 293-294.

    Les Vitraux de Saint-Denis: L'Enfance du Christ.
    In Forty Essays in Honor of Erwin Panofsky. Editor MEISS, Millard,
    New York, 1961, pp. 170-186.

GRODECKI, Louis (Contd.)

Die Glasmalerei um 1400.
In Katalog der Ausstellung 'Europäische Kunst um 1400'.
Vienna, 1962, pp. 221-

Sainte-Chapelle.
Paris, 1962.

La Quatrième Réunion Internationale du Corpus Vitrearum Medii Aevi
et Ses Enseignements.
Bulletin Monumental, vol. 121 (1963), pp. 73-82.

Review of FRODL-KRAFT, Eva, CVMA, Austria, 1, and HELBIG, Jean,
CVMA, Belgium, 1.
Bulletin Monumental, vol. 121 (1963), pp. 214-216.

Chartres.
New York, 1963.

Review of JOHNSON, J.R., Stained Glass Theories of Viollet-le-Duc.
Bulletin Monumental, no. 122 (1964), pp. 108-110.

Problèmes de la Peinture en Champagne Pendant la Seconde Moitié
du Douzième Siècle.
In Romanesque and Gothic Art; Studies in Western Art.
(Acts of the Twentieth International Congress of the History of
Art, I.)
Princeton, 1963, pp. 129-141.

Le Maître de Saint Eustache de la Cathédrale de Chartres.
In Gedenkschrift Enrst Gall, editors KUHN, M., and GRODECKI, L.
Munich, 1965, pp. 171-194.

Review of CVMA (Scandinavia).
Bulletin Monumental, vol. 123 (1965), pp. 358-361.

GRODECKI, Louis (Contd.)

Les Vitraux du XIIe Siècle de Saint-Germer-de-Fly.
Miscellanea pro arte. Festschrift für Hermann Schnitzler,
Dusseldorf (1965), pp. 149-157.

Le Vitrail Roman de Gargilesse (Indre).
Mélanges Offerts à René Crozet, vol. 2 (1966), pp. 953-957.

Les Vitraux de la Cathédrale d'Angers.
(With HAYWARD, Jane.)
Bulletin Monumental, no. 124 (1966), pp. 7-67.

Review of BEER, Ellen, CVMA, Switzerland, III.
Bulletin Monumental, no. 125 (1967), pp. 452-455.

Les Quinze Signes Précurseurs de la Fin du Monde dans les Vitraux
Allemands, Français et Alsaciens.
Kunst des Mittelalters in Sachsen. Festschrift Wolf Schubert.
Weimar, 1967, pp. 292-299.

Les Vitraux de la Cathédrale d'Evreux.
(An exchange of articles with BAUDOT, Marcel, and DUBUC, René.)
Bulletin Monumental, no. 126 (1968), pp. 55-65.

Les Vitraux de la Sainte-Chapelle.
(With CAVINESS, M.H.)
Revue de l'Art, 1-2 (1968), pp. 8-16.

Review of MEULEN, Jan van der, A Logos-Creator at Chartres and its
Copy.
Bulletin Monumental, no. 127 (1969), pp. 43-44.

Colloque du Corpus Vitrearum Medii Aevi (no. 6) (Report of).
Bulletin Monumental, no. 127 (1969), p. 49.

GRODECKI, Louis (Contd.)

Review of FRODL-KRAFT, Eva, Die Glasmalerei . . .
Revue de l'Art, no. 10 (1970), p. 98.

Review of BAUDOT and THIRION's Vitraux . . . d'Evreux, and
BAUDOT and LAFOND's Vitraux . . . de Port-Audemer.
Ibid.

Review of Berühmte Glasmalerein in Europa, by FRENZEL, RODE,
SEIFERT, Von WITZLEBEN, BEYER, and POPESLO.
Ibid.

Review of KRUMMER-SCHROTH, Glasmalereien aus dem Freiburger Munster.
Ibid.

Review of BEEH-LUSTENBERGER, Glasmalerei . . . in Darmstadt.
Ibid.

Nouvelles Découvertes sur les Vitraux de la Cathédrale de Troyes.
In Intuition und Kunstwissenschaft: Festschrift für Hanns
Swarzenski.
Edited by BLOCH, P., BUDDENSIEG, T., HENTZEN, A., and MULLER, T.
Berlin, 1973, pp. 191-203.

'Le Maître du Bon Samaritain' de la Cathédrale de Bourges.
In The Year 1200. A Symposium.
New York, 1975, pp. 339-359.

La Sainte-Chapelle.
Paris, 1975. (2nd, revised, edition.)

Les Plus Anciens Vitraux de Saint-Remi de Reims.
In Beiträge zur Kunst des Mittelalters: Festschrift für Hans Wentzel.
Berlin, 1975, pp. 65-77.

Les Vitraux de Saint-Denis. Etude sur le Vitrail au XIIe Siècle.
t. 1.
(CVMA, France, Série Etudes.)
Paris, 1976.
Reviewed by PERROT, Françoise, Bulletin Monumental, vol. 137 (1979),
pp. 83-85.

Le Vitrail Roman.
Fribourg, 1977.
Reviewed by GRANBOULAN, Anne, Bulletin Monumental, vol. 137 (1979),
pp. 192-194.

Le Style 'Dur' de la Peinture sur Verre en France.
In Akten des 10. Internationalen Colloquiums des CVMA.
Stuttgart, 1977, pp. 26-28.

Esthétique Ancienne et Moderne du Vitrail Roman.
Les Monuments Historiques de la France, no. 1 (1977), pp. 17-30.

Sauvons les Vitraux Anciens.
Les Dossiers de l'Archéologie, no. 26 (Jan.-Feb., 1978), pp. 12-25.

Les Problèmes de l'Origine de la Peinture Gothique et le 'Maître
de Saint Chéron' de la Cathédrale de Chartres.
Revue de l'Art, nos. 40-41 (1978), pp. 43-64.

(With PERROT, Françoise, TARALON, Jean.)
Recensement des Vitraux de Paris, de la Région Parisienne, de la
Picardie, du Nord et du Pas-de-Calais.
CVMA, France, supplementary series, no. 1, Paris, 1978.
Reviewed by BRISAC, Catherine, Bulletin Monumental, vol. 138, no.
1 (1980), pp. 109-111.

(Groombridge)

The John Packer Heraldic Window at Groombridge.
The Connoisseur, (Apr., 1930).

GRUBER, J.

Les Vitraux (Modern Stained Glass at the Paris Exhibition, 1925).
Paris, 1926.

Quelques Aspects de l'Art et de la Technique du Vitrail en France.
(Dernier Tiers du XIIIe Siècle, Premier Tiers du XIVe.)
Travaux des Etudiants du Groupe d'Histoire de l'Art.
Paris, 1927-1928, pp. 71-94.

Le Vitrail Francais.
(With AUBERT, M., CHASTEL, A., GRODECKI, L., LAFOND, J., MATHEY, F.,
TARALON J., VERRIER, J.)
Paris, 1958.
Reviewed by SALET, Francis, Bulletin Monumental, no. 116 (1958),
p. 226.

GRUENKE, Bernard O.

Slab Glass in Architecture.
Stained Glass, vol. 50, no. 1 (Spring, 1955), pp. 9-10.

GRUNDY-NEWMAN, S.A.

Heraldry of Lichfield Cathedral.
(Request for identification of some coats.)
Notes and Queries, series 11, vol. 10 (Dec. 12, 1914), pp. 467.
                                vol. 11 (Jan. 2, 1915), p. 35.

(Grunewald, Matthias)
Mathias Grunewald und die Glasmalerei. By Dr. J.Z.
Diamant, (Dec. 21, 1925), pp. 770-772.

GRUZ, H.

Compositionen für Glasmaler, Glasätzer, u.s.w.
Berlin, 1886.

GRYLLS, Harry

Fourteenth Century Sussex Furnaces.
(Letter to the Editor.)
The Times, Dec. 7, 1932.

GRYLLS, Henry

Descriptive Sketch of the Windows of St. Neot Church.
3rd edition, Devonport, 1844.

(Guengat, Brittany)
Un Vitrail Nurembergeois dans une Eglise Bretonne.
Mémoires de la Société d'Émulation des Côtes-du-Nord, 1953.
Summarised in Bulletin Monumental, vol. 112 (1954), pp. 116-117.

GUERBER, Victor

Essai sur les Vitraux de la Cathédrale de Strasbourg.
Strasbourg, 1848.

GUIBERT, Joseph

Les Dessins d'Archéologie de Roger de Gaignières.
Series II, Vitraux.
Paris, n.d.

GUIFFREY, Jules

La Famille de Jean Cousin, Peintre et Verrier du XVIe Siècle.
Nogent-le-Rotrou, 1882.

Artistes Parisiens des XVIe et XVIIe Siècles.
Paris, 1915.

GUILHERMY, R.F.M.N.

(With VIOLLET-LE-DUC, E.)
Description de Nôtre-Dame, Cathédrale de Paris.
Paris, 1856.

GUILLAUME, P.

Maître Jacques Jouin, Peintre Verrier à Embrun, 1671.
Revue de l'Art Français (June, 1889).

GUILLOT, Marcel

Sur l'Irisation du Verre Antique . . .
Comptes Rendus de l'Académie des Sciences, vol. 198 (1934), pp.
2093-2095.

GUILLUM, Judith D.

Church Windows; Modern Stained Glass.
In Post-War Church Building.
(Editor SHORT, Ernest.)
London, 1948.

GUITARD, A.

Vitraux de Bourges.
Vitraux du XIIIe Siècle de la Cathédrale de Bourges.
(With CLEMENT, S.)
Bourges, 1900.

GULLICK, T.J.

Oil Painting on Glass Including Mirrors, Windows, etc.; with
Remarks upon the Principles of Painting and Decorative Art
Generally.
London, 1892.

GUNTON, S.

History of the Church of Peterburgh.
Peterborough, 1686.

GUTHRIE, J. Gordon

Meditations upon a Theme.
Stained Glass (Spring, 1933).

(Gyles, Henry)
Letters from the Stowe Ms.
The Yorkshire Archaeological Journal, vol. 14 (1898), pp. 422-443.

HABERLEY, Lloyd
    The Antiquary. A Poem Written on Waterperry Church and Decorated
    with Designs from the Glass of the Ancient Windows.
    Long Crendon, 1933.

HABINGTON, Thomas
    The Windows of Malvern Priory Church.
    In A Survey of Worcestershire, editor AMPHLETT, J.
    Vols. 1, 2, Oxford, 1895, 1899.

HABSBURG, Geza von
    Les Vitraux de Lorenzo Ghiberti.
    In 7ᵉ Colloque du Corpus Vitrearum Medii Aevi, Florence ?, (1970),
    pp. 24-26.

HAENDKE, Berthold
    Die schweizerische Malerei in XVI Jahrhundert diesseits der Alpen
    und unter Berücksichtigung der Glasmalerei des Formschnittes und
    des Kupferstichs.
    Arau, 1893.

HAFNER, Albert
    Meisterwerke Schweizerischer Glasmalerei.
    Berlin, 1887-1889.
    (Also American and French editions.)

HAHNLOSER, Hans R.
    Chorfenster und Altäre des Berner Münsters.
    Berne, 1950.
    Reviewed by A.L., The Connoisseur, vol. 129 (March, 1952), pp. 50-51.

    Preface.
    In 8ᵉ Colloque du Corpus Vitrearum Medii Aevi. Compte Rendu.
    Paris ?, 1972, pp. 5-6.

    Organisation Générale du CVMA.
    Ibid., pp. 56-58.

HAINES, Herbert
    Guide to the Cathedral Church of Gloucester.
    Gloucester, 1867.

HALAHAN, Brenda C.
    The Frome Copse Glass-House, Chiddingfold.
    Surrey Archaeological Collections, vol. 34 (1921), pp. 24-31.

    On the Association of Flint Chippings with Fragments of Old Glass
    Found in Mediaeval Glasshouses at Chiddingfold in Surrey.
    J.M.G.P., vol. 1, no. 1 (1924), pp. 11-15.

    Chiddingfold Glass and its Makers in the Middle Ages.
    Transactions of the Newcomen Society, vol. 5 (1924-1925), pp. 77-85.

HALL, E.T., and SCHWEIZER, F.
    X-ray Fluorescence Analysis of Museum Objects: A New Instrument.
    A Non-Dispersive X-ray 'Isoprobe'.
    Archaeometry, vol. 15 (1973), pp. 53-57, 74-76.

(Hallward, Reginald)
    Rum Bottles and Church Windows. By L.D.
    (Contains an account of the work of Reginald Hallward.)
    Daily Sketch, Oct. 15, 1925.

HALLWARD, Reginald
    Stained Glass.
    Reply to letter by VOYSEY, C.A.
    The Builder, vol. 136 (March 1, 1929), p. 413.

    Applied Craftsmanship. V. Firing and Staining Glass.
    The Builder (May 24, 1929).

(Hallward, Reginald)
    Stained Glass Windows, Abberley Hall School Chapel, by Mr. Reginald
    Hallward.
    The Builder (Jan. 6, 1933).

HALLWARD, Reginald
    Stained Glass in England.
    Stained Glass, vol. 34, no. 1 (Spring-Summer, 1939), pp. 5-14.

HAMAND, L.A.
    The Ancient Windows of Great Malvern Priory Church.
    St. Albans, 1947.
    Reviewed in Burlington Magazine, vol. 90 (Jan.-Dec., 1948), p. 183.

    Angel Musicians and their Instruments. Portrayed in the Great
    Malvern Priory Church Windows.
    St. Albans, 1950.

(Hamburg Museum)
    Museum für Kunst und Gewerbe. Meisterwerke mittelalterlicher
    Glasmalerei aus der Sammlung des Reichs-Freiherrn vom Stein.
    Hamburg, 1966.

HAMILTON, Andrew
    Notes on Remains of Ancient Painted Glass in the Churches of
    Rivenhall, Witham, Faulkbourne, Cressing, White Notley, Bradwell,
    Little Braxted, and in the Original Windows of Faulkbourne Hall.
    Transactions of the Essex Archaeological Society, new series, vol. 2,
    1884 (1885), pp. 71-90.

HAMILTON, W.
    The First Twelve Kings and Twenty Knights from the Norman Conquest
    in Armour. Thirty-two Original Coloured Drawings by W. Hamilton,
    R.A.; and Stained on Glass the Same Size, by Francis Eginton of
    Handsworth, near Birmingham, for Fonthill Abbey, Wiltshire, the
    Seat of William Beckford, Esq.
    (n.p., n.d.)

HAMM, Dr. A. Schröder
    Neuere religiöse Glasmalerei.
    Keramische Rundschau, 35th year, no. 26 (June 30, 1927), pp. 416-418.

(Hampp, J. Christopher)
    Catalogue of Sale of Glass in Christie's Room, London.
    June 18, 1808.

    Wer war J.C. Hampp?
    (Letter to the Editor.)
    Diamant (Oct. 21, 1937).

(Hampton Court)
    (Glass by Willement in the Great Hall.)
    The Gentleman's Magazine, vol. 27, new series, part 1 (1847), pp.
    291-293.

HAMY-LONGUESP, Nicole
    Troyes, haut-lieu du Vitrail.
    Les Dossiers de l'Archéologie, no. 26 (Jan.-Feb., 1978), pp. 86-101.

(Hanau)
    Glasgemälde in der Marienkirche zu Hanau.
    Zeitschrift für alte und neue Glasmalerei (1912), p. 35.

HANCOCK, F.

    Notes on the Parish of Selworthy.
    Notes and Queries for Somerset and Dorset, vol. 3 (1893).
    (Glass, pp. 203-204.)

HAND, Charles R.

    The Chancel of Beaumaris Church.
    Archaeologia Cambrensis, vol. 79 (1924), pp. 366-370.

HANSEN, B.A.

    Middelalterlige glasmalerier.
    Hikuin, vol. 1 (1974), pp. 87-96.

HARBIN, E.H. Bates

    Appendix on the Figure of St. Dunstan in a Window of Cothelstone
    Church.
    Proceedings of the Somersetshire Archaeological and Natural History
    Society, vol. 62 for 1916, part 2 (1917), pp. 24-25.

HARCOURT-BATH, William

    'Grand-Queux': Evreux Cathedral.
    (Request for explanation of the term. A window of 1410 is dedicated
    to the 'Grand-Queux de France.')
    Notes and Queries,   series, vol. 147 (Nov. 29, 1924), p. 391.

HARDEN, D.B.

    New Light on Roman and Early Medieval Window-Glass.
    Glastechnische Berichte, 32K (1959), Heft 8, pp. 8-16.

    Domestic Window-Glass, Roman, Saxon, and Medieval.
    In Studies in Building History (Essays in recognition of the work
    of B.H. St. J. O'Neil), editor JOPE, E.M.
    London, 1961.

    The Rothschild Lycurgus Cup: Addenda and Corrigenda.
    Journal of Glass Studies, vol. 5 (1963), pp. 9-17.

    Ancient Glass. I. Pre-Roman.
    Archaeological Journal, (1968), pp. 46-72.

    Ancient Glass. II. Roman.
    Archaeological Journal (1969), pp. 44-77.

    Ancient Glass. III. Post-Roman.
    Ibid., pp. 78-117.

    Medieval Glass in the West.
    Proceedings of the Eighth International Congress on Glass (1969),
    pp. 97-111.

    Anglo-Saxon and Later Medieval Glass in Britain - Some Recent
    Developments.
    Medieval Archaeology, vol. 22 (1978), pp. 1-24.

HARDMAN, John T.

    Note to W.E. Chance and the Revived Manufacture of Coloured Glass.
    J.M.G.P., vol. 5, no. 4 (Oct., 1934), pp. 174-176.

    The Penancer's Window in the Nave of York Minster.
    (A discussion with KNOWLES, J.A.)
    J.M.G.P., vol. 5, no. 4 (Oct., 1934), pp. 177-179.

(Hardman, John T.)

    Obituary.
    J.M.G.P., vol. 13, no. 1 (1960), pp. 365-366.

HARDY, Charles Frederick

    On the Music in the Windows of the Beauchamp Chapel, Warwick.
    Archaeologia, vol. 61 (1909), pp. 583-614.

HARDY, V.

    La Cathédrale Saint-Pierre de Lisieux.
    Paris, 1917.

HARE, N.

    Heraldic Glass Formerly in St. Martin's Church, Liskeard.
    The Antiquary, vol. 14 (1886), pp. 113-116.

HARFORD, Dundas

    On the East Windows of St. Stephen's Church, Norwich.
    Norfolk Archaeology, vol. 15 (1904), pp. 335-348.

(Harlow Church)

    The Armorial Glass and Badges in Harlow Church.
    Transactions of the Essex Archaeological Society, vol. 11 (1910),
    p. 347.

HARMS, Julius, and ORTLIEB, Nora

    Die Ausstellung 'Alte und Neue Glas-und Wandmalerei' im
    nassauischen Landesmuseum zu Wiesbaden.
    Glastechnische Berichte, no. 12 (1934), p. 264.

HARRIES, John

    Discovering Stained Glass.
    Tring, 1968.
    Reviewed by SKEAT, Francis, J.M.G.P., vol. 14, no. 4 (1968-1969), p. 223.

HARRIS, H.A.

    The Mediaeval Glass in Yaxley Church.
    (With WOODFORDE, Christopher.)
    Proceedings of the Suffolk Institute of Archaeology, vol. 21, part 2
    (1932).

HARRISON, F.

    The West Choir Clerestory Windows in York Minster.
    Yorkshire Archaeological Journal, vol. 26 (1922), pp. 353-373.

    The Windows of York Minster.
    Journal of the British Archaeological Association, new series,
    vol. 29 (1923), pp. 96-108.

    The Bedern Chapel, York.
    The Yorkshire Archaeological Journal, vol. 27 (1924), pp. 197-210.

    The Old Glass of St. Michael-le-Belfrey Church, York.
    St. Michael-le-Belfrey Parish Magazine, (July-Dec., 1925).

    Restoration of a Clerestory Window in York Minster.
    Yorkshire Herald, Aug. 6, 1925.

    Lancets in the Transepts of York Minster.
    Yorkshire Herald, Oct. 14, 1925.

    A Yorkshire Archaeological Society Window in York Minster.
    Yorkshire Herald, Oct. 21, 1925.

    York Minster. The Te Deum Windows in the South Transept.
    Yorkshire Herald, Oct. 27, 1925.

    The West Choir Clerestory Windows in York Minster.
    Yorkshire Archaeological Journal, vol. 26.

    The Mediaeval Stained Glass of York Minster.
    (Report of a lecture before the Sheffield Literary and Philosophical
    Society.)
    Yorkshire Herald, Feb. 3, 1926.

    York Minster Windows.
    Yorkshire Herald, June 19, 21, 1926.

HARRISON, F. (Contd.)

St. Martin's Church, Coney Street (York). Some notes on its
history and its ancient glass.
York, 1926.

York Minster.
London, 1927.
(Glass, pp. 121-130.)

The Medieval Stained Glass.
In York Minster Historical Tracts, 627-1927.
Editor THOMPSON, A. Hamilton.
London, 1927. (Unpaginated.)

The Mediaeval Windows of York Minster.
Yorkshire Herald, York Minster 1300th Anniversary Supplement,
June 25, 1927.

The Painted Glass of York.
London, 1927.
(Reviewed in The Times Literary Supplement, Nov. 3, 1927.)

The Painted Glass of York Parish Churches and in the Museum.
London, 1928.

The Preservation of the Minster Windows, 1920-1932.
4th Annual Report of the Friends of York Minster (Spring, 1932),
pp. 46-56.

Treasures of Art. Stained Glass of York Minster.
London, 1937.
Reviewed in Stained Glass, vol. 32, no. 2 (Christmas, 1937), pp. 64-65.

Canterbury Tales Windows in Sheffield Cathedral.
Sheffield Telegraph, Feb. 14, 1939.

The Five Sisters Window.
11th Annual Report of the Friends of York Minster (1939), pp. 14-16.

Medieval Pictorial Art.
J.M.G.P., vol. 8, no. 3 (Apr., 1941), pp. 89-95.

The War and the Medieval Glass of York.
J.M.G.P., vol. 9, no. 1 (1943), pp. 22-23.

The Wanderings of Mediaeval Glass.
(Refutes a letter holding that the York Jesse in the Choir did
not come from New College.)
(Letter to the Editor) Country Life (June 13, 1947), p. 1119.

York Minster Glass.
Letter to The Times, Feb. 23, 1949.

(Harrison, Frederick)
Obituary, by MILNER-WHITE, Eric.
In The Dean's Letter, 31st Annual Report of the Friends of York
Minster (1959), pp. 19-20.

Obituary, by HARRISON, Kenneth.
J.M.G.P., vol. 13, no. 1 (1960), pp. 366-367.

HARRISON, Kenneth
Recent Repairs to the Windows of King's College Chapel, Cambridge.
J.M.G.P., vol. 11, no. 1 (1952), pp. 37-39.

The Windows of King's College Chapel: Notes on their History and
Design.
Cambridge, 1952.

(Harrison, Kenneth)
Review of The Windows of King's College Chapel, Cambridge: Notes on
Their History and Design.
Notes and Queries, vol. 198 (Jan., 1953), p. 43.
J.M.G.P., vol. 11, no. 2 (1953), p. 116.
By A.L., Burlington Magazine, vol. 95 (Jan.-Dec., 1953), pp. 108-109.

HARRISON, Kenneth (Contd.)
An Illustrated Guide to the Windows of King's College Chapel,
Cambridge.
Cambridge, 1953.

Notes on Sixteenth-Century Ornaments. Profile Medallions, True
Lovers' Knots and Roman Lettering.
J.M.G.P., vol. 11, no. 3 (1954), pp. 152-156.

Early Sixteenth Century Glass at Sampford Courtenay, Devon.
J.M.G.P., vol. 11, no. 4 (1955), pp. 204-205.

Obituary of HARRISON, Frederick.
J.M.G.P., vol. 13, no. 1 (1960), pp. 366-367.

HARRISON, Martin
A Burne-Jones Window.
(A long-lost Jesse Tree.)
J.M.G.P., vol. 15, no. 1 (1972-1973), pp. 63-65.

Victorian Stained Glass.
The Connoisseur, vol. 182 (Apr., 1973), pp. 251-254.

The Stained Glass of Lavers and Barraud.
The Connoisseur, vol. 183 (July, 1973), pp. 194-199.

(With WATERS, Bill.)
Burne-Jones.
London, 1973.

In Change and Decay: The Future of Our Churches.
(Editors BINNEY, Marcus, and BURMAN, Peter.)
London, 1977.
(Chapter, Stained Glass, pp. 109-113.)

HARROD, Henry
On Windows in Stained Glass, and Particularly the New West Window of
Norwich Cathedral (by Hedgeland).
The Gentleman's Magazine, vol. 42, new series, part 2 (1854), pp.
574-578.
(These severe criticisms refuted in a letter by A.T., Ibid, vol. 43
new series, part 1 (1855), p. 274.
(HARROD replies, Ibid, p. 385.)

HARTIG, Michael
Albert Figel.
Die Christliche Kunst (March, 1930).

HARTLEY, Walter
Guide Book for Selby Abbey.
Selby, 1957 (almost worthless).

HARVEY, A.S.
Cottingham Church and its Heraldry.
The Yorkshire Archaeological Journal, vol. 40, 1959-1962 (1962),
pp. 265-297.

HARVEY, F.B.
Painted Windows. A Lecture on the New West Window Presented to
Berkhamsted Church by Thomas Whately.
London, 1869.

HARVEY, John H.
The Strange Story of William of Wykham's Stained Glass - the Real
and the Copy.
Illustrated London News (Apr. 1, 1950).

HARVEY, John H. (Contd.)

Review of WOODFORDE, Christopher, Stained Glass of New College, Oxford.
Journal of the British Archaeological Association, 3rd series, vol. 14 (1951), pp. 71-72.

Thurbern's Chantry at Winchester College.
(With CHITTY, Herbert.)
Antiquaries Journal, vol. 42 (1962), pp. 208-225.

Winchester College Stained Glass.
(With KING, Dennis G.)
Part 1. History of the Glass, its Dispersal and Recovery.
Archaeologia, vol. 103, (1971), pp. 149-166.

HARWERTH, W.

Die Glasmalereien. Nach Scheiben aus der Ritterstiftskirche in Wimpfen am Neckar.
Darmstadt, 1923.

HARWOOD, Mary W.

Hastingleigh.
Canterbury (printed), 1952.
(Glass, pp. 9-12.)

HASELOCK, Jeremy, and O'CONNOR, David

The Stained and Painted Glass.
In A History of York Minster.
Oxford, 1977 (reprinted 1979), pp. 313-393.

HASELOFF, Arthur

Eine thüringisch-sächsische Malerschule des 13. Jahrhunderts.
Strasbourg, 1897.

Die Glasgemälde der Elizabethkirk in Marburg.
Berlin, 1907.

Die Glasmalereien in der Kirche zu Breitenfelde und die deutsch-nordischen Künstlerischen Beziehungen im 13. Jahrhundert.
n.p., n.d. (1937).
Reprinted from Schifferer Festschrift.

HASKINS, Charles

Notes on the Church of St. Thomas of Canterbury, Salisbury.
Salisbury, n.d.
(Vestry glass, p. 9.)

(Hassop Hall, Derbyshire)

Notes on the Heraldic Glass Formerly at Warkworth Castle, Banbury, and Now at Hassop Hall, Derbyshire.
By SCOTUS.
Notes and Queries, 5th series, vol. 12 (Oct. 18, 1879), pp. 305-306.
Replied to by CARMICHAEL, C.H., Ibid., (Oct. 25, 1879), pp. 333-334, and by P.P., Ibid. (Dec. 27, 1879), p. 517.

HASWELL, J.F.

Heraldic Glass in Edenhall Church.
Transactions of the Cumberland and Westmorland Antiquarian and Archaeological Society, vol. 15 (1899), pp. 111-113.

The Glass (of Edenhall Church).
Transactions of the Cumberland and Westmorland Antiquarian and Archaeological Society, new series, vol. 13 (1913), pp. 230-233.

HAUCK, Marie-Luise

Die Kirche zu den vierzehn Nothhelfern in Zetting.
Saarheimat (1961), fasc. 9, pp. 1-10.

HAUCK, Marie-Luise (Contd.)

Die spätmittelalterlichen Glasmalereien in Settingen.
Saarbrucker Hefte (1962), pp. 20-29.

Die 'Geburt Christi' von Martin Schongauer auf einem Gemälde in der Metzer Kathedrale.
Saarheimat, X (1966), pp. 346-347.

Glasmalereien von Hermann von Münster im Musée Lorrain in Nancy.
Raggi-Zeitschrift für Kunstgeschichte und Archäologie, vol. 8, no. 2, Basel, 1968, pp. 44-60.

Mittelalterliche Glasmalereien im historischen Museum der Pfalz, Speyer.
Mitteilungen des Historischen Vereins der Pfalz.
Band 67, Spire, 1969, pp. 242-251.

Valentin Busch und seine Beziehungen zu Italien.
In 7e Colloque du Corpus Vitrearum Medii Aevi, Florence ?, 1970, pp. 33-34.

HAUDICQUER DE BLANCOURT, J.

L'Art de la Verrerie.
(Editor JOMBERT, C.)
Paris, 1718.

HAUG, Hans

Notes sur Pierre d'Andlau.
Archives Alsaciennes d'Art et d'Histoire (1936).

La Cathédrale de Strasbourg.
Strasbourg, 1957.

HAVERGAL, F.T.

Description of the Ancient Glass in Credenhill Church, Herefordshire, Representing Archbishop Thomas à Becket and St. Thomas de Cantelupe, Bishop of Hereford.
Walsall, 1884.
Reviewed in The Archaeological Journal, vol. 41, p. 326.

HAWKINS, John S.

A History of the Origin and Establishment of Gothic Architecture . . . and an Enquiry into the Mode of Painting upon Stained Glass, as Practised in the Ecclesiastical Structures of the Middle Ages.
London, 1813.

HAWKE, D.J.

The Medieval Heraldry of York Minster.
S.R. Publishers, 1971.

HAYES, Dagmar

Ervin Bossanyi, The Splendour of Stained Glass.
Canterbury, 1965.

HAYWARD, Jane

Identification and the 'Crucifixion' Window.
Bulletin of the City Art Museum of St. Louis, vol. 42, part 2 (1957), pp. 19-22.

Review of FRANKL, Paul, Peter Hemmel, Glasmaler von Andlau.
Art Bulletin, vol. 40 (March, 1958), pp. 75-78.

Les Vitraux de la Cathédrale d'Angers.
(With GRODECKI, Louis.)
Bulletin Monumental, no. 124 (1966), pp. 7-67.

HAYWARD, Jane (Contd.)

Stained-Glass Windows from the Carmelite Church at Boppard-am-Rhein.
A Reconstruction of the Glazing Program of the North Nave.
Metropolitan Museum Journal, vol. 2 (1969), pp. 75-114.

Medieval Stained Glass from St. Leonhard in Lavanttal at The
Cloisters.
Bulletin of the Metropolitan Museum of Art, new series, vol. 28
(1969-1970), pp. 291-292.

Stained-Glass Windows.
In The Year 1200: A Background Survey.
New York, 1970, pp. 67-84.

Some English Panels in the Metropolitan Museum, New York.
In 8e Colloque du Corpus Vitrearum Medii Aevi, Paris ?, 1972,
pp. 43-44.

Glazed Cloisters and Their Development in the Houses of the
Cistercian Order.
Gesta, vol. 12 (1973), pp. 93-109.

Review of LAFOND, Jean, CVMA, France,IV, part 2.
Art Bulletin, vol. 55 (June, 1973), pp. 293-296.

The Choir Windows of Saint-Serge and Their Glazing Atelier.
Gesta, vol. 15, parts 1 and 2 (1976), pp. 255-264.
(Essays in Honor of Sumner McKnight Crosby.)

HAYWARD, John

Advisory Committees. Notes on Talk to Chairmen and Secretaries.
J.M.G.P., vol. 14, no. 5 (1970-1971), pp. 247-249.

Review of PIPER, John, Stained Glass: Art or Anti-Art.
J.M.G.P., vol. 14, no. 5 (1970-1971), pp. 252-255.

HAYWARD, John (Contd.)

Review of LEWIS, Mostyn, Stained Glass in North Wales up to 1850.
J.M.G.P., vol. 14, no. 5 (1970-1971), p. 266.

Review of WHITE, James, and WYNNE, Michael, Irish Stained Glass.
J.M.G.P., vol. 14, no. 5 (1970-1971), pp. 268-269.

HAYWARD, Lilian H.

Armorial Bearings in Atcham Church.
Transactions of the Shropshire Archaeological Society, vol. 54,
1951-1953 (1953), (Glass, pp. 215-217).

HEAL, Ambrose

Glass-Painter and Writing-Master.
(Request for information about the windows of John Langton of
Stamford.)
Notes and Queries, vol. 155 (Dec. 8, 1928), pp. 406-407.

John Rowell, Plumber and Glazier of Wycombe.
Buckinghamshire Free Press, June 10, 1932.
Reprinted Reading Mercury, July 9, 1932.

HEALES, Alfred

Cranleigh.
Surrey Archaeological Collections, vol. 6 (1879).
(Glass, pp. 29-34.)

Horley Church.
Surrey Archaeological Collections, vol. 7 (1880), pp. 172-173.

Horley Church 'Restoration'.
Ibid., vol. 8 (1883), pp. 240-242.

(Hearst, W.R.)

(Glass from the Hearst collection acquired by the International
Studio Art Corporation.)
Stained Glass, vol. 35, no. 2 (Summer, 1940), pp. 63-64.

(Heat of kiln)

Testing the Heat of the Glass Painter's Kiln.
J.M.G.P., vol. 1, no. 3 (Oct., 1925), pp. 28-29.

HEATON and BUTLER

Illustrated Catalogue of Stained Glass Windows, with Text on
Glass-Staining and Painting.
London (c. 1860).

HEATON, BUTLER and BAYNE

Designs for Works in Stained Glass, Adapted to Ecclesiastic and
Domestic Use.
London, 1864.

(Heaton, Clement)

MOBBS, Robert, Mr.Clement Heaton and His Work.
The Studio, vol. 32 (1904), pp. 212-219.

HEATON, Clement

Precious Windows of Chartres.
R.I.B.A. Journal (1906).

The Origin of the Early Stained Glass in Canterbury Cathedral.
Burlington Magazine, vol. 11 (Apr.-Sept, 1907), pp. 172-176.

Early Stained Glass and Romanesque Architecture at Rheims.
Burlington Magazine, vol. 12 (Oct., 1907-March, 1908), pp. 366-368.

The Art of Stained and Painted Glass.
The American Architect, vol. 101 (1912), pp. 13, 62, 68, 113, 141,
153, 209.
Vol. 102 (   ), pp. 1, 41, 81, 125.

(Heaton, Clement)

Obituary.
Stained Glass, vol. 35, no. 2 (Summer, 1940), pp. 59-62.

HEATON, Maurice

Progressive Steps in the Making of Stained Glass Windows.
The American Architect, (Jan. 20, 1929).

HEATON, Noel

Mediaeval Stained Glass: Its Production and Decay.
Journal of the Royal Society of Arts, vol. 55 (March 15, 1907),
pp. 468-484.

The Production and Decay of Mediaeval Stained Glass.
Nature, vol. 76 (1907), p. 19.

The Foundations of Stained Glass Work.
Journal of the Royal Society of Arts (1910), pp. 454-470.

The Production and Identification of Artificial Precious Stones.
Annual Report of the Smithsonian Institution (1911), pp. 217-234.

Stained Glass.
Journal of the R.I.B.A., 3rd series, vol. 21 (1914), pp. 325-331.

The Process of Decay in Ancient Stained Glass.
Journal of the R.I.B.A. (Aug. 27, 1920).

The Materials of the Medieval Glass Painter.
Journal of the British Society of Master Glass-Painters (1924), pp
16-27.

HEATON, Noel (Contd.)

The Technical Foundations of Stained Glass.
Bulletin of Stained Glass Association of America, vol. 21, no. 8
(Sept., 1926), pp. 7-11.

The Origin and Use of Silver Stain.
Journal of the British Society of Master-Glass-Painters (1947), pp.
9-16.

Ancient and Modern Stained Glass.
J.M.G.P., vol. 10, no. 2 (1949), pp. 74-77.

(Heaton, Noel)

Obituary by SALMOND, H.
J.M.G.P., vol. 12, no. 1 (1956), pp. 70-71.

HECQ, Gaëtan

Un Ancien Vitrail de l'Eglise de Blaton.
Annales de la Société d'Archéologie de Bruxelles, vol. 7 (1893).

HEDGELAND, J.P.

A Description Accompanied by Sixteen Coloured Plates of the Splendid
Decorations Recently Made to the Church of St. Neot, in Cornwall, at
the Sole Expense of the Reverend Richard Gerveys Grylls: by J.P.
Hedgeland.
To which are prefixed some Collections and Translations respecting
St. Neot, and the former state of his church, by Davies Gilbert, M.A.,
P.R.S., F.A.S.
London, 1830.

HEDVALL, J.A., and JAGITSCH, R.

Über das Problem der Zerstörung antiker Gläser.
Transactions of the Chalmers University of Technology, Sweden, no.
19 (1943), pp. 5-33.

HEDVALL, J.A., JAGITSCH, R. and OLSON, G.

Über das Problem der zerstörung antiker Gläser. II. Mitteilung
Über die belegung von Glasoberflächen mit Schutzfilmen.
Transactions of the Chalmers Institute of Technology, no. 118
(1951).
Reprinted from Zeitschrift für Physikal Chemie (1950), pp. 23-24.

HEDVALL, J.A.

Kulturdenkmaler und Materialkenntnis.
Zeitschrift für Metallkunde (Feb., 1952), pp. 34-37.

HEFFRON, Joseph E.

The History of Glass-Making.
Glass Container (New York), vol. 5, no. 6 (Apr., 1926), pp. 14, 15,
18, 26, 30, 32, 34, 36, 38, 40, 44, 46.

HEILBORN, Adolf

Ausstellung von Werken der Glasmalerei Schmidt in Berlin.
Zeitschrift für alte und neue Glasmalerei (1912), p. 51.

Zum Schaffen der Werkstatt J. Schmidt. Zugleich ein Wort über
moderne Glasmalerei-Probleme und verwendungsmöglichkeiten.
Ibid., (1915), pp. 7-25.

HEINEN, Eugen

Dom und Kloster Altenberg.
Dusseldorf, 2nd edition, 1951.

HEINERSDORFF, Gottfried

Die Trennung zwischen Kartonzeichner und Glasmaler. Eine
Entgegnung.
Zeitschrift für alte und neue Glasmalerei (1912), p. 126.
Ausstellung moderner Kirklicher Glasmalereien.
Keramische Rundschau, vol. 21 (1913), p. 141.

HEINERSDORFF, Gottfried

Die Glasmalerei, ihre Technik und ihre Geschichte. Mit einer
Einleitung und einem Anhang über moderne Glasmalerei von Karl
Scheffler.
Berlin, 1914.

HEINIGKE, Otto (Senior)

Rambling Thoughts of a Glassman.
The Craftsman, vol. 3 (1902), pp. 170-182.

(On the stained glass in Holy Trinity, Brooklyn.)
Architectural Review (U.S.A.), (Jan., 1906).

Rambling Thoughts of 'A Glass Man'.
Stained Glass, vol. 30, no. 3 (Winter, 1935-1936), pp. 75-90.
(Reprinted from The Craftsman, Dec., 1902).

Architectural Sympathy in Leaded Glass.
Stained Glass, vol. 32, no. 1 (Spring-Summer, 1937), pp. 5-14.
(Reprinted from The Architectural Review, Aug., 1897.)

HEINIGKE, Otto W.

American Craftsmen and Craftsmanship.
(Letter to the editor praising CONNICK, C.J.)
Stained Glass, vol. 27, no. 1 (Jan., 1932), p. 26.

Louis Comfort Tiffany. (Obituary)
Stained Glass, vol. 27, no. 12 (Dec., 1932), pp. 341-345.

Otto Heinigke.
Stained Glass, vol. 30, no. 3 (Winter, 1935-1936), pp. 71-74.

Leadership.
(An obituary of CONNICK, C.J.)
Stained Glass, vol. 41, no. 1 (Spring, 1946), pp. 20-21.

HEINIGKE, Otto W.

(Letter to the Editor on the whereabouts of some John La Farge
glass.)
J.M.G.P., vol. 13, no. 2 (1961), p. 458.

(Heinigke, Otto W.)

Obituary.
Stained Glass, vol. 63, no. 3 (Autumn, 1968), p. 22.

HEINRICH, W.

On the Yellow Staining of Glass.
Sprechsaal, 64th year, (1931), pp. 868, 890, 915, 932, 951.

HELBIG, Jean

Le Sort de la Peinture sur Verre dans l'Emancipation Progressive
de l'Activité Artistique en Belgie sous le Régime Corporatif.
Revue Belge d'Archéologie et d'Histoire de l'Art, fasc. 2 (1936),
pp. 137-150.

A Propos du Déchiffrement de Quelques Signatures sur nos Anciens
Vitraux.
L'Art et la Vie, (Nov., 1936).

Une Signature de Nicolas Rombouts.
Revue Belge d'Archéologie et d'Histoire de l'Art, fasc. 1 (1937),
pp. 5-10.

Les Plus Anciens Vitraux Conservés en Belgique.
Bulletin des Musées Royaux Bruxelles, 3rd series, vol. 9, no. 1 (1937),
pp. 1-11.

Faveurs et Sévérités du Sort.
Clarté (June, 1937), pp. 5-8.

L'Introduction du Style Renaissance dans nos Vitraux à l'Epoque
Austro-Espagnole.
Bulletin des Musées Royaux Bruxelles, 3rd series, vol. 9, no. 3 (1937),
pp. 49-60.

HELBIG, Jean (Contd.)

Arnold de Nimègue et le Problème de son Identité.
L'Art et la Vie (Sept., 1937).

Origine Anversoise de la Peinture sur Verre Dite à l'Apprêt.
Revue Belge de l'Archéologie et d'Histoire de l'Art, vol. 8,
part 3 (July-Sept., 1938), pp. 197-209.

La Peinture sur Verre dans les Pays-Bas Méridionaux.
Annales de la Société Royale d'Archéologie de Bruxelles, vol. 42
(1938), pp. 147-183.

Peintures sur Verre Revenues d'Angleterre.
Bulletin des Musées Royaux d'Art et d'Histoire. no. 1 (1938), pp. 7-10.

Circulation de Modèles d'Ateliers au XIVe Siècle.
Revue Belge d'Archéologie et d'Histoire de l'Art, vol. 8, part 2
(Apr.-June, 1938), pp. 113-118.

The Bird's-Eye View in Stained Glass of the Middle Ages.
J.M.G.P. vol. 7, no. 3 (Oct., 1938), pp. 110-115.
(Extra list in J.M.G.P., vol. 8, no. 2 (Apr., 1940), p. 76.

The Clemency and Harshness of Fate.
J.M.G.P., vol. 7, no. 4 (Apr., 1939), pp. 160-163.

Nicolas Rombouts, Peintre Verrier et Bourgeois de Bruxelles.
Bulletin de la Société Royale d'Archéologie de Bruxelles, no. 1
(1939), pp. 3-23.

Le Point de Vue Plongeant, dans le Vitrail au Moyen Age.
Revue Belge d'Archéologie et d'Histoire de l'Art, fasc. 2 (1939),
pp. 117-120.

Aperçus sur la Profession de Verrier en Belgique du XIIe au XVIIIe
Siècle.
Verre et Silicates Industriels, vol. 10, nos. 6, 7 (1939), pp. 64-68,
76-79.

A Flemish Armorial Window.
(Attributes Flemish glass in The Cloisters to Nicholas Rombouts.)
(See STEINBERG, S.H., 1939.)
Burlington Magazine, vol. 75 (1939), p. 42.

Une Ancienne Verrière de Gilde Militaire Malinoise.
Bulletin des Musées Royaux d'Art et d'Histoire, no. 3 (1940), pp. 50-60.

'Dépose' de Verrières Historiques.
Bulletin des Musées Royaux d'Art et d'Histoire, no. 6 (1940), p. 137.

Meesterwerken van de glasschilderkunst in de oude Nederlanden.
Antwerp, 1941.

Portraits de Donateurs dans nos Vitraux Anciens.
Revue Belge d'Archéologie et d'Histoire de l'Art, fasc. 1 (1941),
pp. 53-58.

L'Envers de Vieux Vitraux.
Bulletin des Musées Royaux d'Art et d'Histoire, no. 3 (1941), pp.
52-59.

Verrières Héraldiques de la Famille de Charles Quint.
Revue Belge d'Archéologie et d'Histoire de l'Art, fasc. 4 (1941),
pp. 245-262.

Une Verrière Historique à l'Eglise Saint Jacques d'Anvers.
Arc-en-Ciel (Sept. 11, 1941), pp. 8-9.

Confidences de Vieilles Verrières.
Apollo (Nov. 1, 1941), pp. 12-14.

Une Ancienne Verrière de l'Eglise Saint-Pierre d'Anderlecht.
Antwerp, 1942.

De oude glasremen van de Collegiale Sinte-Goedele te Brussel.
Antwerp, 1942.

Oud-Antwerpsche School van Glazeniers.
Antwerp, 1943.

HELBIG, Jean (Contd)

De Glasschilderkunst in Belgie: repertorium en documenten.
(With DOURMONT, R., Van Steenberghe de.)
The Hague, vol. 1, 1943, vol. 2, 1951.
Vol. 1 reviewed by BOOM, A. van der, in Burlington Magazine, vol. 89
(Jan.-Dec., 1947), pp. 109-110.
Vol. 2 reviewed by RACKHAM Bernard, Burlington Magazine, vol. 93
(Jan.-Dec., 1951), p. 365,
and J.M.G.P., vol. 10, no. 1 (1948), pp. 47-49.

Jacques Floris va-t-il enfin se reveler?
Revue Belge d'Archéologie, vol. 14 (1944), pp. 129-139.

Portraits of Donors in Flemish Glass-Painting.
J.M.G.P., vol. 9, no. 3 (1945), pp. 73-77.

L'Iconographie Eucharistique dans le Vitrail Belge.
Antwerp, 1946.

A Survey of Belgian Glass.
Stained Glass, vol. 44, no. 3 (Autumn, 1949), pp. 73-76.

The Craft of the Glass-Painter in Belgium from the 12th to the
18th Century.
J.M.G.P., vol. 10, no. 2 (1949), pp. 61-66.
J.M.G.P., vol. 10, no. 3 (1950), pp. 136-141.

Les Auteurs des Verrières d'Hoogstraten.
Revue Belge d'Archéologie, vol. 18 (1949), pp. 35-52.

De Glazeniers.
Reprinted from Flandria Nostra, n.d. (? 1951).

L'Evolution du Décor Architectural dans le Vitrail Belge Pendant
le Premier Quart du 16e Siècle.
, 1951-1952.

Le Céramique et le Vitrail dans l'Ancien Namurois.
Etudes d'Histoire et Archéologie Namuroises (1952).

Anciennes Verrières de l'Abbaye de Parc.
Bulletin des Musées Royales d'Art et d'Histoire (1958), pp. 71-82.

Les Vitraux Médiévaux Conservés en Belgique, 1200-1500.
(CVMA, Belgium, 1.)
Brussels, 1962.
Reviewed by GRODECKI, Louis, Bulletin Monumental, vol. 121 (1963),
pp. 214-216.

Les Vitraux de la Première Moitié du 16e Siècle Conservés en
Belgique, Province d'Anvers et Flandre.
(CVMA, Belgium 2.)
Brussels, 1968.

HELBIG, Jules

Les Vitraux de l'Ancienne Eglise Abbatiale des Dames Nobles de
Herckenrode.
Bulletin des Commissions Royales d'Art et d'Archéologie, vol. 15
(1877), pp. 366-382.

HELBING, Hugo

Sammlung Lord Sudeley. Schweizer Glasmalereien vorwiegend des 16
und 17 Jahrhunderts.
(Introduction by:)
Hans Lehmann: Die ehemalige Sammlung schweizerischer Glasmalereien
in Toddington Castle.
Munich, 1911.

HELIOT, Pierre

Les Origines et les Débuts de l'Abside Vitrée (11e-13e Siècles).
Wallraf-Richartz Jahrbuch (1968), pp. 89-127.

(Heraldic Glass)

English Armorial Glass. By G.W.M.
(Request for corroboration of identities.)
Notes and Queries, 6th series, vol. 5 (Jan. 21, 1882), pp. 44-45.
Replied to by P.P., Ibid., (March 4, 1882), p. 178.

HERBERGER, Theodor

Die ältesten Glasgemälde im Dome zu Augsburg, mit der Geschichte
des Dombaus in der romanischen Kunstperiode . . .
Augsburg, 1860.

(Herefordshire)

List of Stained-Glass Windows Inserted in Herefordshire Churches
1929-1948, with Names of Designers.
Transactions of the Woolhope Naturalists' Field Club, vol. 33,
1949, 1950, 1951 (1952), p. 88.

HERTEL, Bernhard

Die Glasgemälde des Kölner Domes.
Die Bibelfenster, die Allerheiligenfenster in der Johanneskapelle
und die Königsfenster im Obergaden des hohen Chores.
Berlin, 1925.

(Herzogenbuchsee Church, Switzerland)

Die Bergpredigt. Reproduktion des Originalkartons zu den
Glasmalereien für die Kirche zu Herzogenbuchsee (Schweiz).
Basel, 1914.
(Also in a French version.)

HESS, Robert

Modern Stained Glass in Switzerland.
(Translated by FIVIAN, Lina, from Neue Glasmalerei in der Schweiz,
Basel, 1939.)
Stained Glass, vol. 35, no. 2 (Summer, 1940), pp. 41-47.

HESSE, Karl

Die Glasveredelung.
Leipzig, 1928.

HETTES, Karel

O Ochrane Sklenených Pamatak Pres Odskelnovanim.
Zpravy Pamatkove Pece, no. 14 (1955), pp. 240-245.

HEUDUIN, M.

A Pane of Sixteenth-Century Glass Restored to the Church of Saint
Pierre de Roye.
Bulletin de la Société des Antiquaires de Picardie, part 3 (1934).

HEUSS, Th.

Ausstellung des Kunstlerbundes für Glasmalerei.
Dekorative Kunst München, vol. 14 (Dec., 1911), pp. 129-136.

HEY, C.W.

Catalogue of Drawings from Ancient Glass. Exhibited at the
Arundel Society's Room.
London, 1865.

HEYE, Eva

Die Rundscheiben aus Schloss Erbach in der Skulpturen-Abtalung.
Berliner Museen, 15 (1965), pp. 49-57.

HEYNE, Moritz

Zur Geschichte der deutschen Glasmalerei.
Sprechsaal, vol. 14 (1881), pp. 130, 154.

Die Basler Glasmalerei des 16. Jahrhunderts und die Scheiben des
Basler Schützenhauses.
Basel, 1883.

HIBGAME, F.T.

Artists in Stained Glass.
(Request for a list of artists in the 18th and 19th centuries.)
Notes and Queries, 12th series, vol. 3 (May, 1917), p. 299.
Replied to by MAGRATH, J.R., BENSLY, E., TAPLEY-SOPER, H, Ibid.,
(Aug., 1917), pp. 396-397.

HICKL-SZABO, H.

Stained Glass in Austria.
Journal of the Royal Ontario Museum (Toronto), (1965), pp. 87-92.

HICKMAN, Helen Carew

American Stained Glass in Architecture.
Stained Glass, vol. 49, no. 2 (Summer, 1954), pp. 65-70.

(Hiemer, Edward W.)

Obituary.
Stained Glass, vol. 64, no. 4 (Winter, 1969-1970), pp. 18-20.

HIEMER, George

The Choir Rose Window in Notre Dame, Cathedral, Paris.
Stained Glass, vol. 37, no. 2 (Summer, 1942), pp. 62-64.

(Hiemer, George)

Obituary.
Stained Glass, vol. 50, no. 2 (Summer, 1955), pp. 71-73.

HIGGINS, Walter

Making of a Stained-Glass Window.
Scholastic and Woman Teachers' Chronicle, (Nov. 28, 1929).

HILDBURGH. W.L.

An Alabaster Table of the Annunciation with the Crucifix: a Study
in English Iconography.
Archaeologia, vol. 74 (1924), pp. 203-232.

Some Further Notes on the Crucifix on the Lily.
Antiquaries Journal, vol. 12, no. 1 (Jan., 1932), pp. 24-26.

HILL, D. Ingram

With COUNCER, C.R.
Ancient Heraldic Glass at Wickham Court, West Wickham, Kent.
J.M.G.P., vol. 11, no. 2 (1953), pp. 94-104.

Thirteenth Century Stained Glass for Canterbury Cathedral.
(The Hearst Glass.)
35th Annual Report of the Friends of Canterbury Cathedral (1962),
(centre pages, 1-3).

(Hill, D. Ingram)

Review of Stained Glass in Canterbury Cathedral, by SPENCE, Horace,
36th Annual Report of the Friends of Canterbury Cathedral (1963), p. 24.

HILL, D. Ingram

Additions to the Stained Glass of the Cathedral.
Canterbury Cathedral Chronicle, no. 59 (Autumn, 1964), pp. 36-38.

Storied Windows.
Chough, no. 7 (1964).

The Stained Glass of Canterbury Cathedral.
Canterbury, n.d.

Ancient Heraldic Glass at Knole, Sevenoaks.
Archaeologia Cantiana, vol. 91 (1975), pp. 1-14.

HILLS, A.

Stained Glass Formerly at New Hall.
The Essex Review, vol. 37, no. 145 (Jan., 1928), pp. 66-70.

HIMSWORTH, J.B.

Medieval Stained Glass and Some Places Where It May Be Seen.
Transactions of the Hunterian Archaeological Society, vol. 3, no. 3
(Dec., 1927), pp. 262-263.

HIMSWORTH, J.B.

Some Fragments of Stained Glass in South Yorkshire and Derbyshire.
J.M.G.P., vol. 3, no. 2 (Oct., 1929), pp. 66-73.

Old Stained Glass in South Yorkshire and Derbyshire.
J.M.G.P., vol. 4, no. 2 (Oct., 1931), pp. 65-70.

With JARVIS, A.C.E.
Notes on Old Painted Glass Formerly in St. Luke's Church, Hollis Croft, Sheffield.
J.M.G.P., vol. 9, no. 4 (1946), pp. 110-114.

(Hinton-in-the-Hedges Church)

Hinton-in-the-Hedges Church, Northamptonshire: Glass.
(Grant towards re-leading a window.)
The Pilgrim Trust, 43rd Annual Report (1973), p. 15.

HIRTH, F.

Formenschatz der Renaissance.
4 vols, Munich, 1877-1881.

HOBLEY, Brian

Excavations at the Cathedral and Benedictine Priory of St. Mary, Coventry.
Transactions of the Birmingham and Warwickshire Archaeological Society, vol. 84 (for 1967-1970).
(Excavation and analysis of glass, pp. 96-107.)
(Report on the glass by NEWTON, P.A., pp. 107-111.)
(Report on the glass by PLESTERS, J., p. 111.)

HOCKMAN, William S.

A Layman's Response to Stained Glass.
Stained Glass, vol. 58, no. 3 (Autumn, 1963), pp. 31-37.

HODGE, E.W.

Stained Glass of the Nineteenth Century and Later in the Diocese of Carlisle.
Transactions of the Cumberland and Westmorland Antiquarian and Archaeological Society, new series, vol. 76 (1976), pp. 199-213.

(Some additional Notes.)
Ibid., vol. 77 (1977), pp. 183-184.

HOFF, August

Die religiose Kunst Johann Thorn Prikkers. (Der Weisse Reiter.)
Dusseldorf, 1914.

HOFFMANN, H.

Die Chorfenster der St. Bonifatiuskirche zu Berlin.
Rostock, c. 1927.

HOFMANN, H.

Mosaik und Glasmalerei auf der Juryfreien Kunstschau, Berlin, 1927.
Sprechsaal, 60th year, no. 34 (Aug. 25, 1927), pp. 614-616.

HOGAN, James H.

The Windows in the Great Central Space of Liverpool Cathedral.
Journal of the Society of Glass Technology, vol. 23 (1939), pp. 239-241.

Stained Glass.
Journal of the Royal Society of Arts, vol. 88 (May 3, 1940).
J.M.G.P., vol. 8, no. 3 (Apr., 1941), pp. 109-125.

(Hogan, James H.)

Obituary, by SCOTT, Giles Gilbert.
J.M.G.P., vol. 10, no. 1 (1948), pp. 50-51.

Obituary by TRETHOWAN, Harry.
The Studio, vol. 135 (1948), pp. 156-157.

(Hogan, James H.)

Obituary.
Stained Glass, vol. 43, no. 1 (Spring, 1948), p. 31.

(Holbein, Hans)

Die angeblichen Holbein - Glasgemälde in Augsburg.
Diamant (Nov. 11 1925), pp. 686-688.

Die Glasgemälde Hans Holbeins der älterre im Dome zu Eichstätt in Franken.
Diamant, 48th year, no. 16 (June 1, 1926), pp. 306-307.

HOLDEN, E.W.

Excavations at the Deserted Medieval Village of Hangleton.
Sussex Archaeological Collections, no. 101 (1963).
(Discovery of window glass, p. 110.)

HOLIDAY, Henry

Stained Glass as an Art.
London, 1896.

HOLIDAY, Henry

Design for a Church Window.
Art Journal (1830), p. 31.

The Crucifixion Window in Holy Trinity Church, New York.
Art Journal (1904), pp. 23-24.

(Holiday, Henry)

Decorative Work of Henry Holiday.
International Studio, vol. 37 (Apr., 1909), pp. 106-115.

Obituary.
J.M.G.P., vol. 2, no. 2 (Oct., 1927), pp. 105-106.

(Holland of Warwick)

(Glass by Holland of Warwick in Stratford-on-Avon and elsewhere.)
Art Journal, (1855), p. 218.

HOLLANDE, M.

La Cathédrale de Reims.
Paris, n.d.

HOLLIS, Edwin

Design in Glass Quarry, Sixteenth or Seventeenth Century.
(Request for identification.)
Notes and Queries, vol. 151 (Aug. 14, 1926), p. 117.
Suggested solution given by WARD, Frank, Ibid., (Oct. 16, 1926), p. 283.

HOLLOWAY, A.V.

(On restoring glass at St. Mary's, Shrewsbury.)
(In Recent and Current Work by Members.)
J.M.G.P., vol. 14, no. 3 (1967), pp. 163-174.

(Letter giving an account of his restoration of the Willement windows at Penrhyn Castle.)
J.M.G.P., vol. 14, no. 4 (1968-1969), pp. 215-216.

(Holt, Henry F.)

The Painted Glass at Fairford, Gloucestershire.
(Report of his paper attributing the Fairford windows to Dürer.)
The Times, Aug. 13, 1868.

HOLT, Henry F.

The Painted Glass in Fairford Church, and Albert Dürer.
The Builder, vol. 26 (Aug., 15, 1868), pp. 598-601.
(He repeats and strengthens his statement, Ibid., (Aug. 22, 1868), pp. 615-617.)

HOLT, Henry F. (Contd.)

 The Fairford Windows.
 (Letter to the Editor.)
 The Times, Aug. 19, 1868.

 (On the Fairford glass.)
 (Letter to the Editor.)
 The Standard, Sept. 15, 1868.

 The 'St. Christopher of 1423'.
 (Discussion of Fairford windows.)
 Notes and Queries, 4th series, vol. 2 (Sept. 19, 1868), pp. 265-267.

 The Fairford Windows.
 Notes and Queries, 4th series, vol. 2 (Sept. 26, 1868), pp. 306-307.

 Observations upon Early Engraving and Printing.
 (Connected with the Fairford discussion.)
 Ibid., (Oct. 17, 1868), pp. 361-364.

HONE, Evie Sydney

 Modern Stained Glass in France and Holland.
 Art Notes (Summer, 1940).

(Hone, Evie Sydney)

 Obituary by RIVERS, Elizabeth.
 J.M.G.P., vol. 12, no. 1 (1956), pp. 71-73.

HONEY, W.B.

 Our Stained Glass.
 (Review of READ, Herbert, English Stained Glass.)
 Burlington Magazine, vol. 50 (Jan.-June, 1927), pp. 219-220.

HONORÉ-DUVERGE, Suzanne

 Le Prétendu Vitrail de Charles le Mauvais à la Cathédrale d'Evreux.
 Bulletin Monumental, vol. 101 (1942).

HOOD, Fred

 Merkwürdige GlasgemÄlde.
 St. Lucas (Deutsche Glaser Zeitung), vol. 10 (1899), p. 100.

HOOD, Peter

 The Photography of Stained Glass.
 J.M.G.P., vol. 3, no. 4 (Oct., 1930), pp. 118-122.

HORNABROOK, Charles

 Painted Glass.
 Furniture Gazette, London, vol. 23 (1885), pp. 135, 155.

HORNE, Ethelbert

 A Crucifixion Panel in Wells Cathedral.
 J.M.G.P., vol. 3, no. 1 (Apr., 1929), p. 12.

 Marks on the Glass at Wells.
 (A discussion with ROBINSON, J. Armitage, and KNOWLES, J.A.)
 J.M.G.P., vol. 4, no. 2 (Oct., 1931), pp. 74-77.

 'Scrap' Windows.
 Notes and Queries, vol. 181 (Sept. 20, 1941), p. 164.

(Hornsey Church, Middlesex)

 (Window by David Evans inserted.)
 The Gentleman's Magazine, vol. 4, new series, part 2 (1835), pp. 413-414.

(West Horsley Church, Surrey)

 (Drawings of the old glass exhibited by R.C. Hussey at the Society of Antiquaries.)
 The Gentleman's Magazine, vol. 101, part 1 (1831), p. 163.

HOSKEN, Clifford

 The Recently Discovered Window at Chelsea.
 J.M.G.P., vol. 1, no. 1 (Apr., 1924), pp. 6-10.

 Review of SHERRILL, C.H., Stained Glass Tours in Spain and Flanders.
 J.M.G.P., vol. 1, no. 4 (Apr., 1926), pp. 42-44.

 An Eighteenth Century English Woman Glass-Painter.
 (Eglington Margaret Pearson.)
 The Connoisseur, vol. 69 (May-Aug., 1924), pp. 133-134.

HOTBLACK, J.T.

 The Armorial Bearings of the City of Norwich.
 Norfolk Archaeology, vol. 17 (1910), pp. 245-243.

HOUGHTON, F.T.S.

 On the Sixteenth Century Glass in the Church of St. Neot, Cornwall.
 Transactions of the Birmingham Archaeological Society, vol. 44 for 1918 (1920), pp. 141-142.

HOUSDEN, J.A.J.

 Jesse Window.
 (Flemish, at Wimborne Minster.)
 Notes and Queries, 8th series, vol. 8 (July 27, 1895), p. 75.

(Westminster, House of Lords)

 Painted Glass in the House of Lords.
 Dublin University Magazine, vol. 29 (1846), p. 131.

HOUVET, Emile

 Les Vitraux de la Cathédrale de Chartres.
 4 vols, Chartres, 1926.
 (With DELAPORTE, Yves.)
 Partly translated in Chartres Cathedral, Chartres, 1972.

 Chartres, Ses Vitraux.
 Chartres, n.d.

HOVEY, Walter Reed

 Some Relationships between the Art Motifs of the Pre-Romanesque Period and Early Stained Glass.
 Stained Glass, vol. 35, no. 4 (Winter, 1940), pp. 104-110.

HOWARD, E.G.

 Ancient and Modern Painted Glass.
 National Review, vol. 9 (1887), p. 793.

HOWARD, Frank

 St. Helen's Crown Glass Company. Trade Book of Patterns for Ornamental Windows (Glass), with Designs for Church, Hall, Staircase and Memorial Windows by Frank Howard.
 St. Helens, 1850.

 Stained Glass as a Means of Decoration.
 Civil Engineering and Architectural Journal, vol. 16 (1853), p. 169.

HOWARD, Len

 Stained Glass for the Future.
 Stained Glass, vol. 41, no. 3 (Autumn, 1946), pp. 87-91.

HOWARD, T.W.
    Cost Accounting for Stained Glass Manufacturers.
    National Glass Budget, (Pittsburgh) (June 27, 1925).

HOWSON, Joan
    Wilhelmina Margaret Geddes, (Obituary).
    J.M.G.P., vol. 12, no. 1 (1956), pp. 69-70.

    East Window of South Choir, Newark Parish Church.
    J.M.G.P., vol. 12, no. 4 (1959), pp. 264-269.

    (Letter to the Editor quoting from a letter of LAFOND, Jean, on
    restoration technique.)
    J.M.G.P., vol. 13, no. 2 (1961), p. 457.

(Howson, Joan)
    Obituary, by ROPE, M.E. Aldrich.
    J.M.G.P., vol. 14, no. 2 (1965), pp. 111-112.

HOYLE, Alexander E.
    Stained Glass in the Nave. The Cathedral of St. John the Divine
    (New York).
    The Churchman (New York), (Nov., 1945).

HUBBUCK, Rodney
    Curiosities in English Stained Glass, 1837-1914.
    J.M.G.P., vol. 17, no. 2 (1978-1979), pp. 57-64.

HUBBARD, Hesketh
    Old Stained Glass in England.
    Wonderful Britain, no. 25 (n.d.).

HUBER, Hans
    Glasmalerei im Mittelalter.
    Diamant, vol. 47 (Oct. 1, 1925), pp. 589-590.

    Glas-gemälde im bayerischen Nationalmuseum zu München.
    Diamant, 50th year, no. 24 (Aug. 21, 1928)
                  no. 25 (Sept. 1, 1928).

HUBERT, Jean
    Les Origines de l'Art Français.
    Paris, 1947.

HUCH, Richard
    (Introduction to.)
    Farbenfenster grosser Kathedralen d. 12 u. 13 Jahrhunderts (mit
    Geleitwort v. Ricarda Huch).
    Leipzig, 1937.

HUCHER, Eugène
    Etudes Artistiques et Archéologiques sur le Vitrail de la Rose de
    la Cathédrale du Mans.
    Bulletin Monumental, vol. 14 (1848), pp. 345-

    Calques des Vitraux de la Cathédrale du Mans.
    Paris and Le Mans, 1854-1864.

    Vitraux Peints de la Cathédrale du Mans.
    Paris and Le Mans, 1865.

    Le Vitrail Absidal de Nôtre-Dame de la Cour.
    Bulletin Monumental, vol. 45 (1879), p. 314.

    La Restauration du Vitrail de Beillé (Sarthe) aux Armes de
    Montmorency-Bois-Dauphin.
    Tours, 1883.

    La Restauration de Vitraux de l'Eglise de Soire-le-Château (Nord).
    Bulletin Monumental, vol. 49 (1883), p. 643.
    Reprinted Tours, 1883.

HUDD, Alfred E.
    Some Old Glass from the Temple Church, Bristol, Representing St.
    Katherine of Alexandria, and Other Saints.
    Proceedings of the Clifton Antiquarian Club, vol. 6 (1905), pp. 62-76.

HUDIG, Ferrand
    Quelques Vitraux de 16e Siècle.
    La Revue d'Art, part 24 (1922-1923), pp. 98-112.

HUDLESTON, F., and C.R.
    Medieval Glass in Penrith Church.
    Transactions of the Cumberland and Westmorland Antiquarian and
    Archaeological Society, new series, vol. 51 (1951), pp. 96-102.

HUDSON, Henry A.
    Ancient Glass of the Cathedral Church of Manchester.
    Transactions of the Lancashire and Cheshire Antiquarian Society,
    vol. 25 (1907), pp. 119-145.

HUGHES, H. Harold
    Llanrhychwyn Church and its Painted Windows.
    Archaeologia Cambrensis, vol. 82 (1927), pp. 113-127.

    (Llangadwaladr Church, Anglesey.)
    (Report of a description of the glass.)
    Archaeologia Cambrensis, vol. 85 (1930), pp. 467-468.

    Heraldic Glass at Godney.
    (Of 1839.)
    Notes and Queries for Somerset and Dorset, vol. 20 (1930-1932), pp.
    206-207.

HUGHES, T. Cann
    Stained Glass in Oxford.
    (Request for location of a panel.)
    Notes and Queries, vol. 167 (Sept. 29, 1934), p. 224.

(Hull, Holy Trinity Church)
    (Parmentier's east window removed and the usable part presented to
    Hessle church.)
    The Gentleman's Magazine, vol. 101, part 2 (1831), p. 453.

HULME, E. Wyndham
    On English Mediaeval Window Glass.
    The Antiquary, vol. 43 (1907), pp. 56-59.

    Chapters in the History of Glass Making and Painting in England.
    Utynam's Patent for the Glazing of the King's Chapels, A.D. 1449.
    The Antiquary, vol. 51 (1915), pp. 288, 422.

    Glaziers' Bills at Coldharbour and Westminster, 1485-1531.
    The Antiquary, (Nov., 1915), pp. 422-426.

    John Prudde: King's Glazier.
    Notes and Queries, 12th series, vol. 2 (Dec. 23, 1916), p. 517.

    Barnard Flower, the King's Glazier.
    Notes and Queries, 12th series, no. 4 (Jan., 1918), pp. 19-20.

    Glass-Workers in North Staffordshire.
    (Letter to the Editor.)
    J.M.G.P., vol. 4, no. 1 (Apr., 1931), p. 44.

    Review of T. PAPE's Mediaeval Glass-Workers in North Staffordshire.
    J.M.G.P., vol. 5, no. 4 (Oct., 1934), p. 196.

HULST, Henri D'.
    Kunstglasramen in de collegiale kerk van Sint-Gummarus te Lier.
    Antwerp, 1956.

HUME, Raphael

    A Window in the Chapel of Canterbury School.
    Stained Glass (Sept.,1933).

HUMMEL, Richard

    Chemicals Used in Glass Making.
    Stained Glass, vol. 40, no. 2 (Summer, 1945), pp. 39-47.

    Coloring and Opalescent Agents in Glass.
    Stained Glass, vol. 40, no. 3 (Autumn, 1945), pp. 79-85.

HUMPHREYS, N. Noel

    The Fairford Windows.
    (Letter to the Editor.)
    The Times, Aug. 21, 1868.

(Hungarian Glass-Painting)

    Das neue glasmalerische Ideal in ungarischer Fassung.
    Zeitschrift für alte und neue Glasmalerei (1914), p. 118.

HUNT, Henry

    The Autobiography of Henry Hunt.
    (Stained glass workshop life in England and the U.S.A. in the late
    nineteenth century.)
    Stained Glass, vol. 36, no. 4 (Winter, 1941), pp. 118-122.

HUNT, J.E.

    The Glass in St. Mary's Church, Shrewsbury.
    Shrewsbury, 1951.

HUNT, Thomas F.

    Exemplars of Tudor Architecture adapted to Modern Habitations . . .
    London, 1830.

HUNTER, K.S.

    Sales Catalogue of Elizabethan Panelling and Heraldic Stained Glass
    Windows in 'The Great Chamber' of Gilling Castle.
    (Sotheby and Co.)
    London, 1929.

HÜSGEN, Heinrich S.

    Nachrichten von Franckfurter Künstlern und Kunstsachen, enthaltene
    des Leben und die Wercke . . . Nebst einem Anhang von allem was in
    öffentlichen und Privat-Gebäuden, merckwürdiges von Kunst-Sachen
    zu sehen ist.
    Frankfurt, 1780.
    (Another edition, Frankfurt, 1790.)

HUSSEY, A.

    Notes on the Churches in the Counties of Kent, Sussex and Surrey, etc.
    London, 1852.

HUSSEY, Christopher

    Highcliffe Castle, Hampshire.
    (Glass from Jumièges.)
    Country Life, vol. 91 (1942), pp. 806-808, 844-857, 902-905.

HUSSEY, R.C.

    A Note on Mediaeval Window Casements and Shutters.
    Archaeologia Cantiana, vol. 10 (1876), pp. 90-92.

HUTCHINSON, F.E.

    Medieval Glass at All Soul's College. A History and Description,
    Based upon the Notes of the Late G.M. Rushforth.
    London, 1949.
    Reviewed in J.M.G.P., vol. 10, no. 3 (1950), p. 163.
    Reviewed by READ, Herbert, Burlington Magazine, vol. 92 (Jan.-Dec.,
    1950), p. 55.
    Reviewed in Oxoniensia, vol. 15 for 1950 (1952), pp. 117-118.
    Reviewed by F.G.R., The Connoisseur, vol. 127 (May, 1951), pp. 126-127.

HUTCHINSON, G.P.

    The Devotional Aspect of Stained Glass.
    Ornamental Glass Bulletin, (Chicago)(Jan., 1925).

    Liverpool Stained Glass.
    International Studio (Oct., 1925).

HUTH, Franz

    Glas in Blei. Ein neues Musterwerk.
    Hamburg, 1924.

    Glasses for Art Glazing.
    Diamant, no. 28 (1924).

    The Beginnings of Glass-Painting.
    Diamant, no. 34 (1924).

    History of the Manufacture of Gold Ruby.
    Diamant, no. 1 (1925).

HUTTER, Heribert

    Medieval Stained Glass.
    Translated by M. SHENFIELD.
    London, 1964.

HUTTON, W.H.

    Highways and Byways in Shakespeare's Country.
    London, 1914.
    (A few references to Warwickshire glass.)

HUXLEY, Aldous

    An Artist in Stained Glass.
    (Joep Nicolas.)
    The Studio, vol. 101 (Jan.-June, 1931), pp. 125-128.

(Iconography)

    Zur Typologie der mittelalterlichen Glasgemälde.

    Zeitschrift für alte und neue Glasmalerei (1912), pp. 56-58.

ILG, Albert

    Die Tiroler Glasmalerei 1882-1886.

    Innsbruck, 1886.

IMAGE, Selwyn

    St.Michael and St. Uriel: Designs by Mr. Ford Madox Brown for
Painted Glass.

    Century Guild Hobby-Horse, vol. 5 (July, 1890), pp. 112-119.

(Image, Selwyn)

    The Work of Mr. Selwyn Image. (Part 1.)

    The Studio, vol. 14 (1898), pp. 3-10.

    Obituary.

    J.M.G.P., vol. 3, no. 4 (Oct., 1930), p. 203.

The Importation of Stained Glass Windows Duty Free.

    National Glass Budget, 43rd year, no. 22 (Oct. 1, 1927).

INGLEBY, C.

    Denton and its Glass.

    In Supplement to Blomefield's Norfolk, 1929.

(International Exhibition, London, 1862)

    Stained Glass at the International Exhibition, London, 1862.

    Civil Engineer and Architect's Journal, vol. 25 (1862), p. 321.

(International Exhibition, London, 1872)

    Art Journal Illustrated Catalogue of the International Exhibition,
London, 1872.

    London, 1872.

    (Stained glass, pp. 19, 62.)

JACKSON, E.

    Clifton Hall and its Owners.

    (Clifton church glass now at Swindale described.)

    Transactions of the Cumberland and Westmorland Antiquarian and
Archaeological Society, new series, vol. 12 (1912), pp. 139-140.

JACKSON, Francis M.

    Jesse Window.

    (Request for information about illustrations of them.)

    Notes and Queries, 8th series, vol. 8 (July 13, 1895), pp. 28-29.

    Replied to by BEAZELEY, Alex, Ibid.,(July 27, 1895), p. 75;

    HOUSDEN, J.A.J., Ibid., (July 27, 1895), p. 75;

    COLEMAN, E.H., Ibid., (July 27, 1895), p. 75;

    WARD, C.A., Ibid., (July 27, 1895), p. 75;

    E.L.G. (who denies there ever was one at Salisbury), Ibid., (July
27, 1895), p. 75;

    WALKER, Ben, Ibid, (Aug. 17, 1895), p. 133;

    E.L.G., Ibid, (Aug. 17, 1895), p. 133;

    J.T.F(owler), Ibid, (Aug. 17, 1895), p. 133;

    GOWER, A.F.G. Leveson, Ibid, (Aug. 31, 1895), p. 178;

    MARSHALL, Edward H., Ibid, (Dec. 28, 1895), p. 511.

    (For earlier sequence of correspondence see JESSE Windows.)

JACKSON, Thomas Graham

    Some Account of St. Mary's, the Parish Church of Wimbledon.

    Surrey Archaeological Collections, vol. 34 (1921), pp. 1-14.

JACOBI, R.

    Das Konservierungsverfahren für die Obergadenfenster des Kölner
Domes.

    Kölner Domblatt, no. 9 (1955), pp. 122-130.

    Die Konservierung alter Glasmalereien des Kölner Domes.

    Glastechnische Berichte, no. 30 (1957), pp. 509-514.

    Reprinted Frankfort-am-Main, 1957.

    Fehlurteile, über die Restaurierung der Domfenster-Entgegnung auf
einen Aufsatz von G. Frenzel.

    Kölner Domblatt, nos. 18, 19 (1960), pp. 167-170.

    Ein Konservierungsverfahren für mittelalterliche Glasfenster auf
der Basis der modernen Sicherheitsglastechnik.

    Glas-Email-Keramo-Technik, no. 22 (1971), pp. 172-174.

Inventaire Général des Monuments et des Richesses Artistique de la France.

    No. 1, Brittany (Finistère, Canton Carhaix-Plouger).

    Paris, 1969.

    (First in the series.)

Inventaire Général des Monuments et des Richesses Artistiques de la France.

    Répertoire des Inventaires, Limousin.

    Paris, 1970.

IRONS, E.A.

    North Luffenham Church and North Luffenham Hall.

    10th Annual Report and Transactions of the Rutland Archaeological
and Natural History Society (1913), pp. 53-

ISENBERG, Anita and Seymour

    How to Work in Stained Glass.

    Philadelphia, New York and London, 1972.

    Reviewed by SKEAT, Francis, J.M.G.P., vol. 15, no. 2 (1973-1974),
pp. 73-74.

'ISIS'

    A New Stained Glass Technique.

    The Builder (Jan. 14, 1938).

JADART, Henri

    Le Vitrail de Puiseux et Autres Anciens Vitraux des Eglises du
Départment des Ardennes.

    Dole, 1900.

    Reprinted from Revue Historique d'Ardennes, vol. 7 (1900), pp. 316-337.

(Jade Window)

    It's Worth a Fortune.

    (On a window made out of pure jade given by J.L. Kraft.)

    Stained Glass, vol. 47, no. 3 (Autumn, 1952), p. 111.

JAER, L. de

    Peintres-Verriers Liégois aux 14e et 15e siècles.

    Chronique Archéologique du Pays de Liége, vol. 23, no. 4 (1932),
pp. 83-90.

JAHN, Johannes

    Mittelalterliche Glasmalerei.

    Diamant, 57th year, no. 6 (Feb. 21, 1935).

JAMES, Frances

    A Monumental Jigsaw.

    (On restoring York Minster glass.)

    Stained Glass, vol. 47, no. 3 (Autumn, 1952), pp. 119-120.

JAMES, John

What Price the Cathedrals?
(An attempt to estimate the cost of building Chartres Cathedral, including the glass.)
Transactions of the Ancient Monuments Society, new series, vol. 19 (1972).
(Glass, p. 53.)

JAMES, Lionel

The Five Sisters at York.
(Letter to the Editor.)
The Times, Dec. 2, 1933.

JAMES, M.M.

Chapter 10 (Sculpture, glass, painting) in TILLEY, A. (Editor),
Medieval France: A Companion to French Studies.
Cambridge, 1922.

JAMES, Montague Rhodes

On the Glass in the Windows of the Library at St. Albans Abbey.
Proceedings of the Cambridge Antiquarian Society, vol. 8 (1892-1893),
pp. 213-220.

On Some Fragments of Fifteenth Century Painted Glass from the
Windows of King's College Chapel, Together with Notes upon the
Painted Glass in the Side Chapels.
Proceedings of the Cambridge Antiquarian Society, vol. 9 (1894-1898),
pp. 3-12.

On the Paintings Formerly in the Choir at Peterborough.
(Parallels are shown to exist with the Canterbury glass.)
Proceedings of the Cambridge Antiquarian Society, vol. 9 (1894-1898),
pp. 178-194.

On a Window Recently Releaded in King's College Chapel.
Ibid., pp. 237-241.

A Guide to the Windows of King's College Chapel, Cambridge.
London, 1899.
Reprinted with an appendix by MILNER-WHITE, Eric, Cambridge, 1930.
(Further editions.)

Malvern Priory Church. Suggestions for the Rearrangement of the
Glass.
Cambridge, 1900.

The Verses Formerly Inscribed on Twelve Windows in the Choir of
Christ Church, Canterbury.
Cambridge, 1901.

Description of the Stained Glass in the Windows of Election Hall
(Eton College).
Etoniana (1904), pp. 38-39.

Notes on Glass in Ashridge Chapel.
Grantham, 1906.

Glass.
Contained in The Prayer Book Dictionary, editor HARFORD, H.
Bath, 1925, pp. 390-394.

Emblem of St. Simon the Apostle in All Soul's, Oxford.
Notes and Queries, vol. 151 (Oct. 30, 1926), p. 320.

Glass at Eaton Bishop and Madley.
(Letter to the Editor.)
J.M.G.P., vol. 3, no. 1 (Apr., 1929), p. 47.

Suffolk and Norfolk.
London, 1930 (?).

JAMISON, William

A New Material - for the Stained Glass Industry.
(Epoxy resins.)
Stained Glass, vol. 57, no. 2 (Summer, 1962), pp. 14-18.

JANEAU, Guillaume

Modern Glass.
London, 1931.

JÄNNICKE, Friedrich

Handbuch der Glasmalerei.
Stuttgart, 1890.

JANSEN, Franz

Glasmalereien.
In Kunstschätze der ehemaligen Benediktiner-Abtei Sankt Vitus,
Städtisches Museum, Ausstellung, May-July, 1948, (Cologne.)

(Jarrow Church)

Ancient Glass at Jarrow. By F.H.C(rossley)?
(Request for confirmation of the report of discovery of the
earliest stained glass known in England in The Times, Sept. 11, 1933.)
Notes and Queries, vol. 166 (May 5, 1934), p. 314.
Replied to by FORSE, E.J.G., and COPE, E.E. (May, 19, 1934), p. 354.

JEAVONS, S.A.

Medieval Painted Glass in Staffordshire Churches.
Transactions of the Birmingham Archaeological Society, vol. 68
(1952), pp. 25-73.
Reprinted Oxford, 1952.

JELE, Albert

Die Tiroler Glasmalerei, 1882-1886.
Berichte 25 Jubiläum des Hauses Innsbruck, 1886.

Die Tiroler Glasmalerei, 1886-1893.
Berichte Tätigkeit des Hauses Innsbruck, 1894.

JENKINS, F.L.

Stained Glass Windows for Skibo Castle (Sutherland).
Magazine of Art, vol. 28 (Jan., 1904), pp. 128-136.

JENKINS, Rhys

The Importation of Glass from the Continent into England in the
Middle Ages.
(Letter to the Editor.)
J.M.G.P., vol. 3, no. 1 (Apr., 1929), p. 48.

JENKINS, Rosalie

Stained Glass Craft Old But Thriving.
The Kansas City (Mo.) Times, Dec. 8, 1966.

JERROLD, Walter

Windows from Church at Trier.
Notes and Queries, 10th series, vol. 12 (Aug. 21, 1909), pp. 156-157.

(Jersey)

The New Window at St. Helier's Church, Jersey.
Magazine of Art, vol. 12 (1889), pp. 37, 38.

JERVIS, Henry

Salisbury Glass. An Act of Vandalism in 1790.
(Letter to the Editor.)
The Times, Nov. 7, 1932.

(Jesse Windows)

Jesse Windows. By H. De B. H.
(Request for information.)
Notes and Queries, 7th series, vol. 10 (Aug. 30, 1890), pp. 166-167.

(Contd.)

(Jesse Windows, Contd.)

    Jesse Windows. By H. De B. H.
    Ibid., (Oct. 4, 1890), pp. 274-275.
    Replies by 'St. Swithin', Ibid. (Oct. 4, 1890), p. 275;
    'Boileau', Ibid. (Oct. 4, 1890), p. 275;
    BIRKBECK-TERRY, F.C., Ibid. (Oct. 4, 1890), p. 275;
    W.M.E.F., Ibid. (Oct. 4, 1890), p. 275;
    BUSK, R.H., Ibid. (Nov. 29, 1890), pp. 428-429;
    'Alpha', Ibid. (Nov. 29, 1890), p. 429;
    GOULD, I.C., Ibid. (Nov. 29, 1890), p. 429;
    BRIGGS, Albert E., Ibid. (Nov. 29, 1890), p. 429.
    (For a further sequence of correspondence see JACKSON, Francis M.)

JESSEL, Louis
    Glasmalerei und Kunst Verglasung.
    Moderne Fenster für kirchlichen Zwecke.
    2nd edition, New York, 1896.

JEWERS, A.J.
    Heraldry in the Manor House of North Cadbury, with the Heraldry
    and Monuments in the Church.
    Proceedings of the Somersetshire Archaeological and Natural History
    Society, vol. 36 for 1890, part 2 (1891), pp. 137-167.

JOHNSON, Esther
    Stained Glass as Decorative Art.
    (Reprinted from the Journal of the Royal Architectural Institute
    of Canada, March, 1944.)
    Stained Glass, vol. 40, no. 1 (Spring, 1945), pp. 7-11.

JOHNSON, James R.
    Modern and Mediaeval Stained Glass: A Microscopic Comparison of
    Two Fragments.
    Art Bulletin, vol. 38 (Sept., 1956), pp. 185-186.

    Stained Glass and Imitation Gems.
    Art Bulletin, vol. 39 (Sept., 1957), pp. 221-224.

    The Tree of Jesse Window of Chartres.
    Speculum, vol. 36 (1961), pp. 1-22.

    The Stained Glass Theories of Viollet-le-Duc.
    Art Bulletin, vol. 45 (June, 1963), pp. 121-134.
    Reviewed by GRODECKI, Louis, Bulletin Monumental, no. 122 (1964),
    pp. 108-110.

    The Internal Structure of Medieval Ruby Glass.
    Stained Glass, vol. 59, no. 2 (Summer, 1964), pp. 17-22.

    The Radiance of Chartres. Studies in the Early Stained Glass of
    the Cathedral.
    Columbia University Studies in Art History and Archaeology, no. 4,
    London, 1964.
    Reviewed by BRIDGES, Stephen, Stained Glass, vol. 60, no. 3 (Autumn,
    1965), p. 31.

JOHNSON, Walter
    Stained Glass: Whitby Abbey.
    (Enquiry about fate of fragments known to exist in the late
    seventeenth century.)
    Notes and Queries, 11th series, vol. 7 (Feb. 22, 1913), p. 148.

JOHNSTON, Philip Mainwaring
    West Horsley Church.
    Surrey Archaeological Collections, vol. 22 (1909),
    (Glass, pp. 172-176.)

    Albury Old Church.
    Surrey Archaeological Collections, vol. 34 (1921).
    (Glass by PUGIN, A.W.N., p. 89.)

    New College Glass.
    (Letter to the Editor.)
    The Times, Nov. 19, 1932.

JONAS, Henri
    Le Peintre Hollandais.
    L'Artisan et les Arts Liturgiques (Brussels), no. 1 (1947).

JONES, A.W.
    Obituary.
    Stained Glass, vol. 38, no. 1 (Spring, 1943), p. 32.

JONES, Kenneth H.
    Thirteenth Century Glass at Nackington Church, near Canterbury.
    Archaeologia Cantiana, vol. 50 (1938), pp. 161-162.

JONES, M.C.
    Memorial Window to John Harvard in St. Saviour's Church, Southwark,
    London.
    The Critic (New York), vol. 46 (1905), p. 415.

JONES, P. Thoresby (Revised by HOSKINS, J.P.)
    Stamford. The Story of Six Parish Churches.
    Gloucester, 1960.

JONES, Rowland G.
    (On the destruction of a window in Camberwell Church.)
    (Letter to the Editor.)
    J.M.G.P., vol. 6, no. 4 (Apr., 1937), p. 228.

JONES, W. Bell
    Ancient Stained and Painted Glass in Flintshire.
    Journal of the Flintshire Historical Society, vol. 11 (1924), pp. 1-

JOURDAIN, Francis
    The Heraldic Stained Glass in Ashbourne Church, Derbyshire.
    Journal of the Derbyshire Archaeological and Natural History
    Society, vol. 3 (1881), pp. 90-94.

JOURDAIN, M.
    English Decoration and Furniture of the Early Renaissance, 1500-1650.
    Its Development and Characteristic Form.
    London, 1924.
    (Stained Glass, chapter 8.)

JOYCE, J.G.
    Specimens of the Ancient Stained Glass in Canterbury Cathedral.
    London, 1841.

    The Fairford Windows.
    (Letter to the Editor.)
    The Times, Sept. 28, 1868.

    (On the Stained Glass in Fairford Church, Gloucestershire.)
    (Report of address.)
    The Archaeological Journal, vol. 27 (1870), p. 332.

    The Fairford Windows.
    London, 1872.

    Remarks on the Fairford Windows.
    Transactions of the Bristol and Gloucester Archaeological Society,
    vol. 2 (1877-1878), pp. 53-91.

JUNG, Wilhelm
    Die mittelalterlichen Glasmalereien in der Marienkirche zu Frankfurt
    a.d. Oder.
    Zeitschrift für alte und neue Glasmalerei (1912), p. 47.

JUNG-JOHANN, Arthur
    Two Examples of Middle Rhenish Painted Glass of the Second Half
    of the Twelfth Century in the Wiesbaden Museum.
    Nassauische Heimatblätter, Jahrgang 35.

JUSSELIN, Maurice
    Un Donateur Pour les Verrières de Saint-Père de Chartres au Début
    du 14ᵉ Siècle.
    Bulletin Monumental, vol. 89 (1930), pp. 540-541.

KALLIR, Eva Marie
(Letter to the Editor deprecating much contemporary American
work.)
Stained Glass, vol. 49, no. 2 (Summer, 1954), pp. 79-83.
Replied to by SACHS, Hilda, Stained Glass, vol. 49, nos. 3, 4
(Autumn-Winter, 1954), pp. 127-129.

(Kansas City, Nelson Gallery of Art)
Ancient Glass Acquired by the Nelson Gallery of Art, Kansas City.
Stained Glass, vol. 30, no. 1 (Spring-Summer, 1935), pp. 25-27.

KARAWINA-HSIAO, Erica
From Maui to Mainz.
(A Modern Day Pilgrimage.)
Stained Glass, vol. 51, no. 4 (Winter, 1956-1957), pp. 151-162.

From Maui to Mainz. (Concluded.)
Stained Glass, vol. 52, no. 1 (Spring, 1957), pp. 17-30.

From Hawaii to Holland. A Study in Stained Glass.
Stained Glass, vol. 58, no. 2 (Summer, 1963), pp. 40-43,
        vol. 58, no. 3, pp. 40-51.

(Karlsruhe Glass-Painting Exhibition.)
Deutsche Glasmalerei-Ausstellung in Karlsruhe.
Kunstgewerbliches Blatt, vol. 13 (1901), pp. 1-12, 36-40.

KATZMANN, Volker
Glasmalerei in gotischen Kathedralen.
Tübingen, 1978.

KAUTZCH, Martin
Anfänge der Glasmalerei in Nürnberg und Franken von 1240-1450.
Halle, 1931.

KAYSER, C.E.
St. Christopher as Portrayed in England during the Middle Ages.
The Antiquary, vol. 8 (1883), pp. 193-200.

KÉBERLÉ, B.
Die Glasmalereien in den Langhausfenstern der Florentius-kirche zu
Niederhaslach.
L'Annuaire de la Société d'Histoire et d'Archéologie de Molsheim
et Environs (1971), pp. 15-36.

KEBLE, Edward
Church of St. Mary, Fairford in Gloucestershire. Visitors Handbook.
n.d.

KECK, Henry
Notes - Europe Revisited.
Stained Glass, vol. 42, no. 4 (Winter, 1947), pp. 104-110.

KEGHEL, M. De
Dekorative Malerei auf Glas.
Revue des Produits Chimiques, vol. 27 (1924), pp. 289-294, 365-368.
Reviewed in Chemical Zentralblatt, vol. 11 (1924), p. 1262.

KEHLMANN, Robert
The Stained Glass of Morris and Co.
Glass Art (June, 1975), pp. 26-31.

KELLER, Ferdinand
Die Tapete von Sitten. Ein Beitrag zur Geschichte der Xylographie
mit einigen Bemerkungen.
Mitteilungen der Antiquarischen Gesellschaft in Zurich, 11, 6 (1857),
pp. 140-148.

KELLER, Ferdinand (Contd.)
On a Stained Glass Window in the Abbey Church of Königsfelden.
Proceedings of the Society of Antiquaries, 2nd series, vol. 1
(1859), pp. 378-384.

KELLER, Hans Gustav
Die Jugend Jesu Christi. Sechs Glasgemälde in der Kirche von
Hilterfingen.
Thun, 1935.

Die Passion. Die Glasgemälde des Meisters Hans Noll in der Kirche
von Hilterfingen.
Thun, 1936.

KEMPE, A.J.
Some Account of the Jerusalem Chamber in the Abbey of Westminster,
and of the Painted Glass Remaining Therein.
Archaeologia, vol. 26 (1836), pp. 432-435.

KENDRICK, A.F.
The Cathedral Church of Lincoln.
London, 1898.

KENDRICK, Thomas
(Report of Speech at Annual Dinner of S.B.M.G.P.)
J.M.G.P., vol. 13, no. 4 (1963), pp. 579-580.

KENNEDY, H.A.
Glass Painting.
Journal of the Royal Society of Arts, vol. 39 (1891), p. 591.

Technique in Glass Painting.
The Studio, vol. 1 (1893), pp. 245-247.

(South Kensington Exhibition, 1864)
Exhibition of Stained Glass at South Kensington.
(Announcement.)
Art Journal (1864), p. 58.
Reviewed, Ibid., p. 199.

KENT, Ernest A.
Norwich Guildhall; The Fabric and the Ancient Stained Glass.
Norwich, n.d. (c. 1927).

Stained and Painted Glass in the Guildhall, Norwich.
Norfolk Archaeology, vol. 23 for 1927-1929 (1929), pp. 1-10.

Some Heraldic Glass in Norwich.
J.M.G.P., vol. 4, no. 3 (Apr., 1932), pp. 137-141.

The Seasons in Domestic Glass.
J.M.G.P., vol. 5, no. 1 (Apr., 1933), pp. 19-24.

John Christopher Hampp of Norwich, an Importer of Ancient Glass.
Norfolk Archaeology, vol. 26 for 1935-1937 (1938), pp. 192-196.

John Christopher Hampp of Norwich.
J.M.G.P., vol. 6, no. 4 (Apr., 1937), pp. 191-196.

KENT, William
The Lost Treasures of London.
London, 1947.
(War destruction.)
Reprinted (slightly amplified) in J.M.G.P., vol. 10, no. 1 (1948),
pp. 32-33.

KENYON, J.H.
Some Notes on the Glass Industry in England Prior to 1567, with
Particular Reference to Cullet, Dating, Analysis and Colour.
J.M.G.P., vol. 12, no. 2 (1957), pp. 103-107.

KENYON, J.H. (Contd.)

The Glass Industry of the Weald.
Leicester, 1964.
Reviewed by WOOD, E.S., The Archaeological Journal, vol. 124, (for 1967), pp. 267-269.
Reviewed by FISHER, Albert, J.M.G.P., vol. 14, no. 4 (1968-1969), p. 222.

KERR, Charles

The Painted Windows in the Chapel of St. Nicholas, Haddon Hall, Derbyshire.
Derbyshire Archaeological and Natural History Society, vol. 22 (1900), pp. 30-39.

KERR, Jill

With NEWTON, P.A.
The County of Oxford. A Catalogue of Mediaeval Stained Glass.
(CVMA, Great Britain, vol. 1.)
London, 1979.

KERRY, Charles

The Ancient Painted Window in Hault Hucknall (Great Hucklow) Church, Derbyshire.
Derbyshire Archaeological and Natural History Society, vol. 20 (1898), pp. 40-51.

KEYSER, C.E.

Notes on Some Fifteenth Century Glass in the Church of Wiggenhall St. Mary Magdalene.
Norfolk Archaeology, vol. 16 (1907), pp. 306-319.

Notes on Some Ancient Stained Glass in Sandringham Church, Norfolk.
Norfolk Archaeology, vol. 19 (1917), pp. 122-132.

KIDSON, George

The Armorial Glass at Lacock Abbey.
Notes and Queries, vol. 190 (Feb. 9, 1946), p. 61.

KIESLINGER, Franz

Die Glasmalerei in Oesterreich. Ein Abriss ihrer Geschichte.
Vienna, 1921.

Gotische Glasmalerei in Oesterreich bis 1450.
Zurich, 1928.
Reviewed by RACKHAM, Bernard, Burlington Magazine, vol. 54 (Jan.-June, 1929), pp. 156-157.

A Gothic Stained Glass Window. (From St. Lorenzen.)
Burlington Magazine, vol. 63 (July-Dec., 1933), pp. 87-88.

Glasmalerei in Osterreich.
Vienna, 1947.
Reviewed in Burlington Magazine, vol. 90 (Jan.-Dec., 1948), p. 183.

KILLER, Kaspar

Bericht über die Versuche mit einer elektrischen Glühmuffel zum Einbrennen von Farben in der Glasmalerei.
Allgemeine Glas-und-Keramisch Industrie, vol. 19 (1928), pp. 5-6.

Einiges über Glasmalerfarben.
Glastechnische Berichte, vol. 7 (1929-1930), pp. 317-322.

(Kilndown Church)

Abbildungen der Glasgemälde in der Salvatorkirche zu Kilndown in der Grafschaft Kent.
Copies of Paintings on Glass in Christchurch, Kilndown, in the County of Kent. Executed in the Royal Establishment for Painting on Glass, Munich, by order of Alexander J. Beresford Hope, Esq., M.P.
Published by Franz Eggert, Painter on Glass, Munich.
Reviewed in The Ecclesiologist, vol. 14 (1853), pp. 31-34.

KING, Dennis

The Releading and Rearrangement of Ancient Glass in Bale Church, Norfolk.
J.M.G.P., vol. 8, no. 2 (Apr., 1940), pp. 58-62.

KING, Dennis G.

On Cleaning Stained Glass.
J.M.G.P., vol. 12, no. 4 (1959), pp. 252-253.

A Technical Note; in BINNALL, P.B.G., The East Window of Redbourne Church, Lincolnshire.
J.M.G.P., vol. 13, no. 2 (1961), pp. 408-410.

Problèmes de la Technique et de la Restauration.
(A summary of a discussion between FRODL-KRAFT, Eva, TARALON, Jean, FRENZEL, Gottfried, KING, Dennis.)
Bulletin du Comité International d'Histoire de l'Art (Jan.-June, 1969), p. 8.

Winchester College Stained Glass.
(With HARVEY, John H.)
Part 2: Technical Report on the Restoration of the Glass.
Archaeologia, vol. 103 (1971), pp. 166-177.

The Medieval Stained and Painted Glass.
(With NEWTON, P.A.)
In The Hospital of William Browne, Merchant, Stamford, Lincolnshire. A History and an Account of the Buildings and Stained Glass.
Stamford, n.d.

Stained Glass Tours Around Norfolk Churches.
Norwich, 1974.

The Restoration of the Lady Chapel Stained Glass.
The British Archaeological Association Conference, Medieval Art and Architecture at Ely, for 1976 (1979), p. 98.

Problems with the Ely Glass.
In Akten des 10. Internationalen Colloquiums des CVMA.
Stuttgart, 1977, p. 50.

KING, G.A.

On the Ancient Stained Glass Still Remaining in the Church of St. Peter Hungate, Norwich.
Norfolk Archaeology, vol. 16 (1907), pp. 205-218.

A Description of the Ancient Painted Glass in the Church of St. Peter Mancroft, Norwich.
Norfolk Archaeology, vol. 17 (1910), pp. 194-220.

The Pre-Reformation Painted Glass in St. Andrew's Church, Norwich.
Norfolk Archaeology, vol. 18 (1914). p.293.

KING, W.

The Relation Between English and Flemish Domestic Glass.
International kunsthistorisch congres te Brussel in 1930.
Brussels, 1930.

KINON, N.

Farbige Vorlagen für moderne Verglasungen. 130 Entwürfe von Opalescent-und Messing-Verglasung: für Türen und Fenster, sowie 34 Entwürfe für Paravents auf 30 meist mehrfarbig.
Berlin, 1904.

KINSMAN, J.

Fairford Windows.
Notes and Queries, 4th series, vol. 3 (June 26, 1869), p. 613.

KIPPENBERGER, A.

Granteppichfenster der Elizabethkirche zu Marburg und des zisterzienserklosters Haina.
Festschrift Richard Hamann, Burg bei Magdeburg, 1939.

KIRBY, H.T.

    Ancient Glass at Twycross.
    Burlington Magazine, vol. 82 (Jan.-June, 1943), pp. 124-127.

    The Sixteenth Century Italian Glass in Chadshunt Church.
    Apollo (Sept., 1943), pp. 65-69.

    The Lesser Glass in St. Mary's Church, Warwick.
    Apollo (Feb., 1944), pp. 45-48.

    Thomas Willement: an Heraldic Artist's Note Book.
    Apollo, vol. 43 (1946), pp. 47-48.

    Polar History in a Midland Village.
    J.M.G.P., vol. 9, no. 4 (1946), pp. 115-116.

    Thomas Willement. An Heraldic Glass-Painter's Note Book.
    J.M.G.P., vol. 9, no. 4 (1946), pp. 127-131.

    The Fourteenth Century Winchester Glass at Ettington, Warwickshire.
    J.M.G.P., vol. 10, no. 1 (1948), pp. 17-31.

    Review of WOODFORDE, Christopher, Stained Glass in Somerset.
    J.M.G.P., vol. 10, no. 1 (1948), pp. 49-50.

K(IRBY), H.T.

    The Centenary of a Stained Glass Work.
    (William WARRINGTON's History of Stained Glass.)
    J.M.G.P., vol. 10, no. 2 (1949), p. 82.

KIRBY, H.T.

    Return of the Ettington Glass.
    Country Life (May 12, 1950).

    The Stained Glass Artist - His Mark.
    J.M.G.P., vol. 10, no. 4 (1951), pp. 205-212.

    Review of STETTLER, Michael, Swiss Stained Glass of the Fourteenth
    Century.
    J.M.G.P., vol. 10, no. 4 (1951), pp. 220-221.

    Review of WOODFORDE, Christopher, The Norwich School of Glass-
    Painting.
    J.M.G.P., vol. 10, no. 4 (1951), pp. 221-222.

    Notice of
    Year Book and Livery List of the Worshipful Company of Glaziers (1951).
    J.M.G.P., vol. 11, no. 1 (1952), p. 35.

    Review of WOODFORDE, Christopher, The Stained Glass of New College,
    Oxford.
    J.M.G.P., vol. 11, no. 1 (1952), p. 56.

(KIRBY, H.T. ?)

    Scaffolding and Fixing.
    J.M.G.P., vol. 11, no. 2 (1953), pp. 68-69.

KIRBY, H.T.

    Notice of the Livery List of the Worshipful Company of Glaziers and
    Painters of Glass, (1954).
    J.M.G.P., vol. 11, no. 4 (1955), p. 246.

    Some Warwickshire Medallions of Sixteenth Century Stained Glass.
    J.M.G.P., vol. 12, no. 2 (1957), pp. 127-130.

    The 'Jesse Tree' Motif in Stained Glass. A Comparative Study of
    Some English Examples.
    The Connoisseur, vol. 141 (Feb., 1958), pp. 77-82.

    Editor's Report.
    J.M.G.P., vol. 12, no.3 (1958), pp. 181-182.

KIRBY, H.T. (Contd.)

    The Baptism of St. Christopher. A Unique Piece of Stained Glass.
    (Birtsmorton Church.)
    Apollo.
    Reprinted in J.M.G.P., vol. 12, no. 3 (1958), pp. 196-197.

    Editor's Report.
    J.M.G.P., vol. 12, no. 4 (1959), pp. 255-257.

    The 'Jesse Tree' Motif in Stained Glass. A Comparative Study of
    Some English Examples.
    Part 1, J.M.G.P., vol. 13, no. 1 (1960), pp. 313-320.
    Part 2, J.M.G.P., vol. 13, no. 2 (1961), pp. 434-441.

    Review of ARMITAGE, E. Liddall, Stained Glass.
    J.M.G.P., vol. 13, no. 1 (1960), pp. 374-375.

    Review of BAKER, John, LAMMER Alfred, English Stained Glass.
    J.M.G.P., vol. 13, no. 1 (1960), pp. 375-376, and
    The Connoisseur, vol. 147 (Feb., 1961), pp. 48-49.

    Obituary of Ninian Comper.
    J.M.G.P., vol. 13, no. 2 (1961), pp. 447-448.

    Changes in Stained Glass.
    J.M.G.P., vol. 13, no. 3 (1962), pp. 488-489.

    Obituary of PAWLE, H.L.
    J.M.G.P., vol. 13, no. 3 (1962), pp. 526-527.

    Review of LAFOND, J., and GANDERTON, E.W., Ludlow Stained and
    Painted Glass.
    J.M.G.P., vol. 13, no. 3 (1962), pp. 537-538.

    Clerical Portraits in Stained-Glass: Two Famous Oxfordshire Rectors.
    (At Horley, Oxfordshire.)
    The Antiquaries Journal, vol. 42, (1962), pp. 251-252.

    Clerical Portraits in Stained Glass.
    (An expanded version of the Antiquaries Journal article.)
    J.M.G.P., vol. 13, no. 4 (1963), pp. 565-568.

    The Van Linge Window at Wroxton Abbey, Oxfordshire.
    J.M.G.P., vol. 14, no. 2 (1965), pp. 117-121.

    Review of GOLD, Sidney M., A Short Account of the Life and Work of
    John ROWELL.
    J.M.G.P., vol. 14, no. 2 (1965), p. 136.

    Review of BEYER, Victor, Stained Glass Windows.
    J.M.G.P., vol. 14, no. 2 (1965), p. 136.

(Kirby, H.T.)

    Obituary, by HAYES, C.H.
    J.M.G.P., vol. 14, no. 3 (1967), p. 156.

KIRBY, J. Potter

    York's Painted Glass. Report of Lecture.
    Yorkshire Evening Press, Feb. 8, 1939.

KIRCHOFF, F.

    Report on Stained and Painted Glass.
    In Artisans' Reports to the Royal Society of Arts on the Paris
    Exhibition, 1878.
    London, 1879, pp. 157-164.

KIRK, G.E.

    Beeston Chapelry, Leeds.
    Leeds, n.d.

(Kirkleatham, Yorks.)

    (An account of the glass in the Chapel of Kirkleatham Hospital.)
    News and Notes, J.M.G.P., vol. 6, no. 1 (Apr., 1935), p. 2.

KIRKPATRICK, H.F.

    Dorchester-on-Thames and the Abbey Church of St. Peter and St. Paul.
    Guildford, n.d.
    (Glass, pp. 13-15, unnumbered pages.)

KITSON, Peter

    Lapidary Traditions in Anglo-Saxon England: Part 1, the Background;
    the Old English Lapidary.
    Anglo-Saxon England, 7, 1978, pp. 9-60.

KITSON, Sydney D.

    Barnard Dinninghof, Sixteenth Century Glass-Painter and Architect.
    J.M.G.P., vol. 3, no. 2 (Oct., 1929), pp. 55-58.

KLARIS, Gertrude

    Broadening Horizons for Stained Glass.
    Stained Glass, vol. 42, no. 3 (Autumn, 1947), pp. 83-86.

KLEINSCHMIDT, Beda

    Die Basilika San Francesco in Assisi.
    Berlin, 1915.

KNAPP, George E.C.

    Medieval Glass from Selborne Priory (excavated).
    (Letter to the Editor.)
    J.M.G.P., vol. 12, no. 2 (1957), pp. 163-164.
    Replied to by KNOWLES, J.A. (q.v.).

KNAPPE, Karl Adolf

    Albrecht Dürer und das Bamberger Fenster in St. Sebald in Nürnberg.
    Nuremberg, 1961.

KNIGHT, Emma

    Obituary.
    J.M.G.P., vol. 3, no. 1 (Apr., 1929), p. 45.

KNOEPFLI, A.

    Kunstgeschichte des Bodenseeraumes, vol. 1.
    Constance-Lindau, 1961.

KNOWLES John Alder

    The Technique of Glass-Painting in Mediaeval and Renaissance Times.
    Journal of the Royal Society of Arts, vol. 62 (May 15, 1914), pp.
    568, 585.
    The Antiquary, vol. 10 (1914), pp. 334-340, 419-422.
    Building News, vol. 106 (May 29, 1914), pp. 702-705, 735-739.
    (German translation, Die Technik der Glasmalerei im Mittelalter und
    in der Renaissancezeit, Diamant, vol. 49 (1927), pp. 428-439.)

    A Jesse Window in the South Aisle of the Choir of York Minster.
    Yorkshire Herald, Nov. 9, 1920.
    Reprinted York, 1920.

    John Thornton of Coventry and the Great East Window in York Minster.
    Notes and Queries, 12th series, vol. 7 (Dec. 18, 1920), pp. 481-483.

    (Anonymously.)
    Henry Gyles.
    Architects Journal, vol. 53 (March 9, 1921), p. 281.

    The Cause of Decay in Ancient Stained Glass.
    Architectural Review of London, vol. 49 (1921), pp. 110-112.

KNOWLES, J.A. (Contd.)

    Glass-Painters of York.
    (A sequence of articles in Notes and Queries.)

    The Chamber Family.
    Notes and Queries, 12th series, vol. 8 (Feb. 12, 1921), p. 127.

    The Inglish Family.
    Ibid., (Apr. 23, 1921), pp. 323-325.

    The Shirley Family.
    Ibid. (May 7, 1921), pp. 364-366.

    The Shirwyn Family.
    Ibid. (May 21, 1921), pp. 406-407.

    John Witton.
    Ibid. (June 4, 1921), pp. 442-443.

    The Preston Family.
    Ibid. (June 18, 1921), pp. 485-487.

    The Petty Family.
    Ibid. vol. 9 (July 9, 1921), pp. 21-22.

    Sir John Petty.
    Ibid. (July 23, 1921), pp. 61-64.

    Robert Petty.
    Ibid. (Aug. 6, 1921), pp. 103-104.

    The Thompson Family.
    Ibid. (Aug. 27, 1921), pp. 163-165.

    The Gyles Family.
    Ibid. (Sept. 10, 1921), pp. 204-206.

    Henry Gyles.
    Ibid. (Sept. 24, 1921), pp. 245-247.

    Henry Gyles (Contd.).
    Ibid. (Oct. 1, 1921), pp. 268-270.

    William Peckitt.
    Ibid. (Oct. 22, 1921), pp. 323-325.

    William Peckitt (Contd.).
    Ibid. (Nov. 5, 1921), pp. 363-366.

    William Peckitt (Contd.).
    Ibid. (Nov. 19, 1921), pp. 404-406.

    William Peckitt (Contd.).
    Ibid. (Dec. 3, 1921), pp. 442-444.

    The Barnett Family.
    Ibid. (Dec. 17, 1921), pp. 483-485.

    The Barnett Family (Contd.).
    Ibid. (Dec. 31, 1921), p. 523.

    The Hodgson Family.
    Ibid., vol. 10 (Jan. 21, 1922), pp. 44-45.

    John de Burgh.
    Ibid. (Feb. 4, 1922), pp. 88-89.

    Glass-Painters of York. Chronological List of York Glass-Painters.
    Notes and Queries, 12th series, vol. 10 (March 11, 1922), pp. 184-186;
                                        (March 25, 1922), pp. 222-224.

    The Periodic Plagues of the Second Half of the Fourteenth Century and
    Their Effect on the Art of Glass-Painting.
    Archaeological Journal, vol. 79 (1922), pp. 343-352.
    Translated into German, Diamant, 48th year, no. 30 (Oct. 21, 1926),
    pp. 583-585.

KNOWLES, J.A. (Contd.)

    The Continuity of the Art of Glass Painting in England.
    The Builder, vol. 123 (1922), p. 97.

    Processes and Methods of Mediaeval Glass Painting.
    Journal of the Society of Glass Technology, vol. 6 (1922), pp.
    255-274.

    Cap of Maintenance.
    (In the St. William Window at York.)
    Notes and Queries, series 12, vol. 10 (1922), p. 275.

    Ancient Painted Glass.
    The Architect, vol. 107 (1922), pp. 200-202.

    The Study of Ancient Painted Glass.
    Journal of the Society of Architects, new series, vol. 15 (1922), p. 145.
    The Builder, vol. 122 (1922), pp. 766-767.

    Mediaeval Stained Glass.
    The Builder, vol. 123 (1922), p. 879.

    'Man of Wax'.
    (Votive offering of limb portrayed in St. William Window, York.)
    Notes and Queries, 12th series, vol. 12 (Feb. 3, 1923), p. 95.

    Henry Gyles, Glass Painter of York (1645-1709).
    Walpole Society Annual Volume, no. 11 (1922-1923), pp. 47-72.
    (Reviewed in the Times Literary Supplement, Aug. 16, 1923.)

    The York School of Glasspainting.
    Journal of the British Archaeological Association, new series, vol.
    29 (1923), pp. 109-127.

    The York School of Glass-Painting.
    Architects Journal, vol. 58 (1923), pp. 314-317.
    The Builder, vol. 125 (1923), pp. 294-295.

    Forgeries of Ancient Stained Glass. Methods of their Production
    and Detection.
    Journal of the Royal Society of Arts, vol. 72 (1923), pp. 38-56.
    The Builder, vol. 125 (1923), p. 851.
    Architects' Journal, vol. 59 (1924), pp. 524-526.
    The Connoisseur, vol. 69 (1924), pp. 201-208;
                    vol. 75 (1926), pp. 207-214.

    Sir Joshua Reynolds' Designs for Stained Glass.
    The Builder, vol. 125 (1923), p. 179.

    Note on the Scrope Window in York Minster.
    Yorkshire Archaeological Journal, vol. 27, part 2 (1923), pp. 221-224.

    Sashes or Casement Windows.
    (Letter to the Editor.)
    Architects Journal, vol. 59 (Jan. 9, 1924), p. 128.

    Heraldic Glass at Ockwells.
    (Letter to the Editor.)
    Country Life, vol. 55 (Feb. 2, 1924), p. 183.

    Exhibition of French Painted Glass in London about A.D. 1802.
    Notes and Queries, 13th series, vol. 146 (Apr. 19, 1924), p. 292.

    The Visitation Window in York Minster.
    Notes and Queries, vol. 146, no. 42 (Apr. 19, 1924), p. 292.

    Exhibitions of Painted Glass in London.
    (In the early 18th and 19th centuries.)
    Notes and Queries, 13th series, vol. 146 (May 24, 1924), pp. 374-377.

    The Detection of Forgeries of Old Glass.
    The Connoisseur, vol. 69 (May-Aug., 1924), pp. 201-208.

    The Coloured Glass Used in Mediaeval Windows. Was it Manufactured
    in England?
    Glass, vol. 1, no. 5 (1924), pp. 201-204.

KNOWLES, J.A. (Contd.)

    The East Window of Holy Trinity Church, Goodramgate, York.
    Yorkshire Archaeological Journal, vol. 28 (1924), pp. 1-24.

    Forgeries of Ancient Stained Glass. Methods of Production and
    Detection.
    (Report of Lecture to the Royal Society of Arts.)
    Architects Journal, vol. 59 (1924), pp. 524-526.

    The St. William and St. Cuthbert Windows in York Minster Compared.
    Yorkshire Herald, Jan. 16, 1925.

    Disputes Between English and Foreign Glass-Painters in the Sixteenth
    Century.
    The Antiquaries Journal, vol. 5 (Apr., 1925), pp. 148-157.

    Ancient Glass of All Saints', North Street, York.
    Yorkshire Herald, Aug. 24, 1925.

    Mediaeval Methods of Employing Cartoons for Stained Glass.
    J.M.G.P., vol. 1, no. 3 (Oct., 1925), pp. 35-44.

    Mediaeval Glass in York Minster and Churches.
    Society of Chemical Industries Handbook, Leeds Meeting (1925),
    pp. 136-138.

    The History of Copper Ruby Glass.
    Transactions of the Newcomen Society, vol. 6 (1925-1926), pp. 66-74.

    The History of Copper Ruby Glass.
    National Glass Budget (Jan. 2, 1926), pp. 3, 19, 26.

    Transition from the Mosaic to the Enamel Method of Painting on Glass.
    Antiquaries Journal, vol. 6 (Jan., 1926), pp. 26-35.
    (Translated into German: Der Uebergang von der Mosaik zur
    Schmelzmethode in der Glasmalerei, Diamant, 48th year, no. 13
    (May 1, 1926), pp. 246-248; no. 14 (May 11, 1926), pp. 266-268.)

    Stained Glass.
    (Report of a lecture before the Scottish Ecclesiological Society.)
    Stained Glass Bulletin, vol. 21, no. 1 (Feb. 1926).

    Mittelalterliche Methoden für die Verwendung von Kartons anstatt
    farbigen Glases.
    Diamant (Feb. 11 and 21, 1926).

    The Church of the Glass Painters, St. Helen's Church, York.
    Architecture, vol. 4, no. 10, new series (Feb., 1926), pp. 342-344.

(Knowles, J.A.)

    Notice of article The Transition from the Mosaic to the Enamel Method
    of Painting on Glass, in Memorabilia,
    Notes and Queries, vol. 150 (March 6, 1926), p. 164.

KNOWLES, J.A.

    Streitigkeiten zwischen englischen und fremden Glasmalern im 16.
    Jahrhundert.
    Diamant, 48th year, no. 8 (March 11, 1926);
                    no. 9 (March 21, 1926).

    The Source of the Coloured Glass Used in Mediaeval Stained Glass
    Windows.
    Glass, vol. 3, no. 4 (March, 1926), pp. 157-159;
              no. 5 (Apr., 1926), pp. 201-203;
              no. 7 (June, 1926), pp. 295-296.

    The Source of the Coloured Glass Used in Mediaeval Stained Glass
    Windows.
    National Glass Budget, 41st year, no. 49 (Apr. 3, 1926), pp. 6, 9, 19.

    Imitation Stained Glass, Ancient and Modern.
    J.M.G.P., vol. 1, no. 4 (Apr., 1926), pp. 19-22.

KNOWLES, J.A. (Contd.)

A History of the York School of Glass-Painting.
J.M.G.P., vol. 1, no. 4 (Apr., 1926), pp. 25-41.

A Thirteenth Century Glass-Painting.
(Q.v. READ, Herbert, 1924.)
Burlington Magazine, vol. 48 (Jan.-June, 1926), pp. 143-144.

The Glass of Holy Trinity Church, Goodramgate, York, described by
John A. Knowles on the visit of York Architectural Society.
Yorkshire Herald, July 1, 1926.

Forgeries in Stained Glass.
The Connoisseur, vol. 75 (May-Aug., 1926), pp. 207-214.
Noticed in Memorabilia, Notes and Queries, vol. 151 (Aug. 14, 1926),
p. 109.

Vom Ursprung des in mittelalterlichen Glasmalereifenstern verwendeten
farbigen Glases.
Diamant, 48th year, nos. 18, 19, 20, 22, 23 (July-Aug., 1926).

On Some Seventeenth and Eighteenth Century Designs for Stained Glass
Recently Presented to the Yorkshire Museum.
Yorkshire Philosophical Society Report (1926). pp. 6-8.

A History of the York School of Glass-Painting. Part 2.
J.M.G.P., vol. 1, no. 5 (Oct., 1926), pp. 16-28.

Review of PITCHER, Sydney, Ancient Stained Glass in Gloucestershire
Churches.
J.M.G.P., vol. 1, no. 5 (Oct., 1926), p. 38.

Stained Glass. Is it a Lost Art?
National Glass Budget, 42nd year, no. 26 (Oct. 23, 1926), pp. 16-

On Two Panels of Glass in the Bodleian Library Representing Scenes
from the History of St. Thomas Becket.
Bodleian Quarterly Record, vol. 5, no. 52, (4th quarter, 1926).

Emblem of St. Simon the Apostle in All Soul's, Oxford.
Notes and Queries, vol. 151 (Oct. 30, 1926), pp. 319-320.

Ancient Reduplication and Mass Production of Works of Art.
The Connoisseur, vol. 76 (Sept.-Dec., 1926), pp. 133-142.

Die periodischen Plagen in der zweiten Hälfte des 14 Jahrhunderts
und ihre Wirkungen auf die Glasmalerkunst.
Diamant, 48th year, no. 31 (Nov. 1, 1926), pp. 606-609.

The York Glass-Painters.
In York Minster Historical Tracts, 627-1927.
Edited by THOMPSON, A. Hamilton.
London, 1927 (Unpaginated.)

Mediaeval Cartoons for Stained Glass. How Made and How Used.
Journal of the American Institute of Architects, vol. 15, no. 1
(Jan.,1927), pp. 8-22.

Artistic Craft Gilds of the Middle Ages.
Journal of the Royal Institute of British Architects, vol. 34, no.
8, 3rd series (Feb. 19, 1927), pp. 263-271.

Rise and Progress of the Glass-Painters Craft in Mediaeval England.
Bulletin of the Stained Glass Association of America, vol. 22,
no. 2 (March, 1927);
no. 3 (Apr., 1927);
no. 4 (May, 1927).

Additional Notes on the History of the Worshipful Company of Glaziers.
Antiquaries Journal, vol. 7, no. 3 (July, 1927), pp. 282-293.

Technical Notes on the St. William Window in York Minster.
Proceedings of the Yorkshire Philosophical Society (1927), pp. 10-12.

Glass-Painters' Advertisements.
J.M.G.P., vol. 2, no. 1 (1927), pp. 18-22.
Reprinted in Bulletin of the Stained Glass Association of America,
vol. 24, no. 2 (Feb., 1929).
(Check J.A.K., Notes and Queries, vol. 140, no. 47, (May, 1924).)

KNOWLES, J.A. (Contd.)

A History of the York School of Glass-Painting. Part 3.
J.M.G.P., vol. 2, no. 1 (1927), pp. 30-37.

Mediaeval Stained Glass Designers.
Architects Journal, vol. 66 (July 20, 1927), pp. 94-96.

Mediaeval Processes of Glass Manufacture.
Glass, vol. 4 (July-Sept., 1927).

Die Technik der Glasmalerei im Mittelalter und in der Renaissancezeit.
Diamant, 49th year, nos. 22-32 (Aug. 1-Nov. 11, 1927), pp. 428-430,
464-468, 482-485, 508-509, 553-554, 549-550, 576-578, 592-594, 632-635.

The Ancient Stained Glass in St. Michael's Spurriergate and St.
John's, Micklegate, York.
The Yorkshire Herald, Sept. 1, 1927.

Eighteenth Century Windows in St. Botolph's, Aldersgate.
J.M.G.P., vol. 2, no. 2 (Oct., 1927), pp. 72-73.

A History of the York School of Glass-Painting. Part 5.
J.M.G.P., vol. 2, no. 2 (Oct., 1927), pp. 78-85.

Die Glasmaler von York.
Diamant, 50th year, nos. 8, 9, 10 (March 11-Apr. 1, 1928).

A History of the York School of Glass-Painting. Part 6.
J.M.G.P., vol. 2, no. 3 (Apr., 1928), pp. 136-151.

A History of the York School of Glass-Painting. Part 7.
J.M.G.P., vol. 2, no. 4 (Oct., 1928), pp. 193-209.

A History of the York School of Glass-Painting. Part 7.
J.M.G.P., vol. 3, no. 1 (Apr., 1929), pp. 30-42.

A History of the York School of Glass-Painting. Part 7.
J.M.G.P., vol. 3, no. 2 (Oct., 1929), pp. 85-94.

William Peckitt, Glass-Painter.
Walpole Society, vol. 17 (1929), pp. 45-59.

The York School of Glass-Painting.
British Architect's Conference Handbook, pp. 102-105.
Privately printed, 1929.

Stained Glass in Domestic Use.
Notes and Queries, vol. 158 (March 15, 1930), pp. 189-190.

Stained Glass Sundials.
The Connoisseur, vol. 85 (Jan.-June, 1930), pp. 227-231.
Noticed in Memorabilia, Notes and Queries, vol. 158 (Apr. 12, 1930),
pp. 253-254.

A History of the York School of Glass-Painting. Part 8.
J.M.G.P., vol. 3, no. 3 (Apr., 1930), pp. 123-132.

Ancient Leads for Windows and the Methods of their Manufacture.
J.M.G.P., vol. 3, no. 5 (Apr., 1930), pp. 133-139.

Review of READ, Herbert, Stained Glass, in Encyclopaedia Britannica,
1929 edition.
J.M.G.P., vol. 3, no. 3 (Apr., 1930), p. 140.

On Glass Formerly in the East Window of Holy Trinity Church, Hull.
Privately printed, 1930.

The Film on Ancient Stained Glass.
Journal of the British Society of Master Glass-Painters, vol. 3, no.
4 (Oct., 1930), pp. 181-188.

A History of the York School of Glass-Painting. Part 8.
J.M.G.P., vol. 3, no. 4 (Oct., 1930), pp. 189-199.

KNOWLES, J.A. (Contd.)

A History of the York School of Glass-Painting. Part 9.
J.M.G.P., vol. 4, no. 1 (Apr., 1931), pp. 32-41.

Marks on the Glass at Wells.
(A discussion with ROBINSON, J. Armitage, and HORNE, Ethelbert.)
J.M.G.P., vol. 4, no. 2 (Oct., 1931), pp. 77-80.

A History of the York School of Glass-Painting. Part 9.
J.M.G.P., vol. 4, no. 2 (Oct., 1931), pp. 81-93.

A History of the York School of Glass-Painting. Part 10.
J.M.G.P., vol. 4, no. 3 (Apr., 1932), pp. 146-155.

A History of the York School of Glass-Painting. Part 10.
J.M.G.P., vol. 4, no. 4 (Oct., 1932), pp. 189-202.

The Donors of the St. William Window, York Minster.
(A query.)
Notes and Queries, vol. 163, no. 23 (Dec. 3, 1932), p. 405.

Curiosities of Glass-Painting.
J.M.G.P., vol. 5, no. 1 (Apr., 1933), pp. 27-34.
J.M.G.P., vol. 5, no. 2 (Oct., 1933), pp. 71-79.
Reprinted in Stained Glass, vol. 27 (Autumn, 1933), vol. 28
(Winter, 1933-1934).

A History of the York School of Glass-Painting. Part .
J.M.G.P., vol. 5, no. 1 (Apr., 1933), pp. 37-48.

A History of the York School of Glass-Painting. Part 11.
J.M.G.P., vol. 5, no. 2 (Oct., 1933), pp. 82-92.

A History of the York School of Glass-Painting. Part 12.
J.M.G.P., vol. 5, no. 3 (Apr., 1934), pp. 133-141.

Medieval Stained Glass Designers.
J.M.G.P., vol. 5, no. 3 (Apr., 1934), pp. 142-147.

Review of MOLLET, Ralph, Leaded Glass Work.
J.M.G.P., vol. 5, no. 3 (Apr., 1934), pp. 151-152.

Additional Notes on the St. William Window in York Minster. Part 1.
Proceedings of the Yorkshire Architectural and Yorkshire
Archaeological Society, vol. 1, no. 2 (1934).

The Penancer's Window in the Nave of York Minster.
(A discussion with HARDMAN, J.T.)
J.M.G.P., vol. 5, no. 4 (Oct., 1934), pp. 179-184.

A History of the York School of Glass-Painting. Part 12.
J.M.G.P., vol. 5, no. 4 (Oct., 1934), pp. 187-195.

A History of the York School of Glass-Painting. Parts 13 and 14.
J.M.G.P., vol. 6, no. 1 (Apr., 1935), pp. 32-48.

A History of the York School of Glass-Painting. Part 15.
J.M.G.P., vol. 6, no. 2 (Oct., 1935), pp. 89-99.

Glass-Painters of the Middle Ages.
(Report of Lecture before the Society of Glass Technology.)
Yorkshire Herald, Nov. 7, 1935.

A History of the York School of Glass-Painting. Part 17.
J.M.G.P., vol. 6, no. 3 (Apr., 1936), pp. 152-160.

(The sequence of articles on The York School of Glass-Painting was
reprinted at irregular intervals in Stained Glass, 1929-1950.)

Essays in the History of the York School of Glass-Painting.
London, 1936.
Reviewed by RUSHFORTH, G. McNeil, The Archaeological Journal, vol.
93 (for 1936), pp. 121-123.
Reviewed by RACKHAM, Bernard, Burlington Magazine, vol. 70 (Jan.-
June, 1937), p. 149.

KNOWLES, J.A. (Contd.)

Reviewed by SKINNER, Orin E., Stained Glass, vol. 31, no. 3 (Winter,
1936-1937), pp. 92-97.
Reviewed in The Builder (Jan. 22, 1937).
Reviewed by EDEN, F.S., The Connoisseur, vol. 99 (Jan., 1937), p. 52.
Reviewed in Diamant (Dec. 1, 1937).

Review of RACKHAM, Bernard, Guide to the . . . Stained Glass in
the Victoria and Albert Museum.
J.M.G.P., vol. 6, no. 4 (Apr., 1937), p. 221.

Horace Walpole and his Collection of Stained Glass at Strawberry Hill.
(With a catalogue of the sale of the collection.)
J.M.G.P., vol. 7, no. 1 (Oct., 1937), pp. 45-49.
        vol. 7, no. 2 (Apr., 1938), pp. 100-101.
        vol. 7, no. 3 (Oct., 1938), pp. 131-133.
        vol. 7, no. 4 (Apr., 1939), p. 192.

Stained Glass at the Paris Exhibition.
J.M.G.P., vol. 7, no. 2 (Apr., 1938), pp. 97-99.

(Knowles, J.A.)
(Heraldic Shields for Norwich Cathedral.)
York Gazette, June 3, 1938.

KNOWLES, J.A.
Viollet-le-Duc.
L'Intermédiaire, no. 1901 (Sept. 15, 1938).

Leaded Lights and Ornamental Glazing.
J.M.G.P., vol. 7, no. 3 (Oct., 1938) pp. 134-138.
        vol. 7, no. 4 (Apr., 1939), pp. 184-191.
        vol. 8, no. 1 (Oct., 1939), pp. 18-25.

The Church of the Glass-Painters, St. Helen's Church, York.
J.M.G.P., vol. 7, no. 4 (Apr., 1939), pp. 156-159.

Gild Windows.
J.M.G.P., vol. 7, no. 4 (Apr., 1939), pp. 164-168.

Windows That Tell A Story.
Everybody's Weekly (Apr. 17, 1943).

(Knowles, J.A.)
A Bibliography of Works by John Alder Knowles relating to Ancient
Stained and Painted Glass.)
J.M.G.P., vol. 9, no. 1 (1943), pp. 26-29.

KNOWLES, J.A.
Mathematics and Geometry for Glass-Painters and Lead Light Makers.
J.M.G.P., vol. 10, no. 2 (1949), pp. 92-104.

Bernard van Ling.
(Reply to a letter requesting information about him.)
J.M.G.P., vol. 10, no. 2 (1949), p. 110.

Technical Notes on the St. William Window in York Minster.
Yorkshire Archaeological Journal, vol. 37 for 1948-1951 (1951), pp.
148-161.
Reprinted J.M.G.P., vol. 10, no. 3 (1950), pp. 118-131.

Historical Sketch of the Stained Glass Windows of St. George's Chapel.
J.M.G.P., vol. 10, no. 3 (1950), pp. 132-135.

(KNOWLES, J.A. ?)
Taking Sizes and Templets for Stained Glass Windows.
J.M.G.P., vol. 10, no. 3 (1950), pp. 149-156.

(Knowles, J.A.)
(Lectures in London.)
Yorkshire Evening Press, November 10, 1950.

KNOWLES, J.A.
An Attempt to Determine the Original Arrangement and Contents of the
Windows in the Western Portion of the Choir of York Minster.
The Yorkshire Archaeological Journal, vol. 37 (1951), pp. 442-455.

KNOWLES, J.A. (Contd.)

    Sir Joshua Reynolds' Window in the Ante-Chapel of New College, Oxford.
    J.M.G.P., vol. 10, no. 4 (1951), pp. 189-195.

    Exhibitions of Stained Glass in London.
    J.M.G.P., vol. 11, no. 1 (1952), pp. 44-50.

    Early Nineteenth-Century Ideals and Methods of Restoring Ancient
    Stained Glass. (Part 1.)
    J.M.G.P., vol. 11, no. 2 (1953), pp. 72-79.

    The Price Family of Glass-Painters.
    Antiquaries Journal, vol. 33 (1953), pp. 184-192.

    William Peckitt, Glass-Painter.
    Annual Report of the Yorkshire Architectural and York Archaeological
    Society, (1953-1954, pp. 99-114.

    Stained Glass of Historic Interest in London.
    J.M.G.P., vol. 11, no. 3 (1954), pp. 135-147.
    (See additions and corrections in STEPHENS, Francis, (1956).)

    The West Window, St. Martin-Le-Grand, Coney Street, York.
    The Yorkshire Archaeological Journal, vol. 38 (1955), pp. 148-184.

    The Authorship of the West Window of St. Martin-Le-Grand, Coney
    Street, York.
    J.M.G.P., vol. 11, no. 4 (1955), pp. 193-200.

    Walter Geddes' Booke of Sundry Draughtes, 1615.
    J.M.G.P., vol. 12, no. 1 (1956), pp. 15-21.

(Knowles, J.A.)

    (Receives honorary M.A. at Hull University.)
    Yorkshire Evening Press, May 23, 1957.

    A Manual of Glass-Painting.
    J.M.G.P., vol. 12, no. 2 (1957), pp. 117-126.
            vol. 12, no. 3 (1958), pp. 198-205.
            vol. 13, no. 1 (1960), pp. 349-356.

    The Authorship of the Article 'Vitrail' in Viollet-le-Duc's
    Dictionnaire Raisonné de l'Architecture Française.
    Stained Glass, vol. 52, no. 4 (Winter, 1957-1958), pp. 165-168.

    (On glass excavated at Selborne Priory.)
    (Letter to the Editor.)
    J.M.G.P., vol. 12, no. 2 (1957), pp. 164-165.

    Notes on Some Windows in the Choir and Lady Chapel of York Minster.
    The Yorkshire Archaeological Journal, vol. 39 (1958), pp. 91-118.

    Ancient Stained Glass Lost and Found.
    Stained Glass, vol. 53, no. 3 (Autumn, 1958), pp. 110-111.

    John Thornton of Coventry and the East Window of Great Malvern Priory.
    Antiquaries Journal, vol. 39 (1959), pp. 274-282.

    Cleaning the Outside of Mediaeval Stained Glass Windows.
    J.M.G.P., vol. 12, no. 4 (1959), pp. 251-252.

    Decay of Glass, Lead and Iron of Ancient Stained Glass Windows.
    J.M.G.P., vol. 12, no. 4 (1959), pp. 270-276.

    The History of Copper Ruby Glass.
    J.M.G.P., vol. 13, no. 1 (1960), pp. 357-363.

    Old Exhibitions of Stained Glass.
    Stained Glass, vol. 56, no. 2 (Summer, 1961), pp. 30-31.

(Knowles, J.A.)
    (Death at No. 35, Stonegate, York.)
    Yorkshire Evening Press, November 25, 1961.

    Obituary.
    Yorkshire Evening Press, November 27, 1961.

(Knowles, J.A., Contd.)
    Will.
    Yorkshire Evening Press, May 9, 1962.

    Obituary. By J.E.L.
    J.M.G.P., vol. 13, no. 3 (1962), pp. 527-529.
    (Partly reprinted in Stained Glass, vol. 57, no. 1 (Spring, 1962),
    pp. 22-23.)

KNOWLES, J.A.

    The East Window of St. Michael-le-Belfrey Church, York.
    The Yorkshire Archaeological Journal, vol. 40, for 1959-1962 (1962),
    pp. 145-159.

    An Inquiry into the Date of the Stained Glass in the Chapter House
    at York.
    The Yorkshire Archaeological Journal, vol. 40, for 1959-1962 (1962),
    pp. 451-461.

    The Nostell Priory Collection of Swiss Glass Painting.
    Stained Glass, vol. 57, no. 4 (Winter, 1962-1963), pp. 20-21.

    Foreign Inscriptions on the Glass at Fairford.
    J.M.G.P., vol. 13, no. 4 (1963), pp. 549-553.

(Knowles, J.A.)
    (His working materials, plans, etc., given to the Castle Museum by
    his sister.)
    Yorkshire Evening Press, January 18, 1964.

KNOWLES, J.A.
    Early Nineteenth-Century Ideals and Methods of Restoring Ancient
    Stained Glass. (Part 2.)
    J.M.G.P., vol. 14, no. 1 (1964), pp. 9-16.

    Ancient Stained Glass Collectors.
    Stained Glass, vol. 63, no. 3 (Autumn, 1968), p. 32.

KOCH, Robert
    Louis C. Tiffany, Rebel in Glass.
    New York, 1964.
    Reviewed in Stained Glass, vol. 59, no. 4 (Winter, 1964-1965), p. 33.
    Reviewed in J.M.G.P., vol. 16, no. 1 (1976-1977), pp. 72-74.

KOEPF, H.
    Schwäbische Kunstgeschichte, 2 (Baukunst der Gotik).
    Constance and Stuttgart, 1961.

KOLB, H.
    Glasmalereien des Mittelalters und der Renaissance. Originale
    Aufnahmen.
    Stuttgart, 1884-1889.

KORN, Ulf-Dietrich
    Die romanische Farbverglasung von St. Patrokli in Soest.
    Munster-in-Westphalia, 1967.

    Ursachen und Symptome des Zerfalls mittelalterlicher Glasgemälde.
    Deutsche Zeitschrift für Kunst und Denkmalpflege, vol. 29 (1971),
    pp. 58-74.

    (Glass only by KORN.)
    Konservieren-Restaurieren.
    (Catalogue of exhibition at the Westfälischen Landesmuseum, Münster.
    Munster, 1975.)
    (Glass, pp. 89-108.)

    Die romanischen Glasmalerei Fragmente aus Sieverstedt bei Flensburg.
    Beiträge zur Kunst des Mittelalters. Festschrift für Hans Wentzel.
    Berlin, 1975.

KORN, Ulf-Dietrich (Contd.)

Die Löhner Jesse-Fenster und die Soester Wandmalerei um 1250.
In Akten des 10. Internationalen Colloquiums des CVMA.
Stuttgart, 1977, pp. 22-23.

Zur Restaurierung der Chorfenster der Stiftskirche zu Bücken.
In Akten des 10. Internationalen Colloquiums des CVMA.
Stuttgart, 1977, p. 49.

KRAUS, F.-X.

Kunst und Altertum im Unter-Elsass.
Strasbourg, 1876.

Kunst und Altertum im Ober-Elsass.
Strasbourg, 1884.

Kunst und Altertum im Lothringen.
Strasbourg, 1889.

KRAUS, H.

Notre-Dame. Vanished Medieval Glass.
Gazette des Beaux-Arts, part 2 (1966), pp. 131-148.
Reviewed by GRODECKI, Louis, Bulletin Monumental, no. 125 (1967),
pp. 104-105.

KRUMMER-SCHROTH, Ingeborg

Glasmalereien aus dem Freiburger Münster.
Fribourg-im-Brisgau, 1967.
Reviewed by GRODECKI, Louis, Revue de l'Art, no. 10 (1970), p. 98.

KUHN ——.

Zur Geschichte der Glasmalerei im Mittelalter.
Kunst und Gewerbe (Nuremberg), vol. 12 (1878), pp. 129-

KUHN, John H.

Is New Mural (sic) for Tuskegee Uncle Tom in Stained Glass?
The Record, New Jersey (July 24, 1968).
(See The Singing Windows of Tuskegee, Stained Glass, vol. 64, no. 1,
(Spring, 1969), pp. 26-28.)

KUHNE, Klaus

Beiträge zur Kenntnis mittelalterlicher Gläser.
Silikattechnik, no. 11 (1960), pp. 260-262.

KUNZE, H.

Bestand und Anordnung der Glasgemälde des Strassburger Münsters um
die Mitte des 19 Jahrhunderts und in der Gegenwart.
Strassburger Münsterblatt (1913).

KURTHEN, Josef

Zur Kunst der Steinfelden Kreuzgangfenster. Ein Werkstattbesuch
bei ihren Meister Gerhard Remisch.
Euskirchen, 1941.

LABANDE, L.H.

    Les Primitifs Français. Peintres et Peintres-Verriers de la
Provence Occidentale.
Marseilles, 1932, 2 vols.

(Labouret)

    Labouret's Work in Philadelphia.
Stained Glass, vol. 45, no. 3 (Autumn, 1950), pp. 118-120.

LACAMBRE, Geneviève and Jean

    Les Vitraux de la Chapelle de Carheil. Un Témoignange de l'Art
Officiel au Temps de Louis-Phillippe.
Revue de l'Art, no. 10 (1970), pp. 85-94.

LACHOT, Abbé

    Notice sur les Verrières de l'Eglise de Seurre (Côte d'Or).
Citeaux, 1882.

LACROIX, A.

    Des Couleurs Vitrifiables et de leur Emploi pour la Peinture sur
Porcelaine, Faience, Vitraux, etc.
Paris, 1872.
Translated into English: Practical Instructions for Painting on
China . . . Glass, with Analysis of Vitrifiable Colours.
London, 1874.

LACROIX, Paul

    De la Peinture sur Verre.
Revue des Arts (Bruxelles), vol. 20 (1865), p. 175.

    Les Arts au Moyen Age et a l'Epoque de la Renaissance.
Paris, 1869 (2nd edition).
English version, translated by DAFFORNE, J., The Arts in the Middle
Ages and at the Period of the Renaissance.
London, 1870.

LACY, R.E.

    A Note on the Climate Inside a Medieval Chapel.
(King's College.)
Studies in Conservation, vol. 15 (1970), pp. 65-80.

LAENEN, L.

    Histoire de l'Eglise Métropolitaine de Saint Rombaut à Malines.
Malines, 1920.

(Lafarge, John)

    A New Window by John Lafarge.
International Studio, vol. 15 (Nov., 1901, supplement), p. 36.

    Ames Memorial Church Window by Lafarge.
Current Literature, vol. 31 (Dec., 1901), p. 723.

    Windows, part 3. The Translucent Filling of the Lights.
In STURGIS, Russel, Dictionary of Architecture and Building.
New York, 1902 (Vol. 3, pp. 1067-1091).

    The Spirit of John Lafarge (Senior).
Stained Glass, vol. 39, no. 4 (Winter, 1944), pp. 107-114.

La FARGE, J.

    See Stained Glass Problems in Our Day.

LAFAYE, M.

    Mémoire au Sujet des Vitraux Anciens: Etat où ils se Trouvent Après
le Siége, dans les Eglises de Paris.
Paris, 1871.

LAFOND, Jean

    Un Vitrail d'Engrand Le Prince à Saint-Vincent de Rouen et sa Copie
par Mausse Heurtault à Saint Ouen de Pont-Audemer.
Bulletin de la Société des Amis des Monuments Rouennais (1908), pp.
157-167.

    Etudes sur l'Art du Vitrail en Normandie.
Arnoult de la Pointe, Peintre et Verrier de Nimègue et les Artistes
Etrangers à Rouen aux 15e et 16e Siècles.
Bulletin de la Société des Amis des Monuments Rouennais, for 1911
(1912), pp. 141-172.

    Saint Louis et le Vitrail de Moulineaux.
Journal de Rouen, (March 30, 1919).

    L'Art Chrétien dans Nos Vitraux Normands.
Journal de Rouen (Aug. 24, 29, 1919).
Reprinted Rouen, 1920.

    Les Vitraux de Paris au Petit Palais.
Journal de Rouen
Reprinted in Revue de l'Art Ancien et Moderne (Dec., 1919), pp. 271-276.
Reprinted Rouen, 1919.

    L'Eglise d'Envermeu.
Journal de Rouen (May 4, 1920).

    Etude sur les Vitraux.
In La Cathédrale de Rouen (Abbé LOISEL), Paris, 1924.

    Les Vitraux de l'Ancienne Abbaye de Jumièges. Chapelle de la
Mailleraye-sur-Seine. Eglise Paroissale de Jumièges.
(From JOUEN, Léon, Jumièges.)
Rouen, 1926.
2nd edition, Rouen, 1937.
3rd edition, Rouen, 1954.

    Etudes sur l'Art du Vitrail en Normandie. Arnoult de Nimègue et
son Oeuvre.
Bulletin de la Société des Amis des Monuments Rouennais (1926-1927),
pp. 137-154.

    Etude sur les Vitraux.
In MASSON, A., L'Abbatiale de Saint-Ouen de Rouen.
Paris, 1927.

    Etude sur les Vitraux.
In LEBLOND, V., L'Eglise Saint-Etienne de Beauvais.
Paris, 1929.

    With GUEY, Fernand.
Catalogue de l'Exposition d'Art Religieux Ancien.
Rouen, 1931.

    Etude sur les Vitraux.
In La Cathédrale de Coutances, by COLMET - DAAGE, P.
Paris, 1933.

    Les Vitraux de Saint-Nicaise de Rouen.
In DESCROUT, Chanoine, Saint-Nicaise de Rouen.
Rouen, 1934.
Reprinted in Bulletin de la Société des Amis des Monuments Rouennais,
for 1932 (1934), pp. 115-127.

    Découverte des Vitraux de la Commanderie de Sainte-Vaubourg à
l'Abbaye de Saint-Denis.
Bulletin de la Commission Départementale des Antiquités de la Seine-
Inférieure, vol. 19 (seance du Dec. 10, 1936), pp. 194-196.

    La Cathédrale de Rouen.
Paris, 1936.

LAFOND, Jean (Contd.)

(Reports of addresses on glass given at the summer meeting of the
Royal Archaeological Institute at Rouen.)
Archaeological Journal, vol. 95 for 1938 (1939), pp. 362-409.
(Glass at St. Vincent, Rouen, St. Ouen, Rouen, The Cathedral,
Rouen, by CLAPHAM, A.W.; Caudebec, Louviers, Grand Audely, Ecouis,
Conches, by BAKER, E.; The Cathedral, Beauvais, St. Etienne,
Beauvais, Grisors, Fécamp.)

Romain Buron et les Vitraux de Conches. L'Enigma de l'Inscription
Aldegrevers.
Annuaire Normand (1940-1941), pp. 5-42.

La Resurrection d'un Maître d'Autrefois, le Peintre-Verrier Arnoult
de Nimègue.
In Précis Analytique des Trauvaux de l'Académie des Sciences, Belles-
Lettres et Arts de Rouen Pendant les Années 1940 et 1941.
Rouen, 1942.
Reviewed by RACKHAM, Bernard, Burlington Magazine, vol. 89 (Jan.-
Dec., 1947), pp. 198-200.

Romain Buron et les Vitraux de Conches.
Bayeux, 1942.
(Reprinted from Annuaire Normand, 1940-1941.)

Les Vitraux 'Royaux' du 14e Siècle à la Cathédrale d'Evreux.
Bulletin Monumental, no. 101 (1942), pp. 69-93.

Pratique de la Peinture sur Verre à l'Usage des Curieux, Suivre d'un
Essai Historique sur le Jaune d'Argent, et d'une Note sur les Plus
Anciens Verres Gravés.
Rouen, 1943.
Reviewed by AUBERT, Marcel, Bulletin Monumental, vol. 103 (1945), pp.
298-299.
Reviewed by RACKHAM, Bernard, Burlington Magazine, vol. 89 (Jan.-
Dec., 1947), pp. 198-200.

The Stained Glass Decoration of Lincoln Cathedral in the Thirteenth
Century.
The Archaeological Journal, vol. 103 (for 1946), pp. 119-156.

Vitraux de Rouen, à Propos de la 'Repose' de Saint-Patrice.
Revue Française de l'Elite, 2nd year, no. 8, Paris (May 25, 1948),
pp. 41-45.

Les Vitraux Français du Musée Ariana et l'Ancienne Vitrerie de
Saint-Fargeau (Yonne).
Geneva, vol. 26 (1948), pp. 115-132.

Le Vitrail de François Bohier à Vraiville (Eure).
Bulletin de la Commission des Antiquités de la Seine-Inférieure,
vol. 20 (1949), pp. 84-85.

Review of SCHEIDEGGER, Alfred, Die Berne Glasmalerei . . .
Musées Suisses/Schweizer Museen, no. 3 (March, 1949), pp. 74-75.

Deux Vitraux de Rathausen au Musée Ariana de Genève.
Musées Suisses/Schweizer Museen, vol. 9 (Dec., 1951), pp. 1-9.

Le Vitrail en Normandie de 1250 à 1300.
Bulletin Monumental, vol. 3 (1953), pp. 317-358.

Les Vitraux Anciens de la Cathédrale de Lausanne.
Congrès Archéologique de France, 110e session, Suisse Romande, 1952.
Paris, 1953, pp. 116-132.

Félibien est-il Notre Premier Historien du Vitrail? Les 'Principes
de l'Architecture' et l'Origine de l'Art de la Peinture sur Verre.
Bulletin de la Société de l'Histoire de l'Art Français (1954), pp.
45-60.

La Peinture sur Verre à Jumièges.
Jumièges. Congrès Scientifique du 13e Centenaire.
Rouen, 1954, pp. 529-536.

LAFOND, Jean (Contd.)

Le Vitrail Anglais de Caudebec-en-Caux.
La Revue des Arts, no. 4 (1954), pp. 201-206.

Le Vitrail du 14e Siècle en France.
In L'Art du 14e Siècle en France, edited by LEFRANCOIS-PILLION.
Paris, 1954, pp. 187-238.
Reviewed by RACKHAM, Bernard, Burlington Magazine, vol. 97 (Jan.-
Dec., 1955), p. 357.

Un Vitrail du Mesnil-Villeman (1313) et les Origines du Jaune
d'Argent.
Bulletin de la Société Nationale des Antiquaires de France
(séance du Déc. 8, 1954), pp. 93-95.

L'Immaculée Conception Glorifiée par le Vitrail Normand.
Ecclesia, no. 60 (Dec., 1954), pp. 57-64.

Les vitraux de Sées.
Congrès Archaéologique de France, 111e session, tenue dans l'Orne
en 1953.
Paris, 1955, pp. 59-83.

Review of WOODFORDE, English Stained and Painted Glass.
The Archaeological Journal, vol. 111 (for 1954), pp. 239-241.

Les Vitraux d'Argentan.
Bulletin Monumental, vol. 113 (1955), pp. 259-275.

Le Peintre Verrier Arnoult de Nimègue (Aert Van Oort) et les Débuts
de la Renaissance à Rouen et à Anvers.
Actes du 17e Congrès International de l'Histoire de l'Art, La Haye,
1955, pp. 333-344.

À Propos des Vitraux du 15e Siècle Provenant de l'Eglise Saint-Vincent
et Transférés à la Cathédrale de Rouen.
Revue des Sociétés Savantes de Haute-Normandie, vol. 4 (1956), pp.
37-45.

The English Window at Caudebec-en-Caux.
J.M.G.P., vol. 12, no. 1 (1956), pp. 42-47.

Le Vitrail Civil Français à l'Eglise et au Musée.
n.p., n.d.
Reprinted from Medicine de France, vol. 77 (1956), pp. 16-33.
Reviewed by AUBERT, Marcel, Bulletin Monumental, no. 115 (1957),
pp. 73-74.

La Famille Pinaigrier et le Vitrail Parisien au 16e et au 17e Siècle.
Bulletin de la Société de l'Histoire de l'Art Français (1957), pp.
63-75.

Job et les Musiciens. A Propos d'un Vitrail de Saint-Patrice de
Rouen.
Bulletin de la Société Nationale des Antiquaires de France (1957),
pp. 183-184.

Les Plus Anciens Vitraux de Saint-Patrice de Rouen.
Revue des Sociétés Savantes de Haute-Normandie, Histoire de l'Art, no. 8
(1957), pp. 5-17.

Les Vitraux dits 'Arabes' dans le Monde Byzantin et Musulman.
Bulletin de la Société Nationale des Antiquaires de France (1957),
pp. 54-55.

Review of BEER, Ellen, CVMA (Switzerland, vol. 1).
The Archaeological Journal, vol. 113 for 1956 (1957), pp. 170-172.

Les Vitraux de la Cathédrale Saint-Pierre de Troyes.
Congrès Archéologique de France, no. 113, Troyes, 1955.
Paris, 1957, pp. 29-62.

With CHASTEL, A., AUBERT, M., GRODECKI, L., GRUBER, J.-J., MATHEY, F.,
TARALON, J., VERRIER, J.
Le Vitrail Français.
Paris 1958.
Reviewed by SALET, Francis, Bulletin Monumental, no. 116 (1958), p. 226.

LAFOND, Jean (Contd.)

L'Eglise Saint-Vincent de Rouen et Ses Vitraux.
Actes du Congrès des Sociétés Savantes.
Rouen-Caen, 1956, pp. 59-77.
Reprinted Paris, 1958.

Les Vitraux de l'Abbaye de la Trinité de Fécamp.
L'Abbaye Bénédictine de Fécamp. Ouvrage Scientifique du 13e
Centenaire.
Vol. 3, Fécamp, 1958, pp. 97-120, 253-264.
Reviewed by E.E., J.M.G.P., vol. 13, no. 4 (1963), p. 601.

L'Eglise des Junies (Lot) et Ses Vitraux.
Bulletin de la Société Nationale des Antiquaires de France (1958), p. 28.

Les Vitraux de Saint-Wandrille.
L'Abbaye Saint-Wandrille de Fontenelle, 8, (Christmas, 1958), pp. 19-20.

Les Vitraux de la Cathédrale Saint-Etienne d'Auxerre.
Congrès Archéologique de France.
116e Session, Auxerre, 1958.
Paris, 1959, pp. 60-75.

Les Vitraux de l'Eglise de Cravan.
Ibid., pp. 289-293.

Les Vitraux de l'Eglise Saint-Julien-du-Sault.
Ibid., pp. 365-369.

Les Vitraux de l'Eglise Notre-Dame de Villeneuve-sur-Yonne.
Ibid., pp. 378-382.

Les Vitraux de Notre-Dame et de la Sainte-Chapelle de Paris.
(With AUBERT, M., and GRODECKI, L.)
(CVMA France 1. Département de la Seine 1.)
Paris, 1959.

Vitraux Français en Angleterre: Wilton (12e et 13e Siècles).
Bulletin de la Société Nationale des Antiquaires de France (1959),
pp. 241-243.

Review of 2nd edition of WENTZEL, Hans, Meisterwerke des Glasmalerei.
The Archaeological Journal, vol. 114 for 1957 (1959), pp. 200-201.

Review of FRANKL, Paul, Peter Hemmel, Glasmaler von Andlau.
The Archaeological Journal, vol. 114 for 1957 (1959), pp. 201-203.

Review of RÉAU, L., Les Monuments Détruits de l'Art Français.
L'Oeil, no. 62 (Feb., 1960), p. 55.

Le Commerce des Vitraux Anciens en Angleterre aux 18e et 19e Siècles.
Revue des Sociétés Savantes de Haute-Normandie, Histoire de l'Art
(1960), pp. 5-15.
Reviewed by E.E., J.M.G.P., vol. 13, no. 4 (1963), p. 601.

Le Vitrail 'de Saint Louis' à l'Eglise de Moulineaux (Seine-Maritime).
Festschrift Hans R. Hahnloser.
Basel, 1961, pp. 299-306.

Jean Lescuyer. Un Grand Peintre Verrier de la Renaissance.
Médecine de France, no. 123 (1961), pp. 17-32.

Ludlow Stained and Painted Glass.
(With GANDERTON, E.W.)
Ludlow, 1961.
Reviewed in Bulletin de la Société Nationale des Antiquaires de
France (for 1960), pp. 127-131.
Reviewed by KIRBY, H.T., J.M.G.P., vol. 13, no. 3 (1962), pp. 537-538.

Notre-Dame des Marais et les Vitraux de La Ferté-Bernard.
Congrès Archéologique de France, 119e Session, Maine, 1961.
Paris, 1961, pp. 224-245.

Les Vitraux de Châlons-sur-Marne et de Saint-Quentin et l'Oeuvre de
Mathieu Bléville.
Bulletin de la Société de l'Histoire de l'Art Français (1961), pp. 21-28.

LAFOND, Jean (Contd.)

Review of ARMITAGE, E. Liddall, Stained Glass.
The Archaeological Journal, vol. 116 for 1959 (1961), pp. 271-272.

Review of CVMA (Germany, Band 1).
        CVMA (France, vol. 1).
The Archaeological Journal, vol. 116 for 1959 (1961), pp. 272-274.

Review of BAKER, LAMMER and READ, English Stained Glass.
The Archaeological Journal, vol. 116 for 1959 (1961), pp. 274-276.

Le Christ en Croix de la Cathédrale de Quimper à Castelnau-
Bretenoux (Lot).
Bulletin de la Société Nationale des Antiquaires de France (1962),
pp. 36-38.

La Légende de Saint Georges Dans un Vitrail de La Ferté-Bernard (Sarthe).
Ibid., pp. 151-152.

La Technique du Vitrail, Aperçus Nouveaux.
Art de France, vol. 2 (1962), pp. 242-248.

La Vitrerie de l'Eglise Saint-Michel de Pont-L'Evêque. Une
Victime de la Guerre.
Bulletin de la Société des Antiquaires de Normandie, vol. 56 (1961-
1962), pp. 3-20.

L'Arbre de Jessé d'Engrand Le Prince à Saint-Etienne de Beauvais.
Cahiers de la Céramique, du Verre et des Arts du Feu, no. 30 (1963),
pp. 117-127.

Guillaume de Marcillat et la France.
Scritti in Onore di Mario Salmi.
Rome, 1963. Vol. 3, pp. 147-161.

Les Vitraux de Nôtre-Dame de Louviers.
Nouvelles de l'Eure, no. 15 (1963), pp. 42-46.

With MUSSET, L.
Une Description Inédite des Vitraux de l'Eglise des Jacobins de Caen.
Bulletin de la Société des Antiquaires de Normandie, no. 57 (1963-
1964), pp. 686-693.

The Traffic in Ancient Stained Glass with England in the Eighteenth
and Nineteenth Centuries.
J.M.G.P., vol. 14, no. 1 (1964), pp. 58-67.

Le Vitrail.
Paris, 1966.
Reviewed by ERLANDE-BRANDENBURG, A., Bulletin Monumental, vol. 125
(1967), pp. 124-126.
Reviewed by ARMITAGE, E. Liddall, J.M.G.P., vol. 14, no. 3 (1967),
pp. 178-179.

Article 'Le Vitrail'.
Dictionnaire des Eglises de France.
Paris, 1966.

Les Courtois (Robert, Pierre, et Jean) et les Peintres Verriers de
La Ferté-Bernard.
Mémoires de la Société Nationale des Antiquaires de France, 9th
series, t. 4 (1968), pp. 195-241.

Découverte de Vitraux Historiés du Moyen Age à Constantinople.
Cahiers Archéologiques, vol. 18 (1968), pp. 231-238.

Exposition du Conseil de l'Europe.
L'Europe Gothique 12e-14e Siècle.
(Notices 210-214.)
Paris, 1968.

La Prétendue Invention du 'Plat de Verre' au 14e Siècle et les
Familles de 'Grosse Verrerie' en Normandie.
Revue des Sociétés Savantes de Haute-Normandie, no. 58 (1968),
pp. 1-16.

LAFOND, Jean (Contd.)

Les Verrières de Saint-Jacques de Lisieux Détruites en 1944.
Bulletin de la Société des Antiquaires de Normandie, no. 58 (1965-1966), (Caen, 1969), pp. 213-249.

Was Crown Glass Discovered in Normandy in 1330?
Journal of Glass Studies (1969), pp. 37-38.

Eglises et Vitraux de la Région de Pont-Audemer.
(LAFOND's contribution is Vitraux de l'Arrondissement de Pont-Audemer, pp. 22-47.)
Nouvelles de l'Eure, numéro spécial, 3ᵉ trimestre, (1969).
With BAUDOT, M.

La Cananéene de la Cathédrale de Bayonne et le Vitrail Parisien aux Environs de 1530.
Revue de l'Art, no. 10 (1970), pp. 77-84.

Le Vitrail Civil en France. Un Grand Passé Méconnu.
(Preface to catalogue of the Exhibition Le Vitrail dans la Demeure.)
Rennes, 1970.

Les Vitraux de l'Eglise Saint-Ouen de Rouen.
Vol. 1.
(CVMA France, 4, 2, vol. 1.)
Paris, 1970.
Reviewed by SALET, Francis, Bulletin Monumental, no. 129 (1971), p. 301.

(Lafond, Jean)

(Editorial of number dedicated to Jean Lafond.)
Revue de l'Art, no. 10 (1970), pp. 4-6.

Bibliographie des Travaux Scientifiques de Jean Lafond.
By PERROT, Françoise.
Revue de l'Art, no. 10 (1970), pp. 95-96.

Le Château de Highcliffe, Sculptures des Andelys et de Jumièges, Vitraux de Rouen et de Saint-Denis.
Bulletin de la Société Nationale des Antiquaires de France (1972), pp. 98-106.

Les Vitraux de Saint-Vincent de Rouen et l'Aménagement du Vieux-Marché.
Bulletin des Amis des Monuments Rouennais, for 1958-1970, Rouen (1972), pp. 147-168.

Un Chef-d'oeuvre. Le Vitrail d'Arnoult de Nimègue à l'Eglise Sainte-Foy des Conches.
Cahiers de la Céramique, du Verre et des Arts du Feu, no. 52 (1973), pp. 50-65.

LAISHLEY, A.L.

They Paint in Light.
(On the work of STAMMERS, Harry, and HARVEY, Harry.)
Yorkshire Life Illustrated (June, 1960).

The Stained Glass of York.
York, n.d.

LAKIN, Thomas

The Valuable Receipts of the Late Mr. Thomas Lakin . . . together with the most recent and valuable improvements in the admired art of glass staining and painting.
Edited by the author's widow.
Leeds, 1824.

LAMB. Charles Rollinson

How an American Stained Glass Window is Made.
The Chautauquan (Meadville, Pa.), vol. 29 (1899), pp. 515-521.

LAMB, Frederick Stymetz

Stained Glass in its Relation to Church Ornamentation.
The Catholic World (New York), vol. 74 (1902), pp. 667-677.

The Painted Window.
The Craftsman (Syracuse, U.S.A.), vol. 3 (1903), pp. 341-349.

The Making of a Modern Stained Glass Window: its History and Process, and a Word About Mosaics.
The Craftsman (Syracuse, U.S.A.), vol. 10 (1906), pp. 18-31.

Windows for Plymouth Church, Brooklyn, designed by F.S. Lamb.
International Studio Supplement, vol. 40 (1910), pp. 44-45.

LAMBARDE, Fane

Coats of Arms in Sussex Churches. Part 1.
Sussex Archaeological Collections, vol. 67 (1926), pp. 149-187.
Part 2, Ibid., vol. 68 (1927), pp. 210-240.
Part 3: The Heraldry of Horselunges, Ibid., vol. 69 (1928), pp. 71-75.
Part 4, Ibid., vol. 70 (1929), pp. 134-164.
Part 5, Ibid., vol. 71 (1930), pp. 134-170.
Part 6, Ibid., vol. 72 (1931), pp. 218-242.
Part 7, Ibid., vol. 73 (1932), pp. 102-144.
Part 8, Ibid., vol. 74 (1933), pp. 181-208.
Part 9, Ibid., vol. 75 (1934), pp. 171-189.

LAMBORN, E.A. Greening

The Parish Church.
Oxford, 1929.
(Several subsequent editions.)
(Glass, pp. 144-151.)

Review of the R.C.H.M. Volume for the City of Oxford.
J.M.G.P., vol. 8, no. 3 (Apr., 1941), pp. 109-125.

The Armorial Glass at Wytham.
Notes and Queries, vol. 184 (March 27, 1943), pp. 187-190.

Some Armorial Glass of Northamptonshire.
Notes and Queries, vol. 184 (May 22, 1943), pp. 311-313.

The Armorial Glass of the Enamel Period at Stoke Poges.
J.M.G.P., vol. 9, no. 2 (1944), pp. 32-43.

The Sibyls in Painted Glass.
Notes and Queries, vol. 186 (Apr. 8, 1944), pp. 178-179.

The Armorial Glass at Lacock Abbey.
Notes and Queries, vol. 189 (Dec. 1, 1945), pp. 227-233.
Ibid., vol. 190 (Feb. 9, 1946), pp. 61-62.

Some Sources for the New Papworth.
Notes and Queries, vol. 190 (June 29, 1946), pp. 269-272.

The Armorial Glass at Stanford-on-Avon.
Notes and Queries, vol. 191 (Nov. 2, 1946), pp. 180-185.

The Armorial Glass of the Oxford Diocese, 1250-1850.
Oxford, 1949.
Reviewed in the Journal of the British Archaeological Association, 3rd series, vol. 12 (1949), pp. 99-100.
Reviewed in Oxoniensia, vol. 14 for 1949 (1951), pp. 99-100.
Reviewed in Notes and Queries, vol. 194 (Aug. 20, 1949), pp. 373-374.
Reviewed in J.M.G.P., vol. 10, no. 3 (1950), p. 165.
Reviewed by WOODFORDE, Christopher, Burlington Magazine, vol. 91 (Jan.-Dec., 1949), pp. 264-265.

LAMI DE NOZAN, E.

De la Peinture sur Verre, que doit-elle être au 19ᵉ siècle.
Mémoires de la Société Architectural du Midi, vol. 6 (1852).
Reprinted (revised) Paris, 1863.

LAMONT, Virginia
    French Glassmen of this Century.
    (With CREAGER, Kathryn.)
    Stained Glass, vol. 37, no. 2 (Summer, 1942), pp. 59-61.

LAMORT
    Notice Sur les Vitraux Peints de l'Eglise du Loçon.
    St. Omer, 1846.

(Lamport Hall, Northamptonshire.)
    The Arms of Isham at Lamport Hall, Northamptonshire.
    J.M.G.P., vol. 13, no. 2 (1961), p. 433.

(Lancashire)
    Notes taken in the Churches of Preston, Manchester, Eccles,
    Winwick, Farnworth, Sephton, and Hale, in the County of Lancashire;
    Some by Thomas Chaloner, in or about the year 1591, and others by
    Randle Hohne, in the years 1636 and 1652; and Notes taken at Lea
    Hall, in the same County.
    Edited by RYLANDS J.P.
    Transactions of the Historic Society of Lancashire and Cheshire,
    new series, vol. 14 for 1898 (1900), pp. 203-230.

LANCASTER, Joan C.
    John Thornton of Coventry, Glazier.
    Transactions of the Birmingham Archaeological Society, vol. 74 (1956).
    J.M.G.P., vol. 12, no. 4 (1959), pp. 261-263.

LANCASTER, W.T. (Editor)
    Letters addressed to Ralph Thoresby.
    Thoresby Society's Publications, vol. 21.

(Landelies, Belgium)
    À Propos d'un Vitrail à Landelies. Verrière Votive du Chanoine
    Hubert de Corswarem.
    L'Action d'Art (1913), pp. 50-57.

LANDOLT-WEGENER, Elisabeth
    Die Glasmalereien im Hauptchor der Soester Wiesenkirche.
    Westfalen 13. Sonderheft.
    Munster, 1959.

LANDMANN, T.M.
    Uber Glasmalerei.
    Die Christliche Kunst, 25th year, no. 11 (Aug., 1929).

LANE, Arthur
    Florentine Painted Glass and the Practice of Design.
    Burlington Magazine, vol. 91 (Jan.-Dec., 1949), pp. 43-48.

    New Windows in Canterbury Cathedral.
    The Connoisseur, vol. 143 (Feb., 1959), pp. 40-41.

(Lane, Arthur)
    Obituary, by J.E.L.
    J.M.G.P., vol. 14, no. 1 (1964), pp. 25-26.

LANE, John
    Portraits in Stained Glass.
    (A request for information.)
    Notes and Queries, 12th series, vol. 2 (Aug. 26, 1916), p. 172.
    Replied to by BRABROOK, E., (Sept. 9, 1916), p. 211.
            HARRISON, John, Ibid., p. 211.
            DODGSON, E.S., Ibid., p. 211.
            SPARKE A., Ibid., p. 211.

                                (Contd.)

LANE, John (Contd.)
    Replied to by BARNS, S.J. (Sept. 30, 1916), p. 275.
            CUMMINGS, C.L., Ibid., p. 275-276.
            W.B.H., Ibid., p. 276.
            MAGRATH, J.R. (Oct. 14, 1916), pp. 317-318.
            HIBGAME, F.T., Ibid., p. 318.
            BULL, W., Ibid., p. 318.
            J.T.F., Ibid., p. 318.
            PAGE, J.T. (Oct. 21, 1916), pp. 337-338.
            B.B. (Nov. 4, 1916), p. 374.
            QUARRELL, W.H., Ibid., p. 374.
            HIBGAME, F.T., Ibid., p. 374.
            KEALY, A.G., Ibid., p. 374.
            R.S.B. (Dec. 2, 1916), p. 458.
            DRURY, C., Ibid., p. 458.
            BARKER, A.T., Ibid., p. 458.
            S.R.C., Ibid., p. 458.
            KEALY, A.G. (Dec. 23, 1916), p. 517.
            SUMMERS, M., Ibid., p. 517.
            HIBGAME, F.T., Ibid., p. 517.
            FYNMORE, R.J., vol. 3 (Jan. 6, 1917), p. 15.
            W.A.C. (Jan. 13, 1917), p. 36.
            M.A. (Oxon.), Ibid., p. 36.
            J.T.F. (Jan. 27, 1917), p. 76.
            M.S.T., Ibid., p. 76.
            W.B.H., Ibid., p. 76.
            MILNER-GIBSON-CULLUM, G. (Feb. 3, 1917), pp. 95-96.
            KNOWLES, L., Ibid., p. 96.
            H.S.G. (Feb. 24, 1917), p. 159.
            MILNER-GIBSON-CULLUM, G. (March 10, 1917), p. 198.
            FAWCETT, J.W., Ibid., p. 198.
            CORNER, S., Ibid., pp. 198-199.
            WAINEWRIGHT, J.B. (March 17, 1917), p. 218.
            KEALY, A.G., Ibid., p. 218.
            FYNMORE, A.H.W., Ibid., p. 218.
            BAYLEY, A.R. (Apr. 14, 1917), p. 286.
            HIBGAME, F.T., Ibid., p. 286.
            YEO, W. Curzon, Ibid., p. 286.
            RUSSELL, F.A. (June, 1917), p. 344.
            R. B.-R. (Sept., 1917), pp. 430-431.

LANEY, Al
    Stained Glass Making.
    Popular Science (New York), (Oct., 1942).

LANGARDIÈRE, M. de
    Les Fenêtres de Mésières-en-Brenne (Indre).
    Bulletin Archéologique for 1934-1935 (1938).

LANGE VAN WIJNGAERDEN, C.J.De
    De Goudsche Glazen of geschilderde Kerk-Glasen of Sant Janskerk:
    alsmede de Goudesche Schilders en Glas-Schilders-Kunst.
    S'Gravenhage, 1819.

LANGLOIS, E.H.
    Mémoire sur la Peinture sur Verre, et sur Quelques Vitraux
    Remarquables des Eglises de Rouen.
    Séance de la Société Libre d'Emulation de Rouen (1823), pp. 42-88.

    Essai Historique et Descriptif sur la Peinture sur Verre . . .
    Suivi de la Biographie des plus Célèbres Peintres-Verriers.
    Rouen, 1832.

    Essai Historique et Descriptif sur l'Abbaye de Fontenelle ou de
    Saint-Wandrille.
    Rouen, 1834.

LAROCHE and DEFOSSÉS
    Descriptions des Peintures sur Verre de la Fabrique de L(aroche) et
    D(efossés), Précédé d'une Notice sur l'Art de la Peinture Vitrifiée
    depuis son Origine Jusqu'à nos Jours.
    Brussels, 1841.

(Larsen, Andreas Ruud)
   Obituary.
   Stained Glass, vol. 38, no. 1 (Spring, 1943), pp. 33-34.

LASELLE, Dorothy A.
   Stained Glass by College Students.
   (At Texas State College for Women.)
   Stained Glass, vol. 37, no. 1 (Spring, 1942), pp. 5-13.

LASSALLE, Joseph
   Vitraux Posés dans la Chapelle de Nôtre Dame à St. Pierre de Condom
   par M. L'Abbé Goussard.
   Bulletin de la Comité Historique et Archéologique du Province
   Ecclésiastique d'Auch, vol. 2 (1861), pp. 370-384.

LASSUS, J.B.
   Monographie de la Cathédrale de Chartres.
   Paris, 1842.

   Exposition de l'Industrie. Peinture sur Verre.
   Annales Archéologiques (Paris), vol. 1 (1884), p. 40.

   With DUVAL, Amaury.
   Monographie de la Cathédrale de Chartres.
   (2 vols.), Paris, 1867-1881.

LASTEYRIE, F. de
   Description des Verrières Peintes de la Cathédrale d'Auxerre.
   Annuaire Statistique du Département de l'Yonne, vol. 5, part 3
   (1841), pp. 38-46.

   Histoire de la Peinture sur Verre.
   (2 vols.), Paris, 1838-1857.
   Reviewed by BARESTE, Eugène, Revue 19ᵉ Siècle, (1838), p. 16.

   Quelques Mots sur la Théorie de la Peinture sur Verre.
   Paris, 1852.

   Notice sur les Vitraux de l'Abbaye de Rathausen, Canton du Lucerne.
   Paris, 1856.

   La Peinture sur Verre au 19ᵉ Siècle.
   Gazette des Beaux-Arts, vol. 9 (1861), p. 129.

   Les Peintres Verriers Etrangers à la France, Classés Méthodiquement
   Selon les Pays et l'Epoque où ils ont Vécu.
   Mémoires de la Société des Antiquaires de France (1879),

   Peintres-Verriers Etrangers à la France.
   Paris, 1880.

   Histoire de la Peinture sur Verre d'Après ses Monuments du Pas de
   Calais et du Nord.
   Amiens, 1881.

LATHAM, W.
   Painted Glass from Basingwerk Abbey (in Llanassa Church, Flint).
   The Gentleman's Magazine, vol. 95, part 2 (1825), pp. 401-402.

LATTEUX, L.
   Déscription d'un Vitrail de l'Eglise de Gisors.
   St. Quentin, 1878.

   Mémoire sur les Anciens Vitraux des Départements du Nord et du Pas-
   de-Calais.
   Amiens, 1880.

LAUBER, Joseph
   American Colour Windows.
   Western Architectural Magazine (Minneapolis), (Feb., March, 1907).

   Design in Cathedral Windows.
   Western Architectural Magazine (Minneapolis), (Oct., 1908).

   European Versus American Colour Windows.
   Architectural Record   (New York), vol. 31 (1912), pp. 138-151.

LAUGARDIERE, Abbé De
   Les Vitraux de Saint-Bonnet de Bourges.
   Bulletin Monumental, vol. 91, no. 2 (1932), pp. 247-285.

(Laughlin, Alice D.)
   Obituary.
   Stained Glass, vol. 47, no. 2 (Summer, 1952), p. 82.

LAURENT, E.
   Saint-Germain d'Argentan.
   Argentan, 1859.

LAURENT, Marcel
   Musée du Cinquantenaire. Le Vitrail de Dirick Vellert.
   La Revue d'Art, part 25 (1925), pp. 81-84.

(Lausanne Cathedral)
   Cathédrale de Lausanne - 700ᵉ Anniversaire de la Consécration
   Solenelle. Catalogue de l'Exposition.
   Lausanne, 1975.

(Lauterbach, Franz)
   Obituary.
   Diamant, 55th year, no. 13 (May 1, 1933).

LAUTIER, Claudine
   La Technique du Vitrail.
   Les Dossiers de l'Archéologie, no. 26 (Jan.-Feb., 1978), pp. 26-37.

   With BRISAC, Catherine, BOUCHON, Chantal, ZALUSKA, Yolanta.
   La 'Belle-Verrière' de Chartres.
   Revue de l'Art, no. 46 (1979), pp. 16-24.

LAVANOUX, Maurice
   Stained Glass and Architecture.
   Stained Glass, vol. 27, no. 5 (May, 1932), pp. 146-148.

   The Good Samaritan Window, Bourges Cathedral.
   Stained Glass, vol. 27, no. 7 (July, 1932), pp. 202-205.

   Here and There.
   (Windows installed in Washington, Yale, etc.)
   Stained Glass, vol. 27, no. 10 (Oct., 1932), pp. 287-294.

   Painted Windows.
   The Commonweal (East Strondsburg, Philadelphia), (Oct. 13, 1933).

(Lavanoux, Maurice)
   Obituary.
   Stained Glass, vol. 69, no. 3 (Fall, 1974), p. 30.

LAVERGNE, N.
   Les Vitraux de Claudius Lavergne Placés dans la Cathédrale de
   Beauvais (Chapelle de Sainte-Anne et de St. Joseph).
   Beauvais, 1886.

   Les Vitraux de Claudius Lavergne Placés dans l'Eglise de Saint-Cyr
   au Mont d'Or, Diocèse de Lyon.
   Paris, 1888.

   L'Art des Vitraux.
   Paris, 1891.

LAW, Florence F.
The Parish Church of St. Andrew's, Shalford: its Associations with Families whose Coats of Arms are . . . in the East Window . . .
Colchester, 1898.

LAW, Margaret Lathrop
The Glory that is Glass - Past and Present.
Art and Archaeology, vol. 20, no. 5 (Nov., 1925), pp. 233-242.

(Henry Lawrence Collection Sale)
(Panel of an English Jesse Tree fetches £18,500 in a New York sale. Bought by A.P. Raymond.)
The Times, Jan. 31, 1921.

LAWRENCE, Marion
Maria Regina.
(Iconography of the crowned Madonna.)
Art Bulletin, vol. 7, no. 4 (June, 1925).
(Glass, p. 161.)

LAWSON, Richard
Trinity Windows.
(Mentions their former existence in (now) Manchester Cathedral.)
Notes and Queries, 9th series, vol. 3 (Apr. 15, 1899), pp. 293-294.

(Laxenburg)
54 Wechselausstellung der Österreichischen Galerie zu den Wiener Festwochen. Romantische Glasmalerei in Laxenburg.
Vienna, 1962.

LAZENBY, O.E.
Who Was the Donor of the St. William Window in York Minster?
Ryedale Historian, no. 6 (1972).

(Lead)
Modern American Work in Lead.
(From The Dutch Boy Quarterly.)
J.M.G.P., vol. 3, no. 2 (Oct., 1929), pp. 95-96.

(Leads)
A Machine for Cutting Reinforced Leads.
J.M.G.P., vol. 1, no. 5 (Oct., 1926), pp. 29-30.

LEATHER, G.F.T.
The Flodden Window in the Parish Church of St. Leonard, Middleton, Lancs.
Historians of Berwickshire Naturalists' Club, vol 30, part 1.

LECAPLAIN, Jean
Deux Figures de Putréfiés.
(Vitraux de Saint-Vincent et de Saint-Patrice de Rouen.)
Bulletin de la Société des Amis des Monuments Rouennais (1911), pp. 41-44.

LECHENETIER, A.
Notice sur les Vitraux de l'Eglise Paroissiale de Montfort l'Amaury.
Rambouillet, 1877.

LECHEVALLIER-CHEVIGNARD, Edmond
Projet de Vitrail pour la Cathédrale d'Orléans.
Revue des Arts Décoratifs, vol. 1 (1881), p. 490.

LECLERCQ, E.
Restauration des Vitraux (Ste. Goedele).
Gazette des Beaux-Arts, vol. 11 (1861), pp. 459-462.

LECOCK, G.
Etude sur les Vitraux de la Cathédrale de St. Quentin.
St. Quentin, 1874.

LECOMPTE, Rowan
Hommage à Bossanyi.
Cathedral Age (Washington), L. 3 (1975), p. 17.

LECOMTE, F.
Vitraux des Eglises. 1: Notre Dame.
Laon, 1854.

LEDICHE-DUFLOS, Marie Charles Edouard
Mémoire sur les Vitraux Peints de l'Arrondissement de Clermont (Oise).
Mémoires de la Société des Antiquaires de Picardie, 2nd series, vol. 10 (1850), pp. 93-120.

LEDIT, J.
Cathédrale de Troyes. Les Vitraux.
n.p., n.d. (1972).

LEDRU, A.
La Cathédrale du Mans.
Le Mans, 1923.

LEE, Lawrence
A Perspective on the Care of Historic Glass.
J.M.G.P., vol. 14, no. 5 (1970-1971), pp. 250-251.

The World of Stained Glass.
In Stained Glass, New York, 1976, pp. 8-63.
Reviewed by BRISAC, Catherine, Bulletin Monumental, vol. 136 (1978), pp. 304-306.
Reviewed in J.M.G.P., vol. 15, no. 3 (1974-1975), p. 74, and vol. 16, no. 1 (1976-1977), pp. 67-68.
Reviewed by SKINNER, Orin E., Stained Glass, vol. 71, no. 4 (Winter, 1976-1977), p. 235.

The Appreciation of Stained Glass.
Oxford, 1977.
Reviewed in J.M.G.P., vol. 16, no. 1 (1976-1977), pp. 68-70.

LEE, Ruth Webb
Sandwich Glass.
Framingham Centre, Mass., 1939.

LEES, Thomas
On the Remains of Ancient Glass in the East Window of Greystoke Church.
Transactions of the Cumberland and Westmorland Antiquarian and Archaeological Society, vol. 2 (1876), pp. 375-389.

With FERGUSON, R.S.
On the Remains of Ancient Glass and Woodwork at St. Anthony's Chapel, Cartmel Fell.
Transactions of the Cumberland and Westmorland Antiquarian and Archaeological Society, vol. 2 (1876), pp. 389-399.

LEES-MILNE, James

    The Vyne, Hampshire.
    (National Trust Guide.)
    2nd edition, London, 1961.

LEFÉBURE, Amélie

    Review of LILLICH, M.P., An Early Image of St. Louis.
    Bulletin Monumental, Chronique, vol. 128 (1970), p. 156.

LEFÉBVRE, Casimir

    Peinture sur Porcelaine . . . Suivie de la Peinture sur Verre . . .
    Paris, 1858.

LEFÉVRE, P.

    La Verrerie à Vitres et les Verriers de Belgique de puis le 15ᵉ
    Siecle.
    Charleroi, 1938.

    Documents relatifs aux vitraux de Sainte-Gudule, à Bruxelles, du
    16ᵉ et du 17ᵉ Siècle.
    Revue Belge d'Archéologie et d'Histoire de l'Art, vol. 15 (1945),
    pp. 117-162.

LEFRANÇOIS, G.

    St. Nicolas', Rouen.
    (Inquiry about location of glass sold in 1802.)
    Notes and Queries, 10th series, vol. 12 (July 17, 1909), p. 47.

LEGA-WEEKES, Ethel

    Two St. Katherines in Exeter Cathedral Window.
    Devon and Cornwall Notes and Queries, vol. 18 (1935), pp. 211-213.

LEGGE, T.M.

    A Note on the Stained Glass Windows of Henry A. Payne.
    The Studio, vol. 61 (1914), pp. 128-130.

LEGGE, Thomas

    Trade Guild Windows.
    J.M.G.P., vol. 4, no. 2 (Oct., 1931), pp. 51-64.
    (Taken from the article, The Trade Guild Windows at Chartres, The
    Labour Magazine, vol. 9, no. 11 (March, 1931), with an addendum.)

LEHMANN, Hans

    Die Glasgemälde im Kantonal Museum in Aarau.
    Aarau, 1897.

    With RAHN, J.R.
    Ergänzungen zur Literatur über die Schweizerische Glasmalerei.
    Anzeiger für schweizerische Altertumskunde, new series, vol. 2
    (1900), pp. 69-73.

    Die Glasgemälde in der Aargauischen Kirchen und öffentlichen Gebäuden.
    Anzeiger für schweizerische Altertumskunde, new series, vol. 3
    (1902-1907), pp. 291-303;
    vol. 4, pp. 73-94, 184-197, 306-312;
    vol. 7, pp. 122-138;
    vol. 8, pp. 44-58;
    vol. 9, pp. 230-248.

    Zur Geschichte der Glasmalerei in der Schweiz.
    Zurich, 4 parts, 1906-1912.
    Reprinted from Mitteilungen der antiquarischen Gesellschaft in
    Zürich, vol. 26.

    Die ehemalige Sammlung schweizerischer Glasmalereien in Toddington
    Castle (England).
    Munich, 1911.

LEHMANN, Hans

    Die zerstörten Glasgemälde in der Kirche von Hindelbank.
    Zeitschrift für alte und neue Glasmalerei (1912), p. 13.

    Die Glasmalerei in Bernzum Ende des 15 und Anfang des 16
    Jahrhunderts.
    Anzeiger für schweizerische Altertumskunde (1912-1914).

    Die Kirche zu Jegensdorf und ihre Glasgemälde.
    Festschrift zum Jubilaumsfeier des 400 Jahr. Bestandes.
    Berne, 1915.

    Die zerstörten Glasgemälde in der Kirche von Hindelbank und ihre
    Beziehungen zur Familie von Erlach.
    Berne, c. 1918.

    Zur Geschichte der Glasmalerei in der Schweiz.
    Leipzig, 1925.

    Lukas Zeiner und die Spätgotische Glasmalerei in Zurich.
    Mitteilungen der antiquarischen Gesellschaft in Zurich, band 30,
    heft 2, Zurich (1926).
    Reprinted Zurich, 1926.

    Das ehemalige Cisterzienser Kloster. Maris Stella bei Wettingen und
    seine Glasgemälde.
    Aarau, 1926.

    Zwei zürcher Wappenscheiben.
    Musée National Suisse, Zurich, 38me Rapport Annuel (1929), pp. 73-81.

    Die Glasgemälde im Gemeindehaus zu Unterstammheim.
    Andelfingen, 1932.

    Geschichte der Luzerner Glasmalerei von den Anfängen bis zu Beginn
    des 18. Jahrhunderts.
    Luzern Geschichte und Kultur, vol. 3, no. 5 (1941), pp. 143-151,
    166-172.

    Geschichte der Luzerner Glasmalerei.
    Lucerne, 1942.

LEHMANN, R.

    Die ältere Geschichte des Zisterzienserkloster Dobrilugh in der Lausig.
    Heidelberg, 1916.

LEHMBRUCK, W.

    Hans Acker, Maler und Glasmaler von Ulm.
    Ulm, 1968.

LEIGH, Gertrude

    (Revised by COCHRANE, R.A.)
    The Story of Winchelsea Church.
    15th edition, Gloucester, n.d.
    (Ancient glass, p. 13; glass by STRACHAN, Douglas, pp. 16-22.)

LEIGHTON, W.A.

    Figures in Weston Church, Salop.

    (Enquiry concerning the identity of donor figures formerly in the
    East Window.)

    Notes and Queries, 2nd series, vol. 10 (Aug. 11, 1860), pp. 108-109.

    Replied to by H.S.G., Ibid., (Aug. 25, 1860), p. 155.

(Leipzig)

    A Stained Glass Window in Leipzig.

    (Note.)

    Diamant, no. 20 (1924),

LEISCHING, Julius

    Die amerikanische Glasmalerei.

    St. Lucas (Deutsche Glaser Zeitung), vol. 6 (1895), p. 3.

    Glasmalerei und Kunstverglasung.

    Kunstgewerbebliches, Leipzig, vol. 13 (1902), pp. 107-119.

LEMAYRIE, Jean

    Marc Chagall: Vitraux pour Jérusalem.

    Monte Carlo, 1962.

    The Jerusalem Windows of Marc Chagall.

    (Translated by DESAUTELS, E.)

    New York, 1967.

    Reviewed by LLOYD, J.G., Stained Glass, vol. 64, no. 4 (Winter, 1969-
    1970), pp. 28-29.

LEMONNIER, Henry

    Au Château de Chantilly: la Galerie de Psyché. (Les Vitraux
    Consacrés à Psyché, 16e Siècle.)

    Gazette des Beaux-Arts (May, 1928), pp. 257-267.

LENOIR, Alexandre

    Description Historique et Chronologique des Monumens de Sculpture
    Réunis au Musée des Monumens Français . . . Augmentée . . . d'un
    Traité de la Peinture sur Verre.

    Paris, 1802, 6th edition.

    Musée des Monuments Français; Histoire de la Peinture sur Verre,
    et Description des Vitraux Anciens et Modernes . . .

      Paris, 1803.

    Notice Historique sur l'Ancienne Peinture sur Verre, sur les Moyens
    Pratiqués dans cet Art depuis l'Epoque de son Invention jusqu'à nos
    Jours; et par suite sur Jean Cousin qui a Excellé dans le même Art.

    Paris, 1824.

    Traité Théorique de la Peinture sur Verre.

    Paris, 1846.

    Traité Historique de la Peinture sur Verre.

    (Edited by DUMOULIN, J.-B.)

    Paris, 1856.

LENORMANT, Charles

    Sur l'Auteur des Vitres du Choeur de l'Ancienne Collégiale de Conches.

    Journal de Rouen (Feb. 16, 1855).

(St. Magnus', Lerwick)

    St. Magnus' Episcopal Church, Lerwick: Stained Glass.

    (Grant towards installing Comper windows.)

    The Pilgrim Trust, 42nd Annual Report (1972), p. 16.

LETHABY, W.R.

    Leadwork, Old and Ornamental and for the Most Part English.

    London, 1893.

    Mediaeval Art from the Peace of the Church to the Eve of the
    Renaissance.

    London, 1904.

    (Stained glass, pp. 177-180.)

    Stained Glass Work.

    New York, 1905.

    Westminster Abbey and the King's Craftsmen.

    London, 1906.

    (Glass, pp. 29, 37, 38, 237-239, 299-304.)

    Archbishop Roger's Cathedral at York and its Stained Glass.

    The Archaeological Journal, vol. 72 (1915), pp. 37-48.

    Philip Webb.

    (Contains material on Morris and Burne-Jones.)

    The Builder, (March 6, 1925).

    Westminster Abbey Re-examined.

    London, 1925.

    (Stained glass, pp. 234-254.)

    Early Thirteenth Century Glass at Salisbury Cathedral.

    J.M.G.P., vol. 1, no. 4 (Apr., 1926), pp. 17-18.

LEVETT, N.D.

    Glass Painting in England.

    Dublin University Magazine, vol. 95 (1879), p. 361.

LE VIEIL, P.

    L'Art de la Peinture sur Verre et de la Vitrerie.

    Paris, 1774.

LÉVY, Edmond

    (Plates by CAPRONNIER, J.)

    Histoire de la Peinture sur Verre en Europe, et Particulièrement en
    Belgique.

    (2 parts) Brussels, 1854-1860.

LEWIS, Cécile Francis

    A Practical Handbook on Glass-Painting.

    London, 1929.

LEWIS, H. Mostyn

    Stained Glass in North Wales up to 1850.

    Altrincham, 1970.

    Reviewed by NEWTON, Peter, Archaeologia Cambrensis, vol. 120 (1971),
    pp. 120-121.

    Reviewed by CLIFTON-TAYLOR, Alec, The Connoisseur, vol. 177 (June,
    1971), p. 51.

    Reviewed by HAYWARD, John, J.M.G.P., vol. 14, no. 5 (1970-1971), p. 266.

    Stained Glass in North Wales.

    Archaeologia Cambrensis, vol. 123 (1974), pp. 1-12.

LEWIS, Reury

    First Khaki-Clad Figures in a Stained-Glass Window.

    Notes and Queries, 12th series, vol. 4 (Aug., 1918), p. 214.

LEWIS, Virginia

    Stained Glass in Pittsburgh.

    Pitt (A University of Pittsburgh Quarterly), (Summer, 1946).

    Stained Glass in Pittsburgh.

    Stained Glass, vol. 43, no. 2 (Summer, 1948), pp. 35-46.

    Some Aspects of Stained Glass in Pittsburgh - Past and Present.

    Stained Glass, vol. 56, no. 1 (Spring, 1961), pp. 13-27.

LEXOW, Einar

    Norske glassmalerier frå langstiden.
    Oslo, 1938.

LIEBENAU, T. von

    Die Glasgemälde der ehemaligen Benediktiner-Abtei Muri . . . in
    Aarau.
    Aarau, 1892.

(Liége Cathedral)

    Fragments de Vitrail du 16e Siècle Provenant de la Cathédrale St.
    Lambert. By J.A.
    Chronique Archéologique de Pays de Liége, vol. 3 (1908), pp. 59-60.

(Liége School)

    Un Peintre Verrier Liégeois du 16e Siècle. By J.B.
    Chronique Archéologique du Pays de Liége, vol. 1 (1906), pp. 110-111.

LIGHTFOOT, N.F.

    A Paper on Some Churches in the Deanery of Tavistock.
    Transactions of the Exeter Diocesan Architectural Society, vol. 2
    (1847),
    (Stained Glass at Sydenham Damerell, pp. 58-59.)

LIGHTFOOT. William J.

    Notes on Warehorne Church and its Ancient Stained Glass . . .
    Archaeologia Cantiana, vol. 4 (1861), pp. 97-112.

LILLICH, Meredith Parsons

    Découverte d'un Vitrail Perdu de Saint-Père de Chartres.
    Mémoires de la Société des Antiquaires d'Eure-et-Loir, no. 13 (1964),
    pp. 261-268.

    An Early Image of Saint-Louis.
    Gazette des Beaux-Arts, vol. 75 (1970), pp. 251-256.

    The Band Window: A Theory of Origin and Development.
    Gesta, vol. 9 (1970), pp. 26-33.

    Les Vitraux de la Nef Saint-Père de Chartres: Analyse Stylistique.
    Bulletin des Sociétés Archéologiques d'Eure-et-Loir, Mémoires, no.
    40, 1e trimestre (1971).

    A Redating of the Thirteenth-Century Grisaille Windows of Chartres
    Cathedral.
    Gesta, vol. 11 (1972), pp. 11-18.

    Vitrail Normand du 18e Siècle aux Armes de la Ferrière.
    Archivum Heraldicum   pp. 190-197.

    Les Donateurs de Quelques Vitraux de la Nef de Saint-Père de Chartres.
    Bulletin des Sociétés Archéologiques d'Eure-et-Loir, Mémoires, no.
    46, 3e trimestre (1972).

    Les Vitraux de Saint-Pierre-de-Chartres.
    Les Monuments Historiques de la France, no. 1 (1977), pp. 52-57.

    A Stained Glass Apostle from Sées Cathedral (Normandy) in the
    Victoria and Albert Museum.
    Burlington Magazine, vol. 119 (July, 1977), pp. 497-500.

LILLIE, W.W.

    The Trial of Archbishop Laud.
    J.M.G.P., vol. 8, no. 4 (1942), pp. 137-144.

(Lincoln's Inn, Old Hall)

    Heraldic Glass in the Old Hall, Lincoln's Inn.
    J.M.G.P., vol. 4, no. 1 (Apr., 1931), p. 23.

LIND, Karl

    Uebersicht der noch in Kirchen Niederösterreichs erhaltenen
    Glasmalereien.
    Bernauer Altertums-Ver (Vienna), vol. 27 (1891), pp. 109-129.

    Meisterwerke der kirklichen Glasmalerei. Herausgegeben unter der
    artistischen Leitung von R. Geyling und Alois Löw.
    Vienna, 1894-1897, 1899.

    Ein altes Glasgemälde in der Sammlung der Museums Franscisco-
    Carolinum zu Linz.
    Mitteilungen Kaizerlich-königlicher Zentral-Commission für
    Erforschung von Erhaltung künstlerische und historischer Denkmale,
    year 24 (1898), pp. 208-210.

LINDBLOM, Andreas

    Sveriges Konsthistoria.
    Stockholm, 1940.
    Reviewed by SKEAT, Francis, J.M.G.P., vol. 10, no. 4 (1951), p. 219.

(Van Linge brothers)

    The Works of the Van Linges in Painted Glass.
    The Gentleman's Magazine, vol. 34, new series, part 2 (1850), pp.
    383-387.

(Linge, Bernard Van)

    (His work at Lincoln's Inn. A suggestion that his surname was
    Bernard.)
    The Gentleman's Magazine, vol. 35, new series, part 1 (1851), p. 65.

LINNEMANN, Otto and Rudolf

    Vorbildliche Glasmalereien aus dem Späten Mittelalter und der
    Renaissance. (Aufnahmen der Glasmaler Gebr. Linnemann in
    Frankfurt-am-Main.)
    Berlin, 1911.

LINNEMANN, Otto

    Glasmalerei und Architektur.
    Glastechnische Berichte, 12th year, no. 5 (May, 1934).

    Glasmalerei und Architektur.
    Diamant, 56th year, no. 20 (July 11, 1934).

    Einiges über die Technik der Glasmalerei in Verbindung mit der
    Ausstellung 'Deutsche Wand - und Glasmalerei'.
    Report to Technical Committee no. 4, of the Deutsche Glastechnische
    Gesellschaft, Wiesbaden.
    Glastechnische Berichte, no. 12, (1934), p. 262.

LINNEMANN, Rudolf

    Nochmals 'Die Trennung zwischen Kartonzeichner und Glasmaler'.
    Zeitschrift fur alte und neue Glasmalerei (1912), p. 138.

    Reste heraldischer Glasmalereien in der Wallfahrtskirche zu Wilsnack.
    Ibid., (1914), p. 6.

LINSLEY, G.F.

    A Possible Method of Conserving Ancient Glass.
    In 8e Colloque du Corpus Vitrearum Medii Aevi.
    Paris ?, 1972, p. 51.

LISTER, E.G.

    Westwood Manor House, Wiltshire.
    Country Life, vol. 60, no. 1543 (Aug. 14, 1926), p. 250.

(Kaunas, Lithuania)

    Vitrazo ir Skulpturos Galerija.
    Vilno, 1973.

LJUBINKOVIC, Radivojé

    Sur un Exemplaire de Vitraux du Monastère du Studenica.
    Archaeologia Jugoslavica, no. 3 (1959), pp. 137-141.

LITTLE, Helen D.

    The Five Sisters at York.
    (Letter to the Editor.)
    The Times, Oct. 30, 1933.

(Litton Industries Annual Report)
    (Profusely illustrated with wholly irrelevant coloured photographs
    of stained glass.)
    Beverley Hills ?, 1967.

(Liverpool Cathedral glass)
    Stained Glass.
    (An account of his windows by HOGAN, James.)
    The Studio, vol. 3 (Jan.-June, 1936), pp. 190-193.

LIVET

    Rapport fait à l'Académie de Metz sur les Vitraux Exposés par M.M.
    Maréchal et Gugnon. Le Secret de la Peinture sur Verre, a-t-il été
    Perdu?
    Mémoires de l'Académie de Metz (1843).

(Living persons depicted in stained glass)
    News and Notes, J.M.G.P., vol. 12, no. 4 (1959), p. 239.

(Llanllugan Church, Montgomery)
    (Report of notes given on the east window by Dr. R.A.S. Macalister.)
    Archaeologia Cambrensis, vol. 87 (1932), pp. 460-461.

(Llanrhychwyn Church)
    A Trinity in Stained Glass in Llanrhychwyn Church, North Wales.
    Manchester Guardian, July 5, 1929.

LLOYD, John G.
    Secular Uses for Stained Glass.
    Stained Glass, vol. 56, no. 3 (Autumn, 1961), pp. 4-16.

    Stained Glass is Thriving.
    Glass Digest (Jan., 1962).

    Stained Glass Art Surges to Greatest Growth in History.
    Chicago Construction News (Feb. 23, 1962).

    Stained Glass Faces Crisis.
    American Glass Review (July, 1962).

    Art of Stained Glass Thriving.
    American Glass Review (July, 1963).

    Stained Glass in America.
    Jenkintown, Pennsylvania, 1963.

    Stained Glass for the Older Church.
    Your Church (March-Apr., 1967).

LLOYD-PRITCHARD, M.F., and MARTYN, C.W.
    The Story of Aylsham and Her Parish Church.
    Aylsham, 1950.
    (Glass, p. 10.)

(Lobmeyer, J. and L.)
    100 Jahre Österreichische Glaskunst, Lobmeyr, 1823-1923.
    Vienna, 1925.

LOCKETT, William
    Review of REYNTIENS, Patrick, The Technique of Stained Glass.
    J.M.G.P., vol. 14, no. 4 (1968-1969), p. 221.

LOFFLER, J.
    Reaktionen zwischen Glas und Luftfeuchtigkeit.
    Glastechnische Berichte, vol. 41 (1968), pp. 506-512.

LOFTIE, W.J.
    Notes on Early Glass in Canterbury Cathedral.
    The Archaeological Journal, vol. 33 (1876), pp. 1-14.

LOIRE, Gabriel
    Le Vitrail: Aperçus Historiques, Artistiques et Techniques. D'Apres
    les plus Beaux Vitraux des Eglises et Chapelles de l'Anjou.
    Angers, 1925.

LONDON, H. Stanford
    The Garter Windows in St. George's, Stamford.
    Notes and Queries, vol. 193 (Aug. 21, 1948), p. 367.

(London, Battersea, St. Mary's)
    Seventeenth Century Heraldry and Portraits in St. Mary's, Battersea.
    Daily Chronicle, Jan. 21, 1926.

(London, Lamb's Chapel)
    (Glass-paintings briefly described and illustrated.)
    The Gentleman's Magazine, vol. 53 (1783), p. 27.

(London, St. George's, Hanover Square)
    The Stained Glass at St. George's, Hanover Square.
    (Mentions damage to the windows by suffragettes and their
    restoration by Clayton and Bell.)
    The Connoisseur, vol. 40 (Sept.-Dec., 1914), pp. 96-97.

(London, St. James', Piccadilly)
    St. James', Piccadilly. and Modern Glass Painting.
    (East window by Wailes.)
    The Ecclesiologist, vol. 6 (1846), pp. 46-48.

(London, St. Margaret's, Westminster)
    Stained Glass of St. Margaret, Westminster. By T.W.
    The Ecclesiologist, vol. 3 (1844), pp. 24-26.

(London, St. Mary's, Battersea)
    (Restoration of Van Linge window by John Hayward.)
    J.M.G.P., vol. 15, no. 3 (1974-1975), pp. 64-66.

(London, St. Mary's Lambeth)
    New Stained Glass in St. Mary's, Lambeth.
    The Ecclesiologist, vol. 14 (1853), pp. 107-108.

(London, St. Paul's)
    The Internal Decoration of St. Paul's Cathedral.
    (Contributions to a discussion on the introduction of stained glass
    by COCKERELL, C.S., PENROSE, F.C., Archdeacon HALE, PAPWORTH, J.W.,
    PARRIS, E.T., SCOTT, G.G.)
    The Gentleman's Magazine, vol. 38, new series, part 2 (1852), pp.
    261-269.

(London, Temple Church)

(Willement windows inserted.)

The Gentleman's Magazine, vol. 17, new series, part 1 (1842), pp. 654-655.

The Temple Church, its Interior, Restorations and Decoration, with Plans of the East Windows of the North and South Aisles.
Weale's Quarterly Papers on Architecture, vol. 1, London (1844).

Mr. Winston's New Window at the Temple Church.
The Ecclesiologist, vol. 14 (1853), p. 178.
(Further criticism of Winston.)
Ibid., pp. 293-294.

LONG, E.T.

Ancient Stained Glass in Dorset Churches.
Proceedings of the Dorset Natural History and Antiquaries Field Club, vol. 43 (1923), pp. 45-

Church Notes (on Dorset Churches).
In A Choice of Dorset Churches.
Dorchester, 1967.

(Long Melford Church)

Long Melford Church, Suffolk: Glass.
(A grant to restore and rearrange the windows.)
The Pilgrim Trust, 27th Annual Report (1957), pp. 19-20.

(Lorimer, Robert)

Memorial Stained Glass Windows by Sir R. Lorimer.
(Work executed by STRACHAN, D., PARSONS, K., DAVIS, L., CAMM, W.H., PAYNE, H.)
Country Life, vol. 38 (Nov., 1915), pp. 641-644.

LORIN, C.

Le Panneau de l'Ascenscion de Saint-Pierre de Chartres.
Mémoires de la Société des Antiquaires d'Eure-et-Loir, vol. 1 (1906), pp. 508-514.

LORIN, Felix
8e, 9e et 10e Pardons d'Anne de Bretagne. Le Légende de Saint Yves et les Peintres Verriers.
La Porte du Cimetière de Montfort-l'Amaury.
Versailles, 1908.

LORIN, N.
De la Peinture sur Verre à Propos de l'Exposition de Philadelphie.
Chartres, 1878.

LOTHÉ, Ernest
Les Vitraux du Grand Séminaire de Lille. Vitraux de Paul Turpin Exécutés d'Après les Cartons de P. Pruvost.
Lille, 1937.

LOTTIN, Abbé
Verrières, Peintes de la Nouvelle Eglise d'Ecommoy.
Le Mans, 1845.

Description Iconographique des Vitraux Peints de l'Eglise des Soeurs de la Providence de Ruille sur Loir, Sarthe.
Le Mans, 1858.

LÖW, Alois
Studien über ein Capital der Monumental Glasmalerei.
Berichte Altertums Verein, Wien, vol. 27 (1891), pp. 99-107.

Alte Glasmalereien in Niederösterreich.
Ibid., vol. 3 (1895), pp. 9-28.

LOW, Alois (Contd.)

Die alten Glasgemälde in der Pfarrkirche zu Heiligenblut (Niederösterreich).
Ibid., vol. 33 (1898), pp. 44-46.

Ein altes Glasgemälde in Stift Ardagger.
Ibid., vol. 35 (1900), p. 119-128.

Die alten Glasfenster von St. Stephan in Wien. Beiträge zur Geschichte der Glasmalerei in Wien.
Ibid., vol. 40 (1906), pp. 1-27.

Die St. Lukas-Zeche in Wien Beiträge zur Geschichte der Glasmalerei in Wien.
Ibid., vol. 40 (1907), pp. 163-186.

LOW, Will H.
Old Glass in New Windows.
Scribner's Magazine (Dec., 1888).

LOWE, John
The Medieval English Glazier. A Brief Survey of the Origins of Glass-Painting and the Glazier's Craft from 1200-1500.
J.M.G.P., vol. 13, no. 2 (1961), part 1, pp. 425-432; part 2, vol. 13, no. 3 (1962), pp. 492-508.

Stained Glass at Coventry Cathedral.
J.M.G.P., vol. 13, no. 4 (1963), pp. 585-587.

LOWE, W.F.
The Conservation of Stained Glass.
Aberdeen, 1960.
Also in Studies in Conservation, no. 5, part 4 (1960), pp. 139-149.

Restoration of Morris Windows at the Victoria and Albert Museum.
The Museum Journal, vol. 60, part 5 (1960), p. 121.

LOWE, William
The Conservation of Stained Glass.
J.M.G.P., vol. 13, no. 3 (1962), pp. 468-476.

LOWLAND, Scalion (Pseudonym)
The Schizophrenic Crisis of Scalion Lowland, a Stained Glass Addict, as Told by Himself.
Stained Glass, vol. 46, no. 1 (Spring, 1961), pp. 3-13.

LOWNDES, M.
Composition and Design in Ancient Stained Glass.
The Englishwoman, vol. 20 (1913), p. 10.

LOWTHER BOUCH, C.M.
Notes on Carlisle Cathedral. 1: John of Gaunt and the East Window.
Transactions of the Cumberland and Westmorland Antiquarian and Archaeological Society, new series, vol. 45 (1946), pp. 122-125.

LOXTON, C.A.
First Khaki-Clad Figures in Stained Glass Windows.
Notes and Queries, 12th series, vol. 4 (Sept., 1918), p. 250.

(Lübeck)
Lübeck, die Heimat der Glasmalerei.
Neue Lübeckische Blätter, Jg. 6, no. 46.
Lübeck, 1840.

(Lübeck, Marienkirche)
Die Stiftungen des deutschen Kaisers für die Marienkirche zu Lübeck.
Zeitschrift für alte und neue Glasmalerei (1914), p. 79.

LUBECKER, Pierre

Contemporary Danish Glass-Painting.
J.M.G.P., vol. 11, no. 2 (1953), pp. 89-91.

LÜBKE, Wilhelm

Die Glasgemälde im Kreuzgange zu Kloster Wettingen.
Mittelalterliche antiquitäten Gesellschaft, Zurich, vol. 14, part 5
(1863).

Ueber die alten Glasgemälde der Schweiz.
Zurich, 1866.

Vorschule zum Studium der kirchlichen Kunst des deutschen Mittelalters.
Leipzig, 1866, 5th edition.
English version: Ecclesiastical Art in Germany During the Middle Ages.
Edinburgh and London, 1870.
(Stained glass, pp. 232-237.)

Die Glasgemälde im Chor des Klosters Konigsfelden.
Zurich, 1867.

LUCAS, Arthur

(Letter to the Editor enquiring for information about war damage to
glass.)
J.M.G.P., vol. 8, no. 4 (1942), p. 156.

LUCOT, Abbé

Histoire de St. Memmie. Verrières Historiques de la Chapelle du
Petit Seminaire de St. Memmie-les-Châlons.
Châlons, 1872.

Eglise Notre-Dame en Vaux.
Châlons, 1873.

Verrières de la Cathédrale de Châlons en Général, et plus
Particulièrement les Verrières des Collatéraux.
Châlons, 1884.

L'Ancien Vitrail de Saint Etienne de l'Epoque de la Renaissance
de la Cathédrale de Châlons.
Mémoires de la Société Agriculturale de la Marne (1885).

Les Vitraux de l'Eglise St. Etienne (Cathédrale); Sanctuaire,
Transept, Choeur et Nef Principale.
Ibid., (1885).

St. Etienne et l'Evêque Pierre de Mans. Vitrail de la Cathédrale
de Châlons-sur-Marne.
Mémoires de la Société Nationale des Antiquités de France, vol. 51
(1891).

(Ludlow Church)

(The windows cleaned and repaired by EVANS, David.)
The Gentleman's Magazine, vol. 45, new series, part 1 (1856), p. 393.

LUKENS, Glen

A Window of Glass and Clay.
Stained Glass, vol. 63, no. 3 (Autumn, 1968), pp. 12-15.

LUSH, Frederick

On the System and Principles Pursued by the Gothic Architects, from
the Eleventh to the Fifteenth Centuries Inclusive, in the
Embellishment by Colour of the Architectural Members and Other Parts
of their Religious and Civil Edifices.
The Architectural Magazine (1838), pp. 198-214.

LUTYENS, Sir Edwin

Speech at the Annual Dinner of the British Society of Master Glass-
Painters.
J.M.G.P., vol. 5, no. 2 (Oct., 1933), pp. 93-98.

LUTZ, Jules

Les Verrières de l'Ancienne Eglise Saint Etienne à Mulhouse.
Supplement au Bulletin du Musée Historique de Mulhouse, vol. 29,
Mulhouse (1906).

With PERDRIZET, Paul.
Texte Critique (of 'Speculum Humanae Salvationis') Traduction
Inédité de Jean Mielot (1448).
Les Sources et l'Influence Iconographique Principalement sur l'Art
Alsacien du 14e Siècle.
Avec la Réproduction en 140 Planches du Manuscrit de Sélestat
(Schlettstacht) de la Série Complète des Vitraux de Mulhouse, des
Vitraux de Colmar, de Wissembourg, etc.
Mulhouse, 1907-1909.

LUYNES, Victor de

Exposition Universelle de 1889. Rapport du Jury International.
Classe 19. Cristaux, Verrerie et Vitraux.
Paris, 1889.

(Lyon, Museum)

Catalogue du Musée des Beaux-Arts de la Ville de Lyon.
Lyon, 1894.

LYSONS, Samuel.

Collection of Gloucestershire Antiquities, with Examples in Colour
of the Ancient Stained Glass from the Windows of Churches.
London, 1803.

LYSONS, Daniel and Samuel

Magna Britannia, Being a Concise Topographical Account of the
Several Counties of Great Britain.
6 vols. (all published), London, 1806-1822.

McCLINTON, Katherine Morrison
Stained Glass for the Changing Church.
Stained Glass, vol. 52, no. 3 (Autumn, 1957), pp. 108-112.

McGRATH, Raymond, and FROST, A.C.
Glass in Architecture and Decoration.
London, 1937.
(New revised edition 1961).
Reviewed by THORPE, W.A., Burlington Magazine, vol. 73, July-Dec.,
1938), p. 46.

McKEAN, Hugh F.
Tiffany. A Personal Recollection.
Stained Glass, vol. 63, no. 3 (Autumn, 1968), pp. 24-30.

McLAUGHLIN
A Layman at Chartres.
Stained Glass, vol. 45, no. 3 (Autumn, 1950), pp. 107-111.

MAAS, Arnold
Stained Glass Tours: Puerto Rico.
Stained Glass, vol. 60, no. 3 (Autumn, 1965), pp. 25-29.

MacCAUSLAND, M.B.
On the Making of Stained Glass Windows.
Toronto, 1913.

MacDONALD, M.I.M.
John Scott and Son, of Carlisle, Stained Glass Manufacturers.
Transactions of the Cumberland and Westmorland Antiquarian and
Archaeological Society, new series, vol. 72 (1972), pp. 274-282.

MacKARNESS, George R.
The Merton College Library Windows.
The Ecclesiologist, vol. 19 (1858), pp. 385-387.

MACKAY, Norman A.M.
The Stained Glass in St. John's Kirk, Perth.
J.M.G.P., vol. 16, no. 1 (1976-1977), pp. 35-40.

MACLAGAN, Charles P.D.
The Old Stained Glass of All Saints, North Street, York.
In SHAW, P.J., An Old York Church, All Hallows in North Street: Its
Mediaeval Stained Glass etc.
York (?), 1908.
Published separately, York, 1908.

MACLAGAN, Sir Eric
New Light on the Lady Chapel Windows.
In BRIGHT, Hugh, Lichfield Cathedral: the Lady Chapel Windows.
New and revised edition, 1950.

MACRAY, J.
(Contribution to the discussion on the Fairford Windows.)
Notes and Queries, 4th series, vol. 2 (Sept. 19, 1868), pp. 268-269.

MADER, G., STADL, J., NEUHAUSER, A.
Fensterzeichnungen aus der Tiroler Glasmalerei-anstalt.
Innsbruck, 1866.

(Madley Church)
Madley Church Repairs, etc., in the Seventeenth and Eighteenth
Centuries.
Transactions of the Woolhope Naturalists' Field Club, vol. 35 for
1955-1957 (1958), pp. 308-310.

MAERKER, Karl-Joachim
Frühe thüringisch-sächsische Glasmalereien und ihr Verhältnis zu
Skulptur und Malerei.
In Akten des 10. Internationalen Colloquiums des CVMA.
Stuttgart, 1977, p. 21.

'MAGDALENENSIS'
Glass Painters.
(Request for information about the Price family of glass-painters.
Some information given by the Editor.)
Notes and Queries, 2nd series, vol. 1 (Apr. 26, 1856), p. 337.

(Magdeburg Exhibition)
Ausstellung für moderne Glasmalerei in Magdeburg.
Keramische Rundschau, vol. 20 (1912), p. 131.

MAGINNIS, Charles D.
The Glass Artist in Competition.
Stained Glass, vol. 36, no. 3 (Autumn, 1941), pp. 71-74.

(Maginnis, Charles D.)
Obituary.
Stained Glass, vol. 49, nos. 3 and 4 (Autumn-Winter, 1954), pp. 133-134.

MAGNE, Lucien
Le Vitrail.
Gazette des Beaux-Arts, vol. 31 (1885), pp. 53, 138, 417.

L'Oeuvre des Peintres-Verriers Français. Verrieres des Monuments
Eleves pars les Montmorency-Montmorency, Ecouen, Chantilly.
2 vols., Paris, 1885.

Le Musee du Vitrail. (Au Palais de l'Industrie.)
Gazette des Beaux-Arts (Oct., 1886), pp. 297-311.

Les Vitraux de l'Ancienne Abbaye de Garcy, Departement de Seine-et-
Oise.
Commission des Antiquites et des Arts, vol. 7 (1887), pp. 75-98.

Les Vitraux de Montmorency et d'Ecouen.
Paris, 1888.

Rapport. Classe 67. Vitraux a l'Exposition Universelle Internationale
de 1900 a Paris.
Paris, 1900.

L'Art et les Vitraux Modernes.
L'Art Decoratif, vol. 19 (1906).

Palais du Trocadero, Musee de la Sculpture Comparee, Galerie des
Vitraux.
Paris, 1912.

Le Decor du Verre.
Paris, 1913.
(Vol. 3 of L'Art Applique aux Metiers.)

With MAGNE, H.M.
Decor du Verre; Gobeleterie, Mosaique, Vitrail.
Paris, 1927, 2nd edition.

MAGNIER, M.
Nouveau Manuel Complet de la Peinture sur Verre, sur Porcelaine et
sur Email (with Rebouleau).
Paris, 1868.

MAGRATH, John R.
Pre-Raphaelite Stained Glass.
(Morris Glass at Middleton Cheney, Buckinghamshire.)
Notes and Queries, 12th series, vol. 5 (Apr., 1919), pp. 105-106.

MAGUIRE, John F.
>The Artificial Lighting of Stained Glass.
>Stained Glass, vol. 46, no. 1 (Spring, 1951), pp. 18-26.

MAHN, H.
>Von moderner Lübischer Glasmalerei.
>Diamant, 52nd year, no. 6 (Feb. 21, 1930), pp. 101-102.

MAILLET, Germaine
>La Cathedrale de Chalons-sur-Marne.
>Paris, 1946.

MAINES, Clark
>The Charlemagne Window at Chartres Cathedral: New Considerations on
>Text and Image.
>Speculum, vol. 52 (1977), pp. 801-823.

MALE, Emile
>La Peinture sur Verre en France.
>In Histoire Generale de l'Art.
>Paris, 1905, 1, 2 and 4.

>Quelques Imitations de la Gravure Italienne par les Peintres-Verriers
>du 16^e Siecle.
>In Melanges Offerts a M. Henry Lemonnier.
>Paris, 1913.

>Religious Art in France: Thirteenth Century. A Study in Mediaeval
>Iconography and its Sources of Inspiration.
>London, 1913.
>Reprinted as The Gothic Image, London, 1961.

>L'Art Religieux du 12^e Siecle en France.
>Paris, 1922.

>Copies of Italian Engravings by French Glass-Painters of the
>Sixteenth Century.
>J.M.G.P., vol. 3, no. 2 (Oct., 1929), pp. 74-80.
>See letter to the Editor, J.M.G.P., vol. 3, no. 3 (Apr., 1930), p. 146.

>Twelfth Century Symbolism and Iconography.
>In L'Art Religieux du 12e Siècle en France.
>(Translated by SMITH,F.P.)
>Stained Glass, vol. 38, no. 1 (Spring, 1943), pp. 4-10.
>   vol. 38, no. 3 (Autumn, 1943), pp. 77-82.

>Notre Dame de Chartres.
>Paris, 1948.

(Mâle, Emile)
>Obituary. By AUBERT, Marcel.
>Bulletin Monumental, vol. 113 (1955), pp. 47-49.

MALLET-STEVENS, Robert
>(Foreword by LEON, Paul.)
>Exposition Internationale de 1937. Vitraux Modernes.
>Paris, 1937.

(Malpas, St. Oswald's Church)
>(Windows by Warrington inserted.)
>The Ecclesiologist, vol. 5 (1846), p. 128.

(Great Malvern)
>The Painted Windows in Malvern Church. By J.C.
>The Gentleman's Magazine, 2nd series, vol. 72 (1802), pp. 923-924.

(Great Malvern Glass Illustrated)
>Stones of the Temple. 13. The Windows.
>The Church Builder (1866), pp. 137-147.

(Great Malvern)
>Modern Stained Glass Restored.
>The Times, Nov. 3, 1919.
>The Worcester Herald, Nov. 8, 1919.

>The Windows of Great Malvern Priory.
>(On their removal because of the War.)
>Malvern Gazette, July 28, 1941.
>J.M.G.P., vol. 8, no. 4 (1942), pp. 152-153.

>(Grant towards replacing the windows.)
>The Pilgrim Trust, 15th Annual Report (1945), p. 7.

>(Grant towards the restoration of some of the windows.)
>The Pilgrim Trust, 47th Annual Report (1977), p. 10.

MANCEAU, Abbé
>Explication d'une Verrière de l'Eglise Métropolitaine de Tours.
>Bulletin Monumental, vol. 6 (1840), p. 261.

MANCINI, Giralomo
>Guglielmo de Marcillat, Francese, Insuperato Pittore Sul Vetro.
>Florence, 1909.

MANDACH, C. de
>La Peinture sur Verre en Suisse.
>In MICHEL, André, Histoire de l'Art Depuis les Premiers Temps
>Chrétiens Jusqu'à Nos Jours.
>Paris, 1905.
>Vol. 2, part 1, pp. 397-
>Vol. 3, pp. 392.

>Schweizerische Glasscheiben im Auslande.
>Anzeige für Schweizerische Altertumskunde, new series, vol. 9 (1908),
>pp. 334-340.

MANDER, G.P., and PAPE, T.
>Some Ridware Armorial Glass.
>Staffordshire Historical Collections, new series, vol. 24 (1923),
>pp. 279-290.
>Reprinted London, 1924.

MANNING, C.R.
>Elsing Church.
>Norfolk Archaeology, vol. 6, (1864), p. 200.

(Le Mans, Cathedral)
>Restauration d'une Verrière dans la Cathédrale du Mans Offrant la
>Legende de St. Julien.
>Le Mans, 1841.

>Interprétations Nouvelles de Deux Verrières du 13e Siècle à la
>Cathédrale du Mans d'après un Livre Récent de M. Emile Mâle.
>Revue Historique et Archéologique de Maine (Mamers), vol. 51 (1902),
>pp. 224-236.

MANSELL, M.H.
>The Parish Church of All Saints, Woodchurch, Kent.
>n.p., 1972.
>(Glass, pp. 11-12.)

MANZONI, Luigi
>Appunti e Documenti per l'Arte dei Pinger su Vetro in Perugia nel
>Seculo 15.
>Repertorium Kunstwissenschaft, vol. 26 (1902), pp. 120-132.

MAPPAE CLAVICULA
>Mappae Clavicula. (That is, Little Key of Drawing or Painting.)
>A Manuscript of the Twelfth Century . . . Treating of the Preparation
>of Pigments . . .
>Privately printed, London, 1847.
>See Archaeologia, vol. 32 (1847), pp. 183-244.

MARCHAL

　　Vitraux de Sainte Gudule.
　　Bulletin de l'Académie Royale d'Archéologie de Belgique, vol. 1 (　　),
　　p. 47.

MARCHINI, Giuseppe

　　Le Vetrate Italiane.
　　Milan, 1955.
　　Reviewed by AUBERT, Marcel, Bulletin Monumental, no. 114 (1956), pp.
　　77-78.

　　Italian Stained Glass Windows.
　　London, 1957.
　　Reviewed in J.M.G.P., vol. 12, no. 3 (1959), pp. 227-228.
　　Reviewed in Stained Glass, vol. 56, no. 4 (Winter, 1961-1962), p. 33.

　　Vetri Italiani in America.
　　In Arte in Europa, Miscellanea di Studi in Onore de E. Arslan.
　　Milan, 1966, pp. 431-436.

　　Per la Protezione delle Vetrate in Sito.
　　In 7e Colloque du Corpus Vitrearum Medii Aevi, Florence ?, 1970, p. 42.

　　Le Antiche Vetrate in Italia.
　　In 7e Colloque du Corpus Vitrearum Medii Aevi, Florence ?, 1970, pp.
　　17-23.

　　L'Affaiblissement de la Grisaille le Long des Plombs.
　　In 8e Colloque du Corpus Vitrearum Medii Aevi, Paris ?, 1972, p. 46.

　　Le Vetrate dell' Umbria.
　　(CVMA, Italy, vol. 1.)
　　Rome, 1973.

　　Conservation of Stained Glass in Italy.
　　J.M.G.P., vol. 15, no. 2 (1973-1974), pp. 11-15.

　　A Treatise on Stained Glass.
　　(Letter to the Editor denying any connection with PEZZELLA's
　　edition of Antonio da Pisa.)
　　Burlington Magazine, vol. 119 (May, 1977), p. 355.

MARECHAL, Abbé

　　Vitraux de St. Vincent de Paul (Paris).
　　Annales Archéologiques, vol. 1 (1844), p. 189.

(Marienstern, Saxony)

　　Die Wappenscheiben unter den Glasgemälden zu Marienstern in Sachsen.
　　Zeitschrift fur alte und neue Glasmalerei (1913), p. 70.

MARILLIER, H.C.

　　A Note on the Morris Stained Glass Work.
　　Privately printed, 1913.

MARITAIN, Jacques

　　Art and Scholasticism.
　　(Translated by SCANLAN, J.F.)
　　London, 1930.

MARKS, Richard

　　Medieval Stained Glass in Bedfordshire. Part 1.
　　Bedfordshire Magazine, vol. 15 (Summer, 1976), pp. 179-184.
　　Part 2, Ibid., vol. 15 (Autumn, 1976), pp. 228-233.

　　The Glazing of Fotheringhay Church and College.
　　Journal of the British Archaeological Association, vol. 131 (1978),
　　pp. 79-109.

　　The Glazing of the Collegiate Church of the Holy Trinity, Tattershall
　　(Lincolnshire): A Study of Late Fifteenth Century Glass-Painting
　　Workshops.
　　Archaeologia, vol. 106 (1979), pp. 133-156.

MARQUAND, Allan

　　Two Windows in the Cathedral of Florence.
　　Princeton, 1899.
　　American Journal of Archaeology, 2nd series, vol. 4 (1900), pp. 192-203.

MARQUET, A.

　　La Cathédrale du Mans.
　　Le Mans, n.d.

MARSAUX, Abbé

　　Vitraux de l'Eglise Saint-Martin de Croslay.
　　Mémoires de la Société Historique de Pontoise et du Vexin, vol. 12
　　(1889).

MARSH, David

　　The Comper Windows in Westminster Abbey.
　　London, 1977.

MARSHALL, Edward H.

　　Jesse Windows.
　　(Modern one mentioned at All Saints, Margaret Street, Cavendish Square.)
　　Notes and Queries, 8th series, vol. 8 (Dec. 28, 1895).

MARSHALL, George

　　A Short Account of Freen's Court and Its Former Owners.
　　Transactions of the Woolhope Naturalists' Field Club, for 1914, 1915,
　　1916, 1917, vol. 22 (1918),
　　(Glass, pp. 215-218.)

　　The Church of Leintwardine.
　　Transactions of the Woolhope Naturalists' Field Club, for 1918, 1919,
　　1920, vol. 23 (1921).
　　(Glass, pp. 226, 228-229.)

　　Some Remarks on the Ancient Stained Glass in Eaton Bishop Church,
　　County of Hereford.
　　Transactions of the Woolhope Naturalists' Field Club, for 1921, 1922,
　　1923, vol. 24 (192), pp. 101-114.
　　Ibid. Notes on the Manor of Sugwas in the County of Hereford.
　　(Glass, p. 119.)

　　Ancient Glass in Madley Church, County of Hereford.
　　Transactions of the Woolhope Naturalists' Field Club, for 1924, 1925,
　　1926, vol. 25 (1928), pp. 66-71.

　　Ancient Glass in the Churches of Eaton Bishop and Madley, Herefordshire.
　　J.M.G.P., vol. 2, no. 4 (Oct., 1928), pp. 171-175.

　　Notes on Kingsland Church, Herefordshire.
　　Transactions of the Woolhope Naturalists' Field Club, for 1930, 1931,
　　1932, vol. 27 (1935).
　　(Glass, pp. 22-25.)

　　(Foy Church, Herefordshire. A 1675 copy of the 1630 Sellack Church
　　glass.)
　　Transactions of the Woolhope Naturalists' Field Club, for 1936, 1937,
　　1938, vol. 29 (1940), p. 163.

MARTEAU, Robert

　　Les Vitraux de Chagall, 1957-1970.
　　Paris, 1972.

MARTIMORT, Aimé-Georges

　　A Pointed Criticism of Subject Matter. The Errors of Modern
　　Iconography.
　　(Translated by McCORMICK, N.)
　　Stained Glass, vol. 45, no. 4 (Winter, 1950-1951), pp. 163-169.
　　Replied to by
　　In Defense of 'Modern Iconography'.
　　Stained Glass, vol. 46, no. 3 (Autumn, 1951).

MARTIN, A., and CAHIER, C.
Monographie de la Cathédrale de Bourges.
2 vols., Paris, 1841-1844.

MARTIN, C.
Essai Critique et Descriptif sur les Nouveaux Vitraux de l'Eglise
Nôtre-Dame de Bourg.
Bourg, 1874.

MARTIN, Helene
The Role of the Library in a Stained Glass Studio.
Stained Glass, vol. 62, no. 2 (Summer, 1967), pp. 13-16.

Review of REYNTIENS, Patrick, The Techniques of Stained Glass.
Stained Glass, vol. 62, no. 4 (Winter, 1967-1968), p. 53.

MARTIN, William
London Topography in the Stained Glass Windows of Lincoln's Inn.
Proceedings of the Society of Antiquaries of London, 2nd series,
vol. 28 (1915-1916), pp. 140-146.

MARTINEAU, Chanoine
Saint-Etienne de Bourges.
Paris, 1975.

MARTIRANO, Matthew
Stained Glass Tours: Montreal, with a short excursion into Quebec
Province.
Stained Glass, vol. 62, no. 1 (Spring, 1967), pp. 8-16.

MASON, A.J.
A Guide to the Ancient Glass in Canterbury Cathedral.
Canterbury, 1925.

MATHEWS, Richard
Stained and Leaded Glass Work.
Work, vol. 4 (1892), p. 582.
       vol. 5 (1892), p. 84.
       vol. 6 (1893), p. 148.

Stained and Leaded Glass Work.
The Illustrated Carpenter and Builder (Apr. 16, 1897).

MATTHEWS, E., and Sons
Glass Painting and Staining for Amateurs.
London, 1877.

MATTHIEU,
Verrière à l'Hotel de Ville d 'Enghien.
Annales du Cercle Archaeologique d'Enghien, vol. 4, p. 368.

MATHEWS, Thomas
France - Stained Glass Windows by Gerald Lardeur.
The Future of Religious Art.
Liturgical Arts (Feb., 1967).

MATHEY, F.
With AUBERT, M., CHASTEL, A., GRODECKI, L., GRUBER, J.-J., LAFOND, J.,
TARALON, J., VERRIER, J.
Le Vitrail Français.
Reviewed by SALET, Francis, Bulletin Monumental, no. 116 (1958), p. 226.

MANOURY, Jean
Concerning the Removal of Ancient Windows.
Stained Glass, vol. 31, no. 1 (Spring-Summer, 1936), pp. 3-7.

Report from Chartres.
(About the reported damage to the Chartres glass.)
Stained Glass, vol. 41, no. 1 (Spring, 1946), pp. 28-29.

MAUNOURY, Jean (Contd.)
Chartres Glass Being Replaced.
Stained Glass, vol. 42, no. 4 (Winter, 1947), pp. 113-114.

Etienne Houvet. Obituary.
Stained Glass, vol. 44, no. 2 (Summer, 1949), pp. 63-64.

MAURER, Emil
Die Kunstdenkmaler des Kantons Aargau, vol. 3.
Das Kloster Königsfelden.
Basel, 1949.

MAURER, Mary D.
Imprisoned Sunlight.
Panorama (Kansas City), (Aug., 1937).

The Romance of the Stained Glass Window.
Missouri Club Woman (Dec., 1937).

MAXE-WERLY, L.
Vitraux de Saint-Nicaise de Reims.
Bulletin Archéologique du Comité des Travaux Historiques (1884), p. 122.

MAYER, F.S.
Meisterwerke aus der deutschen Glasmalerei-Ausstellung in Karlsruhe, 1901.
Berlin, and Leipzig, 1903.

MAYERFELS, K. Mayer von
Die Glasmalereien im ehemaligen Kloster Hofen, jetzigem Sommer-
residenzschlosse des Königs von Württemberg.
Schriflen des Vereins der Geschichte des Bodensees (Lindau), 1882.

MAYEUX, Albert
Les Vitraux de Saint-Denis de Jouhet (Indre).
Bulletin Monumental, vol. 82 (1923), pp. 183-

(Meaford, Ontario)
Church Gets Windows of Bomb-Blasted Glass from War-Torn
European Cathedrals.
(Reprinted from the Glass Digest.)
Stained Glass, vol. 42, no. 4 (Winter, 1947), pp. 116-117.

MECHIN, Abbé
Description Iconographique de Trois Verrières de l'Eglise Saint
Martin ès Vignes.
Congrès Archéologique de Troyes (1853).

MEGAW, Arthur H.S.
Notes on Recent Work of the Byzantine Institute in Istanbul.
(Stained glass at the Zeyrek Camii and the Kariye Camii.)
Dumbarton Oaks Papers, vol. 17 (1963), pp. 333-371.

MEGUEN, Clamens and Borderau
Quelques Lignes sur la Peinture sur Verre. Vitraux du 15e Siècle
de l'Eglise de Joué, Maine et Loire.
Angers, 1881.

MEINHOF, Dr.
Paul Schmude und die Glasmalerei der Zukunst.
Diamant, 49th year, no. 22 (Aug. 1, 1927).

MEISS, Millard
Light as Form and Symbol in Some Fifteenth-Century Paintings.
Art Bulletin, vol. 27, no. 3 (Sept., 1945), pp. 175-181.

MEISTER, Abbé

    Les Pinaigrier Peintres Verriers (16e-17e Siècles). Essai
    Genealogique.
    Bulletin Archéologique (1926), pp. 187-200.

MELLOR, Ethel

    Les Lichens Vitricoles et la Détérioration des Vitraux d'Eglise.
    Paris, 1922.

    Lichens and the Action on the Glass and Leadings of Church Windows.
    Nature (Aug. 25, 1923), p. 299, (Oct. 6, 1923), p.

    The Decay of Window Glass from the Point of View of Lichenous Growth.
    Journal of the Society of Glass Technology, vol. 8 (1924), pp. 162-186.

(Mells Church)

    N.p., n.d.
    (Mediaeval glass, glass by Hardman, some made in Mells, 1860, and
    some by Sir William Nicholson.)

MÉLDIZES, Albert

    Les Vitraux de la Cathédrale de Bourges Postérieurs au 13e Siècle.
    Bulletin Archéologique,(1887).

    Vitraux Peints de la Cathédrale de Bourges Postérieurs au 13e Siècle
    avec une Introduction par E. de Beaurepaire.
    Paris, 1891-1897.

MELY, F. de

    Etude Iconographique sur les Vitraux du 13e Siècle de la Cathédrale
    de Chartres.
    Revue de l'Art Chrétien (Lille), (1888), p. 413.

MEMMINGER, K.

    Bemerkungen zu den Naumberger Domfenstern.
    Zeitschrift für alte und neue Glasmalerei (1913), p. 31.

MÉNARD, René Joseph

    Le Vitrail de Troyes.
    L'Art et l'Autel (1903, 1904).

(Meopham, Kent)

    Restoration of the Old Glass at Meopham Church, Kent.
    The Antiquaries Journal, vol. 3 (1923), pp. 155-157.

(Merchant Taylors Company)

    A Sixteenth Century Glass 'Find'. Arms of the Merchant Taylors
    Company.
    The Morning Post, March 11, 1935.

MEREWETHER, Dean

    A Lecture on Stained Glass.
    Archaeologia Cambrensis, first series, vol. 3 (1848), p. 362.

MERLET, L.

    Compte de l'Oeuvre de la Cathédrale de Chartres en 1415-1416.
    Bulletin Archéologique du Comité des Travaux Historiques et
    Scientifiques (1889), pp. 35-94.

    (Editor.)
    Archives Départementales de l'Eure-et-Loir. Inventaire Sommaire.
    Searle, G.
    Chartres, 1890.

MERLO, J.J.

    Nachr. von der Leben und die Werken Kölnischer Künstler.
    Cologne, 1850.

    Die Glasmalerei von 1508.
    In Kölner Dom und ihre Meister.
    Bonn, 1877.

MERLO, J.J. (Contd.)

    Kölnische Künstler in alter und neuer Zeit.
    (Revised and enlarged by FERMINECH-RICHARTZ and KEUSSEN, H.)
    Dusseldorf, 1895.

MERRIFIELD, Mrs.

    Original Treatises Dating from the Twelfth to the Eighteenth
    Centuries on the Arts of Painting.
    2 vols., London, 1849.

MERSON, Olivier

    Les Vitraux.
    Paris, 1896.

    Les Vitraux.
    (Partly translated by DRAKE, Maurice.)
    J.M.G.P., vol. 1, no. 1 (Apr., 1924), pp. 39-44.

MERZ, Walther

    Hans Ulrich Fisch. Ein Beitrag zur Kunstgeschichte des Aargaus.
    Aarau, 1894.

    Führer durch die Klosterkirche zu Königsfelden.
    Aarau, 1913 (3rd edition).

MESNAGE, Abbé

    Les Vitraux de l'Eglise Saint Saturnin de Tours.
    Tours, 1890 (new edition).

MESSENGER, A.W.B.

    The Royal Arms and their Story.
    (Refers to Canterbury glass.)
    Canterbury Cathedral Chronicle, no. 41 (Oct., 1945), pp. 13-21.

    The Royal Heraldry in Exeter Cathedral.
    23rd Annual Report of the Friends of Exeter Cathedral (1953), pp. 18-21.

(Messingham Church)

    Lincolnshire Notes and Queries (Apr., 1927), pp. 86-87.

    Messingham Church, Scunthorpe, Lincolnshire: Glass.
    (Grant to restore the East Window.)
    The Pilgrim Trust, 38th Annual Report (1968), p. 16.

METAIS, L.

    Un Vitrail du 16e Siècle à Courville (Eure-et-Loir).
    Bulletin Archéologique for 1900, (1901), pp. 26-33.

METCALF, Robert M.

    A Stained Glass Tour of Europe.
    Stained Glass, vol. 36, no. 3 (Autumn, 1941), pp. 87-91.

    Beaux Arts Competition. (Program.)
    Stained Glass, vol. 44, no. 2 (Summer, 1949), pp. 39-40.

METCALF, Robert and Gertrude

    Making Stained Glass: A Handbook for the Amateur and the Professional.
    Newton Abbot, 1972.

(Metz Cathedral)

    Gotische Glasgemälde im Dome zu Metz, um 1385.
    Zeitschrift fur alte und neue Glasmalerei (1912), p. 23.

MEULEN, Jan van der

    A Logos-Creator at Chartres and its Copy.
    Journal of the Warburg and Courtauld Institutes (1966), pp. 82-100.
    Reviewed by GRODECKI, Louis, Bulletin Monumental, no. 127 (1969),
    pp. 43-44.

MEUNIER, Ernst
Katholische Kunst in Berlin.
Die Christliche Kunst (Dec., 1930).

MEUNIER, J.J.
Notice sur la Peinture sur Verre Ancienne, la Fabrication des
Couleurs, et la Construction du Four.
Paris, 1842.

MEYER, Hermann
Der Glasmaler Monogrammist A.H. II Hälfte des 16 Jahrhunderts.
Anzeige für Schweizerische Altertumskunde (Zurich), (1879).

Die schweizerische Sitte der Fenster - und Wappenschenkung vom 15
bis 17 Jahrhundert. Nebst Verzeichnis der Zürischer Glasmaler von
1540 an, und Nachweis noch vorhandener arbeiten derselben.
Frauenfeld, 1884.

MEYRICK, F.J.
Fifteenth-Century Glass in the Chancel Window of St. Peter Mancroft,
Norwich.
Norfolk Archaeology, vol. 17 (1910).

Fifteenth-Century Glass in the Chancel Window of St. Peter Mancroft,
Norwich.
(With an introduction by RICHMOND, Sir W.B.)
Norwich, 1911.

Pathos and Humour in a Great Window.
Peasant Arts Guild Paper, no. 27, London (n.d.).

(Michaelhouse)
Notes on the Symbolism of the New Stained Glass Windows,
Michaelhouse Chapel.
Natal, 1954.

(Middleton, St. Leonard's Church)
St. Leonard's Church, Middleton, Lancashire: Flodden Window.
(A grant towards its restoration.)
The Pilgrim Trust, 39th Annual Report (1969), p. 17.

(Further grant towards repair and restoration of the Flodden Window.)
The Pilgrim Trust, 40th Annual Report (1970), p. 14.

MILLAR, A.H.
Stained Glass.
Art Journal (1881), pp. 69-70.

MILLER, Frederick
Pottery and Glass Painting.
Furniture Gazette (1884), no. 1, pp. 19, 49, 92, 173, 234, 344, 397,
461, 521; no. 2, pp. 3, 45, 172, 232, 332, 515.
(1885), pp. 44, 204, 240, 391, 456.
(1886), pp. 189, 227, 298, 364.
(1887), pp. 139, 173.

Glass Painting. A Course of Instruction in the Various Methods
of Painting Glass, and the Principles of Design.
London, 1885.

Reviewed in The Builder, vol. 48 (Apr. 4, 1885), pp. 498-499.

MILLER, Frederick (Contd.)
Notes on a Few Bits of Old Glass.
The Builder (June 20, 1885).

Notes on Glass Painting Work.
Ibid (July 5, 1890).

Art Workers and Recent Productions. Glass Painters.
Art Journal (1895), pp. 150-153.
(Refers to WHALL, C., DAVIS, L., WINSTON, C., WATSON, J.D., RYLAND, H.,
Messrs. GUTHRIE, BURNE-JONES, MORRIS and Co.)

MILNER-WHITE, Eric
'New' Glass in King's Chapel.
The Cambridge Review (Oct. 28, 1921).

'New' Glass in King's Chapel.
The Cambridge Review (Dec. 3, 1924).

The Whichcote Chantry in King's College Chapel.
Ibid., (May 4, 1928).

An Appendix to 'A Guide to the Windows of King's College Chapel,
Cambridge'.
Cambridge, 1930.

How to Choose Stained Glass.
London, n.d.

William Jay Bolton, 1816-1884.
J.M.G.P., vol. 6, no. 4 (Apr., 1937), pp. 212-215.

Chronological List of English Glass Paintings. (Additions.)
(Letter to the Editor.)
J.M.G.P., vol. 6, no. 4 (Apr., 1937), p. 227.

Report on the Windows of Ely Cathedral.
First Annual Report of the Friends of Ely Cathedral (Apr., 1937),
pp. 10-19.

Chronological List of English Glass-Paintings. (Additions.)
(Letter to the Editor.)
J.M.G.P., vol. 7, no. 1 (Oct., 1937), pp. 57-58.

The St. John's Glass.
(Gift of the glass from St. John's, Micklegate.)
17th Annual Report of the Friends of York Minster (1945), p. 3.

Replacement of Windows.
(Appeal for funds.)
Ibid., p. 10.

Ancient Glass from St. John's, Micklegate.
Ibid., pp. 14-21.

The Dean's Letter: Glasswork.
(Replacement and restoration. Use of excavated fragments from
Watton Priory.)
18th Annual Report of the Friends of York Minster (1946), pp. 4-9.

The Return of the Windows.
(Chronicle both of the order of return and the chief changes made.)
Ibid., pp. 28-33.
19th Annual Report (1947), pp. 35-36.
20th Annual Report (1948), pp. 27-36.
21st Annual Report (1949), pp. 30-36.
22nd Annual Report (1950), pp. 27-29.
23rd Annual Report (1951), pp. 31-33.
24th Annual Report (1952), pp. 25-33.
25th Annual Report (1953), pp. 25-37. (Includes completion of
Great East Window.)
26th Annual Report (1954), pp. 20-27.
27th Annual Report (1955), pp. 25-37. (Includes St. William Window.)
28th Annual Report (1956), pp. 36-37.
29th Annual Report (1957), pp. 29-40. (Includes St. Cuthbert Window.)

MILNER-WHITE, Eric (Contd.)

    30th Annual Report of the Friends of York Minster (1958), pp. 31-41.

    31st Annual Report (1959), pp. 37-40.

    32nd Annual Report (1960), pp. 30-35.

    33rd Annual Report (1961), pp. 17-20.

    34th Annual Report (1962), pp. 29-33.

    35th Annual Report (1963), pp. 17-19.

    The Fall of Man.
    (Sixteenth Century French windows acquired. Identified by KNOWLES,
    J.A.)
    19th Annual Report of the Friends of York Minster (1947), pp. 18-21.

    The Adventure of the Great East Window.
    (Its restoration and partial replacement.)
    Ibid., pp. 22-34.

    The Ancient Glass of St. Michael's Spurriergate, York.
    York, 1948.

    The Dean's Letter: Glasswork.
    (Replacement and reconstruction of 'lost' windows.)
    20th Annual Report of the Friends of York Minster (1948), pp. 7-11.

    Re-insertion and Re-dedication of the 'Bombay Window'.
    (Order of Service.)
    Friday, Sept. 24, 1948.
    York, 1948.

    The Dean's Letter.
    (Replacement of glass and acquisition of quarries.)
    21st Annual Report of the Friends of York Minster (1949), pp. 8-11.

    The Cardinal's Glass.
    (Acquisition of glass from the Rochdale collection.)
    Ibid., pp. 22-24.

    The East Window. The Great Apocalypse Series.
    Ibid., pp. 24-30.

    The Windows of York. Restoring the Glories of the Minster's Glass.
    The Times, Feb. 18, 1949.

    All Saints' Church, Upper Poppleton.
    Service of Dedication of a Memorial Window.
    Sunday, July 10, 1949.

    St. Lawrence's Church, Kirby Misperton.
    Service of Dedication of a Memorial Window.
    Saturday, Oct. 1, 1949.

    The Dean's Letter: A Diversity of Gifts.
    (Panels of bottle-glass and a piece of gold pot-metal.)
    22nd Annual Report of the Friends of York Minster (1950), p. 10.

    The Restoration of the East Window of York Minster.
    The Antiquaries Journal, vol. 30 (July-Oct., 1950), pp. 180-184.

    A Service to Welcome Back the Five Sisters Windows at their
    reinsertion, 1950, after the Second World War.
    Dec. 9, 1950.
    York, 1950.

    York Minster's Ancient Glass. A Lost Window Discovered.
    The Times, Feb. 8, 1951.

    The Function of Colour and Design in Stained Glass.
    In Report on the British Colour Council's 6th Designers' Conference,
    held at York, Oct. 8-11, 1951, pp. 11-14.
    London, 1951.

    The Dean's Letter: The Windows.
    23rd Annual Report of the Friends of York Minster (1951), p. 9.

    The Jesse Window in the Nave.
    Ibid., pp. 20-30.
    Reprinted in J.M.G.P., vol. 11, no. 1 (1952), pp. 26-34.

MILNER-WHITE, Eric (Contd.)

    The Resurrection of a Fourteenth-Century Window.
    Burlington Magazine, vol. 94 (Jan.-Dec., 1952), pp. 108-112.

    Service for the Re-dedication of Fourteen Ancient Windows in the
    Nave of York Minster, at the Annual Festival of the Friends of the
    Minster.
    June 30, 1952.
    York, 1952.

    Dedication of a Memorial Window in York Minster.
    July 8, 1952.
    (Glass from Rouen.)
    York, 1952.

    The Dean's Letter: The Windows.
    24th Annual Report of the Friends of York Minster (1952), pp. 11-14.

    A Vanished Window Returns.
    Ibid., pp. 21-24.

    Service of Re-dedication of the Great East Window, 1405-1953, at the
    Annual Festival of the Friends of the Minster.
    June 29, 1953.
    York, 1953.

    The Dean's Letter: The Windows.
    25th Annual Report of the Friends of York Minster (1953), pp. 4-5.

    The Dean's Letter: The Glass - Three Miracles and Three Gifts.
    (Inter alia: reconstruction of glass from St. Martin's, Coney Street;
    completion of a fragmentary St. Christopher with purchased French
    glass. Gifts of sixteenth century French glass and the fragments
    from the Grayling collection.)
    26th Annual Report of the Friends of York Minster (1954), pp. 4-7.

    A Sermon Preached at St. Cyprian's, Regent's Park, London.
    J.M.G.P., vol. 11, no. 3 (1954), pp. 164-166.

    The Dean's Letter: The Glass.
    (Inter alia, gifts of fragments and a French sixteenth century
    window.)
    27th Annual Report of the Friends of York Minster (1955), pp. 10-12.

    A New Window in St. Stephen's Chapel.
    (French glass from Haseley Court, Oxon.)
    Ibid., pp. 21-25.

    Review of WOODFORDE, Christopher, English Stained and Painted Glass.
    Burlington Magazine, vol. 97 (Jan.-Dec., 1955), pp. 262-263.

    Speech at the Building Centre.
    J.M.G.P., vol. 12, no. 2 (1957), pp. 132-134.

    Parish Church of the Ascension, Bitterne Park. Service for the
    Dedication of the Isaac Watts Windows.
    Sunday, Sept. 15, 1957.
    (Windows by A.K. Nicholson Studios.)

    The Dean's Letter: the Windows.
    (Includes the retirement of the glazier Herbert Nowland.)
    29th Annual Report of the Friends of York Minster (1957), pp. 11-13.

    The Dean's Letter: The Windows.
    30th Annual Report of the Friends of York Minster (1958), pp. 16-18.

    (Letter to the Editor supplying some corrections.)
    J.M.G.P., vol. 12, no. 3 (1958), p. 216.

    York Minster. An Index and Guide to the Ancient Windows of the Nave.
    York, 1959.

    Frederick HARRISON, Obituary.
    31st Annual Report of the Friends of York Minster (1959), pp. 19-20.

    (On Harry STAMMERS.)
    The Dean's Letter.
    Ibid., p. 21.

MILNER-WHITE, Eric (Contd.)
A Discovery of Sixteenth Century Glass.
31st Annual Report of the Friends of York Minster (1959), pp. 28-37.

St. Luke's Parish Church York.
Service of Dedication (by MILNER-WHITE) of the Lady Chapel Windows.
(By DOYLE, H.J.)
Sunday, Dec. 6, 1959.
York, 1959.

The Dean's Letter: The Windows.
32nd Annual Report of the Friends of York Minster (1960), pp. 16-17.

Sixteenth Century Glass in York Minster and in the Church of St.
Michael-le-Belfry.
York, 1960.

The Dean's Letter: The Windows and the Pilgrim Trust.
33rd Annual Report of the Friends of York Minster (1961), pp. 5-6.

The Dean's Letter: The Windows.
34th Annual Report of the Friends of York Minster (1962), pp. 9-10.

All Saints' Church, Hovingham. Order for Evensong, Sunday, 30 Sept.,
1962.
(Dedication of an H.J. Stammers window.)

(Milner-White, Eric)
Obituaries.
The Times, June 17, 1963.
The Times, June 20, 1963.

Obituary.
York Civic Trust Annual Report (1962-1963), p. 2.

MILNER-WHITE, Eric
Another Glass Discovery.
35th Annual Report of the Friends of York Minster (1963), pp. 14-16.

(Milner-White, Eric)
(His will.)
Yorkshire Evening News, Feb. 22, 1964.

Obituary. By A.J. McM.
J.M.G.P., vol. 14, no. 1 (1964), pp. 20-23.

Eric Milner-White; A Memoir. By PARE, P.N.
London, 1965.

(L. Minard Collection)
Catalogue des Objets d'Art et Antiquités.
Gard, 1883.
(Painted glass, pp. 120-124.)

MINNOTT, Charles I.
A Group of Stained Glass Roundels at The Cloisters.
Art Bulletin, vol. 43 (Sept., 1971), pp. 237-239.

MINUKHIN, Elrem Abramovich
Vitrazhi.
Riga, 1959.

MINUTOLI, H.C.M. von
Ueber die Anfertigung und die Nutzanwendung der Farbigen Glas bei
den Alten.
Berlin, 1836.

MIRAULT
Rapport sur l'Establissement de Peintures en Email sur Verre, et de
Fabrication de Vitraux Colorés.
Paris, 1839.

MISSET, A.
Lampadius, Lampades, Lampas. Ou, St. Louis et sa Famille Autour
de St. Memmie dans un Vitrail de la Cathédrale de Châlons (en 1258).
Lettre à M. le Chanoine Lucot.
Paris, 1911.

Mittelalterliche Bleiverglasung.
Diamant (Aug. 1, 1925).

MOBBS, Robert
Mr. Clement Heaton and His Work.
The Studio, vol. 32 (1904), pp. 212-219.

Modern Stained Glass.
Architectural Review, vol. 59, no. 353 (Apr., 1926), pp. 200-202.
(Modern Craftsmanship Number.)

(Modern work mistaken for old.)
(A short list of erroneous attributions which have appeared in print.)
News and Notes, J.M.G.P., vol. 13, no. 1 (1960), p. 307.

(Moira, Gerald)
Gerald Moira's Stained-Glass Designs.
The Studio, vol. 18 (1899), pp. 18-24.

(Mold Church, Flint)
Archaeologia Cambrensis, vol. 99 (1947), pp. 344.

MOLINIER, Émile
In Collection Spitzer: Antiquité, Moyen Age, Renaissance.
6 vols, Paris, 1890-1892.
(Les Vitraux, vol. 3, pp. 113-126.)

MOLLET, Ralph
Leaded Glass Work.
London, 1933.

MOLLICA, Peter
Stained Glass Primer.
Vol. 1, Berkeley, 1971.
Vol. 2, Berkeley, 1977.

(Monell Collection)
Fifteenth-Century Glass in the Ambrose Monell Collection.
Bulletin of the Stained Glass Association of America, vol. 25, no. 11
(Nov., 1930).

(Monell Collection auctioned, Nov. 28, 1930)
(Panels from Loise-en-Brie.)
The Connoisseur, vol. 87 (Jan.-June, 1931), p. 68.

MONNERET DE VILLARD, U.
Le Vetrate del Duomo di Milano.
3 vols., Milan, 1918-1920.

La Pittura su Vetro.
In La Corte di Ludovico il Moro.
(Edited by MALAGUZZI-VALERI.)
Milan, 1923.
(Vol. 4, chapter 2.)

MONTFAUÇON, Bernard de

    Les Monumens de la Monarchie Françoise, qui Comprennent l'Histoire
    de France, avec les Figures de Chaque Règne que l'Injure des Temps
    a Epargnées.
    5 vols, Paris, 1729-1733.
    English version, 2 vols, London, 1750.

MONTIER, A.

    Les Vitraux de la Chapelle Saint Firmin à Saint Martin-Saint Firmin.
    Bulletin de la Société des Amis des Arts du Département de l'Eure
    (Evreux), vol. 18 (1903), pp. 33-39.

(Montgomery Castle)

    (Grisaille glass excavated at Montgomery Castle.)
    In The Excavation of the 'New Building' at Montgomery Castle, by
    LEWIS, J.M.
    Archaeologia Cambrensis, vol. 117 (1968), pp. 152-153.

(Montgomery, Walter)

    Obituary.
    J.M.G.P., vol. 2, no. 3 (Apr., 1928), p. 163.

(Montmorency, Rachel de)

    Obituary. By C.D.
    J.M.G.P., vol. 13, no. 4 (1963), pp. 589-590.

(Montreal Museum)

    (French thirteenth century medallion, originally from the Baron de
    St. Levee d'Agnerre Collection, goes to the Montreal Museum.)
    Stained Glass, vol.31, no. 3 (Winter, 1936-1937), pp. 98-99.

(Moor Monkton, Red House School Chapel)

    (Grant to repair the glass in the East Window.)
    40th Annual Report of the Pilgrim Trust (1970), p. 14.
    (Some glass is fourteenth century. Centre light - hexagonal panels
    by Bernard DINNINGHOF (late sixteenth century).)

MOORE, C.H.

    Development and Character of Gothic Architecture.
    New York and London, 1899.
    (Stained glass, chapters 15 and 16.)

MOORE, Peter

    The Stained Glass of Ely Cathedral.
    Ely, 1973.

MORANCE, Abbé

    Notice sur les Verrières de l'Eglise de la Ferté-Bernard (Sarthe).
    Bulletin Monumental, vol. 5 (1839), pp. 497-517.

MORANT, A.W.

    Indications of Date in Architecture . . . Stained Glass, etc.
    London, 1870.
    Reprinted from The Architect, vol.   (1870).

MORGAN, Charles

    Stained Glass. Its History, Development and Application to
    Architecture.
    Amateur Photographer (Aug. 10, 1900).

MORGAN, F.C.

    Painted Glass Window Formerly at the East End of the Choir of
    Hereford Cathedral, being a copy by Charles Backler of Benjamin
    West's Last Supper.
    J.M.G.P., vol. 13, no. 4 (1963), p. 588.

MORGAN, F.C.

    Hereford Cathedral Church Glass.
    2nd edition (revised), 1967.
    1st edition reviewed by MEDCALF, J.E., Notes and Queries, new series,
    vol. 10 (Jan., 1963), p. 3.

MORGAN, Nigel

    Early Grisaille Windows in England.
    In Akten des 10. Internationalen Colloquiums des CVMA.
    Stuttgart, 1977, p. 29.

MORIN, Louis

    Les Travaux d'Achèvement et les Vitraux de l'Eglise Saint-Pantaléon
    de Troyes. Notes sur les Artistes du 17e Siècle qui ont Travaillé
    à Saint-Pantaléon.
    Caen, 1904.
    Reprinted from Comptes Rendus du 69e Congrès Archéologique de France
    (Troyes et Provins), 1902.

MORRIS, G.T. Windyer

    Heraldic Glass at Medland Manor.
    Devon and Cornwall Notes and Queries, vol. 18 (1935), p. 233.

MORRIS, Olivia

    (Letter giving an account of the difficulties of restoring glass in
    Italy.)
    J.M.G.P., vol. 14, no. 4 (1968-1969), p. 216.

MORRIS, Roland

    Modern Leaded Glazing.
    The Builder, no. 4469 (Sept. 28, 1928), p. 504.

    Review of Neue Glasmalkunst.
    J.M.G.P., vol. 4, no. 2 (Oct., 1931), p. 97.

    Modern Treatment of Glass.
    Building (Nov., 1931).

    A Panel of Modern German Stained Glass.
    J.M.G.P., vol. 4, no. 3 (Apr., 1932), p. 156.

    The 1932 Exhibition of Stained Glass at the L.C.C. Central School
    of Arts and Crafts.
    J.M.G.P., vol. 5, no. 1 (Apr., 1933), pp. 25-26.

MORRIS, William

    Glass, Painted and Stained.
    (Article in Chambers' Encyclopaedia.)
    London and Edinburgh, 10 vols, 1860-1868.
    (Several subsequent editions, including
    Philadelphia, 1935.)

    A Note on the Morris Stained Glass Works.
    (Privately printed) London, 1913.

(Morris, William)

    Morris and Company, 1861-1940: A Commemorative Centenary Exhibition.
    (Arts Council of Great Britain.)
    London, 1961.

MORRIS, William

    The Suitability of Stained Glass as a Means of Decoration in Churches.
    J.M.G.P., vol. 6, no. 1 (Apr., 1935), pp. 30-31.
    Translated in Diamant, 57th year, no. 20 (July 11, 1935).

    Stained Glass.
    (Letter to the Editor.)
    Church Times (Aug. 2, 1935).

(Morris, William)
Obituary.
J.M.G.P., vol. 9, no. 3 (1945), p. 98.

MORRIS, William & Co.
Stained Glass Windows.
London, 1953.

MORRISON, Ellen E.
A New Approach to the Making of Medieval Stained Glass.
(A suggested clarification of Theophilus.)
Stained Glass, vol. 63, no. 1 (Spring, 1968), pp. 20-32.
Rebutted in Stained Glass, vol. 63, no. 3 (Autumn, 1968), pp. 34-36.

Le Vitrail Médiéval: le Rôle de la Soie.
Strasbourg, 1970.
Reprinted from Cahiers de l'Art Médiéval, vol. 5, part 3.

MORRISON, Phillips L. (Snr.)
Executing Better Faceted-Stained Glass Panels with Epoxy.
Stained Glass, vol. 65, no. 2 (Summer, 1970), pp. 18-22.

MORSHEAD, T.Y.A.
Old Glass at Salcombe Regis.
Devon and Cornwall Notes and Queries, vol. 8 (1915), p. 97.

MOSCHENROSS, A.
Thann à Travers son Passé.
Rixheim, 1947.

MOUFANG, Wilhelm
Moderne Glasmalerei.
Die Christliche Kunst, 25th year, no. 11 (Aug., 1929).

MUELLER, Wayne P., and FROHBEITER-MUELLER, Jo.
Stained Glass in the Soviet Union.
Stained Glass, vol. 74, no. 3 (Fall, 1979), pp. 223-227.

MUENTZ, Eugène
Guillaume de Marcillat et la Peinture sur Verre en Italie.
Revue des Arts Décoratifs, vol. 11 (1890-1891), pp. 359-374.

MÜHLENBEIN, H.
Alte Glasmalereien in Goslar.
Diamant, 56th year, no. 29 (Oct. 11, 1934).

MÜHLETHALER, Bruno
Kennen wir die Grenzen und Möglichkeiten für die Erhaltung
mittelalterlicher Glasmalereien.
In Akten des 10. Internationalen Colloquiums des CVMA.
Stuttgart, 1977, pp. 37-46.

(Mulhouse)
Les Vitraux Peints de l'Ancienne Eglise Saint-Etienne de Mulhouse.
Bulletin du Musée Historique de Mulhouse, vol. 6 (1881), pp. 95-101.

Exposition des Vitraux Médiévaux de l'Eglise Reformée St. Etienne
de Mulhouse.
Mulhouse, 1948.

MÜLLER, C.G.
Die Glasmalerei in der Gegenwart.
Diamant, 51st year, no. 7 (March 1, 1929), pp. 123-124.

MULLER, E.
Le Vitrail de Saint Pantaléon à la Cathédrale de Noyon.
Revue de l'Art Chrétien (Lille), (1883).

MÜLLER, Franz H.
Beiträge zur deutschen Kunst und Geschichtskunde durch Kunst-Denkmale.
Darmstadt, 1832-1835.

Die St. Katharinenkirche zu Oppenheim. Ein Denkmal deutscher
Kirchenbaukunst aus dem 13. Jahrhundert.
Frankfort am Main, 1853.

MÜLLER, H.
Die Heiligen auf den Glasgemälden im Kreuzgang des Klosters Muri.
Muri, 1958.

MÜLLER, J.H.
Die ältesten Glasgemälde der Kirchen des Kantons Bern.
In Beiträge zur Geschichte der Kunst und des Kunsthandwerks in Bern
in 15, 16 and 17 Jahrhundert.
Berne, 1879.

(Müller, Jean Jacques)
(Letter to the Editor on the work of Müller.)
The Art-Union (1847), p. 262.

MUNDY, P.D.
Armorial Glass in Alstonfield Church, Staffordshire.
Notes and Queries, vol. 186 (March 11, 1944), p. 138.

(Munich Glass-Painting)
Chapters on Painted Glass. 1. The Munich School.
The Ecclesiologist, vol. 7 (1847), pp. 121-125.

(Munich)
Abbildungen der Glasgemälde in der Pfarrkirche der Vorstadt Au.
Munich, 1850.

Zwei Scheiben von Josias Murer in der Kgl. Residenz zu München.
Zeitschrift für alte und neue Glasmalerei (1912), p. 59.

Münchens alte Glasgemälde.
Ibid., p. 60.

(Munnerstadt and Goslar)
Mainfränkische Glasmalerei um 1420. Fenster aus den Kirchen in
Munnerstadt und Iphogen.
and
Romanische Glasfenster aus der Martkirche in Goslar.
(Catalogues.)
Nuremberg, 1975.

MURATOVA, Xenia
Deux Panneaux Inconnus de Vitraux Français du 13e Siècle au Musée
de Kiev.
Revue de l'Art, no. 10 (1970), pp. 63-65.

(Murphy, Thomas J.)
Obituary.
Stained Glass, vol. 51, no. 1 (Spring, 1956), p. 18.

MURRAY, B.H., and EGAN, H.F.
A Color Tour of Europe's New Churches.
Catholic Property Administration (Jan., 1963).

MURRAY, H.
Glass Painting.
Art Journal, vol. 21 (1869), p. 231.

MURRAY, John
Louvain and Malines: Old Painted Glass.
(In St. George's, Hanover Square.)
Notes and Queries, 11th series, vol. 10 (Oct. 17, 1914), p. 318.

Music on Stained Glass Windows.
John O'London's Weekly, vol. 15, no. 366 (Apr. 10, 1926).

MYERS, T.
Report upon the Condition of the Stained Glass in York Churches.
Antiquarian and Architectural Year Book for 1844.
London, 1845, pp. 177-242.
(The pagination of this article is extraordinarily irregular. The
above information is far from a full description but will serve to
locate it.)

NASH, E.J.

A Note on Charles Winston, the Author of 'Ancient Glass Paintings . . .'
(A window executed by him at Farningham Church.)
Archaeologia Cantiana, vol. 50 (1938), pp. 160-161.

(National Union of German Glass-Painters)
(A list of 54 members.)
Diamant. no. 32 (1924).

Report of Second Annual General Meeting.
Diamant, (May 21, 1925).

NEALE, James
The Abbey Church of St. Albans, Hertfordshire.
London, 1877.

NEALE, J.P., and BRAYLEY, E.W.
The History and Antiquities of the Abbey Church of St. Peter,
Westminster.
2 vols., London, 1818-1823.

NEALE, John Mason
Hierologus, or the Church Tourists' Companion.
London, 1843.
(Contains a description of the 'Prick of Conscience' Window, All
Saints', North Street, York.)

Batalha.
The Ecclesiologist, vol. 15 (1854), pp. 223-238.
(The glass atrociously handled, pp. 227-228.)

Nederlandsche Ambachts en Nijverheids-Kunst. 1923-1924.
n.d., n.p.

NEEFFS, E.
Notes sur les Anciennes Verrières de l'Eglise Metropolitaine de
Malines.
Messager des Sciences Historiques de Belgique (Ghent, 1877), pp. 1-27.

NEFF, John Hallmark
Matisse's Forgotten Stained Glass Commission.
Burlington Magazine, vol.114 (Dec., 1972), pp. 867-870.

NELSON, Philip
The Fifteenth-Century Glass in the Church of St. Michael, Ashton-
under-Lyne.
The Archaeological Journal, vol. 70 (1913), pp. 1-10.

Ancient Painted Glass in England, 1170-1500.
London, 1913.
Reviewed in The Antiquary, vol. 49 (1913), p. 476.
Reviewed in Daily News, Jan. 27, 1913.
Reviewed by EDEN, F.S., Notes and Queries, 11th series, vol. 8
(Dec. 20, 1913), pp. 497-498.
Reviewed in Burlington Magazine, vol. 25 (Apr.-Sept., 1914), p. 251.

Ancient Glass from Hale Hall, Lancashire.
Transactions of the Historic Society of Lancashire and Cheshire, vol.
88 for 1936 (1937), pp. 259-260.

Hale Hall Glass.
Ibid., vol. 89 for 1937 (1938), pp. 117-118.

The Ancient Painted Glass from Hale Hall.
Ibid., vol. 90 for 1938 (1939), pp. 203-205.

NEUHAUSER, JELE and Co.
Die Tiroler Glasmalerei und Mosaikanstalt in Innsbruck.
Rückblick des 50 jährigen Gründungsjubiläums 1861-1911.
Innsbruck, 1911.

NEUMANN, Dr., and REDSLOB, Edwin
Das Friedrich Bayer Fenster von Dietz Edzard. Anfsatz über D.E.
von Dr. Neumann . . . Betrachtung über das Fenster von Dr. Redslob.
Berlin, 1925.

NEUMANN, Dr.
Von Deutschen Glas Mosaik.
Glastechnische Berichte, year 3, part 12 (March, 1926), pp. 448-451.

NEUSS, Henri van
Les Vitraux de l'Abbaye des Dames Nobles de Herckenrode.
n.p., 1895.

NEW, Keith
Stained Glass in the Annual Diploma Show at the Royal College of Art.
J.M.G.P., vol. 14, no. 3 (1967), p. 161.

New Work in Stained Glass.
A Symposium.
Contributions by HUNT, H.
              SUMNER, J.R.
              HIEMER, E.W.
              CUMMINGS, H.W.
              BRIDGES, S.
              WILLET, H.L.
Stained Glass, vol. 49, no. 1 (Spring, 1954), pp. 17-21.

(New York)
(St. John the Divine, New York.)
A Great Painted Window.
(By Powell.)
The Connoisseur, vol. 36 (1913), p. 209.

(New York, Calvary Church)
Old Oxford Glass for a New York Church.
(Letter to the Editor, with illustration, describing two windows
supposedly from a demolished building in Oxford.
Stained Glass, vol. 27, no. 9 (Sept., 1932), p. 275.

(New York, Cathedral of St. John the Divine)
A New Window.
Stained Glass, vol. 28 (Winter, 1933-1934), pp. 203-204.

(New York, Kennedy Airport)
The World's Largest Stained Glass Window.
(By Robert SOWERS.)
Stained Glass, vol. 56, no. 3 (Autumn, 1961), pp. 17-23.

(New York, Exhibition at the Van Baarn Galleries, Dec.10-Jan. 31, 1937-1938)
Mediaeval Glass Exhibited in New York.
Stained Glass, vol. 32, no. 3 (Winter, 1937-1938), pp. 97-98.

(Newcastle, St. Peter's Chapel)
(Window by Wailes inserted.)
The Gentleman's Magazine, vol. 21, new series, part 1 (1844), p. 183.

NEWHOFF, Natalie
Fused Glass - 1974.
Stained Glass, vol. 69, nos. 1 and 2 (Spring-Summer, 1974), pp. 8-14.

NEWMAN, Harold

    An Illustrated Dictionary of Glass.
    London, 1977.
    Reviewed in J.M.G.P., vol. 17, no. 2 (1978-1979), pp. 76-77.

(Newington, Bucks.)

    Old Painted Glass.
    (Query concerning the heraldic glass at Merser's House, Newington.)
    Notes and Queries, vol. 1 (Jan. 26, 1850), p. 197.

NEWTON, P.A.

    (Report on excavated glass from Coventry.)
    In Transactions of the Birmingham and Warwickshire Archaeological
    Society, vol. 84 (for 1967-1970), pp. 107-111.

NEWTON, Peter A.

    Review of LEWIS, H. Mostyn, Stained Glass in North Wales up to 1850.
    Archaeologia Cambrensis, vol. 120 (1971), pp. 120-121.

NEWTON, P.A.

    The Medieval Stained and Painted Glass.
    (With KING, D.)
    In The Hospital of William Browne, Merchant, Stamford, Lincolnshire.
    A History and an Account of the Buildings and Stained Glass.
    Stamford, n.d.

    (With KERR, Jill.)
    The County of Oxford. A Catalogue of Medieval Stained Glass.
    (CVMA, Great Britain, vol. 1.)
    London, 1979.

NEWTON, Roy G.

    Some Problems in the Dating of Ancient Glass by Counting the
    Layers in the Weathering Crust.
    Glass Technology, vol. 7 (1966), pp. 22-25.

    Some Further Observations on the Weathering Crusts of Ancient Glass.
    Ibid., vol. 10 (1969), pp. 40-42.

    The Enigma of the Layered Crusts on some Weathered Glasses. A
    Chronological Account of the Investigations.
    Archaeometry, vol. 13 (1971), pp. 1-9.

    Recent Results from Conservation Studies.
    In 8e Colloque du Corpus Vitrearum Medii Aevi.
    Paris ?, 1972, pp. 48-50.

    Cathedral Chemistry - Conserving the Stained Glass.
    Chemistry in Britain, vol. 10, part 3 (1974), pp. 89-91.

    With HEDGES, R.E.M.
    Analysis of Weathered Glass from York Minster.
    Archaeometry, vol. 16 (1974), pp. 244-245.

    The Deterioration and Conservation of Painted Glass: A Critical
    Bibliography.
    (CVMA Great Britain: Occasional Papers, no. 1) London, 1974.
    Reviewed in J.M.G.P., vol. 15, no. 3 (1974-1975), pp. 78-79.

    Recovery of Lost or Faded Decoration on Painted Glass.
    (CVMA, Great Britain, Additional Papers, no. 1.)
    London, 1974, pp. 68-69.

    With GIBSON, Peter.
    A Study on Cleaning Painted and Enamelled Glass in an Ultrasonic Bath.
    (CVMA, Great Britain, Additional Papers, no. 1.)
    London, 1974, pp. 70-78.

NEWTON, R.G. (Contd.)

    With HEDGES, Robert.
    Use of the 'Isoprobe' for Studying the Chemical Composition of Some
    Twelfth Century Glass from York Minster.
    (CVMA, Great Britain, Additional Papers, no. 1.)
    London, 1974, pp. 79-86.

    Recent Impetus in the Study of the Conservation of Medieval Stained
    Glass Windows.
    Glass (Dec., 1974), pp. 405-409.

    Cathedral Chemistry - Conserving Stained Glass.
    Stained Glass, vol. 70, no. 1 (Spring, 1975), pp. 20-25.

    With ILIFFE, C.J.
    Using Triangular Diagrams to Understand the Behaviour of Medieval
    Glasses.
    (Actes du 9e Colloque du CVMA, Paris, Sept. 8-12, 1975.)
    Verres et Réfractaires, numéro spécial, vol. 30, no. 1 (Jan.-Feb.,
    1976), pp. 30-34.

    The Effects of Medieval Glass Paint.
    Stained Glass, vol. 71, no. 4 (Winter, 1976-1977), pp. 226-229.

    Colouring Agents Used by Medieval Glassmakers.
    (Letter to the Editor.)
    Glass Technology, vol. 19, no. 3 (June, 1978), pp. 59-60.

    Coloring Ingredients Used by Medieval Glassmakers.
    Stained Glass, vol. 74, no. 4 (Winter, 1979-1980), pp. 310-311.

NICAISE, Henri
    Jaarboek Antwerpen's Ondheidkondige Kring (1936).

NICHOLS, John Gough
    The Works of the Van Lings in Painted Glass.
    The Gentleman's Magazine (Oct., 1850), pp. 383-387.

    The Armorial Windows Erected in the Reign of Henry VI . . . in
    Woodhouse Chapel . . . in Charnwood Forest, Lincolnshire.
    London, 1860.

(Nicholson, A.K.)
    Church of the Ascension, Bitterne Park, Southampton. The East
    and West Memorial Windows made by A.K. Nicholson. Photographed
    by Sidney Pitcher.
    Privately printed, 1931.

    Church of the Ascension, Bitterne Park, Southampton. The Windows
    of the South Aisle made by A.K. Nicholson. Photographed by Sydney
    Pitcher.
    Privately printed, 1931.

    Obituary.
    J.M.G.P., vol. 7, no. 1 (Oct., 1937), pp. 52-56.

NICHOLSON, Charles
    Architecture and Stained Glass.
    J.M.G.P., vol. 1, no. 2 (Apr., 1925), pp. 5-17.

    Stained Glass.
    Transactions of the St. Paul's Ecclesiological Society, vol. 10
    (1931), pp. 11-18.

NICOLAS, Joep

    The Credo of an Artist.
    Liturgical Arts (New York), (May, 1941).

    Different Approaches to the Arts and Crafts in Europe and America.
    Stained Glass, vol. 39, no. 1 (Spring, 1944), pp. 4-10.

    An Approach to Modern Stained Glass.
    Stained Glass, vol. 39, no. 4 (Winter, 1944), pp. 116-122.

    Stained Glass Making - A Millenial Craft.
    Think (New York), (March, 1945).

    The Arts and Crafts in Europe and America.
    Liturgical Arts (New York), (Nov., 1945).

    See Stained Glass Problems in Our Day.

    So You're Going to be a Stained Glass Man!
    Stained Glass, vol. 44, no. 4 (Winter, 1949), pp. 100-107.

NICOLSON, William

    Diaries (part 2).
    (Description of Henry Gyles' glass-painting.)
    Transactions of the Cumberland and Westmorland Antiquarian and
    Archaeological Society, new series, vol. 2 (1902), pp. 159-160.

NIEPOE, L.

    La Peinture sur Verre à Lyon à propos d'un Nouveau Vitrail dans
    la Chapelle de Fourvière.
    Lyon, 1882.

(Nineteenth Century Windows)

    Gifts of Stained Glass Windows.
    The Church Builder (1862), pp. 14, 58, 166.

NIORÉ, Charles

    Un Vitrail Politique dans l'Eglise de Pont-Sainte-Marie.
    Mémoires de la Société Académique de l'Aube (1895).
    Reprinted Troyes, 1895.

    Les Triomphes de Pétrarque sur un Vitrail de l'Eglise d'Evry (Aube).
    Mémoires de la Société Académique de l'Aube, vol. 61 (1897), pp.
    145-170.

NODET, Victor

    Un Vitrail de l'Eglise de Brou. Titien et Albert Dürer. (Le
    Maître Verrier Reproduit un Dessin du Premier et une Gravure du
    Second dans le Vitrail de l'Assomption.)
    Gazette des Beaux-Arts, vol. 35 (Feb., 1906), pp. 95-112.

    L'Eglise de Brou.
    Paris, 1925.

NOGET-LACOUDRE, M.

    Projet de Vitraux pour la Chapelle du Seminaire de Sommervieu.
    Bulletin Monumental, vol. 25 (1859), p. 629.

NOLLOTH, Henry Edward

    Beverley Minster and its Town.
    (Revised 3rd edition) Rushden, 1952.
    (Glass, p. 19.)

NOPPEN, J.G.

    (Revised by RIGOLD, S.E.)
    The Chapter House, Westminster Abbey.
    H.M.S.O., London, 1952, pp. 19-20.

(Norbury Church)

    Norbury Church, Derbyshire: Glass.
    (A grant towards the restoration of the East Window.)
    The Pilgrim Trust, 41st Annual Report (1971), pp. 14-15.

    Norbury Church, Derbyshire: Glass.
    (Grant to complete the restoration.)
    The Pilgrim Trust, 42nd Annual Report (1972), p. 15.

NORDSTRÖM, Folke

    Peterborough, Lincoln, and the Science of Robert Grosseteste:
    A Study in Thirteenth Century Architecture and Iconography.
    The Art Bulletin, no. 37 (1955), pp. 241-272.

NORMILE, James

    The William Randolph Hearst Collection of Mediaeval and Renaissance
    Stained and Painted Glass.
    (Reprinted from the Los Angeles County Museum Quarterly, (Fall and
    Winter, 1945).)
    Stained Glass, vol. 41, no. 2 (Summer, 1946), pp. 39-44.

NORRIS, Dom Charles

    Stained Glass. An Introduction to its History and Appreciation.
    The Buckfast Abbey Chronicle, vol. 7, no. 1 (March, 1937);
                                     vol. 7, no. 2 (June, 1937).
    Reprinted in J.M.G.P., vol. 7, no. 1 (Oct., 1937), pp. 3-12.
                  J.M.G.P., vol. 7, no. 2 (Apr., 1938), pp. 74-79.
                  J.M.G.P., vol. 7, no. 3 (Oct., 1938), pp. 120-130.

NORRIS, W. Foxley

    The Mediaeval Glass of York Minster.
    Journal of the Society of Glass Technology, vol. 6 (1922), pp. 160-167.

NORTH, T.

    Leicester Ancient Stained Glass.
    Transactions of the Leicestershire Archaeological Society, vol. 4
    (1878), pp. 138-145, 187-190, 199-202, 220-223, 232-242, 250-252,
    254-262.

(Northampton Architectural Society)

    A List of the Architects and Artificers in Church Work.
    Uppingham, 1853.

(Northiam Church)

    Window, Northiam Church, Sussex. Designed and Painted by Mr.
    Reginald Bell.
    The Builder, vol. 135 (Nov. 9, 1928).

NOTT, James

    Historical and Descriptive Notes on the Stained Glass in the Priory
    Church, Great Malvern.
    Malvern, 1869.

    The Stained Glass Windows of Great Malvern Priory Church.
    Journal of the British Archaeological Association, vol. 38 (1882),
    pp. 55-59.

    Malvern Priory Church. Descriptive Accounts of its Ancient Stained
    Glass, etc.
    Malvern, 1895.

    The Great East Window of Gloucester Cathedral. Stray Notes.
    Transactions of the Woolhope Naturalists' Field Club, for 1898, 1899
    vol. 16 (1900), pp. 56, 57.

(Nowland, Herbert)

    (Retirement of a glazier from York Minster.)
    Reprinted from Yorkshire Evening Press.
    News and Notes, J.M.G.P., vol. 12, no. 2 (1957), pp. 95-96.

(Nuremberg, German National Museum)

    Farbige Fenster aus deutschen Kirchen des Mittelalters.

    1. Mainfränkische Glasmalerei um 1420: Fenster aus den Kirchen
    in Münnerstadt und Iphofen.
    Nuremburg, 1974.

    2. Romanische Glasfenster aus der Marktkirche in Goslar.
    Nuremberg, 1975.

(Nuremberg)

    Die Glasmalereien in den Nürnberger gotischen Kirchen St. Sebald
    und St. Lorenz. By H.H.
    Diamant, 48th year, no. 10 (Apr. 1, 1926), pp. 183-186.

NYSON, R.E.

    Stained Glass in Mexico City.
    Stained Glass, vol. 38, no. 3 (Autumn, 1943), pp. 73-76.

OAKESHOTT, Walter

    Review of The Ancient Glass of Canterbury, by RACKHAM, Bernard.
    The Antiquaries Journal, no. 31 (1951), pp. 86-89.

OBERLIES, Frida

    Elektronenoptische Untersuchungen an Verwitterten Glasoberflächen.
    Glastechnische Berichte, no. 29 (1956), pp. 109-120.

O'CONNOR, David E.

    Review of DURST, Hans, Vitraux Anciens en Suisse, Fribourg, 1971.
    J.M.G.P., vol. 15, no. 2 (1973-1974), pp. 75-78.

    Debris from a Medieval Glazier's Workshop.
    Interim Bulletin of the York Architectural Trust, vol. 3, no. 1
    (Aug., 1975), pp. 11-17.

    Excavated Glass from York.
    J.M.G.P., vol. 16, no. 1 (1976-1977), pp. 31-32.

    With HASELOCK, Jeremy.
    The Stained and Painted Glass.
    In A History of York Minster.
    Oxford, 1977 (reprinted 1979), pp. 313-393.

O'CONNOR, John (Jnr.)

    The Lawrence Saint Drawings of Stained Glass Windows.
    Carnegie Magazine (Pittsburgh),(June, 1947).

    Drawings of Ancient Stained Glass Windows.
    Stained Glass, vol. 58, no. 1 (Spring, 1963), pp. 20-26.
    (Reprinted from the Carnegie Magazine.)

O'CONNOR, Michael

    On Painted Glass in Lincoln Cathedral.
    Journal of the British Archaeological Association, vol. 11 (1855),
    pp. 90-94.

OETTLI, Heinz

    The Group of Foreign Stained Glass Windows in Thorney Abbey Church.
    Proceedings of the Cambridge Antiquarian Society, vol. 64 (1973),
    pp. 101-110.

OIDTMANN, Heinrich

    Glasmalerei in ihrer Anwendung auf den Profanbau.
    Berlin, 1874.

    Das Glasmalen für den Profanbau.
    Sprechsaal, vol. 9 (1876), pp. 58, 67, 75.

    Die Glasmalerei als kirkliche Kunst.
    Archiv für kirkliche Bankunst und Kirchenschmuck (1882).

    Die Glasmalerei.
    2 vols, Cologne, 1892-1898.

    Das Einbrennen der Farbe in der Glasmalerei.
    Keramische Rundschau, vol. 1, no. 23 (1893).

    Die alten Glasgemälde in der ehemalige Burg-kapelle, jetzigen
    Pfarrkirche zu Ehrenstein.
    Zu Christliche Kunst, vol. 9 (1896), pp. 65-73.

    Die Schweizer Glasmalerei vom Ausgange des 15 Jahrhundert.
    Zu Christliche Kunst, vol. 12 (1899),
                   vol. 14 (1901).

    Geschichte der Schweizer Glasmalerei.
    Leipzig, 1905.

    Ueber die Instandsetzung alter Glasmalerei.
    Zu Christliche Kunst, vol. 19 (1906), p. 257.

    Die Glasmalerei in alten Frankenlande.
    Leipzig, 1907.
    (Deals particularly with the Hirschvogel family.)

(Oliphant, Francis William)
    Modern Stained Glass.
    (By Oliphant.)
    Art Journal, (1854), p. 208.

OLIPHANT, Francis William
    A Plea for Painted Glass: Being an Inquiry into its Nature,
    Character and Objects; and its Claim as an Art.
    Oxford, 1855.
    Reviewed in The Ecclesiologist, vol. 16 (1855), pp. 159-162.

OLSON, Lynn
    Sculpturing Windows with Cement.
    Stained Glass, vol. 72, no. 2 (Summer, 1977), pp. 92-95.

OOMS-VAN DIESTELHOFF, Jan
    American Stained Glass. As Expressed by a Craftsman from Europe.
    Stained Glass, vol. 58, no. 4 (Winter, 1963-1964), pp. 6-13.

(Opalescent Glass)
    Did John La Farge Invent Opalescent Glass?
    (Letter to the Editor by SCHULER, M., with editorial reply.)
    J.M.G.P., vol. 2, no. 1 (1927), p. 54.

ORGAN, R.M.
    The Safe Storage of Unstable Glass.
    Museums Journal, vol. 56 (1957), pp. 265-272.

ORR, Gertrude
    Historic Stained Glass Windows in the Church of the Presidents.
    (St. John's, Lafayette Square, Washington D.C.)
    (Contains a Winston window.)
    Stained Glass, vol. 56, no. 4 (Winter, 1961-1962), pp. 4-15.

(Ornaments)
    On the Production of Painted Ornaments on Matt Glass.
    Diamant, no. 22 (1924).
OIDTMANN, Heinrich (Contd.)
    Die Glasgemälde des Obergadens im Hochchor des Kölner Domes.
    Zu Christliche Kunst, vol. 22 (1909), pp. 99, 131.

    Die romanische Glasmalereien in der Pfarrkirche St. Kumbert zu Köln.
    Zu Christliche Kunst, vol. 23 (1910), pp. 199-206.

    Die rheinischen Glasmalereien vom 12 bis zum 16 Jahrhundert.
    2 vols., Dusseldorf, 1912-1929.

    Gedichte sind gemalte Fensterscheiben.
    Der Feuerreiter, 4th year, no. 40 (Sept. 29, 1928).

O'KELLY DE GALWAY, Alphonse C.A.
    Notice sur la Peinture sur Verre en Belgique au 19e Siècle.
    Brussels, 1859.

O'KELLY, A.
    Verrières des Environs de Bruxelles.
    Bulletin du Comité Archéologique du Brabant, vol. 1 (1870).

OLDFIELD, Edmund
    On the Portraits of Edward Prince of Wales (afterwards Edward V)
    and his Sisters in the East Window of Little Malvern Church,
    Worcestershire.
    The Archaeological Journal, vol. 22 (1865), pp. 302-325.

OLIN, J.S., THOMPSON, B.A., SAYRE, E.V.
    Characterisation of Medieval Window Glass by Neutron Activation
    Analysis.
    In Developments in Applied Spectroscopy, vol. 10 (1972), pp. 35-55.

ORR, C.B.
    Wright Goodhue, Artist of Glass.
    Boston (Mass.) Evening Transcript, May 16, 1925.

(New Oscott)
    (Window inserted.)
    The Gentleman's Magazine, vol. 10, new series, part 2 (1838), p. 171.

OSTERRATH, Joseph
    Introduction à l'Etude de la Peinture sur Verre.
    Bulletin des Métiers d'Art (Brussels), vols. 1-3 (1902-1904).

OSWALD, Arthur
    Barnard Flower, the King's Glazier.
    J.M.G.P., vol. 11, no. 1 (1952), pp. 8-21.

    The Glazing of the Savoy Hospital.
    J.M.G.P., vol. 11, no. 4 (1955), pp. 224-232.

OTTIN, L.
    L'Art de Faire un Vitrail.
    Paris, 1892.

    Le Vitrail, Son Histoire, Ses Manifestations Diverses.
    Paris, 1896.

OUVERLEAUX-LAGASSE, Felix
    Les Vitraux de l'Ancienne Eglise Abbatiale d'Herckenrode à la
    Cathédrale de Lichfield.
    Bulletin de la Société Royale d'Archéologie de Bruxelles, part 32
    (1926), pp. 89-97.

OWEN, Edward
    Old Stained Glass in St. Beuno's Church, Penmorta.
    Archaeologia Cambrensis, 6th series, vol. 5 (1905), pp. 335-337.

(Oxford, All Souls' College)
    Emblem of St. Simon the Apostle, All Souls', Oxford. By 'Priscilla'.
    (Request for identification.)
    Notes and Queries, vol. 151 (Oct. 9, 1926), p. 260.
    Replied to by GAWTHORP, W.E. (Oct. 23, 1926), p. 302.
                  KNOWLES, J.A. (q.v.), (Oct. 30, 1926), pp. 319-320.
                  JAMES, M.R. (q.v.), Ibid., p. 320.

(Oxford, Merton College)
    Merton Chapel Glass.
    The Times, Jan. 4, 1932.

(Oxford, New College)
    (Three New Windows installed in the north side of the Chapel, Sept.
    24, 1774).
    The Gentleman's Magazine, vol. 44 (1774), p. 490.

    (Piece of Flemish glass presented to New College. Account of
    dispersal of Flemish glass.)
    The Gentleman's Magazine, vol. 56, part 2 (1786), pp. 821-822.

    New College Glass.
    The Times, Nov. 16, 1932.

(Oxford, Wadham College)
    (Window by EVANS, David, inserted.)
    The Gentleman's Magazine, vol. 10, new series, part 2 (1838), pp. 171-
    172.

(Oxford Diocesan Advisory Committee, published for)
    Some Notes on Stained Glass Windows.
    London, 1929.

(Oxford Historical Society)
    Three Oxfordshire Parishes: Kidlington, Tarnton and Begbroke.
    Oxford, 1893.
    (Descriptions of the glass, pp. 55-56, 241-242, 362-363.)

PAATZ, W.
 Die Kirchen von Florenz.
 Frankfurt am Main, 1940-1953.

PAGE, John T.
 Windows from Church at Trier.
 Notes and Queries, 10th series, vol. 12 (Sept. 4, 1909), p. 198.

 St. George's Chapel, Windsor, East Window.
 Notes and Queries, 11th series, vol. 10 (Sept. 26, 1914), p. 256.
 See also FROST, W.A.
   PIERPOINT, R.

PAGET, Elma K.
 Letting in Light.
 J.M.G.P., vol. 12, no. 2 (1957), pp. 97-102.

PAINE, Charles
 The Craft of Stained Glass.
 The Studio, vol. 105 (May, 1933).

Painting with Light.
 Glass Digest, (Aug., 1950).

PALASINSKI, S.
 Polens moderne Glasmalerkunst.
 Zeitschrift für alte und neue Glasmalerei (1913), p. 99.

PALLU, H.
 Dissertation sur l'Antiquité d'une des Verrières de la Cathédrale
 du Mans.
 Bulletin Monumental, vol. 7 (1841), p. 359.

PANOFSKY, Erwin
 Abbot Suger on the Abbey Church of St. Denis and its Art Treasures.
 Princeton, 1946.

PAPE, T.
 Heraldic Glass Memorials of the Sulgrave Washingtons.
 The Connoisseur, vol. 54 (July, 1919), pp. 152-157.

 (With MANDER, G.P.)
 Some Ridware Armorial Glass.
 Staffordshire Historical Collections, new series, vol. 24 (1923), pp.
 279-290.
 Reprinted London, 1924.

 Ancient Glass from Abbots Bromley Manor House. Mary Stuart
 Inscription. An Heraldic Puzzle.
 The Connoisseur, vol. 79 (Dec., 1927), pp. 42-43.

 Early Glass Workers in North Staffordshire.
 J.M.G.P., vol. 3, no. 4 (Oct., 1930), pp. 169-172.
   vol. 4, no. 1 (Apr., 1931), pp. 17-22.

 The Glass Industry in the Burnt Woods (Staffordshire).
 Transactions of the North Staffordshire Field Club, vol. 65 (1930-1931),
 pp. 45-54.
 Reprinted Stoke-on-Trent, 1931.

 Mediaeval Glass-workers in North Staffordshire.
 Transactions of the North Staffordshire Field Club, vol. 68 (1934), pp.
 74-121.
 Reprinted Stoke-on-Trent, 1934.

PARE, Philip Norris
 Eric Milner-White; A Memoir.
 London ?, 1965.

(Paris Exhibition, 1867)
 Artisans' Reports to the Society of Arts on the Paris Universal
 Exhibition, 1867.
 London, 1867.
 (Stained glass, part 1, p. 70.)

 Rapports des Délégations Ouvrières à l'Exposition de 1867.
 3 vols., Paris, 1868.
 (Stained glass, vol. 3.)

 L'Exposition de 1867. Rapports de Jury International.
 13 vols, Paris, 1868.
 (Stained glass, vol. 3.)

 Paris Exhibition, 1867, British Reports.
 6 vols., London, 1868.
 (Vol. 2 contains Report on Glass-Painting, by PARRY, T. Gambier.)

(Paris Universal Exhibition, 1878)
 (Stained glass.)
 The Magazine of Art (1878), p. 190.

(Paris Universal Exhibition, 1889)
 L'Exposition de 1889. Rapports du Jury.
 Paris, 1891.

(Paris Universal Exhibition, 1900)
 L'Exposition de 1900. Rapports du Jury.
 Paris, 1900.

(Paris, Musée des Monumens Français)
 Musée des Monumens Français ou Description Historique et
 Chronologique des Statues en Marbre et en Bronze.
 8 vols., Paris, 1800-1821.
 (Stained glass, vol. 6.)

(Paris, Musée de Sculpture Comparée)
 Galerie des Vitraux Anciens (Musée de Sculpture Comparée). Notice
 Sommaire.
 Paris, 1920.

PARIS, W.F.
 Decorative Elements in Architecture.
 London and New York, 1917.
 (Stained glass, Chapter 9.)

PARKHURST, H.L.
 A Plea for Stained Glass.
 Municipal Affairs, vol. 3 (Dec., 1899), pp. 694-701.

PARMANN, Øistein
 Contemporary Norwegian Stained Glass.
 J.M.G.P., vol. 15, no. 2 (1973-1974), pp. 5-10.

PARRONCHI, Alessandro
 Studi su la Dolce Prospettiva.
 Milan, 1964.
 Contains the following articles:
 La Perspettiva Dantesca.
  Studi Danteschi, 36 (1960).
 Le Fonti di Paulo Uccello.
 I 'Perspettivi Passati'. I 'Filosofi'.
  Paragone, 89 (May, 1957);
   95 (Nov., 1957).
 Le Due Tavole Prospettiche de Brunelleschi.
  Paragone, 107 (Nov., 1958);
   109 (Jan.,1959).
 Le 'Misure Dell'occhio' secondo il Ghiberti.
  Paragone, 133 (Jan., 1961).

(Contd.)

PARRONCHI, Alessandro (Contd.)

    Studi su la Dolce Prospettiva (Contd.).
    Il 'punctum doleur' Della 'Costruzione Legittima'.
        Paragone, 145 (Jan., 1962).
    Leon Battista Albersi as a Painter.
        Burlington Magazine, vol. 104 (July, 1962).
    Sul 'Della Statua' Albertiano.
        Paragone, 133 (Jan., 1961).
    The whole book reviewed by EDGERTON, Samuel, Art Bulletin, vol. 49
    (March, 1967), pp. 77-80.

PARRY, Thomas Gambier

    Glass Painting, Ancient and Modern.
    Civil Engineering and Architectural Journal, vol. 27 (1862), pp. 221,
    253.

    Drawings for Stained Glass by Mr. C. Winston.
    The Ecclesiologist, no. 168 (1865).

    Report on Painting on Glass.
    In Vol. 2, Paris Exhibition, 1867, British Reports.
    London, 1868.

    Report on Mosaic and Painting on Glass.
    In Vol. 1, London International Exhibition, 1871. Official Reports.
    London, 1871.

    With BURCHETT, R.
    (Proposed Exhibition of Stained Glass at South Kensington, 1864.)
    The Ecclesiologist, vol. 24 (1863), pp. 345-346.

    The Art and the Artists of Glass-Painting. Read at the Exhibition of
    the late Mr. Winston's Drawings by the Archaeological Institute, at
    the Rooms of the Arundel Society.
    (Praises WINSTON.)
    The Ecclesiologist, vol. 26 (1865), pp. 143-158.

    Mr. Gambier Parry's Report on the Painting on Glass in the French
    Exhibition.
    The Ecclesiologist, vol. 29 (1868), pp. 204-207.

    Painted Glass in Gloucester Cathedral.
    Furniture Gazette (Feb. 16, Feb. 23, 1884).

    The Ministry of Fine Art to the Happiness of Life.
    Essays on Various Arts.
    London, 1886.

PARSONS, Philip

    The Monuments and Painted Glass of Upwards of One Hundred Churches,
    Chiefly in the Eastern Part of Kent, with an Appendix, containing
    three Churches in other counties. (Hadleigh, Dedham and Lavenham.)
    Canterbury, 1794.

PARVILLÉE, L.

    Architecture et Décoration Turques.
    Paris, 1874.

PASCAUD-GRANBOULAN, Anne

    Le Vitrail de la Vierge à la Trinité de Vendôme.
    L'Information d'Histoire de l'Art, part 3 (1971) pp. 128-132.

(Paterson - Sale Catalogue)

    A Particular of the Cloister: A Beautiful Collection of the Rare Old
    Stained Glass or Painted Glass Exhibiting . . . at Essex House in
    the Strand.
    London, 1773.

PATERSON, James

    Stained Glass.
    London, 1968.

PAUL, Roland W.

    Some Notes on Heraldic Glass in Great Malvern Priory Church.
    Archaeologia, vol. 57 (1901), pp. 353-358.

    (The heraldic glass at St. Mark's Church, Mark, Somerset.)
    Proceedings of the Somersetshire Archaeological and Natural History
    Society, vol. 72, for 1926 (1927), part 1, p. li-lii.

PAULI, Gustav

    Zeichnungen alter Meister in der Kunsthalle zu Hamburg: Niederlander.
    Frankfurt-am-Main, 1924.
    (Contains a drawing by Pieter Aartsen for a window.)

PAULUS, R.

    Der Münchener Glasmaler Paulus Loth, 1605-1642.
    Zeitschrift für alte und neue Glasmalerei (1913), p. 3.

    Münchener Glasmalerwerkstätten von 1550-1650.
    Ibid., p. 109.

PAWLE, H.L.

    (Glass in Hengrave Hall.)
    (Letter to the Editor.)
    J.M.G.P., vol. 11, no. 3 (1954), p. 183.

(Pawle, H.L.)

    Obituary. By KIRBY, H.T.
    J.M.G.P., vol. 13, no. 3 (1962), pp. 526-527.

PAZAUREK, G.

    Alte Züricher Glasmalerei.
    Keramische Rundschau, vol. 34, no. 11 (March 16, 1926), pp. 173, 174.

PEARCE, Walter J.

    The Glazed Windows of Moreton Old Hall, Cheshire.
    J.M.G.P., vol. 8, no. 2 (Apr., 1940), pp. 68-75.

PEARCE, William

    Fourteenth-Century Stained Glass.
    (A query about the position of an Archbishop's ring on a fragment
    in his possession.)
    Notes and Queries, 12th series, no. 1 (Apr. 1, 1916), pp. 267-268.
    (Elucidated, Ibid., pp. 335, 375, 457; 12th series, vol. 2 (Nov. 18,
    1916), pp. 415-416.)

(Pearson, James)

    A Catalogue of the Specimens of Stained Glass, Painted by Mr.
    Pearson . . . also . . . Cartoons by . . . Mr. J.H. Mortimer . . .
    London, 1780.

    (Life of Pearson is in D.N.B., vol. 44.)

PEARSON, James

    On the Art of Staining Glass.
    The Gentleman's Magazine, vol. 85, part 2 (1815), pp. 28-29.

(Pearson, James)

    (On the art of glass-painting as perfected by James PEARSON.)
    Reprinted from The Literary Gazette, in The Gentleman's Magazine,
    vol. 91, part 2 (1821), p. 256.

PEATLING, A.V.

    The Stained Glass of Surrey.
    Surrey Archaeological Society (1924)

    Ancient Stained and Painted Glass in the Churches of Surrey.
    Guildford, 1930.

PECKITT, Harriet

    (Two letters to James DALLAWAY defending her father against strictures
    made in his Observations on English Architecture.)
    The Gentleman's Magazine, vol. 87, part 1 (1817), p. 392.

PECKITT, William

    Biography of William Peckitt, Restorer of the Art of Glass Painting.
    Furniture Gazette, vol. 6 (1877), p. 322.
    Also in D.N.B., vol. 44.

    (Letter from, written 1789.)
    Yorkshire Herald, Oct. 29, 1935.

(Peckitt, William)

    His Secret for Firing Glass.
    Yorkshire Herald, Oct. 30, 1935.

    (An exhibition of his work.)
    Yorkshire Evening Press, Feb. 18, 1975.

PEDERSEN, Harry.

    When Do We Eat?
    (An outcry against American glaziers being reduced to work for the
    W.P.A.)
    Stained Glass, vol. 33, no. 2 (Autumn-Winter, 1938), pp. 47-49.

PEGGE, Samuel

    Brereton Church (in the County of Chester).
    (In a letter to O.S. Brereton.)
    Archaeologia, vol. 9 (1789), pp. 368-369

    Some Observations on the Paintings in the Windows of Brereton Church.
    Archaeologia, vol. 10 (1792), pp. 50-53.

PELINCK, E., and REGTEREN ALTENA, J.Q. van

    Geschilderde Vensters int 1543 in Leiden.
    Oud Holland, vol. 57 (1940), pp. 193 200.

PELLATT, Apsley

    On Stained and Painted Glass.
    Civil Engineering and Architectural Journal, vol. 25 (1862), p. 336.

    A General View of Glass Painting, in Connection with the Jury's
    Report on Stained Glass and Glass Used for Decoration.
    The Builder (Oct. 11, 1862), p. 735.

    Stained Glass and Glass Used for Decoration.
    The Technologist, vol. 4 (1864), p. 90.

PELT, J.-B.

    La Cathédrale de Metz.
    Metz, 1937.

(Pembridge Church)

    Transactions of the Woolhope Naturalists' Field Club, vol. 22 for
    1914, 1915, 1916, 1917 (1918), p. 192.

(Penmorta, Dolbenmaen, Caernarvon)

    The Old Stained Glass.
    Archaeologia Cambrensis, vol. 60 (1905), pp. 147-152.
    (Subsequent correspondence, pp. 335-337.)

(Penna, Edwin)

    Obituary.
    Stained Glass, vol. 39, no. 2 (Summer, 1944), p. 68.

(Pennsylvania Museum)

    The Staley Collection of Stained and Painted Glass.
    The Pennsylvania Museum Bulletin, vol. 18, no. 75 (March, 1923),
    pp. 3-5.

    Catalogue of the Collection of Stained and Painted Glass in the
    Pennsylvania Museum.
    (With a preface by BYE, A.E.)
    Philadelphia, 1925.

PERDRIZET, Paul

    L'Art Symbolique du Moyen Age à propos des Verrières de l'Eglise St.
    Etienne à Mulhouse.
    Bulletin de la Société Industrielle de Mulhouse, vol. 77 (May, 1907),
    pp. 215-236.
    Reprinted Leipzig, 1907.

PEREIRA, H.W.

    Brief Notes on the Heraldry of the Glass and Other Memorials in
    Wells Cathedral.
    Proceedings of the Somersetshire Archaeological and Natural History
    Society, vol. 34 for 1888, part 2 (1889), pp. 40-53.

PERENNES, Canon

    (Glass in the Chapel of Notre Dame du Crann in Spezet.)
    Bulletin d'Histoire et d'Archéologie du Diocèse de Quimper (1930).

    (Glass at La Martyre, near Landerneau.)
    Bulletin d'Histoire et d'Archéologie du Diocèse de Quimper (Sept. 1931).

PEREZ Y JORBA, M.

    With TILLOGA, G., MICHEL, D., and DALLAS, J.P.
    Quelques Aspects du Phénomène de Corrosion des Vitraux Anciens des
    Eglises Françaises.
    Verres et Réfractaires, vol. 29, no. 2 (1975), pp. 53-63.

    With COLLONGUES, R.
    Recherches Récentes sur le Processus de Corrosion des Vitraux.
    In Akten des 10. Internationalen Colloquiums des C.V.M.A.
    Stuttgart, 1977, p. 47.

PERKINS, Jocelyn

    An Abbey Tragedy. Fortunes of the North Rose Window.
    The Times, Sept. 18, 1935.

PERROT, Françoise

    Inventaire Sommaire des Vitraux Déposés dans les Réserves du Musée
    de Cluny.
    L'Information d'Histoire de l'Art, vol. 11, part 2 (May-June, 1966),
    pp. 132-133.

    Notes sur les Arbres de Jesse de Gercy et de Saint-Germain-lès-Corbeil.
    In The Year 1200, New York, 1970.

    Un Panneau de la Vitrerie de la Chapelle de l'Hôtel de Cluny.
    Revue de l'Art, no. 10 (1970), pp. 66-72.

    Compte Rendu.
    (Of the 7th Colloquium of the C.V.M.A.)
    In 7e Colloque du Corpus Vitrearum Medii Aevi.
    Florence ?, 1970, pp. 1-15.

    Bibliographie des Travaux Scientifiques de Jean Lafond.
    Revue de l'Art, no. 10 (1970), pp. 95-96.

    La Rose de Donnemarie-en-Montois.
    Bulletin de la Société d'Histoire et d'Archéologie de Provins, no. 124
    (1970), pp. 53-69.

PERROT, Françoise (Contd.)

Compte Rendu (du 8e Colloque du C.V.M.A.).
8e Colloque du Corpus Vitrearum Medii Aevi.
Paris ?, 1972, pp. 13-33.

Le Vitrail à Rouen.
Rouen, 1972.

Franse kerk-ramen. Vitraux de France.
(Exhibition at the Rijksmuseum, Amsterdam, Dec.,1973-March, 1974.)
Amsterdam, 1973.

With BETTEMBOURG, Jean-Marie
La Restauration des Vitraux de la Façade Occidentale de la Cathédrale
de Chartres.
Verres et Réfractaires, numéro spécial (1976).

Review of WAYMENT, Hilary, C.V.M.A., Great Britain, supplementary
volume 1.
Bulletin Monumental, no. 134 (1976), pp. 161-163.

Le Vitrail de Saint Christophe au Musée de Cluny à Paris.
Begleihefte zum Wallraf-Richartz Jahrbuch. t.1 (1977), pp. 103-105.

Compte Rendu de la Reunion du Comité International du Corpus Vitrearum.
In Akten des 10. Internationalen Colloquiums des C.V.M.A.
Stuttgart, 1977, pp. 55-58.

Les Verrières du 12e Siècle de la Façade, Occidentale /of Chartres7,
Etude Archéologique.
Les Monuments Historiques de France, no. 1 (1977), pp. 42-51.

Chefs d'Oeuvre Méconnus de la Renaissance: Les Vitraux d'Ecouen.
Les Dossiers de l'Archéologie, no. 26 (Jan.-Feb., 1978), pp. 76-85.

Review of GRODECKI, Louis, C.V.M.A., France, serie 'Etudes'. t. 1.
Bulletin Monumental, vol. 137 (1979), pp. 83-85.

With TARALON, Jean, and GRODECKI, Louis.
Recensement des Vitraux de Paris, de la Région Parisienne, de la
Picardie, du Nord et du Pas-de-Calais.
C.V.M.A., France, supplementary series, no. 1.
Paris, 1978.
Reviewed by BRISAC, Catherine, Bulletin Monumental, vol. 138, no. 1
(1980), pp. 109-111.

(Peterborough Cathedral)
History of the Cathedral Church of Peterborough.
Peterborough, 1786 (2nd edition).

PETERS, Charles (Editor)
Home Handicrafts.
London, 1890.
(Stained glass, chapter 3.)

PETHEO, Bela
Manuscript Illuminations and the Modern Stained Glass Painter.
Stained Glass, vol. 69, no. 4 (Winter, 1975), pp. 72-76.

PETIT-GÉRARD, Baptiste
Reflexions sur l'Aspect Général des Vitraux d'Alsace dans leurs
Rapports avec Ceux du Centre de la France.
Congrès Archéologique de France à Strasbourg en 1859, pp. 363-374.

Quelques Etudes sur l'Art Verrier et les Vitraux d'Alsace.
Strasbourg, 1861.

PETTIT, G.W.
A New Style of Ornamental Painting on Glass.
Art Journal, vol. 11 (1849), p. 351.

(Petty, John)
Notes and Queries, 12th series, vol. 9 (1921), pp. 63, 64, 103.

PEVSNER, N.
Colonel Gillum and the Pre-Raphaelites.
Burlington Magazine, vol. 95 (Jan.-Dec., 1953), pp. 78-81.

PFAFF, Konrad
(Introduction by STEPHANY, Erich.)
Ludwig Schaffrath: Stained Glass and Mosaic.
Krefeld, n.d. (? 1977).
Reviewed in J.M.G.P., vol. 17, no. 2 (1978-1979), p. 75.
Reviewed in Stained Glass, vol. 22, no. 4 (Winter, 1977-1978), pp.
253-257.

PFEFFER, Waltraud von
Zur Typologie merovingerzeitlicher Gläser mit Fadenverzierung.
Festschrift des röm.-germ. Zentralmuseum in Mainz zur Feier seines
hundertjahrigen Bestehens.
Mainz, 1952, vol. 3, pp. 147-160.

Fränkisches Glas.
Glastechnische Berichte, vol. 33 (1960), Heft. 4, pp. 136-142.

PFEILL, Karl Gabriel
Bewegung in der Glasmalerei. Neue Bildfenster von Peter Hecker, Köln.
Diamant (Dec. 1, 1937).

PFLEGER, K.
Ehrismanns Glasmalereien in der neuen Magdalenenkirche zu Strassburg.
Zeitschrift für alte und neue Glasmalerei (1913), p. 85.

PFNOR, R.
Ornementation Usuelle de Toutes les Epoques dans les Arts
Industriels . . .
2 vols., Paris, 1867-1868.

PHILIPPE, Joseph
Twentieth Century Vitraux from the Val-Saint-Lambert Glass Works.
J.M.G.P., vol. 15, no. 3 (1974-1975), pp. 39-47.

PHILLIPPS, L.M.
Stained Glass Windows.
The Contemporary Review, vol. 97 (March, 1910), pp. 346-360.

The Living Age.
Ibid., vol. 265 (Apr. 16, 1910), pp. 138-150.

Stained Glass.
The Englishwoman, vol. 20 (1913).

PHILLIPS, Douglas
How to Make a Portable Stained Glass Panel.
American Artist (Dec., 1962).

PHILLIPS, G.S.
Guide to Peterborough Cathedral.
Peterborough, 1853.

(Photography)
Photographing Stained Glass Windows in Churches with a Hand-Camera.
The Amateur Photographer, vol. 91 (Aug. 27, 1941), p. 687.

PIDGEON, Henry
Stained Glass in Ludlow Church, County Salop.
The Gentleman's Magazine, vol. 2, new series, part 2 (1834), pp. 585-
588.

PIEPER, Paul

Das Fenster von Leyden.
Westfalen, 29, pp. 172-188.
Münster, 1951.

PIERCE, Anthony

Observations on Stained Glass Training in Britain and America.
Stained Glass, vol. 63, no. 4 (Winter, 1968-1969), pp. 38-43.

PIERPOINT, Robert

St. George's Chapel, Windsor, East Window.
(Request for information of the fate of the window by West and
Jervais.)
Notes and Queries, 11th series, vol. 10 (Sept. 12, 1914), p. 210.
(See also FROST, W.A.
         PAGE, J.T.)

PIETSCHKE, Friedrich

Die Geheimnisse künstlicher Edelsteine, farbige Flüsse, Emaillen
herzustellen; auch Anweisung über Glasmalerei, u.s.w.
Helmstedt, 1836.

PIGEON, Amédée

Un Vitrail de la Cathédrale de Beauvais Représentant la Vie de
Saint-Martin de Tours.
Gazette des Beaux-Arts (Sept., 1895), pp. 233-242.

PIGGOT, John Jnr.

The Fairford Windows: Albrecht Durer, etc.
Notes and Queries, 4th series, vol. 2 (Aug. 29, 1868), pp. 193-194.
Ibid., (Oct. 31, 1868), p. 429.

(The Pilgrim Trust)

English Stained Glass (1930-1966).
(The work of the Pilgrim Trust in restoring stained glass.)
The Pilgrim Trust, 36th Annual Report (1966), pp. 7-12.

PILLOY, J. and SOCARD, E.

Le Vitrail Carolingien de la Chasse de Séry-lès-Mézières.
Bulletin Monumental, no. 64 (1910), pp. 5-25.

PILLWEIN, Benedikt

Biographische Schilderungen, oder Lexikon Salzburger Künstler,
nebst einen Anhange worin (a) die Glasmalerei auf dem Nonnberge,
(b) die aufgefundenen Alterthümer zu Glas, (c) bei Rosenegger
(d) zu Lory, und (e) bei Norischen zu St. Martin in Lungau,
beschrieben worden.
Salzburg, 1821.

PINE, L.G.

Heraldry in Stained Glass.
J.M.G.P., vol. 11, no. 2 (1953), pp. 105-107.

PIPER, John

Stained Glass: Art or Anti-Art.
London, 1968.
Reviewed by HAYWARD, John, J.M.G.P., vol. 14, no. 5 (1970-1971),
pp. 252-255.

PIQUET, M.O.

Die Glasmalerei im 17 Jahrhundert.
Keramische Rundschau, vol. 13 (1905), nos. 8, 9.

PIRINA, Caterine Gilli

Franceschino Zavattari, Stefano da Pandino, Maffiolo da Cremona,
magistri a Vitriatis e le Vetrate Absidali nel Duomo di Milano.
Arte Antica e Moderna, no. 33 (1966), pp. 25-44.

Michelino da Besozzo and the 'Vecchioni' of the Stained-Glass Window
of S. Giulitta.
Burlington Magazine, vol. 3 (1969), pp. 64-70.

Les Vitraux du 16e Siècle dans l'Abside du Dôme de Milan et les
Gravures du Dürer.
In 7e Colloque du Corpus Vitrearum Medii Aevi.
Florence ?, 1970, p. 29.

The Sixteenth-Century Windows in the Rear Choir of the Duomo in
Milan and Dürer's Engravings.
Burlington Magazine, vol. 114 (1972), pp. 453-456.

The Fifteenth-Century Windows in the Rear Choir of the Duomo in
Milan - 2. Antonio da Pandino and Scenes from the Life of Christ.
Burlington Magazine, vol. 118 (Jan., 1976), pp. 4-14.

PISA, Antonio da

Il Trattato di Antiono da Pisa Sulla Fabbricazione Delle Vetrate
Artistiche, Secolo 14.
Edited by PEZZELLA, Sahatore.
Perugia, 1976.
(See MARCHINI, May, 1977.)

(Pitassi, A. Leo)

Obituary.
Stained Glass, vol. 42, no. 4 (Winter, 1947), pp. 125-126.

PITCHER, Sydney A.

Ancient Stained Glass in Gloucestershire Churches.
Transactions of the Bristol and Gloucestershire Archaeological
Society, vol. 47 (for 1925), pp. 287-345.
Reprinted Gloucester, 1926.

(Pitcher, Sydney)

Mr. Pitcher's Exhibition of Photographs of Stained Glass.
J.M.G.P., vol. 2, no. 3 (Apr., 1928), p. 158.

(Pittsburgh and the Renaissance in Stained Glass.)

The Pittsburgh (Pa.) Press, May 20, 1962.

PLUYM, Willem van der

Max Nauta, Painter and Craftsman in Stained Glass.
The Studio, vol. 141 (1951), pp. 41-43.

POESCHEL, E.

Die romanischen Deckengemälde von Zillis.
Zurich, 1941.

(Poetry and glass)

Werke von Email und Glas in den Dichtungen des Mittelalters. By L.F.
Zeitschrift für alte und neue Glasmalerei (1912), pp. 48-49.

Poetry and Painted Glass.
(An anthology.)
J.M.G.P., vol. 8, no. 1 (Oct., 1939), pp. 36-41.

POGGI, G.

Il Duomo di Firenze.
Berlin, 1909.

(Poitiers - Restoration of the Glass)
   Les Vitraux du 13ᵉ Siècle de la Cathédrale de Poitiers.
   Bulletin de la Société des Antiquaires de l'Ouest (1949).
   Reported in Bulletin Monumental, vol. 108 (1950), p. 223.

PÖLLMAN P. Ansgar
   Beiträge zur Geschichte der Schwäbischen Glasmalerei.
   Zeitschrift für alte und neue Glasmalerei (1913), pp. 1, 32, 44.

   Weltkrieg und Kirchenfenster. Eine Erörterung über die Stellung
   der Glasmalerei im Bauprogramm der deutschen Zukunft. Ein
   Lorbeerkranz auf Franz Xavier Zettler's Grab.
   Munich, 1917.

POLACZEK, Ernst
   Von alter Glasmalerei.
   Kunstgewerbe Elsass-Löthringen, vol. 1 (1901), pp. 32-38.

PONTING, C.E.
   Notes on the Church of St. Mary, Lydiard Tregoze.
   (With additional notes on the glass by GODDARD, E.H.)
   The Wiltshire Archaeological and Natural History Magazine, no. 117
   (June, 1912), pp. 436-444.

POOLE, G. Ayliffe
   With HUGALL, J.W.
   An Historical and Descriptive Guide to York Cathedral and its
   Antiquities.
   York, 1850.

   The Stamford Churches.
   Reports and Papers of the Associated Architectural Societies (1850).

   The Stained Glass in Lowick Church, with Remarks on Glass Painting,
   Old and New.
   Reports and Papers of the Associated Architectural Societies, vol. 6
   (1861), pp. 53-64.

   Painted Glass in Connection with Architecture.
   Ibid., vol. 8 (1865-1866), pp. 134-144.
   Reprinted in The Ecclesiologist, vol. 25 (1864), pp. 251-261.

POOLE, Mrs. Reginald Lane
   Early Seventeenth Century Portraits in Stained Glass at Oxford.
   J.M.G.P., vol. 3, no. 1 (Apr., 1929), pp. 13-20.

POOLE, Stanley Lane
   The Art of the Saracens in Egypt.
   London, 1886.
   (Stained glass, p. 222.)

POPESCO, P.
   Verrière du Bon Samaritain de la Cathédrale de Chartres.
   Cahiers de la Céramique, du Verre et des Arts du Feu, no. 38 (1966),
   pp. 119-140.

   Les Panneaux de Vitrail du 12ᵉ Siècle de l'Eglise Saint-Pierre de
   Chartres.
   Revue de l'Art, vol. 10 (1970), pp. 47-56.

   Die Kathedrale von Chartres.
   Augsburg, 1969.

   La Cathédrale de Chartres.
   Paris, 1970.
   Reviewed by ERLANDE-BRANDENBERG, Alain and Olivier, Bulletin
   Monumental, no. 128 (1970), p. 173.

POPHAM, A.E.
   Notes on Flemish Domestic Glass Painting. Part 1.
   Apollo, vol. 7 (Apr., 1928).

   Notes on Flemish Domestic Glass Painting. Part 2.
   Ibid., vol. 9 (Jan.-June, 1929), p. 155.

   Designs for Stained Glass at Poundisford Park, Taunton, Attributed
   to Aert Claesz, 1498-1562.
   (Pp. 101-102 first published in Old Master Drawings, vol. 2, no. 7
   (Dec. 1927), pp. 37-39.)
   J.M.G.P., vol. 8, no. 3 (Apr., 1941), pp. 101-104.

PORÉE, Abbé
   Notice sur un Vitrail de Sainte-Foy de Conches, Représentant le
   Triomphe de la Sainte Vierge.
   Congrès Archéologique de France à Caen, 1883.
   Tours, 1885.

   La Restauration de l'Eglise de Conches.
   In Semaine Religieuse d'Evreux (1887).
   Reprinted Annuaire de l'Association Normande (session de 1888 à
   Conches).
   Rouen et Caen, 1889.

PORÉE, C.
   La Cathédrale d'Auxerre.
   Paris, 1926.

PORTER, Priscilla Manning
   Heat Fusion of Glass.
   Stained Glass, vol. 69, nos. 1 and 2 (Spring-Summer, 1974), pp. 17-19.

PORTHUSEN, Hermann
   Nachricht von der neuen Erfindung des Hrn. H.P. in Bremen,
   Glasgemälde zu verfertigen, welche nebst einigen Proben in der
   Versammlung der Königl. Gesellschaft d. Wissenschaft zu
   Göttingen, am 5 Jan. 1773 vorgelegt worden.
   Neue Mannigfaltigkeiten (Berlin), Jahr 1 (1774), pp. 271-277.

Portraits in Stained Glass
   Notes and Queries, 12th series, vol. 2 (1916-1917), pp. 172, 211,
   275, 317, 337, 374, 458, 517; vol. 3, pp. 15, 36, 76, 159, 198.

   (A correspondence in Notes and Queries.)
   LANE, John
   Notes and Queries, 12th series, vol. 2 (Aug. 26, 1916), p. 172.
   BRABROOK, E.
   (Sept. 9, 1916), p. 211.
   HARRISON, J.
   (Sept. 9, 1916), p. 211.
   DODGSON, E.S.
   (Sept. 9. 1916), p. 211.
   SPARKE, A.
   (Sept. 9, 1916), p. 211.
   BARNS, S.J.
   (Sept. 30, 1916), p. 275.
   CUMMINGS, C.L.
   (Sept. 30, 1916), pp. 275-276.
   W.B.H.
   (Sept. 30, 1916), p. 276.
   MAGRATH, J.R.
   (Oct. 14, 1916), pp. 317-318.
   HIBGAME, F.T.
   (Oct. 14, 1916), p. 318.
   BULL, W.
   (Oct. 14, 1916), p. 318.
   J.T.F.
   (Oct. 14, 1916), p. 318.
   A.D.G.
   (Oct. 21, 1916), p. 337.

POSTE, Beale
    Remarks on Some Representations of Minstrels in Early Painted Glass,
    Formerly in St. James' Church, Norwich.
    Journal of the British Archaeological Association, vol. 14 (1858),
    pp. 129-131.

POTTIER, André
    Description d'une Verrière de l'Eglise Saint-Vincent de Rouen
    Répresentant une Allégorie Mystique.
    Rouen, 1862.
    (Reprinted from Revue de Normandie.)

POUMON, Emile
    Le Hainaut: Les Vitraux.
    Vilvorde, 1949.

POUSIN, J.A.
    Vitraux d'après les Styles les plus Primitifs, jusqu'à nos Jours.
    Executés par les Procédés, des Anciens Perfectionnés.
    Paris, 1891.

(Powell and Sons, Whitefriars)
    Whitefriars Glass. 250th Anniversary. Opening of Exhibition Today.
    The Times, June 16, 1930.

    Stained Glass Windows for the Great Central Space in Liverpool
    Cathedral . . . some Press Notices on Two Memorable Windows.
    (Designed by HOGAN, James H.)
    London, 1937.

    'Powells' - The Whitefriars Studios.
    J.M.G.P., vol. 13, no. 1 (1960), pp. 321-325.

(Powell and Sons, Exhibition at the Langton Gallery)
    Eighty Years of Whitefriars: Designs for Stained Glass Windows
    From the Studios of Jas. Powell.
    (Exhibition catalogue.)
    London, 1972.

    (Whitefriars and Harry Clarke Studios)
    Studio Closures.
    News and Notes, J.M.G.P., vol. 15, no. 2 (1973-1974), pp. 49-50.

POWELL, A.M.
    The Manufacture of Antique Glass.
    Journal of the British Society of Master Glass-Painters, vol. 9,
    no. 4 (1946), pp. 105-109.

(Powell, Christopher Charles)
    Obituary. By WILKINSON, Alfred L.
    J.M.G.P., vol. 12, no. 1 (1956), pp. 73-74.

POWELL, H.B.
    Ervin Bossanyi, Hon. F.M.G.P., An Appreciation.
    J.M.G.P., vol.   (1974-1975), pp. 4-7.

POWELL, Harry James
    Picture-Windows in New College Ante-Chapel.
    Burlington Magazine, vol. 8 (Feb., 1906), pp. 326-331.

    (On the film on ancient glass.)
    Journal of the Royal Society of Arts (March 15, 1907), p. 481.

    Whitefriars Glass Works.
    The Nineteenth Century, vol. 88 (1920), pp. 851-857.

POWELL, Harry J. (Contd.)
    The Development of Coloured Glass in England.
    Journal of the Society of Glass Technology, vol. 6 (1922), pp. 249-255.

    Glass-Making in England.
    Cambridge, 1923.

POWELL, Hugh
    Kempe and His House.
    J.M.G.P., vol. 14, no. 5 (1970-1971), pp. 239-242.

POWELL, James
    On the Probability of Albert Dürer's Connection with the Stained Glass
    Windows at Fairford.
    Archaeological Journal, vol. 33 (1876), p. 194.
    Also in The Architect, vol. 15 (1876), p. 184.

    Some Details and Technicalities of the Glass Painter's Art.
    The Builder (Feb. 27, 1892).

POWELL, John H.
    Ancient Stained Glass.
    Reports and Papers of the Associated Architectural Societies, vol.
    4 (1857), pp. 161-168.
    Reported in The Ecclesiologist, vol. 18 (1857), pp. 317-318.

POWELL, Joseph
    Albert Dürer and the Fairford Windows.
    (Letter to The Times, Aug. 18, 1875.)
    Replied to by BURTT, Joseph, The Times, Aug. 20, 1875.

    (Report of his paper On the Probability of Albert Dürer's Connection
    with the Stained-Glass Windows of Fairford, and its Restoration by
    WALLER, J.G.)
    The Archaeological Journal, vol. 32 (1875), pp. 194-195.

    Handbook to Fairford Church and its Stained Windows.
    Fairford, 1875.
    (Several subsequent editions; 5th edition revised by TAUNT, H.W.,
    1893.)

    The Fairford Windows and Albert Dürer.
    Notes and Queries, 5th series, vol. 5 (Apr. 1, 1876), pp. 262-263.

POWELL, J.H.
    Highcliffe Castle, near Christchurch, Hampshire.
    Transactions of the Ancient Monuments Society, new series, vol. 15
    (1968).
    (Glass, pp. 91-94.)

POWYS, A.R.
    The Treatment of Window Glazing in the Repair of Ancient Buildings.
    The Builder, vol. 134 (June 1, 1928).

POYNTER, A.
    The Stained Glass in the Sainte Chapelle Royale, Paris.
    London, 1836.

PRATT, H.M.
    Stained Glass Windows.
    The Chautauquan (Meadville, Pa.), vol. 62 (March, 1911), pp. 83-91.

(Preussiche Akademie des Bauwesens, Berlin)

Vorbildliche Glasmalereien aus dem späten Mittelalter und der
Renaissancezeit.
Berlin, 1917.

(Preservation)

Die Konservierung alter Glasgemälde. By H.F.
Zeitschrift für alte und neue Glasmalerei (1912), pp. 6, 68, 72.

PREVOT, A.

Traité Pratique de Peinture, de Cuisson et d'Armature du Vitrail
chez soi, sans Maître, à l'Usage des Amateurs.
Paris, 1882.

(Prew d. Aelteren, Jörg)

Der Augsburger Glasmaler Jörg Prew d. Aelteren.
Diamant, 48th year, no. 25 (Sept. 1, 1926), pp. 484-488.

PRICE, William F.

Notes on the Parish Church of St. Wilfred, Standish.
Transactions of the Historic Society of Lancashire and Cheshire,
new series, vols. 19 and 20 for 1903-1904 (1905).
(Glass, p. 257).

PRIDEAUX, F.B.

Stained Glass in Bamfylde House, Exeter.
Devon and Cornwall Notes and Queries, vol. 15 (1929), pp. 242-243.

PRIESS, F.

Die Glasfenster der Cistercienser-Abteikirche Pforta.
Zeitschrift für Bauwesen (1893), pp. 585-588.

PRIEST, S.C.

Armorial Glass at Bolling Hall.
Bradford Antiquities, new series, vol. 39 (Apr., 1958).

PRISSE D'AVENNES, A.C.T.E.

L'Art Arabe d'après les Monuments du Kaire depuis le 7e Siècle
jusqu'à la fin du 18e.
3 vols., Paris, 1877.

La Décoration Arabe: Décors, Muraux . . . Mosaiques . . . Vitraux, etc.
Paris, 1885.

PROBERT, C.K.

Account of the Painted Glass in Walden Church.
Essex Review (Jan., 1930).

PROST, Bernard

Notice sur les Anciens Vitraux de l'Eglise de St. Julien (Jura) et
Incidemment sur ceux de Notre-Dame de Brou (Ain).
Publications Archéologiques de la Société d'Emulation du Jura,
Lons-le-Saunier, 1885.

PUCKLE, Bertram

Stained Glass Windows and How They Are Made.
Town Crier Magazine (Feb., 1929).

PUTRON, M.E. de

Joan Howson.
J.M.G.P., vol. 16, no. 1 (1976-1977), pp. 46-54.

PÜTZ, W.

Neue Pütz-Glasmalereien ausgestellt in Köln a. Rhein. By D.
Diamant, vol. 36 (1914), p. 4.

PUGH, George Augustus

The Old Glass Windows of Ashton-under-Lyne Parish Church.
Lancashire and Cheshire Antiquarian Society, vol. 20 (1903), pp.
130-138.

PUGIN, Augustus

With WILLSON, E.J.

Specimens of Gothic Architecture . . .
2 vols., London, 1821-1823.

With WILLSON, E.J. (and others, including PUGIN, A.W.N.)
Examples of Gothic Architecture . . .
3 vols., London, 1831-1838.

With KEUX, J. Le, and H. Le.
Essays Accompanying Engraved Specimens of the Architectural
Antiquities of Normandy.
London, 1833.

PUGIN, A.W.N.

Floriated Ornament Specially Adapted for Stained Glass Windows.
London, 1849.

PUREY-CUST, A.P.

The Heraldry of York Minster: A Key to the History of its Builders
and Benefactors, as Shown in its Stained Glass Windows and in the
Carved Work in Stone.
2 vols., Leeds, 1890-1896.

York Minster.
London, 1897.

(Quebec)

Stained Glass in Quebec.
Stained Glass, vol. 43, no. 2 (Summer, 1948), pp. 47-49.

QUENTIN, Charles

Mr. Kempe's Painted Glass Windows.
Art Journal (1900), pp. 344-348.

QUIÉVREUX, François

Les Vitraux de 13e Siècle de l'Abside de la Cathédrale de Bourges.
Bulletin Monumental, (1942), pp. 255-275.

QUINET, Paul

A propos de Vitraux Peints de l'Eglise Sainte Waudru à Mons.
Annales du Cercle Archéologique de Mons, vo. 30 (1901), pp. 223-228.

RAADT, J. Th. De.

Fragments de Verrière au Musée Communal de Bruxelles.
Annales du Cercle Archéologique de Bruxelles, vol. 7 (   ), pp.
228-229.

RABY, F.J.E.

Review of RUSHFORTH, G. McNeil, Medieval Christian Imagery . . .
The Antiquaries Journal, vol. 16, no. 3 (July, 1936).

RACKHAM, Bernard

A Stained Glass Panel from Landshut in the Victoria and Albert Museum.
The Burlington Magazine, vol. 36 (March, 1920), p. 104.

Stained Glass in the Victoria and Albert Museum.
Country Life (March 14, 1925).

A Franconian Glass Panel at South Kensington.
Burlington Magazine, vol. 46 (Jan.-June, 1925), pp. 183-184.

English Glass-Paintings of St. Edmund at South Kensington and
Dorchester.
Burlington Magazine, vol. 47 (July-Dec., 1925), pp. 87-88.

The Italian Annunciation in the Victoria and Albert Museum.
J.M.G.P., vol. 1, no. 3 (Oct., 1925), pp. 24-25.

Glass Painting as an Art for Today.
Art Work, vol. 2, no. 5 (Oct.-Dec., 1925; Jan.-March, 1926; Summer,
1926).

The Glass of Winchester College Chapel.
J.M.G.P., vol. 1, no. 4 (Apr., 1926), pp. 23-24.

Review of LEHMANN, Das ehemalige Cisterzienserklaster Maris Stella
bei Wettingen und seine Glasgemälde.
J.M.G.P., vol. 2, no. 1 (1927), pp. 42-44.

English Importations of Foreign Stained Glass in the Early Nineteenth
Century.
J.M.G.P., vol. 2, no. 2 (Oct., 1927), pp. 86-94.

Bruges Stained Glass.
Daily Telegraph, Nov. 9, 1927.

Review of READ, Herbert, English Stained Glass.
Spectator Literary Supplement (Dec. 4, 1927).

The Early Stained Glass at Canterbury Cathedral.
Burlington Magazine, vol. 52 (Jan.-June, 1928), pp. 33-41.

A Stained Glass Panel from Canterbury.
(Letter to the Editor.)
Burlington Magazine, vol. 52 (Jan.-June, 1928), p. 106.

The Ashridge Stained Glass.
Old Furniture, vol. 5 (Sept., 1928), pp. 33-37.

Review of KIESLINGER Franz, Gotische Glasmalerei in Österreich
bis 1450.
Burlington Magazine, vol. 54 (Jan.-June, 1929), pp. 156-157.

Stained Glass in the Collection of Mr. F.E. Sidney.
1. Swiss Glass.
2. Netherlandish and German Medallions.
Old Furniture, vol. 7 (Aug., 1929), pp. 223-230.
          vol. 8 (Sept., 1929), pp. 13-19.

The Window Decoration of Richard Süssmuth.
The Studio, vol. 98 (1929), p. 814.

Stained Glass Windows by Miss W.M. Geddes.
The Studio, vol. 98 (July-Dec., 1929), p. 682.

The Glass-Painter Lukas Zeiner and his School.
Old Furniture, vol. 8 (Oct., 1929), pp. 54-60.

RACKHAM, Bernard (Contd.)

Austrian Stained Glass at South Kensington.
Burlington Magazine, vol. 56 (Jan.-June, 1930), pp. 291-292.

The Stained Glass in the Chapel of the Holy Blood at Bruges.
From Actes du 12ᵉ Congrès International d'Histoire de l'Art . . .
Brussels (Sept. 20-29, 1930),
Reprinted J.M.G.P., vol. 8, no. 2 (Apr., 1940), pp. 45-50.

Note on a Fifteenth Century Roundel Acquired by the Victoria and
Albert Museum.
The Collector, vol. 11 (Nov., 1930).

The Glass-Paintings of Coventry and its Neighbourhood.
Walpole Society, vol. 19 (1930-1931), pp. 89-110.

(Notice of 'Glass-Paintings of Coventry . . .'.
Memorabilia, Notes and Queries, vol. 161 (Nov. 21, 1931), p. 361.)

The Ancient Stained Glass at Lindsell Church.
Transactions of the Essex Archaeological Society, new series, vol. 20
for 1930-1933 (1933), pp. 73-77.

Review of EDEN, F.S., Ancient Stained and Painted Glass (revised
edition).
Burlington Magazine, vol. 63 (July-Dec., 1933), p. 186.

Notice of WOODFORDE, Christopher, The Mediaeval Glass of St. Peter
Mancroft, Norwich.
Burlington Magazine, vol. 63 (Oct., 1933).

The North Transept Window.
6th Annual Report of the Friends of Canterbury Cathedral (1933),
pp. 32-37.

The Newly Replaced Glass in the Trinity Chapel.
7th Annual Report of the Friends of Canterbury Cathedral (1934),
pp. 29-33.

The Glass Collections of the Victoria and Albert Museum, London.
Journal of the Society of Glass Technology, vol. 18 (1934), pp.
308-322.

The Siege of Canterbury.
Canterbury Cathedral Chronicle, no. 22 (Oct., 1935), pp. 5-6.

Notes on the Glass in the Lord Mayor's Chapel, Bristol.
Transactions of the Bristol and Gloucester Archaeological Society,
vol. 57 (for 1935), pp. 266-268.

A Guide to the Collections of Stained Glass (in the Victoria and
Albert Museum).
London, 1936.
Reviewed by READ, Herbert, Burlington Magazine, vol. 69 (July-Dec., 1936)
p. 47.

Review of KNOWLES, J.A., Essays in the History of the York School
of Glass Painting.
Burlington Magazine, vol. 70 (Jan.-June, 1937), p. 149.

Reviews of HARRISON, F., Stained Glass of York Minster, and of
AUBERT, Marcel, Vitraux des Cathédrales de France.
Burlington Magazine, vol. 72 (Jan.-June, 1938), pp. 98-99.

Review of CONNICK, C.J., Adventures in Light and Colour.
Burlington Magazine, vol. 72 (Jan.-June, 1938), p. 246.

Faces in the Glass: A Study of the Heads.
Canterbury Cathedral Chronicle (1939).

Ancient Stained and Painted Glass. An Address Given . . . to the
Friends of Canterbury Cathedral on June 17, 1939.
Canterbury Cathedral Chronicle (July, 1939), pp. 22-33.

The East Windows of Becket's Crown.
Canterbury Cathedral Chronicle, no. 36 (Aug., 1940), pp. 3-6.

RACKHAM, Bernard (Contd.)

    Genealogical Windows at Canterbury Cathedral.
    (Letter to the Editor.)
    Burlington Magazine, vol. 78 (Jan.-June, 1941), pp. 165-166.

    Further Notes on the Early Glass-Paintings.
    15th Annual Report of the Friends of Canterbury Cathedral (1942),
    pp. 29-31.

    With BATY, C.W.
    The Jesse Window at Llanrhaiadr, Denbighshire. Part 1.
    Burlington Magazine, vol. 80 (Jan.-Dec., 1942), pp. 62-66.
    Part 2, Ibid., pp. 121-124.

    With BATY, C.W.
    The Jesse Window at Llanrhaiadr.
    (Letter to the Editor.)
    Burlington Magazine, vol. 82 (Jan.-June, 1943), p. 51.

    A Seventeenth Century Window at Compton, Surrey.
    J.M.G.P. vol. 8, no. 4 (1942), pp. 133-136.

    Review of ZSCHOKKE, Fridtjof, Die romanischen Glasgemälde des
    Strassburger Munsters.
    Burlington Magazine, vol. 83 (July-Dec., 1943), p. 208.

    The Great West Window.
    16th Annual Report of the Friends of Canterbury Cathedral (1943), pp.
    30-31.
    The Grapes of Eschol.
    Ibid., pp. 31-32.

(Rackham, Bernard)

    A List of Works by Bernard Rackham Relating to Stained and Painted
    Glass.
    J.M.G.P., vol. 9, no. 2 (1944), pp. 61-62.

    The Mariawald-Ashridge Glass.
    Burlington Magazine, vol. 85 (July-Dec., 1944), pp. 266-273.
    Part 2, Ibid., vol. 86 (Jan.-Dec., 1945), pp. 90-94.

    An Early Glass Panel Retrieved.
    17th Annual Report of the Friends of Canterbury Cathedral (1944),
    pp. 15-17.

    Fifteenth Century Glass Panel - St. Catherine of Alexandria.
    Canterbury Cathedral Chronicle, no. 40 (Oct., 1944), pp. 13-14.

(Rackham, Bernard)

    Announcement of the Ancient Glass of Canterbury Cathedral.
    18th Annual Report of the Friends of Canterbury Cathedral (1945),
    pp. 18-19.

RACKHAM, Bernard

    The Dream of King Henry- a Stained Glass Medallion.
    Ibid., pp. 31-32.

    Review of BOOM, A. van der, Ontwikkeling en Karakter der Oude
    Monumentale Glasschilderkunst.
    Burlington Magazine, vol. 89 (Jan.-Dec., 1947), p. 171.

    Review of LAFOND, Jean, 1) La Résurrection d'un Maître d'Autrefois:
    Le Peintre-Verrier Arnoult de Nimègue. 2) Pratique de la Peinture
    sur Verre à l'Usage des Curieux, Suivie d'un Essai Historique sur
    le Jaune d'Argent et d'une Note sur les plus Anciens Verres Gravés.
    Burlington Magazine, vol. 89 (Jan.-Dec., 1947), pp. 198-200.

    Old Glass Reinstated.
    Canterbury Cathedral Chronicle, no. 42 (Oct., 1947), pp. 20-23.

    The Ashridge Stained Glass.
    London, 1948.
    In Journal of the British Archaeological Association, 3rd series,
    vol. 10 (for 1945-1947), pp. 1-22.

RACKHAM, Bernard (Contd.)

    The Crucifixion: A Stained Glass Medallion Reinstated.
    21st Annual Report of the Friends of Canterbury Cathedral (1948), p. 31.

    The East Window of the Chapel of Trinity Hospital, Greenwich.
    J.M.G.P., vol. 10, no. 1 (1948), pp. 4-8.

    Review of AUBERT, Marcel, Le Vitrail en France.
    J.M.G.P., vol. 10, no. 1 (1948), pp. 44-47.
    Also in Burlington Magazine, vol. 90 (Jan.-Dec., 1948), pp. 54-55.

    Review of WOODFORDE, Christopher, Stained Glass in Somerset.
    Burlington Magazine, vol. 90 (Jan.-Dec., 1948), p. 153.

    Review of HELBIG, Jean, De Glasschilderkunst in België. Repertorium
    en Documenten.
    J.M.G.P., vol. 10, no. 1 (1948), pp. 47-49.

    The Dream of King Louis VII. A Medallion in Canterbury Cathedral.
    18th Annual Report of the Friends of Canterbury Cathedral.
    Reprinted in Stained Glass, vol. 43, no. 4 (Winter, 1948), pp. 111-113.

    Florentine Painted Glass.
    (Letter to the Editor.)
    Burlington Magazine, vol. 91 (Jan.-Dec., 1949), p. 114.

    Review of ZSCHOKKE, Fridtjof, Mittelalterliche Bildfenster . . .
    and Medieval Stained Glass of Switzerland.
    Burlington Magazine, vol. 91 (Jan.-Dec., 1949), pp. 117-118.

(Rackham, Bernard)

    Invitation to an exhibition advertising the forthcoming 'Ancient
    Glass of Canterbury Cathedral'.
    (4 page leaflet with illustration.)
    London, n.d. (1949).

    The Ancient Glass of Canterbury Cathedral.
    London, 1949.
    Reviewed by COUNCER, C.R., Archaeologia Cantiana, vol. 63 (1950),
    pp. 156-158.
    Reviewed by MILLAR, E.G., 23rd Annual Report of the Friends of
    Canterbury Cathedral (1950), pp. 24-26.
    Reviewed in J.M.G.P., vol. 10, no. 3 (1950), pp. 163-165.
    Reviewed by READ, Herbert, Burlington Magazine, vol. 92 (Jan.-Dec.,
    1950), p. 55.

    The Stained Glass of Guildford Guildhall.
    Surrey Archaeological Collections, vol. 51 (1950), pp. 97-101.

    The Ancient Glass of Canterbury Cathedral.
    (Letters to the Editor.)
    Burlington Magazine, vol. 92 (1950), p. 357.
                 vol. 93 (1951), pp. 94-95.
    (Q.v. GRODECKI, Louis, Ibid., vol. 92, pp. 294-297; vol. 93, p. 94.)

    Review of HELBIG, J., and DOURMONT, R. van Steenberghe de,
    De Glasschilderkunst in Belgie . . . vol. 2.
    Burlington Magazine, vol. 93 (Jan.-Dec., 1951), p. 365.

    Review of WOODFORDE, Christopher, The Stained Glass of New College,
    Oxford.
    Burlington Magazine, vol. 94 (Jan.-Dec., 1952), pp. 90-91.

    The Resurrection of a Fourteenth-Century Window.
    (Letter to the Editor.)
    (Q.v. MILNER-WHITE, Eric, Ibid., pp. 108-112.)
    Burlington Magazine, vol. 94 (Jan.-Dec., 1952), p. 209.

    The Ancient Windows of Christ's College Chapel, Cambridge.
    The Archaeological Journal, vol. 109 (for 1952), pp. 132-142.

    Supplementary Note on the Windows of Christ's College Chapel, Cambridge.
    Ibid., vol. 110 (for 1953), p. 214.

RACKHAM, Bernard (Contd.)

A Newly Restored Window in the Trinity Chapel.
27th Annual Report of the Friends of Canterbury Cathedral (1954), pp. 14-15.

Review of LAFOND, Jean, (Chapter on Stained Glass in LEFRANÇOIS-PILLON, L.,(editor), L'Art du 14ᵉ Siècle en France.
Burlington Magazine, vol. 97 (Jan.-Dec., 1955), p. 357.

The Stained Glass Windows of Canterbury Cathedral.
Canterbury, 1957.

Review of DRAKE, Wilfred, A Dictionary of Glass-Painters and 'Glasyers' of the Tenth to Eighteenth Centuries.
J.M.G.P., vol. 12, no. 2 (1957), pp. 161-162.

With POINTER, H.W.
The Ancient Stained Glass at St. John's, Stoke-next-Guildford.
Surrey Archaeological Collections, vol. 55 (1958), pp. 18-31.

Stained Glass in France.
(Review of Le Vitrail Français. Contributions by CHASTEL, GRODECKI, GRUBER, AUBERT, LAFOND, TARALON, MATHEY.)
Burlington Magazine, vol. 101 (Jan.-Dec., 1959), pp. 194-197.

Review of WENTZEL, Hans, C.V.M.A., Germany 1.
Burlington Magazine, vol. 101 (Jan.-Dec., 1959), p. 360.

Corrigenda and Addenda to 'The Ancient Glass of Canterbury Cathedral'.
Canterbury Cathedral Chronicle, no. 55 (Oct., 1960), pp. 16-19.

Glass, Stained and Painted.
(Article in Chambers' Encyclopaedia, 1961.)

Mr. Samuel Caldwell. (Obituary,)
Canterbury Cathedral Chronicle, no. 58 (Oct., 1963), p. 10.

Obituary.
37th Annual Report of the Friends of Canterbury Cathedral (1964), centre page 2.

Obituary.
(Reprinted from The Times, Feb. 14, 1964).
J.M.G.P., vol. 14, no. 2 (1965), pp. 108-109.

RADEMACHER, F.

Die deutschen Gläser des Mittelalters.
Berlin, 1933.

Fränkische Gläser aus dem Rheinland.
Bonner Jahrbucher, 147 (1942), pp. 285-344.

RADCLIFFE, G.R.Y.

New College Glass.
(Letter to the Editor.)
The Times, Nov. 17, 1932.

RAGGHIANTI, C.L.

Il Foppa e le Vetriere del Duomo di Milano.
In Critica d'Arte, 6 (1954), pp. 520-

Postilla Foppesca.
In Critica d'Arte, 9 (1955), pp. 285-

RAGUIN, Virginia Chieffo

The Genesis Workshop of the Cathedral of Auxerre and its Parisian Inspiration.
Gesta, vol. 13, part 1 (1974), pp. 27-38.

RAGUIN, Virginia Chieffo (Contd.)

Windows of Saint-Germain-lès-Corbeil: A Traveling Glazing Atelier.
Gesta, vol. 15, parts 1 and 2 (1976).
Essays in Honor of Sumner McKnight Crosby, pp. 265-272.

The Isaiah Master of the Sainte-Chapelle in Burgundy.
Art Bulletin, vol. 59 (Dec., 1977), pp. 483-493.

RAHN, J.R.

Die biblischen Deckengemälde in der Kirche von Zillis im Kanton Graubündten.
Reprinted from Mitteilungen der Antiquarischen Gesellschaft in Zurich, no. 36.
Zurich, 1872.

Geschichte der bildenden Künste in der Schweiz von den ältesten Zeiten bis zum Schlusse des Mittelalters.
Zurich, 1876.

Die Glasgemälde in der Wasserkirche zu Zürich.
Zurich, 1877.

Die Glasgemälde in der Rosette der Kathedrale von Lausanne.
Ein Bild der Welt aus dem 13 Jahrhundert.
Mitteilungen der Antiquarischen Gesellschaft, Zurich, 20, 1879.
French version: La Rose de la Cathédrale de Lausanne.
Lausanne, 1879.

Die Glasgemälde Christoph Maurers im germanischen Museum zu Nürnberg.
Anzeiger für schweizerische Altertumskunde, part 5 (1883).

Die Glasgemälde im Chor der Kirche von St. Saphorin im Kanton Waadt.
Mitteilungen Geschichte Erhalt historische Kunstdenkmaler (Geneva), part 3 (1885).

Die Glasgemälde im gotischen Hause zu Wörlitz. (Gesammelte Studien zur Kunstgeschichte. Eine Festgabe . . . für A. Springer.)
Leipzig, 1885.

Glasgemälde in Muri-Gries bei Bozen.
Anzeiger für schwsizerische Altertumskunde (1888).

Die schweizerischen Glasgemälde in der Vincent 'schen Sammlung in Constanz.
Mitteilungen der Antiquarischen Gesellschaft, Zurich, vol. 22 (1890), pp. 179-263.
Reprinted Zurich, 1890.

Ausstellung von Glasgemälden aus dem Nachlasse des Dichters J.M. Usteri (1763-1829).
Zurich, 1899.

Glasgemälde aus dem Anfang des 16 Jahrhunderts und ihre Vorlagen.
Anzeiger für schweizerische Altertumskunde, new series, vol. 3 (1901), pp. 58-66.

Die Glasgemälde in der Kirche zu Oberkirch bei Frauenfeld.
Mitteilungen: Geschichte-Erhaltung historische Kunstdenkmaler (Geneva), new series, (1901). Section 1.

With LEHMANN, Hans
Ergänzungen zur Litteratur über die schweizerische Glasmalerei.
Anzeiger für schweizerische Altertumskunde, new series, vol. 2 (1900), pp. 69-73.

RALPH, Elizabeth, and EVANS, Henley
St. Mark's, The Lord Mayor's Chapel, Bristol.
Bristol, 1959.
(Glass, pp. 11-25.

RAMBUSCH, Harold
Stained Glass: Its Background and Foreground.
The Glass Industry (March, 1941).

RAMBUSCH, Harold (Contd.)

    The Apprentice Question.
    Stained Glass, vol. 37, no. 1 (Spring, 1942), pp. 22-26.

    Stained Glass.
    The Keystone (Brooklyn), (Oct. 15, 1944).

    See Stained Glass Problems in Our Day.

    Modern Portuguese Stained Glass.
    Stained Glass, vol. 43, no. 1 (Spring, 1948), pp. 5-15.

    L'Affaire Matisse.
    (Letter to the Editor.)
    Stained Glass, vol. 47, no. 2 (Summer, 1952), pp. 76-78.

    An Autobiography.
    Stained Glass, vol. 72, no. 2 (Summer, 1977), pp. 85-88.

    Some Memoirs of a President.
    Stained Glass, vol. 73, no. 4 (Winter, 1978-1979), p. 266.

RAMBUSCH, Robert E.
    Keeping the Craft Alive.
    Stained Glass, vol. 51, no. 1 (Spring, 1956), pp. 4-7.

    American Architecture and American Stained Glass.
    Stained Glass, vol. 52, no. 3 (Autumn, 1957), pp. 113-114.

RAMBUSCH, Robert, BRIDGES, Stephen. GOODMAN, P., ATKINSON, Harry, BATES, Harold.
    Stained Glass as Architects Consider It. (A Symposium.)
    Stained Glass, vol. 59, no. 4 (Winter, 1964-1965), pp. 24-31.

RAMBUSCH, Robert, FREI, Robert, ELSKUS, Albinus
    Contemporary Stained Glass.
    Stained Glass, vol. 60, no. 1 (Spring, 1965), pp. 13-23.

RANQUET, H. du
    Les Vitraux de la Cathédrale de Clermont-Ferrand.
    Clermont, 1932.

RANSOME, D.R.
    The Struggle of the Glaziers Company with the Foreign Glaziers, 1500-
    1550.
    Guildhall Miscellany, vol. 2, no. 1.

RANTON, William L.
    Maintenance and Repair.
    Stained Glass, vol. 44, no. 1 (Spring, 1949), pp. 13-16.

RANTSCH, D.
    Über Erhaltungszustand und Technik der Sakristeifenster von St. Gereon
    in Köln.
    Jahrbuch der rheinischen Denkmalpflege, vol. 22 (1959), pp. 71-86.

(Rathausen)
    Alte Schweizer Glasmalereien aus dem ehemalige Cistercienzer-Kloster
    Rathausen, bei Luzern.
    Zurich, 1899.

RATHE, Kurt
    Eine Kabinetscheibe aus dem Kreise des Hausbuchmeisters.
    Oberrheinische Kunst, 6, pp. 68-71.
    Freiburg, 1934.

RATHOUIS, Edouard
    Le Vitrail Royal de l'Eglise Nôtre-Dame de Saint-Lô (Manche) Restauré
    à la Manufacture de Vitraux Peints du Carmel du Mans par E.R. sous la
    Direction Artistique et Archéologique de E. Hucher.
    Paris, 1873.

RATTNER, Abraham
    ' . . . And There Was Light'.
    Studies by Abraham Rattner for the Stained Glass Window, Chicago
    Loop Synagogue.
    (Foreward by TAYLOR, J.C.)
    (Introduction by FLINT, J.A.)
    (Notes on the Stained Glass Window and the Symbols by RATTNER, A.)
    Washington D.C., 1976.

(Rattner, Abraham)
    Obituary.
    Stained Glass, vol. 73, no. 1 (Spring, 1978), p. 45.

RAULIN, J.
    Les Vitraux Nouveaux de l'Eglise Notre Dame de Mayenne.
    Photogravures d'après les Cartons de Ch. Champigneulle, de Paris.
    Paris, 1894.

RAW, F.
    The Long-Continued Action of Water on Window-Glass: Weathering of
    the Medieval Glass at Wealey Castle, Birmingham.
    Journal of the Society of Glass Technology, vol. 39 (1955), pp. 128-133.

READ, Herbert
    The Labours of the Months: A Series of Stained Glass Roundels.
    Burlington Magazine, vol. 43 (July-Dec., 1923), pp. 167-168.

    A Thirteenth Century Glass-Painting.
    (Acquired for the Victoria and Albert Museum.)
    Burlington Magazine, vol. 45 (July-Dec., 1924), pp. 180-185.

(Read, Herbert)
    Announcement of the forthcoming appearance of English Stained Glass,
    Memorabilia, Notes and Queries, vol. 150 (May 22, 1926), p. 361.

    Review of LEHMANN, . . . Glasmalerei in der Schweiz.
    J.M.G.P., vol. 1, no. 5 (Oct., 1926), pp. 36-37.

    English Stained Glass.
    London, 1926.
    Reviewed by HONEY, W.B., Burlington Magazine, vol. 50 (Jan.-June, 1927),
    pp. 219-220.

    Review of COUTEUR, J.D. le, English Medieval Painted Glass.
    J.M.G.P., vol. 2, no. 4 (Oct., 1928), p. 212.

    Review of BRUCKMANN, F., Deutsche Glasmalkunst.
    J.M.G.P., vol. 2, no. 4 (Oct., 1928), pp. 213-214.

    A Stained Glass Panel from Milan Cathedral.
    Burlington Magazine, vol. 53 (July-Dec., 1928), p. 312.

    Article 'Stained Glass'.
    In Encyclopaedia Britannica, 1929 edition.

    Netherlandish Glasspainters in England in the Fifteenth and Sixteenth
    Centuries.
    12e International kunsthistorisch congres te Brussel in 1930.
    Brussels, 1930, pp. 416-423.

    Modern Stained Glass.
    The Listener, (May 11, 1932).

    Review of RACKHAM, Bernard, A Guide to the Collection of Stained Glass.
    (In the Victoria and Albert Museum.)
    Burlington Magazine, vol. 69 (July-Dec., 1936), p. 47.

    Stained Glass at Canterbury and Oxford.
    (Reviews of RACKHAM, Bernard, The Ancient Glass of Canterbury Cathedral,
    and HUTCHINSON, F.E., Medieval Glass at All Souls' College.)
    Burlington Magazine, vol. 92 (Jan.-Dec., 1950), p. 55.

READ, Herbert (Contd.)
  Review of WENTZEL, Hans, Meisterwerke der Glasmalerei.
  Burlington Magazine, vol. 94 (Jan.-Dec., 1952), pp. 241-242.

  Introduction to BAKER, John, and LAMMER, Alfred, 1960, (q.v.).

READ, L.W.
  English Stained Glass in the Middle Ages.
  The Parents' Review (Apr., 1925).

RÉAU, L.
  Les Monuments Détruits de l'Art Français.
  Paris, 1959.
  Reviewed by LAFOND, Jean, L'Oeil, no. 62 (Feb., 1960), p. 55.

REBOULEAU
  Nouveau Manuel Complet de la Peinture sur Verre, sur Porcelaine et
  sur Email.
  (With M. MAGNIER.)
  Paris, 1868.

REDSLOB, Edwin
  With NEUMANN, Dr.
  Das Friedrich Bayer Fenster von Dietz Edzard. Aufsatz über D.E. von
  Dr. Neumann . . . Betrachtung über das Fenster von Dr. Redslob.
  Berlin, 1925.

  Auftragswille und Werkstattsleistung als Grundfaktoren Künstlerischer
  Arbeit. Ein Betrachtung über ein Glasfenster für Leverkusen vom
  Reichskunstwart.
  Diamant (Nov. 1, 1925).

REDSTONE, Louis G.
  Art in Architecture.
  New York, 1968.

REGAMEY, R.P.
  Cinq Artistes Français au Service du Sanctuaire.
  L'Artisan et les Arts Liturgiques (Brussels), no. 1, (1948).

RÉGNIER, Louis
  Monographie de l'Eglise de Nonancourt et de ses Vitraux.
  Mesnil-sur-l'Estrée, 1894.

REGTEREN-ALTENA, Johan Quiryn van
  Over het Portret bij de gebroeders Crabeth.
  Amsterdam, 1953.
  From Oud-Holland, no. 68.

REICHEL, Oswald J.
  Ancient Heraldic Glass in Slapton Church.
  Devon and Cornwall Notes and Queries, vol. 6 (1911), p. 187.

REIFFENBERG, F.A.F.T. de
  De la Peinture sur Verre aux Pays-Bas, Suivi d'un Mémoire sur
  les Tetatives Faites au Sein de l'Académie pour la Publication des
  Monumens Inédits de l'Histoire Belgique.
  Nouveaux Mémoires de l'Académie Royal (Bruxelles), vol. 7 (1832).

REINAUD DE FONTVERT, J.T.
  Notice sur la Fenêtre Absidiale de l'Eglise Saint Jacques de Malts
  à Aix, et Description de sa Nouvelle Verrière, suivies, d'un Exposé
  Sommaire de l'Histoire et des Procédés de la Peinture sur Verre.
  Mémoires de l'Academie de l'Aix (1862).

REINHARDT, H.
  La Cathédrale de Reims.
  Paris, 1963.

(Reiser, Walter E.)
  Obituary.
  Stained Glass, vol. 31, no. 2 (Autumn, 1936), p. 67.

RENAUD, J.G.N.
  Das Hohlglas des Mittelalters unter besonderer Berücksichtigung der
  neuesten in Holland und anderswo gemachten Funde.
  Glastechnische Berichte, 32K, Heft 8 (1959), pp. 29-33.

RENESSE, Graat Théodore de
  Du Rôle des Armoiries dans les Vitraux.
  Annales de l'Académie Royale d'Archéologie de Belgique, 7th series,
  part 4 (1927), pp. 15-41.

RENOUVIER, J.
  Notice sur la Peinture sur Verre et sur Mur dans le Midi de la France.
  Bulletin Monumental, vol. 5 (1839), pp. 416-424.

REQUIN, Abbé
  Documents Inédits sur les Peintres, Peintres Verriers et
  Enlumineurs d'Avignon au 15e Siècle.
  Paris, 1889.

RÉVILLE, J.B., and LAVALLÉE, J.B.B.
  Vues des Salles du Musée des Monuments Français. Peinture sur Verre.
  Paris, 1816.

REYNOLDS, Joseph G.
  Toward the Ideal Window.
  (REYNOLDS comments on the six 'yardsticks' adopted by the Chapter
  of Washington Cathedral.)
  Stained Glass, vol. 30, no. 2 (Autumn, 1935), pp. 42-48.

  Modern Stained Glass at the Paris Exposition.
  Stained Glass, vol. 32, no. 3 (Winter, 1937-1938), pp. 72-80.

  Stained Glass: Its Spiritual Significance.
  The Cathedral Age (Washington D.C.), (Christmas, 1944).

(Reynolds, Joshua)
  West Window of the Chapel, New College, Oxford, after Pictures
  Painted by Sir J. Reynolds and Executed on Glass by Mr. Jervaise.
  London, 1785.

REYNTIENS, Patrick
  (Report of speech at Annual Dinner of S.B.M.G.P.)
  J.M.G.P., vol. 13, no. 4 (1963), pp. 580-581.

  The Technique of Stained Glass.
  London, 1968.
  Reviewed by LOCKETT, William, J.M.G.P., vol. 14, no. 4 (1968-1969),
  p. 221.
  Reviewed in J.M.G.P., vol. 17, no. 2 (1978-1979), pp. 77-78 (2nd
  edition).

RHEIMS, Gabrielle
  L'Eglise de Saint-Julien-du-Sault (Yonne) et ses Verrières.
  Gazette des Beaux-Arts (Sept.-Oct.,1926), pp. 139-162.

(Rhineland)
  Le Vitrail du 12e Siècle en Rhenanie et en France.
  Bulletin Monumental, vol. 112 (1954), pp. 212-213.

(Rhode Island School of Design)

    (Acquired a panel said to have come from Bourges.)

    Stained Glass, vol. 32, no. 3 (Winter, 1937-1938), pp. 94-95.

RIAÑO, Juan F.

    The Industrial Arts in Spain.

    South Kensington Museum Art Handbook.

    London, 1879.

    (Contains a list of Spanish glass-painters.)

RICE, William Gorham

    A Burne-Jones Window.

    (In St. Peter's, Albany, New York.)

    Stained Glass, vol. 28, no. 3 (Autumn, 1933), p. 165.

RICH, F.D.

    The Twentieth Century Renaissance in Stained Glass.

    The Glass Digest (Aug., 1955).

RICHARDSON, A.E.

    (Speech at the Annual Dinner of the British Society of Master
    Glass-Painters.)

    J.M.G.P., vol. 11, no. 4 (1955), pp. 238-240.

RICK. P.P.

    Kloster Steinfeld.

    Steinfeld, 1949.

RICKMAN, John

    Historical Curiosities Relating to St. Margaret's Church, Westminster.

    London, 1837.

(Rickmansworth, St. Mary's Church)

    (Rediscovery of sixteenth century French glass from Rouen in the
    church.)

    News and Notes, J.M.G.P., vol. 9, no. 3 (1945), p. 70.

RIDGWAY, Maurice Hill

    With LEACH, George B.

    Further Notes on the Glasshouse Site at Kingswood, Delamere, Cheshire.

    Journal of the Chester Archaeological Society, vol. 37, part 1.

    Reprinted, Chester, 1948.

    Coloured Window Glass in Cheshire. Part 1. Fourteenth Century.

    Transactions of the Lancashire and Cheshire Antiquarian Society,

    vol. 59 (1947).

    Reprinted Bristol, 1949.

    Coloured Window Glass in Cheshire. Part 2. 1400-1550.

    Transactions of the Lancashire and Cheshire Antiquarian Society,

    vol. 60 (1948).

    Reprinted Bristol, 1949.

    Grappenhall, Cheshire, Fourteenth Century Glass.

    J.M.G.P., vol. 10, no. 4 (1951), pp. 198-204.

RIFF, A.

    Un Vitrail de 1523 aux Armes de la Ville de Strasbourg.

    Archives Alsaciennes d'Histoire de l'Art, vol. 2 (1923), pp. 77-83.

RIGAL, Juliette

    Deux Dessins de L. Gontier pour des Vitraux de l'Hôtel de l'Arquebuse
    à Troyes.

    Revue du Louvre. vol. 2 (1977).

RIJKSEN, A.A.J.

    Gespiegeld in kerkeglas: Hollands leed en vrengol in de
    glasschilderingen van de St. Janskerk te Gouda.

    Lochern (1948 ?).

    The Stained Glass Windows of St. John's Church, Gouda.

    Gouda, 1948.

(Riom. Glass now at Princeton University Museum.)

    Les Vitraux de Riom.

    La Revue des Arts (1951).

    Cited in Bulletin Monumental, no. 110 (1952), pp. 87-88.

RIORDAN, John A.

    Stained Glass in Cincinnatti.

    Stained Glass, vol. 45, no. 2 (Summer, 1950), pp. 53-57.

RIORDAN, Roger

    American Stained Glass.

    American Arts Review, vol. 2 (1881), Part 1, pp. 229-234;

                                 Part 2, pp. 7-11, 59-64.

(Riordan Studios)

    Artists and Businessmen Too - Riordan Studios.

    Glass Digest (July, 1966).

RITTER, Georges

    Les Vitraux de la Cathédrale de Rouen, 13e, 14e, 15e et 16e Siècles.

    Cognac, 1926.

(Rivenhall)

    Twelfth Century Medallion from the Church of St. Mary and All Saints,

    Rivenhall, Essex. (Coloured plate only.)

    The Studio (Oct., 1925).

ROBAUT, A.

    Trois Cartons pour Vitraux, par Eugène Delacroix.

    L'Art, vol. 17 (1879), p. 193.

ROBERT, Charles

    La Grande Verrière du 13e Siècle, et Autres Vitraux Anciens de la

    Cathédrale de Dol.

    Rennes, n.d. (?).

ROBERT, Karl

    Le Fusain sur Faience. Petit Guide des Peintures Vitrifiables en

    Grisailles pour Servir d'Etudes Préparatoires aux Peintures

    Vitrifiables en Général.

    Paris, 1879.

    La Céramique. Traité Pratique des Peintures Vitrifiables,

    Porcelaine . . . les Vitraux.

    Paris, 1892.

    Le Vitrail Simplifié.

    Paris, 1895.

ROBERTS, William E.

    A Color Comment.

    (Letter to the Editor stating that nineteenth century glass has
    changed colour with age.)

    Stained Glass, vol. 27, no. 3 (March, 1932), pp. 91-94.

    Replied to by SKINNER, Orin, Ibid., p. 96.

ROBERTSON, Manning

    The Craft Revival in Dublin.

    Architecture, vol. 4, no. 10 (Feb., 1926).

ROBINSON, Arnold
    Charles Winston's Experiments in 1850.
    J.M.G.P., vol. 11, no. 4 (1955), pp. 221-223.

(Robinson, Arnold)
    Obituary.
    J.M.G.P., vol. 12, no. 1 (1956), pp. 74-75.

ROBINSON, C.J.
    Stopham.
    Sussex Archaeological Collections, vol. 27 (1877).
    (Glass in church, pp. 61-62.)

ROBINSON, Geoffrey A.K.
    Modern German Glass in Munich.
    J.M.G.P., vol. 13, no. 3 (1962), pp. 477-478.

    Exhibition of Stained Glass Design at Coventry.
    J.M.G.P., vol. 13, no. 4 (1963), pp. 572-573.

    (On restoring glass at St. Thomas', Salisbury, and Banwell, Somerset.)
    (In Recent and Current Work by Members.)
    J.M.G.P., vol. 14, no. 3 (1967), pp. 163-174.

    (Letter giving a brief account of the restoration and moving of glass
    at Lydiard Tregoze.)
    J.M.G.P., vol. 14, no. 4 (1968-1969), p. 216.

ROBINSON, J. Armitage
    The Golden Window at Wells.
    Bath and Wells Diocesan Gazette (Jan., 1924).

    The Windows of the Lady Chapel (of Wells Cathedral).
    Bath and Wells Diocesan Gazette (Dec., 1924).

    The Donors of the Lady Chapel Windows (of Wells Cathedral).
    Bath and Wells Diocesan Gazette (March, 1925).

    The Windows of the Lady Chapel in Wells Cathedral.
    Notes and Queries for Somerset and Dorset, vol. 18 (1926), pp. 121-123.

    Fourteenth Century Glass at Wells.
    Archaeologia, vol. 81 (1931), pp. 85-118.
    (With an Appendix on the chemical analysis of the glass by SCOTT,
    Alexander.)

    Marks on the Glass at Wells.
    (A discussion with KNOWLES, J.A., and HORNE, Ethelbert.)
    J.M.G.P., vol. 4, no. 2 (Oct., 1931), pp. 71-74.

    The Great West Window at Wells.
    J.M.G.P., vol. 4, no. 3 (Apr., 1932), pp. 109-122.

ROBINSON, John
    A Number of Fragments of Glass of Various Ages from Westminster Abbey.
    Proceedings of the Society of Antiquaries of Newcastle, vol. 5 (1899),
    p. 147.

ROBINSON, Joseph
    Conservation and the Ancient Stained Glass.
    Canterbury Cathedral Chronicle, no. 68 (1974), pp. 23-24.

RODBERT
    Vom Stilgesetz der Glasmalerei.
    Diamant (July 21, 1936).

RODE, Herbert
    Der Kölner Dom.
    Augsburg, 1968.

RODE, Herbert (Contd.)
    Die Namen der Meister der Hl. Sippe und von St. Severin.
    Wallgraf-Richartz Jahrbuch, vol. 31 (1969), pp. 249-254.

    Zur datierung des Bibelfensters in der Dreikönigenkapelle des
    Kölner Doms.
    In 7e Colloque du Corpus Vitrearum Medii Aevi.
    Florence ?, 1970, p. 40.

    Die mittelalterlichen Glasmalereien des Kölner Domes.
    Berlin, 1974.
    (C.V.M.A., Germany, vol. 4, part 1.)

RODWELL, W.J.
    (Letter on the Rivenhall glass incorporated in Editorial.)
    J.M.G.P., vol. 17, no. 1 (1978-1979), pp. 5-6.

ROE, R. Gordon
    Quarries.
    The Connoisseur, vol. 67 (Oct., 1923).

    A Stained-Glass Panel for Jesus College, Cambridge: Bishop Alcock's
    Coat of Arms.
    The Connoisseur, vol. 68 (Jan.-Apr., 1924), pp. 34-35.
    (Alternative provenance suggested by WILDRIDGE, T. Tindall, Letter
    to the Editor, Ibid., pp. 219-220.)

    A Relic of the Last Abbot of Bury St. Edmunds.
    (Arms probably from the Abbot's residence.)
    The Connoisseur, vol. 73 (Sept.-Dec., 1925), pp. 36-38.

(Roe, R. Gordon)
    Obituary.
    J.M.G.P., vol. 2, no. 2 (Oct., 1927), pp. 106-107.

ROENN, Kenneth von
    The Stained Glass Movements as Determined by External Influences.
    Stained Glass, vol. 70, no. 1 (Spring, 1975), pp. 27-31.

    Photographing Stained Glass. Part 1.
    Stained Glass, vol. 70, nos. 3, 4 (Fall and Winter, 1975), pp. 107-109.
    (Also see COOK, Leland A.)

ROGERS, Frances, and BEARD, Alice.
    Five Thousand Years of Glass.
    Philadelphia, (n.d.?).

ROGERS, H. Mordant
    Stained Glass from the Sixteenth Century to the Present Day.
    J.M.G.P., vol. 6, no. 3 (Apr., 1936), pp. 132-143.
             vol. 6, no. 4 (Apr., 1937), pp. 199-211.

ROGERS, W.H. Hamilton
    Huyshe; of Lod-huish and Doniford in Somerset and of Sand in Devon.
    (Armorial glass.)
    Proceedings of the Somersetshire Archaeological and Natural History
    Society, vol. 43, for 1897, part 2 (1897), pp. 1-44.

The Role of Stained Glass in Architecture. A Symposium.
    Contributions by WILLET, C., BRIDGES, S., DUQUETTE, W., ZRNICH, B.,
    HILL, R.
    Stained Glass, vol. 63, no. 3 (Autumn, 1968), pp. 17-21.

ROLLASON, A.A.
    Early Glass-Workers at Eccleshall.
    Transactions of the North Staffordshire Field Club, vol. 54 (1922),
    pp. 33-35.

RONDOT, Natalis

Les Artistes et les Maîtres de Métier de Lyon au Quatorzième Siècle.
Lyon, 1882.

Les Peintres-Verriers de Troyes du 14ᵉ et 15ᵉ Siècle.
Revue de l'Art Français (1887).

Les Peintures sur Verre à Lyon du 14ᵉ au 16ᵉ Siècle.
Paris, 1897.

ROOSVAL, Johnny

Medeltida konst i Gotlands fornsal.
Stockholm, 1925.
Reviewed by SKEAT, Francis, J.M.G.P., vol. 10, no. 4 (1951), p. 218.

Medieval Schools of Stained Glass Painting on Gottland.
Gazette des Beaux-Arts, vol. 28 (1945), pp. 193-204.

Der gotländske ciceronen.
Stockholm, 1950.
Reviewed by SKEAT, Francis, J.M.G.P., vol. 10, no. 4 (1951), pp. 217-218.

Gotländsk vitriarius: de medetida gotländska glasmalningarnas bestånd
och historia.
Stockholm, 1950.
Reviewed by AUBERT, Marcel, Bulletin Monumental, vol. 109 (1951),
pp. 230-231.
Reviewed by SKEAT, Francis, J.M.G.P., vol. 10, no. 4 (1951), pp. 218-219.

(Roundel of unknown subject)
(Reproduced, with a request for suggestions.)
The Gentleman's Magazine, vol. 63, part 1 (1793), p. 397.
(A suggestion: the unequal distribution of worldly gifts by Folly, Ibid.,
p. 522.)
(Another suggestion: a saint distributing alms, Ibid., part 2, 1793,
p. 1188.)

RORIMER, James
Two Stained Glass Panels of the Fourteenth Century.
Bulletin of the Stained Glass Association of America, vol. 24, no. 1
(Jan., 1929).

The Cloisters: the Building and the Collection of Medieval Art in
Fort Tryon Park.
New York, 1938.

(Glass from Saint-Germain-des-Prés in the Metropolitan Museum.)
Bulletin of the Metropolitan Museum of Art, (1948), pp. 201-204.

(Letter to the Editor on DRAKE, Wilfred, Dictionary . . .)
J.M.G.P., vol. 12, no. 2 (1957), p. 163.

ROSCOE, E.S.
Fairford Windows.
The Magazine of Art (1881), pp. 437-439.

ROSEN, Carl von
Fensterschmuck der Wallfahrtskirche zu Kentz in Neuvorpommern. Eine
Festschrift.
Stralsund, 1865.

Die Glasgemälde der St. Marienkirche zu Stralsund.
Stralsund, c. 1870.

ROSEN, Edward
The Invention of Eyeglasses.
Journal of the History of Medicine and Allied Sciences, vol. 11
(Jan., 1956), pp. 13-46, (Apr., 1956), pp. 183-218.

ROSS, D.M.
Lewis Foreman Day, Designer and Writer on Stained Glass.
J.M.G.P., vol. 3, no. 1 (Apr., 1929), pp. 5-8.

ROTELLI, L.
Delle Invetriate Dipinte da G. Botti, nel Duomo di Perugia.
Pisa, 1868.

ROTHENBERG, Polly
Creative Stained Glass.
New York, 1973.

ROTHERY, Guy Cadogan
The Fascination of Stained Glass.
Graphic (Dec. 26, 1925).

Stained Glass in the House.
Ideal Home Magazine (Nov., 1927).

(Rottingdean, St. Margaret's Church)
The Parish Church of St. Margaret, Rottingdean.
(Windows by Morris and Burne-Jones.)
Revised edition, Brighton, 1970.

ROUBICEK, Rene
Contemporary Glass.
Stained Glass, vol. 59, no. 3 (Autumn, 1964), pp. 18-23.
(Reprinted from Czechoslovak Glass Review.)

ROUDIÉ, M.P.
Peintres et Verriers à Bordeaux aux 15ᵉ et 16ᵉ Siècles.
Bulletin et Mémoires de la Société Archéologique de Bordeaux,
vol. 59 for 1954-1956, (1958).

L'Eglise de Castelnau-du-Médoc, son Mobilier, son Vitrail.
Revue Historique de Bordeaux et du Département de la Gironde (1964),
pp. 29-40.

(Rouen Glass Lost)
(Windows from the Chapel of the Ursulines in the Château of Phillipe
Auguste at Rouen sent to the New York World's Fair lost.)
Stained Glass, vol. 34, no. 2 (Autumn, 1939), pp. 64-65.

(Rouen)
Vitraux du Château de Rouen.
(Purchased for the Musée de Cluny.)
Revue des Arts, no. 3 (1955), p. 181.

Les Vitraux de Saint-Vincent de Rouen.
Revue des Sociétés Savantes de Haute-Normandie, no. 4 (1956).
(Cited in Bulletin Monumental, no. 115 (1957), pp. 229-230.)

Le Vieux-Marché de Rouen.
Bulletin des Amis des Monuments Rouennais, numéro spécial (1978-1979).
Reviewed by SALET, Francis, Bulletin Monumental, vol. 138, no. 1
(1980), pp. 108-109.

ROUND, J.H.
The Glass in Chichester Cathedral.
Sussex Archaeological Collections, vol. 62 (1921), pp. 203-204.

ROUSSEL, Jules
Album des Vitraux Extraits des Archives du Ministère de l'Instruction
Publique et des Beaux-Arts.
Paris, 1900.

Les Vitraux.
3 vols, Paris, 1903, 1911, 1913.

ROUSSELET, Pacifique
> Histoire et Description de l'Eglise Royale de Brou.
> Paris, 1767.
> (5th edition enlarged by PUVIS, M., Bourg, 1840.)

> Guide Descriptif et Historique du Voyageur à l'Eglise de Brou.
> 9th edition, Bourg, 1876.

ROWE, George
> Ornamental Glazing Quarries, More Especially those in York . . .
> Reports and Papers of the Associated Architectural Societies, vol.
> 11 (1871-1873), pp. 93-107.

> On Stained Glass in the West Window of St. Martin's Church, Coney
> Street, York . . .
> Ibid., vol. 12 (1873-1874), pp. 95-100.

ROWE, J. Brooking
> The Five Wounds in Stained Glass in Sidmouth Church.
> Devon Notes and Queries, vol. 3 (1905), p. 17.

ROYCE, James
> The Firing of Stained Glass.
> J.M.G.P., vol. 10, no. 3 (1950), pp. 157-158.

RUBINSTEIN-BLOCH, Stella
> Catalogue of the Collection of George and Florence Blumenthal, New
> York.
> 4 vols, Paris, 1926-1927 (privately printed).
> (Stained glass in vol. 3.)

(Ruby Glass)
> New Concepts on the Origins of Copper Ruby Glass.
> National Glass Budget (Jan. 27, 1968).

(Ruby Stain)
> (Editorial reply to a query about the existence of the technique.)
> J.M.G.P., vol. 2, no. 1 (1927), pp. 55-56.

RUDDER, Samuel
> The History of Fairford Church, with a Short Introductory Account . . .
> of the Town of Fairford. Chiefly Extracted from the Author's 'New
> History of Gloucestershire'.
> Cirencester, 1780.

RUEDOLF, Alfred
> With LEVASSEUR, Eugène.
> Les Vitraux de la Cathédrale de Rouen.
> Rouen, n.d.

> Gravures qui ont Inspiré les Vitraux de Petiville (Seine-Intérieure).
> Bulletin Monumental, vol. 112 (1954), pp. 196-200.

RUFFER, Veronica
> Stained Glass.
> (Request for information about the early nineteenth century firm of
> Gray and Son.)
> Notes and Queries, vol. 187 (Nov. 4, 1944), pp. 213-214.
> Replied to by W.H.P. (Dec. 2, 1944), p. 261.
> > JARVIS, R.C. (Dec. 30, 1944), p. 304.

A Rule for Taking Measurements Between Mullions, Sash Bars, Etc.
> J.M.G.P., vol. 2, no. 2 (Oct., 1927), p. 95.

RUPPERT, Ph.
> Die Glasmalerei in Konstanz.
> Konstanz. Gewerb-geschichte; Beiträge (1890).

RUSCHER, Alfred
> Die Glasmalerei als Industrie und Exportartikel.
> Die Glashütte (Dresden), vol. 55 (1925), pp. 805-807.

RUSHFORTH, G. McNeil
> Stained Glass from Malvern.
> (Enquiry about Malvern glass moved elsewhere.)
> Notes and Queries, 11th series, vol. 6 (Sept. 7, 1912), p. 188.

> The Stained Glass of Great Malvern Priory Church. Photographed by
> Sydney A. Pitcher, with descriptive notes by G. McN. Rushforth, F.S.A.
> 6 vols., Gloucester, 1916-1935.

> Painted Glass from a House In Leicester.
> Archaeological Journal, vol. 75 (1918), pp. 47-68.

> The Glass of the East Window of the Lady Chapel in Gloucester
> Cathedral.
> Transactions of the Bristol and Gloucestershire Archaeological
> Society, vol. 43 (1921), pp. 191-218.

> The Great East Window of Gloucester Cathedral.
> Ibid., vol. 44 (for 1922), pp. 293-304.

> The Glass in the Quire Clerestory of Tewkesbury Abbey.
> Ibid., vol. 46 (for 1924), pp. 289-324.

> The Painted Glass in the Lord Mayor's Chapel, Bristol.
> Ibid., vol. 49 (for 1927), pp. 301-331.

> The Baptism of St. Christopher.
> (Stained glass formerly in Birtsmorton Church, Worcestershire.)
> Antiquaries Journal, vol. 6, no. 2 (Apr., 1926), pp. 152-158.

> Review of READ, Herbert, English Stained Glass.
> J.M.G.P., vol. 2, no. 1 (1927), pp. 45-48.

> The Painted Windows in the Chapel of the Vyne in Hampshire.
> The Archaeological Journal, 2nd series, vol. 34 (1927), pp. 105-113.

> The Painted Windows in the Chapel of the Vyne in Hampshire.
> Walpole Society, vol. 15 (1927).

> The Painted Glass of Birtsmorton Church.
> Transactions of the Worcestershire Archaeological Society, new
> series, vol. 4 (for 1926-1927), pp. 91-99.

> Review of HARRISON, F., The Painted Glass of York.
> J.M.G.P., vol. 2, no. 3 (Apr., 1928), pp. 152-156.

> Seven Sacraments Compositions in English Medieval Art.
> Antiquaries Journal, vol. 9, no. 2 (Apr., 1929), pp. 83-100.

> Mediaeval Glass in Oriel College Chapel. St. Margaret and the Dragon.
> The Oriel Record, vol. 5, no. 4 (Dec., 1929).
> Reprinted in J.M.G.P., vol. 3, no. 3 (Apr., 1930), pp. 108-111.

> The Sacraments Window in Crudwell Church.
> The Wiltshire Archaeological and Natural History Magazine, no. 152
> (June, 1930), pp. 68-72.

> Report of Lecture - Ancient Stained Glass at Atcham, County Salop.
> Transactions of the Woolhope Naturalists' Field Club, 1927, 1928,
> 1929, vol. 26 (1931), pp. cxv, cxvi.

> Review of EDEN, F.S., Ancient Stained and Painted Glass (2nd edition).
> The Antiquaries Journal, vol. 13, no. 3 (July, 1933), p. 321.

> St. Urith.
> (Glass at Nettlecombe, Somerset.)
> Devon and Cornwall Notes and Queries, vol. 17 (1933), pp. 290-291.

> The Rev. Benjamin Foster and the Windows of St. Neot.
> Devon and Cornwall Notes and Queries, vol. 17 (1933), pp. 224-226.

RUSHFORTH, G. McNeil (Contd.)

Glass in the Trevelyan Chapel, Nettlecombe Church.
Proceedings of the Somersetshire Archaeological and Natural History
Society, vol. 80, for 1934, part 2 (1935), pp. 63-66.

Medieval Christian Imagery as Illustrated by the Painted Windows
of Great Malvern Priory Church.
Oxford, 1936.
Reviewed by BORENIUS, Tancred, The Archaeological Journal, vol. 92
(for 1935), pp. 364-365.
Reviewed by WOODFORDE, Christopher, J.M.G.P., vol. 6, no. 3 (Apr.,
1936), pp. 161-163.
Reviewed by EDEN, F.S., The Connoisseur, vol. 97 (May, 1936), pp. 291-
292.

Great Malvern Priory Church. A Short Account of the Medieval
Painted Windows.
n.p., n.d.

St. Cecilia.
Notes and Queries, vol. 169 (Nov. 30, 1935).
Reprinted with some additions, J.M.G.P., vol. 6, no. 4 (Apr., 1937).

Review of KNOWLES, J.A., Essays in the History of the York School of
Glass-Painting.
The Archaeological Journal, vol. 93 (for 1936), pp. 121-123.

The Windows of the Church of St. Neot, Cornwall.
Exeter, 1937.
(Reprinted from the Transactions of the Exeter Diocesan Architectural
and Archaeological Society, vol. 15 (1937).)

The Bacton Glass at Atcham in Shropshire.
Transactions of the Woolhope Naturalists' Field Club, 1933, 1934, 1935
vol. 28 (1938), pp. 157-162.

Obituary.
The Times, March 31, 1938.

Obituary.
Transactions of the Bristol and Gloucester Archaeological Society,
vol. 59 (for 1937), pp. 344-350.

Obituary.
Burlington Magazine, vol. 72 (Jan.-June, 1938), p. 244.

Obituary. By BAKER, E.P.
J.M.G.P., vol. 7, no. 3 (Oct., 1938), pp. 150-151.

Obituary.
Transactions of the Woolhope Naturalists' Field Club, 1936, 1937, 1938,
vol. 29 (1940), pp. 212-213.

RUSSELL, Harry W.
Notes on the Ancient Stained Glass . . . in the Church of St. Mary,
Great Chart.
Archaeologia Cantiana, vol. 26 (1904), pp. 91-100.

RUSSELL, J. Fuller
Description of the Glass in Fairford Church, Gloucestershire.
The Ecclesiologist, vol. 26 (1865), pp. 286-289.

On the Painted Glass in Fairford Church, Gloucester, and its Claim
to be Considered the Work of Albert Durer.
The Archaeological Journal, vol. 25 (1868), pp. 119-136.

(Rutherford, Rosemary)
Obituary.
J.M.G.P., vol. 15, no. 1 (1972-1973), pp. 26-

RUTTER, David C.
The Wanderings of Old Glass.
(Holds that the York Jesse in the Choir did not come from New
College.)
(Letter to the Editor.)
Country Life (May 23, 1947).
Rebutted by HARRISON, F., (June 13, 1947), p. 969.

RYDBECK, O.
Glass by Emanuel Vigeland in Lund Cathedral.
Rig, vol. 19.

RYE, W.
Some Early English Inscriptions in Norfolk.
London, n.d.

RYLANDS, John, and BEAUMONT, William
An Attempt to Identify the Arms Formerly Existing in the Windows of
the Parish Church and the Austin Friary at Warrington.
Warrington, 1878.

RYLANDS, J. Paul
The Shields of Arms Formerly in the Windows of the Parish Church of
Lymm, County Chester, as Illustrative of the Origin of Several Local
Coats of Arms.
Transactions of the Historic Society of Lancashire and Cheshire,
3rd series, vol. 7 (1879), pp. 1-12.

With BROWN, R.S.
The Armorial Glass at Vale Royal, Spurstow Hall, Utkinton Hall and
Tarporley Rectory in the County of Chester.
The Genealogist, new series, vol. 38 (1921), pp. 1-14, 61-70.
Reprinted, Exeter, 1921.

RYVES, Bruno
Mercurius Rusticus or the Countries Complaint of the Barbarous
Outrages Committed by the Sectaries of this Kingdom.
Oxford, 1646 (also 1647, 1685).
(Also includes BARWICK, Mercurius Belgieus.)

SAAL, E.M. von
  Zur Geschichte der Glasmalerei.
  Keramische Rundschau, vol. 2 (1894), nos. 14-35.

(Saarbrucken)
  A Large Stained-Glass Window for Saarbrucken Church. (Note.)
  Diamant, no. 25 (1924).

SABIN, Arthur
  The Fourteenth Century Heraldic Glass in the Eastern Lady Chapel of
  Bristol Cathedral.
  Antiquaries Journal, vol. 37 (1957), pp. 54-70.

SACKEN, E.F. von
  Archäologischer Wegweiser durch das Viertel unter dem Wiener-Walde
  von Nieder-Osterreich.
  Vienna, 1866.

(St. Christopher)
  Are There Any Known Representations of St. Christopher in Painted
  Glass, If So, Where? (E.A.H.L.)
  Notes and Queries, vol. 5 (March 27, 1852), p. 295.
  Replies (May 22, 1852), pp. 494-496.

SAINT, Lawrence B.
  Old Stained Glass.
  National Glass Budget (Aug. 8, 1925).

  Bits of Old Stained Glass.
  National Glass Budget, 41st year, no. 49 (Apr. 3, 1926), pp. 1, 10.

  (On the Film on Old Stained Glass.)
  Stained Glass Bulletin (May, 1928).

  Stained Glass in the Middle Ages.
  J.M.G.P., vol. 5, no. 3 (Apr., 1934), pp. 117-129.

  Is Stained Glass a Lost Art?
  Bulletin of the American Ceramic Society, vol. 15, no. 11 (Nov., 1936).

(Saint, Lawrence)
  Obituary.
  Stained Glass, vol. 56, no. 2 (Summer, 1961), pp. 6-7, 36.

SAINT, Lawrence
  The Romance of Stained Glass.
  (Excerpts from Memoirs.)
  Part 1, J.M.G.P., vol. 16, no. 1 (1976-1977), pp. 11-30.
  Part 2, J.M.G.P., vol. 17, no. 1 (1978-1979), pp. 37-51.

(Saint Louis Museum)
  Stained Glass in the City Art Museum, Saint Louis.
  Stained Glass, vol. 29, nos. 1-11 (Spring-Summer, 1934).

  Ancient Glass Acquired by the Saint Louis Museum.
  (From La Flèche.)
  Stained Glass, vol. 30, no. 2 (Autumn, 1935), pp. 60-63.

(St. Neot's Church)
  The Ancient Stained Glass Windows in S. Neot's Church, Cornwall.
  The Ecclesiologist, vol. 12 (1851), pp. 49-55.

SALAQUADA, F.
  On the Yellow Staining of Glass.
  Sprechsaal, 65th year (1932), p. 310.

SALET, Francis
  La Cathédrale de Tours.
  Paris, 1949.

  Review of C.V.M.A. (France, vol. 1).
  Bulletin Monumental, no. 117 (1959), pp. 318-319.

  Review of BAKER, John, English Stained Glass.
  (Translated in French by SCHWARZ, A., Paris, 1961.)
  Bulletin Monumental, vol. 120 (1962), pp. 112-113.

  Review of DELAPORTE, Yves, L'Art du Vitrail aux 12e et 13e Siècles.
  Bulletin Monumental, vol. 121 (1963), pp. 301-302.

  Review of LAFOND, Jean, C.V.M.A., France, 4, 2, vol. 1.
  Bulletin Monumental, vol. 129 (1971), p. 301.

  Review of Le Vieux-Marché de Rouen; Bulletin des Amis des Monuments
  Rouennais, numéro spécial (1978-1979).
  Bulletin Monumental, vol. 138, no. 1 (1980), pp. 108-109.

(Salisbury Cathedral)
  'Dowsing' for Old Glass in a Cathedral Town.
  Stained Glass, vol. 28, no. 1 (Spring, 1933), pp. 59-60.

(Salisbury Fragments)
  (On the proposal to send some of the Salisbury fragments to Canada.)
  News and Notes, J.M.G.P., vol. 7, no. 4 (Apr., 1939), p. 153.

(Salisbury Cathedral)
  (Grant towards the restoration of Pearson and Jervais' East Window.)
  The Pilgrim Trust, 48th Annual Report (1978), p. 10.

SALMON, J.
  Letter to the Subscribers to the Stained Glass Windows for Glasgow
  Cathedral.
  Glasgow, 1857.

SALMOND, Hugh
  Martin Travers Pays a Visit.
  J.M.G.P., vol. 14, no. 5 (1970-1971), pp. 263-265.

  Aunt Mabel Asks the Questions.
  (Recollections.)
  J.M.G.P., vol. 15, no. 1 (1972-1973), pp. 66-72.

SALMOND, R.W.
  A Cockney's Lament.
  (Reminiscences of studio life after the First World War.)
  J.M.G.P., vol. 14, no. 4 (1968-1969), pp. 195-196.

  History of English Antique Glass.
  J.M.G.P., vol. 15, no. 1 (1972-1973), pp. 73-79.

SALZMAN, L.F.
  The Glazing of St. Stephen's Chapel, Westminster, 1351-1352.
  Journal of the British Society of Master Glass Painters, vol. 1, no. 4
  (Apr., 1926), pp. 14-18; vol. 5 (Oct., 1926), pp. 29-34; vol. 2, no. 1
  (1927), pp. 38-41.

  Medieval Glazing Accounts.
  J.M.G.P., vol. 2, no. 3 (Apr., 1928), pp. 116-120.
          vol. 2, no. 4 (Oct., 1928), pp. 188-192.
          vol. 3, no. 1 (Apr., 1929), pp. 25-30.

  Building in England down to 1540.
  Oxford, 1952.

SAN CASCIANI, Paul and Paula
  The Stained Glass of Oxford.
  Oxford, 1979.

(San Francisco)

    Grace Cathedral, San Francisco.

    (With a list of stained glass in the San Francisco Bay area.)

    Stained Glass, vol. 63, no. 1 (Spring, 1968), pp. 8-18.

(Sand, Devonshire: Heraldry in the Hall Windows.)

    Proceedings of the Somersetshire Archaeological and Natural History
    Society, vol. 43 (1897), part 2, pp. 17, 31, 33.

SANDALL, Thomas

    (Revised by WRIGHT, Hilary.)

    St. John's Church, Stamford.

    Stamford, 1968.

(Sandhurst, Kent)

    The Parish Church of St. Nicholas, Sandhurst, Kent.

    n.d., n.p.

    (Glass, p. 8.)

SANDLER, Lucy Freeman

    A Follower of Jean Pucelle in England.

    Art Bulletin, vol. 52 (Dec., 1970), pp. 363-372.

    (Influence on English glass-painting, p. 372.)

SANKEY, Edward H., and SCHÜDDEKOPF, Albert W.

    Ancient German Glass in Wragby Church.

    The Yorkshire Archaeological Journal, vol. 13 (1895), pp. 416-439.

SAUNDERS, O.E.

    A History of English Art in the Middle Ages.

    (With a preface by BORENIUS, Tancred.)

    Oxford, 1932.

SAUNIER, Charles

    Le Vitrail dans l'Amérique du Sud.

    Art Décoration, vol. 23 (1908), pp. 53-60.

SAUZAY, Alexandre

    Notice de la Verrerie et des Vitraux. Musée National du Louvre, Paris.

    Paris, 1882.

SAVE, Gaston

    Les Peintres Verriers Nanciens Sous Réné II.

    Nancy, 1897.

SAVOIE, Pierre

    Alfred Werck. Swiss Artist and Craftsman in Stained Glass.

    Swiss Observer, March 7, 1936.

(Saxlingham Nethergate Church)

    Saxlingham Nethergate Church, Norfolk: Glass.

    (A grant towards restoring and rearranging the glass.)

    The Pilgrim Trust, 26th Annual Report (1956), p. 14.

SCHADEN, Adolph von

    Skizzen in der Manier des seligen A.G. Meissner.

    Nuremberg (?), 1829.

SCHAEFER, Karl

    Die Glasmalerei des Mittelalters und der Renaissance im Abriss
    dargestellt.

    Breslau, 1881.

SCHAEFER, Karl (Contd.)

    With ROSSTEUSCHER, A.

    Ornamentale Glasmalereien des Mittelalters und der Renaissance nach
    original Aufnahmen in Farbendruck.

    Berlin, 1888.

    With STIEHL, O.

    Die Mustergiltigen Kirchenbauten des Mittelalters in Deutschland.
    Geometrische und Photographische Aufnahmen, nebst Beispielen der
    originalen Malerei.

    Berlin, 1901.

SCHAPIRO, Meyer

    On the Esthetic Attitude in Romanesque Art.

    In Art and Thought (editor IYER, K.).

    London, 1947.

SCHARF, George

    Artistic Notes on the Windows of King's College Chapel, Cambridge.

    The Archaeological Journal, vol. 12 (1855), pp. 356-373.

    Continuation of Artistic Notes on the Windows of King's College
    Chapel, Cambridge.

    Ibid., vol. 13 (1856), pp. 44-61.

    (Contribution to the discussion on the Fairford Windows.)

    Notes and Queries, 4th series, vol. 2 (Sept. 19, 1868), pp. 267-268.

SCHAUENBURG, Pierre Rielle de

    Mémoire en Réponse à la Question . . . Quelles sont les Verrières les
    plus Importantes Conservées dans les Eglises d'Alsace?

    Paris, 1860.

    (Reprinted from Congrès Archéologique de France, 1860.)

    La Peinture sur Verre. Lecture Faite à la Préfecture du Bas-Rhin.

    Strasbourg, 1865.

SCHEIDEGGER, Alfred

    Die Berner Glasmalerei von 1540 bis 1580.

    Berne-Bümpliz, 1947.

    Reviewed by LAFOND, Jean, Musées Suisses, no. 3 (March, 1949), pp. 74-75.

SCHER, Stephen K.

    Note sur les Vitraux de la Sainte-Chapelle de Bourges.

    Cahiers d'Archéologie et d'Histoire du Berry, no. 35 (1973), pp. 23-44.

SCHEURPFLUG, Dr.

    Bewegung in der Glasmalerei.

    Diamant (July 21, 1939).

SCHIMMEL, C.

    Die Cisterzienser-Abtei Altenburg bei Cöln. Mit historischen
    Erläuterungen.

    Münster, 1832.

SCHINNERER, Johannes

    Katalog der Glasgemälde des bayerischen Nationalmuseums.

    Munich, 1908.

    Die kirchliche Glasmalerei zur Zeit der Spätgotik und Frührenaissance
    in Nürnberg.

    Munich, 1908.

    Die monumentale Glasmalerei zur Zeit der Frührenaissance in Nürnberg.

    Zeitschrift für Christliche Kunst, vol. 6 (1910), pp. 238, 324.

    Scheibenrisse von Jörg Preu d'A.

    Zeitschrift für alte und neue Glasmalerei (1912), p. 50.

    Zur Datierung der Glasmalereien im Regensburger Dom.

    Repertorium Kunstwissenschaft, vol. 37 (1914), p. 197.

(Schloss Mainberg Collection)
Report of Auction.
The Connoisseur, vol. 2 (1902).
(Stained Glass, p. 66.)

SCHMARSOW, A.
Kompositionsgesetze romanischer Glasgemälde in frühgotischen
Kirchenfenstern.
Des 33.Bandes der Abhandlungen der philologisch-historischen Klasse
der Kgl. Sächs Gesellschaft der Wissenschaften.   No. 2.
Leipzig, 1916.

SCHMIDT, Christa
Glasfenster im Naumburger Dom.
Vienna, 1975.

SCHMITT, Rupert
(Reported statement.)
Stained Glass Lags in Europe.
Stained Glass, vol. 42, no. 3 (Autumn, 1947), pp. 79-82.
Reprinted from The Milwaukee Journal (June 1, 1947).

SCHMITZ, Franz
Der Dom zu Coeln, seine Konstruktion und Ausstattung.
2 parts, Cologne, 1867-1876.

SCHMITZ, Hermann
Die deutsche Kirkliche Glasmalerei der neuesten Zeit.
Die Kirche (1912), p. 221.
Ibid., (1913), p. 26.

Die Glasgemälde des Königlichen Kunstgewerbemuseums in Berlin. Mit
einer Einführung in die Geschicte der deutschen Glasmalerei.
2 vols., Berlin, 1913.
Reviewed by VALLANCE, Aymer, Burlington Magazine, vol. 29 (Apr.-Dec.,
1916), pp. 12-15.

Deutsche Glasmalereien der Gotik und Renaissance. Rund-und
Kabinettscheiben.
Munich, 1923.

A Late Fourteenth Century Austrian Glass Painting.
J.M.G.P., vol. 3, no. 4 (Oct., 1930), pp. 166-167.

SCHMUDE, Paul
Kunstlerische Prinzipien in der Glasmalerei.
Diamant, 49th year, no. 35 (Dec. 11, 1927), pp. 686-689.

SCHNEBBELIE, J.
The Antiquaries' Museum.
London, 1791.
(Glass at Walmesford, Whittington, Canterbury Cathedral, Burbach
(Leicestershire).)

SCHNEIDER, Jenny
Die schweizerischen Kabinettscheiben.
Orgaan der Stichting Nederland - Switzerland, Jg. 4. no. 4, pp. 37-40.
Breda, 1953.

Der Basler Bürgermeister Lukas Gebhardt und sein Familie im Spiegel
der Glasmalerei.
Zeitschrift für schweizerische Archaeologie und Kunstgeschichte, 14,
pp. 47-54.
Basel, 1953.

Die Standesscheiben von Lukas Zeiner im Tagsatzungssaal zu Baden
(Schweiz).
Basel, 1954.

Kabinettscheiben des 16. und 17. Jahrhunderts.
Berne, 1956.

SCHNEIDER, Jenny (Contd.)
Zeugnisse schweizerischer Glasmalerei in Amerikanischen Museen.
Zeitschrift für schweizerische Archäologie und Kunstgeschichte, 19,
pp. 94-98.
Basel, 1959.

Konstanzer Glasmalerei im 17 Jahrhundert.
Bodenseebuch, pp. 62-66.
Kreuzlingen, 1960.

Glasgemälde, Katalog der Sammlung des Schweizerischen Landesmuseums
Zurich.
2 vols., Zurich, 1970.

SCHNÜTGEN, Alexander
Kölnisches Glasgemälde des 14 Jahrhunderts.
Zeitschrift für Christliche Kunst (1888).

SCHÖNE, Wolfgang
Austellung mittelalterlicher Glasgemälde in Frankfurt am Main.
Die Glas-Industrie, 36th year (1928), pp. 34-36.

Die berühmten Kappenberger Glasfenster.
Diamant, 50th year, no. 6 (Feb. 21, 1928), pp. 112-113.

Über das Licht in der Malerei.
Berlin, 1954.
Reviewed by NEUMEYER, Alfred, Art Bulletin, vol. 37 (Dec., 1955), pp.
301-304.

SCHOTT, R.
On the Yellow Staining of Glass.
Sprechsaal, 65th year (1932), p. 117.

SCHRINGER, Leo J.
Stained Glass Windows in Catholic Churches.
American Ecclesiastical Review, vol. 46 (March, 1912).

SCHRÖDER. H.
Über die Angreifbarkeit des Glases durch Losungen mit pH-Werten
nahe 7.
Glastechnische Berichte, no. 26 (1953), pp. 91-97.

With KAUFMANN, R.
Schutzschichten für alte Gläser.
In Beiträge zur Angewandten Glasforschung.
(Editor SCHOTT, E.)
Stuttgart, 1959, pp. 355-361.

SCHÜLER, Th.
Das Strassburger Münster.
Strasbourg, 1817 (new edition).

SCHULZE, Johannes
Klöster, Stifte und Hospitaler der Stadt Kassel und Kloster
Weissenstein Register und Urkunden.
Marburg, 1913.

SCHÜRENBERG, L.
Der Dom zu Metz.
Frankfort-am-Main, 1942.

SCOTT, Alexander
Apparent Decay of Ancient Glass at Wells Cathedral.
J.M.G.P., vol. 4, no. 4 (Oct., 1932), p. 171.
(From a paper read before the Royal Society of Arts, Feb. 24, 1931,
The Romance of Museum Restoration.)
(See also his Appendix, on the composition and decay of the Wells
glass, in Archaeologia, vol. 31 (1931), pp. 116-118.)

SCOTT, George Gilbert

(Contribution to a discussion on the place of stained glass in the decoration of St. Paul's Cathedral.)
The Gentleman's Magazine, vol. 38, new series, part 2 (1852), pp. 268-269.

Gleanings from Westminster Abbey.
Oxford and London, 1861.

SCOTT, Judith D.G.

The Artist and the Client.
J.M.G.P., vol. 14, no. 1 (1964), pp. 44-49.

(Letter to the Editor on the Diocesan Advisory Committee System.)
J.M.G.P., vol. 14, no. 2 (1965), pp. 142-143.

SCOTT, S. Cooper

Notes on the New West Windows of St. John Baptist Church (Chester).
Journal of the Chester Archaeological and Historical Society, new series, vol. 4 (1896), pp. 171-177.

SCOTT, William Bell

The Ornamentist, or Artisan's Manual in the Various Branches of Ornamental Art . . .
London, Dublin and Edinburgh, 1845.

Half-hour Lectures on the History and Practice of the Fine and Ornamental Arts.
London, 1861.

SCOTT, William H.

The Story of Selby Abbey.
London, 1899.

SEALE, F.S.P.

(Glass in East Brent Church.)
Proceedings of the Somersetshire Archaeological and Natural History Society, vol. 51 (for 1905), part 1 (1906), pp. 41-42.

SEARS, Taber

Stained Glass Windows.
Art and Progress, vol. 3 (Nov., 1911), pp. 392-397.

SEDDON, George

The History of Stained Glass.
In Stained Glass.
New York, 1976, pp. 64-175.
Reviewed by BRISAC, Catherine, Bulletin Monumental, vol. 136 (1978), pp. 305-306, and in J.M.G.P., vol. 15, no. 3 (1974-1975), p. 74;
Ibid., vol. 16, no. 1 (1976-1977), pp. 67-68.
Reviewed by SKINNER, Orin E., Stained Glass, vol. 71, no. 4 (Winter, 1976-1977), p. 235.

SEDDON, J.P.

What A Memorial Window Should Be.
The Magazine of Art (1890), pp. 67-72.

The Works of P.R.B. in Llandaff Cathedral.
Public Library Journal: Quarterly Magazine of the Cardiff and Penarth Free Public Libraries, (March, June, Sept., 1903).

SEE, Ingram

Stained Glass in St. Louis.
Stained Glass, vol. 65, no. 1 (Spring, 1970), pp. 6-15.

SÉGANGE, L. du Broc de

Les Vitraux de la Cathédrale de Moulins.
Bulletin Monumental, vol. 42 (1876), pp. 142-160, 211-246.

SEIFERT, Hans

Alte und neue Fenster in Ulmer Münster.
Königstein im Taunus, 1962.

With WITZLEBEN, Elisabeth von.
Das Ulmer Münster.
Augsburg, 1968.

(Selby Abbey)

Selby Abbey East Window. An Account of the Window and of the First Restoration of it Before the Fire.
The Builder (Sept. 24, 1892).

Selby Abbey Glass. Panel of Fragments from Jesse Window Inserted in Abbey.
Yorkshire Herald, Oct. 7, 1932.

SELIGMAN, Dorothy C.

A Roundel of Painted Glass Attributed to Lucas van Leyden.
The Connoisseur, vol. 66 (May-Aug., 1923), pp. 13-15.

(Sellock Church, Herefordshire)

Transactions of the Woolhope Naturalists Field Club, vol. 22 for 1914, 1915, 1916, 1917 (1918), p. 119.

SENGER, Felix

Faceted Glass in Architecture.
Stained Glass, vol. 55, no. 4 (Winter, 1960-1961), pp. 4-9.

SENNOTT, Mina

Stained Glass - A Newly Flourishing Technique.
Ciba Journal (Summer, 1966).

(Sens Cathedral)

Deux Vitraux de la Cathédrale de Sens Conservés à Baltimore.
(Walters Art Gallery.)
Bulletin de la Société Archéologique de Sens, for 1939-1943 (1948).
Cited in Bulletin Monumental, vol. 107 (1949), pp. 187-188.

SEPP, J.N.

Ursprung der Glasmaler-Kunst im Kloster Tegernsee.
Munich and Leipzig, 1878.

SEREL, T.

Historical Notes on Saint Cuthbert's Church in the City of Wells.
Wells, 1875.

Notice of Four Stained Glass Shields of Arms and a Monumental Slab in St. Magdalene's Church, Cowgate, Edinburgh.
Proceedings of the Society of Antiquaries of Scotland, vol. 21 (1886-1887), pp. 266-274.

(Sèvres Manufactured Windows)

Notice Explicative des Fenêtres Peints en Vitraux de Coleurs, et des Tableaux Peints sur Glace, Exécutés à la Manufacture Royale de Porcelaine de Sèvres, et Exposés au Louvre le 18 Avril, 1847.
Paris, 1847.

SEWTER, A.C.

William Morris's Designs for Stained Glass.
Architectural Review, vol. 127 (March, 1960), pp. 196-200.

The Place of Charles Winston in the Victorian Revival of the Art of Stained Glass.
Journal of the British Archaeological Association, 3rd series, vol. 24 (1961), pp. 80-91.
Reviewed by A.L.N., J.M.G.P., vol. 13, no. 4 (1963), p. 596.

SEWTER, A.C. (Contd.)

Notes on Morris and Co.'s Domestic Stained Glass.
Journal of the William Morris Society, vol. 1, no. 1 (1961), pp. 22-28.
Reviewed by WILKINSON, A.L., J.M.G.P., vol. 13, no. 4 (1963), p. 596.

D.G. Rossetti's Designs for Stained Glass.
J.M.G.P., vol. 13, no. 2 (1961), pp. 419-424.

Victorian Stained Glass.
Apollo, vol. 76 (1962), pp. 760-765.

Morris Windows at Dedworth.
Architectural Review, vol. 136 (Dec., 1964), pp. 457-458.

With TAYLOR, N.
Morris In Hospital.
(Glass from the Chest Hospital, Ventnor.)
The Architectural Review, vol. 141 (1967), pp. 224-227.

A Check-list of Designs for Stained Glass by Ford Madox Brown.
Journal of the William Morris Society, vol. 2 (Summer, 1968), pp. 19-29.

Notes on Some Burne-Jones Designs for Stained Glass in American
Collections.
Museum Studies (Art Institute of Chicago), vol. 5 (1970), pp. 76-81.

The Stained Glass of William Morris and His Circle. Vol. 1.
New Haven and London, 1974.

The Stained Glass of William Morris and His Circle. A Catalogue.
New Haven and London, 1975.
Reviewed in J.M.G.P., vol. 15, no. 3 (1974-1975), pp. 74-76.
Reviewed by TAYLOR, T.C., Stained Glass, vol. 70, no. 1 (Spring, 1975),
p. 37.
Reviewed by BRIDGES, Stephen, Stained Glass, vol. 71, no. 2 (Summer,
1976), pp. 102-103.

SHARPE, Edmund
Four Letters in Colour in Churches, on Walls and in Windows . . .
London, 1870.
Reprinted from The Builder, vol.   (1870).

SHAW, G.
Weathered Crusts on Ancient Glass.
New Scientist (July 29, 1965), pp. 290-291.

SHAW, H.
The Encyclopaedia of Ornament.
London, 1842.

The Decorative Arts, Ecclesiastical and Civil, of the Middle Ages.
London, 1851.

SHAW, P.J.
An Old York Church, Allhallows in North Street.
York, 1908.

SHAW, Sax
Stained Glass Department of Edinburgh College of Design.
J.M.G.P., vol. 14, no. 1 (1964), pp. 28-30.

SHAW, Stebbing
The History and Antiquities of Staffordshire.
London, 1798-1801.
(Part 2, p. 122, has an account of EGINTON, W.R.)

SHAW, T.
History and Process of Stained Glass.
London (?), 1838.

SHELDON, James
Cathedral Lighting.
Stained Glass, vol. 30, no. 2 (Autumn, 1935), pp. 37-41.

Stained Glass at Washington Cathedral.
Washington D.C., 1936.

The Glory of Stained Glass.
Arts and Decoration (Feb., 1939).

Ralph Adams Cram. An Appreciation.
StainedGlass, vol. 37, no. 4 (Winter, 1942), pp. 106-107.

Symbols in Stained Glass.
The Cathedral Age (Washington D.C.), (Christmas, 1944).

(Sheldon, James)
Obituary. By BURNHAM, Wilbur H.
Stained Glass, vol. 51, no. 1 (Spring, 1956), pp. 15-16.

SHEPPERD, Eugenia
(Letter to the Editor suggesting, among other things, ways of
improving the magazine - much needed at this period.)
Stained Glass, vol. 47, no. 3 (Autumn, 1952), pp. 121-124.

(Sherborne Abbey)
Early Church Glass. Valuable Discovery at Sherborne Abbey.
(Rediscovery of glass removed in 1838)
The Times, Nov. 21, 1923.

Early Church Glass at Sherborne Abbey. A Puzzling Discovery.
The Times, Nov. 22, 1923.

The Abbey Church of St. Mary the Virgin, Sherborne.
Sherborne, 12th edition, 1959.
(Glass, p. 22.)

Sherburn-in-Elmet)
Sherburn-in-Elmet Church, Yorkshire: Glass.
(Grant towards restoring the medieval heraldic glass.)
The Pilgrim Trust, 38th Annual Report (1968), p. 15.

SHERRILL, Charles Hitchcock
Stained Glass Tours in France.
London, 1908.

Stained Glass Tours in England.
London, 1909.

A Stained Glass Tour in Italy.
London, 1913.
Reviewed in Manchester Guardian, July 25, 1913.

Stained Glass Tours in Germany, Austria, and the Rhine Lands.
London, 1927.
Reviewed in the Times Literary Supplement, (Dec. 8, 1927).
Reviewed by EDEN, F.S., The Connoisseur, vol. 79 (Sept.-Dec., 1927),
p. 255.

Stained Glass Tours in Spain and Flanders.
London, 1924.

A Remarkable Panel of Sixteenth Century Stained Glass, Representing
the Temptation of St. Anthony.
J.M.G.P., vol. 2, no. 3 (Apr., 1928), pp. 121-122.

Discovery of the Companion to the Window by William of Marseilles in
the Victoria and Albert Museum.
J.M.G.P., vol. 3, no. 1 (Apr., 1929), pp. 9-11.

SHOBE, Dennis, and BROWN, Jonathan
Light . . . after Forty Years of Darkness.
(Discovery of a collection of von Gerichten windows.)
Stained Glass, vol. 73, no. 3 (Fall, 1978), pp. 183-188.

(Shrewsbury, St. Chad's)

(Window by David Evans inserted.)

The Gentleman's Magazine, vol. 18, new series, part 2 (1842), p. 517.

(Shrigley and Hunt Ltd.)

Soothing Charm of Stained Glass. An Account of the Firm of
Shrigley and Hunt of Lancaster.
The Manchester Guardian, Jan. 10, 1936.

SICOTIÈRE, L. de la

Notice sur les Vitraux de l'Eglise Notre Dame d'Alençon.
Bulletin Monumental, vol. 8 (1842), pp. 105-115.

Le Département de l'Orne, Archéologique et Pittoresque.
Laigle, 1845-1854.

(Sidmouth, St. Nicholas' Church)

(Shield of the Five Wounds preserved in the vestry.)
The Ecclesiologist, vol. 28 (1867), p. 314.

SIGHART, J.

Geschichte der bildenden Kunst im Königreich Bayern.
Munich, 1863.

SIMON, Glyn

Antiquarian Opportunities of a Bishop.
(Presidential Address to the Cambrian Archaeological Association.)
Archaeologia Cambrensis, vol. 115 (1966).
(Contains an account of the restoration of the Llandefalle church
glass, pp. 4-6.)

SIMON, Jacques

Restauration des Verrières de Saint-Remi de Reims.
Les Monuments Historiques de la France, no. 1 (1959), pp. 14-25.

SIMON, Paul

Note sur les Vitraux de la Cathédrale de Reims.
In Congrès Archéologique de France (1911), p. 295.

La Grande Rose de la Cathédrale de Reims.
Reims, 1911.

SIMPSON, Carnegie

Westminster College Chapel, Cambridge. The Gift of Sir W.J. Noble,
Bart., and Lady Noble.
(Descriptive notes on the Douglas Strachan windows.)
Newcastle-on-Tyne, 1926.

SIMPSON, W.S.

Master John Schorn: His Effigy in Painted Glass.
Journal of the British Archaeological Association, vol. 25 (1869), p. 334.

SIMSON, Otto von

The Gothic Cathedral. The Origins of Gothic Architecture and the
Medieval Concept of Order. With an Appendix by Ernst Levy.
London, 1956.
Reviewed by SALET, Francis, Bulletin Monumental, vol. 114 (1956),
pp. 235-236.

SINCLAIR, J.S.

(Revised and enlarged by CROOME W.I.)
The Story of Cirencester Parish Church.
Gloucester, n.d.
Glass, pp. 22-23.

SINCLAIR, M.L.

History and Description of the Windows of the Parish Church of
the House of Commons.
London, 1895.

SINCLAIR, Ludwig (F.X.)

Wilhelmsche Glasmalereien und Kunstverglasungen 1890-1915.
Rottweil, 1915.

SKEAT, Francis W.

Notes on the Salvage of the Damaged Glass of Exeter Cathedral.
J.M.G.P., vol. 9, no. 1 (1943), pp. 15-21.

Review of LINDBLOM, Andreas, Sveriges Kunsthistoria;
ROOSVAL, Johnny, Medeltida Konst i Gotlands fomsal and Den
gotländske ciceronen.
J.M.G.P., vol. 10, no. 4 (1951), pp. 217-219.

The Vanished Glass of Exeter Cathedral.
J.M.G.P., vol. 11, no. 2 (1953), pp. 80-88.

Review of HARRIES, John, Discovering Stained Glass.
J.M.G.P., vol. 14, no. 4 (1968-1969), pp. 223.

The Stained Glass Work of Janos Hajnal.
J.M.G.P., vol. 15, no. 3 (1974-1975), pp. 49-50.

Stained Glass Windows of St. Albans Cathedral.
Chesham, 1977.
Reviewed by ARCHER, Michael, J.M.G.P., vol. 16, no. 1 (1976-1977),
pp. 74-76.
Reviewed by WEIS, Helene, Stained Glass, vol. 72, no. 3 (Fall, 1977),
p. 191.

A Survey of Stained Glass in Museums.
J.M.G.P., vol. 17, no. 2 (1978-1979), pp. 65-72.

SKETCHLEY, Rose E.D.

The Glass of the Great Choir Windows at Dunblane by Louis Davis: a
Memorial to Janet McEwan Younger.
London, 1915.

SKINNER, A.B.

A Stained Glass Window in the Victoria and Albert Museum, London.
Magazine of Art, vol. 27 (May, 1904), pp. 315-317.

SKINNER, Orin E.

Restoring the Stained Glass Treasures of Rheims Cathedral.
The American Architect, vol. 131, no. 2520 (May 5, 1927), pp. 559-63.
Reprinted in Bulletin of the Stained Glass Association of America,
vol. 22, no. 7 (July, 1927).

(Letter to the Editor on the colour changes which are alleged to
have occurred in nineteenth century glass.)
Stained Glass, vol. 27, no. 3 (March, 1932), p. 96.

Review of EDEN, F.S., Ancient Stained and Painted Glass (2nd edition).
Stained Glass, vol. 28, no. 2 (Summer, 1933), pp. 112-13.

SKINNER, Orin E. (Contd.)

    Stained Glass in the City Art Museum of Saint Louis.
    (Derived from articles in the Bulletin of the Museum.)
    Stained Glass, vol. 29, nos. 1-2 (Spring-Summer, 1934), pp. 7-20.

    The Stained Glass of the Brothers Bolton.
    Stained Glass, vol. 31, no. 1 (Spring, 1936).

    Stained Glass in the Toledo Museum of Art.
    Stained Glass, vol. 31, no. 2 (Autumn, 1936), pp. 37-47.

    Review of KNOWLES, J.A., Essays in the History of the York School
    of Glass-Painting.
    Stained Glass, vol. 31, no. 3 (Winter, 1936-1937), pp. 92-97.

    Into the Woods for Mousetraps.
    Liturgical Arts (New York), (Oct., 1938).

    Stained Glass at the New York World's Fair.
    Stained Glass, vol. 34, no. 2 (Autumn, 1939), pp. 51-61.

    Stained Glass Dinner Meeting in New York.
    (Reports of speeches by STOKES, A.P.; BURNHAM, W.H.; REYNOLDS, J.G.;
    SHELDON, James; etc.)
    Stained Glass, vol. 35, no. 1 (Spring, 1940), pp. 14-30.

    Women in Stained Glass.
    (As artists.)
    Stained Glass, vol. 35, no. 4 (Winter, 1940), pp. 113-123.
    Part 2, Ibid., vol. 36, no. 1 (Spring, 1941), pp. 18-25.
    Part 3, Canadian Women in Stained Glass, Ibid., vol. 36, no. 2
    (Summer, 1941), pp. 50-52.
    Part 4, Stained Glass Women in England, Scotland and Ireland, Ibid.,
    vol. 36, no. 4 (Winter, 1941), pp. 106-115.

    Priorities Regulation no. 10 and the Production Code.
    (On the availability of materials in wartime.)
    Stained Glass, vol. 37, no. 2 (Summer, 1942), pp. 91-94.

    Stained Glass Goes to Jail.
    (Prison Chapel Windows in the U.S.A.)
    Stained Glass, vol. 37, no. 2 (Summer, 1942), pp. 95-97.

    Stained Glass Serves in War.
    Stained Glass, vol. 38, no. 1 (Spring, 1943), pp. 12-22.

    Stained Glass Goes to School.
    Stained Glass, vol. 38, no. 4 (Winter, 1943), pp. 108-119.

    Stained Glass Goes to Public Buildings.
    Stained Glass, vol. 39, no. 1 (Spring, 1944), pp. 11-19.

    An American Approach to Arts and Crafts.
    Stained Glass, vol. 39, no. 2 (Summer, 1944), pp. 38-42.

    Stained Glass in all its Inspiring Beauty.
    Church Property Administration (Milwaukee), (Nov.-Dec., 1945).

    An American Approach to Arts and Crafts.
    Liturgical Arts (New York), (Feb., 1946).

(Skinner, Orin E.)

    See 'Stained Glass Problems in Our Day'.

SKINNER, Orin E.

    An Adventurer in Light and Colour.
    (An obituary of CONNICK, C.J.)
    Church Property Administration (Milwaukee), (May-June, 1946).

    The Care and Maintenance of Stained Glass.
    The Homiletic and Pastoral Review (New York), (March, 1947).

SKINNER, Orin E. (Contd)

    The Craft of Color and Light.
    The Homiletic and Pastoral Review (New York), (June, 1947).

    A Visit to Chartres. History of Chartres Cathedral. Lessons to
    be Learned from Chartres. A Short History of Stained Glass Windows.
    American Fabrics, (Winter, 1949-1950).

    Apprentice Competition.
    Stained Glass, vol. 45, no. 1 (Spring, 1950), pp. 6-13.

    Mostly about Editors.
    (Of Stained Glass.)
    Stained Glass, vol. 48, no. 1 (Spring, 1953), pp. 11-16.

    Review of ARMITAGE, E. Liddall, Stained Glass.
    Stained Glass, vol. 55, no. 1 (Spring, 1960), p. 39.

    With BRIDGES, Stephen, FREI, Robert, and others.
    What makes for Good Stained Glass Design? (A Symposium.)
    Stained Glass, vol. 55, no. 4 (Winter, 1960-1961), pp. 16-27.
    Part 2, Ibid., vol. 56, no. 1 (Spring, 1961), pp. 38-47.

    Stained Glass Tours: Boston.
    Stained Glass, vol. 60, no. 2 (Summer, 1965), pp. 7-17.

    In Rebuttal. A New Approach Indeed!
    (Contradicts Ellen E. MORRISON's article in vol. 63, no. 1. (Spring,
    1968).)
    Stained Glass, vol. 63. no. 3 (Autumn, 1968), pp. 34-35.

    Connick in Retrospect.
    Stained Glass, vol. 70, no. 1 (Spring, 1975), pp. 17-19.

    Review of LEE, Lawrence, SEDDON, George, STEPHENS, Francis,
    Stained Glass.
    Stained Glass, vol. 71, no. 4 (Winter, 1976-1977), p. 235.

    An Autobiography.
    Stained Glass, vol. 72, no. 4 (Winter, 1977-1978), pp. 232-235.

    (And others.)
    Mostly About the Magazine.
    (The history of the changing names and formats of Stained Glass.)
    Stained Glass, vol. 73, no. 1 (Spring, 1978), pp. 13-17.

    Mostly About Editors.
    (Of Stained Glass and its predecessors.)
    Stained Glass, vol. 73, no. 2 (Summer, 1978), pp. 113-116.

SMEKENS, T., and HENDRICX, J.L.

    Rapport sur les Verrières de l'Eglise d'Hoogstraeten.
    Bulletin de la Commission des Monuments de la Province d'Anvers,
    part 2 (1863-1886), pp. 355-365.

SMITH, George (and others)

    A Lost Window of Great Bedwyn Church.
    The Wiltshire Archaeological and Natural History Magazine, no. 200
    (June, 1954), pp. 285-288.

SMITH, H. Clifford

    (Elizabethan heraldic panel in verre eglomisé exhibited.)
    With contributions by READ, Hercules, EVANS, Arthur, HOPE, William.
    Proceedings of the Society of Antiquaries, 2nd series, vol. 28 (Nov.,
    1915-June, 1916), pp. 12-15.

SMITH, Herbert L.

    Notes of Brasses, Memorial Windows, and Escutcheons, formerly
    existing in Ashford and Willesbrough Churches.
    Archaeologia Cantiana, vol. 2 (1859), pp. 103-110.

SMITH, John Thomas

Antiquities of Westminster: the Old Palace, St. Stephen's Chapel, etc.
2 vols., London, 1807.

SMITH, M.C.

St. Michael's Windows and Decorations.
(Church of St. Michael and All Angels, New York City.)
International Studio, vol. 33 (Jan., 1908), pp. 97-99.

Thorley Memorial Window.
(Window in Collegiate Church, New York City.)
International Studio, vol. 34 (May, 1908), p. 120.

SMITH, William

Ancient Painted Window of the Early Part of the Sixteenth Century,
in the Possession of Mr. William Smith, Upper Southwick Street,
London, Originally Forming a Portion of One of the Windows in the
Cathedral at Basle.
London, n.d.
(See EVANS, E.T., Notes and Queries, series 7, vol. 5 (June 16, 1888),
pp. 464-465.)

SOCARD, E.

Iconographie de la Verrière de St. Joseph à l'Eglise St. Martin ès
Vignes de Troyes.
Troyes, 1858.

(Soissons)

Une Verrière Démembrée de la Cathédrale de Soissons.
(Partly in the Kunstgewerbe Museum in Berlin, partly in the Pitcairn
Collection. Bryn-Athyn. Pennsylvania.)
Gazette des Beaux-Arts, (1953).
Quoted in Bulletin Monumental, vol. 112 (1954), p. 116.

SOLLOWAY, John

The St. Germanicus Window in Selby Abbey.
Selby, 1914.

Selby Abbey, Past and Present.
Leeds, 1925.

SOLON, Louis Marc Emmanuel

A Contribution towards a Bibliography of the Art of Glass.
Part 1.   Glass-Making and Technology.
Part 2.   Glass-Painting (a) Technology
                         (b) Stained and Painted Glass:
                              Description and Reproduction.
Transactions of the Ceramic Society, vol. 12 (1912-1913), pp.
65-77, 285-324.

SOMMERARD, Alexandre de

Les Arts du Moyen-Age, etc., en ce qui Concerne Principalement le
Palais Romain de Paris, l'Hôtel de Cluny Issu de ses Ruines, et
les Objets d'Art de la Collection Classée dans cet Hôtel.
11 vols., Paris, 1836-1846.

SOMMERARD, E. du

Paris: Musée de Cluny. Catalogue et Description des Objets d'Art . . .
Paris, 1881, 1883.

SOMNER, William

The Antiquities of Canterbury; or a Survey of that Ancient Citie
with the Suburbs and Cathedrall, etc.
London, 1640.
(2nd edition revised and enlarged by BATTELY, Nicholas, London, 1703.)

SOTHEBY'S

Catalogue of the Magnificent Sixteenth Century Stained Glass
Windows from the Chapel of Ashridge, Herts. To be sold by
Messrs. Sotheby & Co. on the 12th July 1928.
London, 1928.

Description of the Elizabethan Panelling and Heraldic Stained
Glass Windows in the Great Chamber, Gilling Castle, Yorkshire.
(Auction sale catalogue.)
London, 1929.

(Sale of panels, some from Warwick Castle.)
News and Notes, J.M.G.P., vol. 15, no. 2 (1973-1974), p. 53.

(Sales in London and New York.)
News and Notes, J.M.G.P., vol. 15, no. 3 (1974-1975), p. 55.

Sale Catalogue for Auction of 23rd March 1976.
Sotheby's Belgravia, London.

(Glass sold recently.)
J.M.G.P., vol. 16, no. 1 (1976-1977), pp. 9-10.

(Sales of stained glass.)
Editorial, J.M.G.P., vol. 17, no. 1 (1978-1979), pp. 7-9.

SOUBIELLE, Abbé

La Chapelle du Petit Seminaire de Larresore.
Paris, 1872.

(South Germany)

Aus der Geschichte der Glasmalerei in Süddeutschland. By H.H.
Diamant (Jan. 11, 1926), pp. 23-25, (Jan. 21, 1926), pp. 43-45.

SOWERS, Robert

The Lost Art, A Survey of One Thousand Years of Stained Glass.
New York, 1954.
Reviewed in Stained Glass, vol. 49, nos. 3 and 4 (Autumn-Winter, 1954),
pp. 131-132.
Reviewed by CRAIG, John, J.M.G.P., vol. 11, no. 4 (1955), pp. 251-252.

Some Thoughts on a Stained Glass Manual for Architects.
Craft Horizons (Nov.-Dec., 1960).

Matisse and Chagall as Craftsmen.
Craft Horizons (Jan.-Feb., 1962).

Stained Glass: An Architectural Art.
London, 1965.
Reviewed by WILLET Muriel C., Stained Glass, vol. 60, no. 4 (Winter,
1965-1966), p. 27.

On the Blues in Chartres.
Art Bulletin, vol. 48 (June, 1966), pp. 218-222.

With WILLET, Crosby.
Stained Glass: A Dialogue.
Faith and Form (Apr., 1968).

New Stained Glass in Germany.
Craft Horizons (May-June, 1969).

Where It's At.
(Stained glass essentially an abstract art.)
Stained Glass, vol. 69, nos. 1 and 2 (Spring-Summer, 1974), pp. 14-17.

SPARKE, Archibald

Pre-Raphaelite Stained Glass.
(A listing.)
Notes and Queries, 12th series, vol. 4 (Dec., 1918), p. 337.
(Another example given by 'St. Swithin' on the same page.)
Further examples given by PAGE, J.T., vol. 5 (March, 1919), p. 74;
H.K. St. J.S., Ibid.; J.R.H., Ibid.; M., Ibid.; MAGRATH, J.R. (q.v.),
(Apr., 1919), pp. 105-106.

SPARROW, Walter Shaw
Christopher Whall and his Influence.
The Studio, vol. 90 (1925), pp. 365-368.

SPEAR, Francis H.
In Fifteen Craftsmen on their Crafts.
London, n.d.

SPENCER, Jeannette Dyer
Les Vitraux de la Sainte Chapelle de Paris.
Paris, 1932.

SPERLING, C.F.D.
Dynes Hall, Great Maplestead.
Transactions of the Essex Archaeological Society, new series, vol. 20
for 1930-1933 (1933).
(Some Tudor painted quarries, p. 6.)

(Spiers, Richard N.)
Obituary.
Stained Glass, vol. 31, no. 2 (Autumn, 1936), pp. 66-67.

SPITZER, Fréderic (Collection)
La Collection Spitzer: Catalogue des Objets d'Art . . . dont la Vente
Publique Aura Lieu à Paris, du 17 Avril au 16 Juin, 1893.
Paris, 1893.

SPRING, R.O.C.
The Stained Glass of Salisbury Cathedral.
Salisbury, 1973.

SPRINGER, Ludwig
Einige Versuche über Glasmalerfarben.
Keramische Rundschau, vol. 34, no. 6 (1926), pp. 85-86;
                          no. 7 (1926), pp. 105-106.

(Springfield, Mass.)
Ancient Glass at Springfield Museum.
Stained Glass, vol. 40, no. 3 (Autumn, 1945), pp. 86-87.

SQUIRE, J.C.
Review of READ, Herbert, English Stained Glass.
The Observer, Jan. 16, 1927.

STABENRATH, Charles de
Vitraux de l'Eglise de Conches.
Revue de Rouen (1840), pp. 74-87.

(Staehelin-Paravicini, A.)
Die Schliffscheiben der Schweiz von A. Staehelin-Paravicini.
Basel, 1926.

STAFFELBACH, Georg
Anna Maria Franziska Pfyffer v. Altishofen - v. Sonnenberg.
Eine unbekannte Hinterglasmalerin.
Innerschweizerisches Jahrbuch für Heimatkunde, 8-10, pp. 89-98.
Lucerne, 1944-1946.

Geschichte der Luzerner Hinterglasmalerei von den Anfängen bis zur
Gegenwart.
Lucerne, 1951.

STAHL, C.J.
Glaserkunst, Glasmalerei und moderne Kunstverglasung: ein Hand-und
Nachschlagebuch.
Vienna, 1912.

Dekorative Glasmalerei, Unterglasmalerei und Malen auf Glas.
Vienna and Leipzig, 1915.

(Stained Glass)
(Observations upon its history. By E.M.S.)
The Gentleman's Magazine, vol. 87, part 1 (1817), pp. 309-

(Anon.)
Stained Glass.
The Ecclesiologist, vol. 3 (1844), pp. 16-20.

(Anon.)
Stained Glass.
The Ecclesiologist, vol. 3 (1844), pp. 107-111.

Thoughts on Stained Glass.
The Ecclesiologist. vol. 15 (1854), pp. 33-36.

Some Remarks on Glass-Painting, No. 1. By G.R.F.
The Ecclesiologist, vol. 17 (1856), pp. 364-367.
No. 2, Ibid., vol. 18 (1857), pp. 73-83.
No. 3, Ibid., pp. 263-271.
No. 4, Ibid., vol. 19 (1858), pp. 1-8, 83-86.
No. 5, Ibid., pp. 352-360.

(Mid-nineteenth century in Britain.)
Visits to Art-Manufactories. No. 2 - Stained Glass.
(Refers to Winston, Powell, Wailes, Willement, Hardman, Bell,
Clayton, Lavers and Barraud.)
Art Journal (1859), pp. 38-40.

Some Modern Church Glass.
Art Journal (Apr., 1901), pp. 120-122.

Stained Glass. An Old Craft with Modern Possibilities.
Arts and Crafts Trader, vol. 1, no. 12

A New Era in Stained Glass with Revolutionary Possibilities.
(B.R. Bayne's invention of fusing pieces of coloured glass together.)
Glass, vol. 7, no. 5 (May, 1930).

The Story of Stained Glass.
Prepared by The Stained Glass Association of America.
Fairfax, Virginia. n.d. (?).

A Revolution in Stained Glass.
(B.R. Bayne's invention of fusing pieces of coloured glass together.)
Architect and Building News (Apr. 4, 1930).

Leading Article, The Times, June 17, 1930.
(On the current position of the art.)

L'Art de Vitrail.
L'Artisan Liturgique, no. 49 (Apr.-June, 1938).
(Special number on glass.)

Stained Glass Windows.
Leading Article. Yorkshire Post, Sept. 17, 1938.
Reprinted in J.M.G.P., vol. 8, no. 1 (Oct., 1939), pp. 3-4.

Stained Glass as Architects Consider It. A Symposium.
Contributions from GOODMAN, P.
                    BRIDGES, S.
                    BATES, H.
                    ATKINSON, H.
                    RAMBUSCH, R.E.
Stained Glass, vol. 59, no. 3 (Autumn, 1964), pp. 8-17.

(Stained Glass, Contd.)

Stained Glass Craftsmanship.
A Discussion by RAMBUSCH, H.W., SKINNER, O.E., D'ASCENSO, N.,
SCHMITT, R.P., PAYNE, G.L., DURHAN, W.J.
Church Property Administration (Mar.-Apr., 1950).

Stained Glass Developments Abroad of Interest in the United States.
National Glass Budget (June 4, 1966).

Stained Glass. Finds in Strange Places.
The Times, Jan. 9, 1934.

Stained Glass in Seminary Chapels.
Stained Glass, vol. 44, no. 1 (Spring, 1949), pp. 4-12.
                vol. 44, no. 2 (Summer, 1949), pp. 52-56.
                vol. 44, no. 4 (Winter, 1949), pp. 108-113.

(Stained Glass Association of America.)
Code of Ethics.
Stained Glass, vol. 36, no. 4 (Winter, 1941), p. 126.

Meeting of Joint Committee, American Stained Glass Craft.
(On the crisis in the U.S. stained-glass trade.)
Stained Glass, vol. 49, nos.3 and 4 (Autumn-Winter, 1954), pp. 112-116.

Forty-Seventh Convention of the Stained Glass Association of America.
(Includes the decision to use the Ketchum public relations organisation
in an attempt to recover ground lost to European imports.)
Stained Glass, vol. 51, no. 2 (Summer, 1956), pp. 42-50.

(Stained Glass Association of America.)
An Index of Stained Glass published.
Stained Glass, vol. 74, no. 1 (Spring, 1979), p.39.

Modern Stained Glass.
(Arts Council Exhibition Catalogue.)
London, 1960.

(Stained Glass, Contd.)

Stained Glass Given New Dimension.
Catholic Institutional Management (May-June, 1969).

(Illuminating stained glass externally by gas.)
Chapters on Painted Glass. 3 - Illuminated Windows.
The Ecclesiologist, vol. 12 (1851), pp. 90-91.

Stained Glass. How to Photograph It.
J.M.G.P., vol. 1, no. 2 (Apr., 1925), pp. 50-51.

Stained Glass Problems in Our Day. A Symposium.
Contributions from La FARGE, J.
                     SKINNER, O.E.
                     WILLET, H.L.
                     NICOLAS, J.
                     RAMBUSCH, H.
Stained Glass, vol. 41, no. 4 (Winter, 1946), pp. 103-124.
(Reprinted from Liturgical Arts, Aug., 1946.).

Stained Glass: Tradition Meets Technology.
Architectural and Engineering News (Nov., 1969).

(Stalin)

Stained Glass for Stalin.
Stained Glass, vol. 43, no. 1 (Spring, 1948), p. 25.

(Stamford, Browne's Hospital)

Browne's Hospital, Stamford, Lincolnshire: Glass.
(Grant to restore the glass.)
The Pilgrim Trust, 31st Annual Report (1961), p. 28.

(Stamford, St. John's)

St.John's Church, Stamford, Lincolnshire: Glass.
(Grant to restore the windows.)
The Pilgrim Trust, 43rd Annual Report (1973), p. 14.

(Stammers, Harry)

MILNER-WHITE, Eric.
(On Harry Stammers.)
The Dean's Letter, 31st Annual Report of the Friends of York Minster
(1959), p. 21.

Obituary. By STAMMERS, Mrs., and NUTTGENS, J.E.
J.M.G.P., vol. 14, no. 4 (1968-1969), pp. 189-190.

STANFORD, H.

The Arms of the Glazier's Guild and the Use of the Grozing Irons in
Heraldry.
Notes and Queries, vol. 172, no. 7, p. 116.

(Stanford-on-Avon Church)

Stanford-on-Avon Church, Northamptonshire: Glass.
(Grant towards repairing two chancel windows.)
The Pilgrim Trust, 38th Annual Report (1968), p. 16.

(Stanton Harcourt)

Stanton Harcourt, A Short History.
Oxford, revised edition, 1964.
(Gives almost no indication of what is to be seen.)

STATZ, Vincent

Glasfenster im gotischen Stile. Entwürfe für Kunstglaser und
Architekten.
Berlin, 2nd edition, 1885.

With UNGEWITTER, G.G.
Gothisches Musterbuch. Mit einer Einleitung von A. Reichesperger.
2 vols., Leipzig, 1856-1861.
English translation by MONICKE, C.H., The Gothic Model Book.
London, 1858.

STAVRIDI, Margaret

Charles Eamer Kempe, Church Decorator for England, America and the
World.
Stained Glass, vol. 74, no. 4 (Winter, 1979-1980), pp. 315-320.

STEBBING, Beatrice

Stained Glass Tour: Oklahoma.
Stained Glass, vol. 62, no. 3 (Autumn, 1967), pp. 12-22.

STEENBERGHE DE DOURMONT, R. van

De Glasschilderkunst in Belgie.
(With HELBIG, Jean.)
The Hague, vol. 1, 1943, vol. 2, 1951.

STEER, Francis W.

The Braybrooke Glass in Saffron Walden Church.
J.M.G.P., vol. 11, no. 3 (1954), pp. 148-151.

Heraldic Glass in the Percy Chapel at Petworth House.
J.M.G.P., vol. 11, no. 4 (1955), pp. 213-220.

Heraldic Glass in Stopham Church, Sussex, England.
New England Historical and Genealogical Register, vol. 112, no. 447.

The Fitzalan Chapel, Arundel.
4th edition, Chichester, 1974.
(Glass, pp. 7-8.)

The Heraldic Glass of Arundel Castle.
J.M.G.P., vol. 16, no. 1 (1976-1977), pp. 56-66.

STEFANAGGI, Marcel

    L'Etat des Recherches en France.
    In 7ᵉ Colloque du Corpus Vitrearum Medii Aevi.
    Florence ?, 1970, pp. 47-48.

STEFFEN, P. Stephan

    Neuentdeckte Reste mittelalterlicher Scheiben in Marienstatt.
    Zeitschrift für alte und neue Glasmalerei (1915), p. 44.

STEIN, Heinrich Friedrich Karl

    Städelsches Kunstinstitut. Ausstellung mittelalterlicher Glasmalereien
    aus Schloss Kappenberg, gesammelt vom Freiherrn vom Stein.
    Frankfort am Main, 1928.

(Vom STEIN Collection)

    Meisterwerke Glasmalerei Mittelalterlicher.
    Museum für kunst und Gewerbe Hamburg. Meisterwerke mittelalterlicher
    Glasmalerei aus der Sammlung des Reichsfreiherrn vom Stein.
    Hamburg, 1966.

STEIN, Otto

    Die alten Glasmalereien in der Reinoldikirche zu Dortmund.
    Dortmund, 1920.

STEINBEISS, Otto

    Entwickelung der Kunstglaserei und Glasmalerei.
    St. Lucas (Deutsche Glaser Zeitung), vol. 9 (1898), pp. 345, 366.

STEINBERG, S.H.

    A Flemish Armorial Window.
    Burlington Magazine, vol. 74 (1939), pp. 218-222.
    (See HELBIG, Jean, Ibid., vol. 75, p. 42.)

STEINBRUCKER, Charlotte

    Hans Baldung Grien als Glasmaler.
    Diamant, 57th year, no. 4 (Feb. 1, 1935).

    Die Glasgemälde im Berliner Schlossmuseum.
    Diamant, 57th year, no. 28 (Oct. 1, 1935).

    Die Glasgemälde im Kaiser-Friedrich-Museum in Berlin.
    Diamant, 58th year, no. 30 (Nov. 11, 1936).

    Melchior Lechter als Glasmaler.
    Diamant (Apr. 21, 1939).

STEPHENS, F.G.

    Mr. Edward Burne-Jones A.R.A. as a Decorative Artist.
    Portfolio, vol. 20 (Nov., 1889), pp. 214-219.

STEPHENS, Francis

    Stained Glass of Historic Interest in London.
    Letter to the Editor (additions and corrections to KNOWLES, q.v.).
    J.M.G.P., vol. 12, no. 1 (1956), p. 84.

    How a Stained-Glass Window is Made and Restored.
    In Stained Glass.
    New York, 1976, pp. 176-194.
    Reviewed by BRISAC, Catherine, Bulletin Monumental, vol. 136 (1978),
    pp. 305-306.

STETTLER. Michael

    Königsfelden, Farbenfenster des 14. Jahrhunderts.
    Laupen near Bern, 1949.

    Swiss Stained Glass of the Fourteenth Century from the Church of
    Koenigsfelden.
    London, 1949.
    Reviewed by KIRBY, H.T., J.M.G.P., vol. 10, no. 4 (1951), pp. 220-222.

    Anciens Vitraux de Suisse. Adaptation Française de P. Grellet.
    Zurich, 1953.

STEVENSON, William J.

    The Romance of Stained Glass.
    Chambers' Journal, 7th series, vol. 5 (Nov. 20, 1915), pp. 810-812.

STEWART-SMITH, D.C.

    Modern Stained Glass.
    Reports and Papers of the Northamptonshire Architectural and
    Archaeological Society, vol. 54 (1948), pp. 2-11.

STIASSNY, Robert

    Hans Baldung Griens Wappenzeichnungen in Coburg.
    Vienna, 1896.

STIDGER, William L.

    Preaching Through Stained Glass.
    Church Management (Cleveland), (Jan., 1948).

STITES. Raymond S.

    Pre-Romanesque Forerunners of the Stained Glass Technique.
    Stained Glass, vol. 36, no. 2 (Summer, 1941), pp. 40-49.

STILLFRIED-RATTONITZ, R.M.B. von

    Alterthümer und Kunstdenkmale des Hauses Hohenzollern.
    3 vols, Berlin, 1838, 67.
    (Stained glass in vol. 2.)

STINTZI, P.

    L'Eglise de Vieux-Thann. Monument Historique et Trésor Artistique.
    Mulhouse, n.d.

STOCKBAUER

    Geschichte der Königlichen Glasmalereianstalt in München.
    Kunst-und Gewerbe Bl. (Nürnberg), vol. 9 (1875), pp. 193, 201.

STOHLMAN, W. Frederick

    Ancient Stained Glass Medallion (Torture of St. George) of the
    Thirteenth Century.
    Art and Archaeology (New York), (Oct., 1925).

(Stoke d'Abernon, St. Mary's Church)

    St. Mary's, Stoke d'Abernon. Dedication of Windows by the Lord
    Bishop of Guildford. (Sunday, July 23, 1950).
    (Fifteenth century Flemish glass, some from the Costessey collection,
    some from Cassiobury Park, Hertfordshire. The windows are briefly
    described.)

    Old Stained Glass at Stoke D'Abernon.
    Country Life, (Nov. 3, 1950).

    St. Mary's, Stoke D'Abernon. A Short Guide to the Ancient Stained
    Glass.
    n.d., n.p.

(Stoke d'Abernon, St. Mary's Church)

St. Mary's, Stoke d'Abernon. A Short Guide.
Revised and enlarged edition, Esher, 1958.
(Glass, pp. 11-12.)

(Stoke-on-Trent)

(Glass by David Evans installed at the new church at Stoke.)
The Gentleman's Magazine, vol. 100, part 1 (1830), pp. 583-584.

(Stoke Poges)

(On the glass in Stoke Poges Church and the 'bicycle' window.)
The Bulletin, (Oct., 1928).

(Stoke Prior, Worcestershire)

Guide to the Architecture of St. Michael's Church, Stoke Prior.
n.d., n.p. (duplicated pamphlet).
(Glass from Malvern, p. 3.)

STOKES, Thomas

W.E. Chance and the Revised Manufacture of Coloured Glass.
J.M.G.P., vol. 5, no. 4 (Oct., 1934), pp. 170-174.

STOKINGER, Josef

Die Technik der Glasmalerei.
Diamant (Dec. 11, 1925), pp. 749-751.
         (Dec. 21, 1925), pp. 769-770.

STOLBERG, August

Tobias Stimmers Malereien an der astronomischen Münsterruhr zu Strassburg.
Strasbourg, 1894.

STOLBERG, August (Contd.)

Tobias Stimmer (1539-1584), sein Leben und seine Werke, mit Beiträgen zur Geschichte der deutschen Glasmalerei im 16. Jahrhundert.
Strasbourg, 1905.

(Stolen Stained Glass Windows)

Disquieting Rumours of Chartres and Rouen.
The Morning Post, Nov. 28, 1933.

(Strachan, Douglas)

Obituary.
Stained Glass, vol. 45, no. 3 (Autumn, 1950), p. 128.

Obituary, by WILSON, William.
J.M.G.P., vol. 11, no. 1 (1952), pp. 52-53.

STRACHAN, L.R.M.

Stained Glass Windows to Fictitious Characters.
Notes and Queries, vol. 171 (Dec. 12, 1936), p. 425.

STRAELEN, Hildegarde van

Studien zur Florentiner Glasmalerei des Trecento und Quattrocento.
Wattenscheid, 1938.

(Strasbourg Exhibition)

Ausstellung von Glasmalereien und Mosaiken in Strassburg.
Zeitschrift für alte und neue Glasmalerei (1912), p. 30.

(Strasbourg)

French Decorate Captain Rorimer.
(For his part in saving the glass removed from the Cathedral by the Germans.)
Stained Glass, vol. 41, no. 2 (Summer, 1946), pp. 64-66.

STRAUB, A.

Mémoire sur les Vitraux de l'Ancienne Collégiale de Haslach et de l'Eglise de Walbourg . . .
Paris, 1860.
Reprinted from Mémoirs de la Congrès Archéologique de France, no. 26, Strasbourg (Aug. 27, 1859), pp. 296-363.

L'Eglise de Vieux-Thaun et ses Vitraux.
Bulletin de la Société pour la conservation des monuments historiques d'Alsace, 2nd series, vol. 9 (1876), pp. 98-107.

STREET, George Edmund

On Glass Painting.
The Ecclesiologist, vol. 13 (1852), pp. 237-247.

(Strelley Church, Notts.)

Old Stained Glass at Strelley, Notts. By A.E.L.L.
(Request for identification of subjects.)
Notes and Queries, 5th series, vol. 6 (Sept. 23, 1876), pp. 248-249.
Replied to by YRAM, Ibid., (Oct. 21, 1876), p. 333.

STRICKLAND, Hilda

Ernest Heasman, Stained Glass Artist.
J.M.G.P., vol. 15, no. 2 (1973-1974), pp. 29-35.

STROHM, Paul

The Imagery of a Missing Window at Great Malvern Priory Church.
Transactions of the Worcestershire Archaeological Society, 3rd series, vol. 1 (1965-1967), pp. 65-68.

STYGER, C.

Glasmaler und Glasgemälde im Lande Schwyz 1465-1680.
Mitteilungen historische vereins Cantons Schwyz (Einsiedeln), (1855).

SUAU, Jean-Pierre

Les Vitraux du 14e Siècle de la Cathédrale de Narbonne.
Narbonne, Archéologie et Histoire, t. 2, Narbonne au Moyen Age.
Montpellier, 1973, pp. 237-269.

SUDELEY, Lord (Auction of Collection)

Katalog der Sammlung Lord Sudeley (Toddington Castle, England) Schweizer Glasmalereien, vorwiegend des 16 und 17 Jahrhunderts.
Munich, 1911.

Zur Versteigerung der Glasgemälde des Lord Sudely am 4 Oktober 1911 in München.
Zeitschrift für alte und neue Glasmalerei (1912), p. 18.

SUDRÉ, Jean Pierre

La Chapelle de Saint Ferdinand.
Paris, 1846.

SUFFLING, E.R.

Handbook on Glass Painting, Staining and Fret Lead Glazing, with a Review of the Style of Ancient Glass.
London, 1890.

SUFFLING, E.R. (Contd.)

Curiosities of Stained Glass Windows.
Pearson's Magazine (1896), pp. 507-511.

A Treatise on the Art of Glass Painting, prefaced with a review of
Ancient Glass.
London, 1902.

(Sundials)

Gläserne Sonnenuhren. By Dr. Z.
Diamant, 48th year, no. 28 (Oct. 1, 1926), pp. 543-544.

(Sunniswald, Switzerland)

Die Glasgemälde der Kirche von Sunniswald.
Bern, 1912.

SUNSHINE, Donald

Stained Glass: When and Where Appropriate.
Stained Glass, vol. 63, no. 2 (Summer, 1968), pp. 8-11.

SUPINO, J.B.

La Basilica di San Francesco.
Bologna, 1924.

L'Arte Nelle Chiese di Bologna.
Bologna, 1932.

Surrey and Sussex Glassmen. The Last of the Line.
The Times, Dec. 30, 1930.

(Sussex)

Coloured Glass in Sussex.
(Letter to the Editor.)
Sussex County Herald, Apr. 28, 1928.

Rare Windows in a Sussex Farm Loft.
Sussex Daily News, May 28, 1937.

SUTER, John Wallace

The Art of Stained Glass.
The Cathedral Age (Autumn, 1948).

SUTTON, Frederick H.

Renaissance Glass.
Reports and Papers of the Associated Architectural Societies, vol. 14
(1877), pp. 52-56.

SVAHN, M.A.

Un Vitrail de l'Eglise des Iffs.
Bulletin de la Société Archéologique du Département d'Ille-et-Vilaine,
(1931).

Le Vitrail de la Chaste Susanne.
Bulletin de la Société Archéologique du Département d'Ille-et-Vilaine,
(1931).
Reprinted Rennes, 1931.

SWAAN, W.

The Gothic Cathedral.
London, 1969.

SWAINE, J.B.

East Window of St. Margaret's, Westminster.
London, 1833.

(Swansea College of Art)

The Department of Stained Glass at the Swansea College of Art.
J.M.G.P., vol. 14, no. 2 (1965), pp. 124-125.

SWEETING, W.D.

Notes on the Parish Churches In and Around Peterborough.
London and Peterborough, 1868.

(Swiss Glass)

Etwas zur Geschichte der Glasmahlerey in der Schweiz.
Hannover Mag   (1765), cols. 1607-1611.

(Auction catalogue.)
Catalogue d'une Collection Suisse de Vitraux Peints, Porcelaines . . .
etc. . . . .
Amsterdam, 1916.

Swiss Glass.
Architectural Review (Apr., 1924).

(Switzerland)

Die Entwicklung der Glasmalerei in der Schweiz. By Prof. N-r.
Diamant, 50th year, no. 28 (Oct. 1, 1928), pp. 581-582.

(Swiss National Exhibition, 1896)

Exposition Nationale Suisse, Genève, 1896. Catalogue de l'Art
Ancien, Groupe 25. Les Vitraux Comprenant les Numéros 1446-1612.
Geneva, 1896.

SWOBODA, K.M.

Zur Frage nach dem Anteil des führenden Meisters am Gesamtkunstwerk
der Kathedrale von Chartres.
Festschrift für Hans R. Hahnloser, Basel, 1961, pp. 37-45.

'THEOPHILUS JUNIOR'
    Towards an Appreciation of Stained Glass.
    Liturgical Arts, vol. 6, 2nd quarter (1937).

THEVENOT, E.H.
    Essai Historique sur le Vitrail . . . dans ses Rapports avec la
    Décoration des Monuments Réligieux depuis le 13ᵉ jusqu'au 19ᵉ Siècle.
    Annales Scientifiques-Littéraires et Industrielles d'Auvergne
    (Sept. - Oct., 1837), p. 424.

THIBAUD, Emile
    De la Peinture sur Verre, ou Notice Historique sur cet Art, dans
    ses Rapports avec la Vitrification.
    Annales Scientifique-Littéraires et Industrielles de l'Auvergne,
    vol. 8 (1835), pp. 667-695.

    Notices Historiques sur les Vitraux Anciens et Modernes, et sur l'Art
    de la Peinture Vitrifiée.
    Clermont-Ferrand, 1838.

    Considerations Historiques et Critiques sur les Vitraux Anciens et
    Modernes et sur la Peinture sur Verre.
    Clermont-Ferrand, and Paris, 1842.

    With DIDRON, Adolphe Napoléon
    Manufacture de Vitraux.
    Paris, 1850.

THOEMEL
    Die Glas-und Wandmalerei in der restaurirten Frauenkirche zu Grimma
    nach Zusammenhang und Bedeutung.
    Grimma, 1890.

THOMAS, Brian, and RICHARDSON, Eileen
    Directory of Master Glass-Painters.
    London, 1972.

THOMAS, J.
    Les Vitraux de Notre Dame de Dijon.
    Dijon, 1898.

THOMAS, J.M.L.
    The High Pavement Chapel, Nottingham; an Interpretation of the
    Chancel Window.
    Nottingham, 1904.

THOMAS, R.G.
    Stained Glass. Its Origin and Application.
    Privately printed, New York, 1922.

THOMAS, W.H.
    Window Making as an Art.
    Munsey's Magazine, vol. 26 (Dec., 1901), pp. 386-395.

    Coloured Glass Windows - the Supremacy of the Modern School.
    International Studio, vol. 29 (Aug., 1906), supplement, pp. xliv-l.

THOMAS, Walter Lloyd
    The Windows of Merchant Taylor's Hall.
    (With FRY, Sir Frederick Morris.)
    Privately printed, 1934.

THOMAS, William
    Antiquitates Prioratus Majoris Malverne.
    London, 1725.

THOMPSON, Bruce Logan
    Some Notes on Windermere Parish Church.
    Transactions of the Cumberland and Westmorland Antiquarian and
    Archaeological Society, new series, vol. 34 (1934).
    (On the glass, p. 32.)

THOMPSON, Harold J.
    Stained Glass - A Liturgical Art.
    Stained Glass, vol. 27, no. 10 (Oct., 1932), pp. 295-299.

THOMPSON, N.P.
    Huish Church. Excavation of the Original Foundations and an Early
    Chapel.
    (Report by NEWTON, P.A., on excavated fragments.)
    The Wiltshire Archaeological and Natural History Magazine, vol. 62,
    (1967), pp. 51-66.

THORMANN, Franz, and MÜLINEN, W.F. von
    Die Glasgemälde der Bernischen Kirchen. Mit Zeichnungen von R. Münger.
    Berne, 1896.

THORNE, W.T.
    Was Coloured Glass Made in Medieval England?
    Journal of the British Society of Master Glass Painters, two parts
    (1956), pp. 9-14, 108-116.

(Thornhill Church)
    Thornhill Church, Yorkshire: Stained Glass.
    (A grant towards the restoration.)
    The Pilgrim Trust, 42nd Annual Report (1972), p. 15.
    (Grant to restore some of the windows.)
    The Pilgrim Trust, 43rd Annual Report (1973), p. 15.

THORNTON, W.
    The Stained Glass of Some Cathedrals and Churches in Normandy.
    Reports of the Northampton Architectural Society, (1848), p. 48.

THORNTON, W. Pugin
    Descriptive and Illustrated Catalogue of Two Old Dutch Painted and
    Stained Windows, in the Royal Museum and Free Library at Canterbury.
    Canterbury, 1899.

(Thuringia)
    Thüringer Glasmaler und Glasschneider des 16-18 Jahrhunderts.
    Glas und Apparat, vol. 12, (1931), p. 207;
                    vol. 13, (1932), pp. 3, 20, 36.

TIBBS, Rodney
    King's College Chapel, Cambridge. The Story and the Renovation.
    Lavenham, 1970.
    (Glass, pp. 61-66.)

(Tiffany Glass)
    A Synopsis of the Exhibit of the Tiffany Glass and Decorating
    Company . . . at the World's Fair . . . Chicago, 1893. With an
    Appendix on Memorial Windows.
    New York, 1893.

    Memorial Windows.
    New York, 1896.

    A Partial List of Windows Designed and Executed by Tiffany Studios.
    New York, c. 1912.

    Memorials in Glass and Stone.
    Baltimore, 1913.

TIFFANY, L.C.

American Art Supreme in Coloured Glass.
Forum, vol. 15 (1893), p. 621.

The Art Work of Louis C. Tiffany.
New York, 1914.

TILLYER, J.

Stained Glass Superseded by the New Process of Vitremanie, for the
Decoration of Windows, etc.
London, c. 1877.

TOESCA, P.

Vetrate Dipinte Fiorentine.
Bollettino d'Arte, vol. 14 (1920).

Storia dell'arte Italiana.
Vol. 1, Turin, 1927.
Vol. 2, Il Trecento, Turin, 1951.

TOKE, N.E.

The Swiss Stained Windows in the Churches of Patrixbourne and Temple
Ewell.
Archaeologia Cantiana, vol. 44 (1932), pp. 229-252.

Stained Glass Windows at Stowting.
Archaeologia Cantiana, vol. 45 (1933), pp. 31-36.

Swiss Glass in Patrixbourne Church.
Archaeologia Cantiana, vol. 45 (1933), pp. 275-276.

Ancient Stained Glass in Bishopsbourne Church, Kent.
Reprinted from Archaeologia Cantiana, vol. 46 (1934), pp. 113-122.
J.M.G.P., vol. 6, no. 3 (Apr., 1936), pp. 112-120.

The Medieval Stained Glass Windows at Upper Hardres.
Archaeologia Cantiana, vol. 47 (1935), pp. 153-165.

Swiss Stained Glass at Temple Ewell.
Archaeologia Cantiana, vol. 51 (1939), pp. 1-8.

TOURNEUR, Abbé

Histoire et description des Vitraux et des Statues de l'Intérieur de
la Cathédrale de Reims.
Reims, 1857.

(Tours, Museum)

Un Vitrail de Bourdichon?
Bulletin de la Société Archéologique de Touraine (1949).
Quoted in Bulletin Monumental, vol. 109 (1951), p. 92.

TOWER, Walter E.

The Re-leading of Ancient Stained Glass.
(Letter to the Editor.)
J.M.G.P., vol. 1, no. 4 (Apr., 1926), pp. 53-54.

TOWNSEND, Horace

American and French Applied Art at the Grafton Galleries.
(Includes Tiffany stained glass.)
The Studio, vol. 17 (1899), pp. 39-44.

TRÄCHSEL, G.

Die Glasmalerei in Bern bis in die Mitte des 17 Jahrhunderts.
Festschrift zur Eröffnung des Kunstmuseums in Bern (1879), pp. 30-42.

Nikl. Manuel (Glasmaler).
Ibid., pp. 43-48.

Hans Jakob Dünz, der ältere Glasmaler, Radirer und Chorweibel.
Ibid., pp. 91-106.

(Travers, Martin)

BLACKHAM, R.J.
Martin Travers, Stained Glass Artist and Beautifier of Churches.
(Obituary.)
J.M.G.P., vol. 10, no. 2 (1949), pp. 106-107.

(Tréguier)

Window Dedicated to St. Ives.
(A modern window in Tréguier Cathedral, Brittany.)
Stained Glass, vol. 31, no. 2 (Autumn, 1936), pp. 48-49.

TREIB, E. Marc

Martin Lipofsky . . . Just Doing His Glass Thing.
Craft Horizons (Sept.-Oct., 1968).

Tremeirchion Church, (Flint)

Archaeologia Cambrensis, vol. 99 (1947), p. 337.

TRESS, Henry John

Periodic Bands in Ruby Glasses.
Journal of the Society of Glass Technology, vol. 38 (1954), pp. 35-37.

TRÉTAIGNE, Baronin de, and VINCENT

(Auction catalogue of collection.)
Auktion der Glasgemälde Sammlung der Baronin de Trétaigne in Paris,
und von Glasgemälden Vincent-Sammlung in Konstanz.
Zurich, 1904.

TREXELL, Margaret M.

New Craftsmen for an Old Art.
Manpower (Oct., 1969).

TRIDON, Abbé

Déscription Iconographique des Trois Principales Verrières de la
Chapelle d'Hervée à la Cathédrale de Troyes.
Troyes, 1849.

(Trier)

Windows in England Brought from Trier (Trèves) and other Places
Abroad.
Notes and Queries, series 10, vol. 12 (1909), pp. 109, 156, 198.

TRIGER, Robert

Les Vitraux des Cathédrales de Bourges et du Mans Postérieurs au
12e Siècle. Note sur un Recent Ouvrage de M. le Marquis Albert des
Meloizes.
Revue Historique et Archéologique de Maine, vol. 45 (1899), pp. 95-98.

(Trinity Windows)

Trinity Windows. By 'St. Swithin'.
(Reply to a request for their locations in England. York ones only
named.)
Notes and Queries, 9th series, vol. 3 (Apr. 15, 1899), p. 293.

Notes and Queries, 9th series, vol. 3 (1899), pp. 28, 187, 293.

TROCHE, N.M.

Vitraux de St. Germain l'Auxerrois à Paris.
Revue Archéologique, vol. 3 (1846-1847), p. 412.

TROLLOPE, Edward
Painted Glass.
(Suggested iconographical schemes.)
Reports and Papers of the Associated Architectural Societies, vol. 9
(1867-1868), pp. 41-56.

TRUMAN, Nevil
The Story of Holme-by-Newark Church and its Founder.
Gloucester and London, 1934.

The Care of Churches.
London, 1935.

Medieval Glass in Holme-by-Newark Church, Notts.
J.M.G.P., vol. 6, no. 1 (Apr., 1935), pp. 4-15.
        vol. 6, no. 2 (Oct., 1935), pp. 80-88.
        vol. 7, no. 1 (Oct., 1937), pp. 20-26.
        vol. 8, no. 3 (Apr., 1941), pp. 105-108.

Medieval Glass in Holme-by-Newark Church, Notts.
Transactions of the Thoroton Society, vol. 39 for 1935 (1936), pp. 92-
118.
Part 2, Ibid., vol. 43 for 1939 (1940), pp. 27-32.

(On glass from Annesley Church, Notts.)
Transactions of the Thoroton Society (1935).

Addlethorpe Church Painted Glass.
Reports and Papers of the Lincolnshire Architectural and
Archaeological Society, vol. 1, new series, part 1, for 1936 (1938),
pp. 23-24.

Ancient Glass in Nottinghamshire. A Survey.
J.M.G.P., vol. 9, no. 2 (1944), pp. 51-60.
        vol. 9, no. 3 (1945), pp. 78-79.
        vol. 9, no. 4 (1946), pp. 132-138.
        vol. 10, no. 2 (1949), pp. 78-80.
        vol. 11, no. 3 (1954), pp. 160-163.
        vol. 11, no. 4 (1955), pp. 206-212.
        vol. 12, no. 1 (1956), pp. 30-35.
        vol. 12, no. 2 (1957), pp. 137-139.

Ancient Glass in Nottinghamshire.
(Reprinted from J.M.G.P.)
Part 1, Transactions of the Thoroton Society, vol. 51 for 1947 (1948),
pp. 50-65.
Part 2, Ibid., vol. 52 for 1948 (1949), pp. 58-68.

(Truman, Nevil)
Obituary.
J.M.G.P., vol. 10, no. 3 (1950), pp. 159-160.
(Reprinted from Nottingham Journal, Apr. 7, 1949).

TRUMAN, Nevil
An Important Discovery at Croxton, Lincs.
Lincolnshire Architectural and Archaeological Society Reports and
Papers.
Reprinted in J.M.G.P., vol. 11, no. 2 (1953), pp. 92-93.

TSCHISCHKA (or ZISKA), Franz
Die Metropolitankirche zu St. Stephan in Wien, mit einer Ansicht
und einem Grundrisse.
Vienna, 1823.

Der St. Stephansdom in Wien und seine alten Denkmale.
8 vols., Vienna, 1832.

TUCCI, Douglas Shand
Ralph Adams Cram, American Medievalist.
Boston, 1975.

(Tunstall Church)
(Sixteenth century glass in East window.)
Transactions of the Cumberland and Westmorland Antiquarian and
Archaeological Society, new series, vol. 5 (1905), p. 280.

(Turkish Stained Glass)
L'Architecture Ottomane.
Constantinople. 1873.

(Contemporary.)
News and Notes, J.M.G.P., vol. 10, no. 3 (1950), pp. 113-114.

TURPIN, Pierre
An Eighteenth Century Artist in Stained Glass.
(Who transferred glass from Selling to Upper Hardres and signed it
in an imitation Lombardic inscription.)
Notes and Queries, 11th series, vol. 12 (Nov. 13, 1915), p. 379.
        12th series, vol. 1 (Feb. 26, 1916), p. 174.
            vol. 2 (Nov. 4, 1916), pp. 374-375.

Representations of the Blessed Trinity.
Notes and Queries, 12th series, vol. 3 (March 24, 1917), pp. 231-232.

Ancient Glass in England - Note 1. An English Fifteenth Century
Roundel.
Burlington Magazine, vol. 30 (Jan.-June, 1917), pp. 214-218.

TWINING, E.W.
The Art and Craft of Stained Glass.
London, 1928.
Reviewed by EDEN, F.S., The Connoisseur, vol. 82 (Sept.-Dec., 1928).

(Twining, Ernest Walter)
Obituary.
J.M.G.P., vol. 12, no. 2 (1957), p. 153.

(Twycross Church, Leicestershire)
(Proposal to return the thirteenth century French glass to France.)
News and Notes, J.M.G.P., vol. 10, no. 2 (1949), p. 60.

(Tyrolean Glass)
Die Tiroler Glasmalerei - Anstalt in Innsbruck.
Die Glashütte, vol. 4 (1874), nos 48, 50.

Die Tiroler Glasmalerei 1875.
Die Glashütte, vol. 5 (1875), pp. 397-401.

Die Tiroler Glasmalerei 1886-1893.
Innsbruck, 1894.

UNDERWOOD, H.J.

    The Church of St. Mary the Virgin at Littlemore, Oxfordshire.
    Oxford, 1845.

(United States of America)

    Stained Glass Association of America.
    24th Annual Meeting at Pittsburgh.
    National Glass Budget, Pittsburgh (June 27, 1925).

    Where to See Windows of Representative Craftsmen in the United States.
    Liturgical Arts, vol. 6, 2nd quarter (1937).

    Stained Glass in the United States.
    (A listing, with descriptions.)
    Stained Glass, vol. 44, no. 2 (Summer, 1949), pp. 47-51.
               vol. 44, no. 3 (Autumn, 1949), pp. 84-88.
               vol. 44, no. 4 (Winter, 1949), pp. 114-120.
               vol. 45, no. 1 (Spring, 1950), pp. 17-26.
               vol. 45, no. 2 (Summer, 1950), pp. 70-75.
               vol. 45, no. 3 (Autumn, 1950), pp. 112-118.
               vol. 45, no. 4 (Winter, 1950-1951), pp. 169-171.
               vol. 46, no. 3 (Autumn, 1951), pp. 107-111.
               vol. 47, no. 1 (Spring, 1952), pp. 24-28.
               vol. 47, no. 3 (Autumn, 1952), pp. 107-110.
               vol. 48, no. 2 (Summer, 1953), pp. 89-96.
               vol. 48, no. 4 (Winter, 1953-1954), pp. 143-150.

UNWIN, Max

    A Treatment for the Preservation of Glass.
    Museums Journal, vol. 51 (1951), p. 10.

(Upwell Church, Cambs.)

    (Handley and Oldfield window inserted.)
    The Gentleman's Magazine, vol. 12, new series, part 2 (1839), p. 400.

URSEAU, Charles

    Les Vitraux de la Renaissance en Anjou.
    Réunion des Sociétés des Beaux-Arts des Départements (1905), pp. 700-703.

    Quelques Détails de la Rose du Croisillon Nord de la Cathédrale d'Angers.
    Réunion des Sociétés des Beaux-Arts des Départements, vol. 36 (1912), pp. 3-9.

    La Cathédrale d'Angers.
    Paris, 1929.

    Un vitrail Angevin du XVIe siecle, La crucifixion de Soulaire.

    Bulletin Monumental, vol. 95 (1936), pp. 223-231.

    Hugues de Chamblancé et les Vitraux de la Nef de la Cathédrale d'Angers.
    Bulletin Monumental, vol. 96 (1937), pp. 327-333.

USHER, Henry

    Glass Painting.
    Reports and Papers of the Associated Architectural Societies, vol. 11 (1871-1872), pp. 57-67.

USTERI, Johann Martin (Collection)

    Ausstellung von Glas-Gemälden aus dem Nachlass des Dichters J.M. Usteri.
    Zurich, 1894.

UYTLEGGINE, V.D.

    Wijd-Beroemde en Vermaerde Glasen Binnen se St. Jans Kerk tut Gouda.
    Gouda, 1699.

VAIL, R.W.G.

'Storied Windows Richly Dight'.
(A study of the lives and works of Evert and Gerritt Duyckinck,
seventeenth century glass-painters in New York.)
New York Historical Society Quarterly, vol. 36, no. 2 (Apr., 1952),

VAIVRE, Jean-Bernard de

Les Armoires de Pierre de Mortain.
Bulletin Monumental, no. 131 (1973), pp. 30-40.
Erratum et addendum (to the above).
Ibid., pp. 161-162.

VALLANCE, Aymer

Church Furnishing and Decoration.
Arts Journal (1890), p. 267.

The Decorative Art of Sir Edward Burne-Jones, Bart.
Easter Art Annual of the Art Journal (1900), pp. 1-16.

British Stained Glass.
The Studio Year Book of Decorative Art (1908),

Sir Edward Burne-Jones' Designs for Painted Glass.
The Studio, vol. 51 (1911), pp. 91-103.

Some Flemish Painted Glass Panels.
Burlington Magazine, vol. 19 (Apr.-Sept., 1911), pp. 189-192.

German Painted Glass.
Burlington Magazine, vol. 29 (Apr.-Dec., 1916), pp. 12-15.
(Review of SCHMITZ, H., Die Glasgemälde des Königlichen
Kunstgewerbemuseums . . .)

An Exhibition of Glass-Paintings.
(The Grosvenor Thomas collection.)
Burlington Magazine, vol. 33 (July-Dec., 1918), pp. 65-73.

The Costessey Collection of Glass.
Burlington Magazine, vol. 35 (July-Dec., 1919), pp. 26-31.
Reprinted as:
Introduction to DRAKE, Maurice, The Costessey Collection of
Stained Glass.
Exeter, 1920.

VALLERY-RADOT, Jean

L'Eglise de la Trinité de Fecamp.
Paris, 1928.

VASSELOT, M. de

Histoire du Portrait en France.
Paris, 1880.
(Stained glass, pp. 67-80.)

VELGE, Henri

La Collégiale des Saints Michel et Gudule à Bruxelles.
Brussels, 1926.

(Vence)

"One Man's Meat . . ."
(On the Matisse windows at Vence.)
Stained Glass, vol. 46, no. 4 (Winter, 1951-1952).

(On Matisse's work at Vence.)
Vogue (Dec., 1951).

(Ventnor, Chest Hospital)

Reynolds-Stephen out of Hospital.
(Glass of the Morris school and by Reynolds-Stephen removed from Ventnor
Chest hospital. Offered to St. Lawrence's Church.)
J.M.G.P., vol. 14, no. 4 (1968-1969), pp. 204-206.

(Ventnor, St. Lawrence)

Ventnor (St. Lawrence) Church, Isle of Wight: Glass.
(Grant towards installing Morris and Morris-influenced glass from
the demolished Chest Hospital in the Church.)
The Pilgrim Trust, 42nd Annual Report (1972), p. 16.

VENTURI, Lionello

Georges Rouault.
New York, 1940.

VERDIER, Phillippe

La Verrière de Saint Vincent à Saint-Germain-des-Prés.
Mémoires Publiées par la Fédération des Sociétés Historiques et
Archéologiques de Paris et de l'Ile-de-France, vol. 9 (1957-1958),
pp. 69-87.

(Fragments from Soissons in the Corcoran Gallery.)
The Corcoran Gallery of Art Bulletin, vol. 10 (Nov., 1958).

The Window of Saint Vincent from the Refectory of the Abbey of
Saint-Germain-des-Prés, 1239-1244.
Journal of the Walters Art Gallery, vols. 25-26 (1962-1963), pp. 38-99.

Témoignages Artistiques des Mariages Franco-Anglais au début du
14e Siècle.
Bulletin Monumental, no. 131 (1973), pp. 137-145.

La Restauration des Vitraux Anciens.
Revue de l'Art, no. 31 (1976), pp. 5-8.

The Medieval Collection of the Montreal Museum of Fine Arts: Stained
Glass from the Lady Chapel, Abbey of St. Germain-des-Prés.
Apollo, no. 171 (1976), pp. 363-364.

VERHAEGEN, Arthur

Vitraux Anciens à l'Eglise de Notre-Dame de Hal.
Bulletin de la Quatorzième Réunion du Gilde de Saint-Thomas et de
Saint-Luc, fasc. 1, Lille-Bruges (1881).

L'Art de la Peinture sur Verre au Moyen Age.
Revue de l'Art Chrétien (1886), pp. 297, 437.

VERNEUIL, M.P.

Les Vitraux de Grasset.
Art et Décoration, vol. 12 (1908), pp. 109-124.

VERRIER, Jean

La Cathédrale de Bourges et ses Vitraux.
Paris, 1942.

Les Vitraux du 12e et du 13e Siècles.
Paris, 1948 (preface).

Panneaux Découverts à la Bonneville-Appetot (Eure).
Bulletin de la Société Nationale des Antiquaires de France (1957),
pp. 74-75.

Le Vitrail Français.
With AUBERT, M., CHASTEL, A., GRODECKI, L., GRUBER, J.-J., LAFOND, J.,
MATHEY, F., TARALON, J.
Paris, 1958.
Reviewed by SALET, Francis, Bulletin Monumental, no. 116 (1958), p. 226.

VERRIER, Jean (Contd.)

Note sur les Vitraux de l'Eglise de la Madeleine de Verneuil.
Nouvelles de l'Eure, no. 12 (1962), pp. 24-29.

(Verrier, Jean)

Obituary. By SALET, Francis.
Bulletin Monumental, vol. 122 (1964), pp. 69-72.

VERRIERES, Georges de

Vitraux de Rouen.
Revue Française de l'Elite, 2nd year, no. 8, Paris (May 25, 1948).

VERRIEST, Léo

Un Vitrail de la Chapelle de Saint Pancrace au Château d'Ath.
Annales du Cercle Royal d'Archéologie d'Ath, vol. 24 (1938), pp. 313, 316.

VEUCLIN, E.

Quelques Mots sur les Vitraux Anciens de l'Eglise Paroisale d'Orbec (Calvados).
Orbec, 1878.

Peintres Verriers et Autres Artistes Habitant la Ville de Dreux au 16e Siècle.
Société des Beaux-Arts des Départements, de 5 au 9 Juin 1900, pp. 139-144.

VICART, Abbé

Mémoires sur les Verrières du Choeur de l'Eglise de Nôtre-Dame-la-Riche de Tours.
Mémoires de la Société Archéologique de Touraine, t. 2 (1845), pp. 148-177.

(Victoria and Albert Museum)

Catalogue of the Exhibition of Stained Glass etc. by British Artists.
London, 1864.

A First List of Examples of Stained and Painted Glass in the United Kingdom Previous to 1820.
London, 1875.

List of Books and Pamphlets in the National Art Library of the South Kensington Museum, Illustrating Glass.
London, 1887.

(Pierpont Morgan gift.)
Collection of Stained Glass.
The Athenaeum, vol. 5 (1919), p. 563.

(Loans of stained glass, including panels from the Costessey collection.)
The Times, March 29, 1920.

(Acquisition of four panels from the Engel-Gros collection.)
The Times, Feb. 27, 1923.

(Acquisition of a panel of thirteenth century glass.)
The Times, Aug. 25, 1924.

(Two panels of Swiss glass stolen.)
The Times, Sept. 2. 1926.
(Returned.)
The Times, Sept. 3, 1926.

Review of the Principle Acquisitions During the Year 1927.
London, 1928, pp. 30-33.

Drawings of Ancient Stained Glass.
(By EDEN, F.S., and SAINT, Lawrence B., exhibited at the Victoria and Albert Museum.)
The Connoisseur, vol. 84 (July-Dec., 1929), p. 60.

(Victoria and Albert Museum, Contd.)

Review of the Principal Acquisitions During the Year 1929.
London, 1930, pp. 24-26, 32-34, 44.

(Two fourteenth-century Austrian panels purchased.)
The Times, May 29, 1930.

Catalogue of an Exhibition in Celebration of the Centenary of William Morris.
London, 1934.

Annual Review.
Swiss and Other Glass Paintings, pp. 16-17 (1934).

Exhibition of Drawings of Stained Glass at the Victoria and Albert Museum, South Kensington.
J.M.G.P., vol. 6, no. 4 (Apr., 1937), pp. 197-198.

A Panel of Painted Glass with the Arms of the D'Avenches Family in the Victoria and Albert Museum.
Illustrated London News (Sept. 18, 1937).

Catalogue of an Exhibition of Victorian and Edwardian Decorative Arts.
London, 1952.

Victorian Church Art Exhibition (Nov., 1971-Jan., 1972). Catalogue.
London, 1971.

(Purchase of the Betley Hall Window.)
J.M.G.P., vol. 16, no. 1 (1976-1977), p. 10.

VIEGEN, Joseph

Balans der moderne Limburgse wand-en glasschilderkunst.
Maastricht, 1955.

VIEIL, Pierre Le

L'Art de la Peinture sur Verre et de la Vitrererie.
Paris, 1774.
German version translated by HARREPETER, J.C., Die Kunst auf Glas . . .
Nuremberg 1779, 1780.

(Vienna, K.K. Oesterreichisches Museum)

K.K. Oesterreichisches Museum fur Kunst und Industrie, Bibliothek. Katalog 12. Glas-fabrikation und Glasmalerei.
Vienna, 1904.

(Vigeland, Emmanuel)

Emmanuel Vigeland.
Paris, 1925.

Obituary. By POLAK, Ada.
J.M.G.P., vol. 10. no. 3 (1950), pp. 160-162.

VIGNÉ, M.

Peinture sur Verre. Considérations Critiques sur cet Art . . .
Paris, 1840.

VIGURS, E.B.

(Sale catalogue of collection.)
A Catalogue of the Highly Valuable and Interesting Collection of the Late E.B. Vigurs, Esq., Comprising Ancient Stained Glass of Rare Beauty, Principally from the Archiepiscopal Palace of Lambeth.
London, 1849.

VILLARD DE HONNECOURT

Sketchbook.
Edited by BOWIE, Theodore.
New York, 1962.

(Tattershall Church)

De Lisle and Dudley MS.
Historical Manuscripts Commission Report, no. 77, vol. 1.
Edited by KINGSFORD, C.L.
London, 1925.

(Tavern Glass-Paintings)

Ueber das Fensterbier.
Zeitschrift für alte und neue Glasmalerei (1912), p. 73.

TARBOX, John E.

A Retrospect: Christopher W. Whall.
Stained Glass, vol. 28, no. 3 (Autumn, 1933), pp. 143-146.

TAYLOR, Arthur

Notes on the Stained Glass at West Wickham, Kent.
Transactions of the St. Paul's Ecclesiological Society, vol. 2
(1886-1890), p. xxxvii.

Mediaeval Stained Glass.
Transactions of the St. Paul's Ecclesiological Society, vol. 2
(1886-1890), pp. 43-46.

TAIT, C.J.

Glass Windows at Doddiscombsleigh.
Notes and Gleanings, vol. 2 (Nov. 15, 1889), pp. 167-169, 192.

TANSEY, Anne

An American "Mediaeval Artist".
(About Thomas Murphy.)
The Messenger of the Sacred Heart (New York), (Dec., 1947).

TARALON, Jean

With AUBERT, M., CHASTEL, A., GRODECKI, L., GRUBER, J.-J.,
LAFOND, J., VERRIER, J.
Le Vitrail Français.
Paris, 1958.
Reviewed by SALET, Francis, Bulletin Monumental, no. 116 (1958), p. 226.

Le Colloque International d'Erfurt et le sauvegarde des Vitraux Anciens.
Les Monuments Historiques de la France (1962), pp. 231-246.

Problèmes de la Technique et de la Restauration.
(A summary of a discussion between FRODL-KRAFT, Eva, TARALON, Jean,
FRENZEL, Gottfried, KING, Dennis.)
Bulletin du Comité International d'Histoire de l'Art (Jan.-June, 1969),
p. 8.

Programme de Recherches sur la Composition des Vitraux et les
Maladies des Verres.
In 7e Colloque du Corpus Vitrearum Medii Aevi.
Florence ?, 1970, pp. 43-46.

Problématique de la Conservation et de la Restauration des Vitraux.
In Les Monuments Historiques de la France, no. 1, Les Vitraux.
Paris, 1977, pp. 2-6, 97-100.

TAYLOR, E.S.

Notices of the Church of Martham, Norfolk, Previous to its
Restoration in 1856.
Norfolk Archaeology, vol. 5 (1859), pp. 168-179.

TAYLOR, J.G.

Our Lady of Battersea.
Chelsea, 1926.

TAYLOR, Jane

A Light on Our Darkness.
(The Gabriel Loire windows at Salisbury Cathedral.)
The Observer, colour supplement, June 8, 1980, pp. 47-48.

TAYLOR, Tom

The Fairford Windows.
(Letter to the Editor, agreeing with HOLT, H.F.)
The Times, Aug. 15, 1868.

The Fairford Windows.
(Letter to the Editor.)
The Times, Aug. 19, 1868.

Albert Dürer and the Fairford Windows.
The Gentleman's Magazine, (Oct., 1868).

The Fairford Windows.
The Builder, vol. 26 (Nov. 7, 1868), p. 845.

Test to Distinguish Ancient Glass From Modern.
(Letter to the Editor from MAUDSON, F.G., and editorial reply.)
J.M.G.P., vol. 1, no. 3 (Oct., 1925), pp. 50-51.
(Letter to the Editor from BELL C.J.)
J.M.G.P., vol. 1, no. 4 (Apr., 1926), p. 52.

TETTAU, W.J. von

Beschreibende Darstellung der älteren Bau-und Kunstdenkmaler der
Stadt Erfurt und des Erfurter Landkreises.
Halle, 1890.

(Tewkesbury)

The Glass of Tewkesbury Abbey Completely Restored.
The Sphere (Apr. 11, 1925).

TEXIER, Jacques R.A.

Histoire de la Peinture sur Verre en Limousin.
Paris, 1847.

Origine de la Peinture sur Verre.
Annales Archéologiques, vol. 10 (1850), pp. 81-89.

(Theft of Stained Glass)

(Widespread thieving in the U.S.A.)
Editorial, Stained Glass, vol. 70, no. 2 (Summer, 1975), pp. 61-62.
(More on the subject.)
Stained Glass, vol. 70, nos. 3 and 4 (Fall and Winter, 1975), p. 130.

THÉOLES, Henri

Le Vitrail de Saint-Anne d'Aptetle Retour de la Papauté d'Avignon à
Rome, 1365.
Avignon, 1924.

THEOPHILUS

De Diuersibus Artibus.
Edited and translated by DODWELL, C.R.
London, 1961.
Translated by HAWTHORNE, J.G., and SMITH, C.S., Chicago. (This
contains a full bibliography of Theophilus.)

VILLASEÑOR, Enrique

    Stained Glass in Mexico.

    Stained Glass, vol. 32, no. 2 (Autumn, 1937), pp. 39-46.

VILLETTE, J.

    Les Vitraux de Chartres.

    Paris, 1964.

VINCENT, C., and P.N. (Collection)

    Catalog der reichhaltigen Glasgemälde und Kunstsammlung der Herrn

    C. u. P.N. Vincent im Capitelsaal in Constanz.

    Constance, 1890.

VINCENT, W.T.

    The Historical Windows in Woolwich Town Hall.

    Transactions of the Woolwich Antiquarian Society, vol. 11 (1905), pp.

    39-62.

VIOLLET-LE-DUC, E.E.

    Description du Chateau de Coucy.

    Paris, n.d.

    With GUILHERMY, R.F.M.N.

    Description de Nôtre-Dame, Cathédrale de Paris.

    Paris, 1856.

    Dictionnaire Raisonné de l'Architecture Française du 11e au 16e Siècle.

    Tome 9, Paris, 1868.

    (Article Vitrail, pp. 373-462.)

    Vitrail.

    Architectural Receuil, vol. 32 (1912), pp. 487-495.

    On the Employment of Couverte on the Windows of Chartres Cathedral.

    J.M.G.P., vol. 5, no. 1 (Apr., 1933), pp. 35-36.

    Reprinted from Mémoires de la Société Archéologique d'Eure et Loire

    (1909), pp. 459-462.

    Vitrail.

    (Translated by HOLLAND, Leicester B.)

    J.M.G.P., vol. 7, no. 1 (Oct., 1937), pp. 29-44.

                no. 2 (Apr., 1938), pp. 80-96.

                no. 3 (Oct., 1938), pp. 139-145.

                no. 4 (Apr., 1939), pp. 169-181.

        vol. 8, no. 1 (Oct., 1939), pp. 5-14.

        vol. 9, no. 3 (1945), pp. 87-92.

        vol. 9, no. 4 (1946), pp. 118-126.

        vol. 10, no. 1 (1948), pp. 36-43.

                 no. 2 (1949), pp. 83-90.

    Vitrail.

    Translated by SMITH, F.P.

    Mediaeval Stained Glass.

    Atlanta, Georgia, 1942.

VISCHER-MERIAN, K.

    Die Glasgemälde in Meiringen und deren Stifter H. Immer von Gilgenberg.

    Beiträge zur vaterländischen Geschichte (Basel), (1887).

Le Vitrail Français.

    Paris, 1958.

    Contributions by AUBERT, M., CHASTEL, A., GRODECKI, L., GRUBER, J.-J.,

    LAFOND, J., MATHEY, F., TARALON, J., VERRIER, J.

    Reviewed by H.H., The Connoisseur, vol. 144 (Dec., 1959), p. 257.

VIVIAN-NEAL, A.W.

    Heraldic Stained Glass at Pitminster.

    Proceedings of the Somersetshire Archaeological and Natural History

    Society, vol. 77 for 1931, part 2 (1932), p. 141.

VIZTELLY, H.

    A History of Champagne. Illustrated by woodcuts.

    London, 1882.

    (Evreux Cathedral, p. 23.)

VOEGLIN, S.

    Die Glasgemälde aus der Stiftsprobstei, der Chorherrenställe und aus dem

    Pfarrhause zu Grossmünster.

    Zurich, 1882.

VOGL, Eduard

    Das Zwei-Plattensystem in der amerikanischen Glasmalerei.

    Diamant, vol. 29 (1907), p. 39.

VOISIN, Auguste

    Notre-Dame du Mans ou Cathédrale de Saint-Julien. Origine, Histoire

    et Description.

    Paris, 1866.

VOISIN Charles Joseph

    Vitraux Légendaires de la Cathédrale de Tournai.

    Paris, 1871, 2nd edition.

    Vitraux de la Chapelle Saint Vincent. Oeuvres Posthumes de

    Monseignor le Vicaire Général Voisin.

    Tournai, 1877.

VOLCKERT, Daniel

    Ausführungen über Technik der Glasmalerei.

    Augsburg, 1758.

VOLLANT, J.

    L'Eglise de Saint-Germain-Lès-Corbeil.

    Paris, 1897.

VORBRUGG, F.

    Fenster-Dekoration.

    Diamant, vol. 29 (1907), p. 657.

VOYSEY, C.F. Annesley

    Stained Glass.

    (Letter to the Editor.)

    The Builder, vol. 136, no. 4491 (March 1, 1929), p. 413.

    Review of PEATLING, A.V., Ancient Stained and Painted Glass in the

    Churches of Surrey.

    J.M.G.P., vol. 4, no. 4 (Oct., 1932), pp. 203-204.

WACKERNAGEL, Wilhelm
    Die Deutsche Glasmalerei. Geschichtlicher Entwurf mit Belegen.
    Leipzig, 1855.

WAERN, Cecilia
    John La Farge, Artist and Writer.
    London, 1896.

    The Industrial Arts of America. II: The Tiffany or Favrile Glass.
    International Studio, vol. 5 (1898), pp. 16-21.

(Wailes, William)
    (Brief account of life.)
    News and Notes, J.M.G.P., vol. 12, no. 3 (1958), pp. 175-176.

WALKER, Ben
    Jesse Windows.
    Notes and Queries, 8th series, vol. 8 (Aug. 17, 1895), p. 133.

(Walker, Leonard)
    Stained Glass for Lahore.
    (By Leonard Walker.)
    The Connoisseur, vol. 59 (Jan.-Apr., 1921), p. 123.

    The Renascence of Stained Glass. By Criticus.
    (On Leonard Walker.)
    The Connoisseur, vol. 63 (May-Aug., 1922), pp. 164-167.

    Stained Glass at Singapore.
    (By Leonard Walker.)
    The Connoisseur, vol. 69 (May-Aug., 1924), p. 117.

WALKER, Leonard
    Some Personal Views on Stained Glass.
    The Builder (Sept. 4, 1925).

(Walker, Leonard)
    The Future of Stained Glass. Mr. Leonard Walker and His Art.
    The Curwen Press, n.d.

    Obituary.
    J.M.G.P., vol. 14, no. 2 (1965), pp. 112-113.

WALLACE-DUNLOP, M.A.
    Glass in the Old World.
    London, 1882.

WALLER, F.S.
    Notes on Old Glass in the Cathedral, Gloucester.
    Rec. Gloucester Cathedral, vol. 2 (1883-1884), pp. 76-78.

WALLER, J.G.
    Painted or Stained Glass from West Wickham Church, Kent; Traced and
    Drawn by J.G. Waller.
    Weale's Quarterly Papers on Architecture, vol. 2 (1844).

    On Ancient Painted Glass in Morley Church.
    Journal of the British Archaeological Association, vol. 8 (1852),
    pp. 28-34.

    The Fairford Windows.
    The Builder, vol. 26 (Oct. 17, 1868), pp. 763-764.
    (Refuted in a letter by B.A.A., who supports HOLT.)
    Ibid., (Oct. 24, 1868), pp. 788-789.
    (WALLER refutes B.A.A.)
    Ibid., (Oct. 31, 1868), p. 806.

WALLER, J.G. (Contd.)
    The Inquiry as to the Fairford Windows.
    Ibid. (Nov. 28, 1868), pp. 879-880.

    Mediaeval Art and the Fairford Windows.
    The Archaeological Journal, vol. 25 (1868), pp. 192-206.

    On Tracings Made Previous to Restoration of some Figures in Painted
    Glass in West Wickham Church, Kent.
    Proceedings of the Society of Antiquaries, 2nd series, vol. 15 (1873),
    pp. 92-96.

(Walpole, Horace)
    DALLAWAY, James; Walpole's Anecdotes of Painting . . . with
    considerable additions by the Rev. J. Dallaway.
    vol. 2, p. 1826.
    Reviewed in The Gentleman's Magazine, vol. 97, part 1 (1827).
    (Stained Glass, pp. 42-43.)

    (Horace Walpole Collection.)
    (Glass sold.)
    The Gentleman's Magazine, vol. 18, new series, part 2 (1842), pp. 603-
    604.

WALPOLE, Horace
    (Sale catalogue of collection.)
    Catalogue of Rare Prints and Illustrated Works Removed from Strawberry
    Hill. To be Sold by Auction. 13th June, 1842. Collected by H. Walpole.
    London, 1842.

WALTER, Joseph
    La Cathédrale de Strasbourg.
    Paris, 1933.

WALTERS, Henry Alburt
    The Significance of Symbolism in Stained Glass.
    Stained Glass, vol. 37, no. 2 (Summer, 1942), pp. 82-85.

WARD, C.A.
    Jesse Window.
    Notes and Queries, 8th series, vol. 8 (July 27, 1895), p. 75.

(Warham, St. Mary's Church)
    St. Mary's Church, Warham, Norfolk: Glass.
    (Grant to cover the restoration and rearrangement of the glass.)
    The Pilgrim Trust, 30th Annual Report (1960), pp. 15-16.

WARING, J.B.
    Arts Connected with Architecture, Illustrated by Examples in Central
    Italy from the Thirteenth to the Fifteenth Century.
    London, 1858.

    Examples of Stained Glass, Fresco Ornament . . . Drawn on Stone and
    Printed in Colours by Vincent Brooks.
    London, 1858.

    Masterpieces of Industrial Art and Sculpture at the International
    Exhibition, 1862 . . .
    3 vols., London, 1863.

    Catalogue of Drawings from Ancient Glass Paintings by the Late Charles
    Winston.
    London, 1865.

    A Record of My Artistic Life.
    London, 1873.

WARNECKE, Fr.

Musterblätter für Künstler und Kunstgewerbtreibende, insbesondere für Glasmaler.
2nd edition, with supplement, Berlin, 1880, 1887.

WARNER, Stephen A.

Lincoln College, Oxford.
London, 1908.
(Glass, pp. 56-59.)

Canterbury Cathedral.
London, 1923.

WARNER, Thomas H.

Stained Glass Windows in Churches.
Church Management (Jan., 1938).

WARREN, H.J.

Fifty-four Years of Glass Craft.
J.M.G.P., vol. 13, no. 4 (1963), pp. 562-564.

WARRINGTON, R.W.

The Italian Annunciation in the Victoria and Albert Museum.
(Letter to the Editor.)
J.M.G.P., vol. 1, no. 2 (Apr., 1925), pp. 54-55.

WARRINGTON, William

The Painted Glass Window in St. James', Piccadilly.
(Letter to the Editor.)
The Builder, no. 181 (July 25, 1846),
Reviewed in The Ecclesiologist, vol. 6 (1846), pp. 104-105.
Replied to by WARRINGTON, The Ecclesiologist, vol. 7 (1847), pp. 38-39.

The History of Stained Glass from the Earliest Period of the Art to the Present Time.
London, 1848.
Noticed in The Archaeological Journal, vol. 6 (1849), pp. 424-434.
Reviewed in Chapters on Stained Glass - no. 2, Warrington and Winston.
The Ecclesiologist, vol. 10 (1850), pp. 81-97.
Replied to by WARRINGTON, Ibid., pp. 251-252.

(Wartime removal of glass in England)
In News and Notes, J.M.G.P., vol. 8, no. 3 (Apr., 1941), pp. 87-88.

(War Damage Commission)
(On the payment by the Commission to replace windows and the amount of replacement desirable.)
News and Notes, J.M.G.P., vol. 9, no. 4 (1946).

WARTMANN, W.

Les Vitraux Suisses au Musée du Louvre. Catalogue Critiqué et Raisonné.
Paris, 1908.

WARTON, T.

Verses on Sir Joshua Reynolds' Painted Window at New College, Oxford.
London, 1782.

(Warwickshire)
Notices of the Churches of Warwickshire.
Warwick, 1847.

(Warwick, Beauchamp Chapel)
(Stained glass in the Beauchamp Chapel.)
Antiquarian and Architectural Year Book for 1844.
London, 1845, pp. 318-322.

(Washington D.C., St. John's Church)
St. John's Church Committee on Stained Glass Windows. Report . . . made to the Vestry, Oct. 16, 1883.
New York, 1883.

Subjects of the Stained Glass Windows in St. John's Church, Washington.
London, privately printed, 1885.

(Washington D.C., Cathedral)
A Guide to Washington Cathedral.
Washington D.C., 1947.
(Glass, pp. 50-61.)

Four New Windows in Washington Cathedral.
Cathedral Age (Summer, 1949).

WATKINS, Alfred

The Strange Story of Wisteston Chapel.
(Glass at Wisteston Court.)
Transactions of the Woolhope Naturalists' Field Club, for 1914, 1915, 1916, 1917, vol. 22 (1918).
Glass, p. 26.

WATKINSON, Ray

William Morris as Designer.
New York, 1968.

WATSON, Arthur

The Early Iconography of the Tree of Jesse.
Oxford, 1934.
Reviewed by B.S.T., The Connoisseur, vol. 95 (Feb., 1935), pp. 111-112.

WATTS, Harvey Maitland

William Willet, 1869-1921.
Stained Glass, vol. 29, no. 3 (Autumn, 1934), pp. 62-65.

WAY. Albert

The Legend of Saint Werstan.
(In the glass at Great Malvern.)
The Archaeological Journal, vol. 2 (1846), pp. 48-65.

Stained Glass at Königsfelden, Switzerland.
The Archaeological Journal, vol. 16 (1859), pp. 339-342.

(The S.S. collar in glass at Thun, Switzerland.)
The Archaeological Journal, vol. 16 (1859), pp. 359-361.

WAYMENT, Hilary G.

The Windows of King's College Chapel and their Relation to French Art.
Actes du 19ᵉ Congrès International d'Histoire de l'Art, (Paris), (8-13 Sept., 1958), pp. 298-304.

Un Chef-d'oeuvre Anglo-Flamand de la Première Renaissance. Les Vitraux de King's College, Cambridge.
Bulletin des Musées Royaux d'Art et d'Histoire, 4th series, (1958), pp. 83-101.

The Use of Engravings in the Design of the Renaissance Windows of King's College Chapel, Cambridge.
Burlington Magazine, vol. 100 (Jan.-Dec., 1958), pp. 378-388.

WAYMENT, Hilary G. (Contd.)

A Rediscovered Master: Adrian van den Houte (c. 1459-1521) and the
Malines/Brussels School.
Oud Holland, vol. 82 (1967), pp. 172-
                vol. 83 (1968), pp. 71-
                vol. 84 (1969), pp. 257-

Bernard Van Orley and Malines: The Dido and Aeneas Tapestries at
Hampton Court.
The Antiquaries Journal, vol. 49 (1969), pp. 367-376.

The Windows of King's College Chapel, Cambridge.
In 7ᵉ Colloque du Corpus Vitrearum Medii Aevi.
Florence ?, 1970, pp. 38-39.

The Windows of King's College Chapel, Cambridge. A Description and
Commentary.
C.V.M.A., Great Britain, supplementary volume 1.
London, 1972.
Reviewed by PERROT, F., Bulletin Monumental, no. 134 (1976), pp. 161-163.

The Stained Glass in the Chapel of the Vyne.
National Trust Studies 1980.
London, 1979, pp. 35-47.

WAYNE, C.S.

Stained Glass.
Potter's American Monthly, vol. 8 (1876), p. 331.

(Wealden Glass)

Visits to the Sites of Old Wealden Glasshouses.
Journal of the Society of Glass Technology, vol. 16, no. 63 (Sept.,
1932), pp. 74-76.

WEALE, John (editor)

Divers Works of Early Masters in Christian Decoration.
2 vols, London, 1846.
(Glass from York, West Wickham, St. George's Chapel, Limbourg, Gouda,
Liège.)

Portfolio, or Selection of Designs of Art, etc.
London, 1858-1859.
(York and Gouda windows.)

WEALE, W.H.J.

Flemish Stained Glass in England.
(Appeal for information to compile a list.)
Notes and Queries, 3rd series, vol. 6 (Dec. 10, 1864), p. 472.
Reply from 'EIRIONNACH' referring to glass at Worsley, nr. Manchester.
Ibid., (Dec. 31, 1864), p. 541.
Reply from   referring to glass in Rugby Chapel.
Ibid., vol. 7 (Feb. 25, 1865), pp. 165-166.
Reply from MACRAY, J., referring to Fairford, inter alia.
Ibid., vol. 7 (Apr.8, 1865), p. 291.

Pierre de Dappere, Peintre-Verrier, 1513-1546.
Le Beffroi, Bruges, III (1866-1870), pp. 288-290.

Stained Glass Windows at Altenberg.
Notes and Queries, 4th series, vol. 8 (Nov. 25, 1871), p. 444.

WEAVER, F.W.

On a Painting of St. Barbara in the Church of St. Lawrence, Cucklington.
Proceedings of the Somersetshire Archaeological and Natural History
Society, vol. 39, part 2 (1893), pp. 43-54.

WEBB, B.

Sketches of Continental Ecclesiology, or Church Notes in Belgium,
Germany and Italy.
London, 1848.

WEBB, Geoffrey

The Relation of Painted Glass to Other Colour-Decoration in English
Churches.
Transactions of the St. Paul's Ecclesiological Society, vol. 7
(1911-1915), pp. 141-144.

(On the film on ancient glass.)
Letter to The Times, Dec. 29, 1925.

Favourite Subjects in York Glass.
(Letter to the Editor criticising Knowles' History of the York
School of Glass Painting, (Apr., 1933).)
J.M.G.P., vol. 5, no. 2 (Oct., 1933), pp. 104-106.

(Webb, Geoffrey)
Obituary. By CROOME, W.I.
J.M.G.P., vol. 11, no. 4 (1955), pp. 243-245.

WEBB, Mary

The Beauty of Colour.
Stained Glass (Nov., 1932).

WEBSTER, Gordon

Douglas Strachan, Ll.D., H.R.S.A.
J.M.G.P., vol. 14, no. 1 (1964), pp. 41-43.

WEDGWOOD, C.V.

Holland's History in Glass. The Windows of St. John's Church, Gouda.
The Geographical Magazine (Apr., 1950).

WEIS, Helene

Some Notes on Early Philadelphia Stained Glass.
Stained Glass, vol. 71, no. 1 (Spring, 1976), pp. 24-27.

Review of SKEAT, F.W., Stained Glass of St. Albans Cathedral.
Stained Glass, vol. 72, no. 3 (Fall, 1977), p. 191.

Review of COWEN, Painton, Rose Windows.
Stained Glass, vol. 74, no. 2 (Summer, 1979), pp. 130-131.

Review of CAVINESS, Madeline H., The Early Stained Glass of
Canterbury Cathedral, circa 1175-1220.
Stained Glass, vol. 74, no. 2 (Summer, 1979), pp. 139-141.

WEISS, Konrad

Die Glasfenster der ehemaligen Minoritenkirche in Regensburg. Als
Versuch über die mittelalterliche Bildnatur.
Munich, 1921.

WEISSENBACH, Hans von

Die Stilgesetze der Glasmalerei.
Nuremberg, 1877.

WEITZMAN, Efrem

A Tour in Light and Colour.
(Modern French and Swiss glass.)
Stained Glass, vol. 52, no. 2 (Summer, 1957), pp. 63-70.

Die Glasmalerei der Zisterzienzer in Deutschland.
In L'Architecture Monastique. Actes et Travaux de la Rencontre
Franco-Allemande des Historiens de l'Art, 1951.
(Special number of the Bulletin des Relations Artistiques France-
Allemagne).
Mainz, May, 1951.

Meisterwerke der Glasmalerei.
Berlin, 1951.
Reviewed by HOTH, Hans, Art Bulletin (June, 1952), pp. 163-165.
Reviewed by READ, Herbert, Burlington Magazine, vol. 94 (Jan.-Dec.,
1952), pp. 241-242.
Review of the second edition, LAFOND, Jean, The Archaeological
Journal, vol. 114 (1957), pp. 200-201.

Die ältesten Farbenfenster in der Oberkirche von San Francesco zu
Assisi und die deutsche Glasmalerei des 13 Jahrhundert.
In Wallraf-Richartz-Jahrbuch.
Cologne, 1952, 14, pp. 45-72.

Das Mutziger Kreuzigungsfenster und verwandte Glasmalereien der
1. Hälfte des 14 Jahrhunderts aus dem Elsass, der Schweiz und
Süddeutschland.
Zeitschrift für Schweizerische Archäologie und Kunstgeschichte,
vol. 14, nos. 3 and 4 (1953), pp. 159-179.

Meisterwerke der Glasmalerei.
2nd edition, Berlin, 1954.

Die Glasmalereien in Schwaben von 1200-1350.
(C.V.M.A., Deutschland, Bd. 1.)
Berlin, 1958.
Reviewed by GRODECKI, Louis, Gazette des Beaux-Arts, (Oct., 1958),
pp. 252-255.
Reviewed by RACKHAM, Bernard, Burlington Magazine, vol. 101 (Jan.-
Dec., 1959), p. 360.

WELLS, G.A.
Goethe's Qualitative Optics.
Journal of the History of Ideas, no. 32 (1971), pp. 617-626.

WELLS, William
Some Notes on the Stained Glass in the Burrell Collection in Glasgow
Art Gallery.
J.M.G.P., vol. 12, no. 4 (1959), pp. 277-280.

(Letter to the editor enquiring for the whereabouts of thirty-three
panels from the Costessey collection.)
J.M.G.P., vol. 14, no. 2 (1965), p. 143.

(Wels, Austria)
Die Welser Glasfenster. Beschreibung ihrer Darstellungen. Beiträge
zu ihrer Geschichte. Zusammengestellt aus Anlass ihrer
Wiedereinsetzung im Jahre 1951 . . .
Wels, 1951.

WENTZE, M.
Meisterwerke der Spätgotischen Glasmalerei in Ulm.
Pantheon, (1968), pp. 255-268.

WENTZEL, Hans
Nordtyska Glasmålningar under 1200 - och 1300 - talen.
Konshistorisk Tidskrift, pp. 18-32.
Stockholm, 1944.

Peter von Andlau. Glasmalereien in der Stiftskirche zu Tübingen.
Berlin, n.d.

Glasmaler und Maler im Mittelalter.
Zeitschrift für Kunstwissenschaft, band 3, Heft 3, 4 (1949), pp. 53-62.

WENTZEL, Hans (Contd.)
Eine Deutsche Glasmalerei-Zeichnung des 14. Jahrhunderts.
Zeitschrift für Kunstwissenschaft, band 12, Heft 3, 4 (1958), pp.
131-140.

Unbekannte mittelalterliche Glasmalereien der Burrell Collection
zu Glasgow.
Pantheon (1961), pp. 105-113.

Die Farbfenster des 13. Jahrhunderts in der Stiftskirche zu Bücken an
der Weser.
Teil 1: Erhaltungszustand.
Niederdeutsche Beitrage zur Kunstgeschichte, Band 1 (1961), pp. 57-72.
Zweiter Teil Ikonographie.
Ibid., Band 2 (1962), pp. 131-151.

Neuerworbene Glasmalereien des Stuttgarter Landesmuseums.
(A work by ANDLAU, Peter.)
Pantheon (1964), pp. 211-219.

Zu Hans von Ulm (Hans Acker).
Zeitschrift für schweizerische Archäologie und Kunstgeschichte,
Band 25, Heft 3 (1968), pp. 138-152.

Sigmaringen-Saulgau-Ulm, Zur Ulmer Glasmalerei extra muros um 1400.
Jahrbuch der Berliner Museen, Band 10 (1968), pp. 101-124.

Eine Glasmalerei-Scheibe aus Boppard.
Pantheon (May-June, 1969), fasc. 3, pp. 177-181.

Glasmalerei am Bodensee im 14 Jahrhundert.
Festschrift A. Knoepfli, 1969.
Unsere Kunst-Denkmäler, Gesellschaft für schweizerische Kunstgeschichte.
Berne. 20 Jahrgang (1969), Heft 3/4, pp. 76-87.

Un Projet de Vitrail au 14e Siècle.
Revue de l'Art, no. 10 (1970), pp. 7-14.

WERCK, Alfred
Stained Glass. A Handbook on the Art of Stained And Painted Glass,
its Origin and Development from the Time of Charlemagne to its
Decadence (850-1650 A.D.).
New York, 1922.

WERE, F.
Heraldry in Tewkesbury Abbey.
(In the glass, pp. 168-170.)
Transactions of the Bristol and Gloucestershire Archaeological
Society, vol. 26 (for 1903).

WERNER, Alfred
Medieval Splendors.
American Artist (Dec., 1966).

WERNER, A.E.
Problems in the Conservation of Glass.
Annales du 1e Congrès des Journées Internationales du Verre.
Liège, 1958, pp. 189-205.

The Care of Glass in Museums.
Museum News Technical Supplement, no. 13 (June, 1966), pp. 45-99.

WERNER, N.
Das "Hornbeck-Fenster" der Benediktuskirche zu Freising.
Beiträge zur Kunst des Mittelalters.
Festschrift für Hans Wentzel.
Berlin, 1975.

WESTLAKE, H.F.
St. Margaret's, Westminster, London. Descriptive and Historical Guide.
London, 1914.

WESTLAKE, Margaret
N.H.J. Westlake, F.S.A.
J.M.G.P., vol. 3, no. 2 (Oct., 1929), pp. 59-65.

WESTLAKE, N.H.J.
Etude sur les Vitraux Peints.
Le Beffroi, vol. 2 (1864-1865), pp. 139-146.

Painting on Glass - 1.
The Magazine of Art (1878), pp. 162-164.

A History of Design in Stained And Painted Glass.
4 vols., London, 1879-1881.

Stained Glass in 1882.
Art Journal, vol. 35 (1883), pp. 84-88.

The Painted Windows at Fairford, Winchester, and King's College,
Cambridge, as Models for Modern Work.
The Builder (Feb. 27, 1892).

WESTMACOTT, Richard Jnr.
(Removal of glass from Gonalston, Notts., to Southwell.)
The Archaeological Journal, vol. 6 (1849), pp. 5, 6, 12.

(Westminster Abbey)
Where the Battle of Britain Glows Forever in Memorial Glass.
Illustrated London News (July 12, 1947).

(Westminster, St. Margaret's Church)
A History and Description of the Caxton Memorial Window in St.
Margaret's Church, Westminster.
London, 1882.

(West Wickham Church, Kent)
(Drawings of old glass by John Swaine exhibited at the Society of
Antiquaries.)
The Gentleman's Magazine, vol. 103, part 1, (1833), p. 161.

WEYDEN, Ernst
Die neuen Glasgemälde im Dome zu Köln; ein Weihegeschenk des Königs
Ludwigs I. von Bayern, beschreiben von E.W.
Cologne, 2nd edition, 1848.

WEYMAN, Henry T.
The Glass in Ludlow Church; also Account of Missing Ludlow Glass.
Ludlow, 1905.

Ludlow Church.
Transactions of the Woolhope Naturalists' Field Club, 1914, 1915,
1916, 1917, vol. 22 (1918), pp. 132-136.

WHALL, Christopher W.
Stained Glass.
The Builder, vol. 60 (1891), pp. 390, 391, 408-411.

Stained Glass Work: A Textbook for Students and Workers in Glass.
London, 1905.

(Whall, Christopher)
Description of an Exhibition to Illustrate the System of Teaching
Stained-Glass Work, Held at 35, Park Walk, Chelsea.
London, 1905.

WHALL, Veronica
Glass, Lead, and - Light.
Stained Glass, vol. 30, no. 1 (Spring-Summer, 1935), pp. 10-14.

Autobiographical Notes.
Stained Glass, vol. 37, no. 2 (Summer, 1942), pp. 51-58.

WHEELER, Mortimer.
The British Academy 1949-1968.
London, 1970.
(Pp. 108-116 deal with the formation of the British section of the
C.V.M.A.)

WHICHCORD, J.
On the Antiquities of Maidstone, and Polychromy of the Middle Ages.
Journal of the British Archaeological Association, vol. 10 (1855),
pp. 32-52.

WHITE, C.H. Evelyn
On William Dowsing's Iconoclastic Visitation of the County of
Cambridge, 1643-1644.
Proceedings of the Cambridge Antiquarian Society (1895-1896), pp. 204-
208.

WHITE, Gleeson
Some Glasgow Designers and Their Work. Part 4, Oscar Paterson.
The Studio, vol. 13 (1898), pp. 12-25.

WHITE, James
Irish Stained Glass.
(With WYNNE, Michael.)
Dublin, 1963.

Irish Stained Glass.
(Report of a lecture.)
J.M.G.P., vol. 14, no. 4 (1968-1969), pp. 197-198.

WHITESIDE, J.
Swindale Chapel.
Transactions of the Cumberland and Westmorland Antiquarian and
Archaeological Society, new series, vol. 1 (1901),
(Glass, pp. 260-261.)

WHITESIDE, Osmond S.
A Preacher Goes to Glass.
Stained Glass, vol.   (Spring-Summer, 1937).

Whitefriars Glass. 250th Anniversary Exhibition.
(Includes an account of the work of James Powell and Sons.)
The Times, June 16, 1930.

WHITTET, G.S.
Carl J. Edwards: Stained Glass Designer.
The Studio, vol. 147 (1954), pp. 10-13.

WHITTOCK, Nathaniel
The Decorative Painters' and Glaziers' Guide; Containing also a
Complete Body of Information on the Art of Staining and Painting on
Glass: Plans for the Erection of Apparatus for Annealing it, etc.
London, 1827. (Supplement, 1832.)

WIBERT, Katherine
Stained Glass in Pittsburgh.
Carnegie Magazine (Dec., 1968).

WICHMANN, E.

   Moderne Glasmalerei. 1 Serie.
   Berlin, 1895.

   Vorlagen für moderne Glasmalerei und Glasätzerei.
   Dusseldorf, 1900.

WICKHAM, W.A.

   Some Notes on Billinge.
   Transactions of the Historic Society of Lancashire and Cheshire,
   new series, vol. 25 for 1909 (1910.)
   (Glass, p. 7.)

(Wiesbaden Exhibition)

   Glasmalereien und Glasmosaik auf der Gewerbe-Ausstellung in Wiesbaden.
   By H.
   Sprechsaal, vol. 42 (1909), p. 433.

WIETHASE, H.

   Der Dom zu Köln. Aufnahmen von A. Schmitz mit historisch
   beschreibendem Text.
   Frankfurt, 1889.

WILD, Christiane Block

   Review of BECKSMANN, Rüdiger, Die Architektonische Rahmung . . .
   Bulletin Monumental, no. 127 (1969), pp. 56-57.

   Le Vitrail de la Vie de la Vierge de Vieux-Thann et sa Place
   dans la Peinture du Rhin Supérieur au XVe Siècle.
   Revue de l'Art, no. 10 (1970), pp. 15-29.

   La Vie de la Vierge et l'Enfance du Christ dans les Vitraux
   de la Cathédrale de Strasbourg.
   Un Oeuvre Exécutée Avant 1331 pour le Bas-coté sud.
   Bulletin de la Société des Amis de la Cathédrale de Strasbourg.
   (1974), pp. 45-53.
   (With an Epilogue by ZSCHOKKE, F., pp. 54-57.)

WILD, J.H.S., and DOYLE, A.I.

   Galilee Glass.
   (From various sources, recently installed in Durham Cathedral.)
   Transactions of the Architectural and Archaeological Society of
   Durham and Northumberland, new series, vol. 3 (1974), p. 111.

WILDE, E.E.

   Shield in 15th Century Window of the Westgate, Winchester.
   (Request for identification.)
   Notes and Queries, vol. 152 (Jan. 15, 1927), p. 45.
   Replied to by C.S.C. (B/C), Ibid. (Jan. 29, 1927), p. 89.
   Further letter by 'Hampshire', vol. 156 (June 1, 1929), p. 397.

WILDENSTEIN, G.

   Quatre Marchés des Peintres Verriers Parisiens.
   (Claude Porcher et Nicholas II Pinaigrier pour les vitraux de la
   chapelle du St. Nom de Jesus à St. Eustache, 1600.)
   Gazette des Beaux-Arts (July-Aug., 1957), pp. 85-88.
   (Material on the Pinaigriers.)

(Wilhelm)

   Wilhelmsche Glasmalereien und Kunstverglasung 1890-1915.
   Rottweil, 1915.

WILKINSON, Alfred L.

   Edward Frampton, 1850-1929. Master Glass Painter.
   J.M.G.P., vol. 11, no. 2 (1953), pp. 70-71.

   Christopher Charles Powell. Obituary.
   J.M.G.P., vol. 12, no. 1 (1956), pp. 73-74.

   Horace Wilkinson. Obituary.
   J.M.G.P., vol. 12, no. 3 (1958), pp. 220-222.

   The Great East Window of the Chapel of Hatfield House.
   J.M.G.P., vol. 12, no. 4 (1959), pp. 245-250.

   Review of SEWTER, A.C., Notes on Morris & Co.'s Domestic Stained Glass.
   Journal of the William Morris Society, vol. 1, no. 1 (1961), pp. 22-28.

   With DRURY, V.J.
   The Conservation of Stained Glass.
   J.M.G.P., vol. 13, no. 4 (1963), pp. 582-584.

   The Works of T. Willement, 1812-1865.
   J.M.G.P., vol. 14, no. 1 (1964), pp. 50-51.

   The Diocesan Advisory Committee System, Faculties and Faculty
   Procedure.
   J.M.G.P., vol. 14, no. 1 (1964), pp. 71-75.

   (Letter on the restoration of the Ruskin window, St. Giles,
   Camberwell, after the war.)
   Quoted in Editorial, J.M.G.P., vol. 16, no. 1 (1976-1977), p. 5.

WILKINSON, Horace

   Fifteenth-Century Stained Glass in Bardwell Church, Suffolk.
   J.M.G.P., vol. 5, no. 4 (Oct., 1934), pp. 159-162.

(Wilkinson, Horace)

   Obituary. By WILKINSON, A.L.
   J.M.G.P., vol. 12, no. 3 (1958), pp. 220-222.

WILKINSON, J.G.

   On Colour and on the Necessity for a General Diffusion of Taste
   Among all Classes.
   London, 1858.

WILL

Schweizerische Glasgemälde in Lichtenthal.
Anzeiger für Schweizerische Altertumskunde (1887).

WILL, Robert

Deux Panneaux Provenant de Neuwiller a Karlsruhe.
Cahiers Alsaciens d'Archéologie, d'Art et d'Histoire (1960), pp. 61-

WILLEMENT, Thomas

Works in Stained Glass Executed by T.W.
Privately printed, 1840.

(Willement, Thomas)

List of Works in Stained Glass by T.W.
Privately printed, 1841 ?.

(Willet, Anne Lee)

Obituary.
Stained Glass, vol. 38, no. 1 (Spring, 1943), pp. 30-31.

WILLET, E. Crosby

The Ministry of Stained Glass.
Journal of the American Society for Church Architecture (Jan., 1963),
p. 10.

WILLET, Henry Lee

Stained Glass Competition.
Stained Glass, vol. 36, no. 3 (Autumn, 1941), pp. 92-98.

Philadelphia Exhibition.
Stained Glass, vol. 37, no. 1 (Spring, 1942), pp. 27-30.

R.A. CRAM, Obituary.
(Editorial notes.)
Stained Glass, vol. 37, no. 4 (Winter, 1942), pp. 103-104.

(Wartime restrictions of the manufacture of stained glass windows.)
Stained Glass, vol. 38, no. 4 (Winter, 1943), pp. 103-107.

(Willet, Henry Lee ? pseud. 'Le Chat')

The Spiritual Aspect of Modern Stained Glass.
Stained Glass, vol. 38, no. 4 (Winter, 1943), pp. 122-125.

WILLET, Henry Lee

See Stained Glass Problems in Our Day.

Stained Glass in Our Time.
(In the U.S.A.)
Stained Glass, vol. 41, no. 3 (Autumn, 1946), pp. 80-86.

(WILLET, Henry Lee ? pseud. 'Le Chat')

Le Chat Meows Again.
Stained Glass, vol. 42, no. 4 (Winter, 1947), pp. 98-103.

WILLET, Henry Lee

The Ministry of Color.
Presbyterian Life (Chicago), (March 27, 1948).

Apprentice Exhibition.
Stained Glass, vol. 43, no. 3 (Autumn, 1948), pp. 75-85.
Another account of this is
Revolution in Stained Glass.
The Charette (Pittsburgh), (Aug., 1948), pp.
Also Stained Glass Exhibits, Made by Apprentices, to Tour Seven Cities.
Labor Information Bulletin (Dec., 1948).

WILLET, Henry Lee (Contd.)

Stained Glass and the Church.
Religion and Life (Autumn, 1949).

With BLENKO, W.H., CUMMINGS, H.W., and others.
Technical Aspects of Stained Glass with Emphasis on Faceted Glass.
(A Symposium.)
Part 1, Stained Glass, vol. 56, no. 3 (Autumn, 1961), pp. 30-39.
Part 2, Ibid., vol. 56, no. 4 (Winter, 1961-1962), pp. 34-45.
Part 3, Ibid., vol. 57, no. 1 (Spring, 1962), pp. 14-21.

Autobiography.
Stained Glass, vol. 73, no. 1 (Spring, 1978), pp. 23-26.

(Interview with TEMME, Norman.)
Mostly About Presidents.
(Of the Stained Glass Association of America.)
Stained Glass, vol. 73, no. 4 (Winter, 1978-1979), pp. 263-265.

WILLET, Muriel Crosby

Religious Exhibition in New York.
(At New York Museum of Contemporary Crafts.)
Stained Glass, vol. 52, no. 3 (Autumn, 1957), pp. 117-120.

WILLET, William

The Art of Stained Glass.
Architecture (1918).

WILLIAMS, E.

Notes on the Painted Glass in Canterbury Cathedral.
(With a Preface by FARRAR, F.W.)
Aberdeen, 1897.

WILLIAMS, Leonard

Arts and Crafts of Older Spain.
3 vols., Edinburgh, 1907.

WILLIAMS, Merritt F.

The Stained Glass of Léon Cathedral.
The Cathedral Age (Autumn, 1948).

WILLIAMS, Yvonne

Some Speculations on the Future of Stained Glass. A Canadian View.
Stained Glass, vol. 39, no. 1 (Spring, 1944), pp. 21-24.

Processes and Craftsmanship in Stained Glass.
Journal of the Royal Architectural Institute of Canada (Toronto),
(Aug., 1946).

WILLIAMSON, Huguley

Some Aspects of the Middle Ages as seen through its Stained Glass.
Stained Glass, vol. 28, no. 3 (Autumn, 1933), pp. 126-134.

WILLIS, Robert, and CLARK, J.W.

The Architectural History of the University of Cambridge, and of
the Colleges of Cambridge and Eton.
4 vols., Cambridge, 1886.

WILLIS, Ronald

(Article on stained glass techniques.)
Yorkshire Evening Press, Dec. 7, 1962.

Stained Glass in York.
Yorkshire Evening Press, July 3, 1976.

WILLSON, E.G., and PUGIN, Augustus
    Specimens of Gothic Architecture . . .
    2 vols., London, 1821-1823.

    With PUGIN, Augustus, and others, including PUGIN, A.W.N.
    Examples of Gothic Architecture . . .
    3 vols., London, 1831-1838.

WILMSHURST, H.
    Notes on Representations and Exhibitions of Painted and Stained Glass,
    with Biographical Notices of Glass-Stainers, Painters on Glass and
    their Work.
    London, n.d. (19th century).

WILSON, Cecil J.
    Exciting New Developments in Epoxy Compounds.
    Stained Glass, vol. 74, no. 1 (Spring, 1979), pp. 29-32.

WILSON, Charles H.
    A Memoir of the Glasgow Cathedral Painted Windows.
    Glasgow, 1864.
    Reviewed in Art Journal (1864), p. 252.

    Descriptive Catalogue of the Painted Glass Windows in Glasgow
    Cathedral.
    Glasgow, 1866.

WILSON, F.R.
    The Glass of Morley Church.
    The Antiquary, vol. 14 (1886), p. 233.

WILSON, H.
    The Work of Sir Edward Burne-Jones, More Especially in Decoration and
    Design.
    Architectural Review, vol. 1 (March-May, 1897), pp. 171-181, 225-233,
    273-281.

WILSON, H.F.
    The Glass at Cartmel Fell and Windermere.
    Transactions of the Cumberland and Westmorland Antiquarian and
    Archaeological Society, new series, vol. 20 (1920), pp. 245-246.

WILSON, H. Weber
    The Controversial History of Residential Stained Glass.
    Stained Glass, vol. 74, no. 3 (Fall, 1979), pp. 228-232.

WILSON, R.A.
    Leaded Lights and Stained Glass.
    Town and Country Houses (Sept., 1927).

WILSON, William
    Cartoon for Stained Glass, 'Christ Washing Peter's Feet'.
    Studio (Nov., 1937).

(Wilson, William)
    Obituary.
    J.M.G.P., vol. 15, no. 1 (1972-1973), pp. 23-24.

WINBOLT, S.E.
    Wealden Glass: The Old Surrey-Sussex Industry.
    Journal of the Society of Glass Technology, vol. 16, no. 63 (Sept., 1932).

    Fourteenth Century Sussex Furnaces.
    (Letter to the Editor.)
    The Times, Nov. 26, 1932.

    Wealden Glass. The Surrey-Sussex Glass Industry. (A.D. 1226-1615.)
    Hove, 1933.

WINBOLT, S.E. (Contd.)
    A Window Glazed with Mediaeval Glass Fragments.
    (In Kirdford Church, Sussex.)
    Journal of the Society of Glass Technology, vol. 18 (1934), p. 307.

(Winchelsea)
    St. Thomas, Winchelsea. The Service of Dedication of a Series of
    Three Windows and an Altar in Memory of the Men of the Cinque Ports . . .
    Who . . . Gave their Lives in the Great War.
    (Windows by Douglas Strachan.)
    Oxford, 1933.

(Winchester Cathedral)
    Winchester Cathedral. Painted Glass in the East Window of the Choir.
    Weale's Quarterly Papers on Architecture, vols, 2, 3 (1844-1845).

    Gift to Winchester Cathedral. Salisbury's Old Glass.
    Daily Telegraph, Nov. 17, 1937.

(Winchester College)
    Rare Glass Back After 121 Years. Famous Panel of a King Restored.
    Gift to Winchester College.
    Daily Telegraph, Sept. 18, 1937.

(Winchester, St. Cross)
    (Old Continental glass recently installed.)
    The Gentleman's Magazine, vol. 100, part 1 (1830), pp. 582-583.

WINCHESTER, H.C., and R.G.'
    Winchester College Hall Windows. A Note.
    Wells, 1931.

What Constitutes a Good Window?
    (Discussion.)
    Stained Glass (Spring-Summer, 1935).

Window in the Hall of the Chartered Institute of Secretaries.
    (Formerly the home of the Worshipful Company of Curriers of the City
    of London.)
    J.M.G.P., vol. 6, no. 1 (Apr., 1935), pp. 28-29.

(Windsor, St. George's Chapel)
    Stained Glass in St. George's Chapel, Windsor.
    (By Willement.)
    The Gentleman's Magazine, vol. 18, new series, part 2 (1842), pp.
    516-517.

    East Window at St. George's Chapel, Windsor.
    Notes and Queries, 11th series, vol. 10 (1910-1915), pp. 210, 218, 256.

WINNIFRITH, John
    St. Peter and St. Paul, Appledore.
    (Printed) Ashford, 1973.
    (Glass, p. 3, unnumbered.)

WINNINGTON, Thomas E.
    Window in Fairford Church.
    Notes and Queries, 3rd series, vol. 10 (Sept. 22, 1866), p. 231.

    Fairford Windows.
    Ibid., 4th series, vol. 2 (Sept. 5, 1868), p. 222.
    Ibid., vol. 3 (Jan. 23, 1869), p. 80.

WINSTANLEY, Herbert
    Speke Hall.
    Transactions of the Historic Society of Lancashire and Cheshire, new
    series, vol. 35 for 1919 (1920).
    (Armorial glass, pp. 15-16.)

WINSTON, Charles

    Painted Glass.
    The Archaeological Journal, vol. 1 (1845), pp. 14-23.

    With F.B.
    Review of CAHIER and MARTIN, Vitraux Peints de Saint Etienne de Bourges.
    The Archaeological Journal, vol. 1 (1845), pp. 169-176.

    (An account of the glass in Mells Church given to the British
    Archaeological Association by WINSTON, Charles.)
    The Gentleman's Magazine, new series, vol. 24, part 2 (1845), p. 287.

    (Report of an account of some painted glass at Mells.)
    The Archaeological Journal, vol. 2 (1846), pp. 202-203.

    (A paper 'On the Painted Glass in the Cathedral and Churches of York'
    given by WINSTON, Charles, to the Archaeological Institute.)
    The Gentleman's Magazine, new series, vol. 26, part 2 (1846), pp.
    294-295.

    (Report of an account of some painted glass at Kingsdown, Kent.)
    The Archaeological Journal, vol. 2 (1846), pp. 188-189.

    (Paper on 'The Stained Glass of Lincoln Cathedral and Southwell
    Minster'given by WINSTON, Charles, to the Archaeological Institute.)
    The Gentleman's Magazine, new series, vol. 30, part 2 (1848), p. 29.

    An Inquiry into the Difference of Style Observable in Ancient Glass
    Paintings, Especially in England: With Hints on Glass Painting.
    By an Amateur.
    2 vols., Oxford, 1847.
    Noticed in The Archaeological Journal, vol. 4 (1847), pp. 165-184.
    Reviewed in The Ecclesiologist, vol. 8 (1848), pp. 106-107.
    Reviewed in Chapters on Stained Glass, no. 2, by WARRINGTON and
    WINSTON. Ibid., vol. 10 (1850), pp. 81-97.

    (Report of an account of the development of ruby glass.)
    The Archaeological Journal, vol. 7 (1850), pp. 187-188.

    (Report of an account of a palimpsest inscription in a window at
    Llanrhaiadr (Denbigh).)
    The Archaeological Journal, vol. 7 (1850), pp. 395-396.

    On a Revived Manufacture of Coloured Glass Used in Ancient Windows.
    The Gentleman's Magazine, new series, vol. 38, part 2 (1852), pp.
    155-159.
    Reprinted from The Builder.

    (A letter on the practice of glass-painting with reference to St.
    Paul's Cathedral.)
    The Gentleman's Magazine, new series, vol. 38. part 2 (1852), p. 265.
    Reprinted from The Builder (Aug. 14, 1852).

    Remarks on the Painted Glass Exhibited by Mr. Lucas.
    The Archaeological Journal, vol. 9 (1852), pp. 100-101.

    (Paper on the Ancient Art of Glass Painting, read to the
    Archaeological Institute.)
    The Gentleman's Magazine, new series, vol. 42, part 2 (1854), pp.
    284-285.

    (An account of the poor state of the glass at North Moreton Church,
    Berks., with an appeal for aid.)
    The Archaeological Journal, vol. 13 (1856), pp. 275-276.

    On the Glazing of the North Rose Window of Lincoln Cathedral.
    The Archaeological Journal, vol. 14 (1857), pp. 211-220.

    (On the repair of the glass at North Moreton Church, Berks., with
    remarks on restoration.)
    The Archaeological Journal, vol. 18 (1861), pp. 152-154.

    (Report of observations on glass in Nettlestead Church, Kent.)
    The Archaeological Journal, vol. 21 (1864), p. 166.
    (See FAUSSET, Thomas Godfrey.)

(Winston, Charles)

    (Proposal to publish his Memoirs . . .)
    The Archaeological Journal, vol. 21 (1864), p. 276.

    (An exhibition of his drawings from March 27-Apr. 8, 1865.)
    The Archaeological Journal, vol. 22 (1865), p. 93.

WINSTON, Charles

    Memoirs Illustrative of the Art of Glass-Painting.
    London, 1865.
    Contains:
    Biographical Memoir,(pp. 1-17).
    Letters on Glass-Painting, (pp. 18-62).
    A Short Notice of the Painted Glass in Winchester and its Neighbourhood,
    (pp. 63-70).
    Reprinted from Proceedings of the Archaeological Institute at
    Winchester (Sept., 1845), London, 1846.
    (Pp. 1-8; each article is separately paged.)
    On the Painted Glass in the Cathedral and Churches of York, (pp. 71-76).
    Reprinted from Proceedings of the Archaeological Institute at York
    (July, 1846), London, 1848.
    (Pp. 18-23; articles irregularly paginated.)
    An Account of the Painted Glass in Lincoln Cathedral and Southwell
    Minster: With Some General Remarks on Glass-Painting, (pp. 77-105).
    Reprinted (and abridged) from Proceedings of the Archaeological
    Institute at Lincoln (July, 1848), London, 1850.
    Pp. 90-124.
    On the Painted Glass at Salisbury, (pp. 106-129).
    Reprinted from Proceedings of the Archaeological Institute at
    Salisbury (July 1849), London, 1851.
    Pp. 135-159.
    On the Painted Glass in New College Chapel and Hall, Oxford, (pp. 130-
    159).
    Reprinted from The Archaeological Journal, vol. 9 (1852), pp. 29-59,
    with a supplementary note, p. 120.
    Also reprinted in Proceedings of the Archaeological Institute at
    Oxford,(June, 1850), London, 1854), pp. 191-220.
    On the Painted Glass at Bristol, Wells, Gloucester and Exeter, (pp.
    160-174).
    Reprinted from Proceedings of the Archaeological Institute at Bristol
    (July-Aug., 1851), London, 1853. Pp. 150-165.
    On a Revived Manufacture of Coloured Glass used in Ancient Windows,
    (pp. 176-185).
    Reprinted from Transactions of the R.I.B.A. (1852), (which also
    includes a discussion on glass-painting.)
    On the Methods of Painting upon Glass, (pp. 186-189).
    Abridged from Transactions of the R.I.B.A. (1853-1854).
    On the Application of Painted Glass to Buildings in Various Styles
    of Architecture, (pp. 190-214).
    Reprinted from Transactions of the R.I.B.A. (1853-1854).
    On the Resemblance Between Mediaeval and Classical Art, as
    Exemplified in the Glass-Paintings of the Twelfth and Thirteenth
    Centuries, (pp. 215-230).
    Reprinted from Transactions of the R.I.B.A. (1856).
    A Lecture on Glass-Painting (1859), (pp. 231-253).
    On a Heraldic Window in the North Aisle of the Nave of York
    Cathedral. (With WALFORD, W.S.), (pp. 256-284).
    Reprinted from The Archaeological Journal, vol. 17 (1860), pp. 22-34,
    132-148.
    A supplementary note to this is in The Archaeological Journal, vol. 20
    (1863), p. 330.
    An Account of the Painted Glass in the East Window of Gloucester
    Cathedral, (pp. 285-311).
    Reprinted from The Archaeological Journal, vol. 20 (1863), pp. 239-253,
    319-330.
    Remarks on the Painted Glass at Lichfield Cathedral, (pp. 312-325).
    Reprinted from The Archaeological Journal, vol. 21 (1864), pp. 193-208.
    The Painted Glass in the Beauchamp Chapel at Warwick, (pp. 326-342).
    Reprinted from The Archaeological Journal, vol. 21 (1864), pp. 302-318.
    A Catalogue of Drawings of Glass-Paintings by the Late Charles Winston,
    (pp. 343-358).

(Winston, Charles)

    Review of Memoirs, (with WILSON, Catalogue of the . . . Windows in
    Glasgow Cathedral).
    Edinburgh Review, (Jan., 1867), pp. 154-186.
    Reviewed in The Ecclesiologist, vol. 27 (1866), pp. 38-39.

    WARING, J.B., Catalogue of Drawings from Ancient Glass Paintings by
    the late Charles Winston.
    London, 1865.

    Review of 2nd edition of An Inquiry . . .
    Notes and Queries, 4th series, vol. 1 (March 21, 1868), p. 283.

    ROBINSON, Arnold, Charles Winston's Experiments in 1850.
    J.M.G.P., vol. 11, no. 4 (1955), pp. 221-223.

    SEWTER, A.C., The Place of Charles Winston in the Victorian Revival
    of the Art of Stained Glass.
    Journal of the Archaeological Association, vol. 24 (1961).
    Reviewed by A.L.N., J.M.G.P., vol. 13, no. 4 (1963), p. 596.

WINTER, A.

    Altération des Surfaces des Verres Anciens.
    7th International Congress on Glass.
    Brussels, 1965. Paper no. 229.

WINTERFELD, Louise von

    Der Glasmaler Mathias Dortmund.
    Westfalen Hefte für Geschichte Kunst und Volkskunde, vol. 20, part 4
    (1937).

    The Glass-Painter, Mathias Dortmund.
    J.M.G.P., vol. 7, no. 3 (Oct., 1938), pp. 116-119.

WINTERICH, Otto

    Time-Savers for a Stained-Glass Studio.
    Stained Glass, vol. 52, no. 1 (Spring, 1957), pp. 6-15.

    New Potentials for Stained Glass.
    Glass Digest (Jan., 1967).

    A Great Year for Stained Glass.
    Glass Digest (Jan., 1968).

    Stained Glass in Architecture Today.
    Catholic Market (Nov.-Dec., 1968).

(Wire Guards)

    (Editorial reply to a query about the date of the introduction of
    wire guards.)
    J.M.G.P., vol. 2, no. 1 (1927), p. 55.

WITHAM, Corine B.

    A Visit to Medieval Europe in America.
    (The Hammond Museum, Gloucester, Mass.)
    Stained Glass, vol. 64, no. 4 (Winter, 1969-1970), pp. 22-24.

(Great Witley Church)

    Great Witley Church, Worcestershire: Painted Glass.
    (A grant to repair three of the more seriously damaged windows.)
    The Pilgrim Trust, 41st Annual Report (1971), p. 13.

    Great Witley Church, Worcestershire: Painted Glass.
    (A grant to complete the restoration.)
    The Pilgrim Trust, 42nd Annual Report (1972), p. 15.

    Great Witley Church, Worcestershire: Painted Glass.
    (Grant towards restoring a further window.)
    The Pilgrim Trust, 43rd Annual Report (1973), p. 13.

WITTE, Fritz

    Wilhelm Puetz, Coeln; ein Wort zur modernen Glasmalerei.
    Zeitschrift für alte und neue Glasmalerei (1914), p. 18.

WITTGENS, F.

    V. Foppa.
    Milan, 1948.

    Vetrate Lombarde.
    In Storia di Milano, vol. 7.
    Treccani, 1956.
    (pp. 829-835.)

WITZLEBEN, Elizabeth von

    Farbwunder deutscher Glasmalerei aus dem Mittelalter.
    Augsburg, 1965.

    Licht und Farbe aus Frankreichs Kathedralen.
    Augsburg, 1966.

    Les Vitraux des Cathédrales de France.
    4th edition, Augsburg, 1968.
    Reviewed by ERLANDE-BRANDENBURG, Alain, Bulletin Monumental, no. 127
    (1969), pp. 179-180.
    Reviewed by DELAPORTE, Yves, Bulletin des Sociétés Archéologiques
    d'Eure-et-Loir, Chronique 3 (1968), p. 38.

    With SEIFERT, Hans.
    Das Ulmer Münster.
    Augsburg, 1968.

    Die Frauenkirche in München.
    Augsburg, 1969.

    Die Scheiben aus St. Cäcilien im Dom zu Köln.
    In 7ᵉ Colloque du Corpus Vitrearum Medii Aevi.
    Florence ?, 1970, pp. 35-37.

    Kölner Bibelfenster des 15. Jahrhunderts in Schottland, England, und
    Amerika.
    Aachener Kunstblätter, vol. 43 (1972), pp. 227-

    Bemalte Glasscheiben: Volkstümliches Leben auf Kabinett-und Bierscheiben.
    Munich, 1977.

(Wolborough, Devonshire)

    Ancient Glass in St. Mary's Church, Wolborough. By F.G.M.
    Devon and Cornwall Notes and Queries, vol. 22 (1946), p. 226.

    Ancient Glass in St. Mary's Church, Wolborough.
    (By RUSSELL, C.A.W., and the editors.)
    Ibid., pp. 261-263.

    Ancient Glass in St. Mary's Church, Wolborough.
    (By PALMER, F.W. Morton.)
    Ibid., p. 276.

WOLF, Jacques

    L'Utilisation du Verre d'Art et les Applications des Vitraux.
    Revue Belge des Industries Verriers, vol. 2, no. 24 (Feb., 1932), pp.
    273-275.

WOLFF, F.

    Ein altes Glasfenster aus der Klosterkirche zu Niepermünster nach
    Hans Baldung Goriens zeichnung.
    Kunstgewerbe in Elsas-Lothringen, year 3 (1902), pp. 141-154.

WOLLASTON, Gerald W.

    Heraldry and Stained Glass.
    J.M.G.P., vol. 10, no. 4 (1951), p. 213.

WOLLASTON, Gerald W. (Contd.)

    The Royal Arms in Churches.
    J.M.G.P., vol. 11, no. 4 (1955), pp. 201-203.

WOOD, Alfred J.

    Note to W.E. Chance and the Revived Manufacture of Coloured Glass.
    J.M.G.P., vol. 5, no. 4 (Oct., 1934), p. 176.

WOOD, G. Bernard

    A Yorkshire Sundial Window.
    (By Henry GYLES, at Tong Hall.)
    (Letter to the Editon)
    Country Life (Feb. 14, 1947), p. 384.

WOOD, Paul W.

    Stained Glass Crafting.
    New York, 1967.

WOODFORDE, Christopher

    Fifteenth-Century Glass in Somerset.
    Journal of the British Society of Master Glass Painters, vol. 4, no. 1
    (Apr., 1931), pp. 5-12.

    Two Unusual Subjects in Ancient Glass in Long Melford Church.
    Proceedings of the Suffolk Institute of Archaeology and Natural
    History, vol. 21, part 1, for 1931 (1932), pp. 63-67.

    The Medieval Glass in Elsing Church, Norfolk.
    J.M.G.P., vol. 4, no. 3 (Apr., 1932), pp. 134-136.

    The Locksley Hall Collection of Stained and Painted Glass.
    London, 1932.

    The Mediaeval Glass in Yaxley Church.
    (With HARRIS, H.A.)
    Proceedings of the Suffolk Institute of Archaeology and Natural History,
    vol. 21, part 2 (1932), pp. 91-98.

    New College Glass.
    (Letter to the Editor.)
    The Times, Nov. 21. 1932.

    Mediaeval Painted Glass in Norfolk.
    Norfolk Archaeology, vol.24 for 1930-1932 (1932), pp. 251-253.

    Mediaeval Painted Glass in East Harling Church.
    Norfolk Archaeology, vol. 24 for 1930-1932 (1932), pp. 254-261.

    The Fifteenth-Century Glass in Blythburgh Church.
    Proceedings of the Suffolk Institute of Archaeology and Natural
    History, vol. 21, part 3 (1933),pp. 232-240.

    Mediaeval Glass Restored to Cawston Church.
    Norfolk Archaeology, vol. 25 for 1932-1934 (1935), pp. 138-139.

    The Mediaeval Painted Glass in North Tuddenham Church, Norfolk.
    Norfolk Archaeology, vol. 25 for 1932-1934 (1935), pp. 220-226.

    Ancient Glass in Lincolnshire. 1. Haydor.
    The Lincolnshire Magazine, vol. 1, no. 3 (Jan.-Feb., 1933).

    Part 3, Tattershall - the History of the Glass.
    Ibid., vol. 1, no. 2 (May-June, 1934), pp. 363-367.
    Part 4, Tattershall - the Glass that Remains.
    Ibid., vol. 2, no. 9 (Jan.-Feb., 1936), pp. 265-267.

    Schools of Glass-Painting in King's Lynn and Norwich in the Middle Ages.
    J.M.G.P., vol. 5, no. 1 (Apr., 1933), pp. 4-18.

    Review of ARMITAGE ROBINSON, J., The Fourteenth-Century Glass at Wells.
    J.M.G.P., vol. 5, no. 1 (Apr., 1933), pp. 49-50.

WOODFORDE, Christopher (Contd.)

    Guide to the Medieval Glass in Lincoln Cathedral.
    London, 1933.

    Further Notes on Ancient Glass in Norfolk and Suffolk.
    J.M.G.P., vol. 5, no. 2 (Oct. 1933), pp. 57-68.

    Obituary of ARMITAGE ROBINSON, J.
    J.M.G.P., vol. 5, no. 2 (Oct., 1933), p. 102.

    The Stained and Painted Glass in Hengrave Hall, Suffolk.
    Proceedings of the Suffolk Institute of Archaeology and Natural
    History, vol. 22, part 1 (1934).

    Essex Glass-Painters in the Middle Ages.
    J.M.G.P., vol. 5, no. 3 (Apr., 1934), pp. 110-115.

    The Medieval Glass of St. Peter Mancroft.
    Norwich, 1934.

    Painted Glass in Saxlingham Nethergate Church, Norfolk.
    J.M.G.P., vol. 5, no. 4 (Oct., 1934), pp. 163-169.

    Glazing Accounts at Little Saxham Hall, Suffolk.
    (Letter to the Editor.)
    J.M.G.P., vol. 5, no. 4 (Oct., 1934), p. 206.

    Foreign Stained and Painted Glass in Norfolk.
    Norfolk Archaeology, vol. 26, for 1935-1937 (1938), pp. 73-84.

    The Medieval Glass in the Churches of St. John the Baptist, Mileham,
    and All Saints' and St. Michael-at-Plea, Norwich.
    Norfolk Archaeology, vol. 26 for 1935-1937 (1938), pp. 164-177.

    Glass-Painters in England Before the Reformation.
    J.M.G.P., vol. 6, no. 2 (Oct., 1935), pp. 62-69.
    Ibid., vol. 6, no. 3 (Apr., 1936), pp. 121-128.

    Ancient Glass in Lincolnshire.
    Lincolnshire Magazine, vol. 2, no. 12 (July-Aug., 1936).

    English Stained and Painted Glass. Eight Centuries of Development.
    Church Assembly News, vol. 13, no. 142 (Jan.-Feb., 1936).

    Review of McNEIL RUSHFORTH, G., Medieval Christian Imagery.
    J.M.G.P., vol. 6, no. 3 (Apr., 1936) pp. 161-163.

    A Group of Fourteenth-Century Windows Showing the Tree of Jesse.
    J.M.G.P., vol. 6, no. 4 (Apr., 1937), pp. 184-190.

    Chronological List of English Glass-Paintings (Additions).
    (Letter to the Editor.)
    J.M.G.P., vol. 6, no. 4 (Apr., 1937), p. 228.

    Review of KNOWLES, J.A., Essays in the History of the York School
    of Glass-Painting.
    Antiquaries Journal, vol. 17, no. 4 (Oct., 1937).

    A Medieval Campaign Against Blasphemy.
    Downside Review, vol. 55 (1937), pp. 357-362.
    Reprinted in J.M.G.P., vol. 7, no. 1 (Oct., 1937), pp. 13-17.

    Franciscan Saints in English Mediaeval Glass and Embroidery.
    Chapter 3 in Franciscan History and Legend in English Mediaeval Art,
    edited by LITTLE, A.G.
    Manchester, 1937.

    Review of McNEIL RUSHFORTH, G., The Windows of the Church of St.
    Neot, Cornwall.
    J.M.G.P., vol. 7, no. 1 (Oct., 1937), pp. 50-51.

    Stained and Painted Glass in England.
    London, 1937.

WOODFORDE, Christopher (Contd.)

    The Fourteenth-Century Glass in North Luffenham Church, Rutland.
    J.M.G.P., vol. 7, no. 2 (Apr., 1938), pp. 69-73.

    Review of Stained Glass of York Minster, with introduction and notes
    by HARRISON, F.
    J.M.G.P., vol. 7, no. 2 (Apr., 1938), pp. 102-103.

    The Medieval Stained Glass of Long Melford Church, Suffolk.
    Journal of the British Archaeological Association, 3rd series, vol.
    3 (1938), pp. 1-63.

    A Further Note on the Medieval Stained Glass at Long Melford,
    Suffolk.
    Journal of the British Archaeological Association, 3rd series, vol.
    4 (1939), pp. 193-196.

    The Painted Glass in Withcote Church.
    Burlington Magazine, vol. 75 (1939), pp. 17-22.

    English Stained Glass and Glass-Painters in the Fourteenth Century.
    Proceedings of the British Academy, vol. 25 (1939).

    Peter Carslegh's Window in Winscombe Church, Somerset.
    J.M.G.P., vol. 8, no. 2 (Apr., 1940), pp. 51-57.

    The Origin of the St. Catherine Window at Clavering.
    Transactions of the Essex Archaeological Society, new series, vol.
    22 for 1936-1939 (1940), pp. 229-231.

    The Medieval Stained Glass of the East Harling and North Tuddenham
    Churches, Norfolk.
    Journal of the British Archaeological Association, 3rd series, vol. 5
    (1940), pp. 1-32.

    The Ancient Glass at Orchardleigh.
    Proceedings of the Somersetshire Archaeological and Natural History
    Society, vol. 86 for 1940, part 2 (1941), pp. 79-85.

    The Passion Window in East Brent Church, Somerset.
    J.M.G.P., vol. 8, no. 3 (Apr., 1941), pp. 96-100.

    Stained Glass in Somerset.
    (A request for information.)
    Notes and Queries for Somerset and Dorset, vol. 23 (1939-1942), pp.
    171-172.

    John Gunthorpe, Dean of Wells, 1472-1498. His Coat-of-Arms, Badges,
    Motto and Monogram.
    J.M.G.P., vol. 9, no. 1 (1943), pp. 2-14.

    Some Medieval English Glazing Quarries Painted with Birds.
    Journal of the British Archaeological Association (1944), pp. 1-11.

    Some Medieval Leaden Ventilating Panels at Wells and Glastonbury.
    J.M.G.P., vol. 9, no. 2 (1944), pp. 44-50.

    Stained Glass Windows in Somerset.
    (A further request for help.)
    Notes and Queries for Somerset and Dorset, vol. 24 (1946), p. 35.

    Stained Glass in Somerset, 1250-1830.
    Oxford, 1946.
    Reviewed by EVANS, Joan, The Archaeological Journal, vol. 105 (for
    1948), p. 96.
    Reviewed by WATKIN, Dom Aelred, The Journal of the British
    Archaeological Association, 3rd series, vol. 10 (for 1945-1947), pp.
    81-83.
    Reviewed in Notes and Queries, vol. 192 (March 22, 1947), p. 130.
    Reviewed by F.G.R., The Connoisseur, vol. 120 (Sept., 1947), p. 65.
    Reviewed in Proceedings of the Somersetshire Archaeological and
    Natural History Society, vol. 92 for 1946, part 2 (1947), pp. 103-104.
    Reviewed by KIRBY, H.T., J.M.G.P., vol. 10, no. 1 (1948), pp. 49-50.

WOODFORDE, Christopher (Contd.)

    Review of LAMBORN, E.A. Greening, The Armorial Glass of the Oxford
    Diocese.
    Burlington Magazine, vol. 91 (Jan.-Dec., 1949), pp. 264-265.

    The Norwich School of Glass-Painting in the Fifteenth Century.
    Oxford, 1950.
    Reviewed in Notes and Queries, vol. 196 (March 31, 1951), pp. 153-154.
    Reviewed by F.G.R., The Connoisseur, vol. 127 (March, 1951), p. 58.
    Reviewed by KIRBY, H.T., J.M.G.P., vol. 10, no. 4 (1951), pp. 221-222.

    The Stained Glass of New College, Oxford.
    Oxford, 1951.
    Reviewed by HARVEY, John, Journal of the British Archaeological
    Association, 3rd series, vol. 14 (1951), pp. 71-72.
    Reviewed in Oxoniensia, vol. 16 for 1951 (1953), pp. 96-98.
    Reviewed by F.G.R., The Connoisseur, vol. 128 (Oct., 1951), p. 125.
    Reviewed by KIRBY, H.T., J.M.G.P., vol. 11, no. 1 (1952), p. 56.
    Reviewed by RACKHAM, Bernard, Burlington Magazine, vol. 94 (Jan.-Dec.,
    1952), pp. 90-91.

    English Stained and Painted Glass.
    Oxford, 1954.
    Reviewed by LAFOND, Jean, The Archaeological Journal, vol. 111 (for
    1954), pp. 239-241.
    Reviewed by CRAIG, John, J.M.G.P., vol. 11, no. 4 (1955), pp. 252-253.
    Reviewed by MILNER-WHITE, Eric, Burlington Magazine, vol. 97 (Jan.-
    Dec., 1955), pp. 262-263.

(Woodforde, Christopher)

    Obituary.
    The Times, Aug. 13, 1962.
    (Reprinted J.M.G.P., vol. 13, no. 4 (1963), pp. 593-595.)

WOODHOUSE, J.C., and NEWLING, W.

    A Short Account of Lichfield Cathedral: More Particularly of the
    Painted Glass with which its Windows are Adorned, etc.
    Lichfield, 1811.
    (Several subsequent editions.)

WOODROFFE, Paul

    The Re-leading of Ancient Stained Glass.
    (Letter to the Editor.)
    J.M.G.P., vol. 1, no. 5 (Oct., 1926).

(Woore, Edward)

    Obituary.
    J.M.G.P., vol. 13, no. 2 (1961), p. 444.

(Wootton Wawen)

    Wootton Wawen Church (R.C.), Warwickshire: Glass.
    (Grant to restore the 1814 window by Samuel Lowe.)
    The Pilgrim Trust, 43rd Annual Report (1973), p. 14.

(Worcester Art Museum, U.S.A.)

    Stained Glass in the Worcester Art Museum.
    Stained Glass, vol. 29, no. 4 (Winter, 1934-1935), pp. 95-105.

(Worcester Cathedral)

    (Adelaide Memorial Window.)
    (Defective colouration pointed out.)
    The Ecclesiologist, vol. 16 (1855), p. 316.
    (PREEDY, F., explains the defect, Ibid., p. 399.)
    (He is rebutted, Ibid., vol. 17 (1856), p. 80.)

World's Fair Focuses Attention on Church Stained Glass Art.
        Worship and Arts (Feb.-March, 1962).

WORMALD, Francis
        Anniversary Address.
        The Antiquaries' Journal, vol. 50 (1970).
        (Refers to the work of the C.V.M.A., pp. 182-183.)

(Wragby Church)
        Wragby Church, Yorkshire: Glass.
        (A grant towards repairing and replacing a window.)
        The Pilgrim Trust, 39th Annual Report (1969), p. 17.

        (Grant to commence the re-leading of the glass.)
        The Pilgrim Trust, 40th Annual Report (1970), p. 14.

        (Grant for the restoration of two further windows.)
        The Pilgrim Trust, 42nd Annual Report (1972), p. 15.

WRIGHT, Georgia Sommers
        Review of The Year 1200: A Symposium.
        Art Bulletin, vol. 59 (March, 1977), pp. 131-133.

WRIGHT, Helen E.
        Memorial Windows of San Francisco.
        Overland Monthly, new series, vol. 43 (Apr., 1904), pp. 332-335.

        The Evolution of a Window.
        Ibid., new series, vol. 43 (May, 1904), pp. 366-369.

WRIGHT, H.E.
        (Letter to the Editor defending opalescent glass.)
        Stained Glass, vol. 27, no. 7 (July, 1932), pp. 219-221.

WRIGHT, Helen Martha
        A Painted Glass Portrait of Sir Hans Sloane.
        (In the possession of the New Jersey Historical Society.)
        Jersey City, 1934.

WROOT, Herbert E.
        Pre-Raphaelite Windows at Bradford.
        (Tristram and Iseult series.)
        The Studio, vol. 72 (1917), pp. 69-73.

WULCKO, C. Tyndall
        Stained Glass in Churches.
        (On objections to it recently put forward by an Anglican bishop.)
        (J.M.G.P., (Apr., 1936), q.v.)
        Notes and Queries, vol. 170 (May 2, 1936), pp. 320-321.

(Wycliffe Church, Yorkshire)
        A Description of the Windows and Stained Glass, etc.
        The Gentleman's Magazine, vol. 82, part 2 (1812), pp. 323-324.

WYNNE, Michael
        (With WHITE, James.)
        Irish Stained Glass.
        Dublin, 1963.
        Reviewed by HAYWARD, John, J.M.G.P., vol. 14, no. 5 (1970-1971), pp.
        268-269.

        Irish Stained Glass.
        Dublin, 1977.

YATES, S.A. Thompson
        Notes, Mainly Concerning Painted Windows, Made During a Journey in
        Italy and Switzerland.
        Liverpool, 1898.

(Yarnton Church)
        Yarnton Church, Oxford: Stained Glass.
        (Grant towards the restoration of the seventeenth century windows.)
        The Pilgrim Trust, 42nd Annual Report (1972), p. 15.

(Yellow Staining of Glass)
        Gelbaetze.
        Sprechsaal, vol. 61 (1928), pp. 769-770.

        On the Yellow Staining of Glass.
        (Abstracts of Articles in Sprechsaal, by HEINRICH, W., SCHOOT, R.,
        SPRINGER, L., SALAQUADA, F.)
        Journal of the Society of Glass Technology, vol. 16, no. 64 (Dec.,
        1932), pp. 479-483.

YERNAUX, Jean
        L'Art du Vitrail au Pays Mosan.
        Liège, 1951.

YOKI
        Vitraux du Jura.
        Moutier, 1969.

        Vitraux Modernes en Suisse.
        Fribourg, 1971.
        Reviewed by PULLEN, Derek, J.M.G.P., vol. 15, no. 2 (1973-1974), pp.
        72-73.

YORK, G.R.
        Initials in Glass Quarries.
        (Request for identification of initials and arms at St. Clement's,
        Norwich; St. Neot's Huntingdon; Puttenham, Hertford.)
        Notes and Queries, vol. 9 (June 3, 1854), p. 515.

(York Glaziers)
        York Memorandum Book. Part 1, 1376-1419. Part 2, 1388-1493.
        a) Des Verrours Glasiourz. b) Glasyers.
        Publications of the Surtees Society, vol. 120, for 1911 (1912), pp.
        50-52.
        Ibid., vol. 125, for 1914 (1915), pp. 208-210.

(York Glaziers' Trust)
        Historic Glass.
        York Civic Trust Annual Report (1966-1967), pp. 27-28.

        Stained Glass - York Glaziers' Trust.
        (A grant to extend the workshop.)
        The Pilgrim Trust, 37th Annual Report (1967), pp. 20-21.

        York Glaziers' Trust. Stained Glass from Parish Churches.
        (Newton Bromswell, Northants.; Thornton, Leics.; Wragby, Yorks.;
        and a grant towards the isoprobe experiments at York University.)
        The Pilgrim Trust, 44th Annual Report (1974), p. 14.

        York Glaziers' Trust: Stained Glass.
        (Goadby Marwood, Leics.; Carlton Scroop, Lincs.; St. Mary's,
        Castlegate, York.)
        The Pilgrim Trust, 45th Annual Report, (1975), p. 16.

        York Glaziers' Trust: Stained Glass from Parish Churches.
        (Helmdon, Northants.; Stanton St. John, Oxfordshire; Ryther, Yorks.)
        The Pilgrim Trust, 46th Annual Report (1976), p. 11.

        York Glaziers' Trust: Stained Glass from Parish Churches.
        (Holy Trinity, Acaster Malbis, York; St. Mary's, Birkin, Yorks.;
        St. Mary's, Weldon, nr. Peterborough.)
        The Pilgrim Trust, 47th Annual Report (1977), p. 10.

York Glazier's Trust: Stained Glass from Parish Churches.
(St. Michael's, Emley, Wakefield; St. Oswald, Kirk Sandal, Sheffield;
All Saints, Normanton; All Saints, Weston, Yorks.; All Saints, Wing,
Bucks.)
The Pilgrim Trust, 48th Annual Report (1978), p. 41.

(York)

(Decision taken to ask for a public subscription of at least £11,000
to remove ancient glass from the churches for the duration.)
Yorkshire Gazette, July 26, 1940; Aug. 9, 1940.

Ancient Glass.
(Various replacements of windows.)
York Civic Trust Annual Report (1948-1949), Article 9.

The Stained Glass of York.
Ibid., (1957-1958), pp. 12-13.

(A research fellowship grant given by the Radcliffe Trust for the
study of York glass.)
Yorkshire Evening Press, March 8, 1973.

(University.)
Installation of Isoprobe Equipment.
News and Notes, J.M.G.P., vol. 15, no. 2 (1973-1974), pp. 50-51.

Heritage of Glass. An Illustrated Appreciation of European Stained
and Painted Glass.
(Announcement of event for the 1973 York Festival.)
York Minster News, no. 1 (June, 1973), p. 5 (unnumbered).

(Pilgrim Trust grant to enable glass to be removed and studied at
York. First window proposed for this to be from St. John the
Baptist, Kirby Wharfe.)
Yorkshire Evening Press, Aug. 6, 1974.

(York Churches)
(A brief listing of the remaining glass.)
The Ecclesiologist, vol. 6 (1846), pp. 97-98.

(York: Appeal for Funds to Remove the Glass.)
English Windows in Danger.
Stained Glass, vol. 35, no. 4 (Winter, 1940), pp. 131-133.

(York Parish Churches)
York Parish Churches: Glass.
(Further grants made.)
The Pilgrim Trust, 19th Annual Report (1949), pp. 11-12.

(York, All Saints, North Street)
Famous Church Window.
(Account of the 'Prick of Conscience' Window.)
Yorkshire Post, Aug. 20, 1931.

All Saints Church, York.
(Grant towards restoring the windows.)
The Pilgrim Trust, 32nd Annual Report (1962), pp. 13-14.

All Saints Church, North Street.
York Civic Trust Annual Report (1965-1966), p. 17.

All Saints, North Street.
Ibid., (1976-1977).
(Glass, p. 5.)

All Saints Church, North Street, York.
York, 1978.

(York, All Saints', Pavement)
(To receive glass from St. Saviour's Church.)
Yorkshire Gazette and Herald, July 9, 1954.

(Patterns made of west window to check whether redundant glass from
elsewhere can be fitted.)
Yorkshire Post, Sept. 2, 1954.

(Glass from St. Saviour's to be dedicated as a memorial to Angelo
Raine.)
Yorkshire Evening Press, Nov. 20, 1957, Nov. 23, 1957, Nov. 25, 1957.

(York, Clifton Church)
(Memorial Windows dedicated.)
Yorkshire Gazette, Dec. 25, 1909.

(York, St. Denys' Church)
St. Denys' Church.
York Civic Trust Annual Report (1974-1975), pp. 20-21.

(York, Garrison Church)
Dedication of East Window in Fulford Barracks.
Yorkshire Evening Press, May 4, 1957, May 6, 1957.

(York, St. Hilda's Church)
(Faculty granted for a window.)
Yorkshire Evening Press, Dec. 13, 1955.

(Dedication of window.)
Yorkshire Evening Press, Feb. 20, 1956.

(York, St. Laurence's Church)
(Dedication of stained glass window.)
Yorkshire Gazette, Sept. 22, 1906.

(Gift of a window.)
Yorkshire Gazette, Oct. 27, 1906.

New Stained Glass Window to Commemorate the Sefton Fearne Family.
Designed by Mr. Harry Harvey.
Yorkshire Evening Press, March 26, 1975.

(York, St. Martin-le-Grand)
Correspondence concerning the West Window. Restoration plan
submitted for approval.
Yorkshire Evening Press, Nov. 15, 1955.

(York, St. Martin's, Coney St.)
(Yorkshire Museum to lend some glass to the church.)
Yorkshire Evening Press, Oct. 24, 1964.

(York, St. Mary, Castlegate)
Account of the Church of St. Mary, Castlegate, York.
York, 1873.

(York, St. Michael-le-Belfrey)
Stained Glass.
York Civic Trust Annual Report (1958-1959), pp. 16-17.

Ancient Glass.
York Civic Trust Annual Report (1959-1960), pp. 14-15.

(York, St. Michael's, Spurriergate)
New Ancient Glass.
York Civic Trust Annual Report (1947-1948), Article 8.

(York, St. Olave's Church)
    (Faculty granted for a window.)
    Yorkshire Gazette, Feb. 19, 1910.

(York, St. Paul's, Holgate)
    (Faculty granted to insert a window.)
    Yorkshire Gazette, Oct. 16, 1909.

(York, Guildhall)
    (Proposal to remove the west window, by Edmund Gyles, and replace it.
    Protests.)
    Yorkshire Gazette, Jan. 17, 1863, Jan. 24, 1863.

    (Stained Glass.)
    Yorkshire Gazette, Oct. 18, 1924.

(York, University)
    (Installation of isoprobe equipment for analysis of glass.)
    Yorkshire Evening Press, Dec. 28, 1973.

(York Minster)
    (Window erected at south end of nave.)
    York Courant, Feb. 21, 1769.

    Description and History of York Cathedral.
    York, 1783, 2nd edition.

    (Window, from St. Nicholas', Rouen, presented by the Earl of Carlisle.)
    York Courant, Nov. 5, 1804.

    (East window to be replaced.)
    Yorkshire Gazette, June 5, 1824.

    Visitors' Guide to York Cathedral with an Account of the Churches in
    York, etc.
    York, 1845.

    (Chapter House windows to be repaired after wind damage.)
    Yorkshire Gazette, June 23, 1855.

    (Chapter House glass restored by Mr. Norton.)
    Yorkshire Gazette, Aug. 11, 1855.

    Exterior of the Five Sisters to be Glazed.
    Yorkshire Gazette, June 29, 1861.

    Four Lancet Windows being made for the North Transept by Clayton & Bell
    in memory of the 51st regiment in India.
    Yorkshire Gazette, March 12, 1864.

    Description of new stained glass windows in the west aisle of the
    North Transept.
    Yorkshire Gazette, Feb. 24, 1866, March 3, 1866.

    Stained Glass in York Minster.
    Description of a part of the Five Sisters' Window - Habakkuk feeding
    Daniel while confined in the lions' den. By G.R.
    With a coloured drawing by KNOWLES, J.W.
    The Yorkshire Architectural Society (Dec., 1873).

    Account of the Restoration of St. Cuthbert's Window, York Minster.
    The Antiquary, vol. 15 (Feb., 1887), p. 78.

    (Notice of restoration of the St. Cuthbert window by J.W. Knowles and
    J.T. Fowler.)
    The Yorkshire Archaeological and Topographical Journal, vol. 10 for
    1887-1889 (1889), pp. 165-166.

    (Window to be installed to the memory of Frank Lockwood.)
    Yorkshire Gazette, June 29, 1901.

(York Minster, Contd.)
    (£50,000 fund opened for Minster glass.)
    Yorkshire Gazette, Nov. 13, 1920.

    (Restoration of the Peter de Dene window as a memorial to Freemasons.)
    Ibid., May 12, 1923.

    (Five Sisters' Window Fund closed at £3,555.19.9.)
    Ibid., June 23, 1923.

    (Window to be restored by Northern Command as a thank-offering for
    victory.)
    Ibid., Oct. 13, 1923.

    Work carried out at the Minster during 1928.
    (Re-leading of windows in the Choir clerestory.)
    1st Annual Report of the Friends of York Minster (June, 1929), pp. 3-4.

    (Unveiling of the newly restored Becket window.)
    Yorkshire Gazette, Oct. 19, 1929.

    Work Carried out at the Minster during 1929.
    (Re-leading of several windows including the Chapter House.)
    2nd Annual Report of the Friends of York Minster (Spring, 1930), pp.
    26-27.

    The Minster Windows.
    (The Chapter House Glass, The Carlisle Window, the Great West Window.)
    Ibid., pp. 35-36.

    Unveiling of the (third) Chapter House Window.
    Summer Report of the Friends of York Minster (1930), pp. 1-3.

    Work Carried out at the Minster during 1930.
    (Re-leading of several windows.)
    3rd Annual Report of the Friends of York Minster (Spring, 1931), pp.
    18-19.

    The Great West Window.
    Ibid., pp. 20-22.

    The Work Upon the Windows. The Process of Preservation.
    Summer Report of the Friends of York Minster (1931), pp. 12-14.

    The Unveiling of the Fifth and Sixth Chapter House Windows.
    Ibid., pp. 16-18.

    The Zouche Chapel East Window.
    Ibid., p. 26.

    Work Carried out at the Minster during 1931.
    (Re-leading.)
    4th Annual Report of the Friends of York Minster (Spring, 1932), pp.
    19-20.

    Restoration Work Carried out during 1932.
    (Re-leading.)
    5th Annual Report of the Friends of York Minster (1933), p. 29.

    Minster Glass, Old or New. By A.D.
    Yorkshire Evening Post, Dec. 15, 1933.

    Glass in the Minster.
    (Proceedings at the Meeting of the Royal Archaeological Institute at
    York.)
    Archaeological Journal, vol. 91 (1935), pp. 360-362.

    Report by Mr. R.C. Green . . . on Restoration Work during 1934.
    (Re-leading of the St. Cuthbert window.)
    7th Annual Report of the Friends of York Minster (1935), pp. 25-26.

    Report by Mr. R.C. Green . . . on the Restoration Work carried out
    during 1935.
    (Re-leading of the St. Cuthbert window.)
    8th Annual Report of the Friends of York Minster (1936), pp. 35-36.

    (Proposal to replace the 1840 glass in the lancets above the Five
    Sisters.)
    11th Annual Report of the Friends of York Minster (1939), pp. 10-11.

Report from the Clerk of the Works. Restoration Work, Jan.-Dec., 1939.
(Removal of the Five Sisters, Great East Window and eighteen others.)
12th Annual Report of the Friends of York Minster (1940), p. 13.

Report from the Clerk of the Works. Restoration Work, Jan.-Dec., 1940.
(Removal of seventeen windows, including St. William, St. Cuthbert, and
Great West Windows.)
13th Annual Report of the Friends of York Minster (1941), p. 13.

Report from the Clerk of the Works. Restoration Work, Jan.-Dec., 1941.
(Removal of twenty-five windows.)
14th Annual Report of the Friends of York Minster (1942), p. 17.

Report from the Clerk of the Works. Restoration Work, Jan.-Dec., 1942.
(Removal of ten windows.)
15th Annual Report of the Friends of York Minster (1943), p. 19.

(Placing of glass from St. John's, Micklegate, in the Minster.)
News and Notes, J.M.G.P., vol. 9, no. 3 (1945), p. 71.

York Minster Glass.
(The restoration work.)
The Pilgrim Trust, 18th Annual Report (1948), pp. 11-13.

Replacement of the 50,000 pieces of glass of the Five Sisters Window
started.
Yorkshire Gazette, Feb. 3, 1950.

(Purchase of some panels of early Tudor glass.)
News and Notes, J.M.G.P., vol. 10, no. 3 (1950), pp. 114-115.

The Minster Glass.
York Civic Trust Annual Report (1951-1952), p. 12 (unnumbered).

(Rededication of the East Window.)
Yorkshire Evening Press, June 30, 1953.

(The Great West Window.)
Ibid., March 14, 1961.

(York Minster and All Saints, North Street.)
The Old Glass of York.
York Civic Trust Annual Report (1961-1962), pp. 12-13.

(Work of replacing the glass nearly completed. Details.)
Yorkshire Evening Press, Nov. 23, 1962.

(Two panels dating c. 1470 found in a cottage window bequeathed to
the Dean and Chapter.)
Ibid., May 14, 1963.

(Five Sisters damaged by vandals.)
Ibid., Feb. 27, 1964.

York Minster Workshops.
(Photograph of window in the glazing department, and a brief account.)
Ibid., Apr. 17, 1964.

(Damage to windows by vandalism.)
36th Annual Report of the Friends of York Minster (1964), p. 4.

(The Monkey's Funeral.)
Yorkshire Evening Press, June 3, 1965.

The Minster Glass-Shop.
38th Annual Report of the Friends of York Minster (1966), p. 8.

The York Glaziers' Trust.
39th Annual Report of the Friends of York Minster (1967), pp. 24-25.

(Great west window to be replaced.)
Yorkshire Evening Press, March 1, 1967.

(Rededication of west window.)
Ibid., July 3, 1967.

York Minster. An Index and Guide to the Windows of the Transepts and
Choir.
York, 1967.

The Great East Window.
York, n.d.

(Glass panel in Montague Bruce memorial window smashed.)
Yorkshire Evening Press, July 1, 1967.

(Two men appear in court.)
Ibid., July 20, 1967, July 24, 1967.

(East window is covered in protective reinforced plastic sheeting
during restoration.)
Yorkshire Evening Press, June 27, 1968.

Minster Notes: The York Glaziers' Trust. York Glass in Paris.
40th Annual Report of the Friends of York Minster (1968), p. 25.

York Minster Glass.
(A grant towards repairing the great West Window.)
The Pilgrim Trust, 38th Annual Report (1968), pp. 16-17.

Stained glass from windows near the east end of the Minster to be
housed in underground chambers used as air raid shelters during the
War, during work on renewing the foundations.
Yorkshire Evening Press, Aug. 27, 1969.

Rose window to be given a 'face-lift'.
Ibid., Sept. 24, 1969.

Three twelfth century windows restored by York Glaziers' Trust to
be exhibited in America.
Ibid., Oct. 13, 1969.

Panel of twelfth century stained glass going to the U.S.A. as part of
an exhibition of European art treasures at the Metropolitan Museum,
New York.
Ibid., Jan. 15, 1970.

Rose window restored.
Ibid., Aug. 27, 1970.

(Gift by the Dean and Chapter of a panel made up from fragments to
Dr. Coggan, Archbishop.)
Yorkshire Evening Press, March 4, 1971.

(Replacement of glass in the South rose.)
43rd Annual Report of the Friends of York Minster (1971), p. 13.

Tracery panels in the north nave clerestory windows now being restored.
Yorkshire Evening Press, Jan. 6, 1972.

York Minster: Nave Clerestory Glass.
(Grant towards restoring the clerestory windows.)
The Pilgrim Trust, 43rd Annual Report (1973), p. 10.

X-rays to Save Minster Glass.
York Minster News, no. 2 (Spring, 1974), p. 7 (unnumbered).

(Experiment to find the best means of ventilating the space between
the old glass and the protective window.)
Yorkshire Evening Press, March 14, 1975.

(Heat sensitive camera produces photos of the stained glass windows in
York Minster, showing the differing temperatures of the glass. Used
in the investigation into the best way of ventilating the space
between the stained glass windows and their outer protective windows.)
Ibid., June 20, 1975.

(All Minster stained glass now back in place for the first time since
the Second World War began in 1939. Stained glass from the
redundant St. Paul's Church, Middlesbrough, placed in the clerestory
immediately to the right of the great East window.)
Ibid., July 26, 1975.

(Exhibition of Minster glass in the Chapter House.)
Ibid., Apr. 13, 1976, Apr. 17, 1976.

(York Minster, Contd.)

(Grant towards the restoration of the remaining clerestory windows.)
The Pilgrim Trust, 48th Annual Report (1978), p. 9.

(Two windows in the South Choir aisle - nos. 16 and 17 - to be used
as trials for rival preservation systems.
Yorkshire Evening Press, Jan. 7, 1978.

(Article on the stained glass of York Minster.)
Ibid., Oct. 8, 1979.

YOUNG, Joseph
Mosaics: Principles and Practice.
New York, 1963.

YOUNG, Mary
Singing Windows.
New York and Nashville, 1962.
Reviewed by ANDERSON, Gwen, Stained Glass, vol. 57, no. 4 (Winter,
1962-1963), p. 37.

ZAKIN, Helen Jackson
French Cistercian Grisaille Glass.
Gesta. vol. 13, part 2 (1974), pp. 17-28.

ZALUSKA, Yolanta, LAUTIER, Claudine, BRISAC, Catherine, BOUCHON, Chantal
La 'Belle-Verriere' de Chartres.
Revue de l'Art, no. 46 (1979), pp. 16-24.

ZIMMETER, Kunibert
Das Glasgemälde im Landesmuseum Ferdinandeum zu Innsbruck.
Museum Ferdinandeum (Innsbruck) Veröffentlichungen, vol. 10, no. 53
(1930).

ZANTNER-BUSCH, Dora
Eine alte Deutsche Kunst. Zur Geschichte der Glasmalerei.
Diamant, 57th year, no.17 (June 11, 1935).

ZEITLER, Julius
Das Arbeitsbild in der Glasmalerei.
Diamant, 51st year, no. 29 (Oct. 11, 1929).

ZELLER, A.
Die Stiftskirche St. Peter zu Wimpfen im Tal. Baugeschichte und
Bauanfnahme, Grundsätze ihrer Wiederherstellung.
Leipzig, 1903.

ZEMP, Josef
Die schweizerische Glasmalerei. Eine kunsthistorische Skizze.
Lucerne, 1890.

ZETTLER, F.X.

Die hervorragendsten Glasgemälde im Königlichen rumänischen Schlosse
Castel Pelesch zu Sinaia.
Munich, 1887.

Vierzig Jahre Glasmalkunst.
Munich, 1910.

Stained Glass Windows Designed and Executed by F.X. Zettler.
Chicago and New York, 1911.

Michael Sigismund Frank. Revivalist of the Art of Glass-Painting in
Germany.
(Translated by Ludwig von Gerichten.)
J.M.G.P., vol. 2, no. 1 (1927), pp. 23-29.

(Zettler, Oscar)

Obituary.
Stained Glass, vol. 48, no. 2 (Summer, 1953), pp. 105-106.

ZHUKOVA, Ariadna

Stained Glass Walls.
U.S.S.R., Apr., 1962.

ZOCCA, E.

Assisi.
Rome, 1936.

ZSCHACKE, F.H.

Goethe und die Glasmalerei.
Diamant (March 21, 1938).

ZSCHACKE, F.H.

Goethe and the Art of Glass Staining.
Journal of the British Society of Master Glass-Painters (1950), pp.
142-146.

ZSCHOKKE, Fridtjof

Die romanischen Glasgemälde des Strassburger Münsters.
Basel, 1942.
Reviewed by RACKHAM, Bernard, Burlington Magazine, vol. 83 (July-Dec,
1943), p. 208.

Alte Glasmalerei der Schweiz.
(Catalogue.)
Zurich ?, 1946.

Vitraux du Moyen-Age en Suisse.
Basel, 1947.

Mittelalterliche Bildfenster der Schweiz. Zehn farbige Tafeln
herausgegeben und eingeleitet von F. Zschokke.
Basle, 1947.
(Translation, Medieval Stained Glass of Switzerland, Ten Colour Plates.
Edited and with an introduction by F. Zschokke.)
London, 1947.

Epilogue (to C. WILD-BLOCK's La Vie de la Vierge . . .).
Bulletin de la Société des Amis de la Cathédrale de Strasbourg, t. 11
(1974), pp. 54-57.

(Zubar, Marco)

The Stained Glass Art of Marco Zubar.
Architects Bulletin, New Jersey (Dec., 1966).

(Zurich)

Wegleitung Kunstgewerbemuseum Zurich.
Zurich, 1946.

ZWIERLEIN, Freiherr von

(Sale catalogue of collection.)
Catalog der Freiherrlich von Zwierlein'schen Kunstsammlungen . . .
gebrannte Glasfenster des 14-18 Jahrhunderts . . . u.s.w.
(Sale Sept. 12-15, 1887.)
Cologne, 1887.

SUPPLEMENT

(Abel Alfons)
Ein Glasmaler besucht Chartres. Alfons Abel.
Diamant, 56th year, no. 19 (July 1, 1934).

BACHER, E. & BRANDESTEIN, H.
Die Mittelalterlichen Glasgemälde in der Steiermark. I,
Graz und Strassengel.
Vienna, Cologne, Graz, 1979.

BARRON, Oswald
A Guide to the Coats of Arms at Montacute House.
n.p., n.d. (4 unnumbered pages).

BECKSMANN, Rüdiger
Die Mittelalterlichen Glasmalereien in Baden und der Pfalz.
Berlin, 1979.

BRADY, D. & SERBAN, W.
Stained Glass. A Guide to Information Sources.
Michigan, 1980.

(Bringmann, Carl)
Zu den Glasgemälden. Von Carl Bringmann aus der Werkstalt
Bringmann & Schmidt in Coburg.
Diamant, 50th year, no. 36 (1928), pp. 742-744.

BUCKINGHAM, F.F.
Doddiscombsleigh. A Short History of the Parish, Incumbents,
Church and Stained Glass Windows.
Yeovil, n.d. (c. 1930).

BUCKLER, J.C. & C.A.
Melbury Bubbe.
Archaeological Journal, vol. 45 (1888)
glass, pp. 367-371.

CAVINESS, M.H. (ed)
Medieval and Renaissance Stained Glass from New England
collections. Catalogue of an Exhibition held at the
Busch-Reisinger Museum, Harvard University.
Medford, 1978.

CAVINESS, M.H. & RAGUIN, V.C.
Another dispersed window from Soissons: A Tree of Jesse
in the Sainte-Chapelle style.
Gesta, vol 20, part 1, 1981, pp. 191-198.

COE, Brian
Stained Glass in England: 1150-1550.
London, 1981.
(Stained glass photography, pp. 135-138.)

COOKE, R.D.
The Churches of Ipplepen & Torbryan.
n.d., n.p.
(Glass, Ipplepen, p. 10.
Torbryan, pp. 27-28)

COUNCER, C.R.
Lost Glass from Kent Churches.
Maidstone, 1980.

DORLING, E.E.
Notes on some Armorial Glass in Salisbury Cathedral.
The Ancestor, no. 4 (Jan 1903)
pp. 120-126.

DORLING, E.E.
Notes on two Nevill Shields at Salisbury.
(In the Hall of John Halle)
The Ancestor, no. 8 (Jan 1904)
pp. 202-204.

DRACHENBERG, E.
Die mittelalterliche Glasmalerei in Erfurt, 2 Dom.
Berlin, 1980.

EARWAKER, Clifford
The Story of St. Peter's, Bexhill.
Bexhill, 1959.
(Subsequent editions 1969, 1977.)
(Glass returned from Walpole's collection, pp. 22-24.
Modern glass, pp. 36-40.)

EDEN, F.C.
(Exhibits panels of fragments, probably from Exeter.)
Proceedings of the Society of Antiquaries, 2nd series, vol. 28.
(Nov., 1915-June, 1916), pp. 102-103.

(Edzard, Dietz)
Das Friedrich-Bayer-Fenster von Diets Edzard. 15s mit vielen
Abbildungen, herausgegeben von den Werkstätten für Mosaik und
Glasmalerei Puhl und Wagner.
Berlin-Treptow, 1927.

EUSTICE, M.
The Windows, Cathedral of St Mary the Virgin, Truro.
(Folding pamphlet.)
St Ives, n.d.

EVANS, S.H.
Prisoners of Conscience Window, Salisbury Cathedral.
London, 1980.

(Ewelme)
Guide to St Mary's Church, Ewelme.
Bath, 1967.
(Glass, pp. 5, 7, 9, 19, 20.)

(Fécamp Abbey)
Fécamp Abbey Stained Glass. Restorer's Alleged Confession.
The Times, Nov. 27, 1933.
Fécamp Abbey Stained Glass.
(Announcement that W.R. Hearst is to return the panels involved.
The Times, Nov 28, 1933.

FINNEY, W.E. St Lawrence
Medieval Games and Gaderyngs at Kinston-upon-Thames.
(Related to a panel of glass formerly at Betley, Staffs.)
J.M.G.P., vol. 6, no. 1 (Apr., 1935), pp. 16-27.
no. 2 (Oct., 1935), pp. 70-79.
no. 3.(Apr., 1936), pp. 144-151.

FRASER, A.C.
The Church of Saint Bartholomew, Brightwell Baldwin.
(n.p., 1981)
Glass, pp. 3-6.

GRASIS, T.
Latviescu Vitrâza.
Riga, 1979.

GRODECKI, Louis
Dix Ans d'activité du Corpus Vitrearum.
Revue de l'Art, no. 51, 1981.
pp. 23-30.

GURDON, W.B.
Restoration considered as a destructive art.
Archaeological Journal, vol. 56 (1899).
Glass, pp. 333-335.

HARRISON, Martin
Victorian Stained Glass (London, 1979).

HAYWARD, Jane

 The Lost Noah Window from Poitiers.
 Gesta, von. 20 part 1, 1981.
 pp. 129-139.

HELBIG, Jean

 Le flux du style Renaissance dans les vitraux Liegeois.
 Revue Belge d'Archeologie, vol. 14 (1944) pp. 69-80.

JOHNSON, Ben

 Stained Glass (of York) in Pevsner, Yorkshire: York and the
 East Riding, London, 1972.
 (pp. 58-67.)

JOHNSON, Ben

 Stained Glass (of York Minster) in Pevsner, Yorkshire and the
 East Riding, London, 1972.
 (pp. 96-105.)

KEYSER, C.E.

 Aldermaston Church, Berkshire.
 Archaeological Journal, vol. 55 (1898).
 Glass, pp. 378-380.

LEHMANN, Hans

 Schweizerische Handzeichnungen und die Frage: Gab es in der
 ersten Hälfte des 16. Jahrhunderts zwei Maler Hans Funk,
 Vater und Sohn, in Bern?
 Anzeiger fur Schweizerische Altertumskunde
 Vol. 31 (1929). pp. 217-226.

LEHMANN, Hans

 Fenster und Wappenschenkungen des luzernischen Amtes Rotenburg
 von 1514-1617.
 Anzeiger fur Schweizerische Altertumskunde
 Vol. 31 (1929). pp. 131-139.

LEHMANN, Hans

 Das alte Schutzenhaus am Platz zu Zurich, sein Fensterschmuck
 und dessen ersteller Jos Murer. Schweizerisches Landesmuseum, Rapport Annuel, 1932
 pp. 43-94.

LEHMANN, Hans

 Grosshans Thomann von Zurich, Glasmaker und Maler (1525-1567)
 Schweizerisches Landesmuseum, Rapport Annuel, 1935.
 pp. 72-97.

LEHMANN, Hans

 Ulrich Ban, der Maler und Glasmaler in Zurich.
 Schweizerisches Landesmuseum, Rapport Annuel, 1936.
 pp. 44-54.

LILLICH, M.

 The Stained Glass of Saint-Père de Chartres.
 Middletown, 1978.

LITTLE, C.T.

 Membra Disjecta: More early stained glass from Troyes
 Cathedral.
 Gesta, vol. 20 part 1, 1981.
 pp. 119-127.

MAXWELL-LYTE, H.

 Heraldic Glass from Lytes Cary.
 The Ancestor, no. 1 (April 1902)
 pp. 104-111.

MILLER, Malcolm

 Chartres Cathedral, The Medieval Stained Glass and Sculpture.
 London, 1980.

(Munich Museum)

 Meisterwerke Alter Glasmalerei. Bayerischen Nationalmuseen.
 Meisterwerke alter deutscher Glasmalerei. Leihgaben des
 Hessischen Landesmuseums, Darmstatd. Scheibenrisse,
 Leihgaben der Kunstammlungen der Veste Coburg und der
 Staatlichen Graphischen Sammlung.
 Munich, 1947.

NEWTON, Peter A.

 Stained glass at Oxford in Sherwood & Pevsner, Oxfordshire,
 London, 1974.
 (pp. 75-90.)

OSBORNE, June

 Stained Glass in England.
 London, 1981.

PAPANICOLAOU, L.M.

 Iconography of the Genesis Window of the Cathedral of Tours.
 Gesta, vol 20, part 1, 1981.
 pp. 179-189.

ROLLET, H.

 Les Maitres de la lumière.
 Paris, 1980.
 Reviewed by Granboulan, Anne, in Bulletin Monumental.
 Vol. 139 part 3, 1981, pp. 202-203.

TODD, John

 Waterperry Church.
 Oxford, 1955 (reprinted 1969).
 (Glass, pp. 12-16.)

TUCKETT, F.F.

 On some Optical Peculiarities of Ancient Painted Glass.
 Transactions of the Clifton Antiquarian Club. 1888?
 pp. 3-12.

TYACK, G.S.

 Church Windows.
 (pp. 137-153 of Antiquities & Curiosities of the Church,
 ed. W Andrews, London, 1897.)

VERNON, T.E.

 Notes on the Parish Church of all Saints, Crudwell, Wilts.
 Melksham, 1957.
 (Glass, pp. 10-13.)

AESTHETIC AND LITURGICAL IMPLICATIONS of Stained Glass, Theories of Colours, etc.

Angel, 1935
Armand, 1936
Armitage, 1949
Ascenzo, 1941
Aubert, 1959
Beaman, 1967
Becksmann, 1967
Beer, 1952, 1965, 1970
Berghoff, 1946
Bridges, 1943, 1965
Bruyne, 1946
Cantore, 1966
Chamberlain, 1855
Chevreul, 1839, 1854
Clark, 1963
Color and Light, 1966-1967, 1967
M.A. Couturier, 1940, 1951
Dahmen, 1922
Dedekam, 1908
Diepolder, 1881
Dvorak, 1918
Edgerton, 1967, 1969
Engels, 1937
W. Field, 1871
Fischer, 1914
Frodl-Kraft, 1962
Gahlen, 1928
Girkon, 1927, 1928
Glass, 1966
Glass-painting, 1898, 1903
Goethe, 1840
Goodhue, 1908
Goodman, 1957
Grinnell, 1946
Grodecki, 1977
Guthrie, 1933
Hamm, 1927
Helbig, 1938, 1939
G.P. Hutchinson, 1925
J.R. Johnson, 1963, 1964
P. Kitson, 1978
F. Lamb, 1902
L. Lee, 1977
Lillich, 1970
Maritain, 1930
Martimort, 1950-1951
Meiss, 1945
Milner-White, 1951

New Work in Stained Glass, 1954
C. Nicholson, 1931
Nicolas, 1941, 1944(2)
Nordström, 1955
Oidtmann, 1882
Oliphant, 1855
Panofsky, 1946
Parronchi, 1964
Petheo, 1975
Pettit, 1849
Piper, 1968
R. Rambusch, Frei, Elskus, 1965
Regamey, 1948
J.G. Reynolds, 1935, 1944
Roenn, 1975
E. Rosen, 1956(2)
Schapiro, 1947
Schmarsow, 1916
Schmude, 1927
Schöne, 1954
J.P. Seddon, 1890
Sharpe. 1870
Simson, 1956
Skinner, 1938
Skinner, Bridges & Frei. 1960-1961. 1961
Sowers, 1965. 1966, 1968. 1974
Stained glass, 1844(2), 1854. 1856,
    1857(2), 1858(2)
The Ecclesiologist's views; 1946, 1969
Steinbeiss, 1898
G.E. Street, 1852
Sunshine, 1968
H.J. Thompson, 1932
Viollet-le-Duc, 1868, 1912, 1933, 1937
    1938(2), 1939(2), 1945, 1946, 1948
    1949, 1942
H.A. Walters, 1942
G. Webb, 1911-1915
G. Wells, 1971
V. Whall, 1935
Whichcord, 1855
J.V. Wilkinson, 1958
H.L. Willet, 1943, 1947
What constitutes a good window? 1935
Winston, 1865
Witzleben, 1966
Wulcko, 1936
Zschacke, 1938, 1950

BIBLIOGRAPHIES

D. Brady & W. Serban, 1980 (S)
G.S. Duncan, 1960
F.S. Eden, 1942
J.A. Knowles, 1943

J. Lafond, 1970
R. Newton, 1974
B. Rackham, 1944
L.M. Solon, 1912-1913

CHEMICAL ANALYSIS of Glasses and Glass Chemistry Generally, Including Corrosion

Angus-Butterworth, 1947
Barff, 1872
Bauer, 1967, 1975, 1976
Bettembourg, 1975, 1976
Brewster, 1863
Brill & Moll, 1961; Brill, 1961(2),
    1963, 1967, 1968, 970, 1972
Charleston, 1960
Chesneau, 1915, 1924
Chevreul, 1863
Collongues, Perez y Jorba, Tilloga
    Dallas, 1976
Collongues, Perez y Jorba, 1977
Collongues, 1977
Cox & Pollard, 1977
Douglas & Isard, 1949

El-Shamy, Lewins & Douglas, 1972
El-Shamy & Douglas, 1972
El-Shamy, 1973
Ernsberger, 1959
Extracts No. 2, 1925
J. Fowler, 1880
Francen & Heine, 1965
Franchet, 1908
Frenzel, 1971(2)
Frodl-Kraft, 1963
Geilmann, 1953, 1954, 1955, 1960, 1962
Glass-painting, 1913
Guillot, 1934
Hall & Schweizer, 1973
Harden, 1963
N. Heaton, 1907(2), 1911, 1920, 1947

Chemical Analysis of Glasses etc. - cont.

Hedvall, Jagitsch & Olson, 1950
Hedvall, 1952
Hummel, 1945(2)
J.R. Johnson, 1956, 1964
Knowles, 1921, 1930, 1959
Korn, 1971
Loffler, 1968
Marchini, 1972
Mellor, 1922, 1923(2), 1924
R. Newton, 1966, 1969, 1971, 1974(2)
    1976, 1976-1977
Olin, Thompson & Sayre, 1972

H.J. Powell, 1907
Raw, 1955
Rodbert, 1936
Saint, 1928
Schröder, 1953, 1959
Scott, 1932
G. Shaw, 1965
Taralon, 1970
Tress, 1954
Viollet-le-Duc, 1933
G. Webb, 1925
Winter, 1965

CISTERCIAN GLASS

Acezat, 1969
Altenberg, 1832, 1871
Anselme, 1972
Aubert, 1947
Berlepsch, 1886
Conyers, 1960
Curling, 1834
Eckert, 1953
Frodl-Kraft, 1965
J. Hayward, 1973
Heinen, 1951

Kippenberger, 1939
Lehmann, 1926
R. Lehmann, 1916
Lübke, 1863
Oberlies, 1956
Priess, 1893
Rathausen, 1899
Schimmel, 1832
Weale, 1871
Wentzel, 1951
Zakin, 1974

CONSERVATION and Restoration Techniques and General Conservation and Repair

Bacher, 1977
Bettembourg, 1972, 1976(2), 1977(2), 1978
Blume, 1978
Bordeaux, 1851
Brill, 1971, 1972(2)
Charles, 1858
Cleaning Old Stained Glass, 1861
Cleaning and Restoration of Museum
    Exhibits, 1926
Cuno, see Hermann
Domaslowski, Kwiatkowski, Torwirt, 1956
Domaslowski, Kwiatkowski, 1962
D. Drake, 1953
V.S. Drury & A.L. Wilkinson, 1963
Duffy, 1972
Egli, (n.d.)
Extracts No. 3, 1925
Frenzel, 1960, 1963, 1968(2)
    1969(2), 1971
Frodl-Kraft, 1969, 1970, 1971,
    1972, 1973, 1975, 1976
P. Gibson & R. Newton, 1974
P. Gibson, 1976
Goslar, 1934, 1935
Grodecki, 1978
F. Harrison, 1932
K. Harrison, 1952
Hedvall & Jagitsch, 1943
Hedvall, Jagitsch & Olson, 1950
Howson, 1961
Hucher, 1883(2)
Jacobi, 1955, 1957, 1960, 1971

F. James, 1952
D. King, 1959, 1969, 1971, 1977
Knowles, 1953, 1959, 1964
Korn, 1975
Lacy, 1970
L. Lee, 1970-1971
Linsley, 1972
W.F. Lowe, 1960(2), 1962
Marchini, 1973-1974
O. Morris, 1968-1969
Mühlethaler, 1977
R. Newton, 1972, 1974(4), 1975
Oidtmann, 1906
Organ, 1957
Perrot & Bettembourg, 1976
Pilgrim Trust, 1966
Preservation, 1912
Ranton, 1949
J. Robinson, 1974
Skinner, 1947
Stephens, 1976
Taralon, 1962, 1969, 1977
Tower, 1926
Truman, 1935
Unwin, 1951
Verdier, 1976
A.E. Werner, 1958, 1966
A. Wilkinson, 1963
Woodroffe, 1926
York, 1973(2), 1973-1974, 1974
    1975(3)

C V M A

Fisher, 1972-1973
Frodl-Kraft, 1963, 1969
Grodecki, 1963, 1969, 1981(S)
Hahnloser, 1972(2)

Perrot, 1970, 1972, 1977
Stefanaggi, 1970
Wheeler, 1970
Wormald, 1970

DIOCESAN ADVISORY COMMITTEES, Faculties etc.

Diocesan Advisory Committees, 1951,
    1968-1969
Eeles, 1944, 1948
Faculty for a window, Faculty, 1962

J. Hayward, 1970-1971
Oxford Diocesan Advisory Committee, 1929
J. Scott, 1964, 1965
A. Wilkinson, 1964

DOMESTIC GLASS and Secular Glazing Generally

Domestic glass, 1930
Eberlein, 1912
F.S. Eden, 1914
Fischer, 1910
Glass-painting, 1884, 1926
A. Godwin, 1895
Goodhue, 1905
Granges, 1864
Harden, 1959, 1961
E.A. Kent, 1933
W. King, 1930

Knowles, 1930
Lafond, 1956, 1970
Lloyd, 1961
Oidtmann, 1874, 1876
Popham, 1928, 1929
Rathe, 1934
Rothery, 1927
Sewter, 1961
Tavern glass-paintings, 1912
H.W. Wilson, 1979
Witzleben, 1977

EXCAVATED GLASS

Berry, 1934 (Sandwich, Mass.)
J. Cook, 1958
Cramp, 1970(2), 1975
Denton (n.d.)
Evetts, 1967
Fixot & Pelletier, 1976
Foy, 1977(2), 1978
Gagniere & Granier, 1968, 1969
Gamlen, 1943-1944, 1974-1975
Hobley, 1970

Holden, 1963
Jarrow, 1934
Knapp, 1957
Knowles, 1957
Montgomery Castle, 1968
P. Newton, 1967-1970
O'Connor, 1975, 1976-1977
Raw, 1955
N.P. Thompson, 1967

EXHIBITIONS

Arts and Crafts Exhibition, 1893, 1906
Azeglio, 1876
Bontempts, 1862, 1868
Brussels. Brussels, 1880
Capronnier, 1880, 1881
Caviness, 1978(S)
Champier, 1884
Chastel, 1953
Cologne, 1914
Connick, 1925(2), 1927
Darcel, 1863, 1864
Delamotte, 1851
Demotte, 1925
Denglar, 1873, 1895
Didron & Clemandot, 1880
Dihl, 1819
W. Drake, 1924
Exhibitions, 1923, 1925, 1937, 1959
  1965, 1972-1973
Farr, 1958
Fine Art Society, 1912
Fischer, 1912, 1913
R. Fletcher, 1924
Geneva International Exhibition, 1927
Germany, 1926
Gerson, 1938
Glass-painting, 1926
Great Exhibition, London, 1851(4)
  1852(2)
Gruber, 1925
Harms & Ortlieb, 1934
Hoffman, 1927
International Exhibitions, London,
  1862, 1872
Karlsruhe Exhibition, 1901
Kensington, 1864
Kirchoff, 1879
Knowles, 1924(2), 1938, 1952, 1961
Lafond, 1931, 1968

Lassus, 1884
Lausanne Cathedral, 1975
N. Lorin, 1878
Luynes, 1889
Magdeburg, 1912
Magne, 1900
Mallet-Stevens, 1937
R. Morris, 1933
W. Morris, 1961
New, 1967
New York, 1937-1938
Paris, 1867, 1868(3), 1878, 1889,
  1900
Parry, 1867, 1863, 1868, 1871
W. Peckitt, 1975
Perrot, 1973
Pitcher, 1928
Rackham, 1949
J.G. Reynolds, 1937-1938
G. Robinson, 1963
Schöne, 1928
Skinner, 1939
Stained glass, 1960
Strasbourg, 1912
Swiss National Exhibition, 1896
Tiffany Glass, 1893
Townsend, 1899
Vallance, 1918
Victoria & Albert Museum, 1929, 1934
  1937, 1952, 1971
Waring, 1863
Whall, 1905
Wiesbaden, 1909
H.L. Willet, 1942
M.C. Willet, 1957
Winston, 1865
World's Fair, 1962
York, 1973, 1976

GLASS MANUFACTURE and Types of Glass

'Antique' glass, 1900
J.C. Bell, 1935
Beltjes, 1948
Berthelot, 1893
Besborodov, (n.d.)
Blenko, 1932, 1933-1934
L.M.A. Butterworth, 1934
Cobb, 1930
Didron & Thibaud, 1850
Directory for the British Glass
  Industry, 1928
Dye, 1948
Flashed Glass, 1927, 1964
J. Fowler, 1880
Glass, 1947, 1967, 1969
Glass-painting, 1912, 1927
Grylls, 1932
Halahan, 1921, 1924, 1924-1925
Harden, 1969
J.T. Hardman, 1934
Heffron, 1926
Hesse, 1928
Hulme, 1907, 1915, 1931
Huth, 1925
J.H. Kenyon, 1957, 1964
Knowles, 1924, 1925-1926, 1926, 1927,
  1960

Lafond, 1961, 1969
R. Lee, 1939
Minutoli, 1836
Mirault, 1839
R. Newton, 1978, 1979-1980
Opalescent glass, 1927
Pape, 1930, 1931(2), 1934
Philippe, 1974-1975
A.M. Powell, 1946
H.J. Powell, 1922, 1923
Ridgway & Leach, 1948
Roberts 1932
Rollason, 1922
Ruby glass, 1968
R.W. Salmond, 1972-1973
Stokes, 1934
Surrey & Sussex Glassmen, 1930
Thorne, 1956
Trexell, 1969
Wealden Glass, 1932
Winbolt, 1932(2), 1933
Winston, 1850, 1852, 1865
Robinson, 1855
A. Wood, 1934
H.E. Wright, 1932

GLASS-PAINTERS and Glass-Painting Firms

Master, A.H. (Swiss)
  Mayer, 1879
Abel, A
  A. Abel, 1934(S)
Acker, H
  Lehmbruck, 1968; Wentzel, 1968
Advertisements of 17th & 18th Century
Glass-painters
  F. Buckley, 1926; Knowles, 1927
Aikman, W
  Buss, 1960
Andlau, P
  See Hemmel, P
Arnold of Nimeguen
  Helbig, 1937; Lafond, 1912,
  1926-1927, 1942, 1955, 1973
Ascenzo, N.D.
  Ascenzo, 1953-1954
Avignon glass-painters
  Requin, 1889
Baillie & Co.
  Baillie, 1875
Baker, C.A.
  Baker, 1936
Baker, J.W.
  J.W. Baker, 1918, 1942
Barnett Family
  Knowles, 1921(2)
Beer, R
  D. Drake, 1963
Bell, R
  M.C.F. Bell, 1951; R. Bell, 1951;
  M. Drake, 1923
Bell, R.A.
  R.A. Bell, 1934
Besozzo, M da
  Pirina, 1969

Betton & Evans
  Couteur, 1920; Coventry, Trinity
  Church, 1834; Dodson, 1920
Biographical notices of glass artists
  Wilmshurst, (n.d.)
Birmingham Glass Painters
  Birmingham Glass Painters, 1886,
  1927, 1928
Blecha, F
  Blecha, 1943
Bleville, M
  Lafond, 1961
Bolton, W.J. & J
  Bolton, W.J. & J., 1936; (W.J. only)
  1944; Milner-White, 1937; Skinner,
  1936
Bordeaux Glass Painters
  Roudié, 1958
Borthwick, A.E.
  Borthwick, 1926
Bossanyi, E
  Benezé, 1930; Bickersteth, 1959;
  Bossanyi, 1935(2), 1974, 1975, 1979;
  W.G. Frank, 1968; Hayes, 1965;
  Michaelhouse, 1954; H.B. Powell,
  1974-1975
Boston Stained Glass Craftsmen
  Connick, 1933
Brangwyn, F
  Brangwyn, 1899
Bridges, S
  Bridges, 1977
Bringmann & Schmidt
  R. Morris, 1932
Brinley, D.P.
  Brinley, 1926

Brown, Ford Madox
  Image, 1890; Sewter, 1968
Burd, C.M.
  Dorr, 1914
Burges, W
  Cardiff Castle, 1977
Burgh, J de
  Knowles, 1922
Burgkmaier, H
  Burgkmaier, 1912
Burne-Jones, E
  M. Harrison, 1972-1973, 1973;
  see Lethaby, 1925, Philip Webb;
  Miller, 1895; Sewter, 1970;
  F.G. Stephens, 1889; Vallance, 1900,
  1911; H. Wilson, 1897; Wroot, 1917
Busch, V
  Hauck, 1970
Caine, O
  Buzas, 1950
Caldwell, S
  Caldwell, S., 1950, 1951, 1952, 1958,
  1964; Rackham, 1963
Campendonk
  Engels, 1959, 1966
Capronnier, J.B.
  Capronnier, 1892
Caspar, H and Gallati, H.B.
  Boesch, 1936
Caumont, J. de
  Caumont, 1928
Chagall, M
  D. Adams, 1974; Chagall, 1961; Freund,
  1963; Genauer, 1962; Lemayrie, 1962,
  1967; Marteau, 1972; Sowers, 1962
Chamber Family
  Chamber Family, 1921 (Knowles, 1921)
Chipping Campden group
  Clarke, 1931
Cingria, A
  Cingria, 1946
Claesz, A
  Popham, 1927, 1941
Clarke, H
  Bowe, 1978-1979; Cartwright, 1933
Clayton & Bell
  Clayton & Bell, 1932, 1933;
  G.W. Clayton, 1956, 1958
Collins
  Collins, 1828
Comper, Ninian
  Comper, 1961
Connick, C.J.
  Connick, 1925(2), 1930, 1932, 1946;
  Heinigke, 1932, 1946; Skinner,
  1946, 1975
Courtois, J
  Giraudet, 1880; (R.P. & J. Courtois)
  Lafond, 1968
Cousin, J
  Charles, 1873; Cousin, 1873;
  Guiffrey, 1882
Cox & Sons
  Cox & Sons, 1865, 1870
Crabeth Brothers
  Regteren-Altena, 1953
Cram, R.A.
  Connick, 1942; Sheldon, 1942;
  Tucci, 1975; H.L. Willet, 1942
Cremona, M da
  Pirina, 1966
Dappere, P. de
  W.H.J. Weale, 1866-70
Dassel family
  Dassel, 1903, 1906
Davies, A.J.
  Davies, 1954

Day, L.F.
  Ross, 1929
Decorchement, F
  Despreaux, 1939
Delacroix, E
  Robaut, 1879
A Dictionary of Glass-painters and
'Glasyers' of the Tenth to the
Eighteenth Centuries
  W. Drake, 1955
Dinninghof, B
  S.D. Kitson, 1929
Dombet, G
  Boyer, 1958
Dortmund, M
  Winterfeld, 1937, 1938
Drake, D
  Drake, Daphne, 1923(4)
Drake, F
  Drake, F., 1920(4)
Drake, M
  Bishop, 1951; D. Drake, 1930, 1932
  M. Drake, 1917, 1923(18), 1974-1975
Drake, W
  W. Drake, 1949; F.S. Eden, 1930
Dreux glass-painters
  Veuclin, 1900
Drury, A.J.
  A.J. Drury, 1940
Dünz, H.J.
  Trachsel, 1879
Durer, A
  Knappe, 1961; Pirina, 1970, 1972;
  James Povell, 1876(2); Joseph Powell,
  1875(2), 1876; J.F. Russell, 1868;
  Tom Taylor, 1868
Duyckinck, E. & G.
  Vail, 1952
The Master E.S.
  Cohn, 1937

Easton, G
  Easton, 1964
Eden, F.C.
  Croome, 1963
Edwards, C.J.
  Whittet, 1954
Eginton, F
  Aitken, 1872; F. Eginton, 1805(2),
  1814, 1823, 1905, 1879(2);
  Hamilton, (n.d.)
Eginton, W.R.
  W.R. Eginton, 1806, 1818, 1819-1822;
  Shaw Stebbing, 1798-1801
Eighteenth and Nineteenth Century artists
  Hibgame, 1917
English Mediaeval glazier's bills
  Hulme, 1915
English Mediaeval glaziers
  Woodforde, 1935, 1936
Ennis, G.P.
  G.P. Ennis, 1936(2)
Eyck, C
  C. Eyck, 1973-1974
Figel, A
  Hartig, 1930
Fisch, H.V.
  Merz, 1894
Floris, J
  Helbig, 1944(S)
Flower, B
  Chitty, 1917; Couteur, 1916, 1918;
  Hulme, 1918; Oswald, 1952
Foppa, V
  Wittgens, 1948
Foreign glass-painters working in France
  Lasteyrie, 1879, 1880
Forseth, E
  E. Forseth, 1952
Forsyth, J.D.
  J.D. Forsyth, 1927

Fouquet, J
  Fiot, 1970
Frampton, E
  E. Frampton, 1929; A. Wilkinson, 1953
Frank, M.S.
  F.X. Zettler, 1927
Frei, E. & Frei, E. Jnr
  E. Frei, 1942, 1948, 1967
Twentieth Century French glass-painters
  Creager & Mont, 1942
Gascoyne, A
  A. Gascoyne, 1928
Geddes, Walter
  Knowles, 1956
Geddes, Wilhelmina
  W.M. Geddes, 1956, 1962; Rackham, 1929
Gerichten, L. von
  Gerichten, 1945; Shobe, 1978
Geyling
  Geyling Firm, 1973-74;
  Lind, 1894-1897, 1899
Ghiberti
  Habsburg, 1970
Glass-Painters, 1750-1780
  Glass-Painters, 1960, 1961, 1962
Gontier, L
  Babeau, 1888; Rigal, 1977
Goodhue, H.E.
  Coburn, 1910; R.A. Cram, 1932;
  Orr, 1925
Gray & Co.
  Ruffer, 1944
Greiner, F
  Glass-painting, 1928
Grien, H.B.
  Fischer, 1913; H.B. Grien, 1959;
  Steinbrucker, 1935; Stiassny, 1896
Grunewald
  Grunewald, 1925
Gyles, H
  Brighton, 1968, 1977;
  Denton-in-Wharfedale, 1968;
  Gyles, 1898; Knowles, 1921;
  (Gyles family) Knowles, 1921(3),
  1922-1923; W. Nicolson, 1902;
  G. Wood, 1947
Hajnal, J
  Skeat, 1974-1975
Hallward, R
  Hallward, 1925
Hardman Studios
  Feeny, 1970-1971
Hardman, J.T.
  J.T. Hardman, 1960
Harvey, H
  Laishley, 1960
Heasman, E
  Strickland, 1973-1974
Heaton, C
  Mobbs, 1904; C. Heaton, 1940
Heaton & Butler
  Heaton & Butler, 1860
Heaton, Butler & Bayne
  Heaton, Butler & Bayne, 1864
Hecker, P
  Pfeill, 1937
Hedgeland
  Ely, 1858; Harrod, 1854, 1855
Heinigke, O. & O.W.
  Beaudry, 1952; Heinigke, 1935-1936,
  1968
Hemmel, P
  Becksmann, 1970; Frankl, 1956;
  Haug, 1936; Wentzel, (n.d.), 1964

Hermann
  Abel, 1865; Hauck, 1968
Hiemer, E.W. & G
  Hiemer, 1955, 1969-1970
Hirschvogel family
  Oidtmann, 1907
Hodgson family
  Knowles, 1922
Hogan, J.H.
  Hogan, 1948(3)
Holbein
  Cohn, 1939, Holbein, 1925,
  1926
Holiday, H
  Holiday, 1890, 1904, 1909
  1927
Holland of Warwick
  Holland, 1855
Hone, E
  Farr, 1958; Hone, 1956
Houte, A. van den
  Wayment, 1967, 1968, 1969
Howard, F
  F. Howard, 1850
Howson, J
  J. Howson, 1965; Putron,
  1976-1977
Hunt, H
  H. Hunt, 1941
Image, S
  S. Image, 1898, 1930
Inglish family
  Knowles, 1921
Jacob von Köln
  Fischer, 1910
Jones, A.W.
  A.W. Jones, 1943
Jouin, J
  Guillaume, 1889
Kempe, C.E.
  H. Powell, 1970-1971; Quentin, 1900;
  Stavridi, 1979-1980
Knight, E
  E. Knight, 1929
Labouret
  Labouret, 1950
La Farge, J
  H.B. Adams, 1975; Downs,
  1945; Heinigke, 1961; Lafarge,
  1901(2), 1902, 1944; Waern, 1896
Langton, J
  Heal, 1928
Larcher & Hermannowske
  Bertrand, 1845
Lardeur, G
  T. Mathews, 1967
Laroche and Defossés
  Laroche & Defossés, 1841
Larsen, A.R.
  A.R. Larsen, 1943
Laughlin, A.D.
  A.D. Laughlin, 1952
Lauterbach, F
  F. Lauterbach, 1933
Lavergne, C
  N. Lavergne, 1886, 1888
Lavers & Barraud
  M. Harrison, 1973
Lechter, M
  Steinbrucker, 1939

Lecuyer, J
  Bourges, 1947; Lafond, 1961
Liège glass-painters
  Jaer, 1932
Van Linge Brothers
  Knowles, 1949; Linge, 1850,
  1851; London, 1974-1975;
  Nichols, 1850
Lipofsky, M
  Treib, 1968
Lixheim, T. von
  Frankl, 1957
Lorimer, R
  R. Lorimer, 1915
Loth, P
  Paulus, 1913
Lucas
  Winston, 1852
Lucas van Leyden
  W.S. Gibson, 1970; Seligman, 1923
Lyon glass-painters
  Rondot, 1882, 1897
Manuel, N
  Trachsel, 1879
Marcillat, G. de
  Germain, 1886; Lafond, 1963;
  Mancini, 1909; Muentz, 1890-1891;
  Sherrill, 1929
Maréchal, C.L.
  Atalone, 1911; Livet, 1843
Matisse, H
  Neff, 1972; H. Rambusch, 1952;
  Sowers, 1962; Vence, 1951-1952,
  1951
Mediaeval Stained Glass Designers
  Knowles, 1927, 1934, 1935
Meissner, A.G.
  Schaden, 1829
Miller, Beale & Hider Limited
  Broad, 1978-1979
Moira, G
  G. Moira, 1899
Montgomery, W
  W. Montgomery, 1928
Montmorency, R. de
  R. de Montmorency, 1963
Morris, William
  See Lethaby, Philip Webb, 1925;
  W.F. Lowe, 1960; Sewter, 1960,
  1961, 1964, 1967, 1974, 1975;
  Victoria and Albert Museum, 1934;
  Watkinson, 1968; Wroot, 1917
Morris & Co
  Goshawk & Bennet, 1958; Kehlmann,
  1975; Marillier, 1913; Miller,
  1895; W. Morris, 1913, 1961
Morris, W
  W. Morris, 1945, 1953
Müller, J.J.
  J.J. Müller, 1847
Murphy, T.J.
  T.J. Murphy, 1956; Tansey, 1947
Nancy glass-painters
  Save, 1897
Nauta, M
  Pluym, 1951
Neuhauser, Jele & Co.
  Neuhauser, 1911
Nicholas le Pot
  Fayolle, 1907
Nicholson, A.K.
  Nicholson, 1931(2), 1937

Nicolas, J
  Dutch Art of Today, 1937; Huxley,
  1931; Nicolas, 1941, 1949
Nowland, H
  Milner-White, 1957; Nowland,
  1957
Oliphant, F.W.
  F.W. Oliphant, 1854, 1855
Orley, B. van
  Wayment, 1969
Ortkens, A
  Boom, 1949
Pandino, A da
  Pirina, 1976
Pandino, S da
  Pirina, 1966
Parisian artists of the sixteenth
and seventeenth centuries.
  Guiffrey, 1915
Paterson, O
  G. White, 1898
Poulson, C
  Canavan, 1969
Pawle, H.L.
  H.L. Pawle, 1962
Payne, H.A.
  T.M. Legge, 1914
Pearson, E.M.
  Hosken, 1924
Pearson, J
  J. Pearson, 1780, 1821
Peckitt, W
  Brighton, 1967-1968, 1969,
  1974-1975; Denton-in-Wharfedale,
  1968; Knowles, 1921(4), 1929,
  1953-1954; H. Peckitt, 1817;
  W. Peckitt, 1877, 1935(2), 1975
Pedigrees of Families of Glass-Painters
  W. Drake, 1934
Penna, E
  E. Penna, 1944
Perreal, J
  Bancel, 1885; Dufay, 1864
Petty family
  Knowles, 1921(3)
Pfyffer von Altishofen von
Sonnenberg
  Staffelbach, 1944-1946
Pinaigrier family
  Brochard, 1938; Doublet de
  Boisthibault, 1854; Lafond,
  1957; Meister, 1926;
  Wildenstein, 1957
Pisa, A da
  A da Pisa, 1976
Pitassi, A.L.
  A.L. Pitassi, 1947
Powell & Co., Whitefriar's Studios
  Gordon-Christian, 1968;
  Powell & Sons, 1930, 1937, 1960,
  1972, 1973-1974; C.C. Powell,
  1956; H.J. Powell, 1920;
  Whitefriar's Glass, 1930;
  A. Wilkinson, 1956

Preston family
  Knowles, 1921
Prew d Aelteren, J
  J. Prew d Aelteren, 1926;
  Schinnerer, 1912
Price family
  Knowles, 1953; 'Magdalensis',
  1856
Prudde, J
  Chitty, 1917; Couteur, 1916;
  Hulme, 1916
Pucelle, J
  Sandler, 1970
Putz, W
  Fischer, 1935, Putz, 1914;
  Witte, 1914
Rambusch, H
  H. Rambusch, 1977, 1978-1979
Rattner, A
  A. Rattner, 1978
Redslob, E
  Neumann & Redslob, 1925;
  Redslob, 1925
Reiser, W.E.
  W.E. Reiser, 1936
Reynolds, J
  Knowles, 1923
Rinderspacher, E
  Fischer, 1913
Riordan Studios
  Riordan Studios, 1966
Robinson, A
  A. Robinson, 1956
Rombouts, N
  Helbig, 1937
Rosetti, D.G.
  Sewter, 1961
Rouault, G
  M.A. Couturier, 1947; Venturi, 1940
Rowell, J
  Gold, 1965; Heal, 1932
Ruskin, J
  Bridges, 1974-1975; A. Wilkinson,
  1976-1977
Rutherford, R
  R. Rutherford, 1972-1973
Saint, L
  J. O'Connor, 1947, 1963; L. Saint,
  1961, 1976-1977, 1978-1979
Salmond, H
  H. Salmond, 1972-1973
Salmond, R.W.
  R.W. Salmond, 1968-1969
Schaffrath, L
  Pfaff, 1977
Schmidt, J
  Heilborn, 1912, 1915
Schmude, P
  Meinhof, 1927
Schongauer, M
  Hauck, 1966
Scott & Son
  MacDonald, 1972
Sèvres windows
  Sèvres, 1847
Sheldon, J
  J. Sheldon, 1956
Shirley Family
  Knowles, 1921
Shirwyn Family
  Knowles, 1921
Shrigley & Hunt Ltd
  Shrigley & Hunt, 1936
Signatures of Artists
  H.T. Kirby, 1951
Skinner, O
  O. Skinner, 1977-1978

Spanish glass-painters
  Codala, 1944; Riaño, 1879
Spiers, R.N
  R.N. Spiers, 1936
Stammers, H
  Laishley, 1960; Milner-White, 1959;
  H. Stammers, 1968-1969
Stimmer, T
  Stolberg, 1894, 1905
Strachan, D
  D. Strachan, 1950, 1952; Webster, 1964
Süssmuth, R
  Rackham, 1929
Thomas of Oxford
  Couteur, 1918
Thompson Family
  Knowles, 1921
Thorn-Prikker, J
  Hoff, 1914
Thornton, J
  Knowles, 1920, 1959; J. Lancaster, 1956
Tiffany, L.C
  Heinigke, 1932; Koch, 1964; McKean, 1968;
  Tiffany Glass, 1893, 1896, 1912, 1913,
  1914; Waern, 1898
Touraine glass-painters
  Giradet, 1885
Tournai glass-painters
  Goovaerts, 1896; Grange & Cloquet, 1889
Travers, M
  Blackham, 1949; Crawford, 1965;
  H. Salmond, 1970-1971
Twining, E.W.
  E.W. Twining, 1957
Vellert, D
  Beets, 1906, 1907, 1908, 1912, 1922, 1925;
  Bye, 1929; Gluck, 1901; Laurent, 1925
Vigeland, E
  Rydbeck; Vigeland, 1925, 1950
Villiet, M.J
  L. Couture, 1862
Wailes
  Crosthwaite, 1849; Ely, 1850, 1857
  London, St. James, 1846; Newcastle, 1844;
  Wailes, 1958
Walburg Master
  Becksmann, 1975
Walker, Leonard
  L. Walker, 1921, 1922, 1924, 1925, (n.d.),
  1965
Waring, J.B
  J.B. Waring, 1873
Warrington, W
  Ely, 1850(2); Malpas, 1846;
  W. Warrington, 1846, 1848, 1850
Webb, G
  G. Webb, 1955
Werck, A
  Savoie, 1936
Whall, C
  Connick, 1926; Miller, 1895; Sparrow, 192
  Tarbox, 1933; Whall, 1891, 1905(2)
Whall, V
  V. Whall, 1942
Wild, H
  Frankl, 1912
Wilhelm,
  Wilhelm, 1915
Wilkinson, H
  A. Wilkinson, 1958
Willement, T
  Crosby Hall, 1834; Curling, 1834;
  Hampton Court, 1847; Holloway, 1968-1969;
  H.T. Kirby, 1946, 1949; London, Temple Chu
  1842; A. Wilkinson, 1964; Willement, 184C
  1841; Windsor, 1842
Willet, H.L
  H.L. Willet, 1978

Glass-painters and glass-painting firms - cont.

Willet, W
  Watts, 1934
Willet, A
  A. Willet, 1943
Wilson, W
  W. Wilson, 1937, 1972-1973
Winston, C
  London, Temple Church, 1853;
  Miller, 1895; Nash, 1938; Orr,
  1961-1962; Parry, 1865(2);
  A. Robinson, 1955; Sewter, 1961;
  Waring, 1865; Winston, 1864, 1865(2)
Witton, J
  Knowles, 1921
Woore, E
  E. Woore, 1961
Women (artists) in stained glass
  Skinner, 1940, 1941(3)

York glass painters. A chronological list
  Knowles, 1922(2), York glaziers, 1912, 1915
Yoors, E
  Dey, 1942
Zavattari, F
  Pirina, 1966
Zeiner, Lucas
  Lehmann, 1926; Rackham, 1929;
  Schneider, 1954
Zettler, O & F.X.
  Bassermann-Jordan, 1908; Fischer,1910;
  Pöllman, 1917; F.X. Zettler, 1911;
  O. Zettler, 1953
Zubar, M
  M. Zubar, 1966

GLASS-PAINTERS' ASSOCIATIONS, Organisations, Trading Difficulties etc.

America

Almy, 1953
Apprenticeship, 1949
A Career in Stained Glass. Career.., 1967
Columbus Guild, 1933-1934
H. Cummings, 1945, 1946
Governmental relations, 1954
T.W. Howard, 1925 (cost accounting)
Importation of Stained Glass windows
  duty free, 1927
Maginnis, 1941

Metcalf, 1949
Pedersen, 1938
Pierce, 1968-1969
H. Rambusch, 1942
R. Rambusch, 1956
Shepperd, 1952
Skinner, 1940, 1942, 1950, 1953, 1978(2)
Stained Glass, 1941, 1954, 1956, 1979
United States, 1925
H.L. Willet, 1941, 1943, 1948(3), 1978-1979

England

Arnold, 1916
Ashdown, 1919
R. Bell, 1930
British Society of Master Glass-Painters
Couteur, 1917 (Repeal of a 1483 act)
Customs duties, 1933
M. Drake, 1908
Fisher, 1970-1971

H.T. Kirby, 1952, 1954, 1958, 1959
Knowles, 1927(2)
Pierce, 1968-1969
Ransome
Reyntiens, 1963
Richardson, 1955
Swansea College of Art, 1965
Thomas & Richardson, 1972

France

Bavillet, 1947

Charavay, 1879

Germany

Association of German Glass-Painting, 1912
German Glass-Painters association, 1911
National Union of German Glass-Painters,
  1924, 1925

Ruscher, 1925
Glass-Painting, 1926 (2)

Grisaille

Amé, 1853, 1854
Brisac, 1977
Brockington, 1933
Frenzel, 1960
Geuer, 1882

Glass-painting, 1928
Grisaille, 1936
Lillich, 1972
Montgomery Castle, 1968
N. Morgan, 1977

HERALDIC GLASS & heraldry

England

Andrews, 1943
Apedale
Atkinson, 1871
Bain, 1868-1870, 1878
Barron (n.d.) (S)
Batten, 1909
Battersby, 1929-1930
Beard, 1939
Beaumont & Rylands, 1878
Bell, C.F., 1953
Benton, 1926, 1930
Bingley, 1931
Boumphrey, 1972, 1973(2), 1974(2), 1975
Bradford, 1911
Brighton, 1960
Bromley, 1907
W. Brown, 1913
Butcher, 1921
Clarke, 1930
Cock, 1931
Collier & Lawrence, 1921, 1924, 1929
Mrs Collier, 1908
E. Cope, 1922, 1923, 1928, 1935
Couteur, 1918
Dixon, 1923, 1924, 1925
Dorling, 1903(S), 1904(S), 1912
D. Drake, 1935
M. Drake, 1905, 1907, 1909
W. Drake, 1911(2), 1913(4), 1915
Duleep Singh, 1904
F.S. Eden, 1926, 1927, 1928(2), 1929,
  1930(3), 1931, 1932, 1934, 1936(2)
  1937, 1938(3), 1940(2), 1941, 1942(2)
Edgcote, 1969
C.J. Evans, 1879, 1886
Evetts, 1959
Eydon, 1969
Feeny, 1957
Field, 1934
F. Fulford, 1911, 1913
R. Gibbs, 1905, 1909(3)
Gilling Castle, 1929, 1939, 1953
Glasgow Museum, 1962
N.W. Graves, 1941
E. Green, 1899
Groombridge, 1930
Grundy-Newman, 1914, 1915
Hare, 1886
Harlow, 1910
A.S. Harvey, 1962
Hassop Hall, 1879
Haswell, 1899
Hawke, 1971
L. Hayward, 1953
Heraldic glass, 1882

Hill, 1953, 1975
Hotblack, 1910
Hughes, 1930-1932
Jewers, 1891
F. Jourdain, 1881
E.A. Kent, 1932
Kidson, 1946
Knowles, 1924, 1938
Lambarde, 1926, 1927, 1928, 1929, 1930
  1931, 1932, 1933, 1934
Lamborn, 1943(2), 1944, 1945, 1946, 1949
Lamport Hall, 1961
F. Law, 1898
Lincoln's Inn, 1931
London, 1926
Lowther Bouch, 1946
Mander & Pape, 1923
Maxwell-Lyte, 1902(S)
Merchant Taylors Company, 1935
Messenger, 1945, 1953
G.T. Morris, 1935
Mundy, 1944
Nelson, 1937, 1938, 1939
Nichols, 1860
Pape, 1919, 1923, 1927
Paul, 1901, 1927
Pawle, 1954
W.J. Pearce, 1940
Pereira, 1889
Pine, 1953
Prideaux, 1929
Priest, 1958
Purey-Cust, 1890-1896
Rackham, 1950
Riff, 1923
R.G. Roe, 1924, 1925
W.H. Rogers
Rylands & Brown, 1921
Sabin, 1957
Sand, 1897
Serel, 1886-1887
H.C. Smith, 1915-1916
Sotheby's, 1929
Stanford,
  (arms of the Glazier's Guild and
   use of grozing irons in heraldry)
Steer, 1954, 1955, 1976-1977
Were, 1903
Westminster Abbey, 1947 (R.A.F.
  Squadron badges)
Wilde, 1927
Winstanley, 1920
Winston, 1860
Wollaston, 1951, 1955
Woodforde, 1934, 1943

Belgium

Donnet, 1911
Glass-Painting, 1774
Helbig, 1939, 1941

Renesse, 1927
Steinberg, 1939

France

Hucher, 1883
Lillich

Vaivre, 1973

Germany

R. Linneman, 1914

Switzerland

Lehmann, 1929

ICONOGRAPHY (Selected Entries)

General
M & W Drake, 1916; Iconography, 1912; Trollope, 1867-1868

Blessed James of Ulm
Bridges, 1937, 1969; H. Cummings, 1949; Ganay, 1932.

Crucifix with Lily
Hildburgh, 1924, 1932

Emblematic windows
Emblematic stained glass, 1787

The Eucharist
Helbig, 1946

Edward the Confessor
Brindley, 1915

The Five Wounds
J. Rowe, 1905

Franciscan Saints
Woodforde, 1937

Immaculate Conception
Lafond, 1954

Jesse Windows
Beazeley, 1895; Becksmann, 1969, 1975; Bridges, 1950; Briggs, 1890; Busk, 1890; Caviness, 1975; Coleman, 1907; Connick, 1932; Delaporte, 1932; Dodson, 1926; Gower, 1895; F. Harrison, 1947; M. Harrison, 1972-73; Housden, 1895; F.M. Jackson, 1895; Jesse Windows, 1890(10); J.R. Johnson, 1961; H.T. Kirby, 1958, 1960, 1961; Knowles, 1920; Korn, 1977; Lafond, 1963; H. Lawrence collection sale, 1921; E. Marshall, 1895; Milner-White, 1951 1952; Perrot, 1970; Rackham, 1942(2), 1943; Selby Abbey, 1932; Walker, 1895; Ward, 1895; Watson, 1934; Woodforde, 1937

Last fifteen days of the world
J.T. Fowler, 1915; Gee, 1969; Grodecki, 1967; J.M. Neale, 1843

Mediaeval Campaign against Blasphemy
Woodforde, 1937

IMITATION GEMSTONES and Stained Glass
Artificial gemstones, 1880   J.R. Johnson, 1957
N. Heaton, 1911   P. Kitson, 1978

IMPORTATION of Continental Glass to England
J.C. Hampp, 1808, 1937; R. Jenkins, 1929; E.A. Kent, 1937, 1938; Lafond, 1960, 1964; Rackham, 1927

LEADS AND LEADWORK
Glass-painting, 1925; Knowles, 1930, 1938, 1939(2), 1949; Lead, 1929; Leads, 1926; Lethaby, 1893; R. Mathews, 1892(2), 1893, 1897; Mittelalterliche Bleiverglasung, 1925; Mollet, 1933; R. Morris, 1928; R. Wilson, 1927; Woodforde, 1944; Woodroffe, 1926

MISCELLANEA

Carved glass	Bridges, 1955
Continental windows donated by Englishmen in the fifteenth century	Donora, 1957
Copies of Italian engravings in French sixteenth century glass	Male, 1913, 1929
Curiosities in English Stained Glass	Hubbuck, 1978-1979; Knowles, 1933; Suffling, 1896

Music Iconography
Chatwin, 1931; Gardner, 1975; Hardy, 1909; Music,... 1926; Poste, 1858

Notes on Sixteenth Century ornament, profile medallions, true lover's knots and Roman lettering
K. Harrison, 1954; Schaefer, 1888

Position of Archbishop's Ring
W. Pearce, 1916

St. Christopher
Collier,   Kayser, 1883; H.T. Kirby, 1958; St. Christopher, 1852

St. Ives
F. Lorin, 1908

St. Louis
Breton, 1880

St. Nicholas
Birch, 1886, 1888

St. Thomas à Becket
Borenius, 1932

Ships
Brindley & Moore, 1910; Brindley, 1911, 1912, 1914, 1915

The Seven Sacraments
Rushforth, 1929, 1930

The Sibyls
Lamborn, 1944

Susanna and the Elders
Svahn, 1931

Theophilus the Penitent
Fryer, 1935

Torture of St. George
Stohlman, 1925

The Trinity
Couteur, 1917; Llanrhychwyn, 1929; Trinity Windows, 1899(2); Turpin, 1917

Virgin with two children
J. Fowler, 1871

Virgin crowned
Lawrence, 1925

Miscellanea - cont.

Cylinder window	Cylinder window, 1966
Disputes between English and Foreign glass-painters in the sixteenth century	Knowles, 1925
Divining for old glass	Ransome 1933(2)
Duplication and mass production of ancient windows	Knowles, 1926
First Khaki-clad figures in stained glass	R. Lewis, 1918; Loxton, 1918
Gild windows	Knowles, 1939; Legge, 1931
Goethe and glass-painting	Gahlen, 1928; Zschacke, 1938, 1950
How to choose stained glass	Milner-White, (n.d.)
Illuminating stained glass externally by gas	Stained glass, 1851
Illustrated dictionary of glass	Newman, 1977
Jade Window	Jade Window, 1952
Means of describing disordered windows	J. Fowler, 1875
Modern Knights in stained glass	Goodyear, 1926
Modern work mistaken for old; some attributions which have appeared in print	Modern work..... 1960
Le Moyen Age Fantastique	Baltrusaitis, 1955
Oil painting on glass	Gullick, 1892
Old glass in new windows	W.H. Low, 1888
Plague in the fourteenth century and its effect on glass-painting	Knowles, 1922
Plan for the study and description of mediaeval stained glass	Goodall, 1965
Polar history in a Midland village	H.T. Kirby, 1946
The Role of the Library in a stained glass studio	H. Martin, 1967
The Schizophrenic crisis of Scalion Lowland, a stained glass addict	Lowland, 1961
Sculptured plain glass recommended	Athoe, 1936
Secular pedigree windows	F.S. Eden, 1937
Some aspects of the middle ages seen through stained glass	Williamson, 1933
Some optical peculiarities of ancient painted glass	Tuckett, 1888(S)
Stained glass for Stalin	Stalin, 1948
Stained glass found in strange places	Stained glass, 1934
Stained glass in poetry	Foulkes, 1969; Haberley, 1933; Poetry, 1912, 1939; Warton, 1782
Stained glass windows to Fictitious Characters	Oidtmann, 1928 Ardagh, 1936 Athoe, 1936 W. Gill, 1937 L. Strachan, 1936
Test to distinguish ancient glass from modern	Test........1925, 1926
'Times' leader on the current position of the art	Stained glass, 1930
Trial of Archbishop Laud (Reference to glass)	Lillie, 1942
Uncle Tom in stained glass?	J.H. Kuhn, 1968
A window of glass and clay	Lukens, 1968
Windows composed of fragments	Brockwell, 1941; Horne, 1941
Windows representing Raleigh	Brushfield, 1907 Crane, 1938

NINETEENTH CENTURY STAINED GLASS (General)

Binnall, 1968-1970
M. Harrison, 1973, 1979(S)
Lami de Nozan, 1852
Lasteyrie, 1861
Levett, 1879
Nineteenth century windows, 1862

Northampton Architectural Society,
  1853 (a list of church artificers)
Parry, 1862
Sewter, 1962
Sparke, 1918
Stained glass, 1859
N.H.J. Westlake, 1883

PHOTOGRAPHY of Stained Glass

B. Coe, 1981(S)
L. Cook, 1975
P. Hood, 1930
Photography, 1941

Pitcher, 1928
Roenn, 1975
Stained glass, 1925

PORTRAITS in Glass

(Of Richard III) Benton & Lewer, 1923
(Of Henry VI) Brown, 1973
Fischer, 1913
H.T. Kirby, 1962, 1963
J. Lane, 1916 (a whole correspondence)
Lefébure, 1970
Lillich, 1970

Living persons depicted, 1959

London, 1926
Oldfield, 1865
R.L. Poole, 1929
Portraits in Stained Glass, 1916(13)
Simpson, 1869
Vasselot, 1880
H.M. Wright, 1934

PRE-MEDIAEVAL GLASS

Formigé, 1934
Harden, 1959, 1961, 1963, 1968, 1969(2),
  1978

Stites, 1941

PROTECTION OF WINDOWS (including removal during wartime)

Aubert, 1936
Chartres, 1936, 1938, 1939
Eeles, 1943
F. Harrison, 1943
Helbig, 1940
Malvern, 1941
Marchini, 1970

Maunoury, 1936
Strasbourg, 1946
Wartime removal of glass in
  England, 1941
Wire guards, 1927
York, 1940(3)

QUARRIES

Franks, 1849
Hollis, 1926
R.G. Roe, 1923
G. Rowe, 1871-1873

Sperling, 1933
Woodforde, 1944
G. York, 1854

RENAISSANCE GLASS - General Accounts of

General

Bryans, 1910; W. Butterworth, 1928, 1932;
  Dilke, 1879; Hirth, 1877-1881; Picquet,
  1905; Sutton, 1877

Belgium

Helbig, 1937

England

M. Jourdain, 1924

France

Brieger, 1938

Germany

Amsler & Ruthardt, 1895;
  Friedlander, 1898

Spain

Alcaide, 1970

U.S.A.

Friedley, 1913

REQUESTS FOR IDENTIFICATION of scenes, portraits, etc.

W. Drake, 1924, 1925

Roundel, 1793

ROSE WINDOWS

Beer, 1952, 1970
Cowen, 1979
Dykes-Bower, 1978-1979
Frodl-Kraft, 1967
Gates, 1933

Hiemer, 1942
Perkins, 1935
Perrot, 1970
Rahn, 1879
P. Simon, 1911

SALES AND COLLECTIONS (not in public museums) of stained glass

General

Frodl-Kraft, 1965

Acezat collection	Acezat, 1969
Ancient stained glass collectors	Knowles, 1968
Ashridge Park Collection	Ashridge Park, 1928
Bazely Collection	Bazely, 1897
Blumenthal Collection	Rubinstein-Bloch, 1926-1927
Chabot-Karlen Collection sale	Chabot-Karlen, 1898
Chester Cathedral glass sale	Chester Cathedral, 1817
Christies Limited	Christies, 1808, 1816, 1820, 1921,
	1931, 1974, 1975, 1979
Comyns	Comyns, 1804
Costessey Collection	M. Drake & A. Vallance, 1920;
	Stoke d'Abernon, 1950; W. Wells, 1965
Craigwell House, Bognor	Craigwell House, 1932
Derschau Collection	Derschau, 1825
Engel-Gros Collection Sale	Engel-Gros Collection, 1922; Ganz, 1925
Foreign glass (purchased for various	Foreign glass, 1807
locations in England)	
Gilling Castle Sale	Hunter, 1929
Goldman Collection	Bye, 1929
Grayling Collection (fragments go to	Milner-White, 1954
York Minster)	
Hearst Collection	Canterbury Cathedral, 1960, 1961;
	Hearst, 1940; Normile, 1945, 1946
Heilbronner Collection Sale	Sherrill, 1928
Highgate Old Hall	F.S. Eden, 1934
Henry Lawrence Collection Sale	Lawrence, 1921
Legge Collection	Extracts, 1, 1925
Locksley Hall Collection	Woodforde, 1932
Mainberg Collection	Schloss Mainberg, 1902
L. Minard Collection	Minard, 1883
Monell Collection	Monell, 1930, 1931
Paterson Collection Sale	Paterson, 1773
Sale in Norwich and London in 1804	Catalogue..............1956
St. Levee d'Agnerre Collection	Montreal Museum, 1936-1937
F.E. Sydney Collection	Rackham, 1929(2)
Sotheby's	Sotheby's, 1928, 1929, 1973-1974,
	1974-1975; 1976, 1976-1977;
	1978-1979
Spitzer Collection	Molinier, 1890-1892; Spitzer, 1893
Stein Collection	Stein, 1928, 1966
Sudeley Castle Sale	Sudeley, 1911, 1912
Swiss Glass	Swiss Glass, 1916
Trétaigne Collection Sale	Trétaigne, 1904
Usteri Collection	Rahn, 1899; Usteri, 1894
Vigurs Collection Sale	Vigurs, 1849
Vincent Collection	Vincent, 1890
Horace Walpole Collection and Sale	Knowles, 1937, 1938(2), 1939;
	Walpole, 1842(2)
Zweierlein Collection	Zweierlein, 1887

SCHOLARS (Obituaries, etc)

M. Aubert	Aubert, 1963	W. Foxley-Norris	Foxley-Norris, 1938
J. Browne	Benson, 1818, 1926	E.W. Ganderton	Ganderton, 1964
J.D. le Couteur	Couteur, 1925	L. Grodecki	Caviness, 1979
M.A. Couturier	Couturier, 1953-1954	F. Harrison	F. Harrison, 1959
Drake Family	See entry under		K. Harrison, 1960
	Glass-Painters		Milner-White, 1959
F.C. Eeles	Eeles, 1955(2)	N. Heaton	Salmond, 1956
Felibien des Avaux	Lafond, 1954	E. Houvet	Maunoury, 1949
W. Fowler	Ball, 1869; Binnall,	H.T. Kirby	H.T. Kirby, 1967
	1928; J.T. Fowler,	J.A. Knowles	Knowles, 1957, 1961(2),
	1907; J. Fowler, 1834		1962(2), 1964
	1869; W. Fowler, 1888	J. Lafond	Lafond, 1970

Scholars (Obituaries, etc) - cont.

A. Lane	A. Lane, 1964	N. Truman	Truman, 1950
M. Lavanoux	Lavanoux, 1974	J. Verrier	Verrier, 1964
E. Mâle	Aubert, 1955	Viollet-le-Duc	Knowles, 1938,
E. Milner-White	Milner-White, 1954		1957-1958
	1957, 1963(3),	N.H.J. Westlake	M. Westlake, 1929
	1964(2); Pare, 1965	C. Winston	See entry under
B. Rackham	Rackham, 1964, 1965		Glass-Painters
R.G. Roe	Roe, 1927	C. Woodforde	Woodforde, 1962
G. McN.Rushforth	Rushforth, 1938(4)		
	1940		
R. Thoresby	W. Lancaster		

STAINED GLASS - GENERALISED ACCOUNTS

Adam, 1894
Aloi, 1950
C. Anderson, 1850-1851
D. Anderson, 1885
Andrae, 1880
Angus-Butterworth, 1961
Archer, 1979
Armitage, 1959
Art Workers' Guild, 1967
Ballantine, 1912
Beck, 1953-1954
M.C.F. Bell, 1970-1971
R. Bell, 1930
R.A. Bell, 1922
Betjeman, 1956
Bles, 1925
Bostock, 1928(2), 1929
Burges, 1865
Burgess, 1914
Burnham, 1945, 1946
W. Butterworth, 1926
Byrne, 1948
Camm, 1890
Carpenter, 1892
Claudel, 1949
Connick, 1924, 1927(2), 1929, 1930,
  1931, 1932, 1937, 1938(4), 1939(2)
  1940(2), 1941, 1942, 1944(4), 1945,
  1946
Cooley, 1966
C. Cooper, 1847
W. Cope, 1882, 1897
Cowell, 1944
E.C. Cram, 1938
R.A. Cram, 1924
Crotti, 1947
Crozier, 1923
Currivan, 1944
Dignity without the dust of Ancients,
  1962
Eckhardt, 1962(2)
F.S. Eden, 1935
Edwards, 1951, 1956
Fish, 1966
Fischer, 1913, 1915
Fitchfield, 1908
J.T. Fowler, 1912
Francis, 1962
Francotte, 1888
Frank, 1924-1925
Frei, 1965-1966
Frei, Rambusch & Elskus, 1965
Gahlen, 1930, 1936
Ganderton, 1964
Gaudin, 1924
Gérin, 1875
Glass-painting, 1834, 1878, 1879, 1880,
  1883, 1890, 1904(2), 1911, 1915, 1912
  1933(2)

Goodhart-Rendel, 1939
Grafly, 1946
C. Heaton, 1912
N. Heaton, 1910, 1914, 1949
Heinersdorff, 1913
Heinigke, 1902, 1935-1936
Hockman, 1963
Hogan, 1940
Holiday, 1896
Hornabrook, 1885
E.G. Howard, 1887
L. Howard, 1946
Huth, 1924
M.R. James, 1925
Janeau, 1931
R. Jenkins, 1966
Jessel, 1896
E. Johnson, 1945
Karawina-Hsiao, 1956-1957, 1957, 1963(2)
T. Kendrick, 1963
Klaris, 1947
Knowles, 1926(2), 1943
F. Lamb, 1903
Landmann, 1929
Lavanoux, 1933
Lavergne, 1891
M. Law, 1925
Lenoir, 1802, 1803, 1856
McClinton, 1957
Magne, 1885, 1906, 1913, 1927
M. Maurer, 1937(2)
Merewether, 1937(2)
Merewether, 1848
Millar, 1881
Modern Stained Glass, 1926
Morant, 1870
Morris, W. 1860-1868
Moufang, 1929
C. Muller, 1929
H. Murray, 1869
New work in stained glass, 1954
Dom Norris, 1937(3), 1938(2)
Oidtmann, 1892-1898
Osterrath, 1902-1904
Paget, 1957
Paine, 1950
Parkhurst, 1899
Parry, 1886
Paterson, 1968
Pellatt, 1862(2), 1864
Phillipps, 1910(2), 1913
Pousin, 1891
J.H. Powell, 1857
Pratt, 1911
Rackham, 1925, 1926(2), 1961
H. Rambusch, 1941, 1944
Read, 1929, 1932
Rich, F.D.
F. Rogers & Beard

Stained Glass - Generalised Accounts - cont.

H.M. Rogers, 1936, 1937
Rothenberg, 1973
Rothery, 1925
Saint, 1925, 1926, 1936
Sears, 1911
Seddon, 1976
Sennott, 1966
Sheldon, 1935, 1939, 1944
Skinner, 1942, 1943(2), 1944, 1945, 1947
Sowers, 1954
Stained glass, 1817, 1901, 1938
Stevenson, 1915
Stewart-Smith, 1948
Stidger, 1948
Suter, 1948
A. Taylor, 1886-1890
R.G. Thomas, 1922
W.H. Thomas, 1901, 1906

Tyack, 1897(S)
Usher, 1871-1872
Vallance, 1908
Wallace-Dunlop, 1882
T.H. Waring, 1938
Wayne, 1876
M. Webb, 1932
A. Werner, 1966
C. Whall, 1891
O. Whiteside, 1937
Wichmann, 1895, 1900
E.C. Willet, 1963
H.L. Willet, 1948
W. Willet, 1918
Y. Williams, 1944
Winterich, 1967
M. Young, 1962

STAINED GLASS AND ARCHITECTURE

The Architect looks..........., 1953
Ballantine, 1845
Bassuk, 1963
Bielenberg, 1930
Bridges, Goodman, Atkinson, Rambusch,
  Bates, 1965
Buttress, 1976-1977
R.A. Cram, 1925, 1939
H. Cummings, 1946
J. Cummings, 1955
Dahmen, 1922
Becksmann, 1977
F.C. Eden, 1931(2)
Felibien des Avaux, 1676
Fischer, 1913(3)
Foxley-Norris, 1927
Frodl-Kraft, 1956
Froidevaux, 1977
Gahlen, 1929
Gailhabaud, 1858
Glass-painting, 1884, 1907
Grodecki, 1949, 1951
Guillum, 1948
Heaton, 1908
Heinigke, 1937
Heliot, 1968
Hickman, 1954
F. Howard, 1853
T.F. Hunt, 1830
R.C. Hussey, 1876

Lavanoux, 1932
Linneman, 1934(2)
Lush, 1838
Lutyens, 1933
McGrath & Frost, 1937
Maguire, 1951
C. Moore, 1899
C. Morgan, 1900
R. Morris, 1931
W. Morris, 1935
C. Nicholson, 1925
W.F. Paris, 1917
G.A. Poole, 1865-1866
Powys, 1928
R. Rambusch, 1957
Redstone, 1968
Role of Stained Glass in Architecture,
  1968
Senger, 1960-1961
Sowers, 1960, 1965
Swaan, 1969
Vallance, 1890
Voysey, 1929
Whichcord, 1855
Winston, 1865
Winterich, 1968
Wolf, 1932

STAINED GLASS SUNDIALS

Knowles, 1930
Sundials, 1926

G. Wood, 1947

STAINED GLASS TECHNIQUE - including design problems, Historical and Modern

Alcaide, 1967
Alder, 1931
Almy, 1949
Amman, 1938
Apligny, 1779
Arendt, 1904
Armitage, 1959
Art's Master-piece...., 1697
Ashley, 1801
J. Barnard, 1865, 1874
W. Barnard, 1863
Batissier, 1843, 1845
Barrow, 1735
Beckmann, 1782-1805
J.C. Bell, 1925

M.C.F. Bell, 1954
Béthune, 1900-1905
Biver, 1913, 1930(2), 1931
Blenko, Willet, Cummings et al.
  1961, 1961-1962, 1962
Bontemps, 1845, 1868
Boom, 1949
Bridges, Frei, Skinner et al.
  1960-1961, 1961
S.L. Brown, 1928
Bruck, 1902
Bruner, 1969
Buckeridge, 1858
Burnham, 1924, 1935
Butler, 1937-1938

Stained Glass Technique - including design problems, Historical and Modern - cont.

Cassell, 1870-1872, 1892-1895
Champigneulle, 1895
Champollion-Figeac, 1851
Chance Bros., n.d. 1855
Chesneau, 1933
Connick, 1932
Copper Wire Ties, 1945
Couteur, 1925
Couverte, 1933
Cowles, 1908
Craftsman's Portfolio, 1927
Davis & Middlemas 1969
Day, 1898
Decoration without burning in,
Decoration, 1924
Delamotte, 1870-1872
Demotte, 1934
Deneux, 1929
Designs....... 1910-1912
Divine & Blachford, 1940
Dixon, 1869
M. Drake, 1923, 1928
T. Drake, 1870
A. Duncan, 1974-1975
Duthie, 1908
F.S. Eden, 1927
Eitelberger von Edelberg, 1871
Electric Kilns, 1925, 1934
Erikson, 1974
S. Evans, 1862
Firing, 1955
Fischer, 1913, 1914
Franchet, 1908(2)
A.C. Freeman, 1930
Frei, 1955, 1958, 1960-1961, 1961
J. French, 1975
Frodl-Kraft, 1962, 1970
Fromberg, 1844
Furnace for firing, 1917
Gahlen, 1930, 1936
Gerrard, 1925
Glass cutting, 1944, 1945, 1969-1970
Glass-painting, 1754(2), 1831, 1836
   1839, 1846, 1875, 1877, 1898, 1901,
   1902, 1903, 1907, 1911, 1912, 1915,
   1927
A. Godwin, 1895
G. Godwin, 1840
Gruber, 1927-1928
Gruenke, 1955
Gruz, 1886
Hallward, 1929
Haudicquer de Blancourt, 1718
Hawkins, 1813
Heat of Kiln, 1925
M. Heaton, 1929
N. Heaton, 1924, 1926
Heinersdorff, 1912, 1914
Heinrich, 1931
Heuss, 1911
Higgins, 1929
Huth, 1924(2)
Isenberg. 1972
Isis, 1938
Jamison 1962 (epoxy resins)
Jannicke, 1890
Keghel, 1924
Kennedy, 1891, 1893
Killer, 1928, 1929-1930
Kinon, 1904
H.T. Kirby, 1953
Knowles, 1914, 1922, 1925, 1926(2),
   1927, 1949, 1950, 1957, 1958, 1960
Kuhne, 1960
A. Lacroix, 1872
P. Lacroix, 1865
Lafond, 1943, 1954, 1962, 1968
Lakin, 1824
C. Lamb, 1899
F. Lamb, 1906

Laney, 1942
Langlois, 1832
Lasteyrie, 1852
Lauber, 1908
Lautier, 1978
Lefebvre, 1858
Leisching, 1902
Lenoir, 1824, 1846
Lethaby, 1905
Le Vieil, 1774
C.F. Lewis, 1929
Linnemann, 1934
R. Linnemann, 1912
Lowndes, 1913
MacCausland, 1913
Magnier & Rebouleau, 1868
Mappae Clavicula, 1847
R. Mathews, 1892(2), 1893, 1897
E. Matthews, 1877
Merrifield, 1849
R. & G. Metcalf, 1972
J. Meunier, 1842
Miller, 1884, 1885(2), 1886, 1887, 1890
Mirault, 1839
Mollica, 1971, 1977
E. Morrison, 1968, 1970
P. Morrison, 1970
Newhoff, 1974
Nicolas, 1945
Oidtmann, 1893
Olson, 1977
Ornaments, 1924
Ottin, 1892
Paine, 1933
J. Pearson, 1815
Peters, 1890
D. Phillips, 1962
Pietschke, 1836
Pisa, 1976
Porter, 1974
Porthusen, 1774
J. Powell, 1892
Prévot, 1882
Puckle, 1929
A.W.N. Pugin, 1849
Reyntiens, 1968
K. Robert, 1879, 1892, 1895
A. Robinson, 1955
Royce, 1950
Ruby stain, 1927
Rule for taking measurements between
   Mullions....... 1927
Saal, 1894
Salaquada, 1932
Scheurpflug, 1939
Schott, 1932
W.B. Scott, 1845, 1861
T. Shaw, 1838
Spear, (n.d.)
Springer, 1926(2)
Stahl, 1912, 1915
Stained glass, 1908, 1911(2), 1930(2)
   1938, 1950, 1969
Statz, 1856-1861, 1885
Stephens, 1976
Stokinger, 1925(2)
Suffling, 1890, 1902
Theophilus, 1961
Thibaud, 1842
Thibaud & Didron, 1850
Tillyer, 1877
Twining, 1928
Viollet-le-Duc, 1933
Vogl, 1907
Volckert, 1758
Vorbrugg, 1907

Stained Glass Technique - including design problems, Historical and Modern - cont.

Warnecke, 1880, 1887
Weissenbach, 1877
Wentzel, 1970
N.H.J. Westlake, 1878
Whall, 1905
Whittock, 1827
Y. Williams, 1946
R. Willis, 1962

C.J. Wilson, 1979
Winston, 1865
Winterich, 1957
P. Wood, 1967
Yellow Staining, 1928, 1932
J. Young, 1963
Zantner-Busch, 1935

VANDALISM (licensed and unlicensed), war damage and rescue, thefts, forgeries etc.

Ancient French treasures, 1944
Atrocious offer made by a glass stainer,
   1845
S. Baker, 1932;
Blatherwycke, 1964
Blume, 1978
Canterbury Cathedral, 1940, 1946
Destruction of painted glass, 1911
Disappearance of windows, 1956
Dowsing's Journal, 1876
M. Drake, 1923
F.S. Eden, 1932
Frenzel, 1977
Gurdon, 1899(S)
M. Harrison, 1977
Helbig, 1937, 1939
Jervis, 1932
R.G. Jones, 1937
W. Kent, 1947

Knowles, 1923 (rp. 1923, 1924(2), 1926),
   1926, 1958
Lafaye, 1871
Lafond, 1961-1962, 1969
London, 1914
Lucas, 1942
Maunoury, 1946
Meaford, 1947
J.M. Neale, 1854
O'Kelly de Galway, 1859
Réau, 1959
Rouen glass lost, 1939
Ryves, 1646
(Stolen Stained Glass) Stolen Stained
   Glass......, 1933
Theft of Stained Glass, 1975(2)
Victoria and Albert Museum, 1926(2)
York, 1964, 1967(3)
Strasbourg, 1946
War Damage Commission, 1946
C.H. White, 1895-1896

TOPOGRAPHICAL INDEX

ENGLAND

General

Arnold & Saint, 1913
Baddeley, 1903
Baker & Lammer, 1960, 1978
Boase, 1953
Brieger, 1957
Bumpus, 1899-1901
Carter, 1780-1794, 1815
Chronological List of English
    Glass-paintings of known date
    (also see Milner-White, 1937(2)
    & Woodforde, 1937)
Coe, 1981 (S)
Couteur, 1926
Crossley, 1936, 1941
Dallaway, 1800, 1806, 1826
Day, 1883
M. Drake, 1912
W. Drake, 1937(2), (additions to
    the Chronological List of English
    Glass-Paintings)
F.S. Eden, 1913(2)
J. Evans, 1949
Fenn, 1932
W. Fowler, 1804, 1809, 1824
J. Gilbert, 1842

Godwin, 1840
Gomme, 1817
Hallward, 1939
Harries, 1968
Hey, 1865
Himsworth, 1927
Hubbard (n.d.)
Knowles, 1922(5), 1927(3)
Lamborn, 1929
J. Lowe, 1961, 1962
D. & S. Lysons, 1806-1822
Milner-White, 1937(2)
Nelson, 1913
Osborne, 1981(S)
A. Pugin, 1821-1823, 1831-1838
Read, 1926, 1960, 1925
Salzman, 1928(2), 1929
Saunders, 1932
Sherrill, 1909
Verdier, 1973
Walpole, Horace, 1826
Warren, 1963
Winston, 1845, 1847, 1854
Woodforde, 1935, 1936(2), 1937(2),
    1954

English Museums

General

Skeat, 1978-1979
Birmingham Museum.   Birmingham Museum, 1895
Bowes Museum, Barnard Castle.   Boesch, 1936
Canterbury Museum.   Canterbury, 1899
Edinburgh.   Royal Scottish Museum.   Gould, 1931
Glasgow Museum, Burrell Collection.   Glasgow Museum, 1947, 1962, 1965, 1977;
                            W. Wells, 1959; Wentzel, 1961
Victoria & Albert Museums.   Day, 1903, Extracts No. 4, 1925; Knowles, 1926;
                            Rackham, 1920, 1925(4), 1930(2), 1934, 1936;
                            Read, 1924; Skinner, 1904; Victoria & Albert
                            Museum, 1864, 1875, 1887, 1919, 1920, 1923, 1924
                            1926(2), 1927, 1929, 1930(2), 1934(2), 1937, 1952,
                            1971, 1976-1977; R. Warrington, 1925.

Bedfordshire
    General   Marks, 1976
    Chicksands.   Gamlen, 1974-1975

Berkshire
    General   F.S. Eden, 1942
    Abingdon (County Hall)   Abingdon, 1939
    Aldermaston   Keyser, 1898 (S)
    Arborfield   Arborfield
    Hurst House   E. Cope, 1922
    North Moreton   Winston, 1856, 1861
    Ockwells Manor E. Green, 1899; Knowles, 1924
    Windsor. St. George's
    Chapel   W. Drake, 1942; Frost, 1914; Knowles, 1950;
                    Page, 1914; Pierpoint, 1914; Weale, 1846;
                    Windsor, 1842, 1910-1915

Buckinghamshire
    Eton College   M.R. James, 1904
    Middleton Cheney   Magrath, 1919
    Newington   Newington, 1850
    Notley Abbey   Gamlen, 1943-1944, 1974-1975
    Stoke Poges   J.T. Fowler, 1903; Lamborn, 1944; Stoke Poges, 1928

Cambridgeshire
    General   Willis & Clark, 1886
    Christ's College   Rackham, 1952, 1953
    Jesus College   Jesus College, 1853; R.G. Roe, 1924
    King's College Chapel   Beets, 1908; Bolton, 1854, 1855; Brindley & Moore, 1910;
                            Cambridge, King's College, 1852; T.J.P. Carter, 1867;
                            C.J. Evans, 1886; K. Harrison, 1952(2), 1953;
                            M.R. James, 1894-1898(2), 1899; Lacy, 1970; Milner-White,
                            1921, 1924, 1928, 1930; Scharf, 1855, 1856; Tibbs, 1970;
                            Wayment, 1958(3), 1970, 1972; N.H.J. Westlake, 1892.

Cambridgeshire - cont.

Peterhouse   Cambridge, St. Peter's College, 1855, 1858
Trinity   Cambridge, Trinity College, 1853
University Library Clark, 1904
Westminster College Simpson, 1926
Ely.   Prebendal house Ely, 1788
       Cathedral   Ely, 1850, 1851, 1853, 1857, 1858, 1862, 1972,
                         1975, 1976, 1976-1977; D. King, 1977, 1979;
                         Milner-White, 1937; P. Moore, 1973.
Thorney Abbey   Oettli, 1973
Upwell   Upwell, 1839

Channel Islands

St. Helier   Jersey, 1889

Cheshire
    General   Ridgway, 1947, 1948
    Bramall Hall   F.S. Eden, 1931
    Brereton   Pegge, 1789, 1792
    Chester Cathedral,
        Chapter House   Chester Cathedral, 1817
    Chester, St. John Baptist S.C. Scott, 1896
    Farndon   Farndon, 1926, 1935
    Grappenhall   Ridgway, 1951
    Lymm   Rylands, 1879
    Malpas   Malpas, 1846
    Moreton Old Hall   W.J. Pearce, 1940
    St. Mary-on-the-Hill Barber, 1904
    Spurstow Hall   Rylands & Brown, 1921
    Tarporley Rectory   Rylands & Brown, 1921
    Thornton Hough   Burlison & Grylls, 1926
    Utkinton Hall   Rylands & Brown, 1921
    Vale Royal   Rylands & Brown, 1921

Cornwall
    General   Boreham, 1957
                Dobie, 1932
    Cotehele   Condy, 1850
    Liskeard   Hare, 1886
    St. Neots   Bourke, 1974-1976; Forster, 1786; D. Gilbert,
                        1830-1831; (see also Hedgeland, 1830) Grylls,
                        1844; Houghton, 1920; Rushforth, 1933, 1937;
                        St. Neots, 1851
    Truro   Eustice, (n.d.) (S)

Cumberland and Westmorland
    General   Hodge, 1976, 1977
    Barrow-in-Furness   Boumphrey & Melville, 1973
    Bowness-on-Windermere Collier, 1897; Eeles, 1950
    Calder Abbey   Fair, 1954
    Carlisle Cathedral Eeles, 1926; Ferguson, 1876; Field, 1934;
                        Lowther Bouch, 1946
    Cartmel Fell   J.T. Fowler, 1912; Lees & Ferguson, 1876;
                        H.F. Wilson, 1920
    Conishead Priory   Boumphrey, 1973
    Crosthwaite   Crosthwaite, 1849
    Edenhall   Haswell, 1899, 1913
    Graythwaite Hall   Boumphrey, 1974
    Greystoke   Lees, 1876
    Holker Hall   Boumphrey, 1974
    Levens Hall   Boumphrey, 1972
    Penrith   Hudleston, 1951
    Rydal Hall   Boumphrey, 1975
    Swindale   E. Jackson, 1912; Whiteside, 1901
    Temple Sowerby   Batten, 1909
    Tunstall   Tunstall, 1905
    Ulverston   Boumphrey, 1973
    Windermere   Clowes, Hughes & Bailey, 1874; Ferguson, 1880;
                        B.L. Thompson, 1934
    Witherslack   Brighton, 1971

Derbyshire
    General   Himsworth, 1929, 1931
    Ashbourne   F. Jourdain, 1881
    Haddon Hall   C. Kerr, 1900
    Hassop Hall   Hassop Hall, 1879
    Hault Hucknall   Kerry, 1898

Essex - cont.

Roothing	Christy, 1903
Saffron Walden	Steer, 1954
Thaxted	Brindley, 1911
Walden	Probert, 1930
White Notley	Hamilton, 1885
Witham	Hamilton, 1885

Gloucestershire and Bristol

General	Lysons, 1803; Pitcher, 1925
Bagendon	Bagendon, 1924
Bledington	Cubitt, 1877; Cutts, 1882-1883
Bristol, Cathedral	Sabin, 1957; Winston, 1865
Lord Mayor's Chapel	Barker, 1892; Rackham, 1935; Ralph & Evans, 1959; Rushforth, 1927
St. Mary Redcliffe	Cottle, 1957
St. Stephen	Bathurst, 1958
Temple Church	Hudd, 1905
Buckland	Barnard, 1923
Cirencester	Beeby, 1916; Croome, 1964; Sinclair, (n.d.)
Deerhurst	E. Gilbert, 1956
Didbrook	Didbrook, 1900
Fairford	Bates, 1868; Bigland, 1791; Carbonell, 1893, 1908; J.R. Clayton, 1868; Cubitt, 1877; S. Evans, 1864; Fairford, 1835, 1864, 1866, 1868(4), 1869, 1871, 1875, 1876, 1891, 1945, 1949; Farmer, 1933; Holt, 1868(8); Humphreys, 1868; Joyce, 1868, 1870, 1872, 1877-1878; Keble (n.d.); Kinsman, 1869; Knowles, 1963; Macray, 1868; Piggot, 1868(2); James Powell, 1876(2); Joseph Powell, 1875(3), 1876; Roscoe, 1881; Rudder, 1780; J.F. Russell, 1865, 1868; Scharf, 1868; Tom Taylor, 1868(4); J.G. Waller, 1868(5); N.H.J. Westlake, 1892; Winnington, 1866, 1868, 1869
Gloucester Cathedral	Dancey, 1911; Grimké-Drayton, 1915; Haines, 1867; Nott, 1900; Rushforth, 1921, 1922; F. Waller, 1883-1884; Winston, 1865(2)
Preston-on-Stour	Batt and New, 1876
Prinknash	Baddeley, 1927, 1928
Tewkesbury	Bannister, (n.d.); Brice, 1963; Extracts No. 5, 1925; Rushforth, 1924; Tewkesbury, 1925; Were, 1903
Toddington	Baddeley, 1900; Helbing, 1911; Lehmann, 1911

Hampshire

Basingstoke	Blacking, 1948
Bitterne Park	Milner-White, 1957; A.K. Nicholson, 1931(2)
Boldre	Boldre, 1953
Highcliffe Castle	C. Hussey, 1942; Lafond, 1972; J.H. Powell, 1968
Selborne	Knapp, 1957; Knowles, 1957
Timsbury	Couteur, 1923
Ventnor	Sewter, 1967; Ventnor, 1968-1969, 1972
The Vyne	Chute, 1888; Lees-Milne, 1961; Rushforth, 1927(2); Wayment, 1979
Winchester (general)	Couteur, 1920; F.S. Eden, 1942; N.H.J. Westlake, 1892; Winston, 1865
Winchester Cathedral	O.B. Carter, 1845; Chitty, 1918(2); Fragments, 1941; Winchester Cathedral, 1844-1845, 1937
Winchester College	Briggs, 1890; Chitty, 1918, 1920; Chitty and Harvey, 1962; Couteur, 1920, 1923; Dodson, 1920; M. Drake, 1920; J.H. Harvey, 1950; J.H. Harvey & D. King, 1971; H.T. Kirby, 1948, 1950; Rackham, 1926; Rutter, 1947; Winchester College, 1937; H.C. Winchester, 1931
Winchester, West Gate	E. Cope, 1923; Wilde, 1927
Winchester St. Cross	Winchester St. Cross, 1830

Herefordshire

General	Herefordshire, 1949, 1950, 1952
Credenhill	Havergal, 1884
Eaton Bishop	Eaton Bishop, 1968; M.R. James, 1929; G. Marshall, 1924, 1928
Goodrich	Goodrich, 1918
Hereford Cathedral	F.S. Eden, 1925; F.C. Morgan, 1963, 1967
Foy	G. Marshall, 1940
Freen's Court	G. Marshall, 1918
Kingsland	G. Marshall, 1935
Leintwardine	G. Marshall, 1921

Derbyshire - cont.

Morley	Bailey, 1886; J.G. Waller, 1852; F. Wilson, 1886
Norbury	Bailey, 1882, 1883; Bowman & Hadfield, 1844; Norbury, 1971, 1972
Stavely	Brighton, 1960

Devonshire

General	Binnall, 1968-1970; Cornelius, 1947; Cotton, 1890; Cresswell, 1908, 1911, 1912, 1921
Ashton	M. Adams, 1899; M. Drake, 1905, 1907
Beer, Bovey House	W. Drake, 1913
Bicton	Bicton, 1850
Bradninch	Bradninch, 1911
Cadbury	Chard, 1925; Cresswell, 1925; Rushforth, 1929
Cheriton Bishop, Medland Manor	D. Drake, 1935; G.T. Morris, 1935
Churston Ferrers	M. Adams, 1904
Clyst St. George	Ellacombe, 1867
Dartmouth	M. Drake, 1909; R. Gibbs, 1909(2)
Diddiscombsleigh	Buckingham, 1925, (n.d.S); M. Drake, 1913; Rushforth, 1929; Tait, 1889
East Ogwell	M. Adams, 1900
Exeter, Bamfylde House	W. Drake, 1911, 1913; Prideaux, 1929
Exeter Cathedral	Allen, 1950; Bell, 1953; Coffin, 1772; D. Drake, 1933; F. Drake, 1879; M. Drake, 1909, 1912, 1913, 1922; W. Drake, 1913(2); M. Drury, 1949, 1951, 1952; F.C. Eden, 1915-1916(S); Exeter Cathedral, 1797, 1830, 1879, 1888, 1921, 1935, 1947; C. Fox, 1952; J.L. Fulford, 1847; R. Gibbs, 1905, 1909; Lega-Weekes, 1935; Skeat, 1943, 1953; Winston, 1865
Ipplepen	Cooke, (n.d.) (S)
Littleham	E.V. Freeman, 1879
Paignton	R. Gibbs, 1905
Polsloe Priory	Clarke, 1905
Salcombe Regis	W. Drake, 1915; Morshead, 1915
Samford Courtenay	K. Harrison, 1955
Sand	Sand, 1897
Sidmouth	J. Rowe, 1905; Sidmouth, 1867
Slapton	W. Drake, 1911; F. Fulford, 1911, 1913, Reichel, 1911
Sydenham Damerel	N. Lightfoot, 1847
Torbryan	Cooke, (n.d.) (S)
Upton Pyne	M. Drake, 1911
Wolborough	Wolborough, 1946(3)

Dorset

General	Long, 1923, 1967
Bradford Peverell	Barnes, 1891
Ibberton	Baigent, 1885
Melbury Bubbe	Buckler, 1888(S)
Sherborne	Gibb, 1971; Sherborne, 1923(2), 1959
Wimborne	Housden, 1895

Essex

General	Bacon, 1921; Benton, 1923; Butcher, 1921; F.S. Eden, 1910(3), 1911, 1925, 1936, 1939, 1940(2); Woodforde, 1934
Belhus	F.S. Eden, 1929
Bicknacre	Benton, 1930
Bradwell	Hamilton, 1885
Clavering	Benton, 1926; Eeles, 1923; Ffytche, 1922; Woodforde, 1940
Colchester	F.S. Eden, 1928(2)
Cressing	Hamilton, 1885
Dedham	Parsons, 1794
Faulkbourne	Hamilton, 1885
Great Maplestead, Dynes Hall	Sperling, 1933
Harlow	Bradford, 1911; Harlow, 1910
Horham Hall	F.S. Eden, 1932
Lindsell	Rackham, 1933
Little Braxted	Hamilton, 1885
Little Easton	Archer, 1977
Maldon	Brookes, 1929; F.S. Eden, 1914
Margaretting	Bacon, 1918, 1925
New Hall	Hills, 1928
Pebmarsh, Stanley Hall	Bayley & Steer, 1958
Rivenhall	F.S. Eden, 1925; Fragments, 1941; Hamilton, 1885; Rivenhall, 1925; Rodwell, 1978-1979

Herefordshire - cont.

Madley	Clarke, 1918; M.R. James, 1929; Madley, 1958; G. Marshall, 1928(2)
Pembridge	Pembridge, 1918
Ross-on-Wye	Beattie, n.d.
Sellock	Sellock, 1918
Sugwas	G. Marshall, 1924
Walterstone	Allt-yr-ynis, 1911, 1921
Wisteston Chapel	Watkins, 1918

Hertfordshire

Ashridge Park	M.R. James, 1906; Rackham, 1928, 1944, 1945, 1948; Sotheby's, 1928
Berkhamsted	F.B. Harvey, 1869
Cassiobury Park	Stoke d'Abernon, 1950
Hatfield House	A. Wilkinson, 1959
Himsdon	H.C. Gibbs, 1915
King's Langley	Gamlen, 1974-1975
New Barnet, Abbey Folk Park	Abbey Folk Park, 1934, 1939
Rickmansworth	Rickmansworth, 1945
St. Albans (general)	Gamlen, 1974-1975; M.R. James, 1892-1893; J. Neale, 1877; Skeat, 1977

Kent

General	Councer, 1980(S); Hussey, 1852; Parsons, 1794
Appledore	Cock, 1931; Cock & Humphry, 1938; Winnifrith, 1973
Ashford	H.L. Smith, 1859
Bishopsbourne	Toke, 1934
Boughton Aluph	Boughton Aluph (n.d.); Councer, 1938
Canterbury Cathedral	Bickersteth, 1959; Burman, 1972-1973; J.M.C. Caldwell, 1931; Canterbury Cathedral, 1850, 1887, 1915, 1928, 1929(2), 1930, 1931, 1932(2), 1933(3), 1935, 1936(2), 1937, 1939(3), 1940(2), 1941, 1946, 1949, 1950, 1960, 1961, 1973, 1974, 1978(2); Caviness, 1965, 1971, 1972 1973, 1974, 1975, 1977(2); Councer, 1952; Couteur, 1911; Crum, 1930; Evetts, 1939, 1941(2); Farrar, 1897; Fergusson, 1975; Gostling, 1774; M. Green, 1975; Grodecki, 1950, 1951; Heaton, 1908; Hill, 1962, 1963, 1964(2); Joyce, 1841; A. Lane, 1959; Loftie, 1876; Mason, 1925; Messenger, 1945, 1953; Rackham, 1928(2), 1933, 1934, 1935, 1939(2), 1940, 1941, 1942, 1943(2), 1944(2), 1945(2), 1947, 1948(2), 1949, 1950, 1951, 1954, 1957, 1960; J. Robinson, 1974; Schnebbelie, 1791; Somner, 1640; S. Warner, 1923; E. Williams, 1897
Canterbury Museum	Canterbury, 1899; W.P. Thornton, 1899
Canterbury School	Hume, 1933
Challock	Challock (n.d.)
Chartham	Chartham, 1954
Chilham	Councer, 1945
Cranbrook	Councer, 1971
Eastwell	Councer, 1946
Farningham	Nash, 1938
Gillingham	Councer, 1948, 1949
Great Chart	H. Russell, 1904
Hastingleigh	Harwood, 1952
Kilndown	Eggert, 1852
Kingsdown	Winston, 1846
Knole	Hill, 1975
Lullingstone	Councer, 1971
Maidstone	Winchcord, 1855
Meopham	Meopham, 1923
Mereworth	Councer, 1962
Mersham	Councer, 1936
Nackington	K.H. Jones, 1938
Nettlestead	Ball, 1909; Fausset, 1864-1865; Winston, 1864
Patrixbourne	Toke, 1932, 1933
Petham	Councer & Hill, 1952
Sandhurst	Sandhurst (n.d.)
Selling	Turpin, 1915, 1916(2)
Stowting	Toke, 1933
Temple Ewell	Toke, 1932, 1939
Teynham	Councer, 1940
Upper Hardres	Toke, 1935; Turpin, 1915, 1916(2)
Warehorne	W. Lightfoot, 1861
Wateringbury	Griffin, 1935
Westbere	Brock, 1887
Westwell	Griffin, 1935

Kent - cont.

West Wickham	Councer, 1949, 1953; Hill, 1953; A. Taylor, 1886-1890; J.G. Waller, 1844, 1873; Weale, 1846; West Wickham, 1833
Willesborough	Garner, 1971; H.L. Smith, 1859
Woodchurch	Bourne, 1938

Lancashire

General	Glynne, 1891, 1894; Lancashire, 1900
Amounderness	Cheetham, 1915
Ashton-under-Lyne	Nelson, 1913; Pugh, 1903
Billinge	Wickham, 1910
Cartmel Priory	Cartmel Priory, 1963; Dickinson (n.d.)
Crosby Hall	Crosby Hall, 1834; Curling, 1834
Hale Hall	Nelson, 1937, 1938, 1939
Healey Hall	Barritt, 1791, 1973
Liverpool	G.P. Hutchinson, 1925
Liverpool Cathedral	Gordon, 1937; Hogan, 1939; Liverpool, 1936; Powell & Sons, 1937
Manchester Cathedral	Hudson, 1907; Lawson, 1899
Middleton	Leather; Middleton, 1969, 1970
Ormskirk	Bromley, 1907
Speke Hall	Winstanley, 1920
Standish	Price, 1905
Warrington	Beaumont & Rylands, 1878
Worsley	Billington, 1954

Leicestershire

Leicester	D. Clarke, 1962; J. Fowler, 1873; North, 1878; Rushforth, 1918
Stoke Golding	Boissier, 1844
Twycross	H.T. Kirby, 1943; Twycross, 1949
Withcote	Woodforde, 1939

Lincolnshire

Boston	Boston (n.d.)
Croxton	Truman, 1953
Haydor	Woodforde, 1933
Lincoln Minster	Binnal, 1966; A. Kendrick, 1898; Lafond, 1946; M. O'Connor, 1855; Winston, 1848, 1857, 1865 Woodforde, 1933
Messingham	Binnall, 1931; Messingham, 1927, 1968
Redbourne	Binnall, 1961
Stamford	Dixon, 1923, 1924, 1925; P.T. Jones, 1960; King & Newton, (n.d.); H.S. London, 1948; G.A. Poole, 1850; Sandall, 1968; Stamford, 1961, 1973
Tattershall	Binnall, 1938, 1962; E.L. Grange, 1889; Marks, 1979; Tattershall, 1 9.2 5 ; Woodforde, 1934-1936
Woodhouse Chapel	Nichols, 1860

London & Middlesex

General	J. Cook, 1958; F.S. Eden, 1914, 1925, 1939; Knowles, 1954; F. Stephens, 1956
Battersea	London, 1926, 1974-1975; J.G. Taylor, 1926
Camberwell	Camberwell, 1860; R.G. Jones, 1937; A. Wilkinson, 1976-1977
Chelsea Old Church	Chelsea, 1922(2); M. Drake, 1922(3); Hosken, 1924
Chiswick	M. Gilbert, 1932
Greenwich Hospital	Rackham, 1948
Hampton Court	Hampton Court, 1847
Highgate, Old Hall	F.S. Eden, 1934
Hornsey	Hornsey, 1835
Laleham	F.S. Eden, 1927
Merchant Taylor's Hall	Fry & Thomas, 1934
Savoy Hospital	Oswald, 1955
Worshipful Company of Curriers	Window, 1935
Gray's Inn	F.S. Eden, 1936(2), 1937, 1938, 1939
Lincoln's Inn	Lincoln's Inn, 1931; W. Martin, 1915-1916
Lambeth Palace	Vigurs, 1849
Woolwich Town Hall	W.T. Vincent, 1905
Lamb's Chapel	London, 1783
St. Botolph's, Aldersgate	Knowles, 1927
St. George's, Hanover Sq.	Gower, 1895; London, 1914; J. Murray, 1914
St. James', Piccadilly	London, 1846; Warrington, 1846
St. Mary's Lambeth	London, 1853
St. Saviour's, Southwark	M.C. Jones, 1905
Temple Church	Essex & Smirke, 1844-1845; London, 1842, 1844, 1853
St. Paul's	London, 1852; G.G. Scott, 1852, Winston, 1852

London and Middlesex - cont.

Westminster, St. Margaret's	Birch, 1886-1890; G.J.B. Fox, 1931; London, 1844; Rickman, 1837; M. Sinclair, 1895; Swaine, 1833; H.F. Westlake, 1914; Westminster, St. Margaret's, 1882
Westminster Abbey	F.S. Eden, 1924, 1927; Eeles, 1978-1979; Hulme, 1915; Kempe, 1836; Lethaby, 1906, 1925; Marsh, 1977; Neale & Brayley, 1818-1823; Noppen, 1952; Perkins, 1935; J. Robinson, 1899; G.G. Scott, 1861; Westminster Abbey, 1947
Old Houses of Parliament	Brayley & Britton, 1836; J. Smith, 1807
St Stephen's Chapel	Salzman, 1926(2), 1927; J. Smith, 1807
New Houses of Parliament	Feeny, 1957; Westminster, 1846

Norfolk

General	Bryant, (n.d.); M.R. James, 1930; D. King, 1974; Rye, (n.d.); Woodforde, 1933, 1938, 1950
Aylsham	Lloyd - Pritchard & Martyn, 1950
Bale	D. King, 1940
Buckenham	Duleep Singh, 1904
Cawston	Woodforde, 1935
Denton	Ingleby, 1929
Earsham	Acomb, 1929
East Harling	East Harling, 1945; Woodforde, 1932, 1940
Elsing	Manning, 1864; Woodforde, 1932
King's Lynn	Woodforde, 1933
Martham	E. Taylor, 1859
Mileham	Woodforde, 1938
North Tuddenham	Woodforde, 1935, 1940
Norwich (general)	Woodforde, 1933
Norwich, Cathedral	C.J. Evans, 1879; Harrod, 1854; Knowles, 1938
Norwich, All Saints	Woodforde, 1938
St. Andrew's	G. King, 1914
St. James'	Poste, 1858
St. Michael at Plea	Woodforde, 1938
St. Peter Hungate	G. King, 1907
St. Peter Mancroft	G. King, 1910; Meyrick, 1910, 1911; Woodforde, 1934
St. Stephen's	Harford, 1904
Norwich, secular	Hotblack, 1910; E.A. Kent, 1927, 1929, 1932, 1933
Sandringham	Keyser, 1917
Saxlingham Nethergate	Woodforde, 1934
Warham	Warham, 1960
Wiggenhall St. Mary	Keyser, 1907

Northamptonshire

General	Lamborn, 1943
Barnwell	Barnwell, 1973
Blatherwycke	Blatherwycke, 1964
Cosgrove	Andrews, 1943
Edgcote	Edgcote, 1969
Eydon	Eydon, 1969
Fotheringay	Marks, 1978
Hinton-in-the-Hedges	Hinton-in-the-Hedges, 1973
Lamport Hall	Lamport Hall, 1961
Lowick	G.A. Poole, 1861
Peterborough Cathedral	Gunton, 1686; M.R. James, 1894-1898; Peterborough, 1786; Phillips, 1853; Sweeting, 1868
Stanford-on-Avon	F.S. Eden, 1930; Lamborn, 1946; Stanford-on-Avon, 1968
Sulgrave	Pape, 1919

Northumberland and Durham

General	Evetts, 1942
Barnard Castle, Bowes Museum	Boesch, 1936
Durham Cathedral	C.H. Fowler, 1876; Wilde & Doyle, 1974
Earsdon	Evetts, 1959
Jarrow	Jarrow, 1934
Lanchester	J.T. Fowler, 1915
Newcastle-on-Tyne	Bertram, Thompson & Hunter Blair, 1922; Newcastle, 1844
Tynemouth	Evetts, 1967

Nottinghamshire

General	H. Gill, 1917; Truman, 1944, 1945, 1946, 1948, 1949(2), 1954, 1955, 1956, 1957
Addlethorpe	Truman, 1938
Annesley	Truman, 1935
Beauvale	Boulay Hill, 1909
Chilwell House	Chilwell House, 1915

Nottinghamshire- cont.

Gonalston	Westmacott, 1849
Holme-by-Newark	Truman, 1934, 1935(2), 1937, 1940, 1941
Newark	Howson, 1959
Nottingham	J.M.L. Thomas, 1904
Southwell	Westmacott, 1849; Winston, 1848, 1965
Strelley	Strelley, 1876

Oxfordshire

General	Boucher, 1918, 1932; Hughes, 1934; J. Kerr & P. Newton, 1979; Lamborn, 1949
Adderbury	Faulkner, 1852
Begbroke	Oxford Historical Society, 1893
Brightwell Baldwin	Fraser, 1981 (S)
Crowmarsh	Crowmarsh, 1866
Dorchester	Best, (n.d.); Dorchester, 1846, 1969; Kirkpatrick, (n.d.); Rackham, 1925
Ewelme	Ewelme, 1967 (S)
Hasely Court	Milner-White, 1955
Horley	H.T. Kirby, 1962, 1963
Kidlington	Oxford Historical Society, 1893
Littlemore	Underwood, 1845
Oxford General	F.S. Eden, 1938; Grinling, 1883; P. Newton, 1974(S); R.L. Poole, 1929; San Casciani, 1979
All Souls' College	F. Hutchinson, 1949; M.R. James, 1926; Knowles, 1926; Oxford, All Souls', 1926
Balliol College	Arnold, 1914
Bodleian Library	Knowles, 1926
Lincoln College	S. Warner, 1908
Merton College	Garrod, 1931; MacKarness, 1858; Oxford, Merton College, 1932
New College	P.M. Johnston, 1932; Knowles, 1951; Oxford, New College, 1774, 1786, 1932; H.J. Powell, 1906; Radcliffe, 1932; J. Reynolds, 1785; Warton, 1782; Winston, 1865; Woodforde, 1932, 1951
Oriel College	Rushforth, 1929
Wadham College	Oxford, Wadham College, 1838
Stanton Harcourt	Stanton Harcourt, 1964
Tarnton	Oxford Historical Society, 1893
Waterperry	Haberley, 1933; Todd, 1955 (S)
Wroxton Abbey	H.T. Kirby, 1965
Wytham	Lamborn, 1943
Yarnton	Yarnton, 1972

Rutland

Ayston	Ayston, 1973
North Luffenham	Irons, 1913; Woodforde, 1938

Scotland

Bothwell	Bain, 1868-1870
Douglas, Lanarkshire	Gould, 1929
Dunblane	Sketchley, 1915
Edinburgh	Edinburgh, 1857, 1868; Serel, 1886-1887; Sax Shaw, 1964
Glasgow Cathedral	Adam, 1898; Annan, 1867; Bliss, 1956; Glasgow Cathedral, 1856, 1862, 1864; Salmon, 1857; C.H. Wilson, 1864, 1866
Lerwick (Shetland)	Lerwick, 1972
Murthly, Perthshire	J.G. Graham & A. Christie, 1850
Perth	Mackay, 1976-1977
Skibo, Sutherland	F. Jenkins, 1904

Shropshire

Atcham	Atcham, 1898, 1916; L. Hayward, 1953; Rushforth, 1931, 1938
Battlefield	W.G.D. Fletcher, 1903
Ellesmere	Ellesmere, 1829
Kinlet	Blakeway, 1908
Ludlow	Ganderton & Lafond, 1961; Ludlow, 1856; Pidgeon, 1834; Weyman, 1905, 1918
Shrewsbury, St. Mary's	Cologne Glass, 1860; J. Fowler, 1873; Holloway, 1967; J.E. Hunt, 1951
Shrewsbury, St. Chad's	Shrewsbury, 1842
Weston	Leighton, 1860

Somerset

General — Woodforde, 1931, 1939-1942, 1946 (2)

Alford	Eeles, 1935
Banwell	Banwell, 1860; G. Robinson, 1967
Bath Abbey	Brakspear, (n.d.)
Cothelstone	Harbin, 1917
Cucklington	Weaver, 1893
East Brent	Eeles, 1930; Seale, 1906; Woodforde, 1941
Farleigh Hungerford	Eeles, 1935
Godney	Hughes, 1930-1932
Lytes Cary	Maxwell-Lyte, 1902 (S)
Mark	Paul, 1927
Mells	Mells, (n.d.); Winston, 1845, 1846
Montacute House	Barron, (n.d.)(S); C.J. Bates, 1887
Nettlecombe	Rushforth, 1933, 1935
North Cadbury	Jewers, 1891
Orchardleigh	Woodforde, 1941
Pitminster	Vivian-Neal, 1932
Poundisford Park	Popham, 1927, 1941
Selworthy	Hancock, 1893
Wells Cathedral	Chester, 1856; Davis, 1809; Horne, 1929, 1931; Knowles, 1931; Pereira, 1889; J.A. Robinson, 1924(2), 1926, 1931(2), 1932; Winston, 1865
Wells, St. Cuthberts	Serel, 1875
Winscombe	Eeles, 1930; Woodforde, 1940

Staffordshire

General — Jeavons, 1952

Abbots Bromley	Pape, 1927
Alstonfield	Mundy, 1944
Apedale	Apedale
Betley Hall	Bridgeman, 1923; Victoria & Albert Museum, 1976-1977
Litchfield Cathedral	Bamps, 1874; Bright, 1932, 1950; Grundy-Newman, 1914, 1915; Maclagen, 1950; Ouverleaux-Lagass, 1926; Winston, 1865; Woodhouse & Newling, 1811 (Also see Belgium, Herckenrode)
Ridware	Mander & Pape, 1923
Stoke-on-Trent	Stoke-on-Trent, 1830

Suffolk

General — H.R. Barker, 1907; M.R. James, 1930; Woodforde, 1932, 1933

Bardwell	Bardwell, 1825; H. Wilkinson, 1934
Blythburgh	Woodforde, 1933
Bury St. Edmunds	Bury, 1925; F.S. Eden, 1925; R.G. Rowe, 1925
Culford Manor	Culford Manor, 1935
Gislingham	Gislingham, 1928, 1928-1929
Hadleigh	Parsons, 1794
Hengrave Hall	Pawle, 1954; Woodforde, 1934
Herringfleet	J. Fowler, 1875
Lavenham	Parsons, 1794
Little Saxham Hall	Woodforde, 1938
Long Melford	Birch, 1884; Couteur, 1927; Long Melford, 1957; Woodforde, 1932, 1938, 1939
Yaxley	Harris & Woodforde, 1932

Surrey

General — F.S. Eden, 1940(2), 1941; Hussey, 1852; Peatling, 1924, 1930

Albury	P.M. Johnston, 1921
Buckland	Buckland, ; E. Clay, 1933
Chiddingfold	Cobb, 1930
Compton	J.L. André, 1895; Rackham, 1942
Cranleigh	Bingley, 1931; Heales, 1879
Epsom	Epsom, 1825-1826
Guildford, Sutton Place	Godfrey, 1913;
Guildhall	Rackham, 1950
Horley	Heales, 1880, 1883
Kingston-upon-Thames	Finny, 1926, 1935(2)(S), 1936(S)
Ockham	Bloxam, 1937
Shalford	F. Law, 1898
Stoke d'Abernon	Stoke d'Abernon, 1950(2), (n.d.), 1958
Stoke-next-Guildford	Rackham, 1958
West Horsley	West Horsley, 1831; P.M. Johnston, 1909
Wimbledon	T.G. Jackson, 1921

Sussex

General — Hussey, 1852; Lambarde, 1926, 1927; Sussex, 1928, 1937

Arundel Castle	Arundel, 1817, 1838; Steer, 1974, 1976-1977
Battle	J.L. André, 1899; F.S. Eden, 1930
Bexhill	Earwaker, 1959(S)
Brightling	Alexander, 1902
Chichester	Round, 1921
Groombridge	Groombridge, 1930
Hamsey	Godfrey, 1950-1953
Hangleton	Holden, 1963
Horselunges	Lambarde, 1928, 1929, 1930, 1931, 1932, 1933, 1934
Kirdford	Winbolt, 1934
Lancing College Chapel	Dykes-Bower, 1978-1979
Northiam	Northiam, 1928
Pagham	F.S. Eden, 1930
Petworth	Steer, 1955
Rottingdean	Rottingdean, 1970
Stopham	C. Robinson, 1877; Steer
Winchelsea	Leigh, (n.d.); Winchelsea, 1933

Wales

General — (N. Wales) H.M. Lewis, 1970, 1974

Basingwerk Abbey (Flint)	Latham, 1825
Cardiff Castle	Cardiff Castle, 1977
Cilcain (Flint)	Cilcain, 1947
Diserth (Flint)	Diserth, 1947
Flint (general)	W.B. Jones, 1924
Gresford (Denbigh)	Gresford, 1935
Llanassa (Flint)	Latham, 1825
Llandaff Cathedral	J.P. Seddon, 1903
Llandefalle	Simon, 1966
Llangadwaladr (Anglesey)	Hughes, 1930
Llanllugan (Montgomery)	Llanllugan, 1932
Llanrhaiadr	Rackham & Baty, 1942(2); Rackham, 1943; Winston, 1850
Llanrhychwyn	Hughes, 1927; Llanrhychwyn, 1929
Mold (Flint)	Mold, 1947
Montgomery Castle	Montgomery Castle, 1968
Penmorta (Caernarvon)	Owen, 1905; Penmorta, 1905
Tremeirchion (Flint)	Tremeirchion, 1947

Warwickshire

General — Hutton, 1914; H.T. Kirby, 1957; Rackham, 1930-1931; Warwickshire, 1847

Chadshunt	H.T. Kirby, 1943
Compton Verney	Compton Verney, 1954, 1955; F.S. Eden, 1931
Coventry (general)	Rackham, 1930-1931
Coventry Cathedral	Chatwin, 1950; Hobley, 1970; J. Lowe, 1963; P. Newton, 1967-1970
Coventry, Trinity Church	Coventry, 1834
Ettington	H.T. Kirby, 1948, 1950 (also see Winchester College)
Kinwarton	Chatwin, 1938
New Oscott	New Oscott, 1838
Upper Shuckburgh	F.S. Eden, 1932
Warwick, St. Mary's	Bentley, 1931; Chatwin, 1931; C.F. Hardy, 1909; H.T. Kirby, 1944; Warwick, 1845; Winston, 1865
Warwick Castle	Sotheby's, 1973-1974
Weoley Castle	Raw, 1955
Wixford	Chatwin, 1933
Wootton Wawen	Wootton Wawen, 1973

Wiltshire

General — Battersby, 1929-1930; Goddard, 1943

Crudwell	Rushforth, 1929, 1930; Vernon, 1957 (S)
Edington	Edington, 1958, 1970
Fonthill Abbey	Britton, 1823; Hamilton, (n.d.)
Great Bedwyn	G. Smith, 1954
Lacock	Kidson, 1946; Lamborn, 1946
Lydiard Tregoze	Goddard, 1912; Ponting, 1912; G. Robinson, 1968-1969
Marlborough	Fragments, 1932
Salisbury Cathedral	S. Baker, 1932; Dorling, 1903 (S), 1912; S. Evans, 1980 (S); J.M.S. Fletcher, 1930; Jervis, 1932; Lethaby, 1926; Salisbury, 1933, 1939, 1978; Spring, 1973; J. Taylor, 1980; Winchester Cathedral, 1937; Winston, 1865

Wiltshire - cont.

Salisbury, St. Edmunds	Burn, 1869
Salisbury, St. Thomas	Haskins, (n.d.); G. Robinson, 1967
Salisbury, Hall of John Halle	Dorling, 1904 (S); Mrs Collier, 1908
Westwood Manor	Lister, 1926
Wilton	W.E. Drury, 1959; Lafond, 1959

Worcestershire

General	M.A. Green, 1934, 1935, 1936, 1939, 1941, 1943, 1945, 1946, 1947, 1948
Abberley	Hallward, 1933
Birtsmorton	H.T. Kirby, 1958; Rushforth, 1926, 1926-1927
Evesham Abbey	See Gloucestershire, Preston-on-Stour
Great Malvern	Deane, 1914; J.T. Fowler, 1883-1884; Habington, 1895, 1899; Hamand, 1947, 1950; M.R. James, 1900; Knowles, 1959; Malvern, 1802, 1866, 1919, 1941, 1945, 1977; Nott, 1869, 1882, 1895; Paul, 1901; Rushforth, 1912, 1916-1935, 1936, (n.d.); Stoke Prior (n.d.); Strohm, 1965-1967; W. Thomas, 1725; Way, 1846
Great Witley	Great Witley, 1971, 1972, 1973
Little Malvern	Oldfield, 1865
Ripple	E.F. Gray, 1967
Stoke Prior	Stoke Prior, (n.d.)
Worcester Cathedral	Binnall, 1973-1974; Worcester Cathedral, 1855
Worcester, The Commandery	Bailey, 1893

Yorkshire

General	Heraldry in the Deanery of Harthill. Collier & Lawrence, 1921
	" " " " " Ryedale " " 1924
	" " " " " Cleveland " " 1924
	" " " " " Richmond " " 1924
	" " " " " Catterick " " 1929
	Himsworth, 1929, 1931
Beverley Minster	Beverley Minster, 1943; Brown, 1973(2); Nolloth, 1952
Birkin	Birkin, 1977
Bolling Hall	Priest, 1958
Bradford	Wroot, 1917
Brighouse	J. Fowler, 1872
Cottingham	A.S. Harvey, 1962
Denton-in-Wharfedale	Denton-in-Wharfedale, 1968
Dewsbury	Chadwick, 1898; J. Fowler, 1873
Elland	J.W. Clay, 1889
Gilling Castle	Bilson, 1907(2), 1922; Gilling, 1929, 1939, 1953; Hunter, 1929; Sotheby's, 1929
Harrogate	A.A. Gibson, 1928
Hovingham	Milner-White, 1962
Hull	Hull, 1831; Knowles, 1930
Ingleby Arncliffe	W. Brown, 1913
Kirby Misperton	Milner-White, 1949
Kirby Sigston	W. Brown, 1913
Kirkleatham	Kirkleatham, 1935
Leeds, Beeston Chapelry	Kirk, (n.d.)
Methley	J. Fowler, 1870, 1873
Moor Monkton	Moor Monkton, 1970
Nostell	Boesch, 1936(2), 1937, 1960; Knowles, 1962-1963
Pickering	Beard, 1939
Scarborough	Destrée, 1896
Selby	J. Fowler, 1879; Hartley, 1957; W.H. Scott, 1899; Selby Abbey, 1892, 1932; Solloway, 1914, 1925
Sheffield	F. Harrison, 1939; Himsworth, 1946
Sherburn-in-Elmet	Sherburn-in-Elmet, 1968
Thornhill	J. Fowler, 1870; Thornhill, 1972, 1973
Tong Hall	G. Wood, 1947
Upper Poppleton	Milner-White, 1949
Whitby	Fragments, 1941; W. Johnson, 1913
Wragby	Fragments, 1941; Sankey & Schüddekopf, 1895; Wragby, 1969, 1970, 1972
Wycliffe	Wycliffe, 1812

York (General)	
Bell, 1844	Laishley, (n.d.)
Benson, 1915	Myers, 1845
Connick, 1932	O'Connor, 1975, 1976-1977
Davies, 1880	G.A. Poole, 1850
F. Drake, 1736	G. Rowe, 1871-1873
P. Gibson, 1972	Weale, 1846, 1858-1859
F. Harrison, 1927, 1928	G. Webb, 1933
Johnson, 1972(S)	R. Willis, 1976
J.P. Kirby, 1939	Winston, 1846, 1865
Knowles, 1923(2), 1925,	York, 1846, 1948-1949

Yorkshire - cont.

York (General) - cont.	Knowles (cont.)	York (cont.)
	1926(2), 1927, 1928(2)	1957-1958, 1949
	1929(3), 1930(2),	
	1931(2), 1932(2),	
	1933(2), 1934(2),	
	1935(2), 1936(2)	

York Minster	Benson, 1893, 1915, 1916; Brockington, 1933; Browne, 1838-1847, 1848, 1915, 1917, Clements, Davies, 1870; Dickins, 1936; F.S. Eden, 1933; Feilden, (n.d.); J. Fowler, 1875; J.T. Fowler, 1877, 1891; T.W. French, 1971, 1975; Gent, 1762; P. Gibson, 1972, 1973, 1976, 1979; W.J. Green, 1946, 1947, 1948, 1949, 1950, 1951, 1952, 1953, 1954, 1955, 1959, 1962, 1963, 1964, 1965, 1966; J.T. Hardman, 1934; F. Harrison, 1922(2), 1923, 1925(5), 1926(2), 1927(4), 1932, 1937, 1939, 1947, 1949; Haselock & O'Connor, 1977; Hawke, 1971; F. James, 1952; L. James, 1933; Johnson, 1972(S); Knowles, 1920(2), 1922, 1923(2), 1924, 1925(2), 1927, 1932, 1934(2), 1951(2), 1958, 1962; Lazenby, 1972; Lethaby, 1915; Little, 1933; Milner-White, 1945(3), 1946, 1947(3), 1948(3), 1949(5), 1950(4), 1951(4),1952(6), 1953(3), 1954, 1955, 1956, 1957(2), 1958(3), 1959(3), 1960(3), 1961(2), 1962(2), 1963(2); W.F. Norris, 1922; Purey-Cust, 1890-1896, 1897; Rackham, 1952; Rutter, 1947; York Minster, 1769, 1783, 1804, 1824, 1845, 1855(2), 1861, 1864, 1866, 1873, 1887, 1889, 1901, 1920, 1923(3), 1929(2), 1930(3), 1931(5), 1932, 1933(2), 1935(2), 1936, 1939, 1940, 1941, 1942, 1943, 1945, 1948, 1950(2), 1951-1952, 1953, 1961, 1961-1962, 1962, 1963, 1964(3), 1965, 1966, 1967(7), 1968(3), 1969(3), 1970(2), 1971(2), 1972, 1973, 1974, 1975(3), 1976, 1978(2), 1979

York Churches

All Saints, North Street	Gee, 1969; Knowles, 1925; Maclagan, 1908; J.M. Neale, 1843; P. Shaw, 1908; York, 1931, 1962, 1965-1966, 1976-1977, 1978
All Saints, Pavement	York, 1954(2), 1957
Bedern Chapel	F. Harrison, 1924
Clifton Church	York, 1909
Garrison Church	York, 1957
Holy Trinity, Goodramgate	Gayner, 1905; Knowles, 1924, 1926
St. Denys	York, 1974-1975
St. Helen's	Knowles, 1926, 1939
St. Hilda's	York, 1955, 1956
St. John's, Micklegate	W.J. Green, 1945; Knowles, 1927; Milner-White, 1945(2)
St. Laurence's	York, 1906(2), 1975
St. Luke's	Milner-White, 1959
St. Martin's, Coney Street	F. Harrison, 1926; Knowles, 1955(2); Milner-White, 1954; G. Rowe, 1873-1874; York, 1964
St. Martin-cum-Gregory	Beach, 1927
St. Martin-le-Grand	York, 1955
St. Mary, Castlegate	York, 1873
St. Michael's Spurriergate	Knowles, 1927; Milner-White, 1948; York, 1947-1948
St. Michael-le-Belfrey	F. Harrison, 1925; Knowles, 1962; Milner-White, 1960; York, 1958-1959, 1959-1960
St. Olave's	York, 1910
St. Paul's, Holgate	York, 1909

York, Secular

Gray's Court	Brighton, 1966
Guildhall	Brighton, 1977; Cooper, 1931; York, 1863(2), 1924
Museum	F. Harrison, 1928; Knowles, 1926
Old Council Chamber	Brighton, 1974-1975

York Glazier's Trust

	York Glazier's Trust, 1966-1967, 1967, 1974, 1975, 1976, 1977, 1978
York	1974

TOPOGRAPHICAL INDEX

EUROPE

General

Beyer, 1963
Boom, 1960
Calkins, 1979
Capronnier & Levy, 1860
Cassie, 1956
Charles, 1860
Cole, 1976
Day, 1882(3), 1886, 1887(3),
    1897, 1910-1911
Didron, 1863, 1864
J. Evans, 1931
Fischer, 1937(2)
Gessert, 1839
Glass-painting, 1927
Grodecki, 1962, 1977
Hansen, 1974
Jane Hayward, 1970
Hovey, 1940
Huber, 1925
Huch, 1937
Hutter, 1964
Jahn, 1935
Katzmann, 1978
Keck, 1947
Knowles, 1926
P. Lacroix, 1869

Lasteyrie, 1838-1857
L. Lee, 1976
Lethaby, 1904
Levy, 1854-1860
Merson, 1896, 1924
Metcalf, 1941
Murray & Egan, 1963
Ottin, 1896
Polaczek, 1901
Saint, 1934
Schaefer, 1881
Schmitt, 1947
Schmitz, 1923
H. Shaw, 1842, 1851
Thevenot, 1837
Thibaud, 1835-1838, 1842
Verhaegen, 1886
Waring, 1858
W. Warrington, 1848
Wentzel, 1949, 1951, 1954
Werck, 1922
N.H.J. Westlake, 1864-1865,
    1879-1881

AUSTRIA

General

Austrian Glass-Paintings, 1930
Fähngruber, 1896
Frodl-Kraft, 1959
Glass-Painting, 1939
Hickl-Szabo, 1965
Kieslinger, 1921, 1928, 1947

Lind, 1891
Lobmeyer, 1925
Löw, 1891, 1895
Mandach, 1908
Sacken, 1866
Sherrill, 1927

Ardagger   Löw, 1900
Graz   Bacher, 1972; Bacher & Brandestein, 1979(S)
Heiligenblut   Löw, 1898
Heiligenkreuz   Camesina, 1857, 1859; Frodl-Kraft, 1967
Hindelbank   Lehmann, 1912, 1918
Karnten   Frodl, 1950
Langenlois   Fischer, 1910
Laxenburg   Laxenburg, 1962
Leoben   Frodl-Kraft, 1971
Rein   Schmitz, 1930
St. Lorenzen   Kieslinger, 1933
Salzburg area   Pillwein, 1821
Spitz   Bacher, 1967
Strassengel   Bacher & Brandestein, 1979 (S); Frodl-Kraft, 1967
Tyrolean Glass Painting Ilg, 1886; Jale, 1886, 1894; Mader, Stadl,
                Neuhauser, 1866; Neuhauser, Jele & Co., 1911;
                Tyrolean Glass, 1874, 1875, 1894
Vienna   Frodl-Kraft, 1952, 1962; Löw, 1906, 1907;
                Tschischka, 1823, 1832
Weitau   Garber, 1928
Wels   Wels, 1951

Museums

Innsbruck, 1930
Lind, 1890

Vienna, 1904

BELGIUM

General

Bamps, 1905
Belgium, 1882
Bemden, 1970, 1974-1975
Boom, 1944, 1947, 1950
Chambon, 1955
Clemen, 1923
Coussemaker, 1860
Cuypers, 1914
Delville, 1912, 1928

Donnet, 1911
Helbig, 1936(2), 1937(3), 1938(4), 1939,
    1941(2), 1943, 1945, 1949(2), 1951(2),
    1962, 1968
Lévy, 1854-1860
O'Kelly de Galway, 1859
Reiffenberg, 1832
B. Webb, 1848
Yernaux, 1951

Belgium - cont.

Flemish Glass in England

Cole, 1973-1974   Vallance, 1911
Flemish glass, 1864-1865, 1965   W.H.J. Weale, 1864
Read, 1930

Belgium

Anderlecht   Helbig, 1942
Antwerp   Baar, 1938; Blomme, 1891; Bosschere, 1905, 1908;
                Burbure, 1854; Cauwenberghs, 1891; Donnet, 1924;
                Friedlander, 1918; Helbig, 1941, 1943; Nicaise, 1936
Blaton   Hecq, 1893
Bruges   Derliegher, 1954; Gaillard, 1846; Rackham, 1930
Brussels   Brussels, 1975; Bruyn, 1871, 1872(2); Graul, 1923;
                Helbig, 1942; Leclercq, 1861; Lefevre, 1945;
                Marchal,   ; O'Kelly, 1870; Raadt,   ;
                Velge, 1926
Charleroi   Close, 1928
Enghien   Matthieu
Flêtre   Coussemaker (n.d.)
Hainault   Poumon, 1949
Hal   Verhaegen, 1881
Hasselt   Daniels, 1927
Herckenrode   Bamps, 1874; Bright, 1932, 1950; Helbig, 1877;
                Neuss, 1895; Ouverleaux-Lagasse, 1926
Hoogstraten   Helbig, 1949; Smekens & Hendricx, 1863-1886
Landelies   Landelies, 1913
Liège   Casteele, 1890; Didier-Lamboray, 1965; Helbig,
                1944(S); Jaer, 1932; Liège, 1906, 1908; Weale, 1846
Lierre   Bosschere, 1908; Hulst, 1956
Limburg   Viegen, 1955; Weale, 1846
Louvain   F.S. Eden, 1914; Even, 1870
Malines   F.S. Eden, 1914; Helbig, 1940; Laenen, 1920;
                Neeffs, 1877; Wayment, 1967, 1968, 1969(2)
Mons   Dornon, 1887; Quinet, 1901
Namur   Helbig, 1952
Parc   Caumont, 1928; Goffaerts, 1891; Helbig, 1958
Tournai   Anstaing, 1855; Capronnier, 1848; Deschamps
                & D'Anstaing, 1848; Goovaerts, 1896; Grange &
                Cloquet, 1889; Voisin, 1871, 1877
Vitres   Lefévre, 1938

Byzantine glass

Grabar, 1971; Megaw, 1963

CANADA

Montreal.   Martirano, 1967
Montreal Museum.   Montreal, 1936-1937
Meaford, Ontario.   Meaford, 1947
Quebec.   Quebec, 1948

CZECHOSLOVAKIA

Roubicek, 1964

DENMARK

Lubecker, 1953

FRANCE

General Accounts

Arnold & Saint, 1913
Assier, 1866
Aubert, 1936, 1937, 1939, 1946, 1947,
    1948, (with Grodecki, Chastel, Gruber,
    Lafond, Mathey, Taralon, Verrier) 1958
Barrelet, 1953
Batissier, 1843
Bourasse, Manceau, Marchand, 1851
Bushnell, 1914
Claudel, 1936
Connick, 1923, 1924(3)
Coulton, 1939
Delaporte, 1963
Fenwick, 1885
Fischer, 1914
Fisher, 1962
Foy, 1977, 1978
France; Modern Stained Glass, 1960
Gaignières, 1914 (also see Guibert)
Gaudin, 1928
Grodecki, 1947, 1951, 1953, 1961,
    1977, 1978

Gruber, 1927-1928
Hone, 1940
Hubert, 1947
Hudig, 1922-1923
M.M. James, 1922
Labande, 1932
Lafond, 1939, 1954, 1966(2)
Lamont, 1942
Male, 1905, 1913, 1922, 1943(2)
Montfaucon, 1729-1733
Renouvier, 1839
Rollet, 1980(5)
Roussel, 1900, 1903, 1911, 1913
Schauenburg, 1865
Sherrill, 1908
Texier, 1850
Verdier, 1973
Verrier, 1948
Weitzman, 1957
Witzleben, 1966, 1968
Yernaux, 1951
Yoki, 1969

Abbéville — Delignières, 1901

Aix — Boyer, 1958; Reinaud de Fontvert, 1862

Notre-Dame d'Alençon — Despierres, 1891; Grodecki, 1953; Sicotière, 1842

Alsace — J.C. Bell, 1932; Bruck, 1901, 1902; F.X. Kraus, 1876, 1884; Lutz & Perdrizet, 1907-1909; Petit-Gerard, 1859, 1861; Schauenburg, 1860; Wentzel, 1953

Amiens — Amiens, 1925; G. Durand, 1889, 1901, 1914; A.P.M. Gilbert, 1833

Angers — Barbier de Montault, 1887; Denais, 1907; Farcy, 1910; Grodecki & Hayward, 1966; Urseau, 1912, 1929, 1937

Anjou — Loire, 1925; Urseau, 1905

Argentan — Antoine, 1913; Cerf, 1856; Lafond, 1955; Laurent, 1859

Assy — Assy Church, 1950, 1951; Bernier, 1949

Ath — Verriest, 1938

Auch — Canéto, 1857; Carsalade du Pont, 1897; L. Couture, 1862

Auppegard — Brindley, 1912

Auxerre — Auxerre, 1932; Bonneau, 1885; Fourrey, 1929; Gahlen, 1931; Lafond, 1959; Lasteyrie, 1841; C. Porée, 1926; Raguin, 1974

Avignon — Gagnière & Granier, 1968, 1969; Théoles, 1924

Bayonne — Andral, 1925; Cuzacq, 1954; Lafond, 1970

Beauvais (Cathedral) — Barraud, 1850, 1855, 1856; Gérin, 1879; Lavergne, 1886; Pigeon, 1895

(St. Etienne) — Lafond, 1929, 1963

Beillé — Hucher, 1883

Beine — Beine, 1926

Besançon — Gaudin, 1895, 1905

St. Lomer de Blois — Blois, 1949

Bonlieu — Brisac, 1977

Bonneville-Appetot — Verrier, 1957

Bordeaux — Roudié, 1958

Bourg — C. Martin, 1874

Bourges (Cathedral) — Barreau, 1863; Beaurepaire, 1897, 1898; Bourges, 1941-1943, 1947; Cahier & Martin, 1841-1844; Clement & Guitard, 1900; Connick, 1932; Girardot & Durand, 1849, 1861; Grodecki, 1948, 1975; Lavanoux, 1932; Meldizes, 1887, 1891-1897; Quiévreux, 1942; Rhode Island, 1937-1938; Triger, 1899; Verrier, 1942

Bourges (St. Etienne) — St. Etienne de Bourges, 1960; Martineau, 1975

(St. Chapelle) — Scher, 1973

Brienne-le Château — Bayeux, 1903

Brittany — André, 1878; Barthélemy, 1849; Mussat, Gruber, Barrie, Moirez-Dubief, 1977; Couffon, 1975; Couffon & Le Bars, 1969; Doble, 1932; Inventaire Général des Monuments ......, 1969

Brou — Angoulvent, P.J., 1930; Bancel, 1885; Baux, 1844; Bidet, 1959; Didron, 1842, 1864; Nodet, 1906, 1925; Rousselet, 1767, 1876

Caen — Lafond & Musset, 1963- 1964

Carcassonne — Carcassonne, 1875

Carheil — Lacambre, 1970

Castelneau-Bretenoux — Lafond, 1962

Castelneau-du-Medoc — Roudié, 1964

Caudebec-en-Caux — Lafond, 1954, 1956

Caylus — Galabert, 1881

Chālons-sur-Marne — Barthélemy, 1856-1857; Chālons-sur-Marne, 1954; Didron, 1863(2); Grodecki, 1954, 1958; Lafond, 1961; Lucot, 1884, 1885(2), 1891; Maillet, 1946; Misset, 1911

Champagne — Chaubry, 1857; Gaussen, 1861; Grodecki, 1963

Champigny — Chalons, 1885

Champres-Froges — Brisac, 1973

Chantilly — Lemonnier, 1928; Magne, 1885

Chartres — H. Adams, 1905; Arthur, (n.d.); Aubert, 1923, 1936, 1952; Boisthibault, 1857-1858; Brisac, Bouchon, Lautier, Zaluska, 1979; Brunet,   ; Bulteau, 1850, 1872, 1887; Castelnuovo, 1965; Chartres, 1936, 1938, 1939, 1951; Connick, 1927, 1932(4); Delaporte & Houvet, 1926, 1932(3), 1943; Dierick,

Chartres - cont. — 1955, 1961; P. Durand, 1867-1881; Frankl, 1963; H.B. Graham, 1962; Grimme, 1961; Grodecki, 1948, 1963, 1965, 1978; Heaton, 1906; Houvet, 1926, n.d.; J. James, J.R. Johnson, 1961, 1964, 1972; Lassus, 1842, 1867-1881; Lillich, 1972; McLaughlin, 1950; Maines, 1977; Male, 1948; Manoury, 1946, 1947; Mely, 1888; Merlet, 1889, 1890; Meulen, 1966; M. Miller, 1980(S); Perrot & Bettembourg, 1976; Perrot, 1977; Popesco, 1966, 1969, 1970; Skinner, 1949-1950; Sowers, 1966; Stolen Stained Glass, 1933; Swoboda, 1961; Villette, 1964

Chartres, St. Père — Jusselin, 1930; Lillich, 1964, 1971, 1972, 1978

Chartres, St. Pierre — Lillich, 1977; C. Lorin, 1906; Popesco, 1970

Clermont — Lediche-Duflos, 1850

Clermont-Ferrand — Chardon du Ranquet, 1932

Colmont — Alleaume, 1897

Conches — Bouillet, 1888; Lafond, 1940-1941, 1973; Lenormant, 1855; Poree, 1885, 1889; Stabenrath, 1840

Condom — Lassalle, 1861

Côtes-du-Nord — Couffon, 1935

Coucy — Viollet-le-Duc. (n.d.)

Courville — Métais, 1901

Coutances — Cacheux, 1933; Fournée, 1964; Lafond, 1933

Crann in Spezet — Perennes, 1930

Cravan — Ame, 1854; Lafond, 1959

Croslay — Marsaux, 1889

Croth — Bonnenfant, n.d.

Dieppe Area — Cochet, 1846-1850

Dijon — Culleton, 1897; Fyot, 1934; Thomas, 1898

Dol — Eagle, 1929; C. Robert, (n.d.)

Donnemarie-en-Montois — Perrot, 1970

Dreux — Veuclin, 1900

Ecommoy — Lottin, 1845

Ecouen — Baillargeat, 1951; Magne, 1885, 1888; Perrot, 1978

Envermeau — Lafond, 1920

Evreux — Baudot, 1967, 1968; Beucher, 1978; Bonnenfant, 1939; Dubuc, 1968; Evreux, 1893; Grodecki, 1957, 1968; Harcourt-Bath, 1924; Honoré-Duverge, 1942; Lafond, 1942; Viztelly, 1882

Evry — Nioré, 1897

Favières — Gatouillat, 1978

Fécamp — Aubert, 1928; Caviness, 1963; Fecamp, 1933(2),(2), (S), 1933-1934, 1936; Lafond, 1958; Vallery-Radot, 1928

Fontenelle — Langlois, 1834

Ganagobie — Fixot & Pelletier, 1976; Foy, 1977

Garcy — Magne, 1887; Perrot, 1970

Gargilesse — Grodecki, 1966

Gisors — Latteux, 1878

Grand-Andely — Didron, 1862

Grasset — Verneuil, 1908

Guengat — Guengat, 1953

L'Huitre — Bernard, 1897

Iffs — Svahn, 1931

Joué — C. & B. Meguen, 1881

Jouhet — Mayeux, 1923

Junies — Alauzier, 1962; Lafond, 1958

Jumièges — C. Hussey, 1942; Lafond, 1926, 1954

La Ferté-Bernard — Charles, 1851, 1857; Lafond, 1961, 1962; Morance, 1839

La Flèche — Saint Louis Museum, 1935

La Martyre, near Landerneau — Perennes, 1931

Laon — Florival & Midoux, 1882-1891; Lecomte, 1854

Larresore — Soubielle, 1872

Lehon — Fouére-Macé, 1897

Le Mans — Aubert, 1954; Fleury, n.d.; Grodecki, 1961; Hucher, 1848, 1854-1864, 1865; Ledru, 1923; Mans, 1841, 1902; Marquet, (n.d.); Pallu, 1841; Triger, 1899; Trinick, 1936; Voisin, 1866

Lille — Lothé, 1937

Limoges — Gauthier & Marcheix, 1964; Inventaire Général...... (of the Limousin) 1970; Texier, 1847

Lisieux — Devilie, 1917; V. Hardy, 1917; Lafond, 1969

Locon — Lamort, 1846

Loise-en-Brie — Monell collection, 1931

Departement du Lot   Crazannes, 1841
Lothringen   F.X. Kraus, 1889
Louviers   Lafond, 1963
Luneville   Demnise, 1855
Lyon   Bégule, 1880, 1911; Brisac, 1977, 1978;
                            Niepoe, 1882; Rondot, 1882, 1897
Martigny   Delaporte, 1941
Meaux   Allou, 1871
Melun   Barrault, 1964
Metz   Aubert, 1931; Bégin, 1843; Birglin, 1877; Hauck,
                            1966; Metz, 1912; Pelt, 1937; Schürenberg, 1942
Mézières-en-Brenne   Laugardière, 1938
Montfort L'Amaury   Dion, 1902; Lechenetier, 1877
Montmorency   Magne, 1888
Mont St. Michel   Corroyer, 1877
Montoire   Charles, 1879
St. Pierre de Montrelais   Bourdeaut
Moret   Didon, 1954
Mouchamps   Dugast - Matinfeux, 1861
Moulineaux   Lafond, 1961
Moulins   Ségange, 1876
Nancy   Save, 1897
Narbonne   Suau, 1973
Nonancourt   Régnier, 1894
Nord & Pas de Calais   Lasteyrie, 1881; Latteux, 1880; Perrot,
                            Taralon & Grodecki, 1978
Normandy   Lafond, 1919, 1926-1927, 1953; A. Pugin, 1833;
                            W. Thornton, 1848
Notre-Dame de la Cour   Hucher, 1879
Notre-Dame de Mayenne   Raulin, 1894
Noyon   E. Muller, 1883
Obazine   Brisac, 1977
Orbec   Veuclin, 1878
Orléans   Bailiet, 1919; Lechevallier-Chevignard, 1881
Orne   Sicotière, 1845-1854
Paris Area   Perrot, Taralon & Grodecki, 1978
Paris, Notre-Dame   Aubert, Grodecki & Lafond, 1959; Frankl, 1957;
                            Guilhermy & Viollet-le-Duc, 1856; Hiemer, 1942;
                            H. Kraus, 1966; Viollet-le-Duc, 1856
Paris (Ste. Chapelle)   Aubert, 1957; Aubert & Grodecki & Lafond, 1959;
                            Caviness & Grodecki, 1968; Caviness, 1971;
                            Decloux & Doury, 1865; Dyer-Spencer, 1932;
                            Grodecki, 1962, 1975; Poynter, 1836; Spencer, 1932
Paris, St. Denis   Grodecki, 1951, 1952, 1961(2), 1976; Lafond, 1936;
                            Panofsky, 1946
Paris, Chapel of St.
  Ferdinand   Sudré, 1846
Paris, St. Germain
  L'Auxerrois   Troche, 1946-1947
Paris, St. Germain-des-Pres Grodecki, 1956, 1957; Verdier, 1957-1958, 1962-
                            1963, 1976
Paris, Saint-Odile   Despréaux, 1939
Paris, Saint Vincent de Paul Maréchal, 1844
Paris, Petit Palais   Lafond, 1919
Petiville   Ruedolf, 1954
Picardy   Cauton & Hainsselin, 1956; G. Durand, 1908;
                            Perrot & Taralon & Grodecki, 1978
Poitiers   Auber, 1849, 1932; Barbier de Montault, 1885;
                            Bidaut, 1951; Connick, 1932; Crozet, 1934;
                            Fillon, 1844; Grinnell, 1946; Grodecki, 1948, 1951;
                            Hayward, 1981 (S); Poitiers, 1949
Pont-Audemer   Baudot & Lafond, 1969; Lafond, 1908
Pont-L'Evêque   Lafond, 1961-1962
Pont-Sainte-Marie   Nioré, 1895
Puiseaux (and Ardennes
  generally)   Jadart, 1900
Quimper   Lafond, 1962
Reims   Demaison, 1954; Gosset, 1894; Heaton, 1908;
                            Hollande, n.d.; Reinhardt, 1963; P. Simon, 1911(2)
                            Skinner, 1927; Tourneur, 1857
Reims, St. Nicaise   Maxe-Werly, 1884
Reims, St. Remi   Grodecki, 1975; J. Simon, 1959
Riom   Riom, 1951

Rouen
  General   Langlois, 1823; Lefrançois, 1909; Perrot, 1972;
                            Rickmansworth, 1945; Stolen Stained Glass, 1933;
                            Verrieres, 1948
  Cathedral   Lafond, 1924, 1936, 1956; Ritter, 1926;
                            Ruedolf & Levasseur, (n.d.)
  St. Nicaise   Lafond, 1934
  St. Ouen   Lafond, 1927
  St. Patrice   Baudry, 1896; Lafond, 1948, 1957(2); Lecaplain, 1911
  St. Vincent   Baudry, 1875; Lafond, 1908, 1956, 1972;
                            Lecaplain, 1911; Pottier, 1862; Rouen, 1956
  Château de Rouen   Rouen, 1939, 1955
  Vieux-Marché de Rouen   Rouen, 1978-1979
Ruille sur Loir   Lottin, 1858
Saint-Antoine en Dauphiné   Dassy, 1844
Saint-Bris   Bonneau, 1899
Saint-Cyr au Mont d'Or   Lavergne, 1888
Saint-Fargeau (Yonne)   Lafond, 1948
Saint-Germain-lès-Corbeil   Perrot, 1970; Raguin, 1976; Vollant, 1897
Saint-Germer   Besnard, 1913; Boeswilwald, 1862; Grodecki, 1965
Saint-Julien (Jura)   Prost, 1885
Saint-Julien-du-Sault   Lafond, 1959; Rheims, 1926
Saint-Lô   Rathouis, 1873
St. Martin de Montmorency   Baillargeat
St. Martin ès Vignes   Méchin, 1853
St. Martin-St. Firmin   Montier, 1903
St. Memmie-les-Châlons   Lucot, 1872
St. Pierre de Roye   Heuduin, 1934
St. Quentin   Lafond, 1961; Lecock, 1874
St. Serge   Jane Hayward, 1976
St. Wandrille   Aubert, 1927; Lafond, 1958; Langlois, 1834
Sainte-Chapelle (Burgundy) Raguin, 1977
Savoie (general)   Dufour & Mugnier, 1894
Sées   Lafond, 1955
Sélestat   Adam & Bannier, 1968
Senlis   Gérin, 1864
Sens   Sens, 1948
Séry-les-Mézières   Pilloy & Socard, 1910
Seurre   Lachot, 1882
Soire-le-Château   Hucher, 1883
Soissons   Caviness & Raguin, 1981(S); Grodecki, 1953, 1960;
                            Soissons, 1953; Verdier, 1958
Sommervieu   Noget-Lacoudre, 1859
Soulaire   Urseau, 1936
Strasbourg
  (Cathedral and general)   Beyer, 1956; with Haug, Ahne, Will, Reiger, 1957,
                            1957, 1960(2), with Ahne, 1960, 1967, 1969, 1970(2),
                            1971, 1972, 1977; Cames, 1964; Frankl, 1960;
                            Guerber, 1848; Haug, 1957; Kunze, 1913; Pfleger,
                            1913; Riff, 1923; Schüler, 1817; Walter, 1933;
                            Zschokke, 1942, 1974
Sully-sur-Loire   Cochard, 1907
Thann   Moschenross, 1947; Stintzi, (n.d.); Straub, 1876
Tours   Boissonot, 1920, 1936; Bourassé, Manceau, Marchand,
                            1849, 1855; Fiot, 1970; Manceau, 1840;
                            Papanicolaou, 1981(S); Salet, 1949
Tours, St. Saturnin   Mesnage, 1890
Tours, Notre-Dame-la-Riche Vicart, 1845
Touraine   Giraudet, 1885
Treguier   Barthélemy, 1847; Tréguier, 1936
Troyes   Babeau, 1881; Bibolet, 1959; Biver, 1925;
                            Coffinet, 1858; Grodecki, 1961, 1973; Hamy-Longuesp,
                            1978; Lafond, 1957; Ledit, 1972; Little, 1981(S);
                            Menard, 1903, 1904; Rondot, 1887; Tridon, 1849
St. Martin es Vignes   Socard, 1858
St. Pantaléon   Morin, 1904
Hôtel de L'Arquebuse   Rigal, 1977
Vaux   Lucot, 1873
Vence   Vence, 1951-1952, 1951
Vendôme   Pascaud - Granboulan, 1971
Verneuil   Verrier, 1962
Villefranche-sur-Saone   Bégule, 1906
Villeneuve-sur-Yonne   Lafond, 1959
Vraiville   Lafond, 1949

Museums
Louvre   Sauzay, 1882; Wartmann, 1908
Lyon   Lyon, 1894
Musée de Cluny   Bamps, 1905; Perrot, 1966, 1970, 1977; Rouen,
                            1955; A. de Sommerard, 1881, 1883; E. du Sommerard,
                            1836-1846

France - cont.

Musée des Monumens Francais	Paris, 1800-1821; Reville & Levallée, 1816
Musée de Sculpture Comparée	Paris, 1920
Nancy	Hauck, 1968
Palais de L'Industrie	Magne, 1886
Palais du Trocadero	Magne, 1900
Rouen	Breton, 1881
Strasbourg	Beyer, 1965
Tours	Tours, 1949

GERMANY

General

Badermann, 1931
Baiet, 1912
Becksmann, 1968, 1970, 1975
Beyer, 1963
Bruckmann, 1927
Figel, 1924-1925
Fischer, 1913(4), 1914
Frankl, 1911
Gahlen, 1929
Gehrig, 1927
Germany, 1926, 1929
Glass-painting, 1895, 1896, 1935
Grodecki, 1951
Heyne, 1881
Kolb, 1884-1889
Kuhn, 1878
Linneman, 1911
Lübke, 1866
Maerker, 1977

F. Müller, 1832-1835
Neumann, 1926
Oidtmann, 1912-1929
Pfeffer, 1952, 1960
Preussiche Akademie, 1917
Rademacher, 1933, 1942
Schaefer, 1901
Sherrill, 1927
Sighart, 1863
L. Sinclair, 1915
South Germany, 1926(2)
Sowers, 1969
Stained glass, 1900
Wackernagel, 1855
B. Webb, 1848
Wentzel, 1951, 1953, 1958, 1970
Witzleben, 1965
F.X. Zettler, 1910

Germany

Altenberg	Altenberg, 1832, 1871; Curling, 1834; Eckert, 1953; Heinen, 1951; Schimmel, 1832; W.H.J. Weale, 1871
Augsburg	Binder, Lieb & Roth, 1965; Boeckler, 1943; Fischer, 1912; Friesenegger, 1930; Herberger, 1860
Baden	Becksmann, 1979(S)
Berlin	Hoffman, 1927; E. Meunier, 1930
Boppard	J. Hayward, 1969; Wentzel, 1969
Brandenburg	Fischer, 1910
Breitenfeld	Haseloff, 1937
Bücken	Korn, 1977; Wentzel, 1961, 1962
Cologne	Boisserée, 1821; 1842-1843; Cologne, 1860, 1868, 1925, 1926, 1947; Essenwein, 1891; Fischer, 1891; Hertel, 1925; Jacobi, 1955, 1957, 1960; Merlo, 1850, 1877, 1895; Oidtmann, 1909, 1910; Rantsch, 1959; Rode, 1968, 1969, 1970, 1974; Schmitz, 1867-1876; Schnütgen, 1888; Weyden, 1848; Wiethase, 1889; Witzleben, 1970, 1972
Constance	Becksmann, 1968; Rahn, 1890; Ruppert, 1890; Schneider, 1960
Darmstadt	Gerstung, 1923
Dobrilugh	R. Lehmann, 1916
Dortmund	Stein, 1920
Dresden	Bruck, 1912
Ehrenstein	Oidtmann, 1896
Erbendorf	Blocherer, 1924-1925
Erfurt	Brueckner & Haetge, 1927; Drachenberg, Maerker & Schmidt, 1976; Drachenberg, 1980(S); Erfurt, 1912; Frodl-Kraft, 1963; Goern, 1961; Tettau, 1890
Frankfurt am Main	Husgen, 1780
Frankfurt a.d. Oder	Jung, 1912
Freiburg	Anderes, 1963; Becksmann, 1969, 1975; Geiges, 1901-1905, 1908, 1931; Graevenitz, 1934; Krummer-Schroth, 1967
Freising	N. Werner, 1975
Goslar	Gahlen, 1934; Goslar, 1934, 1935; Mühlenbein, 1934; Munnerstadt, 1975; Nuremberg, 1975
Grimma	Thoemel, 1890
Hamburg	Pauli, 1924
Hanau	Hanau, 1912
Haina	Kippenberger, 1939
Haslach	Straub, 1860
Herzogenbuchsee	Herzogenbuchsee, 1914

Germany - cont.

Hofen	Mayerfels, 1882
Iphofen	Nuremberg, 1974
Kappenberg	Schöne, 1928
Karlsruhe	Mayer, 1903
Kassel	Schulze, 1913
Kentz	C. Rosen, 1865
Klosterneuburg	Frodl-Kraft, 1963
Leipzig	Leipzig, 1924
Löhne	Korn, 1977
Lorsch	Frodl-Kraft, 1969; Gerke, 1948
Lübeck	Enns, 1978; Lubeck, 1840, 1914; Mahn, 1930
Marburg	Haseloff, 1907; Kippenberger, 1939
Mariawald	Goerke, 1932; M.R. James, 1906; Rackham, 1928, 1944, 1945, 1948
Marienburg	Fischer, 1914; Gahlen, 1935
Marienstatt	Steffen, 1915
Marienstern	Marienstern, 1913
Mulhouse	Lutz, 1906; Lutz & Perdrizet, 1907-1909; Mulhouse, 1881, 1948; Perdrizet, 1907
Munich	Eggert, 1845; Fischer, 1891, 1910, 1912, 1913; Frankl, 1932; Munich, 1847, 1850, 1912(2); Paulus, 1913(2); G. Robinson, 1962; Stockbauer, 1875; Witzleben, 1969
Munnerstadt	Munnerstadt, 1975; Nuremberg, 1974
Naumberg	Memminger, 1913; Schmidt, 1975
Neuwiller	R. Will, 1960
Niederhaslach	Keberlé, 1971
Niepermunster	Wolff, 1902
Nuremberg	Doppelmayr, 1730; Frenzel, 1961, 1967, 1968(2), 1969; Kautzch, 1931; Knappe, 1961; Nuremberg, 1926; Schinnerer, 1908, 1910
Oppenheim	F. Müller, 1853
Pfalz	Becksmann, 1979
Pforta	Priess, 1893
Regensburg	Schinnerer, 1914; Weiss, 1921
Rhineland	Fischer, 1914
Saarbrucken	Saarbrucken, 1924
Settingen	Hauck, 1961, 1962
Sieverstedt	Korn, 1975
Soest	Korn, 1967; Landolt-Wegener, 1959
Steinfeld	Kurthen, 1941; Rick, 1949
Stralsund	C. Rosen, 1870
Stuttgart	Becksmann, 1970
Swabia	Fischer, 1910(2); Frankl, 1912; Koepf, 1961; Pollmann, 1913; Wentzel, 1958
Tergensee	Sepp, 1878
Thuringia	Haseloff, 1897; Thuringia, 1931, 1932
Trier	F.S. Eden, 1909; Jerrold, 1909; Page, 1909; Trier, 1909
Ulm	Seifert, 1962; Seifert & Witzleben, 1968; Wentzel, 1968(2); Witzleben, 1968
Walburg	Straub, 1860
Wiesbaden	Ficker, 1912
Wilsnack	R. Linnemann, 1914
Wimpfen	Harwerth, 1923; Zeller, 1903
Wörlitz	Rahn, 1885
Xanten	Fischer, 1910

Museums

Berlin	Beck, 1900; Berlepsch, 1911-1915, 1913; Heye, 1965; Steinbrucker, 1935, 1936; Stillfried-Rattonitz, 1838
Cologne	Jansen, 1948
Darmstadt	Back, 1923; Beeh-Lustenberger, 1967; Darmstadt, 1932
Hamburg	Hamburg, 1966
Krefeld, Bremen Collection	Bremen
Mainz	Pfeffer, 1952
Munich	Huber, 1928(2); Munich Museum, 1947(S); Schinnerer, 1908; Schmitz, 1913
Munster	Becksmann, 1977
Nuremberg	Nuremberg, 1884, 1974, 1975; Rahn, 1883
Speyer	Hauck, 1969
Stuttgart	Wentzel, 1964
Weisbaden	Jung-Johann

HOLLAND

General
Hone, 1940
Jonas, 1947

Nederlandshe Ambachts........(n.d.)
Renaud, 1959

Gouda — Bridges, 1950; Coleman, 1901; Gouda, 1790, 1845, 1913, (n.d.); Lange van Wyngaerden, 1819; Rijksen, 1948(2); Uytleggine, 1699; Weale, 1846, 1858-1859; Wedgwood, 1950

Leiden — Pelinck & Regteren Altena, 1940

HUNGARY

Bodnar, 1971
Danko, 1880

Fischer, 1914
Hungarian glass-painting, 1914

IRELAND

General
Colum & David, 1932
J. Graves, 1849
Robertson, 1926

White & Wynne, 1963
White, 1968-1969
Wynne, 1977

Kilkenny — Buckley, M.J.C., 1896

ITALY

General
Boom, 1949
Marchini, 1955, 1957, 1966, 1970
O. Morris, 1968-1969
Sherrill, 1913
Toesca, 1927, 1951

Waring, 1858
B. Webb, 1848
Wittgens, 1956
Yates, 1898

Aosta — Brizio, 1956
Assisi — Giusto, 1911; Kleinschmidt, 1915; Supino, 1924; Wentzel, 1952; Zocca, 1936
Bologna — Supino, 1932
Bozen — Rahn, 1888
Florence — Carli, 1946; Cohn, 1959; Florence, 1870; A. Lane, 1949; Marquand, 1899; Paatz, 1940-1953; Poggi, 1909; Rackham, 1949; Straelen, 1938; Toesca, 1920
Milan — Brivio, 1973; F.C. Eden, 1927(2); Monneret de Villard, 1918-1920, 1923; Pirina, 1966, 1969, 1970, 1972, 1976; Ragghianti, 1954, 1955; Read, 1928
Orvieto — Fumi, 1891
Perugia — Bombe, 1914; Manzoni, 1902; Rotelli, 1868
Ravenna — Bovini, 1965; Cecchelli, 1930
Umbria, 1973
Venice — V. Frenzel, 1970

YUGOSLAVIA

Ljubinkovic, 1959

LITHUANIA

Budrys, 1968
Grasis, 1979(S)

Lithuania, 1973

MONACO

Fourès, 1882

NORTH AFRICA AND THE LEVANT

Anselme de Puysaye, 1909
Bon, 1884
Egypt, 1961
Lafond, 1957, 1968

Parvillée, 1874
S.L. Poole, 1886
Prisse d'Avennes, 1877, 1885
Turkish stained glass, 1873, 1950

POLAND

Brzuski, 1926
Buczkowski, 1958
Buek, 1912

Essenwein, 1869
Fischer, 1913
Hettes, 1955

PORTUGAL

General
H. Rambusch, 1948

Batalha — J.M. Neale, 1854

RUMANIA

F.X. Zettler, 1887

SOVIET UNION

Derewitsky, 1897-1898
Minukhin, 1959
Mueller & Frohbeiter-Muller, 1979
Muratova, 1970

Stalin, 1948
Stieglitz Museum, Carbonier, 1893
Zhukova, 1962

SCANDINAVIA

Andersson, 1965, 1972-1973
Aubert, 1923, 1938
Brochmann, 1966
Lexow, 1938

Lindblom, 1940
Parmann, 1973-1974
Roosval, 1925, 1945, 1950(2)
Wentzel, 1944

SOUTH AMERICA

General
Saunier, 1908

GUATEMALA

Berndt, 1945

MEXICO

Nyson, 1943

Villaseñor, 1937

PUERTO RICO

Maas, 1965

SPAIN

General
Alcaide, 1970
Bueno, 1942

Sherrill, 1924
L. Williams, 1907

Granada — Alcaide, 1973
Léon — Arenas, 1976; M. Williams, 1948
Seville — Alcaide, 1969
Valencia — Cuesta, 1958

Museums
Dorregaray, 1871-1876

SWITZERLAND

General
Beer, 1956, 1963
Berlepsch, 1886
Boesch, 1955
Dodgson, 1901
M. Drake, 1912 (appendix), 1922 (on miniature windows)
Dürst, 1971
Fischer, 1912
Gantner, 1947
P. Ganz, 1906
P.L. Ganz, 1966
Haendke, 1893
Hafner, 1887-1889
Hess, 1940
F. Keller, 1857
Lehmann & Rahn, 1900
Lehmann, 1906-1912, 1925
Lübke, 1866

Mandach, 1905, 1908
Meyer, 1884
Oidtmann, 1899, 1901, 1905
Rahn, 1876, 1901
Schneider, 1953, 1956, (in American museums) 1959
Staehelm-Paravicini, 1926
Stettler, 1953
Styger, 1855
Swiss glass, 1765, 1924, 1928
Wartmann, 1908
Weitzman, 1957
Wentzel, 1953
Yates, 1898
Yoki, 1971
Zemp, 1890
Zschokke, 1946, 1947(2)

Switzerland
Aarau — Liebenau, 1892
The Aargau — Lehmann, 1902-1907
Baden — Schneider, 1954
Basel — Basel, (n.d.); Burckhardt, 1885, 1915; Ganz, 1904; Glazer, 1937; Heyne, 1883; Schneider, 1953; W. Smith, (n.d.)
Berne — Beer, 1965; Hahnloser, 1950; Lehmann, 1912-1914, 1929(5); J. Müller, 1879; Scheidegger, 1947; Thormann & Münnen, 1896; Trächsel, 1879
Bodensee — Detzel, 1891; Knoepfli, 1961; Wentzel, 1969
Frauenfeld — Rahn, 1901
Geneva — Blavignac, 1853
Grossmünster — Voeglin, 1882
Hautrive — Beer, 1958
Hilterfingen — H. Keller, 1935-1936
Hindelbank — Lehmann, 1912, 1918
Jegensdorf — Lehmann, 1915

Konigsfelden — Beer, 1965; F. Keller, 1859; Lübke, 1867; Maurer, 1949; Merz, 1913; Stettler, 1949(2); Way, 1859

Lausanne — Bach, Blondel & Bovy, 1942; Bach, 1944; Beer, 1952, 1970; Chamorel & Naef, 1929; Chamorel, 1929; Lafond, 1953; Lausanne, 1975; Rahn, 1879

Lavanttal — J. Hayward, 1969-70

Lichtenthal — Will, 1887

Lucerne — Lehmann, 1929(S), 1942

Meiringen — Vischer-Merian, 1887

Muri — H. Müller, 1958

Payerne — Beer, 1966

Rathausen — Lafond, 1951; Lasteyrie, 1856; Rathausen, 1899

St. Saphorin — Rahn, 1885

Schaffhausen — Baeschlin, 1880; Fischer, 1913

Sunniswald — Sunniswald, 1912

Thun — Way, 1859

Unterstammheim — Lehmann, 1932

Wettingen — Berlepsch, 1886; Lehmann, 1926; Lübke, 1863

Zillis — Poeschel, 1941; Rahn, 1872

Zurich — Lehmann, 1926, 1929(S), 1932(S), 1935(S), 1936(S); Pazaurek, 1926; Rahn, 1877

Swiss Museums

Brisac, 1980   Lafond, 1948, 1951
Burckhardt, 1885   Lehmann, 1897
Egli, 1925   Schneider, 1970
Ganz, 1901   Zurich, 1946

UNITED STATES OF AMERICA

General

Charles, 1915   Leisching, 1895
Craig, 1954   Lloyd, 1962(3), 1963(2), 1967
D.V. Drury, 1963   Nicolas, 1945
Elskus, Rambusch & Frei, 1965   Ooms-van-Diestelhoff, 1963-1964;
Kallir, 1954   R. Riordan, 1881
Lauber, 1907, 1912   Schringer, 1912
Lavanoux, 1932   Skinner, 1944, 1946
Stained glass, 1949(3), 1966   H.L. Willet, 1946
United States, 1937, 1949(3), 1950-1951,   Winterich, 1968
1951, 1952(2), 1953, 1953-1954

Atlanta — English, 1965-1966
Baltimore — Baltimore, 1888
Boston — Skinner, 1965
Chicago — Frueh, 1979; Rattner, 1976
Cincinnatti — J. Riordan, 1950
Conyers, Georgia — Conyers, 1960
Cranwell, Lenox (Mass.) — Cranwell, 1967-1968
Detroit — Detroit, 1943
New York — Connick, 1932; Gates, 1943; Heinigke, 1906; Holiday, 1904; Hoyle, 1945; F. Lamb, 1910; New York, 1913, 1932, 1933-1934, 1961; Rice, 1933; M. Smith, 1908(2)
Oklahoma — Stebbing, 1967
Pittsburgh — Adlow, 1938; Ascenzo, 1932; Connick, 1941; V. Lewis, 1946, 1948, 1961; Pittsburgh, 1962; Wibert, 1968
Rhode Island School of Design — Rhode Island, 1937-1938
Ronaele Manor — Clarke, 1930; F.S. Eden, 1927, 1930(2)
St. Louis — See, 1970
San Francisco — Connick, 1934; San Francisco, 1968; H. Wright, 1904
Texas State College — Laselle, 1942
Tuskegee — J.H. Kuhn, 1968
Washington D.C. — Bayless, 1975; Burnham, 1942, 1943(2); Orr, 1961-1962; Sheldon, 1936; Washington, D.C., 1883, 1885, 1947, 1949

Museums

Brabazon, 1914
The Cloisters. Bridges, 1938
Minnott, 1971
Corcoran Gallery. Rorimer, 1938
M.H. De Young Museum. Verder, 1958
N.W. Graves, 1940. Hammond Museum, Gloucester, Mass. Witham, 1969-1970.
Metropolitan Museum. Cary, 1932.
Nelson Gallery of Art, Kansas City. Kansas City, 1935

Jane Hayward, 1972
Rorimer, 1929, 1948. Pennsylvania Museum. Flick, 1925
Pennsylvania, 1923, 1925. Princeton University Museum, Graham, 1962
Riom, 1951. St. Louis Museum. Hayward, 1957
St. Louis, 1934, 1935
Skinner, 1934. Springfield Museum (Mass.) Springfield, 1945

Toledo Museum (Ohio). Skinner, 1936

Worcester Museum. Worcester Art Museum, 1934-1935